Documents of Revolution: Common Sense, The Complete Federalist and Anti-Federalist Papers, The Articles of Confederation, The Articles of Confederation, The U. S. Constitution, The Bill of Rights

- Alexander Hamilton
- Thomas Jefferson
- John Jay

CONTENTS

AbouT Author 1
   Alexander Hamilton...1
   Thomas Jefferson 2
   John Jay 3

COMMON SENSE; Addressed to the INHABITANTS of AMERICA, ...4
   INTRODUCTION. 5
   OF THE ORIGIN AND DESIGN OF GOVERNMENT IN GENERAL, WITH CONCISE REMARKS ON THE ENGLISH CONSTITUTION. 5
   OF MONARCHY AND HEREDITARY SUCCESSION..8
   THOUGHTS ON THE PRESENT STATE OF AMERICAN AFFAIRS. 11
   OF THE PRESENT ABILITY OF AMERICA, WITH SOME MISCELLANEOUS REFLEXIONS.   17
   APPENDIX..22
   Historical Context 27
   On Common Sense...29

THE DECLARATION OF INDEPENDENCE OF THE UNITED STATES OF AMERICA 30
Articles of Confederation (1777) 34
THE FEDERALIST PAPERS..38
About The Federlist Papers...39
   Federalist Paper No. 1. General Introduction 41
      For the Independent Journal. Saturday, October 27, 1787...41
   Federalist Paper No. 2. Concerning Dangers from Foreign Force and Influence 42
      For the Independent Journal. Wednesday, October 31, 1787...42
   Federalist Paper No. 3. The Same Subject Continued (Concerning Dangers From Foreign Force and Influence) 44
      For the Independent Journal. Saturday, November 3, 1787..44
   Federalist Paper No. 4. The Same Subject Continued (Concerning Dangers From Foreign Force and Influence) 46
      For the Independent Journal. Wednesday, November 7, 1787..46
   Federalist Paper No. 5. The Same Subject Continued (Concerning Dangers From Foreign Force and Influence) 47
      For the Independent Journal. Saturday, November 10, 1787 47
   Federalist Paper No. 6. Concerning Dangers from Dissensions Between the States   49
      For the Independent Journal. Wednesday, November 14, 1787......................................49
   Federalist Paper No. 7. The Same Subject Continued (Concerning Dangers from Dissensions Between the States) 52
      For the Independent Journal. Thursday, November 15, 1787..52
   Federalist Paper No. 8. The Consequences of Hostilities Between the States ...55
      From the New York Packet. Tuesday, November 20, 1787..55
   Federalist Paper No. 9. The Union as a Safeguard Against Domestic Faction and Insurrection 57

Documents of Revolution

For the Independent Journal. Wednesday, November 21, 1787 57

Federalist Paper No. 10. The Same Subject Continued (The Union as a Safeguard Against Domestic Faction and Insurrection) 59

From the Daily Advertiser. Thursday, November 22, 1787. 59

Federalist Paper No. 11. The Utility of the Union in Respect to Commercial Relations and a Navy   62

For the Independent Journal. Saturday, November 24, 1787 62

Federalist Paper No. 12. The Utility of the Union In Respect to Revenue 65

From the New York Packet. Tuesday, November 27, 1787. 65

Federalist Paper No. 13. Advantage of the Union in Respect to Economy in Government   68

For the Independent Journal. Wednesday, November 28, 1787 68

Federalist Paper No. 14. Objections to the Proposed Constitution From Extent of Territory Answered   70

From the New York Packet. Friday, November 30, 1787. 70

Federalist Paper No. 15. The Insufficiency of the Present Confederation to Preserve the Union   72

For the Independent Journal. Saturday, December 1, 1787 72

Federalist Paper No. 16. The Same Subject Continued (The Insufficiency of the Present Confederation to Preserve the Union) 75

From the New York Packet. Tuesday, December 4, 1787 75

Federalist Paper No. 17. The Same Subject Continued (The Insufficiency of the Present Confederation to Preserve the Union) 77

For the Independent Journal. Wednesday, December 5, 1787 77

Federalist Paper No. 18. The Same Subject Continued (The Insufficiency of the Present Confederation to Preserve the Union) 78

For the New York Packet. Friday, December 7, 1787 78

Federalist Paper No. 19. The Same Subject Continued (The Insufficiency of the Present Confederation to Preserve the Union) 81

For the Independent Journal. Saturday, December 8, 1787 81

Federalist Paper No. 20. The Same Subject Continued (The Insufficiency of the Present Confederation to Preserve the Union) 83

From the New York Packet. Tuesday, December 11, 1787 83

Federalist Paper No. 21. Other Defects of the Present Confederation 85

For the Independent Journal. Wednesday, December 12, 1787 85

Federalist Paper No. 22. The Same Subject Continued (Other Defects of the Present Confederation)   87

From the New York Packet. Friday, December 14, 1787. 87

Federalist Paper No. 23. The Necessity of a Government as Energetic as the One Proposed to the Preservation of the Union 90

From the New York Packet. Tuesday, December 18, 1787 90

Documents of Revolution

Federalist Paper No. 24. The Powers Necessary to the Common Defense Further Considered 92

For the Independent Journal. Wednesday, December 19, 1787 92

Federalist Paper No. 25. The Same Subject Continued (The Powers Necessary to the Common Defense Further Considered) 94

From the New York Packet. Friday, December 21, 1787. 94

Federalist Paper No. 26. The Idea of Restraining the Legislative Authority in Regard to the Common Defense Considered. 96

For the Independent Journal. Saturday, December 22, 1788 96

Federalist Paper No. 27. The Same Subject Continued (The Idea of Restraining the Legislative Authority in Regard to the Common Defense Considered) 99

From the New York Packet. Tuesday, December 25, 1787. 99

Federalist Paper No. 28. The Same Subject Continued (The Idea of Restraining the Legislative Authority in Regard to the Common Defense Considered) 100

For the Independent Journal. Wednesday, December 26, 1787 100

Federalist Paper No. 29. Concerning the Militia 102

From the New York Packet. Wednesday, January 9, 1788 102

Federalist Paper No. 30. Concerning the General Power of Taxation 105

From the New York Packet. Friday, December 28, 1787. 105

Federalist Paper No. 31. The Same Subject Continued (Concerning the General Power of Taxation) 107

From the New York Packet. Tuesday, January 1, 1788. 107

Federalist Paper No. 32. The Same Subject Continued (Concerning the General Power of Taxation) 109

From The Independent Journal. Wednesday, January 2, 1788. 109

Federalist Paper No. 33. The Same Subject Continued (Concerning the General Power of Taxation) 111

From The Independent Journal. Wednesday, January 2, 1788. 111

Federalist Paper No. 34. The Same Subject Continued (Concerning the General Power of Taxation) 112

From The Independent Journal. Saturday, January 5, 1788. 112

Federalist Paper No. 35. The Same Subject Continued (Concerning the General Power of Taxation) 115

For the Independent Journal. Saturday, January 5, 1788 115

Federalist Paper No. 36. The Same Subject Continued (Concerning the General Power of Taxation) 117

From the New York Packet. Tuesday, January 8, 1788. 117

Federalist Paper No. 37. Concerning the Difficulties of the Convention in Devising a Proper Form of Government. 119

From the Daily Advertiser. Friday, January 11, 1788. 119

Federalist Paper No. 38. The Same Subject Continued, and the Incoherence of the Objections to the New Plan Exposed. 122

From The Independent Journal. Saturday, January 12, 1788. 122

Documents of Revolution

Federalist Paper No. 39. The Conformity of the Plan to Republican Principles 126
- For the Independent Journal. Wednesday, January 16, 1788 126

Federalist Paper No. 40. On the Powers of the Convention to Form a Mixed Government Examined and Sustained. 128
- For the New York Packet. Friday, January 18, 1788 128

Federalist Paper No. 41. General View of the Powers Conferred by The Constitution 132
- For the Independent Journal. Saturday, January 19, 1788 132

Federalist Paper No. 42. The Powers Conferred by the Constitution Further Considered 135
- From the New York Packet. Tuesday, January 22, 1788 135

Federalist Paper No. 43. The Same Subject Continued (The Powers Conferred by the Constitution Further Considered) 138
- For the Independent Journal. Wednesday, January 23, 1788 138

Federalist Paper No. 44. Restrictions on the Authority of the Several States .. 141
- From the New York Packet. Friday, January 25, 1788 141

Federalist Paper No. 45. The Alleged Danger From the Powers of the Union to the State Governments. 144
- Considered For the Independent Journal. Saturday, January 26, 1788 144

Federalist Paper No. 46. The Influence of the State and Federal Governments Compared 146
- From the New York Packet. Tuesday, January 29, 1788 146

Federalist Paper No. 47. The Particular Structure of the New Government and the Distribution of Power Among Its Different Parts. 148
- For the Independent Journal. Wednesday, January 30, 1788 148

Federalist Paper No. 48. These Departments Should Not Be So Far Separated as to Have No Constitutional Control Over Each Other. 151
- From the New York Packet. Friday, February 1, 1788 151

Federalist Paper No. 49. Method of Guarding Against the Encroachments of Any One Department of Government by Appealing to the People Through a Convention. 153
- For the Independent Journal. Saturday, February 2, 1788 153

Federalist Paper No. 50. Periodical Appeals to the People Considered 154
- From the New York Packet. Tuesday, February 5, 1788 154

Federalist Paper No. 51. The Structure of the Government Must Furnish the Proper Checks and Balances Between the Different Departments 156
- For the Independent Journal. Wednesday, February 6, 1788 156

Federalist Paper No. 52. The House of Representatives 158
- From the New York Packet. Friday, February 8, 1788 158

Federalist Paper No. 53. The Same Subject Continued (The House of Representatives) 159
- For the Independent Journal. Saturday, February 9, 1788 159

Documents of Revolution

Federalist Paper No. 54. The Apportionment of Members Among the States .162

   From the New York Packet. Tuesday, February 12, 1788...162

Federalist Paper No. 55. The Total Number of the House of Representatives.164

   For the Independent Journal. Wednesday, February 13, 1788...164

Federalist Paper No. 56. The Same Subject Continued (The Total Number of the House of Representatives)   166

   For the Independent Journal. Saturday, February 16, 1788. 166

Federalist Paper No. 57. The Alleged Tendency of the New Plan to Elevate the Few at the Expense of the Many Considered in Connection with Representation...167

   From the New York Packet. Tuesday, February 19, 1788...167

Federalist Paper No. 58. Objection That The Number of Members Will Not Be Augmented as the Progress of Population Demands. 169

   Considered For the Independent Journal Wednesday, February 20, 1788...169

Federalist Paper No. 59. Concerning the Power of Congress to Regulate the Election of Members   171

   From the New York Packet. Friday, February 22, 1788...171

Federalist Paper No. 60. The Same Subject Continued (Concerning the Power of Congress to Regulate the Election of Members)...174

   From The Independent Journal. Saturday, February 23, 1788. 174

Federalist Paper No. 61. The Same Subject Continued (Concerning the Power of Congress to Regulate the Election of Members)...176

   From the New York Packet. Tuesday, February 26, 1788. 176

Federalist Paper No. 62. The Senate...178

   For the Independent Journal. Wednesday, February 27, 1788 178

Federalist Paper No. 63. The Senate Continued...180

   For the Independent Journal. Saturday, March 1, 1788 180

Federalist Paper No. 64. The Powers of the Senate...183

   From The Independent Journal. Wednesday, March 5, 1788. 183

Federalist Paper No. 65. The Powers of the Senate Continued...185

   From the New York Packet. Friday, March 7, 1788. 185

Federalist Paper No. 66. Objections to the Power of the Senate To Set as a Court for Impeachments Further Considered. 187

   From The Independent Journal. Saturday, March 8, 1788. 187

Federalist Paper No. 67. The Executive Department...190

   From the New York Packet. Tuesday, March 11, 1788...190

Federalist Paper No. 68. The Mode of Electing the President...191

   From The Independent Journal. Wednesday, March 12, 1788. 191

Federalist Paper No. 69. The Real Character of the Executive...194

Documents of Revolution

From the New York Packet. Friday, March 14, 1788. 194

Federalist Paper No. 70. The Executive Department Further Considered........ 196

From The Independent Journal. Saturday, March 15, 1788.. 196

Federalist Paper No. 71. The Duration in Office of the Executive 199

From the New York Packet. Tuesday, March 18, 1788. 199

Federalist Paper No. 72. The Same Subject Continued, and Re-Eligibility of the Executive Considered. 201

From The Independent Journal. Wednesday, March 19, 1788.. 201

Federalist Paper No. 73. The Provision For The Support of the Executive, and the Veto Power 203

From the New York Packet. Friday, March 21, 1788. 203

Federalist Paper No. 74. The Command of the Military and Naval Forces, and the Pardoning Power of the Executive. 205

From the New York Packet. Tuesday, March 25, 1788. 205

Federalist Paper No. 75. The Treaty-Making Power of the Executive 206

For the Independent Journal. Wednesday, March 26, 1788... 206

Federalist Paper No. 76. The Appointing Power of the Executive 208

From the New York Packet. Tuesday, April 1, 1788. 208

Federalist Paper No. 77. The Appointing Power Continued and Other Powers of the Executive Considered. 211

From The Independent Journal. Wednesday, April 2, 1788. 211

Federalist Paper No. 78. The Judiciary Department.. 213

From McLEAN'S Edition, New York. Wednesday, May 28, 1788.. 213

Federalist Paper No. 79. The Judiciary Continued 215

From MCLEAN's Edition, New York. Wednesday, May 28, 1788 215

Federalist Paper No. 80. The Powers of the Judiciary 216

From McLEAN's Edition, New York. Wednesday, May 28, 1788.. 216

Federalist Paper No. 81. The Judiciary Continued, and the Distribution of the Judicial Authority. 219

From McLEAN's Edition, New York. Wednesday, May 28, 1788... 219

Federalist Paper No. 82. The Judiciary Continued... 223

From McLEAN's Edition, New York. Wednesday, May 28, 1788 223

Federalist Paper No. 83. The Judiciary Continued in Relation to Trial by Jury 225

From MCLEAN's Edition, New York. Wednesday, May 28, 1788 225

Federalist Paper No. 84. Certain General and Miscellaneous Objections to the Constitution Considered and Answered. 230

From McLEAN's Edition, New York. Wednesday, May 28, 1788 230

Federalist Paper No. 85. Concluding Remarks.. 234

From MCLEAN's Edition, New York. Wednesday, May 28, 1788 234
The ANTI-FEDERALIST Papers 237
The ANTI-FEDERALIST Papers 238

- Anti-Federalist Paper No. 1 238
- Anti-Federalist Paper No. 2 239
- Anti-Federalist Paper No. 3 241
- Anti-Federalist Paper No. 4 242
- Anti-Federalist Paper No. 5 244
- Anti-Federalist Paper No. 6 245
- Anti-Federalist Paper No. 7 246
- Anti-Federalist Paper No. 8 247
- Anti-Federalist Paper No. 9 248
- Anti-Federalist Paper No. 10 250
- Anti-Federalist Paper No. 11 252
- Anti-Federalist Paper No. 12 253
- Anti-Federalist Paper No. 13 255
- Anti-Federalist Paper No. 14 257
- Anti-Federalist Paper No. 15 259
- Anti-Federalist Paper No. 16 260
- Anti-Federalist Paper No. 17 261
- Anti-Federalist Paper No. 18-20 263
- Anti-Federalist Paper No. 18-20(part II) 264
- Anti-Federalist Paper No. 21 267
- Anti-Federalist Paper No. 22 269
- Anti-Federalist Paper No. 23 271
- Anti-Federalist Paper No. 24 274
- Anti-Federalist Paper No. 25(part II) 275
- Anti-Federalist Paper No. 26 278
- Anti-Federalist Paper No. 27 280
- Anti-Federalist Paper No. 28 281
- Anti-Federalist Paper No. 29 283
- Anti-Federalist Paper No. 30-31 285
- Anti-Federalist Paper No. 32 286
- Anti-Federalist Paper No. 33 288
- Anti-Federalist Paper No. 34 290
- Anti-Federalist Paper No. 35 291
- Anti-Federalist Paper No. 36 292
- Anti-Federalist Paper No. 37 294
- Anti-Federalist Paper No. 38 296
- Anti-Federalist Paper No. 39 298
- Anti-Federalist Paper No. 40 300
- Anti-Federalist Paper No. 41-43 302
- Anti-Federalist Paper No. 41-43 (Part II) (Richard Henry Lee) 305
- Anti-Federalist Paper No. 44 307
- Anti-Federalist Paper No. 45 309
- Anti-Federalist Paper No. 46 311
- Anti-Federalist Paper No. 47 312
- Anti-Federalist Paper No. 48 315
- Anti-Federalist Paper No. 49 316
- Anti-Federalist Paper No. 50 318

Anti-Federalist Paper No. 51 320
Anti-Federalist Paper No. 53 324
Anti-Federalist Paper No. 54 325
Anti-Federalist Paper No. 55 327
Anti-Federalist Paper No. 56 329
Anti-Federalist Paper No. 57 330
Anti-Federalist Paper No. 58 333
Anti-Federalist Paper No. 59 334
Anti-Federalist Paper No. 60 336
Anti-Federalist Paper No. 61 337
Anti-Federalist Paper No. 62 338
Anti-Federalist Paper No. 63 341
Anti-Federalist Paper No. 64 343
Anti-Federalist Paper No. 65 345
Anti-Federalist Paper No. 66 347
Anti-Federalist Paper No. 67 347
Anti-Federalist Paper No. 68 349
Anti-Federalist Paper No. 69 350
Anti-Federalist Paper No. 70 352
Anti-Federalist Paper No. 71 352
Anti-Federalist Paper No. 72 353
Anti-Federalist Paper No. 73 354
Anti-Federalist Paper No. 74 356
Anti-Federalist Paper No. 75 357
An Antifederalist View of The Appointing Power Under The Constitution 358
Anti-Federalist Paper No. 78-79 361
Anti-Federalist Paper No. 80 363
Anti-Federalist Paper No. 81 365
Anti-Federalist Paper No. 82 369
Anti-Federalist Paper No. 83 371
Anti-Federalist Paper No. 84 372
Anti-Federalist Paper No. 85 375

THE CONSTITUTION OF THE UNITED STATES OF AMERICA, 1787 378

Article I 378
ARTICLE II 384
ARTICLE III 386
ARTICLE IV 387
ARTICLE V 388
ARTICLE VI 388
ARTICLE VII 389

The United States Bill of Rights. 393

I 393
II 393
III 393
IV 393
V 394
VI 394

VII	394
VIII	394
IX	394
X	394

ABOUT AUTHOR

Alexander Hamilton

Alexander Hamilton (/ˌælɪɡˈzændər ˈhæməltən/, January 11, 1755 or 1757 – July 12, 1804) was an American statesman, politician, legal scholar, military commander, lawyer, banker, and economist. He was one of the Founding Fathers of the United States. He was an influential interpreter and promoter of the U.S. Constitution, as well as the founder of the nation's financial system, the Federalist Party, the United States Coast Guard, and the New York Post newspaper. Hamilton continued his legal and business activities in New York City, and was active in ending the legality of the international slave trade. Vice President Burr ran for governor of New York State in 1804, and Hamilton campaigned against him as unworthy.

Thomas Jefferson

Thomas Jefferson (April 13, 1743 – July 4, 1826) was an American statesman, diplomat, lawyer, architect, philosopher, and Founding Father who served as the third president of the United States from 1801 to 1809. He had previously served as the second vice president of the United States between 1797 and 1801. The principal author of the Declaration of Independence, Jefferson was a proponent of democracy, republicanism, and individual rights, motivating American colonists to break from the Kingdom of Great Britain and form a new nation; he produced formative documents and decisions at both the state and national level.

John Jay

John Jay (December 23, 1745 – May 17, 1829)[1] was an American statesman, patriot, diplomat, Founding Father of the United States, abolitionist, negotiator and signatory of the Treaty of Paris of 1783, second Governor of New York, and the first Chief Justice of the United States (1789–1795). He directed U.S. foreign policy for much of the 1780s and was an important leader of the Federalist Party after the ratification of the United States Constitution in 1788. A proponent of strong, centralized government, Jay worked to ratify the United States Constitution in New York in 1788. He was a co-author of The Federalist Papers along with Alexander Hamilton and James Madison, and wrote five of the 85 essays. After the establishment of the new federal government, Jay was appointed by President George Washington the first Chief Justice of the United States, serving from 1789 to 1795.

Documents of Revolution

COMMON SENSE; ADDRESSED TO THE INHABITANTS OF AMERICA,

On the following interesting

SUBJECTS

1. Of the Origin and Design of Government in general,

with concise Remarks on the English Constitution.

2. Of Monarchy and Hereditary Succession
3. Thoughts on the present State of American Affairs
4. Of the present Ability of America, with some miscellaneous Reflections

Man knows no Master save creating HEAVEN
Or those whom choice and common good ordain.
   THOMSON.

PHILADELPHIA

Printed and sold by W. & T. Bradford, February 14, 1776.

MDCCLXXVI

INTRODUCTION.

Perhaps the sentiments contained in the following pages, are not yet sufficiently fashionable to procure them general favor; a long habit of not thinking a thing wrong, gives it a superficial appearance of being right, and raises at first a formidable outcry in defense of custom. But the tumult soon subsides. Time makes more converts than reason.

As a long and violent abuse of power, is generally the Means of calling the right of it in question (and in Matters too which might never have been thought of, had not the Sufferers been aggravated into the inquiry) and as the King of England hath undertaken in his own Right, to support the Parliament in what he calls Theirs, and as the good people of this country are grievously oppressed by the combination, they have an undoubted privilege to inquire into the pretensions of both, and equally to reject the usurpation of either.

In the following sheets, the author hath studiously avoided every thing which is personal among ourselves. Compliments as well as censure to individuals make no part thereof. The wise, and the worthy, need not the triumph of a pamphlet; and those whose sentiments are injudicious, or unfriendly, will cease of themselves unless too much pains are bestowed upon their conversion.

The cause of America is in a great measure the cause of all mankind. Many circumstances hath, and will arise, which are not local, but universal, and through which the principles of all Lovers of Mankind are affected, and in the Event of which, their Affections are interested. The laying a Country desolate with Fire and Sword, declaring War against the natural rights of all Mankind, and extirpating the Defenders thereof from the Face of the Earth, is the Concern of every Man to whom Nature hath given the Power of feeling; of which Class, regardless of Party Censure, is the

AUTHOR

P.S. The Publication of this new Edition hath been delayed, with a View of taking notice (had it been necessary) of any Attempt to refute the Doctrine of Independance: As no Answer hath yet appeared, it is now presumed that none will, the Time needful for getting such a Performance ready for the Public being considerably past.

Who the Author of this Production is, is wholly unnecessary to the Public, as the Object for Attention is the Doctrine itself, not the Man. Yet it may not be unnecessary to say, That he is unconnected with any Party, and under no sort of Influence public or private, but the influence of reason and principle.

Philadelphia, February 14, 1776

OF THE ORIGIN AND DESIGN OF GOVERNMENT IN GENERAL, WITH CONCISE REMARKS ON THE ENGLISH CONSTITUTION.

Some writers have so confounded society with government, as to leave little or no distinction between them; whereas they are not only different, but have different origins. Society is produced by our wants, and government by our wickedness; the former promotes our happiness positively by uniting our affections, the latter negatively by restraining our vices. The one encourages intercourse, the other creates distinctions. The first a patron, the last a punisher.

Society in every state is a blessing, but government even in its best state is but a necessary evil; in its worst state an intolerable one; for when we suffer, or are exposed to the same miseries by a government, which we might expect in a country without government, our calamity is heightened by reflecting that we furnish the means by which we suffer. Government, like dress, is the badge of lost innocence; the palaces of kings are built on the ruins of the bowers of paradise. For were the impulses of conscience clear, uniform, and irresistibly obeyed, man would need no other lawgiver; but that not being the case, he finds it necessary to surrender up a part of his property to furnish means for the protection of the rest; and this he is induced to do by the same prudence which in every other case advises him out of two evils to choose the least. Wherefore, security being the true design and end of government, it unanswerably follows that whatever form thereof appears most likely to ensure it to us, with the least expence and greatest benefit, is preferable to all others.

In order to gain a clear and just idea of the design and end of government, let us suppose a small number of persons settled in some sequestered part of the earth, unconnected with the rest, they will then represent the first peopling of any country, or of the world. In this state of natural liberty, society will be their first thought. A thousand motives will excite them thereto, the strength of one man is so unequal to his wants, and his mind so unfitted for perpetual solitude, that he is soon obliged to seek assistance and relief of another, who in his turn requires the same. Four or five united would be able to raise a tolerable dwelling in the midst of a wilderness, but one man might labour out of the common period of life without accomplishing any thing; when he had felled his timber he could not remove it, nor erect it after it was removed; hunger in the mean time would urge him from his work, and every different want call him a different way. Disease, nay even misfortune would be death, for though neither might be mortal, yet either would disable him from living, and reduce him to a state in which he might rather be said to perish than to die.

Thus necessity, like a gravitating power, would soon form our newly arrived emigrants into society, the reciprocal blessings of which, would supersede, and render the obligations of law and government unnecessary while they remained perfectly just to each other; but as nothing but heaven is impregnable to vice, it will unavoidably happen, that in proportion as they surmount the first difficulties of emigration, which bound them together in a common cause, they will begin to relax in their duty and attachment to each other; and this remissness, will point out the necessity, of establishing some form of government to supply the defect of moral virtue.

Some convenient tree will afford them a State-House, under the branches of which, the whole colony may assemble to deliberate on public matters. It is more than probable that their first laws will have the title only of **Regulations**, and be enforced by no other penalty than public disesteem. In this first parliament every man, by natural right, will have a seat.

But as the colony increases, the public concerns will increase likewise, and the distance at which the members may be separated, will render it too inconvenient for all of them to meet on every occasion as at first, when their number was small, their habitations near, and the public concerns few and trifling. This will point out the convenience of their consenting to leave the legislative part to be managed by a select number chosen from the whole body, who are supposed to have the same concerns at stake which those who appointed them, and who will act in the same manner as the whole body would act were they present. If the colony continue increasing, it will become necessary to augment the number of the representatives, and that the interest of every part of the colony may be attended to, it will be found best to divide the whole into convenient parts, each part sending its proper number; and that the elected might never form to themselves an interest separate from the electors, prudence will point out the propriety of having elections often; because as the elected might by that means return and mix again with the general body of the electors in a few months, their fidelity to the public will be secured by the prudent reflexion of not making a rod for themselves. And as this frequent interchange will establish a common interest with every part of the community, they will mutually and naturally support each other, and on this (not on the unmeaning name of king) depends the strength of government, and the happiness of the governed.

Here then is the origin and rise of government; namely, a mode rendered necessary by the inability of moral virtue to govern the world; here too is the design and end of government, viz. freedom and security. And however our eyes may be dazzled with show, or our ears deceived by sound; however prejudice may warp our wills, or interest darken our understanding, the simple voice of nature and of reason will say, it is right.

I draw my idea of the form of government from a principle in nature, which no art can overturn, viz. that the more simple any thing is, the less liable it is to be disordered; and the easier repaired when disordered; and with this maxim in view, I offer a few remarks on the so much boasted constitution of England. That it was noble for the dark and slavish times in which it was erected, is granted. When the world was over run with tyranny the least remove therefrom was a glorious rescue. But that it is imperfect, subject to convulsions, and incapable of producing what it seems to promise, is easily demonstrated.

Absolute governments (tho' the disgrace of human nature) have this advantage with them, that they are simple; if the people suffer, they know the head from which their suffering springs, know likewise the remedy, and are not bewildered by a variety of causes and cures. But the constitution of England is so exceedingly complex, that the nation may suffer for years together without being able to discover in which part the fault lies, some will say in one and some in another, and every political physician will advise a different medicine.

I know it is difficult to get over local or long standing prejudices, yet if we will suffer ourselves to examine the component parts of the English constitution, we shall find them to be the base remains of two ancient tyrannies, compounded with some new republican materials.

First.—The remains of monarchical tyranny in the person of the king.

Secondly.—The remains of aristocratical tyranny in the persons of the peers.

Thirdly.—The new republican materials, in the persons of the commons, on whose virtue depends the freedom of England.

The two first, by being hereditary, are independent of the people; wherefore in a constitutional sense they contribute nothing towards the freedom of the state.

To say that the constitution of England is a union of three powers reciprocally checking each other, is farcical, either the words have no meaning, or they are flat contradictions.

To say that the commons is a check upon the king, presupposes two things:

First.—That the king is not to be trusted without being looked after, or in other words, that a thirst for absolute power is the natural disease of monarchy.

Secondly.—That the commons, by being appointed for that purpose, are either wiser or more worthy of confidence than the crown.

But as the same constitution which gives the commons a power to check the king by withholding the supplies, gives afterwards the king a power to check the commons, by empowering him to reject their other bills; it again supposes that the king is wiser than those whom it has already supposed to be wiser than him. A mere absurdity!

There is something exceedingly ridiculous in the composition of monarchy; it first excludes a man from the means of information, yet empowers him to act in cases where the highest judgment is required. The state of a king shuts him from the world, yet the business of a king requires him to know it thoroughly; wherefore the different parts, by unnaturally opposing and destroying each other, prove the whole character to be absurd and useless.

Some writers have explained the English constitution thus; the king, say they, is one, the people another; the peers are an house in behalf of the king; the commons in behalf of the people; but this hath all the distinctions of a house divided against itself; and though the expressions be pleasantly arranged, yet when examined they appear idle and ambiguous; and it will always happen, that the nicest construction that words are capable of, when applied to the description of some thing which either cannot exist, or is too incomprehensible to be within the compass of description, will be words of sound only, and though they may amuse the ear, they cannot inform the mind, for this explanation includes a previous question, viz. How came the king by a power which the people are afraid to trust, and always obliged to check? Such a power could not be the gift of a wise people, neither can any power, which needs checking, be from God; yet the provision, which the constitution makes, supposes such a power to exist.

But the provision is unequal to the task; the means either cannot or will not accomplish the end, and the whole affair is a felo de se; for as the greater weight will always carry up the less, and as all the wheels of a machine are put in motion by one, it only remains to know which power in the constitution has the most weight, for that will govern; and though the others, or a part of them, may clog, or, as the phrase is, check the rapidity of its motion, yet so long as they cannot stop it, their endeavors will be ineffectual; the first moving power will at last have its way, and what it wants in speed is supplied by time.

That the crown is this overbearing part in the English constitution needs not be mentioned, and that it derives its whole consequence merely from being the giver of places and pensions is self-evident, wherefore, though we have been wise enough to shut and lock a door against absolute monarchy, we at the same time have been foolish enough to put the crown in possession of the key.

The prejudice of Englishmen, in favour of their own government by king, lords and commons, arises as much or more from national pride than reason. Individuals are undoubtedly safer in England than in some other countries, but the will of the king is as much the law of the land in Britain as in France, with this difference, that instead of proceeding directly from his mouth, it is handed to the people under the more formidable shape of an act of parliament. For the fate of Charles the first, hath only made kings more subtle—not more just.

Wherefore, laying aside all national pride and prejudice in favour of modes and forms, the plain truth is, that it is wholly owing to the constitution of the people, and not to the constitution of the government that the crown is not as oppressive in England as in Turkey.

An inquiry into the constitutional errors in the English form of government is at this time highly necessary, for as we are never in a proper condition of doing justice to others, while we continue under the influence of some leading partiality, so neither are we capable of doing it to ourselves while we remain fettered by any obstinate prejudice. And as a man, who is attached to a prostitute, is unfitted to choose or judge of a wife, so any prepossession in favour of a rotten constitution of government will disable us from discerning a good one.

OF MONARCHY AND HEREDITARY SUCCESSION.

Mankind being originally equals in the order of creation, the equality could only be destroyed by some subsequent circumstance; the distinctions of rich, and poor, may in a great measure be accounted for, and that without having recourse to the harsh ill sounding names of oppression and avarice. Oppression is often the consequence, but seldom or never the means of riches; and though avarice will preserve a man from being necessitously poor, it generally makes him too timorous to be wealthy.

But there is another and greater distinction for which no truly natural or religious reason can be assigned, and that is, the distinction of men into **kings** and **subjects**. Male and female are the distinctions of nature, good and bad the distinctions of heaven; but how a race of men came into the world so exalted above the rest, and distinguished like some new species, is worth enquiring into, and whether they are the means of happiness or of misery to mankind.

In the early ages of the world, according to the scripture chronology, there were no kings; the consequence of which was there were no wars; it is the pride of kings which throw mankind into confusion. Holland without a king hath enjoyed more peace for this last century than any of the monarchial governments in Europe. Antiquity favors the same remark; for the quiet and rural lives of the first patriarchs hath a happy something in them, which vanishes away when we come to the history of Jewish royalty.

Government by kings was first introduced into the world by the Heathens, from whom the children of Israel copied the custom. It was the most prosperous invention the Devil ever set on foot for the promotion of idolatry. The Heathens paid divine honors to their deceased kings, and the christian world hath improved on the plan by doing the same to their living ones. How impious is the title of sacred majesty applied to a worm, who in the midst of his splendor is crumbling into dust!

As the exalting one man so greatly above the rest cannot be justified on the equal rights of nature, so neither can it be defended on the authority of scripture; for the will of the Almighty, as declared by Gideon and the prophet Samuel, expressly disapproves of government by kings. All anti-monarchical parts of scripture have been very smoothly glossed over in monarchical governments, but they undoubtedly merit the attention of countries which have their governments yet to form. "Render unto Cæsar the things which are Cæsar's" is the scripture doctrine of courts, yet it is no support of monarchical government, for the Jews at that time were without a king, and in a state of vassalage to the Romans.

Near three thousand years passed away from the Mosaic account of the creation, till the Jews under a national delusion requested a king. Till then their form of government (except in extraordinary cases, where the Almighty interposed) was a kind of republic administred by a judge and the elders of the tribes. Kings they had none, and it was held sinful to acknowledge any being under that title but the Lord of Hosts. And when a man seriously reflects on the idolatrous homage which is paid to the persons of Kings, he need not wonder, that the Almighty ever jealous of his honor, should disapprove of a form of government which so impiously invades the prerogative of heaven.

Monarchy is ranked in scripture as one of the sins of the Jews, for which a curse in reserve is denounced against them. The history of that transaction is worth attending to.

The children of Israel being oppressed by the Midianites, Gideon marched against them with a small army, and victory, thro' the divine interposition, decided in his favour. The Jews elate with success, and attributing it to the generalship of Gideon, proposed making him a king, saying, Rule thou over us, thou and thy son and thy son's son. Here was temptation in its fullest extent; not a kingdom only, but an hereditary one, but Gideon in the piety of his soul replied, I will not rule over you, neither shall my son rule over you. **The Lord shall rule over you.** Words need not be more explicit; Gideon doth not decline the honor, but denieth their right to give it; neither doth he compliment them with invented declarations of his thanks, but in the positive stile of a prophet charges them with disaffection to their proper Sovereign, the King of heaven.

About one hundred and thirty years after this, they fell again into the same error. The hankering which the Jews had for the idolatrous customs of the Heathens, is something exceedingly unaccountable; but so it was, that laying hold of the misconduct of Samuel's two sons, who were entrusted with some secular concerns, they came in an abrupt and clamorous manner to Samuel, saying, Behold thou art old, and thy sons walk not in thy ways, now make us a king to judge us like all other nations. And here we cannot but observe that their motives were bad, viz. that they might be like unto other nations, i.e. the Heathens, whereas their true glory laid in being as much unlike them as possible. But the thing displeased Samuel when they said, Give us a king to judge us; and Samuel prayed unto the Lord, and the Lord said unto Samuel, Hearken unto the voice of the people in all that they say unto thee, for they have not rejected thee, but they have rejected me, THAT I SHOULD NOT REIGN OVER THEM. According to all the works which they have done since the day that I brought them up out of Egypt, even unto this day; wherewith they have forsaken me and served other Gods; so do they also unto thee. Now therefore hearken unto their voice, howbeit, protest solemnly unto them and shew them the manner of the king that shall reign over them, i.e. not of any particular king, but the general manner of the kings of the earth, whom Israel was so eagerly copying after. And notwithstanding the great distance of time and difference of manners, the character is still in fashion. And Samuel told all the words of the Lord unto the people, that asked of him a king. And he said, This shall be the manner of the king that shall reign over you; he will take your sons and appoint them for himself, for his chariots, and to be his horsemen, and some shall run before his chariots (this description agrees with the present mode of impressing men) and he will appoint him captains over thousands and captains over fifties, and will set them to ear his ground and to reap his harvest, and to make his instruments of war, and instruments of his chariots; and he will take your daughters to be confectionaries, and to be cooks and to be bakers (this describes the expence and luxury as well as the oppression of kings) and he will take your fields and your olive yards, even the best of them, and give them to his servants; and he will take the tenth of your feed, and of your vineyards, and give them to his officers and to his servants (by which we see that bribery, corruption and favoritism are the standing vices of kings) and he will take the tenth of your men servants, and your maid servants, and your goodliest young men and your asses, and put them to his work; and he will take the tenth of your sheep, and ye shall be his servants, and ye shall cry out in that day because of your king which ye shall have chosen, AND THE LORD WILL NOT HEAR YOU IN THAT DAY. This accounts for the continuation of monarchy; neither do the characters of the few good kings which have lived since, either sanctify the title, or blot out the sinfulness of the origin; the high encomium given of David takes no notice of him officially as a king, but only as a man after God's own heart. Nevertheless the People refused to obey the voice of Samuel, and they said, Nay, but we will have a king over us, that we may be like all the nations, and that our king may judge us, and go out before us, and fight our battles. Samuel continued to reason with them, but to no purpose; he set before them their ingratitude, but all would not avail; and seeing them fully bent on their folly, he cried out, I will call unto the Lord, and he shall send thunder and rain (which then was a punishment, being in the time of wheat harvest) that ye may perceive and see that your wickedness is great which ye have done in the sight of the Lord, IN ASKING YOU A KING. So Samuel called unto the Lord, and the Lord sent thunder and rain that day, and all the people greatly feared the Lord and Samuel. And all the people said unto Samuel, Pray for thy servants unto the Lord thy God that we die not, for WE HAVE ADDED UNTO OUR SINS THIS EVIL, TO ASK A KING. These portions of scripture are direct and positive. They admit of no equivocal construction. That the Almighty hath here entered his protest against monarchical government is true, or the scripture is false. And a man hath good reason to believe that there is as much of king-craft, as priest-craft, in withholding the scripture from the public in Popish countries. For monarchy in every instance is the Popery of government.

To the evil of monarchy we have added that of hereditary succession; and as the first is a degradation and lessening of ourselves, so the second, claimed as a matter of right, is an insult and an imposition on posterity. For all men being originally equals, no one by birth could have a right to set up his own family in perpetual preference to all others for ever, and though himself might deserve some decent degree of honors of his cotemporaries, yet his descendants might be far too unworthy to inherit them. One of the strongest natural proofs of the folly of hereditary right in kings, is, that nature disapproves it, otherwise she would not so frequently turn it into ridicule by giving mankind an ass for a lion.

Secondly, as no man at first could possess any other public honors than were bestowed upon him, so the givers of those honors could have no power to give away the right of posterity, and though they might say "We choose you for our head," they could not, without manifest injustice to their children, say "that your children and your children's children shall reign over ours for ever." Because such an unwise, unjust, unnatural compact might (perhaps) in the next succession put them under the government of a rogue or a fool. Most wise men, in their private sentiments, have ever treated hereditary right with contempt; yet it is one of those evils, which when once established is not easily removed; many submit from fear, others from superstition, and the more powerful part shares with the king the plunder of the rest.

This is supposing the present race of kings in the world to have had an honorable origin; whereas it is more than probable, that could we take off the dark covering of antiquity, and trace them to their first rise, that we should find the first of them nothing better than the principal ruffian of some restless gang, whose savage manners or pre-eminence in subtility obtained him the title of chief among plunderers; and who by increasing in power, and extending his depredations, over-awed the quiet and defenceless to purchase their safety by frequent contributions. Yet his electors could have no idea of giving hereditary right to his descendants, because such a perpetual exclusion of themselves was incompatible with the free and unrestrained principles they professed to live by. Wherefore, hereditary succession in the early ages of monarchy could not take place as a matter of claim, but as something casual or complimental; but as few or no records were extant in those days, and traditional history stuffed with fables, it was very easy, after the lapse of a few generations, to trump up some superstitious tale, conveniently timed, Mahomet like, to cram hereditary right down the throats of the vulgar. Perhaps the disorders which threatened, or seemed to threaten, on the decease of a leader and the choice of a new one (for elections among ruffians could

Documents of Revolution

not be very orderly) induced many at first to favor hereditary pretensions; by which means it happened, as it hath happened since, that what at first was submitted to as a convenience, was afterwards claimed as a right.

England, since the conquest, hath known some few good monarchs, but groaned beneath a much larger number of bad ones; yet no man in his senses can say that their claim under William the Conqueror is a very honorable one. A French bastard landing with an armed banditti, and establishing himself king of England against the consent of the natives, is in plain terms a very paltry rascally original.—It certainly hath no divinity in it. However, it is needless to spend much time in exposing the folly of hereditary right; if there are any so weak as to believe it, let them promiscuously worship the ass and lion, and welcome. I shall neither copy their humility, nor disturb their devotion.

Yet I should be glad to ask how they suppose kings came at first? The question admits but of three answers, viz. either by lot, by election, or by usurpation. If the first king was taken by lot, it establishes a precedent for the next, which excludes hereditary succession. Saul was by lot, yet the succession was not hereditary, neither does it appear from that transaction there was any intention it ever should. If the first king of any country was by election, that likewise establishes a precedent for the next; for to say, that the right of all future generations is taken away, by the act of the first electors, in their choice not only of a king, but of a family of kings for ever, hath no parrallel in or out of scripture but the doctrine of original sin, which supposes the free will of all men lost in Adam; and from such comparison, and it will admit of no other, hereditary succession can derive no glory. For as in Adam all sinned, and as in the first electors all men obeyed; as in the one all mankind were subjected to Satan, and in the other to Sovereignty; as our innocence was lost in the first, and our authority in the last; and as both disable us from reassuming some former state and privilege, it unanswerably follows that original sin and hereditary succession are parellells. Dishonorable rank! Inglorious connexion! Yet the most subtile sophist cannot produce a juster simile.

As to usurpation, no man will be so hardy as to defend it; and that William the Conqueror was an usurper is a fact not to be contradicted. The plain truth is, that the antiquity of English monarchy will not bear looking into.

But it is not so much the absurdity as the evil of hereditary succession which concerns mankind. Did it ensure a race of good and wise men it would have the seal of divine authority, but as it opens a door to the foolish, the wicked, and the improper, it hath in it the nature of oppression. Men who look upon themselves born to reign, and others to obey, soon grow insolent; selected from the rest of mankind their minds are early poisoned by importance; and the world they act in differs so materially from the world at large, that they have but little opportunity of knowing its true interests, and when they succeed to the government are frequently the most ignorant and unfit of any throughout the dominions.

Another evil which attends hereditary succession is, that the throne is subject to be possessed by a minor at any age; all which time the regency, acting under the cover of a king, have every opportunity and inducement to betray their trust. The same national misfortune happens, when a king worn out with age and infirmity, enters the last stage of human weakness. In both these cases the public becomes a prey to every miscreant, who can tamper successfully with the follies either of age or infancy.

The most plausible plea, which hath ever been offered in favour of hereditary succession, is, that it preserves a nation from civil wars; and were this true, it would be weighty; whereas, it is the most barefaced falsity ever imposed upon mankind. The whole history of England disowns the fact. Thirty kings and two minors have reigned in that distracted kingdom since the conquest, in which time there have been (including the Revolution) no less than eight civil wars and nineteen rebellions. Wherefore instead of making for peace, it makes against it, and destroys the very foundation it seems to stand on.

The contest for monarchy and succession, between the houses of York and Lancaster, laid England in a scene of blood for many years. Twelve pitched battles, besides skirmishes and sieges, were fought between Henry and Edward. Twice was Henry prisoner to Edward, who in his turn was prisoner to Henry. And so uncertain is the fate of war and the temper of a nation, when nothing but personal matters are the ground of a quarrel, that Henry was taken in triumph from a prison to a palace, and Edward obliged to fly from a palace to a foreign land; yet, as sudden transitions of temper are seldom lasting, Henry in his turn was driven from the throne, and Edward recalled to succeed him. The parliament always following the strongest side.

This contest began in the reign of Henry the Sixth, and was not entirely extinguished till Henry the Seventh, in whom the families were united. Including a period of 67 years, viz. from 1422 to 1489.

In short, monarchy and succession have laid (not this or that kingdom only) but the world in blood and ashes. 'Tis a form of government which the word of God bears testimony against, and blood will attend it.

If we inquire into the business of a king, we shall find that in some countries they have none; and after sauntering away their lives without pleasure to themselves or advantage to the nation, withdraw from the scene, and leave their successors to tread the same idle round. In absolute monarchies the whole weight of business, civil and military, lies on the king; the children of

Israel in their request for a king, urged this plea "that he may judge us, and go out before us and fight our battles." But in countries where he is neither a judge nor a general, as in England, a man would be puzzled to know what is his business.

The nearer any government approaches to a republic the less business there is for a king. It is somewhat difficult to find a proper name for the government of England. Sir William Meredith calls it a republic; but in its present state it is unworthy of the name, because the corrupt influence of the crown, by having all the places in its disposal, hath so effectually swallowed up the power, and eaten out the virtue of the house of commons (the republican part in the constitution) that the government of England is nearly as monarchical as that of France or Spain. Men fall out with names without understanding them. For it is the republican and not the monarchical part of the constitution of England which Englishmen glory in, viz. the liberty of choosing a house of commons from out of their own body—and it is easy to see that when republican virtue fails, slavery ensues. Why is the constitution of England sickly, but because monarchy hath poisoned the republic, the crown hath engrossed the commons?

In England a king hath little more to do than to make war and give away places; which in plain terms, is to impoverish the nation and set it together by the ears. A pretty business indeed for a man to be allowed eight hundred thousand sterling a year for, and worshipped into the bargain! Of more worth is one honest man to society and in the sight of God, than all the crowned ruffians that ever lived.

THOUGHTS ON THE PRESENT STATE OF AMERICAN AFFAIRS.

In the following pages I offer nothing more than simple facts, plain arguments, and common sense; and have no other preliminaries to settle with the reader, than that he will divest himself of prejudice and prepossession, and suffer his reason and his feelings to determine for themselves; that he will put on, or rather that he will not put off, the true character of a man, and generously enlarge his views beyond the present day.

Volumes have been written on the subject of the struggle between England and America. Men of all ranks have embarked in the controversy, from different motives, and with various designs; but all have been ineffectual, and the period of debate is closed. Arms, as the last resource, decide the contest; the appeal was the choice of the king, and the continent hath accepted the challenge.

It hath been reported of the late Mr. Pelham (who tho' an able minister was not without his faults) that on his being attacked in the house of commons, on the score, that his measures were only of a temporary kind, replied "they will last my time." Should a thought so fatal and unmanly possess the colonies in the present contest, the name of ancestors will be remembered by future generations with detestation.

The sun never shined on a cause of greater worth. 'Tis not the affair of a city, a country, a province, or a kingdom, but of a continent—of at least one eighth part of the habitable globe. 'Tis not the concern of a day, a year, or an age; posterity are virtually involved in the contest, and will be more or less affected, even to the end of time, by the proceedings now. Now is the seed time of continental union, faith and honor. The least fracture now will be like a name engraved with the point of a pin on the tender rind of a young oak; the wound will enlarge with the tree, and posterity read it in full grown characters.

By referring the matter from argument to arms, a new æra for politics is struck; a new method of thinking hath arisen. All plans, proposals, &c. prior to the nineteenth of April, i.e. to the commencement of hostilities, are like the almanacks of the last year; which, though proper then, are superseded and useless now. Whatever was advanced by the advocates on either side of the question then, terminated in one and the same point, viz. a union with Great-Britain; the only difference between the parties was the method of effecting it; the one proposing force, the other friendship; but it hath so far happened that the first hath failed, and the second hath withdrawn her influence.

As much hath been said of the advantages of reconciliation, which, like an agreeable dream, hath passed away and left us as we were, it is but right, that we should examine the contrary side of the argument, and inquire into some of the many material injuries which these colonies sustain, and always will sustain, by being connected with, and dependant on Great-Britain. To examine that connexion and dependance, on the principles of nature and common sense, to see what we have to trust to, if separated, and what we are to expect, if dependant.

I have heard it asserted by some, that as America hath flourished under her former connexion with Great-Britain, that the same connexion is necessary towards her future happiness, and will always have the same effect. Nothing can be more fallacious than this kind of argument. We may as well assert that because a child has thrived upon milk, that it is never to have meat, or that the first twenty years of our lives is to become a precedent for the next twenty. But even this is admitting more than is true, for I answer roundly, that America would have flourished as much, and probably much more, had no European power had any thing to do with her. The commerce, by which she hath enriched herself are the necessaries of life, and will always have a market while eating is the custom of Europe.

But she has protected us, say some. That she has engrossed us is true, and defended the continent at our expence as well as her own is admitted, and she would have defended Turkey from the same motive, viz. the sake of trade and dominion.

Alas, we have been long led away by ancient prejudices, and made large sacrifices to superstition. We have boasted the protection of Great-Britain, without considering, that her motive was interest not attachment; that she did not protect us from our enemies on our account, but from her enemies on her own account, from those who had no quarrel with us on any other account, and who will always be our enemies on the same account. Let Britain wave her pretensions to the continent, or the continent throw off the dependance, and we should be at peace with France and Spain were they at war with Britain. The miseries of Hanover last war ought to warn us against connexions.

Documents of Revolution

It has lately been asserted in parliament, that the colonies have no relation to each other but through the parent country, i.e. that Pennsylvania and the Jerseys, and so on for the rest, are sister colonies by the way of England; this is certainly a very round-about way of proving relationship, but it is the nearest and only true way of proving enemyship, if I may so call it. France and Spain never were, nor perhaps ever will be our enemies as Americans, but as our being the subjects of Great-Britain.

But Britain is the parent country, say some. Then the more shame upon her conduct. Even brutes do not devour their young, nor savages make war upon their families; wherefore the assertion, if true, turns to her reproach; but it happens not to be true, or only partly so, and the phrase parent or mother country hath been jesuitically adopted by the king and his parasites, with a low papistical design of gaining an unfair bias on the credulous weakness of our minds. Europe, and not England, is the parent country of America. This new world hath been the asylum for the persecuted lovers of civil and religious liberty from every part of Europe. Hither have they fled, not from the tender embraces of the mother, but from the cruelty of the monster; and it is so far true of England, that the same tyranny which drove the first emigrants from home, pursues their descendants still.

In this extensive quarter of the globe, we forget the narrow limits of three hundred and sixty miles (the extent of England) and carry our friendship on a larger scale; we claim brotherhood with every European christian, and triumph in the generosity of the sentiment.

It is pleasant to observe by what regular gradations we surmount the force of local prejudice, as we enlarge our acquaintance with the world. A man born in any town in England divided into parishes, will naturally associate most with his fellow parishioners (because their interests in many cases will be common) and distinguish him by the name of neighbour; if he meet him but a few miles from home, he drops the narrow idea of a street, and salutes him by the name of townsman; if he travel out of the county, and meet him in any other, he forgets the minor divisions of street and town, and calls him countryman, i.e. county-man; but if in their foreign excursions they should associate in France or any other part of Europe, their local remembrance would be enlarged into that of Englishmen. And by a just parity of reasoning, all Europeans meeting in America, or any other quarter of the globe, are countrymen; for England, Holland, Germany, or Sweden, when compared with the whole, stand in the same places on the larger scale, which the divisions of street, town, and county do on the smaller ones; distinctions too limited for continental minds. Not one third of the inhabitants, even of this province, are of English descent. Wherefore I reprobate the phrase of parent or mother country applied to England only, as being false, selfish, narrow and ungenerous.

But admitting, that we were all of English descent, what does it amount to? Nothing. Britain, being now an open enemy, extinguishes every other name and title: And to say that reconciliation is our duty, is truly farcical. The first king of England, of the present line (William the Conqueror) was a Frenchman, and half the Peers of England are descendants from the same country; therefore, by the same method of reasoning, England ought to be governed by France.

Much hath been said of the united strength of Britain and the colonies, that in conjunction they might bid defiance to the world. But this is mere presumption; the fate of war is uncertain, neither do the expressions mean any thing; for this continent would never suffer itself to be drained of inhabitants, to support the British arms in either Asia, Africa, or Europe.

Besides what have we to do with setting the world at defiance? Our plan is commerce, and that, well attended to, will secure us the peace and friendship of all Europe; because, it is the interest of all Europe to have America a free port. Her trade will always be a protection, and her barrenness of gold and silver secure her from invaders.

I challenge the warmest advocate for reconciliation, to shew, a single advantage that this continent can reap, by being connected with Great Britain. I repeat the challenge, not a single advantage is derived. Our corn will fetch its price in any market in Europe, and our imported goods must be paid for buy them where we will.

But the injuries and disadvantages we sustain by that connection, are without number; and our duty to mankind at large, as well as to ourselves, instruct us to renounce the alliance: Because, any submission to, or dependance on Great-Britain, tends directly to involve this continent in European wars and quarrels; and sets us at variance with nations, who would otherwise seek our friendship, and against whom, we have neither anger nor complaint. As Europe is our market for trade, we ought to form no partial connection with any part of it. It is the true interest of America to steer clear of European contentions, which she never can do, while by her dependence on Britain, she is made the make-weight in the scale of British politics.

Europe is too thickly planted with kingdoms to be long at peace, and whenever a war breaks out between England and any foreign power, the trade of America goes to ruin, because of her connection with Britain. The next war may not turn out like the last, and should it not, the advocates for reconciliation now will be wishing for separation then, because, neutrality in that case, would be a safer convoy than a man of war. Every thing that is right or natural pleads for separation. The blood of the slain, the weeping voice of nature cries, **'Tis time to part**. Even the distance at which the Almighty hath placed England and America, is a strong and natural proof, that the authority of the one, over the other, was never the design of Heaven. The time likewise at which the continent was discovered, adds weight to the argument, and the manner in which it was peopled encreases the force of it. The reformation was preceded by the discovery of America, as if the Almighty graciously meant to open a sanctuary to the persecuted in future years, when home should afford neither friendship nor safety.

The authority of Great-Britain over this continent, is a form of government, which sooner or later must have an end: And a serious mind can draw no true pleasure by looking forward, under the painful and positive conviction, that what he calls "the present constitution" is merely temporary. As parents, we can have no joy, knowing that this government is not sufficiently lasting to ensure any thing which we may bequeath to posterity: And by a plain method of argument, as we are running the next generation into debt, we ought to do the work of it, otherwise we use them meanly and pitifully. In order to discover the line of our duty rightly, we should take our children in our hand, and fix our station a few years farther into life; that eminence will present a prospect, which a few present fears and prejudices conceal from our sight.

Though I would carefully avoid giving unnecessary offence, yet I am inclined to believe, that all those who espouse the doctrine of reconciliation, may be included within the following descriptions. Interested men, who are not to be trusted; weak men, who cannot see; prejudiced men, who will not see; and a certain set of moderate men, who think better of the European world than it deserves; and this last class, by an ill-judged deliberation, will be the cause of more calamities to this continent, than all the other three.

It is the good fortune of many to live distant from the scene of sorrow; the evil is not sufficient brought to their doors to make them feel the precariousness with which all American property is possessed. But let our imaginations transport us for a few moments to Boston, that seat of wretchedness will teach us wisdom, and instruct us for ever to renounce a power in whom we can have no trust. The inhabitants of that unfortunate city, who but a few months ago were in ease and affluence, have now, no other alternative than to stay and starve, or turn out to beg. Endangered by the fire of their friends if they continue within the city, and plundered by the soldiery if they leave it. In their present condition they are prisoners without the hope of redemption, and in a general attack for their relief, they would be exposed to the fury of both armies.

Men of passive tempers look somewhat lightly over the offences of Britain, and, still hoping for the best, are apt to call out, "Come, come, we shall be friends again, for all this." But examine the passions and feelings of mankind, Bring the doctrine of reconciliation to the touchstone of nature, and then tell me, whether you can hereafter love, honour, and faithfully serve the power that hath carried fire and sword into your land? If you cannot do all these, then are you only deceiving yourselves, and by your delay bringing ruin upon posterity. Your future connection with Britain, whom you can neither love nor honour, will be forced and unnatural, and being formed only on the plan of present convenience, will in a little time fall into a relapse more wretched than the first. But if you say, you can still pass the violations over, then I ask, Hath your house been burnt? Hath your property been destroyed before your face? Are your wife and children destitute of a bed to lie on, or bread to live on? Have you lost a parent or a child by their hands, and yourself the ruined and wretched survivor? If you have not, then are you not a judge of those who have. But if you have, and still can shake hands with the murderers, then are you unworthy of the name of husband, father, friend, or lover, and whatever may be your rank or title in life, you have the heart of a coward, and the spirit of a sycophant.

This is not inflaming or exaggerating matters, but trying them by those feelings and affections which nature justifies, and without which, we should be incapable of discharging the social duties of life, or enjoying the felicities of it. I mean not to exhibit horror for the purpose of provoking revenge, but to awaken us from fatal and unmanly slumbers, that we may pursue determinately some fixed object. It is not in the power of Britain or of Europe to conquer America, if she do not conquer herself by delay and timidity. The present winter is worth an age if rightly employed, but if lost or neglected, the whole continent will partake of the misfortune; and there is no punishment which that man will not deserve, be he who, or what, or where he will, that may be the means of sacrificing a season so precious and useful.

It is repugnant to reason, to the universal order of things to all examples from former ages, to suppose, that this continent can longer remain subject to any external power. The most sanguine in Britain does not think so. The utmost stretch of human wisdom cannot, at this time, compass a plan short of separation, which can promise the continent even a year's security. Reconciliation is now a fallacious dream. Nature hath deserted the connexion, and Art cannot supply her place. For, as Milton wisely expresses, "never can true reconcilement grow where wounds of deadly hate have pierced so deep."

Every quiet method for peace hath been ineffectual. Our prayers have been rejected with disdain; and only tended to convince us, that nothing flatters vanity, or confirms obstinacy in Kings more than repeated petitioning—and nothing hath contributed more than that very measure to make the Kings of Europe absolute: Witness Denmark and Sweden. Wherefore, since nothing but blows will do, for God's sake, let us come to a final separation, and not leave the next generation to be cutting throats, under the violated unmeaning names of parent and child.

To say, they will never attempt it again is idle and visionary, we thought so at the repeal of the stamp-act, yet a year or two undeceived us; as well may we suppose that nations, which have been once defeated, will never renew the quarrel.

As to government matters, it is not in the power of Britain to do this continent justice: The business of it will soon be too weighty, and intricate, to be managed with any tolerable degree of convenience, by a power, so distant from us, and so very ignorant of us; for if they cannot conquer us, they cannot govern us. To be always running three or four thousand miles with a tale or a petition, waiting four or five months for an answer, which when obtained requires five or six more to explain it in, will in a few years be looked upon as folly and childishness—There was a time when it was proper, and there is a proper time for it to cease.

Small islands not capable of protecting themselves, are the proper objects for kingdoms to take under their care; but there is something very absurd, in supposing a continent to be perpetually governed by an island. In no instance hath nature made the satellite larger than its primary planet, and as England and America, with respect to each other, reverses the common order of nature, it is evident they belong to different systems: England to Europe, America to itself.

I am not induced by motives of pride, party, or resentment to espouse the doctrine of separation and independance; I am clearly, positively, and conscientiously persuaded that it is the true interest of this continent to be so; that every thing short of that is mere patchwork, that it can afford no lasting felicity,—that it is leaving the sword to our children, and shrinking back at a time, when, a little more, a little farther, would have rendered this continent the glory of the earth.

As Britain hath not manifested the least inclination towards a compromise, we may be assured that no terms can be obtained worthy the acceptance of the continent, or any ways equal to the expence of blood and treasure we have been already put to.

The object, contended for, ought always to bear some just proportion to the expence. The removal of North, or the whole detestable junto, is a matter unworthy the millions we have expended. A temporary stoppage of trade, was an inconvenience, which would have sufficiently ballanced the repeal of all the acts complained of, had such repeals been obtained; but if the whole continent must take up arms, if every man must be a soldier, it is scarcely worth our while to fight against a contemptible ministry only. Dearly, dearly, do we pay for the repeal of the acts, if that is all we fight for; for in a just estimation, it is as great a folly to pay a Bunker-hill price for law, as for land. As I have always considered the independancy of this continent, as an event, which sooner or later must arrive, so from the late rapid progress of the continent to maturity, the event could not be far off. Wherefore, on the breaking out of hostilities, it was not worth the while to have disputed a matter, which time would have finally redressed, unless we meant to be in earnest; otherwise, it is like wasting an estate on a suit at law, to regulate the trespasses of a tenant, whose lease is just expiring. No man was a warmer wisher for reconciliation than myself, before the fatal nineteenth of April 1775, but the moment the event of that day was made known, I rejected the hardened, sullen tempered Pharaoh of England for ever; and disdain the wretch, that with the pretended title of **father of his people** can unfeelingly hear of their slaughter, and composedly sleep with their blood upon his soul.

But admitting that matters were now made up, what would be the event? I answer, the ruin of the continent. And that for several reasons.

First. The powers of governing still remaining in the hands of the king, he will have a negative over the whole legislation of this continent. And as he hath shewn himself such an inveterate enemy to liberty, and discovered such a thirst for arbitrary power; is he, or is he not, a proper man to say to these colonies, "You shall make no laws but what I please." And is there any inhabitant in America so ignorant, as not to know, that according to what is called the present constitution, that this continent can make no laws but what the king gives leave to; and is there any man so unwise, as not to see, that (considering what has happened) he will suffer no law to be made here, but such as suit his purpose. We may be as effectually enslaved by the want of laws in America, as by submitting to laws made for us in England. After matters are made up (as it is called) can there be any doubt, but the whole power of the crown will be exerted, to keep this continent as low and humble as possible? Instead of going forward we shall go backward, or be perpetually quarrelling or ridiculously petitioning.—We are already greater than the king wishes us to be, and will he not hereafter endeavour to make us less? To bring the matter to one point. Is the power who is jealous of our prosperity, a proper power to govern us? Whoever says No to this question is an independant, for independancy means no more, than, whether we shall make our own laws, or whether the king, the greatest enemy this continent hath, or can have, shall tell us "there shall be no laws but such as I like."

But the king you will say has a negative in England; the people there can make no laws without his consent. In point of right and good order, there is something very ridiculous, that a youth of twenty-one (which hath often happened) shall say to several millions of people, older and wiser than himself, I forbid this or that act of yours to be law. But in this place I decline this sort of reply, though I will never cease to expose the absurdity of it, and only answer, that England being the King's residence, and America not so, makes quite another case. The king's negative here is ten times more dangerous and fatal than it can be in England, for there he will scarcely refuse his consent to a bill for putting England into as strong a state of defence as possible, and in America he would never suffer such a bill to be passed.

America is only a secondary object in the system of British politics, England consults the good of this country, no farther than it answers her own purpose. Wherefore, her own interest leads her to suppress the growth of ours in every case which doth not promote her advantage, or in the least interferes with it. A pretty state we should soon be in under such a second-hand government, considering what has happened! Men do not change from enemies to friends by the alteration of a name: And in order to shew that reconciliation now is a dangerous doctrine, I affirm, that it would be policy in the king at this time, to repeal the acts for the sake of reinstating himself in the government of the provinces; in order, that **he may accomplish by craft and subtilty, in the long run, what he cannot do by force and violence in the short one.** Reconciliation and ruin are nearly related.

Secondly. That as even the best terms, which we can expect to obtain, can amount to no more than a temporary expedient, or a kind of government by guardianship, which can last no longer than till the colonies come of age, so the general face and state of things, in the interim, will be unsettled and unpromising. Emigrants of property will not choose to come to a country whose form of government hangs but by a thread, and who is every day tottering on the brink of commotion and disturbance; and numbers of the present inhabitants would lay hold of the interval, to dispense of their effects, and quit the continent.

But the most powerful of all arguments, is, that nothing but independance, i.e. a continental form of government, can keep the peace of the continent and preserve it inviolate from civil wars. I dread the event of a reconciliation with Britain now, as it is more than probable, that it will be followed by a revolt somewhere or other, the consequences of which may be far more fatal than all the malice of Britain.

Thousands are already ruined by British barbarity; (thousands more will probably suffer the same fate) Those men have other feelings than us who have nothing suffered. All they now possess is liberty, what they before enjoyed is sacrificed to its service, and having nothing more to lose, they disdain submission. Besides, the general temper of the colonies, towards a British government, will be like that of a youth, who is nearly out of his time; they will care very little about her. And a government which cannot preserve the peace, is no government at all, and in that case we pay our money for nothing; and pray what is it that Britain can do, whose power will be wholly on paper, should a civil tumult break out the very day after reconciliation? I have heard some men say, many of whom I believe spoke without thinking, that they dreaded an independance, fearing that it would produce civil wars. It is but seldom that our first thoughts are truly correct, and that is the case here; for there are ten times more to dread from a patched up connexion than from independance. I make the sufferers case my own, and I protest, that were I driven from house and home, my property destroyed, and my circumstances ruined, that as man, sensible of injuries, I could never relish the doctrine of reconciliation, or consider myself bound thereby.

The colonies have manifested such a spirit of good order and obedience to continental government, as is sufficient to make every reasonable person easy and happy on that head. No man can assign the least pretence for his fears, on any other grounds, than such as are truly childish and ridiculous, viz. that one colony will be striving for superiority over another.

Where there are no distinctions there can be no superiority, perfect equality affords no temptation. The republics of Europe are all (and we may say always) in peace. Holland and Swisserland are without wars, foreign or domestic: Monarchical governments, it is true, are never long at rest; the crown itself is a temptation to enterprizing ruffians at home; and that degree of pride and insolence ever attendant on regal authority, swells into a rupture with foreign powers, in instances, where a republican government, by being formed on more natural principles, would negociate the mistake.

If there is any true cause of fear respecting independance, it is because no plan is yet laid down. Men do not see their way out—Wherefore, as an opening into that business, I offer the following hints; at the same time modestly affirming, that I have no other opinion of them myself, than that they may be the means of giving rise to something better. Could the straggling thoughts of individuals be collected, they would frequently form materials for wise and able men to improve into useful matter.

Let the assemblies be annual, with a President only. The representation more equal. Their business wholly domestic, and subject to the authority of a Continental Congress.

Let each colony be divided into six, eight, or ten, convenient districts, each district to send a proper number of delegates to Congress, so that each colony send at least thirty. The whole number in Congress will be at least 390. Each Congress to sit and to choose a president by the following method. When the delegates are met, let a colony be taken from the whole thirteen colonies by lot, after which, let the whole Congress choose (by ballot) a president from out of the delegates of that province. In the next Congress, let a colony be taken by lot from twelve only, omitting that colony from which the president was taken in the former Congress, and so proceeding on till the whole thirteen shall have had their proper rotation. And in order that nothing may pass into a law but what is satisfactorily just, not less than three fifths of the Congress to be called a majority.— He that will promote discord, under a government so equally formed as this, would have joined Lucifer in his revolt.

But as there is a peculiar delicacy, from whom, or in what manner, this business must first arise, and as it seems most agreeable and consistent that it should come from some intermediate body between the governed and the governors, that is, between the Congress and the people, let a **Continental Conference** be held, in the following manner, and for the following purpose.

A committee of twenty-six members of Congress, viz. two for each colony. Two members from each House of Assembly, or Provincial Convention; and five representatives of the people at large, to be chosen in the capital city or town of each province, for, and in behalf of the whole province, by as many qualified voters as shall think proper to attend from all parts of the province for that purpose; or, if more convenient, the representatives may be chosen in two or three of the most populous parts thereof. In this conference, thus assembled, will be united, the two grand principles of business, knowledge and power. The members of Congress, Assemblies, or Conventions, by having had experience in national concerns, will be able and useful counsellors, and the whole, being impowered by the people, will have a truly legal authority.

The conferring members being met, let their business be to frame a **Continental Charter**, or Charter of the United Colonies; (answering to what is called the Magna Charta of England) fixing the number and manner of choosing members of Congress, members of Assembly, with their date of sitting, and drawing the line of business and jurisdiction between them: (Always remembering, that our strength is continental, not provincial:) Securing freedom and property to all men, and above all things, the free exercise of religion, according to the dictates of conscience; with such other matter as is necessary for a charter to contain. Immediately after which, the said Conference to dissolve, and the bodies which shall be chosen comfortable to the said charter, to be the legislators and governors of this continent for the time being: Whose peace and happiness, may God preserve, Amen.

Should any body of men be hereafter delegated for this or some similar purpose, I offer them the following extracts from that wise observer on governments Dragonetti. "The science" says he "of the politician consists in fixing the true point of happiness and freedom. Those men would deserve the gratitude of ages, who should discover a mode of government that contained the greatest sum of individual happiness, with the least national expense.

Dragonetti on virtue and rewards."

But where says some is the King of America? I'll tell you Friend, he reigns above, and doth not make havoc of mankind like the Royal Brute of Britain. Yet that we may not appear to be defective even in earthly honors, let a day be solemnly set apart for proclaiming the charter; let it be brought forth placed on the divine law, the word of God; let a crown be placed thereon, by which the world may know, that so far as we approve of monarchy, that in America **the law is king**. For as in absolute governments the King is law, so in free countries the law ought to be King; and there ought to be no other. But lest any ill use should afterwards arise, let the crown at the conclusion of the ceremony be demolished, and scattered among the people whose right it is.

A government of our own is our natural right: And when a man seriously reflects on the precariousness of human affairs, he will become convinced, that it is infinitely wiser and safer, to form a constitution of our own in a cool deliberate manner, while we have it in our power, than to trust such an interesting event to time and chance. If we omit it now, some Massanello [1] may hereafter arise, who laying hold of popular disquietudes, may collect together the desperate and the discontented, and by assuming to themselves the powers of government, may sweep away the liberties of the continent like a deluge. Should the government of America return again into the hands of Britain, the tottering situation of things, will be a temptation for some desperate adventurer to try his fortune; and in such a case, what relief can Britain give? Ere she could hear the news, the fatal business might be done; and ourselves suffering like the wretched Britons under the oppression of the Conqueror. Ye that oppose independance now, ye know not what ye do; ye are opening a door to eternal tyranny, by keeping vacant the seat of government. There are thousands, and tens of thousands, who would think it glorious to expel from the continent, that barbarous and hellish power, which hath stirred up the Indians and Negroes to destroy us, the cruelty hath a double guilt, it is dealing brutally by us, and treacherously by them.

Documents of Revolution

[1] Thomas Anello, otherwise Massanello, a fisherman of Naples, who after spiriting up his countrymen in the public market place, against the oppressions of the Spaniards, to whom the place was then subject, prompted them to revolt, and in the space of a day became king.

To talk of friendship with those in whom our reason forbids us to have faith, and our affections wounded through a thousand pores instruct us to detest, is madness and folly. Every day wears out the little remains of kindred between us and them, and can there be any reason to hope, that as the relationship expires, the affection will increase, or that we shall agree better, when we have ten times more and greater concerns to quarrel over than ever?

Ye that tell us of harmony and reconciliation, can ye restore to us the time that is past? Can ye give to prostitution its former innocence? Neither can ye reconcile Britain and America. The last cord now is broken, the people of England are presenting addresses against us. There are injuries which nature cannot forgive; she would cease to be nature if she did. As well can the lover forgive the ravisher of his mistress, as the continent forgive the murders of Britain. The Almighty hath implanted in us these unextinguishable feelings for good and wise purposes. They are the guardians of his image in our hearts. They distinguish us from the herd of common animals. The social compact would dissolve, and justice be extirpated the earth, or have only a casual existence were we callous to the touches of affection. The robber, and the murderer, would often escape unpunished, did not the injuries which our tempers sustain, provoke us into justice.

O ye that love mankind! Ye that dare oppose, not only the tyranny, but the tyrant, stand forth! Every spot of the old world is overrun with oppression. Freedom hath been hunted round the globe. Asia, and Africa, have long expelled her—Europe regards her like a stranger, and England hath given her warning to depart. O! receive the fugitive, and prepare in time an asylum for mankind.

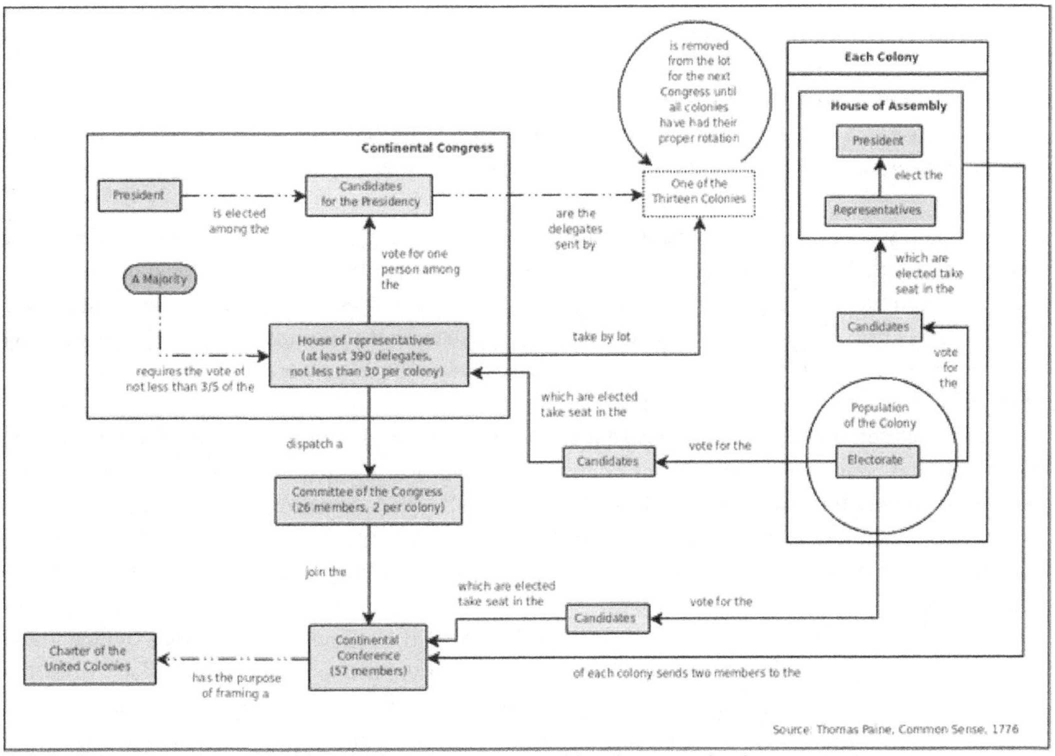

Constitution of the United States as proposed by Thomas Paine in Common Sense

OF THE PRESENT ABILITY OF AMERICA, WITH SOME MISCELLANEOUS REFLEXIONS.

I have never met with a man, either in England or America, who hath not confessed his opinion, that a separation between the countries, would take place one time or other: And there is no instance, in which we have shewn less judgment, than in endeavouring to describe, what we call, the ripeness or fitness of the Continent for independance.

As all men allow the measure, and vary only in their opinion of the time, let us, in order to remove mistakes, take a general survey of things, and endeavour, if possible, to find out the very time. But we need not go far, the inquiry ceases at once, for, the time hath found us. The general concurrence, the glorious union of all things prove the fact.

It is not in numbers, but in unity, that our great strength lies; yet our present numbers are sufficient to repel the force of all the world. The Continent hath, at this time, the largest body of armed and disciplined men of any power under Heaven; and is just arrived at that pitch of strength, in which no single colony is able to support itself, and the whole, when united, can accomplish the matter, and either more, or, less than this, might be fatal in its effects. Our land force is already sufficient, and as to naval affairs, we cannot be insensible, that Britain would never suffer an American man of war to be built, while the continent remained in her hands. Wherefore, we should be no forwarder an hundred years hence in that branch, than we are now; but the truth is, we should be less so, because the timber of the country is every day diminishing, and that, which will remain at last, will be far off and difficult to procure.

Were the continent crowded with inhabitants, her sufferings under the present circumstances would be intolerable. The more sea port towns we had, the more should we have both to defend and to lose. Our present numbers are so happily proportioned to our wants, that no man need be idle. The diminution of trade affords an army, and the necessities of an army create a new trade.

Debts we have none; and whatever we may contract on this account will serve as a glorious memento of our virtue. Can we but leave posterity with a settled form of government, an independant constitution of its own, the purchase at any price will be cheap. But to expend millions for the sake of getting a few vile acts repealed, and routing the present ministry only, is unworthy the charge, and is using posterity with the utmost cruelty; because it is leaving them the great work to do, and a debt upon their backs, from which they derive no advantage. Such a thought is unworthy a man of honor, and is the true characteristic of a narrow heart and a pedling politician.

The debt we may contract doth not deserve our regard if the work be but accomplished. No nation ought to be without a debt. A national debt is a national bond; and when it bears no interest, is in no case a grievance. Britain is oppressed with a debt of upwards of one hundred and forty millions sterling, for which she pays upwards of four millions interest. And as a compensation for her debt, she has a large navy; America is without a debt, and without a navy; yet for the twentieth part of the English national debt, could have a navy as large again. The navy of England is not worth, at this time, more than three millions and an half sterling.

The first and second editions of this pamphlet were published without the following calculations, which are now given as a proof that the above estimation of the navy is just. See Entic's naval history, intro. page 56.

The charge of building a ship of each rate, and furnishing her with masts, yards, sails and rigging, together with a proportion of eight months boatswain's and carpenter's sea-stores, as calculated by Mr. Burchett, Secretary to the navy.

	£ [pounds sterling]
For a ship of 100 guns =	35,553
90 =	29,886

80	=	23,638
70	=	17,785
60	=	14,197
50	=	10,606
40	=	7,558
30	=	5,846
20	=	3,710

And from hence it is easy to sum up the value, or cost rather, of the whole British navy, which in the year 1757, when it was at its greatest glory consisted of the following ships and guns:

Ships.	Guns.	Cost of one.	Cost of all.
		Cost in £ [pounds sterling]	
6	100	35,553	213,318
12	90	29,886	358,632
12	80	23,638	283,656
43	70	17,785	764,755
35	60	14,197	496,895
40	50	10,606	424,240
45	40	7,558	340,110
58	20	3,710	215,180
85	Sloops, bombs and fireships, one with another, at	2,000	170,000

Cost	3,266,786
Remains for Guns	233,214
	3,500,000

No country on the globe is so happily situated, or so internally capable of raising a fleet as America. Tar, timber, iron, and cordage are her natural produce. We need go abroad for nothing. Whereas the Dutch, who make large profits by hiring out their ships of war to the Spaniards and Portuguese, are obliged to import most of the materials they use. We ought to view the building a fleet as an article of commerce, it being the natural manufactory of this country. It is the best money we can lay out. A navy when finished is worth more than it cost. And is that nice point in national policy, in which commerce and protection are united. Let us build; if we want them not, we can sell; and by that means replace our paper currency with ready gold and silver.

In point of manning a fleet, people in general run into great errors; it is not necessary that one fourth part should be sailors. The Terrible privateer, Captain Death, stood the hottest engagement of any ship last war, yet had not twenty sailors on board, though her complement of men was upwards of two hundred. A few able and social sailors will soon instruct a sufficient number of active landmen in the common work of a ship. Wherefore, we never can be more capable to begin on maritime matters than now, while our timber is standing, our fisheries blocked up, and our sailors and shipwrights out of employ. Men of war, of seventy and eighty guns were built forty years ago in New-England, and why not the same now? Ship-building is America's greatest pride, and in which, she will in time excel the whole world. The great empires of the east are mostly inland, and consequently excluded from the possibility of rivalling her. Africa is in a state of barbarism; and no power in Europe, hath either such an extent of coast, or such an internal supply of materials. Where nature hath given the one, she has withheld the other; to America only hath she been liberal of both. The vast empire of Russia is almost shut out from the sea; wherefore, her boundless forests, her tar, iron, and cordage are only articles of commerce.

In point of safety, ought we to be without a fleet? We are not the little people now, which we were sixty years ago; at that time we might have trusted our property in the streets, or fields rather; and slept securely without locks or bolts to our doors or windows. The case now is altered, and our methods of defence, ought to improve with our increase of property. A common pirate, twelve months ago, might have come up the Delaware, and laid the city of Philadelphia under instant contribution, for what sum he pleased; and the same might have happened to other places. Nay, any daring fellow, in a brig of fourteen or sixteen guns, might have robbed the whole Continent, and carried off half a million of money. These are circumstances which demand our attention, and point out the necessity of naval protection.

Some, perhaps, will say, that after we have made it up with Britain, she will protect us. Can we be so unwise as to mean, that she shall keep a navy in our harbours for that purpose? Common sense will tell us, that the power which hath endeavoured to subdue us, is of all others, the most improper to defend us. Conquest may be effected under the pretence of friendship; and ourselves, after a long and brave resistance, be at last cheated into slavery. And if her ships are not to be admitted into our harbours, I would ask, how is she to protect us? A navy three or four thousand miles off can be of little use, and on sudden emergencies, none at all. Wherefore, if we must hereafter protect ourselves, why not do it for ourselves? Why do it for another?

The English list of ships of war, is long and formidable, but not a tenth part of them are at any one time fit for service, numbers of them not in being; yet their names are pompously continued in the list, if only a plank be left of the ship: and not a fifth part, of such as are fit for service, can be spared on any one station at one time. The East and West Indies, Mediterranean, Africa, and other parts over which Britain extends her claim, make large demands upon her navy. From a mixture of prejudice and inattention, we have contracted a false notion respecting the navy of England, and have talked as if we should have the whole of it to encounter at once, and for that reason, supposed, that we must have one as large; which not being instantly practicable, have been made use of by a set of disguised Tories to discourage our beginning thereon. Nothing can be farther from truth than this; for if America had only a twentieth part of the naval force of Britain, she would be by far an over match for her; because, as we neither have, nor claim any foreign dominion, our whole force would be employed on our own coast, where we should, in the long run, have two to one the advantage of those who had three or four thousand miles to sail over, before they could attack us, and the same distance to return in order to refit and recruit. And although Britain by her fleet, hath a check over our trade to Europe, we have as large a one over her trade to the West-Indies, which, by laying in the neighbourhood of the Continent, is entirely at its mercy.

Some method might be fallen on to keep up a naval force in time of peace, if we should not judge it necessary to support a constant navy. If premiums were to be given to merchants, to build and employ in their service ships mounted with twenty, thirty, forty or fifty guns, (the premiums to be in proportion to the loss of bulk to the merchants) fifty or sixty of those ships, with a few guardships on constant duty, would keep up a sufficient navy, and that without burdening ourselves with the evil so loudly complained of in England, of suffering their fleet, in time of peace to lie rotting in the docks. To unite the sinews of commerce and defense is sound policy; for when our strength and our riches play into each other's hand, we need fear no external enemy.

In almost every article of defense we abound. Hemp flourishes even to rankness, so that we need not want cordage. Our iron is superior to that of other countries. Our small arms equal to any in the world. Cannon we can cast at pleasure. Saltpetre and gunpowder we are every day producing. Our knowledge is hourly improving. Resolution is our inherent character, and courage hath never yet forsaken us. Wherefore, what is it that we want? Why is it that we hesitate? From Britain we can expect nothing but ruin. If she is once admitted to the government of America again, this Continent will not be worth living in. Jealousies will be always arising; insurrections will be constantly happening; and who will go forth to quell them? Who will venture his life to reduce his own countrymen to a foreign obedience? The difference between Pennsylvania and Connecticut, respecting some unlocated lands, shews the insignificance of a British government, and fully proves, that nothing but Continental authority can regulate Continental matters.

Another reason why the present time is preferable to all others, is, that the fewer our numbers are, the more land there is yet unoccupied, which instead of being lavished by the king on his worthless dependants, may be hereafter applied, not only to the discharge of the present debt, but to the constant support of government. No nation under heaven hath such an advantage as this.

The infant state of the Colonies, as it is called, so far from being against, is an argument in favour of independance. We are sufficiently numerous, and were we more so, we might be less united. It is a matter worthy of observation, that the more a country is peopled, the smaller their armies are. In military numbers, the ancients far exceeded the moderns: and the reason is evident. For trade being the consequence of population, men become too much absorbed thereby to attend to anything else. Commerce diminishes the spirit, both of patriotism and military defence. And history sufficiently informs us, that the bravest achievements were always accomplished in the non-age of a nation. With the increase of commerce, England hath lost its spirit. The city of London, notwithstanding its numbers, submits to continued insults with the patience of a coward. The more men have to lose, the less willing are they to venture. The rich are in general slaves to fear, and submit to courtly power with the trembling duplicity of a Spaniel.

Youth is the seed time of good habits, as well in nations as in individuals. It might be difficult, if not impossible, to form the Continent into one government half a century hence. The vast variety of interests, occasioned by an increase of trade and population, would create confusion. Colony would be against colony. Each being able might scorn each other's assistance: and while the proud and foolish gloried in their little distinctions, the wise would lament, that the union had not been formed before. Wherefore, the present time is the true time for establishing it. The intimacy which is contracted in infancy, and the friendship which is formed in misfortune, are, of all others, the most lasting and unalterable. Our present union is marked with both these characters: we are young and we have been distressed; but our concord hath withstood our troubles, and fixes a memorable area for posterity to glory in.

The present time, likewise, is that peculiar time, which never happens to a nation but once, viz. the time of forming itself into a government. Most nations have let slip the opportunity, and by that means have been compelled to receive laws from their conquerors, instead of making laws for themselves. First, they had a king, and then a form of government; whereas, the articles or charter of government, should be formed first, and men delegated to execute them afterward: but from the errors of other nations, let us learn wisdom, and lay hold of the present opportunity—To begin government at the right end.

When William the Conqueror subdued England, he gave them law at the point of the sword; and until we consent, that the seat of government, in America, be legally and authoritatively occupied, we shall be in danger of having it filled by some fortunate ruffian, who may treat us in the same manner, and then, where will be our freedom? where our property?

As to religion, I hold it to be the indispensable duty of all government, to protect all conscientious professors thereof, and I know of no other business which government hath to do therewith. Let a man throw aside that narrowness of soul, that selfishness of principle, which the niggards of all professions are so unwilling to part with, and he will be at once delivered of his fears on that head. Suspicion is the companion of mean souls, and the bane of all good society. For myself, I fully and conscientiously believe, that it is the will of the Almighty, that there should be diversity of religious opinions among us: It affords a larger field for our Christian kindness. Were we all of one way of thinking, our religious dispositions would want matter for probation; and on this liberal principle, I look on the various denominations among us, to be like children of the same family, differing only, in what is called, their Christian names.

In page forty, I threw out a few thoughts on the propriety of a Continental Charter, (for I only presume to offer hints, not plans) and in this place, I take the liberty of re-mentioning the subject, by observing, that a charter is to be understood as a bond of solemn obligation, which the whole enters into, to support the right of every separate part, whether of religion, personal freedom, or property. A firm bargain and a right reckoning make long friends.

In a former page I likewise mentioned the necessity of a large and equal representation; and there is no political matter which more deserves our attention. A small number of electors, or a small number of representatives, are equally dangerous. But if the number of the representatives be not only small, but unequal, the danger is increased. As an instance of this, I mention the following; when the Associators petition was before the House of Assembly of Pennsylvania; twenty-eight members only were present, all the Bucks county members, being eight, voted against it, and had seven of the Chester members done the same, this whole province had been governed by two counties only, and this danger it is always exposed to. The unwarrantable stretch likewise, which that house made in their last sitting, to gain an undue authority over the delegates of that province, ought to warn the people at large, how they trust power out of their own hands. A set of instructions for the Delegates were put together, which in point of sense and business would have dishonoured a schoolboy, and after being approved by a few, a very few without doors, were carried into the House, and there passed in behalf of the whole colony; whereas, did the whole colony know, with what ill-will that House hath entered on some necessary public measures, they would not hesitate a moment to think them unworthy of such a trust.

Immediate necessity makes many things convenient, which if continued would grow into oppressions. Expedience and right are different things. When the calamities of America required a consultation, there was no method so ready, or at that time so proper, as to appoint persons from the several Houses of Assembly for that purpose; and the wisdom with which they have proceeded hath preserved this continent from ruin. But as it is more than probable that we shall never be without a **Congress**, every well wisher to good order, must own, that the mode for choosing members of that body, deserves consideration. And I put it as a question to those, who make a study of mankind, whether representation and election is not too great a power for one and the same body of men to possess? When we are planning for posterity, we ought to remember, that virtue is not hereditary.

It is from our enemies that we often gain excellent maxims, and are frequently surprised into reason by their mistakes. Mr. Cornwall (one of the Lords of the Treasury) treated the petition of the New-York Assembly with contempt, because that House, he said, consisted but of twenty-six members, which trifling number, he argued, could not with decency be put for the whole. We thank him for his involuntary honesty. [1]

[1] Those who would fully understand of what great consequence a large and equal representation is to a state, should read Burgh's political disquisitions.

To Conclude, however strange it may appear to some, or however unwilling they may be to think so, matters not, but many strong and striking reasons may be given, to shew, that nothing can settle our affairs so expeditiously as an open and determined declaration for independance. Some of which are,

First.—It is the custom of nations, when any two are at war, for some other powers, not engaged in the quarrel, to step in as mediators, and bring about the preliminaries of a peace: but while America calls herself the Subject of Great-Britain, no power, however well disposed she may be, can offer her mediation. Wherefore, in our present state we may quarrel on for ever.

Secondly.—It is unreasonable to suppose, that France or Spain will give us any kind of assistance, if we mean only, to make use of that assistance for the purpose of repairing the breach, and strengthening the connection between Britain and America; because, those powers would be sufferers by the consequences.

Thirdly.—While we profess ourselves the subjects of Britain, we must, in the eye of foreign nations, be considered as rebels. The precedent is somewhat dangerous to their peace, for men to be in arms under the name of subjects; we, on the spot, can solve the paradox: but to unite resistance and subjection, requires an idea much too refined for common understanding.

Fourthly.—Were a manifesto to be published, and despatched to foreign courts, setting forth the miseries we have endured, and the peaceable methods we have ineffectually used for redress; declaring, at the same time, that not being able, any longer, to live happily or safely under the cruel disposition of the British court, we had been driven to the necessity of breaking off all connections with her; at the same time, assuring all such courts of our peaceable disposition towards them, and of our desire of entering into trade with them: Such a memorial would produce more good effects to this Continent, than if a ship were freighted with petitions to Britain.

Under our present denomination of British subjects, we can neither be received nor heard abroad: The custom of all courts is against us, and will be so, until, by an independance, we take rank with other nations.

These proceedings may at first appear strange and difficult; but, like all other steps which we have already passed over, will in a little time become familiar and agreeable; and, until an independance is declared, the Continent will feel itself like a man who continues putting off some unpleasant business from day to day, yet knows it must be done, hates to set about it, wishes it over, and is continually haunted with the thoughts of its necessity.

APPENDIX.

Since the publication of the first edition of this pamphlet, or rather, on the same day on which it came out, the King's Speech made its appearance in this city. Had the spirit of prophecy directed the birth of this production, it could not have brought it forth, at a more seasonable juncture, or a more necessary time. The bloody mindedness of the one, shew the necessity of pursuing the doctrine of the other. Men read by way of revenge. And the Speech, instead of terrifying, prepared a way for the manly principles of Independance.

Ceremony, and even, silence, from whatever motive they may arise, have a hurtful tendency, when they give the least degree of countenance to base and wicked performances; wherefore, if this maxim be admitted, it naturally follows, that the King's Speech, as being a piece of finished villainy, deserved, and still deserves, a general execration both by the Congress and the people. Yet, as the domestic tranquillity of a nation, depends greatly, on the chastity of what may properly be called **national manners**, it is often better, to pass some things over in silent disdain, than to make use of such new methods of dislike, as might introduce the least innovation, on that guardian of our peace and safety. And, perhaps, it is chiefly owing to this prudent delicacy, that the King's Speech, hath not, before now, suffered a public execution. The Speech if it may be called one, is nothing better than a wilful audacious libel against the truth, the common good, and the existence of mankind; and is a formal and pompous method of offering up human sacrifices to the pride of tyrants. But this general massacre of mankind, is one of the privileges, and the certain consequence of Kings; for as nature knows them not, they know not her, and although they are beings of our own creating, they know not us, and are become the gods of their creators. The Speech hath one good quality, which is, that it is not calculated to deceive, neither can we, even if we would, be deceived by it. Brutality and tyranny appear on the face of it. It leaves us at no loss: And every line convinces, even in the moment of reading, that He, who hunts the woods for prey, the naked and untutored Indian, is less a Savage than the King of Britain.

Sir John Dalrymple, the putative father of a whining jesuitical piece, fallaciously called, "The Address of the people of **England** to the inhabitants of **America**," hath, perhaps, from a vain supposition, that the people here were to be frightened at the pomp and description of a king, given, (though very unwisely on his part) the real character of the present one: "But" says this writer, "if you are inclined to pay compliments to an administration, which we do not complain of," (meaning the Marquis of Rockingham's at the repeal of the Stamp Act) "it is very unfair in you to withhold them from that prince, by whose **nod alone** they were permitted to do any thing." This is toryism with a witness! Here is idolatry even without a mask: And he who can calmly hear, and digest such doctrine, hath forfeited his claim to rationality—an apostate from the order of manhood; and ought to be considered—as one, who hath not only given up the proper dignity of man, but sunk himself beneath the rank of animals, and contemptibly crawls through the world like a worm.

However, it matters very little now, what the king of England either says or does; he hath wickedly broken through every moral and human obligation, trampled nature and conscience beneath his feet; and by a steady and constitutional spirit of insolence and cruelty, procured for himself an universal hatred. It is now the interest of America to provide for herself. She hath already a large and young family, whom it is more her duty to take care of, than to be granting away her property, to support a power who is become a reproach to the names of men and christians—**Ye**, whose office it is to watch over the morals of a nation, of whatsoever sect or denomination ye are of, as well as ye, who are more immediately the guardians of the public liberty, if ye wish to preserve your native country uncontaminated by European corruption, ye must in secret wish a separation—But leaving the moral part to private reflection, I shall chiefly confine my farther remarks to the following heads.

First. That it is the interest of America to be separated from Britain.

Secondly. Which is the easiest and most practicable plan, **reconciliation** or **independance**? with some occasional remarks.

In support of the first, I could, if I judged it proper, produce the opinion of some of the ablest and most experienced men on this continent; and whose sentiments, on that head, are not yet publicly known. It is in reality a self-evident position: For no nation in a state of foreign dependance, limited in its commerce, and cramped and fettered in its legislative powers, can ever arrive at any material eminence. America doth not yet know what opulence is; and although the progress which she hath made stands unparalleled in the history of other nations, it is but childhood, compared with what she would be capable of arriving at, had she, as she ought to have, the legislative powers in her own hands. England is, at this time, proudly coveting what would do her no good, were she to accomplish it; and the Continent hesitating on a matter, which will be her final ruin if neglected. It is the commerce and not the conquest of America, by which England is to be benefited, and that would in a great measure continue, were the countries as independant of each other as France and Spain; because in many articles, neither can go to a better market. But it is the independance of this country of Britain or any other, which is now the main and only object worthy of contention, and which, like all other truths discovered by necessity, will appear clearer and stronger every day.

First. Because it will come to that one time or other.

Secondly. Because, the longer it is delayed the harder it will be to accomplish.

I have frequently amused myself both in public and private companies, with silently remarking, the specious errors of those who speak without reflecting. And among the many which I have heard, the following seems the most general, viz. that had this rupture happened forty or fifty years hence, instead of now, the Continent would have been more able to have shaken off the dependance. To which I reply, that our military ability, at this time, arises from the experience gained in the last war, and which in forty or fifty years time, would have been totally extinct. The Continent, would not, by that time, have had a General, or even a military officer left; and we, or those who may succeed us, would have been as ignorant of martial matters as the ancient Indians: And this single position, closely attended to, will unanswerably prove, that the present time is preferable to all others. The argument turns thus—at the conclusion of the last war, we had experience, but wanted numbers; and forty or fifty years hence, we should have numbers, without experience; wherefore, the proper point of time, must be some particular point between the two extremes, in which a sufficiency of the former remains, and a proper increase of the latter is obtained: And that point of time is the present time.

The reader will pardon this digression, as it does not properly come under the head I first set out with, and to which I again return by the following position, viz.

Should affairs be patched up with Britain, and she to remain the governing and sovereign power of America, (which, as matters are now circumstanced, is giving up the point intirely) we shall deprive ourselves of the very means of sinking the debt we have, or may contract. The value of the back lands which some of the provinces are clandestinely deprived of, by the unjust extention of the limits of Canada, valued only at five pounds sterling per hundred acres, amount to upwards of twenty-five millions, Pennsylvania currency; and the quit-rents at one penny sterling per acre, to two millions yearly.

It is by the sale of those lands that the debt may be sunk, without burthen to any, and the quit-rent reserved thereon, will always lessen, and in time, will wholly support the yearly expence of government. It matters not how long the debt is in paying, so that the lands when sold be applied to the discharge of it, and for the execution of which, the Congress for the time being, will be the continental trustees.

I proceed now to the second head, viz. Which is the easiest and most practicable plan, **reconciliation** or **independance**; with some occasional remarks.

> He who takes nature for his guide is not easily beaten out of his argument, and on that ground, I answer generally—That *INDEPENDANCE* being a *SINGLE SIMPLE LINE*, contained within ourselves; and reconciliation, a matter exceedingly perplexed and complicated, and in which, a treacherous capricious court is to interfere, gives the answer without a doubt.

The present state of America is truly alarming to every man who is capable of reflexion. Without law, without government, without any other mode of power than what is founded on, and granted by courtesy. Held together by an unexampled concurrence of sentiment, which, is nevertheless subject to change, and which every secret enemy is endeavouring to dissolve. Our present condition, is, Legislation without law; wisdom without a plan; constitution without a name; and, what is strangely astonishing, perfect Independance contending for dependance. The instance is without a precedent; the case never existed before; and who can tell what may be the event? The property of no man is secure in the present unbraced system of things. The mind of the multitude is left at random, and seeing no fixed object before them, they pursue such as fancy or opinion starts. Nothing is criminal; there is no such thing as treason; wherefore, every one thinks himself at liberty to act as he pleases. The Tories dared not have assembled offensively, had they known that their lives, by that act, were forfeited to the laws of the state. A line of distinction should be drawn, between, English soldiers taken in battle, and inhabitants of America taken in arms. The first are prisoners, but the latter traitors. The one forfeits his liberty, the other his head.

Notwithstanding our wisdom, there is a visible feebleness in some of our proceedings which gives encouragement to dissensions. The Continental Belt is too loosely buckled. And if something is not done in time, it will be too late to do any thing, and we shall fall into a state, in which, neither Reconciliation nor Independance will be practicable. The king and his worthless adherents are got at their old game of dividing the Continent, and there are not wanting among us, Printers, who will be busy in spreading specious falsehoods. The artful and hypocritical letter which appeared a few months ago in two of the New-York papers, and likewise in two others, is an evidence that there are men who want either judgment or honesty.

Documents of Revolution

It is easy getting into holes and corners and talking of reconciliation: But do such men seriously consider, how difficult the task is, and how dangerous it may prove, should the Continent divide thereon. Do they take within their view, all the various orders of men whose situation and circumstances, as well as their own, are to be considered therein. Do they put themselves in the place of the sufferer whose all is already gone, and of the soldier, who hath quitted all for the defence of his country. If their ill judged moderation be suited to their own private situations only, regardless of others, the event will convince them, that "they are reckoning without their Host."

Put us, say some, on the footing we were on in sixty-three: To which I answer, the request is not now in the power of Britain to comply with, neither will she propose it; but if it were, and even should be granted, I ask, as a reasonable question, By what means is such a corrupt and faithless court to be kept to its engagements? Another parliament, nay, even the present, may hereafter repeal the obligation, on the pretence, of its being violently obtained, or unwisely granted; and in that case, Where is our redress?—No going to law with nations; cannon are the barristers of Crowns; and the sword, not of justice, but of war, decides the suit. To be on the footing of sixty-three, it is not sufficient, that the laws only be put on the same state, but, that our circumstances, likewise, be put on the same state; Our burnt and destroyed towns repaired or built up, our private losses made good, our public debts (contracted for defence) discharged; otherwise, we shall be millions worse than we were at that enviable period. Such a request, had it been complied with a year ago, would have won the heart and soul of the Continent—but now it is too late, "The Rubicon is passed."

Besides, the taking up arms, merely to enforce the repeal of a pecuniary law, seems as unwarrantable by the divine law, and as repugnant to human feelings, as the taking up arms to enforce obedience thereto. The object, on either side, doth not justify the means; for the lives of men are too valuable to be cast away on such trifles. It is the violence which is done and threatened to our persons; the destruction of our property by an armed force; the invasion of our country by fire and sword, which conscientiously qualifies the use of arms: And the instant, in which such a mode of defence became necessary, all subjection to Britain ought to have ceased; and the independancy of America, should have been considered, as dating its æra from, and published by, the first musket that was fired against her. This line is a line of consistency; neither drawn by caprice, nor extended by ambition; but produced by a chain of events, of which the colonies were not the authors.

I shall conclude these remarks, with the following timely and well intended hints. We ought to reflect, that there are three different ways, by which an independancy may hereafter be effected; and that one of those three, will one day or other, be the fate of America, viz. By the legal voice of the people in Congress; by a military power; or by a mob: It may not always happen that our soldiers are citizens, and the multitude a body of reasonable men; virtue, as I have already remarked, is not hereditary, neither is it perpetual. Should an independancy be brought about by the first of those means, we have every opportunity and every encouragement before us, to form the noblest purest constitution on the face of the earth. We have it in our power to begin the world over again. A situation, similar to the present, hath not happened since the days of Noah until now. The birthday of a new world is at hand, and a race of men, perhaps as numerous as all Europe contains, are to receive their portion of freedom from the event of a few months. The Reflexion is awful—and in this point of view, How trifling, how ridiculous, do the little, paltry cavellings, of a few weak or interested men appear, when weighed against the business of a world.

Should we neglect the present favorable and inviting period, and an Independance be hereafter effected by any other means, we must charge the consequence to ourselves, or to those rather, whose narrow and prejudiced souls, are habitually opposing the measure, without either inquiring or reflecting. There are reasons to be given in support of Independance, which men should rather privately think of, than be publicly told of. We ought not now to be debating whether we shall be independant or not, but, anxious to accomplish it on a firm, secure, and honorable basis, and uneasy rather that it is not yet began upon. Every day convinces us of its necessity. Even the Tories (if such beings yet remain among us) should, of all men, be the most solicitous to promote it; for, as the appointment of committees at first, protected them from popular rage, so, a wise and well established form of government, will be the only certain means of continuing it securely to them. Wherefore, if they have not virtue enough to be **Whigs**, they ought to have prudence enough to wish for Independence.

In short, Independance is the only **Bond** that can tye and keep us together. We shall then see our object, and our ears will be legally shut against the schemes of an intriguing, as well, as a cruel enemy. We shall then too, be on a proper footing, to treat with Britain; for there is reason to conclude, that the pride of that court, will be less hurt by treating with the American states for terms of peace, than with those, whom she denominates, "rebellious subjects," for terms of accommodation. It is our delaying it that encourages her to hope for conquest, and our backwardness tends only to prolong the war. As we have, without any good effect therefrom, withheld our trade to obtain a redress of our grievances, let us now try the alternative, by independantly redressing them ourselves, and then offering to open the trade. The mercantile and reasonable part in England, will be still with us; because, peace with trade, is preferable to war without it. And if this offer be not accepted, other courts may be applied to.

On these grounds I rest the matter. And as no offer hath yet been made to refute the doctrine contained in the former editions of this pamphlet, it is a negative proof, that either the doctrine cannot be refuted, or, that the party in favour of it are too numerous to be opposed. **Wherefore**, instead of gazing at each other with suspicious or doubtful curiosity; let each of us, hold out to his neighbour the hearty hand of friendship, and unite in drawing a line, which, like an act of oblivion shall bury in forgetfulness every former dissension. Let the names of Whig and Tory be extinct; and let none other be heard among us, than those of a good citizen, an open and resolute friend, and a virtuous supporter of the **rights** of **mankind** and of the FREE AND INDEPENDANT STATES OF AMERICA.

Documents of Revolution

To the Representatives of the Religious Society of the People called Quakers, or to so many of them as were concerned in publishing the late piece, entitled "The Ancient Testimony and Principles of the People called Quakers renewed, with Respect to the King and Government, and touching the Commotions now prevailing in these and other parts of America addressed to the People in General."

The Writer of this, is one of those few, who never dishonours religion either by ridiculing, or cavilling at any denomination whatsoever. To God, and not to man, are all men accountable on the score of religion. Wherefore, this epistle is not so properly addressed to you as a religious, but as a political body, dabbling in matters, which the professed Quietude of your Principles instruct you not to meddle with.

As you have, without a proper authority for so doing, put yourselves in the place of the whole body of the Quakers, so, the writer of this, in order to be on an equal rank with yourselves, is under the necessity, of putting himself in the place of all those, who, approve the very writings and principles, against which your testimony is directed: And he hath chosen this singular situation, in order, that you might discover in him that presumption of character which you cannot see in yourselves. For neither he nor you can have any claim or title to Political Representation.

When men have departed from the right way, it is no wonder that they stumble and fall. And it is evident from the manner in which ye have managed your testimony, that politics, (as a religious body of men) is not your proper Walk; for however well adapted it might appear to you, it is, nevertheless, a jumble of good and bad put unwisely together, and the conclusion drawn therefrom, both unnatural and unjust.

The two first pages, (and the whole doth not make four) we give you credit for, and expect the same civility from you, because the love and desire of peace is not confined to Quakerism, it is the natural, as well the religious wish of all denominations of men. And on this ground, as men labouring to establish an Independant Constitution of our own, do we exceed all others in our hope, end, and aim. Our plan is peace for ever. We are tired of contention with Britain, and can see no real end to it but in a final separation. We act consistently, because for the sake of introducing an endless and uninterrupted peace, do we bear the evils and burthens of the present day. We are endeavoring, and will steadily continue to endeavour, to separate and dissolve a connexion which hath already filled our land with blood; and which, while the name of it remains, will be the fatal cause of future mischiefs to both countries.

We fight neither for revenge nor conquest; neither from pride nor passion; we are not insulting the world with our fleets and armies, nor ravaging the globe for plunder. Beneath the shade of our own vines are we attacked; in our own houses, and on our own lands, is the violence committed against us. We view our enemies in the character of Highwaymen and Housebreakers, and having no defence for ourselves in the civil law, are obliged to punish them by the military one, and apply the sword, in the very case, where you have before now, applied the halter—Perhaps we feel for the ruined and insulted sufferers in all and every part of the continent, with a degree of tenderness which hath not yet made its way into some of your bosoms. But be ye sure that ye mistake not the cause and ground of your Testimony. Call not coldness of soul, religion; nor put the Bigot in the place of the Christian.

O ye partial ministers of your own acknowledged principles. If the bearing arms be sinful, the first going to war must be more so, by all the difference between wilful attack and unavoidable defence. Wherefore, if ye really preach from conscience, and mean not to make a political hobby-horse of your religion, convince the world thereof, by proclaiming your doctrine to our enemies, for they likewise bear **arms**. Give us proof of your sincerity by publishing it at St. James's, to the commanders in chief at Boston, to the Admirals and Captains who are piratically ravaging our coasts, and to all the murdering miscreants who are acting in authority under **him** whom ye profess to serve. Had ye the honest soul of Barclay [1] ye would preach repentance to your king; Ye would tell the Royal Wretch his sins, and warn him of eternal ruin. Ye would not spend your partial invectives against the injured and the insulted only, but, like faithful ministers, would cry aloud and spare none. Say not that ye are persecuted, neither endeavour to make us the authors of that reproach, which, ye are bringing upon yourselves; for we testify unto all men, that we do not complain against you because ye are Quakers, but because ye pretend to be and are **not** Quakers.

[1] "Thou hast tasted of prosperity and adversity; thou knowest what it is to be banished thy native country, to be over-ruled as well as to rule, and set upon the throne; and being oppressed thou hast reason to know how hateful the oppressor is

both to God and man: If after all these warnings and advertisements, thou dost not turn unto the Lord with all thy heart, but forget him who remembered thee in thy distress, and give up thyself to follow lust and vanity, surely great will be thy condemnation.—Against which snare, as well as the temptation of those who may or do feed thee, and prompt thee to evil, the most excellent and prevalent remedy will be, to apply thyself to that light of Christ which shineth in thy conscience, and which neither can, nor will flatter thee, nor suffer thee to be at ease in thy sins."

—Barclay's address to Charles II.

Alas! it seems by the particular tendency of some part of your testimony, and other parts of your conduct, as if, all sin was reduced to, and comprehended in, the act of bearing arms, and that by the people only. Ye appear to us, to have mistaken party for conscience; because, the general tenor of your actions wants uniformity: And it is exceedingly difficult to us to give credit to many of your pretended scruples; because, we see them made by the same men, who, in the very instant that they are exclaiming against the mammon of this world, are nevertheless, hunting after it with a step as steady as Time, and an appetite as keen as Death.

The quotation which ye have made from Proverbs, in the third page of your testimony, that, "when a man's ways please the Lord, he maketh even his enemies to be at peace with him"; is very unwisely chosen on your part; because, it amounts to a proof, that the king's ways (whom ye are desirous of supporting) do not please the Lord, otherwise, his reign would be in peace.

I now proceed to the latter part of your testimony, and that, for which all the foregoing seems only an introduction, viz.

"It hath ever been our judgment and principle, since we were called to profess the light of Christ Jesus, manifested in our consciences unto this day, that the setting up and putting down kings and governments, is God's peculiar prerogative; for causes best known to himself: And that it is not our business to have any hand or contrivance therein; nor to be busy bodies above our station, much less to plot and contrive the ruin, or overturn of any of them, but to pray for the king, and safety of our nation, and good of all men: That we may live a peaceable and quiet life, in all godliness and honesty; under the government which God is pleased to set over us."—If these are really your principles why do ye not abide by them? Why do ye not leave that, which ye call God's Work, to be managed by himself? These very principles instruct you to wait with patience and humility, for the event of all public measures, and to receive that event as the divine will towards you. Wherefore, what occasion is there for your political testimony if you fully believe what it contains: And the very publishing it proves, that either, ye do not believe what ye profess, or have not virtue enough to practise what ye believe.

The principles of Quakerism have a direct tendency to make a man the quiet and inoffensive subject of any, and every government which is set over him. And if the setting up and putting down of kings and governments is God's peculiar prerogative, he most certainly will not be robbed thereof by us; wherefore, the principle itself leads you to approve of every thing, which ever happened, or may happen to kings as being his work. **Oliver Cromwell** thanks you. **Charles**, then, died not by the hands of man; and should the present Proud Imitator of him, come to the same untimely end, the writers and publishers of the Testimony, are bound, by the doctrine it contains, to applaud the fact. Kings are not taken away by miracles, neither are changes in governments brought about by any other means than such as are common and human; and such as we are now using. Even the dispersion of the Jews, though foretold by our Saviour, was effected by arms. Wherefore, as ye refuse to be the means on one side, ye ought not to be meddlers on the other; but to wait the issue in silence; and unless ye can produce divine authority, to prove, that the Almighty who hath created and placed this new world, at the greatest distance it could possibly stand, east and west, from every part of the old, doth, nevertheless, disapprove of its being independant of the corrupt and abandoned court of Britain, unless I say, ye can shew this, how can ye on the ground of your principles, justify the exciting and stirring up the people "firmly to unite in the abhorrence of all such writings, and measures, as evidence a desire and design to break off the happy connexion we have hitherto enjoyed, with the kingdom of Great-Britain, and our just and necessary subordination to the king, and those who are lawfully placed in authority under him." What a slap of the face is here! the men, who in the very paragraph before, have quietly and passively resigned up the ordering, altering, and disposal of kings and governments, into the hands of God, are now, recalling their principles, and putting in for a share of the business. Is it possible, that the conclusion, which is here justly quoted, can any ways follow from the doctrine laid down? The inconsistency is too glaring not to be seen; the absurdity too great not to be laughed at; and such as could only have been made by those, whose understandings were darkened by the narrow and crabby spirit of a despairing political party; for ye are not to be considered as the whole body of the Quakers but only as a factional and fractional part thereof.

Here ends the examination of your testimony; (which I call upon no man to abhor, as ye have done, but only to read and judge of fairly;) to which I subjoin the following remark; "That the setting up and putting down of kings," most certainly mean, the making him a king, who is yet not so, and the making him no king who is already one. And pray what hath this to do in the present case? We neither mean to set up nor to put down, neither to make nor to unmake, but to have nothing to do with them. Wherefore, your testimony in whatever light it is viewed serves only to dishonor your judgement, and for many other reasons had better have been let alone than published.

First, Because it tends to the decrease and reproach of all religion whatever, and is of the utmost danger to society, to make it a party in political disputes.

Secondly, Because it exhibits a body of men, numbers of whom disavow the publishing political testimonies, as being concerned therein and approvers thereof.

Thirdly, Because it hath a tendency to undo that continental harmony and friendship which yourselves by your late liberal and charitable donations hath lent a hand to establish; and the preservation of which, is of the utmost consequence to us all.

And here without anger or resentment I bid you farewell. Sincerely wishing, that as men and christians, ye may always fully and uninterruptedly enjoy every civil and religious right; and be, in your turn, the means of securing it to others; but that the example which ye have unwisely set, of mingling religion with politics, may be disavowed and reprobated by every inhabitant of **America**.

F I N I S.

Documents of Revolution

HISTORICAL CONTEXT

Paine has a claim to the title The Father of the American Revolution, which rests on his pamphlets, especially Common Sense, which crystallized sentiment for independence in 1776. It was published in Philadelphia on January 10, 1776, and signed anonymously "by an Englishman". It became an immediate success, quickly spreading 100,000 copies in three months to the two million residents of the 13 colonies. During the course of the American Revolution, a total of about 500,000 copies were sold, including unauthorized editions. Paine's original title for the pamphlet was Plain Truth, but Paine's friend, pro-independence advocate Benjamin Rush, suggested Common Sense instead.

The pamphlet came into circulation in January 1776, after the Revolution had started. It was passed around and often read aloud in taverns, contributing significantly to spreading the idea of republicanism, bolstering enthusiasm for separation from Britain, and encouraging recruitment for the Continental Army. Paine provided a new and convincing argument for independence by advocating a complete break with history. Common Sense is oriented to the future in a way that compels the reader to make an immediate choice. It offers a solution for Americans disgusted with and alarmed at the threat of tyranny.

Paine's attack on monarchy in Common Sense is essentially an attack on George III. Whereas colonial resentments were originally directed primarily against the king's ministers and Parliament, Paine laid the responsibility firmly at the king's door. Common Sense was the most widely read pamphlet of the American Revolution. It was a clarion call for unity against the corrupt British court, so as to realize America's providential role in providing an asylum for liberty. Written in a direct and lively style, it denounced the decaying despotisms of Europe and pilloried hereditary monarchy as an absurdity. At a time when many still hoped for reconciliation with Britain, Common Sense demonstrated to many the inevitability of separation.

Paine was not on the whole expressing original ideas in Common Sense, but rather employing rhetoric as a means to arouse resentment of the Crown. To achieve these ends, he pioneered a style of political writing suited to the democratic society he envisioned, with Common Sense serving as a primary example. Part of Paine's work was to render complex ideas intelligible to average readers of the day, with clear, concise writing unlike the formal, learned style favored by many of Paine's contemporaries. Scholars have put forward various explanations to account for its success, including the historic moment, Paine's easy-to-understand style, his democratic ethos, and his use of psychology and ideology.

Common Sense was immensely popular in disseminating to a very wide audience ideas that were already in common use among the elite who comprised Congress and the leadership cadre of the emerging nation, who rarely cited Paine's arguments in their public calls for independence.The pamphlet probably had little direct influence on the Continental Congress' decision to issue a Declaration of Independence, since that body was more concerned with how declaring independence would affect the war effort. One distinctive idea in Common Sense is Paine's beliefs regarding the peaceful nature of republics; his views were an early and strong conception of what scholars would come to call the democratic peace theory.

Loyalists vigorously attacked Common Sense; one attack, titled Plain Truth (1776), by Marylander James Chalmers, said Paine was a political quack and warned that without monarchy, the government would "degenerate into democracy". Even some American revolutionaries objected to Common Sense; late in life John Adams called it a "crapulous mass". Adams disagreed with the type of radical democracy promoted by Paine (that men who did not own property should still be allowed to vote and hold public office) and published Thoughts on Government in 1776 to advocate a more conservative approach to republicanism.

Sophia Rosenfeld argues that Paine was highly innovative in his use of the commonplace notion of "common sense". He synthesized various philosophical and political uses of the term in a way that permanently impacted American political thought. He used two ideas from Scottish Common Sense Realism: that ordinary people can indeed make sound judgments on major political issues, and that there exists a body of popular wisdom that is readily apparent to anyone. Paine also used a notion of "common sense" favored by philosophes in the Continental Enlightenment. They held that common sense could refute the claims of traditional institutions. Thus, Paine used "common sense" as a weapon to delegitimize the monarchy and overturn prevailing conventional wisdom. Rosenfeld concludes that the phenomenal appeal of his pamphlet resulted from his synthesis of popular and elite elements in the independence movement.

According to historian Robert Middlekauff, Common Sense became immensely popular mainly because Paine appealed to widespread convictions. Monarchy, he said, was preposterous and it had a heathenish origin. It was an institution of the devil. Paine pointed to the Old Testament, where almost all kings had seduced the Israelites to worship idols instead of God. Paine also denounced aristocracy, which together with monarchy were "two ancient tyrannies." They violated the laws of nature, human reason, and the "universal order of things," which began with God. That was, Middlekauff says, exactly what most Americans wanted to hear. He calls the Revolutionary generation "the children of the twice-born". because in their childhood they had experienced the Great Awakening, which, for the first time, had tied Americans together, transcending denominational and ethnic boundaries and giving them a sense of patriotism.

ON COMMON SENSE

"No writer has exceeded Paine in ease and familiarity of style, in perspicuity of expression, happiness of elucidation, and in simple and unassuming language."

Thomas Jefferson

"A pamphlet called 'Commonsense' makes a great noise. One of the vilest things that ever was published to the world. Full of false representations, lies, calumny, and treason, whose principles are to subvert all Kingly Governments and erect an Independent Republic."

Nicholas Cresswell

"I dreaded the effect so popular a pamphlet might have among the people, and determined to do all in my Power to counteract the effect of it."

John Adams

"Its effects were sudden and extensive upon the American mind. It was read by public men."

Dr. Benjamin Rush

"Have you read the pamphlet Common Sense? I never saw such a masterful performance.... In short, I own myself convinced, by the arguments, of the necessity of separation."

General Charles Lee

THE DECLARATION OF INDEPENDENCE OF THE UNITED STATES OF AMERICA

When in the Course of human events, it becomes necessary for one people to dissolve the political bands which have connected them with another, and to assume, among the Powers of the earth, the separate and equal station to which the Laws of Nature and of Nature's God entitle them, a decent respect to the opinions of mankind requires that they should declare the causes which impel them to the separation.

We hold these truths to be self-evident, that all men are created equal, that they are endowed by their Creator with certain unalienable Rights, that among these are Life, Liberty, and the pursuit of Happiness. That to secure these rights, Governments are instituted among Men, deriving their just powers from the consent of the governed, That whenever any Form of Government becomes destructive of these ends, it is the Right of the People to alter or to abolish it, and to institute new Government, laying its foundation on such principles and organizing its powers in such form, as to them shall seem most likely to effect their Safety and Happiness. Prudence, indeed, will dictate that Governments long established should not be changed for light and transient causes; and accordingly all experience hath shown, that mankind are more disposed to suffer, while evils are sufferable, than to right themselves by abolishing the forms to which they are accustomed. But when a long train of abuses and usurpations, pursuing invariably the same Object evinces a design to reduce them under absolute Despotism, it is their right, it is their duty, to throw off such Government, and to provide new Guards for their future security. —Such has been the patient sufferance of these Colonies; and such is now the necessity which constrains them to alter their former Systems of Government. The history of the present King of Great Britain is a history of repeated injuries and usurpations, all having in direct object the establishment of an absolute Tyranny over these States. To prove this, let Facts be submitted to a candid world.

He has refused his Assent to Laws, the most wholesome and necessary for the public good.

He has forbidden his Governors to pass Laws of immediate and pressing importance, unless suspended in their operation till his Assent should be obtained; and when so suspended, he has utterly neglected to attend to them.

He has refused to pass other Laws for the accommodation of large districts of people, unless those people would relinquish the right of Representation in the Legislature, a right inestimable to them and formidable to tyrants only.

He has called together legislative bodies at places unusual, uncomfortable, and distant from the depository of their Public Records, for the sole purpose of fatiguing them into compliance with his measures.

He has dissolved Representative Houses repeatedly, for opposing with manly firmness his invasions on the rights of the people.

He has refused for a long time, after such dissolutions, to cause others to be elected; whereby the Legislative Powers, incapable of Annihilation, have returned to the People at large for their exercise; the State remaining in the mean time exposed to all the dangers of invasion from without, and convulsions within.

He has endeavoured to prevent the population of these States; for that purpose obstructing the Laws of Naturalization of Foreigners; refusing to pass others to encourage their migration hither, and raising the conditions of new Appropriations of Lands.

He has obstructed the Administration of Justice, by refusing his Assent to Laws for establishing Judiciary Powers.

He has made judges dependent on his Will alone, for the tenure of their offices, and the amount and payment of their salaries.

He has erected a multitude of New Offices, and sent hither swarms of Officers to harass our People, and eat out their substance.

He has kept among us, in times of peace, Standing Armies without the Consent of our legislatures.

He has affected to render the Military independent of and superior to the Civil Power.

He has combined with others to subject us to a jurisdiction foreign to our constitution, and unacknowledged by our laws; giving his Assent to their Acts of pretended legislation:

For quartering large bodies of armed troops among us:

For protecting them, by a mock Trial, from Punishment for any Murders which they should commit on the Inhabitants of these States:

For cutting off our Trade with all parts of the world:

For imposing taxes on us without our Consent:

For depriving us, in many cases, of the benefits of Trial by Jury:

For transporting us beyond Seas to be tried for pretended offences:

For abolishing the free System of English Laws in a neighbouring Province, establishing therein an Arbitrary government, and enlarging its Boundaries so as to render it at once an example and fit instrument for introducing the same absolute rule into these Colonies:

For taking away our Charters, abolishing our most valuable Laws, and altering fundamentally the Forms of our Governments:

For suspending our own Legislatures, and declaring themselves invested with Power to legislate for us in all cases whatsoever.

He has abdicated Government here, by declaring us out of his Protection and waging War against us.

He has plundered our seas, ravaged our Coasts, burnt our towns, and destroyed the lives of our people.

He is at this time transporting large armies of foreign mercenaries to compleat the works of death, desolation and tyranny, already begun with circumstances of Cruelty & perfidy scarcely paralleled in the most barbarous ages, and totally unworthy of the Head of a civilized nation.

He has constrained our fellow Citizens taken Captive on the high Seas to bear Arms against their Country, to become the executioners of their friends and Brethren, or to fall themselves by their Hands.

He has excited domestic insurrections amongst us, and has endeavoured to bring on the inhabitants of our frontiers, the merciless Indian Savages, whose known rule of warfare, is an undistinguished destruction of all ages, sexes and conditions.

In every stage of these Oppressions We have Petitioned for Redress in the most humble terms: Our repeated Petitions have been answered only by repeated injury. A Prince, whose character is thus marked by every act which may define a Tyrant, is unfit to be the ruler of a free People.

Nor have We been wanting in attention to our British brethren. We have warned them from time to time of attempts by their legislature to extend an unwarrantable jurisdiction over us. We have reminded them of the circumstances of our emigration and settlement here. We have appealed to their native justice and magnanimity, and we have conjured them by the ties of our common kindred to disavow these usurpations, which would inevitably interrupt our connections and correspondence. They too have been deaf to the voice of justice and of consanguinity. We must, therefore, acquiesce in the necessity, which denounces our Separation, and hold them, as we hold the rest of mankind, Enemies in War, in Peace Friends.

We, therefore, the Representatives of the United States of America, in General Congress, Assembled, appealing to the Supreme Judge of the world for the rectitude of our intentions, do, in the Name, and by the Authority of the good People of these Colonies, solemnly publish and declare, That these United Colonies are, and of Right ought to be Free and Independent States; that they are Absolved from all Allegiance to the British Crown, and that all political connection between them and the State of Great Britain, is and ought to be totally dissolved; and that as Free and Independent States, they have full Power to levy War, conclude Peace, contract Alliances, establish Commerce, and to do all other Acts and Things which Independent States may of right do. And for the support of this Declaration, with a firm reliance on the Protection of Divine Providence, we mutually pledge to each other our Lives, our Fortunes and our sacred Honor.

Documents of Revolution

ARTICLES OF CONFEDERATION (1777)

To all to whom these Presents shall come, we, the undersigned Delegates of the States affixed to our Names send greeting. Whereas the Delegates of the United States of America in Congress assembled did on the fifteenth day of November in the year of our Lord One Thousand Seven Hundred and Seventy seven, and in the Second Year of the Independence of America agree to certain articles of Confederation and perpetual Union between the States of Newhampshire, Massachusetts-bay, Rhodeisland and Providence Plantations, Connecticut, New York, New Jersey, Pennsylvania, Delaware, Maryland, Virginia, North Carolina, South Carolina, and Georgia in the Words following, viz. "Articles of Confederation and perpetual Union between the States of Newhampshire, Massachusetts-bay, Rhodeisland and Providence Plantations, Connecticut, New York, New Jersey, Pennsylvania, Delaware, Maryland, Virginia, North Carolina, South Carolina, and Georgia.

Article I. The Stile of this confederacy shall be, "The United States of America."

Article II. Each state retains its sovereignty, freedom and independence, and every Power, Jurisdiction and right, which is not by this confederation expressly delegated to the United States, in Congress assembled.

Article III. The said states hereby severally enter into a firm league of friendship with each other, for their common defence, the security of their Liberties, and their mutual and general welfare, binding themselves to assist each other, against all force offered to, or attacks made upon them, or any of them, on account of religion, sovereignty, trade, or any other pretence whatever.

Article IV. The better to secure and perpetuate mutual friendship and intercourse among the people of the different states in this union, the free inhabitants of each of these states, paupers, vagabonds and fugitives from Justice excepted, shall be entitled to all privileges and immunities of free citizens in the several states; and the people of each state shall have free ingress and regress to and from any other state, and shall enjoy therein all the privileges of trade and commerce, subject to the same duties, impositions and restrictions as the inhabitants thereof respectively, provided that such restrictions shall not extend so far as to prevent the removal of property imported into any state, to any other State of which the Owner is an inhabitant; provided also that no imposition, duties or restriction shall be laid by any state, on the property of the united states, or either of them.

If any Person guilty of, or charged with, treason, felony, or other high misdemeanor in any state, shall flee from Justice, and be found in any of the united states, he shall upon demand of the Governor or executive power of the state from which he fled, be delivered up, and removed to the state having jurisdiction of his offence.

Full faith and credit shall be given in each of these states to the records, acts and judicial proceedings of the courts and magistrates of every other state.

Article V. For the more convenient management of the general interests of the united states, delegates shall be annually appointed in such manner as the legislature of each state shall direct, to meet in Congress on the first Monday in November, in every year, with a power reserved to each state to recall its delegates, or any of them, at any time within the year, and to send others in their stead, for the remainder of the Year.

No State shall be represented in Congress by less than two, nor by more than seven Members; and no person shall be capable of being delegate for more than three years, in any term of six years; nor shall any person, being a delegate, be capable of holding any office under the united states, for which he, or another for his benefit receives any salary, fees or emolument of any kind.

Each State shall maintain its own delegates in a meeting of the states, and while they act as members of the committee of the states.

Documents of Revolution

In determining questions in the united states, in Congress assembled, each state shall have one vote.

Freedom of speech and debate in Congress shall not be impeached or questioned in any Court, or place out of Congress, and the members of congress shall be protected in their persons from arrests and imprisonments, during the time of their going to and from, and attendance on congress, except for treason, felony, or breach of the peace.

Article VI. No State, without the Consent of the united States, in congress assembled, shall send any embassy to, or receive any embassy from, or enter into any conferrence, agreement, alliance, or treaty, with any King prince or state; nor shall any person holding any office of profit or trust under the united states, or any of them, accept of any present, emolument, office, or title of any kind whatever, from any king, prince, or foreign state; nor shall the united states, in congress assembled, or any of them, grant any title of nobility.

No two or more states shall enter into any treaty, confederation, or alliance whatever between them, without the consent of the united states, in congress assembled, specifying accurately the purposes for which the same is to be entered into, and how long it shall continue.

No State shall lay any imposts or duties, which may interfere with any stipulations in treaties, entered into by the united States in congress assembled, with any king, prince, or State, in pursuance of any treaties already proposed by congress, to the courts of France and Spain.

No vessels of war shall be kept up in time of peace, by any state, except such number only, as shall be deemed necessary by the united states, in congress assembled, for the defence of such state, or its trade; nor shall any body of forces be kept up, by any state, in time of peace, except such number only as, in the judgment of the united states, in congress assembled, shall be deemed requisite to garrison the forts necessary for the defence of such state; but every state shall always keep up a well regulated and disciplined militia, sufficiently armed and accounted, and shall provide and constantly have ready for use, in public stores, a due number of field pieces and tents, and a proper quantity of arms, ammunition, and camp equipage.

No State shall engage in any war without the consent of the united States in congress assembled, unless such State be actually invaded by enemies, or shall have received certain advice of a resolution being formed by some nation of Indians to invade such State, and the danger is so imminent as not to admit of a delay till the united states in congress assembled, can be consulted: nor shall any state grant commissions to any ships or vessels of war, nor letters of marque or reprisal, except it be after a declaration of war by the united states in congress assembled, and then only against the kingdom or State, and the subjects thereof, against which war has been so declared, and under such regulations as shall be established by the united states in congress assembled, unless such state be infested by pirates, in which case vessels of war may be fitted out for that occasion, and kept so long as the danger shall continue, or until the united states in congress assembled shall determine otherwise.

Article VII. When land forces are raised by any state, for the common defence, all officers of or under the rank of colonel, shall be appointed by the legislature of each state respectively by whom such forces shall be raised, or in such manner as such state shall direct, and all vacancies shall be filled up by the state which first made appointment.

Article VIII. All charges of war, and all other expenses that shall be incurred for the common defence or general welfare, and allowed by the united states in congress assembled, shall be defrayed out of a common treasury, which shall be supplied by the several states, in proportion to the value of all land within each state, granted to or surveyed for any Person, as such land and the buildings and improvements thereon shall be estimated, according to such mode as the united states, in congress assembled, shall, from time to time, direct and appoint. The taxes for paying that proportion shall be laid and levied by the authority and direction of the legislatures of the several states within the time agreed upon by the united states in congress assembled.

Article IX. The united states, in congress assembled, shall have the sole and exclusive right and power of determining on peace and war, except in the cases mentioned in the sixth article - of sending and receiving ambassadors - entering into treaties and alliances, provided that no treaty of commerce shall be made, whereby the legislative power of the respective states shall be restrained from imposing such imposts and duties on foreigners, as their own people are subjected to, or from prohibiting the exportation or importation of any species of goods or commodities whatsoever - of establishing rules for deciding, in all cases, what captures on land or water shall be legal, and in what manner prizes taken by land or naval forces in the service of the united Sates, shall be divided or appropriated - of granting letters of marque and reprisal in times of peace - appointing courts for the trial of piracies and felonies committed on the high seas; and establishing courts; for receiving and determining finally appeals in all cases of captures; provided that no member of congress shall be appointed a judge of any of the said courts.

The united states, in congress assembled, shall also be the last resort on appeal, in all disputes and differences now subsisting, or that hereafter may arise between two or more states concerning boundary, jurisdiction, or any other cause whatever; which authority shall always be exercised in the manner following. Whenever the legislative or executive authority, or lawful agent of any state in controversy with another, shall present a petition to congress, stating the matter in question, and praying for a hearing, notice thereof shall be given, by order of congress, to the legislative or executive authority of the other state in controversy, and a day assigned for the appearance of the parties by their lawful agents, who shall then be directed to appoint, by joint consent, commissioners or judges to constitute a court for hearing and determining the matter in question: but if they cannot agree, congress shall name three persons out of each of the united states, and from the list of such persons each party shall alternately strike out one, the petitioners beginning, until the number shall be reduced to thirteen; and from that number not less than seven, nor more than nine names, as congress shall direct, shall, in the presence of congress, be drawn out by lot, and the persons whose names shall be so drawn, or any five of them, shall be commissioners or judges, to hear and finally determine the controversy, so always as a major part of the judges, who shall hear the cause, shall agree in the determination: and if either party shall neglect to attend at the day appointed, without showing reasons which congress shall judge sufficient, or being present, shall refuse to strike, the congress shall proceed to nominate three persons out of each State, and the secretary of congress shall strike in behalf of such party absent or refusing; and the judgment and sentence of the court, to be appointed in the manner before prescribed, shall be final and conclusive; and if any of the parties shall refuse to submit to the authority of such court, or to appear or defend their claim or cause, the court shall nevertheless proceed to pronounce sentence, or judgment, which shall in like manner be final and decisive; the judgment or sentence and other proceedings being in either case transmitted to congress, and lodged among the acts of congress, for the security of the parties concerned: provided that every commissioner, before he sits in judgment, shall take an oath to be administered by one of the judges of the supreme or superior court of the State where the cause shall be tried, "well and truly to hear and determine the matter in question, according to the best of his judgment, without favour, affection, or hope of reward: "provided, also, that no State shall be deprived of territory for the benefit of the united states.

All controversies concerning the private right of soil claimed under different grants of two or more states, whose jurisdictions as they may respect such lands, and the states which passed such grants are adjusted, the said grants or either of them being at the same time claimed to have originated antecedent to such settlement of jurisdiction, shall, on the petition of either party to the congress of the united states, be finally determined, as near as may be, in the same manner as is before prescribed for deciding disputes respecting territorial jurisdiction between different states.

The united states, in congress assembled, shall also have the sole and exclusive right and power of regulating the alloy and value of coin struck by their own authority, or by that of the respective states - fixing the standard of weights and measures throughout the united states - regulating the trade and managing all affairs with the Indians, not members of any of the states; provided that the legislative right of any state, within its own limits, be not infringed or violated - establishing and regulating post-offices from one state to another, throughout all the united states, and exacting such postage on the papers passing through the same, as may be requisite to defray the expenses of the said office - appointing all officers of the land forces in the service of the united States, excepting regimental officers - appointing all the officers of the naval forces, and commissioning all officers whatever in the service of the united states; making rules for the government and regulation of the said land and naval forces, and directing their operations.

The united States, in congress assembled, shall have authority to appoint a committee, to sit in the recess of congress, to be denominated, "A Committee of the States," and to consist of one delegate from each State; and to appoint such other committees and civil officers as may be necessary for managing the general affairs of the united states under their direction - to appoint one of their number to preside; provided that no person be allowed to serve in the office of president more than one year in any term of three years; to ascertain the necessary sums of money to be raised for the service of the united states, and to appropriate and apply the same for defraying the public expenses; to borrow money or emit bills on the credit of the united states, transmitting every half year to the respective states an account of the sums of money so borrowed or emitted, - to build and equip a navy - to agree upon the number of land forces, and to make requisitions from each state for its quota, in proportion to the number of white inhabitants in such state, which requisition shall be binding; and thereupon the legislature of each state shall appoint the regimental officers, raise the men, and clothe, arm, and equip them, in a soldier-like manner, at the expense of the united states; and the officers and men so clothed, armed, and equipped, shall march to the place appointed, and within the time agreed on by the united states, in congress assembled; but if the united states, in congress assembled, shall, on consideration of circumstances, judge proper that any state should not raise men, or should raise a smaller number than its quota, and that any other state should raise a greater number of men than the quota thereof, such extra number shall be raised, officered, clothed, armed, and equipped in the same manner as the quota of such state, unless the legislature of such state shall judge that such extra number cannot be safely spared out of the same, in which case they shall raise, officer, clothe, arm, and equip, as many of such extra number as they judge can be safely spared. And the officers and men so clothed, armed, and equipped, shall march to the place appointed, and within the time agreed on by the united states in congress assembled.

The united states, in congress assembled, shall never engage in a war, nor grant letters of marque and reprisal in time of peace, nor enter into any treaties or alliances, nor coin money, nor regulate the value thereof nor ascertain the sums and expenses necessary for the defence and welfare of the united states, or any of them, nor emit bills, nor borrow money on the credit of the united states, nor appropriate money, nor agree upon the number of vessels of war to be built or purchased, or the number of land or sea forces to be raised, nor appoint a commander in chief of the army or navy, unless nine states assent to the same, nor shall a question on any other point, except for adjourning from day to day, be determined, unless by the votes of a majority of the united states in congress assembled.

The congress of the united states shall have power to adjourn to any time within the year, and to any place within the united states, so that no period of adjournment be for a longer duration than the space of six Months, and shall publish the Journal of their proceedings monthly, except such parts thereof relating to treaties, alliances, or military operations, as in their judgment require secrecy; and the yeas and nays of the delegates of each State, on any question, shall be entered on the Journal, when it is desired by any delegate; and the delegates of a State, or any of them, at his or their request, shall be furnished with a transcript of the said Journal, except such parts as are above excepted, to lay before the legislatures of the several states.

Article X. The committee of the states, or any nine of them, shall be authorized to execute, in the recess of congress, such of the powers of congress as the united states, in congress assembled, by the consent of nine states, shall, from time to time, think expedient to vest them with; provided that no power be delegated to the said committee, for the exercise of which, by the articles of confederation, the voice of nine states, in the congress of the united states assembled, is requisite.

Article XI. Canada acceding to this confederation, and joining in the measures of the united states, shall be admitted into, and entitled to all the advantages of this union: but no other colony shall be admitted into the same, unless such admission be agreed to by nine states.

Article XII. All bills of credit emitted, monies borrowed, and debts contracted by or under the authority of congress, before the assembling of the united states, in pursuance of the present confederation, shall be deemed and considered as a charge against the united States, for payment and satisfaction whereof the said united states and the public faith are hereby solemnly pledged.

Article XIII. Every State shall abide by the determinations of the united states, in congress assembled, on all questions which by this confederation are submitted to them. And the Articles of this confederation shall be inviolably observed by every state, and the union shall be perpetual; nor shall any alteration at any time hereafter be made in any of them, unless such alteration be agreed to in a congress of the united states, and be afterwards con-firmed by the legislatures of every state.

And Whereas it hath pleased the Great Governor of the World to incline the hearts of the legislatures we respectively represent in congress, to approve of, and to authorize us to ratify the said articles of confederation and perpetual union, Know Ye, that we, the undersigned delegates, by virtue of the power and authority to us given for that purpose, do, by these presents, in the name and in behalf of our respective constituents, fully and entirely ratify and confirm each and every of the said articles of confederation and perpetual union, and all and singular the matters and things therein contained. And we do further solemnly plight and engage the faith of our respective constituents, that they shall abide by the determinations of the united states in congress assembled, on all questions, which by the said confederation are submitted to them. And that the articles thereof shall be inviolably observed by the states we respectively represent, and that the union shall be perpetual. In Witness whereof, we have hereunto set our hands, in Congress. Done at Philadelphia, in the State of Pennsylvania, the ninth Day of July, in the Year of our Lord one Thousand seven Hundred and Seventy eight, and in the third year of the Independence of America.

Documents of Revolution

THE FEDERALIST PAPERS

By

Alexander Hamilton,
John Jay

James Madison

Under the pseudonym "Publius"

Documents of Revolution

ABOUT THE FEDERLIST PAPERS

The Federalist (later known as The Federalist Papers) is a collection of 85 articles and essays written by Alexander Hamilton, James Madison, and John Jay under the pseudonym "Publius" to promote the ratification of the United States Constitution. The first 77 of these essays were published serially in the Independent Journal, the New York Packet, and The Daily Advertiser between October 1787 and April 1788. A two-volume compilation of these 77 essays and eight others was published as The Federalist: A Collection of Essays, Written in Favour of the New Constitution, as Agreed upon by the Federal Convention, September 17, 1787 by publishing firm J. & A. McLean in March and May 1788. The collection was commonly known as The Federalist until the name The Federalist Papers emerged in the 20th century.

"Federalist No. 10" is generally regarded as the most important of the 85 articles from a philosophical perspective. In it, Madison discusses the means of preventing rule by majority faction and advocates a large, commercial republic. This is complemented by "Federalist No. 14", in which Madison takes the measure of the United States, declares it appropriate for an extended republic, and concludes with a memorable defense of the constitutional and political creativity of the Federal Convention. In "Federalist No. 84", Hamilton makes the case that there is no need to amend the Constitution by adding a Bill of Rights, insisting that the various provisions in the proposed Constitution protecting liberty amount to a "bill of rights". "Federalist No. 78", also written by Hamilton, lays the groundwork for the doctrine of judicial review by federal courts of federal legislation or executive acts. "Federalist No. 70" presents Hamilton's case for a one-man chief executive. In "Federalist No. 39", Madison presents the clearest exposition of what has come to be called "Federalism". In "Federalist No. 51", Madison distills arguments for checks and balances in an essay often quoted for its justification of government as "the greatest of all reflections on human nature."

According to historian Richard B. Morris, the essays that make up The Federalist Papers are an "incomparable exposition of the Constitution, a classic in political science unsurpassed in both breadth and depth by the product of any later American writer"

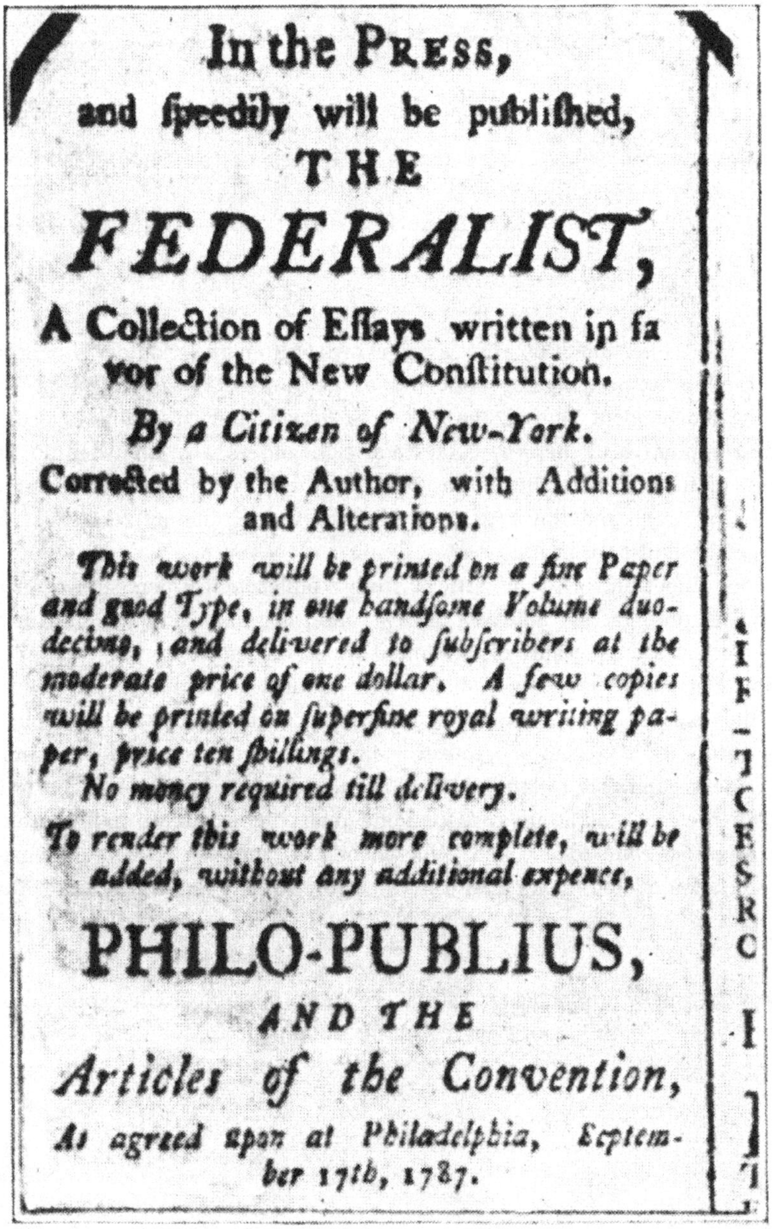

In the PRESS,
and speedily will be published,
THE
FEDERALIST,
A Collection of Essays written in favor of the New Constitution.

By a Citizen of New-York.

Corrected by the Author, with Additions and Alterations.

This work will be printed on a fine Paper and good Type, in one handsome Volume duodecimo, and delivered to subscribers at the moderate price of one dollar. A few copies will be printed on superfine royal writing paper, price ten shillings.

No money required till delivery.

To render this work more complete, will be added, without any additional expence,

PHILO-PUBLIUS,
AND THE
Articles of the Convention,

As agreed upon at Philadelphia, September 17th, 1787.

FEDERALIST PAPER NO. 1. GENERAL INTRODUCTION

For the Independent Journal. Saturday, October 27, 1787

HAMILTON

To the People of the State of New York:

AFTER an unequivocal experience of the inefficacy of the subsisting federal government, you are called upon to deliberate on a new Constitution for the United States of America. The subject speaks its own importance; comprehending in its consequences nothing less than the existence of the UNION, the safety and welfare of the parts of which it is composed, the fate of an empire in many respects the most interesting in the world. It has been frequently remarked that it seems to have been reserved to the people of this country, by their conduct and example, to decide the important question, whether societies of men are really capable or not of establishing good government from reflection and choice, or whether they are forever destined to depend for their political constitutions on accident and force. If there be any truth in the remark, the crisis at which we are arrived may with propriety be regarded as the era in which that decision is to be made; and a wrong election of the part we shall act may, in this view, deserve to be considered as the general misfortune of mankind.

This idea will add the inducements of philanthropy to those of patriotism, to heighten the solicitude which all considerate and good men must feel for the event. Happy will it be if our choice should be directed by a judicious estimate of our true interests, unperplexed and unbiased by considerations not connected with the public good. But this is a thing more ardently to be wished than seriously to be expected. The plan offered to our deliberations affects too many particular interests, innovates upon too many local institutions, not to involve in its discussion a variety of objects foreign to its merits, and of views, passions and prejudices little favorable to the discovery of truth.

Among the most formidable of the obstacles which the new Constitution will have to encounter may readily be distinguished the obvious interest of a certain class of men in every State to resist all changes which may hazard a diminution of the power, emolument, and consequence of the offices they hold under the State establishments; and the perverted ambition of another class of men, who will either hope to aggrandize themselves by the confusions of their country, or will flatter themselves with fairer prospects of elevation from the subdivision of the empire into several partial confederacies than from its union under one government.

It is not, however, my design to dwell upon observations of this nature. I am well aware that it would be disingenuous to resolve indiscriminately the opposition of any set of men (merely because their situations might subject them to suspicion) into interested or ambitious views. Candor will oblige us to admit that even such men may be actuated by upright intentions; and it cannot be doubted that much of the opposition which has made its appearance, or may hereafter make its appearance, will spring from sources, blameless at least, if not respectable—the honest errors of minds led astray by preconceived jealousies and fears. So numerous indeed and so powerful are the causes which serve to give a false bias to the judgment, that we, upon many occasions, see wise and good men on the wrong as well as on the right side of questions of the first magnitude to society. This circumstance, if duly attended to, would furnish a lesson of moderation to those who are ever so much persuaded of their being in the right in any controversy. And a further reason for caution, in this respect, might be drawn from the reflection that we are not always sure that those who advocate the truth are influenced by purer principles than their antagonists. Ambition, avarice, personal animosity, party opposition, and many other motives not more laudable than these, are apt to operate as well upon those who support as those who oppose the right side of a question. Were there not even these inducements to moderation, nothing could be more ill-judged than that intolerant spirit which has, at all times, characterized political parties. For in politics, as in religion, it is equally absurd to aim at making proselytes by fire and sword. Heresies in either can rarely be cured by persecution.

And yet, however just these sentiments will be allowed to be, we have already sufficient indications that it will happen in this as in all former cases of great national discussion. A torrent of angry and malignant passions will be let loose. To judge from the conduct of the opposite parties, we shall be led to conclude that they will mutually hope to evince the justness of their opinions, and to increase the number of their converts by the loudness of their declamations and the bitterness of their invectives. An enlightened zeal for the energy and efficiency of government will be stigmatized as the offspring of a temper fond of despotic power and hostile to the principles of liberty. An over-scrupulous jealousy of danger to the rights of the people, which is more commonly the fault of the head than of the heart, will be represented as mere pretense and artifice, the stale bait for popularity at the expense of the public good. It will be forgotten, on the one hand, that jealousy is the usual concomitant of love, and that the noble enthusiasm of liberty is apt to be infected with a spirit of narrow and illiberal distrust. On the other hand, it will be equally forgotten that the vigor of government is essential to the security of liberty; that, in the contemplation of a sound and well-informed judgment, their interest can never be separated; and that a dangerous ambition more often lurks behind the specious mask of zeal for the rights of the people than under the forbidden appearance of zeal for the firmness and efficiency of government. History will teach us that the former has been found a much more certain road to the introduction of despotism than the latter, and that of those men who have overturned the liberties of republics, the greatest number have begun their career by paying an obsequious court to the people; commencing demagogues, and ending tyrants.

In the course of the preceding observations, I have had an eye, my fellow-citizens, to putting you upon your guard against all attempts, from whatever quarter, to influence your decision in a matter of the utmost moment to your welfare, by any impressions other than those which may result from the evidence of truth. You will, no doubt, at the same time, have collected from the general scope of them, that they proceed from a source not unfriendly to the new Constitution. Yes, my countrymen, I own to you that, after having given it an attentive consideration, I am clearly of opinion it is your interest to adopt it. I am convinced that this is the safest course for your liberty, your dignity, and your happiness. I affect not reserves which I do not feel. I will not amuse you with an appearance of deliberation when I have decided. I frankly acknowledge to you my convictions, and I will freely lay before you the reasons on which they are founded. The consciousness of good intentions disdains ambiguity. I shall not, however, multiply professions on this head. My motives must remain in the depository of my own breast. My arguments will be open to all, and may be judged of by all. They shall at least be offered in a spirit which will not disgrace the cause of truth.

I propose, in a series of papers, to discuss the following interesting particulars:

THE UTILITY OF THE UNION TO YOUR POLITICAL PROSPERITY THE INSUFFICIENCY OF THE PRESENT CONFEDERATION TO PRESERVE THAT UNION THE NECESSITY OF A GOVERNMENT AT LEAST EQUALLY ENERGETIC WITH THE ONE PROPOSED, TO THE ATTAINMENT OF THIS OBJECT THE CONFORMITY OF THE PROPOSED CONSTITUTION TO THE TRUE PRINCIPLES OF REPUBLICAN GOVERNMENT ITS ANALOGY TO YOUR OWN STATE CONSTITUTION and lastly, THE ADDITIONAL SECURITY WHICH ITS ADOPTION WILL AFFORD TO THE PRESERVATION OF THAT SPECIES OF GOVERNMENT, TO LIBERTY, AND TO PROPERTY.

In the progress of this discussion I shall endeavor to give a satisfactory answer to all the objections which shall have made their appearance, that may seem to have any claim to your attention.

It may perhaps be thought superfluous to offer arguments to prove the utility of the UNION, a point, no doubt, deeply engraved on the hearts of the great body of the people in every State, and one, which it may be imagined, has no adversaries. But the fact is, that we already hear it whispered in the private circles of those who oppose the new Constitution, that the thirteen States are of too great extent for any general system, and that we must of necessity resort to separate confederacies of distinct portions of the whole.(1) This doctrine will, in all probability, be gradually propagated, till it has votaries enough to countenance an open avowal of it. For nothing can be more evident, to those who are able to take an enlarged view of the subject, than the alternative of an adoption of the new Constitution or a dismemberment of the Union. It will therefore be of use to begin by examining the advantages of that Union, the certain evils, and the probable dangers, to which every State will be exposed from its dissolution. This shall accordingly constitute the subject of my next address.

PUBLIUS

1. The same idea, tracing the arguments to their consequences, is held out in several of the late publications against the new Constitution.

FEDERALIST PAPER NO. 2. CONCERNING DANGERS FROM FOREIGN FORCE AND INFLUENCE

For the Independent Journal. Wednesday, October 31, 1787

JAY

To the People of the State of New York:

WHEN the people of America reflect that they are now called upon to decide a question, which, in its consequences, must prove one of the most important that ever engaged their attention, the propriety of their taking a very comprehensive, as well as a very serious, view of it, will be evident.

Nothing is more certain than the indispensable necessity of government, and it is equally undeniable, that whenever and however it is instituted, the people must cede to it some of their natural rights in order to vest it with requisite powers. It is well worthy of consideration therefore, whether it would conduce more to the interest of the people of America that they should, to all general purposes, be one nation, under one federal government, or that they should divide themselves into separate confederacies, and give to the head of each the same kind of powers which they are advised to place in one national government.

It has until lately been a received and uncontradicted opinion that the prosperity of the people of America depended on their continuing firmly united, and the wishes, prayers, and efforts of our best and wisest citizens have been constantly directed to that object. But politicians now appear, who insist that this opinion is erroneous, and that instead of looking for safety and happiness in union, we ought to seek it in a division of the States into distinct confederacies or sovereignties. However extraordinary this new doctrine may appear, it nevertheless has its advocates; and certain characters who were much opposed to it formerly, are at present of the number. Whatever may be the arguments or inducements which have wrought this change in the sentiments and declarations of these gentlemen, it certainly would not be wise in the people at large to adopt these new political tenets without being fully convinced that they are founded in truth and sound policy.

It has often given me pleasure to observe that independent America was not composed of detached and distant territories, but that one connected, fertile, wide-spreading country was the portion of our western sons of liberty. Providence has in a particular manner blessed it with a variety of soils and productions, and watered it with innumerable streams, for the delight and accommodation of its inhabitants. A succession of navigable waters forms a kind of chain round its borders, as if to bind it together; while the most noble rivers in the world, running at convenient distances, present them with highways for the easy communication of friendly aids, and the mutual transportation and exchange of their various commodities.

With equal pleasure I have as often taken notice that Providence has been pleased to give this one connected country to one united people—a people descended from the same ancestors, speaking the same language, professing the same religion, attached to the same principles of government, very similar in their manners and customs, and who, by their joint counsels, arms, and efforts, fighting side by side throughout a long and bloody war, have nobly established general liberty and independence.

This country and this people seem to have been made for each other, and it appears as if it was the design of Providence, that an inheritance so proper and convenient for a band of brethren, united to each other by the strongest ties, should never be split into a number of unsocial, jealous, and alien sovereignties.

Similar sentiments have hitherto prevailed among all orders and denominations of men among us. To all general purposes we have uniformly been one people each individual citizen everywhere enjoying the same national rights, privileges, and protection. As a nation we have made peace and war; as a nation we have vanquished our common enemies; as a nation we have formed alliances, and made treaties, and entered into various compacts and conventions with foreign states.

A strong sense of the value and blessings of union induced the people, at a very early period, to institute a federal government to preserve and perpetuate it. They formed it almost as soon as they had a political existence; nay, at a time when their habitations were in flames, when many of their citizens were bleeding, and when the progress of hostility and desolation left little room for those calm and mature inquiries and reflections which must ever precede the formation of a wise and well-balanced government for a free people. It is not to be wondered at, that a government instituted in times so inauspicious, should on experiment be found greatly deficient and inadequate to the purpose it was intended to answer.

Documents of Revolution

This intelligent people perceived and regretted these defects. Still continuing no less attached to union than enamored of liberty, they observed the danger which immediately threatened the former and more remotely the latter; and being persuaded that ample security for both could only be found in a national government more wisely framed, they as with one voice, convened the late convention at Philadelphia, to take that important subject under consideration.

This convention composed of men who possessed the confidence of the people, and many of whom had become highly distinguished by their patriotism, virtue and wisdom, in times which tried the minds and hearts of men, undertook the arduous task. In the mild season of peace, with minds unoccupied by other subjects, they passed many months in cool, uninterrupted, and daily consultation; and finally, without having been awed by power, or influenced by any passions except love for their country, they presented and recommended to the people the plan produced by their joint and very unanimous councils.

Admit, for so is the fact, that this plan is only RECOMMENDED, not imposed, yet let it be remembered that it is neither recommended to BLIND approbation, nor to BLIND reprobation; but to that sedate and candid consideration which the magnitude and importance of the subject demand, and which it certainly ought to receive. But this (as was remarked in the foregoing number of this paper) is more to be wished than expected, that it may be so considered and examined. Experience on a former occasion teaches us not to be too sanguine in such hopes. It is not yet forgotten that well-grounded apprehensions of imminent danger induced the people of America to form the memorable Congress of 1774. That body recommended certain measures to their constituents, and the event proved their wisdom; yet it is fresh in our memories how soon the press began to teem with pamphlets and weekly papers against those very measures. Not only many of the officers of government, who obeyed the dictates of personal interest, but others, from a mistaken estimate of consequences, or the undue influence of former attachments, or whose ambition aimed at objects which did not correspond with the public good, were indefatigable in their efforts to persuade the people to reject the advice of that patriotic Congress. Many, indeed, were deceived and deluded, but the great majority of the people reasoned and decided judiciously; and happy they are in reflecting that they did so.

They considered that the Congress was composed of many wise and experienced men. That, being convened from different parts of the country, they brought with them and communicated to each other a variety of useful information. That, in the course of the time they passed together in inquiring into and discussing the true interests of their country, they must have acquired very accurate knowledge on that head. That they were individually interested in the public liberty and prosperity, and therefore that it was not less their inclination than their duty to recommend only such measures as, after the most mature deliberation, they really thought prudent and advisable.

These and similar considerations then induced the people to rely greatly on the judgment and integrity of the Congress; and they took their advice, notwithstanding the various arts and endeavors used to deter them from it. But if the people at large had reason to confide in the men of that Congress, few of whom had been fully tried or generally known, still greater reason have they now to respect the judgment and advice of the convention, for it is well known that some of the most distinguished members of that Congress, who have been since tried and justly approved for patriotism and abilities, and who have grown old in acquiring political information, were also members of this convention, and carried into it their accumulated knowledge and experience.

It is worthy of remark that not only the first, but every succeeding Congress, as well as the late convention, have invariably joined with the people in thinking that the prosperity of America depended on its Union. To preserve and perpetuate it was the great object of the people in forming that convention, and it is also the great object of the plan which the convention has advised them to adopt. With what propriety, therefore, or for what good purposes, are attempts at this particular period made by some men to depreciate the importance of the Union? Or why is it suggested that three or four confederacies would be better than one? I am persuaded in my own mind that the people have always thought right on this subject, and that their universal and uniform attachment to the cause of the Union rests on great and weighty reasons, which I shall endeavor to develop and explain in some ensuing papers. They who promote the idea of substituting a number of distinct confederacies in the room of the plan of the convention, seem clearly to foresee that the rejection of it would put the continuance of the Union in the utmost jeopardy. That certainly would be the case, and I sincerely wish that it may be as clearly foreseen by every good citizen, that whenever the dissolution of the Union arrives, America will have reason to exclaim, in the words of the poet: "FAREWELL! A LONG FAREWELL TO ALL MY GREATNESS."

PUBLIUS

FEDERALIST PAPER NO. 3. THE SAME SUBJECT CONTINUED (CONCERNING DANGERS FROM FOREIGN FORCE AND INFLUENCE)

For the Independent Journal. Saturday, November 3, 1787

JAY

To the People of the State of New York:

IT IS not a new observation that the people of any country (if, like the Americans, intelligent and wellinformed) seldom adopt and steadily persevere for many years in an erroneous opinion respecting their interests. That consideration naturally tends to create great respect for the high opinion which the people of America have so long and uniformly entertained of the importance of their continuing firmly united under one federal government, vested with sufficient powers for all general and national purposes.

The more attentively I consider and investigate the reasons which appear to have given birth to this opinion, the more I become convinced that they are cogent and conclusive.

Among the many objects to which a wise and free people find it necessary to direct their attention, that of providing for their SAFETY seems to be the first. The SAFETY of the people doubtless has relation to a great variety of circumstances and considerations, and consequently affords great latitude to those who wish to define it precisely and comprehensively.

At present I mean only to consider it as it respects security for the preservation of peace and tranquillity, as well as against dangers from FOREIGN ARMS AND INFLUENCE, as from dangers of the LIKE KIND arising from domestic causes. As the former of these comes first in order, it is proper it should be the first discussed. Let us therefore proceed to examine whether the people are not right in their opinion that a cordial Union, under an efficient national government, affords them the best security that can be devised against HOSTILITIES from abroad.

The number of wars which have happened or will happen in the world will always be found to be in proportion to the number and weight of the causes, whether REAL or PRETENDED, which PROVOKE or INVITE them. If this remark be just, it becomes useful to inquire whether so many JUST causes of war are likely to be given by UNITED AMERICA as by DISUNITED America; for if it should turn out that United America will probably give the fewest, then it will follow that in this respect the Union tends most to preserve the people in a state of peace with other nations.

The JUST causes of war, for the most part, arise either from violation of treaties or from direct violence. America has already formed treaties with no less than six foreign nations, and all of them, except Prussia, are maritime, and therefore able to annoy and injure us. She has also extensive commerce with Portugal, Spain, and Britain, and, with respect to the two latter, has, in addition, the circumstance of neighborhood to attend to.

It is of high importance to the peace of America that she observe the laws of nations towards all these powers, and to me it appears evident that this will be more perfectly and punctually done by one national government than it could be either by thirteen separate States or by three or four distinct confederacies.

Because when once an efficient national government is established, the best men in the country will not only consent to serve, but also will generally be appointed to manage it; for, although town or country, or other contracted influence, may place men in State assemblies, or senates, or courts of justice, or executive departments, yet more general and extensive reputation for talents and other qualifications will be necessary to recommend men to offices under the national government,—especially as it will have the widest field for choice, and never experience that want of proper persons which is not uncommon in some of the States. Hence, it will result that the administration, the political counsels, and the judicial decisions of the national government will be more wise, systematical, and judicious than those of individual States, and consequently more satisfactory with respect to other nations, as well as more SAFE with respect to us.

Because, under the national government, treaties and articles of treaties, as well as the laws of nations, will always be expounded in one sense and executed in the same manner,—whereas, adjudications on the same points and questions, in thirteen States, or in three or four confederacies, will not always accord or be consistent; and that, as well from the variety of independent courts and judges appointed by different and independent governments, as from the different local laws and interests which may affect and influence them. The wisdom of the convention, in committing such questions to the jurisdiction and judgment of courts appointed by and responsible only to one national government, cannot be too much commended.

Because the prospect of present loss or advantage may often tempt the governing party in one or two States to swerve from good faith and justice; but those temptations, not reaching the other States, and consequently having little or no influence on the national government, the temptation will be fruitless, and good faith and justice be preserved. The case of the treaty of peace with Britain adds great weight to this reasoning.

Because, even if the governing party in a State should be disposed to resist such temptations, yet as such temptations may, and commonly do, result from circumstances peculiar to the State, and may affect a great number of the inhabitants, the governing party may not always be able, if willing, to prevent the injustice meditated, or to punish the aggressors. But the national government, not being affected by those local circumstances, will neither be induced to commit the wrong themselves, nor want power or inclination to prevent or punish its commission by others.

So far, therefore, as either designed or accidental violations of treaties and the laws of nations afford JUST causes of war, they are less to be apprehended under one general government than under several lesser ones, and in that respect the former most favors the SAFETY of the people.

As to those just causes of war which proceed from direct and unlawful violence, it appears equally clear to me that one good national government affords vastly more security against dangers of that sort than can be derived from any other quarter.

Because such violences are more frequently caused by the passions and interests of a part than of the whole; of one or two States than of the Union. Not a single Indian war has yet been occasioned by aggressions of the present federal government, feeble as it is; but there are several instances of Indian hostilities having been provoked by the improper conduct of individual States, who, either unable or unwilling to restrain or punish offenses, have given occasion to the slaughter of many innocent inhabitants.

The neighborhood of Spanish and British territories, bordering on some States and not on others, naturally confines the causes of quarrel more immediately to the borderers. The bordering States, if any, will be those who, under the impulse of sudden irritation, and a quick sense of apparent interest or injury, will be most likely, by direct violence, to excite war with these nations; and nothing can so effectually obviate that danger as a national government, whose wisdom and prudence will not be diminished by the passions which actuate the parties immediately interested.

But not only fewer just causes of war will be given by the national government, but it will also be more in their power to accommodate and settle them amicably. They will be more temperate and cool, and in that respect, as well as in others, will be more in capacity to act advisedly than the offending State. The pride of states, as well as of men, naturally disposes them to justify all their actions, and opposes their acknowledging, correcting, or repairing their errors and offenses. The national government, in such cases, will not be affected by this pride, but will proceed with moderation and candor to consider and decide on the means most proper to extricate them from the difficulties which threaten them.

Besides, it is well known that acknowledgments, explanations, and compensations are often accepted as satisfactory from a strong united nation, which would be rejected as unsatisfactory if offered by a State or confederacy of little consideration or power.

In the year 1685, the state of Genoa having offended Louis XIV., endeavored to appease him. He demanded that they should send their Doge, or chief magistrate, accompanied by four of their senators, to FRANCE, to ask his pardon and receive his terms. They were obliged to submit to it for the sake of peace. Would he on any occasion either have demanded or have received the like humiliation from Spain, or Britain, or any other POWERFUL nation?

PUBLIUS

FEDERALIST PAPER NO. 4. THE SAME SUBJECT CONTINUED (CONCERNING DANGERS FROM FOREIGN FORCE AND INFLUENCE)

For the Independent Journal. Wednesday, November 7, 1787

JAY

To the People of the State of New York:

MY LAST paper assigned several reasons why the safety of the people would be best secured by union against the danger it may be exposed to by JUST causes of war given to other nations; and those reasons show that such causes would not only be more rarely given, but would also be more easily accommodated, by a national government than either by the State governments or the proposed little confederacies.

But the safety of the people of America against dangers from FOREIGN force depends not only on their forbearing to give JUST causes of war to other nations, but also on their placing and continuing themselves in such a situation as not to INVITE hostility or insult; for it need not be observed that there are PRETENDED as well as just causes of war.

It is too true, however disgraceful it may be to human nature, that nations in general will make war whenever they have a prospect of getting anything by it; nay, absolute monarchs will often make war when their nations are to get nothing by it, but for the purposes and objects merely personal, such as thirst for military glory, revenge for personal affronts, ambition, or private compacts to aggrandize or support their particular families or partisans. These and a variety of other motives, which affect only the mind of the sovereign, often lead him to engage in wars not sanctified by justice or the voice and interests of his people. But, independent of these inducements to war, which are more prevalent in absolute monarchies, but which well deserve our attention, there are others which affect nations as often as kings; and some of them will on examination be found to grow out of our relative situation and circumstances.

With France and with Britain we are rivals in the fisheries, and can supply their markets cheaper than they can themselves, notwithstanding any efforts to prevent it by bounties on their own or duties on foreign fish.

With them and with most other European nations we are rivals in navigation and the carrying trade; and we shall deceive ourselves if we suppose that any of them will rejoice to see it flourish; for, as our carrying trade cannot increase without in some degree diminishing theirs, it is more their interest, and will be more their policy, to restrain than to promote it.

In the trade to China and India, we interfere with more than one nation, inasmuch as it enables us to partake in advantages which they had in a manner monopolized, and as we thereby supply ourselves with commodities which we used to purchase from them.

The extension of our own commerce in our own vessels cannot give pleasure to any nations who possess territories on or near this continent, because the cheapness and excellence of our productions, added to the circumstance of vicinity, and the enterprise and address of our merchants and navigators, will give us a greater share in the advantages which those territories afford, than consists with the wishes or policy of their respective sovereigns.

Spain thinks it convenient to shut the Mississippi against us on the one side, and Britain excludes us from the Saint Lawrence on the other; nor will either of them permit the other waters which are between them and us to become the means of mutual intercourse and traffic.

From these and such like considerations, which might, if consistent with prudence, be more amplified and detailed, it is easy to see that jealousies and uneasinesses may gradually slide into the minds and cabinets of other nations, and that we are not to expect that they should regard our advancement in union, in power and consequence by land and by sea, with an eye of indifference and composure.

The people of America are aware that inducements to war may arise out of these circumstances, as well as from others not so obvious at present, and that whenever such inducements may find fit time and opportunity for operation, pretenses to color and justify them will not be wanting. Wisely, therefore, do they consider union and a good national government as necessary to put and keep them in SUCH A SITUATION as, instead of INVITING war, will tend to repress and discourage it. That situation consists in the best possible state of defense, and necessarily depends on the government, the arms, and the resources of the country.

As the safety of the whole is the interest of the whole, and cannot be provided for without government, either one or more or many, let us inquire whether one good government is not, relative to the object in question, more competent than any other given number whatever.

One government can collect and avail itself of the talents and experience of the ablest men, in whatever part of the Union they may be found. It can move on uniform principles of policy. It can harmonize, assimilate, and protect the several parts and members, and extend the benefit of its foresight and precautions to each. In the formation of treaties, it will regard the interest of the whole, and the particular interests of the parts as connected with that of the whole. It can apply the resources and power of the whole to the defense of any particular part, and that more easily and expeditiously than State governments or separate confederacies can possibly do, for want of concert and unity of system. It can place the militia under one plan of discipline, and, by putting their officers in a proper line of subordination to the Chief Magistrate, will, as it were, consolidate them into one corps, and thereby render them more efficient than if divided into thirteen or into three or four distinct independent companies.

What would the militia of Britain be if the English militia obeyed the government of England, if the Scotch militia obeyed the government of Scotland, and if the Welsh militia obeyed the government of Wales? Suppose an invasion; would those three governments (if they agreed at all) be able, with all their respective forces, to operate against the enemy so effectually as the single government of Great Britain would?

We have heard much of the fleets of Britain, and the time may come, if we are wise, when the fleets of America may engage attention. But if one national government, had not so regulated the navigation of Britain as to make it a nursery for seamen—if one national government had not called forth all the national means and materials for forming fleets, their prowess and their thunder would never have been celebrated. Let England have its navigation and fleet—let Scotland have its navigation and fleet—let Wales have its navigation and fleet—let Ireland have its navigation and fleet—let those four of the constituent parts of the British empire be be under four independent governments, and it is easy to perceive how soon they would each dwindle into comparative insignificance.

Apply these facts to our own case. Leave America divided into thirteen or, if you please, into three or four independent governments—what armies could they raise and pay—what fleets could they ever hope to have? If one was attacked, would the others fly to its succor, and spend their blood and money in its defense? Would there be no danger of their being flattered into neutrality by its specious promises, or seduced by a too great fondness for peace to decline hazarding their tranquillity and present safety for the sake of neighbors, of whom perhaps they have been jealous, and whose importance they are content to see diminished? Although such conduct would not be wise, it would, nevertheless, be natural. The history of the states of Greece, and of other countries, abounds with such instances, and it is not improbable that what has so often happened would, under similar circumstances, happen again.

But admit that they might be willing to help the invaded State or confederacy. How, and when, and in what proportion shall aids of men and money be afforded? Who shall command the allied armies, and from which of them shall he receive his orders? Who shall settle the terms of peace, and in case of disputes what umpire shall decide between them and compel acquiescence? Various difficulties and inconveniences would be inseparable from such a situation; whereas one government, watching over the general and common interests, and combining and directing the powers and resources of the whole, would be free from all these embarrassments, and conduce far more to the safety of the people.

But whatever may be our situation, whether firmly united under one national government, or split into a number of confederacies, certain it is, that foreign nations will know and view it exactly as it is; and they will act toward us accordingly. If they see that our national government is efficient and well administered, our trade prudently regulated, our militia properly organized and disciplined, our resources and finances discreetly managed, our credit re-established, our people free, contented, and united, they will be much more disposed to cultivate our friendship than provoke our resentment. If, on the other hand, they find us either destitute of an effectual government (each State doing right or wrong, as to its rulers may seem convenient), or split into three or four independent and probably discordant republics or confederacies, one inclining to Britain, another to France, and a third to Spain, and perhaps played off against each other by the three, what a poor, pitiful figure will America make in their eyes! How liable would she become not only to their contempt but to their outrage, and how soon would dear-bought experience proclaim that when a people or family so divide, it never fails to be against themselves.

PUBLIUS

FEDERALIST PAPER NO. 5. THE SAME SUBJECT CONTINUED (CONCERNING DANGERS FROM FOREIGN FORCE AND INFLUENCE)

For the Independent Journal. Saturday, November 10, 1787

JAY

To the People of the State of New York:

QUEEN ANNE, in her letter of the 1st July, 1706, to the Scotch Parliament, makes some observations on the importance of the UNION then forming between England and Scotland, which merit our attention. I shall present the public with one or two extracts from it: "An entire and perfect union will be the solid foundation of lasting peace: It will secure your religion, liberty, and property; remove the animosities amongst yourselves, and the jealousies and differences betwixt our two kingdoms. It must increase your strength, riches, and trade; and by this union the whole island, being joined in affection and free from all apprehensions of different interest, will be ENABLED TO RESIST ALL ITS ENEMIES." "We most earnestly recommend to you calmness and unanimity in this great and weighty affair, that the union may be brought to a happy conclusion, being the only EFFECTUAL way to secure our present and future happiness, and disappoint the designs of our and your enemies, who will doubtless, on this occasion, USE THEIR UTMOST ENDEAVORS TO PREVENT OR DELAY THIS UNION."

It was remarked in the preceding paper, that weakness and divisions at home would invite dangers from abroad; and that nothing would tend more to secure us from them than union, strength, and good government within ourselves. This subject is copious and cannot easily be exhausted.

The history of Great Britain is the one with which we are in general the best acquainted, and it gives us many useful lessons. We may profit by their experience without paying the price which it cost them. Although it seems obvious to common sense that the people of such an island should be but one nation, yet we find that they were for ages divided into three, and that those three were almost constantly embroiled in quarrels and wars with one another. Notwithstanding their true interest with respect to the continental nations was really the same, yet by the arts and policy and practices of those nations, their mutual jealousies were perpetually kept inflamed, and for a long series of years they were far more inconvenient and troublesome than they were useful and assisting to each other.

Should the people of America divide themselves into three or four nations, would not the same thing happen? Would not similar jealousies arise, and be in like manner cherished? Instead of their being "joined in affection" and free from all apprehension of different "interests," envy and jealousy would soon extinguish confidence and affection, and the partial interests of each confederacy, instead of the general interests of all America, would be the only objects of their policy and pursuits. Hence, like most other BORDERING nations, they would always be either involved in disputes and war, or live in the constant apprehension of them.

The most sanguine advocates for three or four confederacies cannot reasonably suppose that they would long remain exactly on an equal footing in point of strength, even if it was possible to form them so at first; but, admitting that to be practicable, yet what human contrivance can secure the continuance of such equality? Independent of those local circumstances which tend to beget and increase power in one part and to impede its progress in another, we must advert to the effects of that superior policy and good management which would probably distinguish the government of one above the rest, and by which their relative equality in strength and consideration would be destroyed. For it cannot be presumed that the same degree of sound policy, prudence, and foresight would uniformly be observed by each of these confederacies for a long succession of years.

Whenever, and from whatever causes, it might happen, and happen it would, that any one of these nations or confederacies should rise on the scale of political importance much above the degree of her neighbors, that moment would those neighbors behold her with envy and with fear. Both those passions would lead them to countenance, if not to promote, whatever might promise to diminish her importance; and would also restrain them from measures calculated to advance or even to secure her prosperity. Much time would not be necessary to enable her to discern these unfriendly dispositions. She would soon begin, not only to lose confidence in her neighbors, but also to feel a disposition equally unfavorable to them. Distrust naturally creates distrust, and by nothing is good-will and kind conduct more speedily changed than by invidious jealousies and uncandid imputations, whether expressed or implied.

The North is generally the region of strength, and many local circumstances render it probable that the most Northern of the proposed confederacies would, at a period not very distant, be unquestionably more formidable than any of the others. No sooner would this become evident than the NORTHERN HIVE would excite the same ideas and sensations in the more southern parts of America which it formerly did in the southern parts of Europe. Nor does it appear to be a rash conjecture that its young swarms might often be tempted to gather honey in the more blooming fields and milder air of their luxurious and more delicate neighbors.

They who well consider the history of similar divisions and confederacies will find abundant reason to apprehend that those in contemplation would in no other sense be neighbors than as they would be borderers; that they would neither love nor trust one another, but on the contrary would be a prey to discord, jealousy, and mutual injuries; in short, that they would place us exactly in the situations in which some nations doubtless wish to see us, viz., FORMIDABLE ONLY TO EACH OTHER.

From these considerations it appears that those gentlemen are greatly mistaken who suppose that alliances offensive and defensive might be formed between these confederacies, and would produce that combination and union of wills of arms and of resources, which would be necessary to put and keep them in a formidable state of defense against foreign enemies.

When did the independent states, into which Britain and Spain were formerly divided, combine in such alliance, or unite their forces against a foreign enemy? The proposed confederacies will be DISTINCT NATIONS. Each of them would have its commerce with foreigners to regulate by distinct treaties; and as their productions and commodities are different and proper for different markets, so would those treaties be essentially different. Different commercial concerns must create different interests, and of course different degrees of political attachment to and connection with different foreign nations. Hence it might and probably would happen that the foreign nation with whom the SOUTHERN confederacy might be at war would be the one with whom the NORTHERN confederacy would be the most desirous of preserving peace and friendship. An alliance so contrary to their immediate interest would not therefore be easy to form, nor, if formed, would it be observed and fulfilled with perfect good faith.

Nay, it is far more probable that in America, as in Europe, neighboring nations, acting under the impulse of opposite interests and unfriendly passions, would frequently be found taking different sides. Considering our distance from Europe, it would be more natural for these confederacies to apprehend danger from one another than from distant nations, and therefore that each of them should be more desirous to guard against the others by the aid of foreign alliances, than to guard against foreign dangers by alliances between themselves. And here let us not forget how much more easy it is to receive foreign fleets into our ports, and foreign armies into our country, than it is to persuade or compel them to depart. How many conquests did the Romans and others make in the characters of allies, and what innovations did they under the same character introduce into the governments of those whom they pretended to protect.

Let candid men judge, then, whether the division of America into any given number of independent sovereignties would tend to secure us against the hostilities and improper interference of foreign nations.

PUBLIUS

FEDERALIST PAPER NO. 6. CONCERNING DANGERS FROM DISSENSIONS BETWEEN THE STATES

For the Independent Journal. Wednesday, November 14, 1787

HAMILTON

Documents of Revolution

To the People of the State of New York:

THE three last numbers of this paper have been dedicated to an enumeration of the dangers to which we should be exposed, in a state of disunion, from the arms and arts of foreign nations. I shall now proceed to delineate dangers of a different and, perhaps, still more alarming kind—those which will in all probability flow from dissensions between the States themselves, and from domestic factions and convulsions. These have been already in some instances slightly anticipated; but they deserve a more particular and more full investigation.

A man must be far gone in Utopian speculations who can seriously doubt that, if these States should either be wholly disunited, or only united in partial confederacies, the subdivisions into which they might be thrown would have frequent and violent contests with each other. To presume a want of motives for such contests as an argument against their existence, would be to forget that men are ambitious, vindictive, and rapacious. To look for a continuation of harmony between a number of independent, unconnected sovereignties in the same neighborhood, would be to disregard the uniform course of human events, and to set at defiance the accumulated experience of ages.

The causes of hostility among nations are innumerable. There are some which have a general and almost constant operation upon the collective bodies of society. Of this description are the love of power or the desire of pre-eminence and dominion—the jealousy of power, or the desire of equality and safety. There are others which have a more circumscribed though an equally operative influence within their spheres. Such are the rivalships and competitions of commerce between commercial nations. And there are others, not less numerous than either of the former, which take their origin entirely in private passions; in the attachments, enmities, interests, hopes, and fears of leading individuals in the communities of which they are members. Men of this class, whether the favorites of a king or of a people, have in too many instances abused the confidence they possessed; and assuming the pretext of some public motive, have not scrupled to sacrifice the national tranquillity to personal advantage or personal gratification.

The celebrated Pericles, in compliance with the resentment of a prostitute,(1) at the expense of much of the blood and treasure of his countrymen, attacked, vanquished, and destroyed the city of the SAMMIANS. The same man, stimulated by private pique against the MEGARENSIANS,(2) another nation of Greece, or to avoid a prosecution with which he was threatened as an accomplice of a supposed theft of the statuary Phidias,(3) or to get rid of the accusations prepared to be brought against him for dissipating the funds of the state in the purchase of popularity,(4) or from a combination of all these causes, was the primitive author of that famous and fatal war, distinguished in the Grecian annals by the name of the PELOPONNESIAN war; which, after various vicissitudes, intermissions, and renewals, terminated in the ruin of the Athenian commonwealth.

The ambitious cardinal, who was prime minister to Henry VIII., permitting his vanity to aspire to the triple crown,(5) entertained hopes of succeeding in the acquisition of that splendid prize by the influence of the Emperor Charles V. To secure the favor and interest of this enterprising and powerful monarch, he precipitated England into a war with France, contrary to the plainest dictates of policy, and at the hazard of the safety and independence, as well of the kingdom over which he presided by his counsels, as of Europe in general. For if there ever was a sovereign who bid fair to realize the project of universal monarchy, it was the Emperor Charles V., of whose intrigues Wolsey was at once the instrument and the dupe.

The influence which the bigotry of one female,(6) the petulance of another,(7) and the cabals of a third,(8) had in the contemporary policy, ferments, and pacifications, of a considerable part of Europe, are topics that have been too often descanted upon not to be generally known.

To multiply examples of the agency of personal considerations in the production of great national events, either foreign or domestic, according to their direction, would be an unnecessary waste of time. Those who have but a superficial acquaintance with the sources from which they are to be drawn, will themselves recollect a variety of instances; and those who have a tolerable knowledge of human nature will not stand in need of such lights to form their opinion either of the reality or extent of that agency. Perhaps, however, a reference, tending to illustrate the general principle, may with propriety be made to a case which has lately happened among ourselves. If Shays had not been a DESPERATE DEBTOR, it is much to be doubted whether Massachusetts would have been plunged into a civil war.

But notwithstanding the concurring testimony of experience, in this particular, there are still to be found visionary or designing men, who stand ready to advocate the paradox of perpetual peace between the States, though dismembered and alienated from each other. The genius of republics (say they) is pacific; the spirit of commerce has a tendency to soften the manners of men, and to extinguish those inflammable humors which have so often kindled into wars. Commercial republics, like ours, will never be disposed to waste themselves in ruinous contentions with each other. They will be governed by mutual interest, and will cultivate a spirit of mutual amity and concord.

Documents of Revolution

Is it not (we may ask these projectors in politics) the true interest of all nations to cultivate the same benevolent and philosophic spirit? If this be their true interest, have they in fact pursued it? Has it not, on the contrary, invariably been found that momentary passions, and immediate interest, have a more active and imperious control over human conduct than general or remote considerations of policy, utility or justice? Have republics in practice been less addicted to war than monarchies? Are not the former administered by MEN as well as the latter? Are there not aversions, predilections, rivalships, and desires of unjust acquisitions, that affect nations as well as kings? Are not popular assemblies frequently subject to the impulses of rage, resentment, jealousy, avarice, and of other irregular and violent propensities? Is it not well known that their determinations are often governed by a few individuals in whom they place confidence, and are, of course, liable to be tinctured by the passions and views of those individuals? Has commerce hitherto done anything more than change the objects of war? Is not the love of wealth as domineering and enterprising a passion as that of power or glory? Have there not been as many wars founded upon commercial motives since that has become the prevailing system of nations, as were before occasioned by the cupidity of territory or dominion? Has not the spirit of commerce, in many instances, administered new incentives to the appetite, both for the one and for the other? Let experience, the least fallible guide of human opinions, be appealed to for an answer to these inquiries.

Sparta, Athens, Rome, and Carthage were all republics; two of them, Athens and Carthage, of the commercial kind. Yet were they as often engaged in wars, offensive and defensive, as the neighboring monarchies of the same times. Sparta was little better than a wellregulated camp; and Rome was never sated of carnage and conquest.

Carthage, though a commercial republic, was the aggressor in the very war that ended in her destruction. Hannibal had carried her arms into the heart of Italy and to the gates of Rome, before Scipio, in turn, gave him an overthrow in the territories of Carthage, and made a conquest of the commonwealth.

Venice, in later times, figured more than once in wars of ambition, till, becoming an object to the other Italian states, Pope Julius II. found means to accomplish that formidable league,(9) which gave a deadly blow to the power and pride of this haughty republic.

The provinces of Holland, till they were overwhelmed in debts and taxes, took a leading and conspicuous part in the wars of Europe. They had furious contests with England for the dominion of the sea, and were among the most persevering and most implacable of the opponents of Louis XIV.

In the government of Britain the representatives of the people compose one branch of the national legislature. Commerce has been for ages the predominant pursuit of that country. Few nations, nevertheless, have been more frequently engaged in war; and the wars in which that kingdom has been engaged have, in numerous instances, proceeded from the people.

There have been, if I may so express it, almost as many popular as royal wars. The cries of the nation and the importunities of their representatives have, upon various occasions, dragged their monarchs into war, or continued them in it, contrary to their inclinations, and sometimes contrary to the real interests of the State. In that memorable struggle for superiority between the rival houses of AUSTRIA and BOURBON, which so long kept Europe in a flame, it is well known that the antipathies of the English against the French, seconding the ambition, or rather the avarice, of a favorite leader,(10) protracted the war beyond the limits marked out by sound policy, and for a considerable time in opposition to the views of the court.

The wars of these two last-mentioned nations have in a great measure grown out of commercial considerations,—the desire of supplanting and the fear of being supplanted, either in particular branches of traffic or in the general advantages of trade and navigation, and sometimes even the more culpable desire of sharing in the commerce of other nations without their consent.

The last war but between Britain and Spain sprang from the attempts of the British merchants to prosecute an illicit trade with the Spanish main. These unjustifiable practices on their part produced severity on the part of the Spaniards toward the subjects of Great Britain which were not more justifiable, because they exceeded the bounds of a just retaliation and were chargeable with inhumanity and cruelty. Many of the English who were taken on the Spanish coast were sent to dig in the mines of Potosi; and by the usual progress of a spirit of resentment, the innocent were, after a while, confounded with the guilty in indiscriminate punishment. The complaints of the merchants kindled a violent flame throughout the nation, which soon after broke out in the House of Commons, and was communicated from that body to the ministry. Letters of reprisal were granted, and a war ensued, which in its consequences overthrew all the alliances that but twenty years before had been formed with sanguine expectations of the most beneficial fruits.

From this summary of what has taken place in other countries, whose situations have borne the nearest resemblance to our own, what reason can we have to confide in those reveries which would seduce us into an expectation of peace and cordiality between the members of the present confederacy, in a state of separation? Have we not already seen enough of the fallacy and extravagance of those idle theories which have amused us with promises of an exemption from the imperfections, weaknesses and evils incident to society in every shape? Is it not time to awake from the deceitful dream of a golden age, and to adopt as a practical maxim for the direction of our political conduct that we, as well as the other inhabitants of the globe, are yet remote from the happy empire of perfect wisdom and perfect virtue?

Let the point of extreme depression to which our national dignity and credit have sunk, let the inconveniences felt everywhere from a lax and ill administration of government, let the revolt of a part of the State of North Carolina, the late menacing disturbances in Pennsylvania, and the actual insurrections and rebellions in Massachusetts, declare—!

So far is the general sense of mankind from corresponding with the tenets of those who endeavor to lull asleep our apprehensions of discord and hostility between the States, in the event of disunion, that it has from long observation of the progress of society become a sort of axiom in politics, that vicinity or nearness of situation, constitutes nations natural enemies. An intelligent writer expresses himself on this subject to this effect: "NEIGHBORING NATIONS (says he) are naturally enemies of each other unless their common weakness forces them to league in a CONFEDERATE REPUBLIC, and their constitution prevents the differences that neighborhood occasions, extinguishing that secret jealousy which disposes all states to aggrandize themselves at the expense of their neighbors."(11) This passage, at the same time, points out the EVIL and suggests the REMEDY.

PUBLIUS

1. Aspasia, vide "Plutarch's Life of Pericles."
2. Ibid.
3. Ibid.
4. Ibid. Phidias was supposed to have stolen some public gold, with the connivance of Pericles, for the embellishment of the statue of Minerva.
5. Worn by the popes.
6. Madame de Maintenon.
7. Duchess of Marlborough.
8. Madame de Pompadour.
9. The League of Cambray, comprehending the Emperor, the King of France, the King of Aragon, and most of the Italian princes and states.
10. The Duke of Marlborough.
11. Vide "Principes des Negociations" par l'Abbé de Mably.

FEDERALIST PAPER NO. 7. THE SAME SUBJECT CONTINUED (CONCERNING DANGERS FROM DISSENSIONS BETWEEN THE STATES)

For the Independent Journal. Thursday, November 15, 1787

HAMILTON

To the People of the State of New York:

IT IS sometimes asked, with an air of seeming triumph, what inducements could the States have, if disunited, to make war upon each other? It would be a full answer to this question to say—precisely the same inducements which have, at different times, deluged in blood all the nations in the world. But, unfortunately for us, the question admits of a more particular answer. There are causes of differences within our immediate contemplation, of the tendency of which, even under the restraints of a federal constitution, we have had sufficient experience to enable us to form a judgment of what might be expected if those restraints were removed.

Territorial disputes have at all times been found one of the most fertile sources of hostility among nations. Perhaps the greatest proportion of wars that have desolated the earth have sprung from this origin. This cause would exist among us in full force. We have a vast tract of unsettled territory within the boundaries of the United States. There still are discordant and undecided claims between several of them, and the dissolution of the Union would lay a foundation for similar claims between them all. It is well known that they have heretofore had serious and animated discussion concerning the rights to the lands which were ungranted at the time of the Revolution, and which usually went under the name of crown lands. The States within the limits of whose colonial governments they were comprised have claimed them as their property, the others have contended that the rights of the crown in this article devolved upon the Union; especially as to all that part of the Western territory which, either by actual possession, or through the submission of the Indian proprietors, was subjected to the jurisdiction of the king of Great Britain, till it was relinquished in the treaty of peace. This, it has been said, was at all events an acquisition to the Confederacy by compact with a foreign power. It has been the prudent policy of Congress to appease this controversy, by prevailing upon the States to make cessions to the United States for the benefit of the whole. This has been so far accomplished as, under a continuation of the Union, to afford a decided prospect of an amicable termination of the dispute. A dismemberment of the Confederacy, however, would revive this dispute, and would create others on the same subject. At present, a large part of the vacant Western territory is, by cession at least, if not by any anterior right, the common property of the Union. If that were at an end, the States which made the cession, on a principle of federal compromise, would be apt when the motive of the grant had ceased, to reclaim the lands as a reversion. The other States would no doubt insist on a proportion, by right of representation. Their argument would be, that a grant, once made, could not be revoked; and that the justice of participating in territory acquired or secured by the joint efforts of the Confederacy, remained undiminished. If, contrary to probability, it should be admitted by all the States, that each had a right to a share of this common stock, there would still be a difficulty to be surmounted, as to a proper rule of apportionment. Different principles would be set up by different States for this purpose; and as they would affect the opposite interests of the parties, they might not easily be susceptible of a pacific adjustment.

In the wide field of Western territory, therefore, we perceive an ample theatre for hostile pretensions, without any umpire or common judge to interpose between the contending parties. To reason from the past to the future, we shall have good ground to apprehend, that the sword would sometimes be appealed to as the arbiter of their differences. The circumstances of the dispute between Connecticut and Pennsylvania, respecting the land at Wyoming, admonish us not to be sanguine in expecting an easy accommodation of such differences. The articles of confederation obliged the parties to submit the matter to the decision of a federal court. The submission was made, and the court decided in favor of Pennsylvania. But Connecticut gave strong indications of dissatisfaction with that determination; nor did she appear to be entirely resigned to it, till, by negotiation and management, something like an equivalent was found for the loss she supposed herself to have sustained. Nothing here said is intended to convey the slightest censure on the conduct of that State. She no doubt sincerely believed herself to have been injured by the decision; and States, like individuals, acquiesce with great reluctance in determinations to their disadvantage.

Those who had an opportunity of seeing the inside of the transactions which attended the progress of the controversy between this State and the district of Vermont, can vouch the opposition we experienced, as well from States not interested as from those which were interested in the claim; and can attest the danger to which the peace of the Confederacy might have been exposed, had this State attempted to assert its rights by force. Two motives preponderated in that opposition: one, a jealousy entertained of our future power; and the other, the interest of certain individuals of influence in the neighboring States, who had obtained grants of lands under the actual government of that district. Even the States which brought forward claims, in contradiction to ours, seemed more solicitous to dismember this State, than to establish their own pretensions. These were New Hampshire, Massachusetts, and Connecticut. New Jersey and Rhode Island, upon all occasions, discovered a warm zeal for the independence of Vermont; and Maryland, till alarmed by the appearance of a connection between Canada and that State, entered deeply into the same views. These being small States, saw with an unfriendly eye the perspective of our growing greatness. In a review of these transactions we may trace some of the causes which would be likely to embroil the States with each other, if it should be their unpropitious destiny to become disunited.

The competitions of commerce would be another fruitful source of contention. The States less favorably circumstanced would be desirous of escaping from the disadvantages of local situation, and of sharing in the advantages of their more fortunate neighbors. Each State, or separate confederacy, would pursue a system of commercial policy peculiar to itself. This would occasion distinctions, preferences, and exclusions, which would beget discontent. The habits of intercourse, on the basis of equal privileges, to which we have been accustomed since the earliest settlement of the country, would give a keener edge to those causes of discontent than they would naturally have independent of this circumstance. WE SHOULD BE READY TO DENOMINATE INJURIES THOSE THINGS WHICH WERE IN REALITY THE JUSTIFIABLE ACTS OF INDEPENDENT SOVEREIGNTIES CONSULTING A DISTINCT INTEREST. The spirit of enterprise, which characterizes the commercial part of America, has left no occasion of displaying itself unimproved. It is not at all probable that this unbridled spirit would pay much respect to those regulations of trade by which particular States might endeavor to secure exclusive benefits to their own citizens. The infractions of these regulations, on one side, the efforts to prevent and repel them, on the other, would naturally lead to outrages, and these to reprisals and wars.

The opportunities which some States would have of rendering others tributary to them by commercial regulations would be impatiently submitted to by the tributary States. The relative situation of New York, Connecticut, and New Jersey would afford an example of this kind. New York, from the necessities of revenue, must lay duties on her importations. A great part of these duties must be paid by the inhabitants of the two other States in the capacity of consumers of what we import. New York would neither be willing nor able to forego this advantage. Her citizens would not consent that a duty paid by them should be remitted in favor of the citizens of her neighbors; nor would it be practicable, if there were not this impediment in the way, to distinguish the customers in our own markets. Would Connecticut and New Jersey long submit to be taxed by New York for her exclusive benefit? Should we be long permitted to remain in the quiet and undisturbed enjoyment of a metropolis, from the possession of which we derived an advantage so odious to our neighbors, and, in their opinion, so oppressive? Should we be able to preserve it against the incumbent weight of Connecticut on the one side, and the co-operating pressure of New Jersey on the other? These are questions that temerity alone will answer in the affirmative.

The public debt of the Union would be a further cause of collision between the separate States or confederacies. The apportionment, in the first instance, and the progressive extinguishment afterward, would be alike productive of ill-humor and animosity. How would it be possible to agree upon a rule of apportionment satisfactory to all? There is scarcely any that can be proposed which is entirely free from real objections. These, as usual, would be exaggerated by the adverse interest of the parties. There are even dissimilar views among the States as to the general principle of discharging the public debt. Some of them, either less impressed with the importance of national credit, or because their citizens have little, if any, immediate interest in the question, feel an indifference, if not a repugnance, to the payment of the domestic debt at any rate. These would be inclined to magnify the difficulties of a distribution. Others of them, a numerous body of whose citizens are creditors to the public beyond proportion of the State in the total amount of the national debt, would be strenuous for some equitable and effective provision. The procrastinations of the former would excite the resentments of the latter. The settlement of a rule would, in the meantime, be postponed by real differences of opinion and affected delays. The citizens of the States interested would clamour; foreign powers would urge for the satisfaction of their just demands, and the peace of the States would be hazarded to the double contingency of external invasion and internal contention.

Suppose the difficulties of agreeing upon a rule surmounted, and the apportionment made. Still there is great room to suppose that the rule agreed upon would, upon experiment, be found to bear harder upon some States than upon others. Those which were sufferers by it would naturally seek for a mitigation of the burden. The others would as naturally be disinclined to a revision, which was likely to end in an increase of their own incumbrances. Their refusal would be too plausible a pretext to the complaining States to withhold their contributions, not to be embraced with avidity; and the non-compliance of these States with their engagements would be a ground of bitter discussion and altercation. If even the rule adopted should in practice justify the equality of its principle, still delinquencies in payments on the part of some of the States would result from a diversity of other causes—the real deficiency of resources; the mismanagement of their finances; accidental disorders in the management of the government; and, in addition to the rest, the reluctance with which men commonly part with money for purposes that have outlived the exigencies which produced them, and interfere with the supply of immediate wants. Delinquencies, from whatever causes, would be productive of complaints, recriminations, and quarrels. There is, perhaps, nothing more likely to disturb the tranquillity of nations than their being bound to mutual contributions for any common object that does not yield an equal and coincident benefit. For it is an observation, as true as it is trite, that there is nothing men differ so readily about as the payment of money.

Laws in violation of private contracts, as they amount to aggressions on the rights of those States whose citizens are injured by them, may be considered as another probable source of hostility. We are not authorized to expect that a more liberal or more equitable spirit would preside over the legislations of the individual States hereafter, if unrestrained by any additional checks, than we have heretofore seen in too many instances disgracing their several codes. We have observed the disposition to retaliation excited in Connecticut in consequence of the enormities perpetrated by the Legislature of Rhode Island; and we reasonably infer that, in similar cases, under other circumstances, a war, not of PARCHMENT, but of the sword, would chastise such atrocious breaches of moral obligation and social justice.

The probability of incompatible alliances between the different States or confederacies and different foreign nations, and the effects of this situation upon the peace of the whole, have been sufficiently unfolded in some preceding papers. From the view they have exhibited of this part of the subject, this conclusion is to be drawn, that America, if not connected at all, or only by the feeble tie of a simple league, offensive and defensive, would, by the operation of such jarring alliances, be gradually entangled in all the pernicious labyrinths of European politics and wars; and by the destructive contentions of the parts into which she was divided, would be likely to become a prey to the artifices and machinations of powers equally the enemies of them all. Divide et impera(1) must be the motto of every nation that either hates or fears us.(2)

PUBLIUS

1. Divide and command.

2. In order that the whole subject of these papers may as soon as possible be laid before the public, it is proposed to publish them four times a week—on Tuesday in the New York Packet and on Thursday in the Daily Advertiser.

FEDERALIST PAPER NO. 8. THE CONSEQUENCES OF HOSTILITIES BETWEEN THE STATES

From the New York Packet. Tuesday, November 20, 1787.

HAMILTON

To the People of the State of New York:

ASSUMING it therefore as an established truth that the several States, in case of disunion, or such combinations of them as might happen to be formed out of the wreck of the general Confederacy, would be subject to those vicissitudes of peace and war, of friendship and enmity, with each other, which have fallen to the lot of all neighboring nations not united under one government, let us enter into a concise detail of some of the consequences that would attend such a situation.

War between the States, in the first period of their separate existence, would be accompanied with much greater distresses than it commonly is in those countries where regular military establishments have long obtained. The disciplined armies always kept on foot on the continent of Europe, though they bear a malignant aspect to liberty and economy, have, notwithstanding, been productive of the signal advantage of rendering sudden conquests impracticable, and of preventing that rapid desolation which used to mark the progress of war prior to their introduction. The art of fortification has contributed to the same ends. The nations of Europe are encircled with chains of fortified places, which mutually obstruct invasion. Campaigns are wasted in reducing two or three frontier garrisons, to gain admittance into an enemy's country. Similar impediments occur at every step, to exhaust the strength and delay the progress of an invader. Formerly, an invading army would penetrate into the heart of a neighboring country almost as soon as intelligence of its approach could be received; but now a comparatively small force of disciplined troops, acting on the defensive, with the aid of posts, is able to impede, and finally to frustrate, the enterprises of one much more considerable. The history of war, in that quarter of the globe, is no longer a history of nations subdued and empires overturned, but of towns taken and retaken; of battles that decide nothing; of retreats more beneficial than victories; of much effort and little acquisition.

In this country the scene would be altogether reversed. The jealousy of military establishments would postpone them as long as possible. The want of fortifications, leaving the frontiers of one state open to another, would facilitate inroads. The populous States would, with little difficulty, overrun their less populous neighbors. Conquests would be as easy to be made as difficult to be retained. War, therefore, would be desultory and predatory. PLUNDER and devastation ever march in the train of irregulars. The calamities of individuals would make the principal figure in the events which would characterize our military exploits.

This picture is not too highly wrought; though, I confess, it would not long remain a just one. Safety from external danger is the most powerful director of national conduct. Even the ardent love of liberty will, after a time, give way to its dictates. The violent destruction of life and property incident to war, the continual effort and alarm attendant on a state of continual danger, will compel nations the most attached to liberty to resort for repose and security to institutions which have a tendency to destroy their civil and political rights. To be more safe, they at length become willing to run the risk of being less free.

The institutions chiefly alluded to are STANDING ARMIES and the correspondent appendages of military establishments. Standing armies, it is said, are not provided against in the new Constitution; and it is therefore inferred that they may exist under it.(1) Their existence, however, from the very terms of the proposition, is, at most, problematical and uncertain. But standing armies, it may be replied, must inevitably result from a dissolution of the Confederacy. Frequent war and constant apprehension, which require a state of as constant preparation, will infallibly produce them. The weaker States or confederacies would first have recourse to them, to put themselves upon an equality with their more potent neighbors. They would endeavor to supply the inferiority of population and resources by a more regular and effective system of defense, by disciplined troops, and by fortifications. They would, at the same time, be necessitated to strengthen the executive arm of government, in doing which their constitutions would acquire a progressive direction toward monarchy. It is of the nature of war to increase the executive at the expense of the legislative authority.

The expedients which have been mentioned would soon give the States or confederacies that made use of them a superiority over their neighbors. Small states, or states of less natural strength, under vigorous governments, and with the assistance of disciplined armies, have often triumphed over large states, or states of greater natural strength, which have been destitute of these advantages. Neither the pride nor the safety of the more important States or confederacies would permit them long to submit to this mortifying and adventitious superiority. They would quickly resort to means similar to those by which it had been effected, to reinstate themselves in their lost pre-eminence. Thus, we should, in a little time, see established in every part of this country the same engines of despotism which have been the scourge of the Old World. This, at least, would be the natural course of things; and our reasonings will be the more likely to be just, in proportion as they are accommodated to this standard.

These are not vague inferences drawn from supposed or speculative defects in a Constitution, the whole power of which is lodged in the hands of a people, or their representatives and delegates, but they are solid conclusions, drawn from the natural and necessary progress of human affairs.

It may, perhaps, be asked, by way of objection to this, why did not standing armies spring up out of the contentions which so often distracted the ancient republics of Greece? Different answers, equally satisfactory, may be given to this question. The industrious habits of the people of the present day, absorbed in the pursuits of gain, and devoted to the improvements of agriculture and commerce, are incompatible with the condition of a nation of soldiers, which was the true condition of the people of those republics. The means of revenue, which have been so greatly multiplied by the increase of gold and silver and of the arts of industry, and the science of finance, which is the offspring of modern times, concurring with the habits of nations, have produced an entire revolution in the system of war, and have rendered disciplined armies, distinct from the body of the citizens, the inseparable companions of frequent hostility.

There is a wide difference, also, between military establishments in a country seldom exposed by its situation to internal invasions, and in one which is often subject to them, and always apprehensive of them. The rulers of the former can have no good pretext, if they are even so inclined, to keep on foot armies so numerous as must of necessity be maintained in the latter. These armies being, in the first case, rarely, if at all, called into activity for interior defense, the people are in no danger of being broken to military subordination. The laws are not accustomed to relaxations, in favor of military exigencies; the civil state remains in full vigor, neither corrupted, nor confounded with the principles or propensities of the other state. The smallness of the army renders the natural strength of the community an overmatch for it; and the citizens, not habituated to look up to the military power for protection, or to submit to its oppressions, neither love nor fear the soldiery; they view them with a spirit of jealous acquiescence in a necessary evil, and stand ready to resist a power which they suppose may be exerted to the prejudice of their rights.

The army under such circumstances may usefully aid the magistrate to suppress a small faction, or an occasional mob, or insurrection; but it will be unable to enforce encroachments against the united efforts of the great body of the people.

In a country in the predicament last described, the contrary of all this happens. The perpetual menacings of danger oblige the government to be always prepared to repel it; its armies must be numerous enough for instant defense. The continual necessity for their services enhances the importance of the soldier, and proportionably degrades the condition of the citizen. The military state becomes elevated above the civil. The inhabitants of territories, often the theatre of war, are unavoidably subjected to frequent infringements on their rights, which serve to weaken their sense of those rights; and by degrees the people are brought to consider the soldiery not only as their protectors, but as their superiors. The transition from this disposition to that of considering them masters, is neither remote nor difficult; but it is very difficult to prevail upon a people under such impressions, to make a bold or effectual resistance to usurpations supported by the military power.

The kingdom of Great Britain falls within the first description. An insular situation, and a powerful marine, guarding it in a great measure against the possibility of foreign invasion, supersede the necessity of a numerous army within the kingdom. A sufficient force to make head against a sudden descent, till the militia could have time to rally and embody, is all that has been deemed requisite. No motive of national policy has demanded, nor would public opinion have tolerated, a larger number of troops upon its domestic establishment. There has been, for a long time past, little room for the operation of the other causes, which have been enumerated as the consequences of internal war. This peculiar felicity of situation has, in a great degree, contributed to preserve the liberty which that country to this day enjoys, in spite of the prevalent venality and corruption. If, on the contrary, Britain had been situated on the continent, and had been compelled, as she would have been, by that situation, to make her military establishments at home coextensive with those of the other great powers of Europe, she, like them, would in all probability be, at this day, a victim to the absolute power of a single man. It is possible, though not easy, that the people of that island may be enslaved from other causes; but it cannot be by the prowess of an army so inconsiderable as that which has been usually kept up within the kingdom.

Documents of Revolution

If we are wise enough to preserve the Union we may for ages enjoy an advantage similar to that of an insulated situation. Europe is at a great distance from us. Her colonies in our vicinity will be likely to continue too much disproportioned in strength to be able to give us any dangerous annoyance. Extensive military establishments cannot, in this position, be necessary to our security. But if we should be disunited, and the integral parts should either remain separated, or, which is most probable, should be thrown together into two or three confederacies, we should be, in a short course of time, in the predicament of the continental powers of Europe—our liberties would be a prey to the means of defending ourselves against the ambition and jealousy of each other.

This is an idea not superficial or futile, but solid and weighty. It deserves the most serious and mature consideration of every prudent and honest man of whatever party. If such men will make a firm and solemn pause, and meditate dispassionately on the importance of this interesting idea; if they will contemplate it in all its attitudes, and trace it to all its consequences, they will not hesitate to part with trivial objections to a Constitution, the rejection of which would in all probability put a final period to the Union. The airy phantoms that flit before the distempered imaginations of some of its adversaries would quickly give place to the more substantial forms of dangers, real, certain, and formidable.

PUBLIUS

1. This objection will be fully examined in its proper place, and it will be shown that the only natural precaution which could have been taken on this subject has been taken; and a much better one than is to be found in any constitution that has been heretofore framed in America, most of which contain no guard at all on this subject.

FEDERALIST PAPER NO. 9. THE UNION AS A SAFEGUARD AGAINST DOMESTIC FACTION AND INSURRECTION

For the Independent Journal. Wednesday, November 21, 1787

HAMILTON

To the People of the State of New York:

A FIRM Union will be of the utmost moment to the peace and liberty of the States, as a barrier against domestic faction and insurrection. It is impossible to read the history of the petty republics of Greece and Italy without feeling sensations of horror and disgust at the distractions with which they were continually agitated, and at the rapid succession of revolutions by which they were kept in a state of perpetual vibration between the extremes of tyranny and anarchy. If they exhibit occasional calms, these only serve as short-lived contrast to the furious storms that are to succeed. If now and then intervals of felicity open to view, we behold them with a mixture of regret, arising from the reflection that the pleasing scenes before us are soon to be overwhelmed by the tempestuous waves of sedition and party rage. If momentary rays of glory break forth from the gloom, while they dazzle us with a transient and fleeting brilliancy, they at the same time admonish us to lament that the vices of government should pervert the direction and tarnish the lustre of those bright talents and exalted endowments for which the favored soils that produced them have been so justly celebrated.

From the disorders that disfigure the annals of those republics the advocates of despotism have drawn arguments, not only against the forms of republican government, but against the very principles of civil liberty. They have decried all free government as inconsistent with the order of society, and have indulged themselves in malicious exultation over its friends and partisans. Happily for mankind, stupendous fabrics reared on the basis of liberty, which have flourished for ages, have, in a few glorious instances, refuted their gloomy sophisms. And, I trust, America will be the broad and solid foundation of other edifices, not less magnificent, which will be equally permanent monuments of their errors.

But it is not to be denied that the portraits they have sketched of republican government were too just copies of the originals from which they were taken. If it had been found impracticable to have devised models of a more perfect structure, the enlightened friends to liberty would have been obliged to abandon the cause of that species of government as indefensible. The science of politics, however, like most other sciences, has received great improvement. The efficacy of various principles is now well understood, which were either not known at all, or imperfectly known to the ancients. The regular distribution of power into distinct departments; the introduction of legislative balances and checks; the institution of courts composed of judges holding their offices during good behavior; the representation of the people in the legislature by deputies of their own election: these are wholly new discoveries, or have made their principal progress towards perfection in modern times. They are means, and powerful means, by which the excellences of republican government may be retained and its imperfections lessened or avoided. To this catalogue of circumstances that tend to the amelioration of popular systems of civil government, I shall venture, however novel it may appear to some, to add one more, on a principle which has been made the foundation of an objection to the new Constitution; I mean the ENLARGEMENT of the ORBIT within which such systems are to revolve, either in respect to the dimensions of a single State or to the consolidation of several smaller States into one great Confederacy. The latter is that which immediately concerns the object under consideration. It will, however, be of use to examine the principle in its application to a single State, which shall be attended to in another place.

The utility of a Confederacy, as well to suppress faction and to guard the internal tranquillity of States, as to increase their external force and security, is in reality not a new idea. It has been practiced upon in different countries and ages, and has received the sanction of the most approved writers on the subject of politics. The opponents of the plan proposed have, with great assiduity, cited and circulated the observations of Montesquieu on the necessity of a contracted territory for a republican government. But they seem not to have been apprised of the sentiments of that great man expressed in another part of his work, nor to have adverted to the consequences of the principle to which they subscribe with such ready acquiescence.

When Montesquieu recommends a small extent for republics, the standards he had in view were of dimensions far short of the limits of almost every one of these States. Neither Virginia, Massachusetts, Pennsylvania, New York, North Carolina, nor Georgia can by any means be compared with the models from which he reasoned and to which the terms of his description apply. If we therefore take his ideas on this point as the criterion of truth, we shall be driven to the alternative either of taking refuge at once in the arms of monarchy, or of splitting ourselves into an infinity of little, jealous, clashing, tumultuous commonwealths, the wretched nurseries of unceasing discord, and the miserable objects of universal pity or contempt. Some of the writers who have come forward on the other side of the question seem to have been aware of the dilemma; and have even been bold enough to hint at the division of the larger States as a desirable thing. Such an infatuated policy, such a desperate expedient, might, by the multiplication of petty offices, answer the views of men who possess not qualifications to extend their influence beyond the narrow circles of personal intrigue, but it could never promote the greatness or happiness of the people of America.

Referring the examination of the principle itself to another place, as has been already mentioned, it will be sufficient to remark here that, in the sense of the author who has been most emphatically quoted upon the occasion, it would only dictate a reduction of the SIZE of the more considerable MEMBERS of the Union, but would not militate against their being all comprehended in one confederate government. And this is the true question, in the discussion of which we are at present interested.

So far are the suggestions of Montesquieu from standing in opposition to a general Union of the States, that he explicitly treats of a confederate republic as the expedient for extending the sphere of popular government, and reconciling the advantages of monarchy with those of republicanism.

"It is very probable," (says he(1)) "that mankind would have been obliged at length to live constantly under the government of a single person, had they not contrived a kind of constitution that has all the internal advantages of a republican, together with the external force of a monarchical government. I mean a CONFEDERATE REPUBLIC."

"This form of government is a convention by which several smaller STATES agree to become members of a larger ONE, which they intend to form. It is a kind of assemblage of societies that constitute a new one, capable of increasing, by means of new associations, till they arrive to such a degree of power as to be able to provide for the security of the united body."

"A republic of this kind, able to withstand an external force, may support itself without any internal corruptions. The form of this society prevents all manner of inconveniences."

"If a single member should attempt to usurp the supreme authority, he could not be supposed to have an equal authority and credit in all the confederate states. Were he to have too great influence over one, this would alarm the rest. Were he to subdue a part, that which would still remain free might oppose him with forces independent of those which he had usurped and overpower him before he could be settled in his usurpation."

"Should a popular insurrection happen in one of the confederate states the others are able to quell it. Should abuses creep into one part, they are reformed by those that remain sound. The state may be destroyed on one side, and not on the other; the confederacy may be dissolved, and the confederates preserve their sovereignty."

"As this government is composed of small republics, it enjoys the internal happiness of each; and with respect to its external situation, it is possessed, by means of the association, of all the advantages of large monarchies."

I have thought it proper to quote at length these interesting passages, because they contain a luminous abridgment of the principal arguments in favor of the Union, and must effectually remove the false impressions which a misapplication of other parts of the work was calculated to make. They have, at the same time, an intimate connection with the more immediate design of this paper; which is, to illustrate the tendency of the Union to repress domestic faction and insurrection.

A distinction, more subtle than accurate, has been raised between a CONFEDERACY and a CONSOLIDATION of the States. The essential characteristic of the first is said to be, the restriction of its authority to the members in their collective capacities, without reaching to the individuals of whom they are composed. It is contended that the national council ought to have no concern with any object of internal administration. An exact equality of suffrage between the members has also been insisted upon as a leading feature of a confederate government. These positions are, in the main, arbitrary; they are supported neither by principle nor precedent. It has indeed happened, that governments of this kind have generally operated in the manner which the distinction taken notice of, supposes to be inherent in their nature; but there have been in most of them extensive exceptions to the practice, which serve to prove, as far as example will go, that there is no absolute rule on the subject. And it will be clearly shown in the course of this investigation that as far as the principle contended for has prevailed, it has been the cause of incurable disorder and imbecility in the government.

The definition of a CONFEDERATE REPUBLIC seems simply to be "an assemblage of societies," or an association of two or more states into one state. The extent, modifications, and objects of the federal authority are mere matters of discretion. So long as the separate organization of the members be not abolished; so long as it exists, by a constitutional necessity, for local purposes; though it should be in perfect subordination to the general authority of the union, it would still be, in fact and in theory, an association of states, or a confederacy. The proposed Constitution, so far from implying an abolition of the State governments, makes them constituent parts of the national sovereignty, by allowing them a direct representation in the Senate, and leaves in their possession certain exclusive and very important portions of sovereign power. This fully corresponds, in every rational import of the terms, with the idea of a federal government.

In the Lycian confederacy, which consisted of twenty-three CITIES or republics, the largest were entitled to THREE votes in the COMMON COUNCIL, those of the middle class to TWO, and the smallest to ONE. The COMMON COUNCIL had the appointment of all the judges and magistrates of the respective CITIES. This was certainly the most, delicate species of interference in their internal administration; for if there be any thing that seems exclusively appropriated to the local jurisdictions, it is the appointment of their own officers. Yet Montesquieu, speaking of this association, says: "Were I to give a model of an excellent Confederate Republic, it would be that of Lycia." Thus we perceive that the distinctions insisted upon were not within the contemplation of this enlightened civilian; and we shall be led to conclude, that they are the novel refinements of an erroneous theory.

PUBLIUS

1. "Spirit of Laws," vol. i., book ix., chap. i.

FEDERALIST PAPER NO. 10. THE SAME SUBJECT CONTINUED (THE UNION AS A SAFEGUARD AGAINST DOMESTIC FACTION AND INSURRECTION)

From the Daily Advertiser. Thursday, November 22, 1787.

MADISON

To the People of the State of New York:

AMONG the numerous advantages promised by a well constructed Union, none deserves to be more accurately developed than its tendency to break and control the violence of faction. The friend of popular governments never finds himself so much alarmed for their character and fate, as when he contemplates their propensity to this dangerous vice. He will not fail, therefore, to set a due value on any plan which, without violating the principles to which he is attached, provides a proper cure for it. The instability, injustice, and confusion introduced into the public councils, have, in truth, been the mortal diseases under which popular governments have everywhere perished; as they continue to be the favorite and fruitful topics from which the adversaries to liberty derive their most specious declamations. The valuable improvements made by the American constitutions on the popular models, both ancient and modern, cannot certainly be too much admired; but it would be an unwarrantable partiality, to contend that they have as effectually obviated the danger on this side, as was wished and expected. Complaints are everywhere heard from our most considerate and virtuous citizens, equally the friends of public and private faith, and of public and personal liberty, that our governments are too unstable, that the public good is disregarded in the conflicts of rival parties, and that measures are too often decided, not according to the rules of justice and the rights of the minor party, but by the superior force of an interested and overbearing majority. However anxiously we may wish that these complaints had no foundation, the evidence, of known facts will not permit us to deny that they are in some degree true. It will be found, indeed, on a candid review of our situation, that some of the distresses under which we labor have been erroneously charged on the operation of our governments; but it will be found, at the same time, that other causes will not alone account for many of our heaviest misfortunes; and, particularly, for that prevailing and increasing distrust of public engagements, and alarm for private rights, which are echoed from one end of the continent to the other. These must be chiefly, if not wholly, effects of the unsteadiness and injustice with which a factious spirit has tainted our public administrations.

By a faction, I understand a number of citizens, whether amounting to a majority or a minority of the whole, who are united and actuated by some common impulse of passion, or of interest, adversed to the rights of other citizens, or to the permanent and aggregate interests of the community.

There are two methods of curing the mischiefs of faction: the one, by removing its causes; the other, by controlling its effects.

There are again two methods of removing the causes of faction: the one, by destroying the liberty which is essential to its existence; the other, by giving to every citizen the same opinions, the same passions, and the same interests.

It could never be more truly said than of the first remedy, that it was worse than the disease. Liberty is to faction what air is to fire, an aliment without which it instantly expires. But it could not be less folly to abolish liberty, which is essential to political life, because it nourishes faction, than it would be to wish the annihilation of air, which is essential to animal life, because it imparts to fire its destructive agency.

The second expedient is as impracticable as the first would be unwise. As long as the reason of man continues fallible, and he is at liberty to exercise it, different opinions will be formed. As long as the connection subsists between his reason and his self-love, his opinions and his passions will have a reciprocal influence on each other; and the former will be objects to which the latter will attach themselves. The diversity in the faculties of men, from which the rights of property originate, is not less an insuperable obstacle to a uniformity of interests. The protection of these faculties is the first object of government. From the protection of different and unequal faculties of acquiring property, the possession of different degrees and kinds of property immediately results; and from the influence of these on the sentiments and views of the respective proprietors, ensues a division of the society into different interests and parties.

The latent causes of faction are thus sown in the nature of man; and we see them everywhere brought into different degrees of activity, according to the different circumstances of civil society. A zeal for different opinions concerning religion, concerning government, and many other points, as well of speculation as of practice; an attachment to different leaders ambitiously contending for pre-eminence and power; or to persons of other descriptions whose fortunes have been interesting to the human passions, have, in turn, divided mankind into parties, inflamed them with mutual animosity, and rendered them much more disposed to vex and oppress each other than to co-operate for their common good. So strong is this propensity of mankind to fall into mutual animosities, that where no substantial occasion presents itself, the most frivolous and fanciful distinctions have been sufficient to kindle their unfriendly passions and excite their most violent conflicts. But the most common and durable source of factions has been the various and unequal distribution of property. Those who hold and those who are without property have ever formed distinct interests in society. Those who are creditors, and those who are debtors, fall under a like discrimination. A landed interest, a manufacturing interest, a mercantile interest, a moneyed interest, with many lesser interests, grow up of necessity in civilized nations, and divide them into different classes, actuated by different sentiments and views. The regulation of these various and interfering interests forms the principal task of modern legislation, and involves the spirit of party and faction in the necessary and ordinary operations of the government.

No man is allowed to be a judge in his own cause, because his interest would certainly bias his judgment, and, not improbably, corrupt his integrity. With equal, nay with greater reason, a body of men are unfit to be both judges and parties at the same time; yet what are many of the most important acts of legislation, but so many judicial determinations, not indeed concerning the rights of single persons, but concerning the rights of large bodies of citizens? And what are the different classes of legislators but advocates and parties to the causes which they determine? Is a law proposed concerning private debts? It is a question to which the creditors are parties on one side and the debtors on the other. Justice ought to hold the balance between them. Yet the parties are, and must be, themselves the judges; and the most numerous party, or, in other words, the most powerful faction must be expected to prevail. Shall domestic manufactures be encouraged, and in what degree, by restrictions on foreign manufactures? are questions which would be differently decided by the landed and the manufacturing classes, and probably by neither with a sole regard to justice and the public good. The apportionment of taxes on the various descriptions of property is an act which seems to require the most exact impartiality; yet there is, perhaps, no legislative act in which greater opportunity and temptation are given to a predominant party to trample on the rules of justice. Every shilling with which they overburden the inferior number, is a shilling saved to their own pockets.

It is in vain to say that enlightened statesmen will be able to adjust these clashing interests, and render them all subservient to the public good. Enlightened statesmen will not always be at the helm. Nor, in many cases, can such an adjustment be made at all without taking into view indirect and remote considerations, which will rarely prevail over the immediate interest which one party may find in disregarding the rights of another or the good of the whole.

The inference to which we are brought is, that the CAUSES of faction cannot be removed, and that relief is only to be sought in the means of controlling its EFFECTS.

If a faction consists of less than a majority, relief is supplied by the republican principle, which enables the majority to defeat its sinister views by regular vote. It may clog the administration, it may convulse the society; but it will be unable to execute and mask its violence under the forms of the Constitution. When a majority is included in a faction, the form of popular government, on the other hand, enables it to sacrifice to its ruling passion or interest both the public good and the rights of other citizens. To secure the public good and private rights against the danger of such a faction, and at the same time to preserve the spirit and the form of popular government, is then the great object to which our inquiries are directed. Let me add that it is the great desideratum by which this form of government can be rescued from the opprobrium under which it has so long labored, and be recommended to the esteem and adoption of mankind.

By what means is this object attainable? Evidently by one of two only. Either the existence of the same passion or interest in a majority at the same time must be prevented, or the majority, having such coexistent passion or interest, must be rendered, by their number and local situation, unable to concert and carry into effect schemes of oppression. If the impulse and the opportunity be suffered to coincide, we well know that neither moral nor religious motives can be relied on as an adequate control. They are not found to be such on the injustice and violence of individuals, and lose their efficacy in proportion to the number combined together, that is, in proportion as their efficacy becomes needful.

From this view of the subject it may be concluded that a pure democracy, by which I mean a society consisting of a small number of citizens, who assemble and administer the government in person, can admit of no cure for the mischiefs of faction.

Documents of Revolution

A common passion or interest will, in almost every case, be felt by a majority of the whole; a communication and concert result from the form of government itself; and there is nothing to check the inducements to sacrifice the weaker party or an obnoxious individual. Hence it is that such democracies have ever been spectacles of turbulence and contention; have ever been found incompatible with personal security or the rights of property; and have in general been as short in their lives as they have been violent in their deaths. Theoretic politicians, who have patronized this species of government, have erroneously supposed that by reducing mankind to a perfect equality in their political rights, they would, at the same time, be perfectly equalized and assimilated in their possessions, their opinions, and their passions.

A republic, by which I mean a government in which the scheme of representation takes place, opens a different prospect, and promises the cure for which we are seeking. Let us examine the points in which it varies from pure democracy, and we shall comprehend both the nature of the cure and the efficacy which it must derive from the Union.

The two great points of difference between a democracy and a republic are: first, the delegation of the government, in the latter, to a small number of citizens elected by the rest; secondly, the greater number of citizens, and greater sphere of country, over which the latter may be extended.

The effect of the first difference is, on the one hand, to refine and enlarge the public views, by passing them through the medium of a chosen body of citizens, whose wisdom may best discern the true interest of their country, and whose patriotism and love of justice will be least likely to sacrifice it to temporary or partial considerations. Under such a regulation, it may well happen that the public voice, pronounced by the representatives of the people, will be more consonant to the public good than if pronounced by the people themselves, convened for the purpose. On the other hand, the effect may be inverted. Men of factious tempers, of local prejudices, or of sinister designs, may, by intrigue, by corruption, or by other means, first obtain the suffrages, and then betray the interests, of the people. The question resulting is, whether small or extensive republics are more favorable to the election of proper guardians of the public weal; and it is clearly decided in favor of the latter by two obvious considerations:

In the first place, it is to be remarked that, however small the republic may be, the representatives must be raised to a certain number, in order to guard against the cabals of a few; and that, however large it may be, they must be limited to a certain number, in order to guard against the confusion of a multitude. Hence, the number of representatives in the two cases not being in proportion to that of the two constituents, and being proportionally greater in the small republic, it follows that, if the proportion of fit characters be not less in the large than in the small republic, the former will present a greater option, and consequently a greater probability of a fit choice.

In the next place, as each representative will be chosen by a greater number of citizens in the large than in the small republic, it will be more difficult for unworthy candidates to practice with success the vicious arts by which elections are too often carried; and the suffrages of the people being more free, will be more likely to centre in men who possess the most attractive merit and the most diffusive and established characters.

It must be confessed that in this, as in most other cases, there is a mean, on both sides of which inconveniences will be found to lie. By enlarging too much the number of electors, you render the representatives too little acquainted with all their local circumstances and lesser interests; as by reducing it too much, you render him unduly attached to these, and too little fit to comprehend and pursue great and national objects. The federal Constitution forms a happy combination in this respect; the great and aggregate interests being referred to the national, the local and particular to the State legislatures.

The other point of difference is, the greater number of citizens and extent of territory which may be brought within the compass of republican than of democratic government; and it is this circumstance principally which renders factious combinations less to be dreaded in the former than in the latter. The smaller the society, the fewer probably will be the distinct parties and interests composing it; the fewer the distinct parties and interests, the more frequently will a majority be found of the same party; and the smaller the number of individuals composing a majority, and the smaller the compass within which they are placed, the more easily will they concert and execute their plans of oppression. Extend the sphere, and you take in a greater variety of parties and interests; you make it less probable that a majority of the whole will have a common motive to invade the rights of other citizens; or if such a common motive exists, it will be more difficult for all who feel it to discover their own strength, and to act in unison with each other. Besides other impediments, it may be remarked that, where there is a consciousness of unjust or dishonorable purposes, communication is always checked by distrust in proportion to the number whose concurrence is necessary.

Hence, it clearly appears, that the same advantage which a republic has over a democracy, in controlling the effects of faction, is enjoyed by a large over a small republic,—is enjoyed by the Union over the States composing it. Does the advantage consist in the substitution of representatives whose enlightened views and virtuous sentiments render them superior to local prejudices and schemes of injustice? It will not be denied that the representation of the Union will be most likely to possess these requisite endowments. Does it consist in the greater security afforded by a greater variety of parties, against the event of any one party being able to outnumber and oppress the rest? In an equal degree does the increased variety of parties comprised within the Union, increase this security. Does it, in fine, consist in the greater obstacles opposed to the concert and accomplishment of the secret wishes of an unjust and interested majority? Here, again, the extent of the Union gives it the most palpable advantage.

The influence of factious leaders may kindle a flame within their particular States, but will be unable to spread a general conflagration through the other States. A religious sect may degenerate into a political faction in a part of the Confederacy; but the variety of sects dispersed over the entire face of it must secure the national councils against any danger from that source. A rage for paper money, for an abolition of debts, for an equal division of property, or for any other improper or wicked project, will be less apt to pervade the whole body of the Union than a particular member of it; in the same proportion as such a malady is more likely to taint a particular county or district, than an entire State.

In the extent and proper structure of the Union, therefore, we behold a republican remedy for the diseases most incident to republican government. And according to the degree of pleasure and pride we feel in being republicans, ought to be our zeal in cherishing the spirit and supporting the character of Federalists.

PUBLIUS

FEDERALIST PAPER NO. 11. THE UTILITY OF THE UNION IN RESPECT TO COMMERCIAL RELATIONS AND A NAVY

For the Independent Journal. Saturday, November 24, 1787

HAMILTON

To the People of the State of New York:

THE importance of the Union, in a commercial light, is one of those points about which there is least room to entertain a difference of opinion, and which has, in fact, commanded the most general assent of men who have any acquaintance with the subject. This applies as well to our intercourse with foreign countries as with each other.

There are appearances to authorize a supposition that the adventurous spirit, which distinguishes the commercial character of America, has already excited uneasy sensations in several of the maritime powers of Europe. They seem to be apprehensive of our too great interference in that carrying trade, which is the support of their navigation and the foundation of their naval strength. Those of them which have colonies in America look forward to what this country is capable of becoming, with painful solicitude. They foresee the dangers that may threaten their American dominions from the neighborhood of States, which have all the dispositions, and would possess all the means, requisite to the creation of a powerful marine. Impressions of this kind will naturally indicate the policy of fostering divisions among us, and of depriving us, as far as possible, of an ACTIVE COMMERCE in our own bottoms. This would answer the threefold purpose of preventing our interference in their navigation, of monopolizing the profits of our trade, and of clipping the wings by which we might soar to a dangerous greatness. Did not prudence forbid the detail, it would not be difficult to trace, by facts, the workings of this policy to the cabinets of ministers.

If we continue united, we may counteract a policy so unfriendly to our prosperity in a variety of ways. By prohibitory regulations, extending, at the same time, throughout the States, we may oblige foreign countries to bid against each other, for the privileges of our markets. This assertion will not appear chimerical to those who are able to appreciate the importance of the markets of three millions of people—increasing in rapid progression, for the most part exclusively addicted to agriculture, and likely from local circumstances to remain so—to any manufacturing nation; and the immense difference there would be to the trade and navigation of such a nation, between a direct communication in its own ships, and an indirect conveyance of its products and returns, to and from America, in the ships of another country. Suppose, for instance, we had a government in America, capable of excluding Great Britain (with whom we have at present no treaty of commerce) from all our ports; what would be the probable operation of this step upon her politics? Would it not enable us to negotiate, with the fairest prospect of success, for commercial privileges of the most valuable and extensive kind, in the dominions of that kingdom? When these questions have been asked, upon other occasions, they have received a plausible, but not a solid or satisfactory answer. It has been said that prohibitions on our part would produce no change in the system of Britain, because she could prosecute her trade with us through the medium of the Dutch, who would be her immediate customers and paymasters for those articles which were wanted for the supply of our markets. But would not her navigation be materially injured by the loss of the important advantage of being her own carrier in that trade? Would not the principal part of its profits be intercepted by the Dutch, as a compensation for their agency and risk? Would not the mere circumstance of freight occasion a considerable deduction? Would not so circuitous an intercourse facilitate the competitions of other nations, by enhancing the price of British commodities in our markets, and by transferring to other hands the management of this interesting branch of the British commerce?

A mature consideration of the objects suggested by these questions will justify a belief that the real disadvantages to Britain from such a state of things, conspiring with the pre-possessions of a great part of the nation in favor of the American trade, and with the importunities of the West India islands, would produce a relaxation in her present system, and would let us into the enjoyment of privileges in the markets of those islands elsewhere, from which our trade would derive the most substantial benefits. Such a point gained from the British government, and which could not be expected without an equivalent in exemptions and immunities in our markets, would be likely to have a correspondent effect on the conduct of other nations, who would not be inclined to see themselves altogether supplanted in our trade.

Documents of Revolution

A further resource for influencing the conduct of European nations toward us, in this respect, would arise from the establishment of a federal navy. There can be no doubt that the continuance of the Union under an efficient government would put it in our power, at a period not very distant, to create a navy which, if it could not vie with those of the great maritime powers, would at least be of respectable weight if thrown into the scale of either of two contending parties. This would be more peculiarly the case in relation to operations in the West Indies. A few ships of the line, sent opportunely to the reinforcement of either side, would often be sufficient to decide the fate of a campaign, on the event of which interests of the greatest magnitude were suspended. Our position is, in this respect, a most commanding one. And if to this consideration we add that of the usefulness of supplies from this country, in the prosecution of military operations in the West Indies, it will readily be perceived that a situation so favorable would enable us to bargain with great advantage for commercial privileges. A price would be set not only upon our friendship, but upon our neutrality. By a steady adherence to the Union we may hope, erelong, to become the arbiter of Europe in America, and to be able to incline the balance of European competitions in this part of the world as our interest may dictate.

But in the reverse of this eligible situation, we shall discover that the rivalships of the parts would make them checks upon each other, and would frustrate all the tempting advantages which nature has kindly placed within our reach. In a state so insignificant our commerce would be a prey to the wanton intermeddlings of all nations at war with each other; who, having nothing to fear from us, would with little scruple or remorse, supply their wants by depredations on our property as often as it fell in their way. The rights of neutrality will only be respected when they are defended by an adequate power. A nation, despicable by its weakness, forfeits even the privilege of being neutral.

Under a vigorous national government, the natural strength and resources of the country, directed to a common interest, would baffle all the combinations of European jealousy to restrain our growth. This situation would even take away the motive to such combinations, by inducing an impracticability of success. An active commerce, an extensive navigation, and a flourishing marine would then be the offspring of moral and physical necessity. We might defy the little arts of the little politicians to control or vary the irresistible and unchangeable course of nature.

But in a state of disunion, these combinations might exist and might operate with success. It would be in the power of the maritime nations, availing themselves of our universal impotence, to prescribe the conditions of our political existence; and as they have a common interest in being our carriers, and still more in preventing our becoming theirs, they would in all probability combine to embarrass our navigation in such a manner as would in effect destroy it, and confine us to a PASSIVE COMMERCE. We should then be compelled to content ourselves with the first price of our commodities, and to see the profits of our trade snatched from us to enrich our enemies and persecutors. That unequaled spirit of enterprise, which signalizes the genius of the American merchants and navigators, and which is in itself an inexhaustible mine of national wealth, would be stifled and lost, and poverty and disgrace would overspread a country which, with wisdom, might make herself the admiration and envy of the world.

There are rights of great moment to the trade of America which are rights of the Union—I allude to the fisheries, to the navigation of the Western lakes, and to that of the Mississippi. The dissolution of the Confederacy would give room for delicate questions concerning the future existence of these rights; which the interest of more powerful partners would hardly fail to solve to our disadvantage. The disposition of Spain with regard to the Mississippi needs no comment. France and Britain are concerned with us in the fisheries, and view them as of the utmost moment to their navigation. They, of course, would hardly remain long indifferent to that decided mastery, of which experience has shown us to be possessed in this valuable branch of traffic, and by which we are able to undersell those nations in their own markets. What more natural than that they should be disposed to exclude from the lists such dangerous competitors?

This branch of trade ought not to be considered as a partial benefit. All the navigating States may, in different degrees, advantageously participate in it, and under circumstances of a greater extension of mercantile capital, would not be unlikely to do it. As a nursery of seamen, it now is, or when time shall have more nearly assimilated the principles of navigation in the several States, will become, a universal resource. To the establishment of a navy, it must be indispensable.

To this great national object, a NAVY, union will contribute in various ways. Every institution will grow and flourish in proportion to the quantity and extent of the means concentred towards its formation and support. A navy of the United States, as it would embrace the resources of all, is an object far less remote than a navy of any single State or partial confederacy, which would only embrace the resources of a single part. It happens, indeed, that different portions of confederated America possess each some peculiar advantage for this essential establishment. The more southern States furnish in greater abundance certain kinds of naval stores—tar, pitch, and turpentine. Their wood for the construction of ships is also of a more solid and lasting texture. The difference in the duration of the ships of which the navy might be composed, if chiefly constructed of

Southern wood, would be of signal importance, either in the view of naval strength or of national economy. Some of the Southern and of the Middle States yield a greater plenty of iron, and of better quality. Seamen must chiefly be drawn from the Northern hive. The necessity of naval protection to external or maritime commerce does not require a particular elucidation, no more than the conduciveness of that species of commerce to the prosperity of a navy.

An unrestrained intercourse between the States themselves will advance the trade of each by an interchange of their respective productions, not only for the supply of reciprocal wants at home, but for exportation to foreign markets. The veins of commerce in every part will be replenished, and will acquire additional motion and vigor from a free circulation of the commodities of every part. Commercial enterprise will have much greater scope, from the diversity in the productions of different States. When the staple of one fails from a bad harvest or unproductive crop, it can call to its aid the staple of another. The variety, not less than the value, of products for exportation contributes to the activity of foreign commerce. It can be conducted upon much better terms with a large number of materials of a given value than with a small number of materials of the same value; arising from the competitions of trade and from the fluctuations of markets. Particular articles may be in great demand at certain periods, and unsalable at others; but if there be a variety of articles, it can scarcely happen that they should all be at one time in the latter predicament, and on this account the operations of the merchant would be less liable to any considerable obstruction or stagnation. The speculative trader will at once perceive the force of these observations, and will acknowledge that the aggregate balance of the commerce of the United States would bid fair to be much more favorable than that of the thirteen States without union or with partial unions.

It may perhaps be replied to this, that whether the States are united or disunited, there would still be an intimate intercourse between them which would answer the same ends; this intercourse would be fettered, interrupted, and narrowed by a multiplicity of causes, which in the course of these papers have been amply detailed. A unity of commercial, as well as political, interests, can only result from a unity of government.

There are other points of view in which this subject might be placed, of a striking and animating kind. But they would lead us too far into the regions of futurity, and would involve topics not proper for a newspaper discussion. I shall briefly observe, that our situation invites and our interests prompt us to aim at an ascendant in the system of American affairs. The world may politically, as well as geographically, be divided into four parts, each having a distinct set of interests. Unhappily for the other three, Europe, by her arms and by her negotiations, by force and by fraud, has, in different degrees, extended her dominion over them all. Africa, Asia, and America, have successively felt her domination. The superiority she has long maintained has tempted her to plume herself as the Mistress of the World, and to consider the rest of mankind as created for her benefit. Men admired as profound philosophers have, in direct terms, attributed to her inhabitants a physical superiority, and have gravely asserted that all animals, and with them the human species, degenerate in America—that even dogs cease to bark after having breathed awhile in our atmosphere.(1) Facts have too long supported these arrogant pretensions of the Europeans. It belongs to us to vindicate the honor of the human race, and to teach that assuming brother, moderation. Union will enable us to do it. Disunion will will add another victim to his triumphs. Let Americans disdain to be the instruments of European greatness! Let the thirteen States, bound together in a strict and indissoluble Union, concur in erecting one great American system, superior to the control of all transatlantic force or influence, and able to dictate the terms of the connection between the old and the new world!

PUBLIUS "Recherches philosophiques sur les Americains."

FEDERALIST PAPER NO. 12. THE UTILITY OF THE UNION IN RESPECT TO REVENUE

From the New York Packet. Tuesday, November 27, 1787.

HAMILTON

To the People of the State of New York:

THE effects of Union upon the commercial prosperity of the States have been sufficiently delineated. Its tendency to promote the interests of revenue will be the subject of our present inquiry.

The prosperity of commerce is now perceived and acknowledged by all enlightened statesmen to be the most useful as well as the most productive source of national wealth, and has accordingly become a primary object of their political cares. By multiplying the means of gratification, by promoting the introduction and circulation of the precious metals, those darling objects of human avarice and enterprise, it serves to vivify and invigorate the channels of industry, and to make them flow with greater activity and copiousness. The assiduous merchant, the laborious husbandman, the active mechanic, and the industrious manufacturer,—all orders of men, look forward with eager expectation and growing alacrity to this pleasing reward of their toils. The often-agitated question between agriculture and commerce has, from indubitable experience, received a decision which has silenced the rivalship that once subsisted between them, and has proved, to the satisfaction of their friends, that their interests are intimately blended and interwoven. It has been found in various countries that, in proportion as commerce has flourished, land has risen in value. And how could it have happened otherwise? Could that which procures a freer vent for the products of the earth, which furnishes new incitements to the cultivation of land, which is the most powerful instrument in increasing the quantity of money in a state—could that, in fine, which is the faithful handmaid of labor and industry, in every shape, fail to augment that article, which is the prolific parent of far the greatest part of the objects upon which they are exerted? It is astonishing that so simple a truth should ever have had an adversary; and it is one, among a multitude of proofs, how apt a spirit of ill-informed jealousy, or of too great abstraction and refinement, is to lead men astray from the plainest truths of reason and conviction.

The ability of a country to pay taxes must always be proportioned, in a great degree, to the quantity of money in circulation, and to the celerity with which it circulates. Commerce, contributing to both these objects, must of necessity render the payment of taxes easier, and facilitate the requisite supplies to the treasury. The hereditary dominions of the Emperor of Germany contain a great extent of fertile, cultivated, and populous territory, a large proportion of which is situated in mild and luxuriant climates. In some parts of this territory are to be found the best gold and silver mines in Europe. And yet, from the want of the fostering influence of commerce, that monarch can boast but slender revenues. He has several times been compelled to owe obligations to the pecuniary succors of other nations for the preservation of his essential interests, and is unable, upon the strength of his own resources, to sustain a long or continued war.

But it is not in this aspect of the subject alone that Union will be seen to conduce to the purpose of revenue. There are other points of view, in which its influence will appear more immediate and decisive. It is evident from the state of the country, from the habits of the people, from the experience we have had on the point itself, that it is impracticable to raise any very considerable sums by direct taxation. Tax laws have in vain been multiplied; new methods to enforce the collection have in vain been tried; the public expectation has been uniformly disappointed, and the treasuries of the States have remained empty. The popular system of administration inherent in the nature of popular government, coinciding with the real scarcity of money incident to a languid and mutilated state of trade, has hitherto defeated every experiment for extensive collections, and has at length taught the different legislatures the folly of attempting them.

No person acquainted with what happens in other countries will be surprised at this circumstance. In so opulent a nation as that of Britain, where direct taxes from superior wealth must be much more tolerable, and, from the vigor of the government, much more practicable, than in America, far the greatest part of the national revenue is derived from taxes of the indirect kind, from imposts, and from excises. Duties on imported articles form a large branch of this latter description.

Documents of Revolution

In America, it is evident that we must a long time depend for the means of revenue chiefly on such duties. In most parts of it, excises must be confined within a narrow compass. The genius of the people will ill brook the inquisitive and peremptory spirit of excise laws. The pockets of the farmers, on the other hand, will reluctantly yield but scanty supplies, in the unwelcome shape of impositions on their houses and lands; and personal property is too precarious and invisible a fund to be laid hold of in any other way than by the imperceptible agency of taxes on consumption.

If these remarks have any foundation, that state of things which will best enable us to improve and extend so valuable a resource must be best adapted to our political welfare. And it cannot admit of a serious doubt, that this state of things must rest on the basis of a general Union. As far as this would be conducive to the interests of commerce, so far it must tend to the extension of the revenue to be drawn from that source. As far as it would contribute to rendering regulations for the collection of the duties more simple and efficacious, so far it must serve to answer the purposes of making the same rate of duties more productive, and of putting it into the power of the government to increase the rate without prejudice to trade.

The relative situation of these States; the number of rivers with which they are intersected, and of bays that wash there shores; the facility of communication in every direction; the affinity of language and manners; the familiar habits of intercourse;—all these are circumstances that would conspire to render an illicit trade between them a matter of little difficulty, and would insure frequent evasions of the commercial regulations of each other. The separate States or confederacies would be necessitated by mutual jealousy to avoid the temptations to that kind of trade by the lowness of their duties. The temper of our governments, for a long time to come, would not permit those rigorous precautions by which the European nations guard the avenues into their respective countries, as well by land as by water; and which, even there, are found insufficient obstacles to the adventurous stratagems of avarice.

In France, there is an army of patrols (as they are called) constantly employed to secure their fiscal regulations against the inroads of the dealers in contraband trade. Mr. Neckar computes the number of these patrols at upwards of twenty thousand. This shows the immense difficulty in preventing that species of traffic, where there is an inland communication, and places in a strong light the disadvantages with which the collection of duties in this country would be encumbered, if by disunion the States should be placed in a situation, with respect to each other, resembling that of France with respect to her neighbors. The arbitrary and vexatious powers with which the patrols are necessarily armed, would be intolerable in a free country.

If, on the contrary, there be but one government pervading all the States, there will be, as to the principal part of our commerce, but ONE SIDE to guard—the ATLANTIC COAST. Vessels arriving directly from foreign countries, laden with valuable cargoes, would rarely choose to hazard themselves to the complicated and critical perils which would attend attempts to unlade prior to their coming into port. They would have to dread both the dangers of the coast, and of detection, as well after as before their arrival at the places of their final destination. An ordinary degree of vigilance would be competent to the prevention of any material infractions upon the rights of the revenue. A few armed vessels, judiciously stationed at the entrances of our ports, might at a small expense be made useful sentinels of the laws. And the government having the same interest to provide against violations everywhere, the co-operation of its measures in each State would have a powerful tendency to render them effectual. Here also we should preserve by Union, an advantage which nature holds out to us, and which would be relinquished by separation. The United States lie at a great distance from Europe, and at a considerable distance from all other places with which they would have extensive connections of foreign trade. The passage from them to us, in a few hours, or in a single night, as between the coasts of France and Britain, and of other neighboring nations, would be impracticable. This is a prodigious security against a direct contraband with foreign countries; but a circuitous contraband to one State, through the medium of another, would be both easy and safe. The difference between a direct importation from abroad, and an indirect importation through the channel of a neighboring State, in small parcels, according to time and opportunity, with the additional facilities of inland communication, must be palpable to every man of discernment.

It is therefore evident, that one national government would be able, at much less expense, to extend the duties on imports, beyond comparison, further than would be practicable to the States separately, or to any partial confederacies. Hitherto, I believe, it may safely be asserted, that these duties have not upon an average exceeded in any State three per cent. In France they are estimated to be about fifteen per cent., and in Britain they exceed this proportion.(1) There seems to be nothing to hinder their being increased in this country to at least treble their present amount. The single article of ardent spirits, under federal regulation, might be made to furnish a considerable revenue. Upon a ratio to the importation into this State, the whole quantity imported into the United States may be estimated at four millions of gallons; which, at a shilling per gallon, would produce two hundred thousand pounds. That article would well bear this rate of duty; and if it should tend to diminish the consumption of it, such an effect would be equally favorable to the agriculture, to the economy, to the morals, and to the health of the society. There is, perhaps, nothing so much a subject of national extravagance as these spirits.

What will be the consequence, if we are not able to avail ourselves of the resource in question in its full extent? A nation cannot long exist without revenues. Destitute of this essential support, it must resign its independence, and sink into the degraded condition of a province. This is an extremity to which no government will of choice accede. Revenue, therefore, must be had at all events. In this country, if the principal part be not drawn from commerce, it must fall with oppressive weight upon land. It has been already intimated that excises, in their true signification, are too little in unison with the feelings of the people, to admit of great use being made of that mode of taxation; nor, indeed, in the States where almost the sole employment is agriculture, are the objects proper for excise sufficiently numerous to permit very ample collections in that way. Personal estate (as has been before remarked), from the difficulty in tracing it, cannot be subjected to large contributions, by any other means than by taxes on consumption. In populous cities, it may be enough the subject of conjecture, to occasion the oppression of individuals, without much aggregate benefit to the State; but beyond these circles, it must, in a great measure, escape the eye and the hand of the tax-gatherer. As the necessities of the State, nevertheless, must be satisfied in some mode or other, the defect of other resources must throw the principal weight of public burdens on the possessors of land. And as, on the other hand, the wants of the government can never obtain an adequate supply, unless all the sources of revenue are open to its demands, the finances of the community, under such embarrassments, cannot be put into a situation consistent with its respectability or its security. Thus we shall not even have the consolations of a full treasury, to atone for the oppression of that valuable class of the citizens who are employed in the cultivation of the soil. But public and private distress will keep pace with each other in gloomy concert; and unite in deploring the infatuation of those counsels which led to disunion.

PUBLIUS

1. If my memory be right they amount to twenty per cent.

FEDERALIST PAPER NO. 13. ADVANTAGE OF THE UNION IN RESPECT TO ECONOMY IN GOVERNMENT

For the Independent Journal. Wednesday, November 28, 1787

HAMILTON

To the People of the State of New York:

As CONNECTED with the subject of revenue, we may with propriety consider that of economy. The money saved from one object may be usefully applied to another, and there will be so much the less to be drawn from the pockets of the people. If the States are united under one government, there will be but one national civil list to support; if they are divided into several confederacies, there will be as many different national civil lists to be provided for—and each of them, as to the principal departments, coextensive with that which would be necessary for a government of the whole. The entire separation of the States into thirteen unconnected sovereignties is a project too extravagant and too replete with danger to have many advocates. The ideas of men who speculate upon the dismemberment of the empire seem generally turned toward three confederacies—one consisting of the four Northern, another of the four Middle, and a third of the five Southern States. There is little probability that there would be a greater number. According to this distribution, each confederacy would comprise an extent of territory larger than that of the kingdom of Great Britain. No well-informed man will suppose that the affairs of such a confederacy can be properly regulated by a government less comprehensive in its organs or institutions than that which has been proposed by the convention. When the dimensions of a State attain to a certain magnitude, it requires the same energy of government and the same forms of administration which are requisite in one of much greater extent. This idea admits not of precise demonstration, because there is no rule by which we can measure the momentum of civil power necessary to the government of any given number of individuals; but when we consider that the island of Britain, nearly commensurate with each of the supposed confederacies, contains about eight millions of people, and when we reflect upon the degree of authority required to direct the passions of so large a society to the public good, we shall see no reason to doubt that the like portion of power would be sufficient to perform the same task in a society far more numerous. Civil power, properly organized and exerted, is capable of diffusing its force to a very great extent; and can, in a manner, reproduce itself in every part of a great empire by a judicious arrangement of subordinate institutions.

The supposition that each confederacy into which the States would be likely to be divided would require a government not less comprehensive than the one proposed, will be strengthened by another supposition, more probable than that which presents us with three confederacies as the alternative to a general Union. If we attend carefully to geographical and commercial considerations, in conjunction with the habits and prejudices of the different States, we shall be led to conclude that in case of disunion they will most naturally league themselves under two governments. The four Eastern States, from all the causes that form the links of national sympathy and connection, may with certainty be expected to unite. New York, situated as she is, would never be unwise enough to oppose a feeble and unsupported flank to the weight of that confederacy. There are other obvious reasons that would facilitate her accession to it. New Jersey is too small a State to think of being a frontier, in opposition to this still more powerful combination; nor do there appear to be any obstacles to her admission into it. Even Pennsylvania would have strong inducements to join the Northern league. An active foreign commerce, on the basis of her own navigation, is her true policy, and coincides with the opinions and dispositions of her citizens. The more Southern States, from various circumstances, may not think themselves much interested in the encouragement of navigation. They may prefer a system which would give unlimited scope to all nations to be the carriers as well as the purchasers of their commodities. Pennsylvania may not choose to confound her interests in a connection so adverse to her policy. As she must at all events be a frontier, she may deem it most consistent with her safety to have her exposed side turned towards the weaker power of the Southern, rather than towards the stronger power of the Northern, Confederacy. This would give her the fairest chance to avoid being the Flanders of America. Whatever may be the determination of Pennsylvania, if the Northern Confederacy includes New Jersey, there is no likelihood of more than one confederacy to the south of that State.

Nothing can be more evident than that the thirteen States will be able to support a national government better than one half, or one third, or any number less than the whole. This reflection must have great weight in obviating that objection to the proposed plan, which is founded on the principle of expense; an objection, however, which, when we come to take a nearer view of it, will appear in every light to stand on mistaken ground.

If, in addition to the consideration of a plurality of civil lists, we take into view the number of persons who must necessarily be employed to guard the inland communication between the different confederacies against illicit trade, and who in time will infallibly spring up out of the necessities of revenue; and if we also take into view the military establishments which it has been shown would unavoidably result from the jealousies and conflicts of the several nations into which the States would be divided, we shall clearly discover that a separation would be not less injurious to the economy, than to the tranquillity, commerce, revenue, and liberty of every part.

PUBLIUS

FEDERALIST PAPER NO. 14. OBJECTIONS TO THE PROPOSED CONSTITUTION FROM EXTENT OF TERRITORY ANSWERED

From the New York Packet. Friday, November 30, 1787.

MADISON

To the People of the State of New York:

WE HAVE seen the necessity of the Union, as our bulwark against foreign danger, as the conservator of peace among ourselves, as the guardian of our commerce and other common interests, as the only substitute for those military establishments which have subverted the liberties of the Old World, and as the proper antidote for the diseases of faction, which have proved fatal to other popular governments, and of which alarming symptoms have been betrayed by our own. All that remains, within this branch of our inquiries, is to take notice of an objection that may be drawn from the great extent of country which the Union embraces. A few observations on this subject will be the more proper, as it is perceived that the adversaries of the new Constitution are availing themselves of the prevailing prejudice with regard to the practicable sphere of republican administration, in order to supply, by imaginary difficulties, the want of those solid objections which they endeavor in vain to find.

The error which limits republican government to a narrow district has been unfolded and refuted in preceding papers. I remark here only that it seems to owe its rise and prevalence chiefly to the confounding of a republic with a democracy, applying to the former reasonings drawn from the nature of the latter. The true distinction between these forms was also adverted to on a former occasion. It is, that in a democracy, the people meet and exercise the government in person; in a republic, they assemble and administer it by their representatives and agents. A democracy, consequently, will be confined to a small spot. A republic may be extended over a large region.

To this accidental source of the error may be added the artifice of some celebrated authors, whose writings have had a great share in forming the modern standard of political opinions. Being subjects either of an absolute or limited monarchy, they have endeavored to heighten the advantages, or palliate the evils of those forms, by placing in comparison the vices and defects of the republican, and by citing as specimens of the latter the turbulent democracies of ancient Greece and modern Italy. Under the confusion of names, it has been an easy task to transfer to a republic observations applicable to a democracy only; and among others, the observation that it can never be established but among a small number of people, living within a small compass of territory.

Such a fallacy may have been the less perceived, as most of the popular governments of antiquity were of the democratic species; and even in modern Europe, to which we owe the great principle of representation, no example is seen of a government wholly popular, and founded, at the same time, wholly on that principle. If Europe has the merit of discovering this great mechanical power in government, by the simple agency of which the will of the largest political body may be concentred, and its force directed to any object which the public good requires, America can claim the merit of making the discovery the basis of unmixed and extensive republics. It is only to be lamented that any of her citizens should wish to deprive her of the additional merit of displaying its full efficacy in the establishment of the comprehensive system now under her consideration.

As the natural limit of a democracy is that distance from the central point which will just permit the most remote citizens to assemble as often as their public functions demand, and will include no greater number than can join in those functions; so the natural limit of a republic is that distance from the centre which will barely allow the representatives to meet as often as may be necessary for the administration of public affairs. Can it be said that the limits of the United States exceed this distance? It will not be said by those who recollect that the Atlantic coast is the longest side of the Union, that during the term of thirteen years, the representatives of the States have been almost continually assembled, and that the members from the most distant States are not chargeable with greater intermissions of attendance than those from the States in the neighborhood of Congress.

That we may form a juster estimate with regard to this interesting subject, let us resort to the actual dimensions of the Union. The limits, as fixed by the treaty of peace, are: on the east the Atlantic, on the south the latitude of thirty-one degrees, on the west the Mississippi, and on the north an irregular line running in some instances beyond the forty-fifth degree, in others falling as low as the forty-second. The southern shore of Lake Erie lies below that latitude. Computing the distance between the thirty-first and forty-fifth degrees, it amounts to nine hundred and seventy-three common miles; computing it from thirty-one to forty-two degrees, to seven hundred and sixty-four miles and a half. Taking the mean for the distance, the amount will be eight hundred and sixty-eight miles and three-fourths. The mean distance from the Atlantic to the Mississippi does not probably exceed seven hundred and fifty miles. On a comparison of this extent with that of several countries in Europe, the practicability of rendering our system commensurate to it appears to be demonstrable. It is not a great deal larger than Germany, where a diet representing the whole empire is continually assembled; or than Poland before the late dismemberment, where another national diet was the depositary of the supreme power. Passing by France and Spain, we find that in Great Britain, inferior as it may be in size, the representatives of the northern extremity of the island have as far to travel to the national council as will be required of those of the most remote parts of the Union.

Favorable as this view of the subject may be, some observations remain which will place it in a light still more satisfactory.

In the first place it is to be remembered that the general government is not to be charged with the whole power of making and administering laws. Its jurisdiction is limited to certain enumerated objects, which concern all the members of the republic, but which are not to be attained by the separate provisions of any. The subordinate governments, which can extend their care to all those other subjects which can be separately provided for, will retain their due authority and activity. Were it proposed by the plan of the convention to abolish the governments of the particular States, its adversaries would have some ground for their objection; though it would not be difficult to show that if they were abolished the general government would be compelled, by the principle of self-preservation, to reinstate them in their proper jurisdiction.

A second observation to be made is that the immediate object of the federal Constitution is to secure the union of the thirteen primitive States, which we know to be practicable; and to add to them such other States as may arise in their own bosoms, or in their neighborhoods, which we cannot doubt to be equally practicable. The arrangements that may be necessary for those angles and fractions of our territory which lie on our northwestern frontier, must be left to those whom further discoveries and experience will render more equal to the task.

Let it be remarked, in the third place, that the intercourse throughout the Union will be facilitated by new improvements. Roads will everywhere be shortened, and kept in better order; accommodations for travelers will be multiplied and meliorated; an interior navigation on our eastern side will be opened throughout, or nearly throughout, the whole extent of the thirteen States. The communication between the Western and Atlantic districts, and between different parts of each, will be rendered more and more easy by those numerous canals with which the beneficence of nature has intersected our country, and which art finds it so little difficult to connect and complete.

A fourth and still more important consideration is, that as almost every State will, on one side or other, be a frontier, and will thus find, in regard to its safety, an inducement to make some sacrifices for the sake of the general protection; so the States which lie at the greatest distance from the heart of the Union, and which, of course, may partake least of the ordinary circulation of its benefits, will be at the same time immediately contiguous to foreign nations, and will consequently stand, on particular occasions, in greatest need of its strength and resources. It may be inconvenient for Georgia, or the States forming our western or northeastern borders, to send their representatives to the seat of government; but they would find it more so to struggle alone against an invading enemy, or even to support alone the whole expense of those precautions which may be dictated by the neighborhood of continual danger. If they should derive less benefit, therefore, from the Union in some respects than the less distant States, they will derive greater benefit from it in other respects, and thus the proper equilibrium will be maintained throughout.

I submit to you, my fellow-citizens, these considerations, in full confidence that the good sense which has so often marked your decisions will allow them their due weight and effect; and that you will never suffer difficulties, however formidable in appearance, or however fashionable the error on which they may be founded, to drive you into the gloomy and perilous scene into which the advocates for disunion would conduct you. Hearken not to the unnatural voice which tells you that the people of America, knit together as they are by so many cords of affection, can no longer live together as members of the same family; can no longer continue the mutual guardians of their mutual happiness; can no longer be fellow citizens of one great, respectable, and flourishing empire. Hearken not to the voice which petulantly tells you that the form of government recommended for your adoption is a novelty in the political world; that it has never yet had a place in the theories of the wildest projectors; that it rashly attempts what it is impossible to accomplish. No, my countrymen, shut your ears against this unhallowed language. Shut your hearts against the poison which it conveys; the kindred blood which flows in the veins of American citizens, the mingled blood which they have shed in defense of their sacred rights, consecrate their Union, and excite horror at the idea of their becoming aliens, rivals, enemies. And if novelties are to be shunned, believe me, the most alarming of all novelties, the most wild of all projects, the most rash of all attempts, is that of rendering us in pieces, in order to preserve our liberties and promote our happiness. But why is the experiment of an extended republic to be rejected, merely because it may comprise what is new? Is it not the glory of the people of America, that, whilst they have paid a decent regard to the opinions of former times and other nations, they have not suffered a blind veneration for antiquity, for custom, or for names, to overrule the suggestions of their own good sense, the knowledge of their own situation, and the lessons of their own experience? To this manly spirit, posterity will be indebted for the possession, and the world for the example, of the numerous innovations displayed on the American theatre, in favor of private rights and public happiness. Had no important step been taken by the leaders of the Revolution for which a precedent could not be discovered, no government established of which an exact model did not present itself, the people of the United States might, at this moment have been numbered among the melancholy victims of misguided councils, must at best have been laboring under the weight of some of those forms which have crushed the liberties of the rest of mankind. Happily for America, happily, we trust, for the whole human race, they pursued a new and more noble course. They accomplished a revolution which has no parallel in the annals of human society. They reared the fabrics of governments which have no model on the face of the globe. They formed the design of a great Confederacy, which it is incumbent on their successors to improve and perpetuate. If their works betray imperfections, we wonder at the fewness of them. If they erred most in the structure of the Union, this was the work most difficult to be executed; this is the work which has been new modelled by the act of your convention, and it is that act on which you are now to deliberate and to decide.

PUBLIUS

FEDERALIST PAPER NO. 15. THE INSUFFICIENCY OF THE PRESENT CONFEDERATION TO PRESERVE THE UNION

For the Independent Journal. Saturday, December 1, 1787

HAMILTON

To the People of the State of New York.

IN THE course of the preceding papers, I have endeavored, my fellow citizens, to place before you, in a clear and convincing light, the importance of Union to your political safety and happiness. I have unfolded to you a complication of dangers to which you would be exposed, should you permit that sacred knot which binds the people of America together be severed or dissolved by ambition or by avarice, by jealousy or by misrepresentation. In the sequel of the inquiry through which I propose to accompany you, the truths intended to be inculcated will receive further confirmation from facts and arguments hitherto unnoticed. If the road over which you will still have to pass should in some places appear to you tedious or irksome, you will recollect that you are in quest of information on a subject the most momentous which can engage the attention of a free people, that the field through which you have to travel is in itself spacious, and that the difficulties of the journey have been unnecessarily increased by the mazes with which sophistry has beset the way. It will be my aim to remove the obstacles from your progress in as compendious a manner as it can be done, without sacrificing utility to despatch.

In pursuance of the plan which I have laid down for the discussion of the subject, the point next in order to be examined is the "insufficiency of the present Confederation to the preservation of the Union." It may perhaps be asked what need there is of reasoning or proof to illustrate a position which is not either controverted or doubted, to which the understandings and feelings of all classes of men assent, and which in substance is admitted by the opponents as well as by the friends of the new Constitution. It must in truth be acknowledged that, however these may differ in other respects, they in general appear to harmonize in this sentiment, at least, that there are material imperfections in our national system, and that something is necessary to be done to rescue us from impending anarchy. The facts that support this opinion are no longer objects of speculation. They have forced themselves upon the sensibility of the people at large, and have at length extorted from those, whose mistaken policy has had the principal share in precipitating the extremity at which we are arrived, a reluctant confession of the reality of those defects in the scheme of our federal government, which have been long pointed out and regretted by the intelligent friends of the Union.

We may indeed with propriety be said to have reached almost the last stage of national humiliation. There is scarcely anything that can wound the pride or degrade the character of an independent nation which we do not experience. Are there engagements to the performance of which we are held by every tie respectable among men? These are the subjects of constant and unblushing violation. Do we owe debts to foreigners and to our own citizens contracted in a time of imminent peril for the preservation of our political existence? These remain without any proper or satisfactory provision for their discharge. Have we valuable territories and important posts in the possession of a foreign power which, by express stipulations, ought long since to have been surrendered? These are still retained, to the prejudice of our interests, not less than of our rights. Are we in a condition to resent or to repel the aggression? We have neither troops, nor treasury, nor government.(1) Are we even in a condition to remonstrate with dignity? The just imputations on our own faith, in respect to the same treaty, ought first to be removed. Are we entitled by nature and compact to a free participation in the navigation of the Mississippi? Spain excludes us from it. Is public credit an indispensable resource in time of public danger? We seem to have abandoned its cause as desperate and irretrievable. Is commerce of importance to national wealth? Ours is at the lowest point of declension. Is respectability in the eyes of foreign powers a safeguard against foreign encroachments? The imbecility of our government even forbids them to treat with us. Our ambassadors abroad are the mere pageants of mimic sovereignty. Is a violent and unnatural decrease in the value of land a symptom of national distress? The price of improved land in most parts of the country is much lower than can be accounted for by the quantity of waste land at market, and can only be fully explained by that want of private and public confidence, which are so alarmingly prevalent among all ranks, and which have a direct tendency to depreciate property of every kind. Is private credit the friend and patron of industry? That most useful kind which relates to borrowing and lending is reduced within the narrowest limits, and this still more from an opinion of insecurity than from the scarcity of money. To shorten an enumeration of particulars which can afford neither pleasure nor instruction, it may in general be demanded, what indication is there of national disorder, poverty, and insignificance that could befall a community so peculiarly blessed with natural advantages as we are, which does not form a part of the dark catalogue of our public misfortunes?

This is the melancholy situation to which we have been brought by those very maxims and councils which would now deter us from adopting the proposed Constitution; and which, not content with having conducted us to the brink of a precipice, seem resolved to plunge us into the abyss that awaits us below. Here, my countrymen, impelled by every motive that ought to influence an enlightened people, let us make a firm stand for our safety, our tranquillity, our dignity, our reputation. Let us at last break the fatal charm which has too long seduced us from the paths of felicity and prosperity.

It is true, as has been before observed that facts, too stubborn to be resisted, have produced a species of general assent to the abstract proposition that there exist material defects in our national system; but the usefulness of the concession, on the part of the old adversaries of federal measures, is destroyed by a strenuous opposition to a remedy, upon the only principles that can give it a chance of success. While they admit that the government of the United States is destitute of energy, they contend against conferring upon it those powers which are requisite to supply that energy. They seem still to aim at things repugnant and irreconcilable; at an augmentation of federal authority, without a diminution of State authority; at sovereignty in the Union, and complete independence in the members. They still, in fine, seem to cherish with blind devotion the political monster of an imperium in imperio. This renders a full display of the principal defects of the Confederation necessary, in order to show that the evils we experience do not proceed from minute or partial imperfections, but from fundamental errors in the structure of the building, which cannot be amended otherwise than by an alteration in the first principles and main pillars of the fabric.

The great and radical vice in the construction of the existing Confederation is in the principle of LEGISLATION for STATES or GOVERNMENTS, in their CORPORATE or COLLECTIVE CAPACITIES, and as contradistinguished from the INDIVIDUALS of which they consist. Though this principle does not run through all the powers delegated to the Union, yet it pervades and governs those on which the efficacy of the rest depends. Except as to the rule of appointment, the United States has an indefinite discretion to make requisitions for men and money; but they have no authority to raise either, by regulations extending to the individual citizens of America. The consequence of this is, that though in theory their resolutions concerning those objects are laws, constitutionally binding on the members of the Union, yet in practice they are mere recommendations which the States observe or disregard at their option.

It is a singular instance of the capriciousness of the human mind, that after all the admonitions we have had from experience on this head, there should still be found men who object to the new Constitution, for deviating from a principle which has been found the bane of the old, and which is in itself evidently incompatible with the idea of GOVERNMENT; a principle, in short, which, if it is to be executed at all, must substitute the violent and sanguinary agency of the sword to the mild influence of the magistracy.

There is nothing absurd or impracticable in the idea of a league or alliance between independent nations for certain defined purposes precisely stated in a treaty regulating all the details of time, place, circumstance, and quantity; leaving nothing to future discretion; and depending for its execution on the good faith of the parties. Compacts of this kind exist among all civilized nations, subject to the usual vicissitudes of peace and war, of observance and non-observance, as the interests or passions of the contracting powers dictate. In the early part of the present century there was an epidemical rage in Europe for this species of compacts, from which the politicians of the times fondly hoped for benefits which were never realized. With a view to establishing the equilibrium of power and the peace of that part of the world, all the resources of negotiation were exhausted, and triple and quadruple alliances were formed; but they were scarcely formed before they were broken, giving an instructive but afflicting lesson to mankind, how little dependence is to be placed on treaties which have no other sanction than the obligations of good faith, and which oppose general considerations of peace and justice to the impulse of any immediate interest or passion.

If the particular States in this country are disposed to stand in a similar relation to each other, and to drop the project of a general DISCRETIONARY SUPERINTENDENCE, the scheme would indeed be pernicious, and would entail upon us all the mischiefs which have been enumerated under the first head; but it would have the merit of being, at least, consistent and practicable Abandoning all views towards a confederate government, this would bring us to a simple alliance offensive and defensive; and would place us in a situation to be alternate friends and enemies of each other, as our mutual jealousies and rivalships, nourished by the intrigues of foreign nations, should prescribe to us.

But if we are unwilling to be placed in this perilous situation; if we still will adhere to the design of a national government, or, which is the same thing, of a superintending power, under the direction of a common council, we must resolve to incorporate into our plan those ingredients which may be considered as forming the characteristic difference between a league and a government; we must extend the authority of the Union to the persons of the citizens,—the only proper objects of government.

Government implies the power of making laws. It is essential to the idea of a law, that it be attended with a sanction; or, in other words, a penalty or punishment for disobedience. If there be no penalty annexed to disobedience, the resolutions or commands which pretend to be laws will, in fact, amount to nothing more than advice or recommendation. This penalty, whatever it may be, can only be inflicted in two ways: by the agency of the courts and ministers of justice, or by military force; by the COERCION of the magistracy, or by the COERCION of arms. The first kind can evidently apply only to men; the last kind must of necessity, be employed against bodies politic, or communities, or States. It is evident that there is no process of a court by which the observance of the laws can, in the last resort, be enforced. Sentences may be denounced against them for violations of their duty; but these sentences can only be carried into execution by the sword. In an association where the general authority is confined to the collective bodies of the communities, that compose it, every breach of the laws must involve a state of war; and military execution must become the only instrument of civil obedience. Such a state of things can certainly not deserve the name of government, nor would any prudent man choose to commit his happiness to it.

There was a time when we were told that breaches, by the States, of the regulations of the federal authority were not to be expected; that a sense of common interest would preside over the conduct of the respective members, and would beget a full compliance with all the constitutional requisitions of the Union. This language, at the present day, would appear as wild as a great part of what we now hear from the same quarter will be thought, when we shall have received further lessons from that best oracle of wisdom, experience. It at all times betrayed an ignorance of the true springs by which human conduct is actuated, and belied the original inducements to the establishment of civil power. Why has government been instituted at all? Because the passions of men will not conform to the dictates of reason and justice, without constraint. Has it been found that bodies of men act with more rectitude or greater disinterestedness than individuals? The contrary of this has been inferred by all accurate observers of the conduct of mankind; and the inference is founded upon obvious reasons. Regard to reputation has a less active influence, when the infamy of a bad action is to be divided among a number than when it is to fall singly upon one. A spirit of faction, which is apt to mingle its poison in the deliberations of all bodies of men, will often hurry the persons of whom they are composed into improprieties and excesses, for which they would blush in a private capacity.

In addition to all this, there is, in the nature of sovereign power, an impatience of control, that disposes those who are invested with the exercise of it, to look with an evil eye upon all external attempts to restrain or direct its operations. From this spirit it happens, that in every political association which is formed upon the principle of uniting in a common interest a number of lesser sovereignties, there will be found a kind of eccentric tendency in the subordinate or inferior orbs, by the operation of which there will be a perpetual effort in each to fly off from the common centre. This tendency is not difficult to be accounted for. It has its origin in the love of power. Power controlled or abridged is almost always the rival and enemy of that power by which it is controlled or abridged. This simple proposition will teach us how little reason there is to expect, that the persons intrusted with the administration of the affairs of the particular members of a confederacy will at all times be ready, with perfect good-humor, and an unbiased regard to the public weal, to execute the resolutions or decrees of the general authority. The reverse of this results from the constitution of human nature.

If, therefore, the measures of the Confederacy cannot be executed without the intervention of the particular administrations, there will be little prospect of their being executed at all. The rulers of the respective members, whether they have a constitutional right to do it or not, will undertake to judge of the propriety of the measures themselves. They will consider the conformity of the thing proposed or required to their immediate interests or aims; the momentary conveniences or inconveniences that would attend its adoption. All this will be done; and in a spirit of interested and suspicious scrutiny, without that knowledge of national circumstances and reasons of state, which is essential to a right judgment, and with that strong predilection in favor of local objects, which can hardly fail to mislead the decision. The same process must be repeated in every member of which the body is constituted; and the execution of the plans, framed by the councils of the whole, will always fluctuate on the discretion of the ill-informed and prejudiced opinion of every part. Those who have been conversant in the proceedings of popular assemblies; who have seen how difficult it often is, where there is no exterior pressure of circumstances, to bring them to harmonious resolutions on important points, will readily conceive how impossible it must be to induce a number of such assemblies, deliberating at a distance from each other, at different times, and under different impressions, long to co-operate in the same views and pursuits.

In our case, the concurrence of thirteen distinct sovereign wills is requisite, under the Confederation, to the complete execution of every important measure that proceeds from the Union. It has happened as was to have been foreseen. The measures of the Union have not been executed; the delinquencies of the States have, step by step, matured themselves to an extreme, which has, at length, arrested all the wheels of the national government, and brought them to an awful stand. Congress at this time scarcely possess the means of keeping up the forms of administration, till the States can have time to agree upon a more substantial substitute for the present shadow of a federal government. Things did not come to this desperate extremity at once. The causes which have been specified produced at first only unequal and disproportionate degrees of compliance with the requisitions of the Union. The greater deficiencies of some States furnished the pretext of example and the temptation of interest to the complying, or to the least delinquent States. Why should we do more in proportion than those who are embarked with us in the same political voyage? Why should we consent to bear more than our proper share of the common burden? These were suggestions which human selfishness could not withstand, and which even speculative men, who looked forward to remote consequences, could not, without hesitation, combat. Each State, yielding to the persuasive voice of immediate interest or convenience, has successively withdrawn its support, till the frail and tottering edifice seems ready to fall upon our heads, and to crush us beneath its ruins.

PUBLIUS

1. "I mean for the Union."

FEDERALIST PAPER NO. 16. THE SAME SUBJECT CONTINUED (THE INSUFFICIENCY OF THE PRESENT CONFEDERATION TO PRESERVE THE UNION)

From the New York Packet. Tuesday, December 4, 1787.

HAMILTON

To the People of the State of New York:

THE tendency of the principle of legislation for States, or communities, in their political capacities, as it has been exemplified by the experiment we have made of it, is equally attested by the events which have befallen all other governments of the confederate kind, of which we have any account, in exact proportion to its prevalence in those systems. The confirmations of this fact will be worthy of a distinct and particular examination. I shall content myself with barely observing here, that of all the confederacies of antiquity, which history has handed down to us, the Lycian and Achaean leagues, as far as there remain vestiges of them, appear to have been most free from the fetters of that mistaken principle, and were accordingly those which have best deserved, and have most liberally received, the applauding suffrages of political writers.

This exceptionable principle may, as truly as emphatically, be styled the parent of anarchy: It has been seen that delinquencies in the members of the Union are its natural and necessary offspring; and that whenever they happen, the only constitutional remedy is force, and the immediate effect of the use of it, civil war.

It remains to inquire how far so odious an engine of government, in its application to us, would even be capable of answering its end. If there should not be a large army constantly at the disposal of the national government it would either not be able to employ force at all, or, when this could be done, it would amount to a war between parts of the Confederacy concerning the infractions of a league, in which the strongest combination would be most likely to prevail, whether it consisted of those who supported or of those who resisted the general authority. It would rarely happen that the delinquency to be redressed would be confined to a single member, and if there were more than one who had neglected their duty, similarity of situation would induce them to unite for common defense. Independent of this motive of sympathy, if a large and influential State should happen to be the aggressing member, it would commonly have weight enough with its neighbors to win over some of them as associates to its cause. Specious arguments of danger to the common liberty could easily be contrived; plausible excuses for the deficiencies of the party could, without difficulty, be invented to alarm the apprehensions, inflame the passions, and conciliate the good-will, even of those States which were not chargeable with any violation or omission of duty. This would be the more likely to take place, as the delinquencies of the larger members might be expected sometimes to proceed from an ambitious premeditation in their rulers, with a view to getting rid of all external control upon their designs of personal aggrandizement; the better to effect which it is presumable they would tamper beforehand with leading individuals in the adjacent States. If associates could not be found at home, recourse would be had to the aid of foreign powers, who would seldom be disinclined to encouraging the dissensions of a Confederacy, from the firm union of which they had so much to fear. When the sword is once drawn, the passions of men observe no bounds of moderation. The suggestions of wounded pride, the instigations of irritated resentment, would be apt to carry the States against which the arms of the Union were exerted, to any extremes necessary to avenge the affront or to avoid the disgrace of submission. The first war of this kind would probably terminate in a dissolution of the Union.

This may be considered as the violent death of the Confederacy. Its more natural death is what we now seem to be on the point of experiencing, if the federal system be not speedily renovated in a more substantial form. It is not probable, considering the genius of this country, that the complying States would often be inclined to support the authority of the Union by engaging in a war against the non-complying States. They would always be more ready to pursue the milder course of putting themselves upon an equal footing with the delinquent members by an imitation of their example. And the guilt of all would thus become the security of all. Our past experience has exhibited the operation of this spirit in its full light. There would, in fact, be an insuperable difficulty in ascertaining when force could with propriety be employed. In the article of pecuniary contribution, which would be the most usual source of delinquency, it would often be impossible to decide whether it had proceeded from disinclination or inability. The pretense of the latter would always be at hand. And the case must be very flagrant in which its fallacy could be detected with sufficient certainty to justify the harsh expedient of compulsion. It is easy to see that this problem alone, as often as it should occur, would open a wide field for the exercise of factious views, of partiality, and of oppression, in the majority that happened to prevail in the national council.

It seems to require no pains to prove that the States ought not to prefer a national Constitution which could only be kept in motion by the instrumentality of a large army continually on foot to execute the ordinary requisitions or decrees of the government. And yet this is the plain alternative involved by those who wish to deny it the power of extending its operations to individuals. Such a scheme, if practicable at all, would instantly degenerate into a military despotism; but it will be found in every light impracticable. The resources of the Union would not be equal to the maintenance of an army considerable enough to confine the larger States within the limits of their duty; nor would the means ever be furnished of forming such an army in the first instance. Whoever considers the populousness and strength of several of these States singly at the present juncture, and looks forward to what they will become, even at the distance of half a century, will at once dismiss as idle and visionary any scheme which aims at regulating their movements by laws to operate upon them in their collective capacities, and to be executed by a coercion applicable to them in the same capacities. A project of this kind is little less romantic than the monster-taming spirit which is attributed to the fabulous heroes and demi-gods of antiquity.

Even in those confederacies which have been composed of members smaller than many of our counties, the principle of legislation for sovereign States, supported by military coercion, has never been found effectual. It has rarely been attempted to be employed, but against the weaker members; and in most instances attempts to coerce the refractory and disobedient have been the signals of bloody wars, in which one half of the confederacy has displayed its banners against the other half.

The result of these observations to an intelligent mind must be clearly this, that if it be possible at any rate to construct a federal government capable of regulating the common concerns and preserving the general tranquillity, it must be founded, as to the objects committed to its care, upon the reverse of the principle contended for by the opponents of the proposed Constitution. It must carry its agency to the persons of the citizens. It must stand in need of no intermediate legislations; but must itself be empowered to employ the arm of the ordinary magistrate to execute its own resolutions. The majesty of the national authority must be manifested through the medium of the courts of justice. The government of the Union, like that of each State, must be able to address itself immediately to the hopes and fears of individuals; and to attract to its support those passions which have the strongest influence upon the human heart. It must, in short, possess all the means, and have aright to resort to all the methods, of executing the powers with which it is intrusted, that are possessed and exercised by the government of the particular States.

To this reasoning it may perhaps be objected, that if any State should be disaffected to the authority of the Union, it could at any time obstruct the execution of its laws, and bring the matter to the same issue of force, with the necessity of which the opposite scheme is reproached.

The plausibility of this objection will vanish the moment we advert to the essential difference between a mere NON-COMPLIANCE and a DIRECT and ACTIVE RESISTANCE. If the interposition of the State legislatures be necessary to give effect to a measure of the Union, they have only NOT TO ACT, or TO ACT EVASIVELY, and the measure is defeated. This neglect of duty may be disguised under affected but unsubstantial provisions, so as not to appear, and of course not to excite any alarm in the people for the safety of the Constitution. The State leaders may even make a merit of their surreptitious invasions of it on the ground of some temporary convenience, exemption, or advantage.

But if the execution of the laws of the national government should not require the intervention of the State legislatures, if they were to pass into immediate operation upon the citizens themselves, the particular governments could not interrupt their progress without an open and violent exertion of an unconstitutional power. No omissions nor evasions would answer the end. They would be obliged to act, and in such a manner as would leave no doubt that they had encroached on the national rights. An experiment of this nature would always be hazardous in the face of a constitution in any degree competent to its own defense, and of a people enlightened enough to distinguish between a legal exercise and an illegal usurpation of authority. The success of it would require not merely a factious majority in the legislature, but the concurrence of the courts of justice and of the body of the people. If the judges were not embarked in a conspiracy with the legislature, they would pronounce the resolutions of such a majority to be contrary to the supreme law of the land, unconstitutional, and void. If the people were not tainted with the spirit of their State representatives, they, as the natural guardians of the Constitution, would throw their weight into the national scale and give it a decided preponderancy in the contest. Attempts of this kind would not often be made with levity or rashness, because they could seldom be made without danger to the authors, unless in cases of a tyrannical exercise of the federal authority.

If opposition to the national government should arise from the disorderly conduct of refractory or seditious individuals, it could be overcome by the same means which are daily employed against the same evil under the State governments. The magistracy, being equally the ministers of the law of the land, from whatever source it might emanate, would doubtless be as ready to guard the national as the local regulations from the inroads of private licentiousness. As to those partial commotions and insurrections, which sometimes disquiet society, from the intrigues of an inconsiderable faction, or from sudden or occasional illhumors that do not infect the great body of the community the general government could command more extensive resources for the suppression of disturbances of that kind than would be in the power of any single member. And as to those mortal feuds which, in certain conjunctures, spread a conflagration through a whole nation, or through a very large proportion of it, proceeding either from weighty causes of discontent given by the government or from the contagion of some violent popular paroxysm, they do not fall within any ordinary rules of calculation. When they happen, they commonly amount to revolutions and dismemberments of empire. No form of government can always either avoid or control them. It is in vain to hope to guard against events too mighty for human foresight or precaution, and it would be idle to object to a government because it could not perform impossibilities.

PUBLIUS

FEDERALIST PAPER NO. 17. THE SAME SUBJECT CONTINUED (THE INSUFFICIENCY OF THE PRESENT CONFEDERATION TO PRESERVE THE UNION)

For the Independent Journal. Wednesday, December 5, 1787

HAMILTON

To the People of the State of New York:

AN OBJECTION, of a nature different from that which has been stated and answered, in my last address, may perhaps be likewise urged against the principle of legislation for the individual citizens of America. It may be said that it would tend to render the government of the Union too powerful, and to enable it to absorb those residuary authorities, which it might be judged proper to leave with the States for local purposes. Allowing the utmost latitude to the love of power which any reasonable man can require, I confess I am at a loss to discover what temptation the persons intrusted with the administration of the general government could ever feel to divest the States of the authorities of that description. The regulation of the mere domestic police of a State appears to me to hold out slender allurements to ambition. Commerce, finance, negotiation, and war seem to comprehend all the objects which have charms for minds governed by that passion; and all the powers necessary to those objects ought, in the first instance, to be lodged in the national depository. The administration of private justice between the citizens of the same State, the supervision of agriculture and of other concerns of a similar nature, all those things, in short, which are proper to be provided for by local legislation, can never be desirable cares of a general jurisdiction. It is therefore improbable that there should exist a disposition in the federal councils to usurp the powers with which they are connected; because the attempt to exercise those powers would be as troublesome as it would be nugatory; and the possession of them, for that reason, would contribute nothing to the dignity, to the importance, or to the splendor of the national government.

But let it be admitted, for argument's sake, that mere wantonness and lust of domination would be sufficient to beget that disposition; still it may be safely affirmed, that the sense of the constituent body of the national representatives, or, in other words, the people of the several States, would control the indulgence of so extravagant an appetite. It will always be far more easy for the State governments to encroach upon the national authorities than for the national government to encroach upon the State authorities. The proof of this proposition turns upon the greater degree of influence which the State governments if they administer their affairs with uprightness and prudence, will generally possess over the people; a circumstance which at the same time teaches us that there is an inherent and intrinsic weakness in all federal constitutions; and that too much pains cannot be taken in their organization, to give them all the force which is compatible with the principles of liberty.

The superiority of influence in favor of the particular governments would result partly from the diffusive construction of the national government, but chiefly from the nature of the objects to which the attention of the State administrations would be directed.

It is a known fact in human nature, that its affections are commonly weak in proportion to the distance or diffusiveness of the object. Upon the same principle that a man is more attached to his family than to his neighborhood, to his neighborhood than to the community at large, the people of each State would be apt to feel a stronger bias towards their local governments than towards the government of the Union; unless the force of that principle should be destroyed by a much better administration of the latter.

This strong propensity of the human heart would find powerful auxiliaries in the objects of State regulation.

The variety of more minute interests, which will necessarily fall under the superintendence of the local administrations, and which will form so many rivulets of influence, running through every part of the society, cannot be particularized, without involving a detail too tedious and uninteresting to compensate for the instruction it might afford.

Documents of Revolution

There is one transcendant advantage belonging to the province of the State governments, which alone suffices to place the matter in a clear and satisfactory light,—I mean the ordinary administration of criminal and civil justice. This, of all others, is the most powerful, most universal, and most attractive source of popular obedience and attachment. It is that which, being the immediate and visible guardian of life and property, having its benefits and its terrors in constant activity before the public eye, regulating all those personal interests and familiar concerns to which the sensibility of individuals is more immediately awake, contributes, more than any other circumstance, to impressing upon the minds of the people, affection, esteem, and reverence towards the government. This great cement of society, which will diffuse itself almost wholly through the channels of the particular governments, independent of all other causes of influence, would insure them so decided an empire over their respective citizens as to render them at all times a complete counterpoise, and, not unfrequently, dangerous rivals to the power of the Union.

The operations of the national government, on the other hand, falling less immediately under the observation of the mass of the citizens, the benefits derived from it will chiefly be perceived and attended to by speculative men. Relating to more general interests, they will be less apt to come home to the feelings of the people; and, in proportion, less likely to inspire an habitual sense of obligation, and an active sentiment of attachment.

The reasoning on this head has been abundantly exemplified by the experience of all federal constitutions with which we are acquainted, and of all others which have borne the least analogy to them.

Though the ancient feudal systems were not, strictly speaking, confederacies, yet they partook of the nature of that species of association. There was a common head, chieftain, or sovereign, whose authority extended over the whole nation; and a number of subordinate vassals, or feudatories, who had large portions of land allotted to them, and numerous trains of INFERIOR vassals or retainers, who occupied and cultivated that land upon the tenure of fealty or obedience, to the persons of whom they held it. Each principal vassal was a kind of sovereign, within his particular demesnes. The consequences of this situation were a continual opposition to authority of the sovereign, and frequent wars between the great barons or chief feudatories themselves. The power of the head of the nation was commonly too weak, either to preserve the public peace, or to protect the people against the oppressions of their immediate lords. This period of European affairs is emphatically styled by historians, the times of feudal anarchy.

When the sovereign happened to be a man of vigorous and warlike temper and of superior abilities, he would acquire a personal weight and influence, which answered, for the time, the purpose of a more regular authority. But in general, the power of the barons triumphed over that of the prince; and in many instances his dominion was entirely thrown off, and the great fiefs were erected into independent principalities or States. In those instances in which the monarch finally prevailed over his vassals, his success was chiefly owing to the tyranny of those vassals over their dependents. The barons, or nobles, equally the enemies of the sovereign and the oppressors of the common people, were dreaded and detested by both; till mutual danger and mutual interest effected a union between them fatal to the power of the aristocracy. Had the nobles, by a conduct of clemency and justice, preserved the fidelity and devotion of their retainers and followers, the contests between them and the prince must almost always have ended in their favor, and in the abridgment or subversion of the royal authority.

This is not an assertion founded merely in speculation or conjecture. Among other illustrations of its truth which might be cited, Scotland will furnish a cogent example. The spirit of clanship which was, at an early day, introduced into that kingdom, uniting the nobles and their dependants by ties equivalent to those of kindred, rendered the aristocracy a constant overmatch for the power of the monarch, till the incorporation with England subdued its fierce and ungovernable spirit, and reduced it within those rules of subordination which a more rational and more energetic system of civil polity had previously established in the latter kingdom.

The separate governments in a confederacy may aptly be compared with the feudal baronies; with this advantage in their favor, that from the reasons already explained, they will generally possess the confidence and good-will of the people, and with so important a support, will be able effectually to oppose all encroachments of the national government. It will be well if they are not able to counteract its legitimate and necessary authority. The points of similitude consist in the rivalship of power, applicable to both, and in the CONCENTRATION of large portions of the strength of the community into particular DEPOSITORIES, in one case at the disposal of individuals, in the other case at the disposal of political bodies.

A concise review of the events that have attended confederate governments will further illustrate this important doctrine; an inattention to which has been the great source of our political mistakes, and has given our jealousy a direction to the wrong side. This review shall form the subject of some ensuing papers.

PUBLIUS

FEDERALIST PAPER NO. 18. THE SAME SUBJECT CONTINUED (THE INSUFFICIENCY OF THE PRESENT CONFEDERATION TO PRESERVE THE UNION)

For the New York Packet. Friday, December 7, 1787

MADISON, with HAMILTON

To the People of the State of New York:

AMONG the confederacies of antiquity, the most considerable was that of the Grecian republics, associated under the Amphictyonic council. From the best accounts transmitted of this celebrated institution, it bore a very instructive analogy to the present Confederation of the American States.

The members retained the character of independent and sovereign states, and had equal votes in the federal council. This council had a general authority to propose and resolve whatever it judged necessary for the common welfare of Greece; to declare and carry on war; to decide, in the last resort, all controversies between the members; to fine the aggressing party; to employ the whole force of the confederacy against the disobedient; to admit new members. The Amphictyons were the guardians of religion, and of the immense riches belonging to the temple of Delphos, where they had the right of jurisdiction in controversies between the inhabitants and those who came to consult the oracle. As a further provision for the efficacy of the federal powers, they took an oath mutually to defend and protect the united cities, to punish the violators of this oath, and to inflict vengeance on sacrilegious despoilers of the temple.

In theory, and upon paper, this apparatus of powers seems amply sufficient for all general purposes. In several material instances, they exceed the powers enumerated in the articles of confederation. The Amphictyons had in their hands the superstition of the times, one of the principal engines by which government was then maintained; they had a declared authority to use coercion against refractory cities, and were bound by oath to exert this authority on the necessary occasions.

Very different, nevertheless, was the experiment from the theory. The powers, like those of the present Congress, were administered by deputies appointed wholly by the cities in their political capacities; and exercised over them in the same capacities. Hence the weakness, the disorders, and finally the destruction of the confederacy. The more powerful members, instead of being kept in awe and subordination, tyrannized successively over all the rest. Athens, as we learn from Demosthenes, was the arbiter of Greece seventy-three years. The Lacedaemonians next governed it twenty-nine years; at a subsequent period, after the battle of Leuctra, the Thebans had their turn of domination.

It happened but too often, according to Plutarch, that the deputies of the strongest cities awed and corrupted those of the weaker; and that judgment went in favor of the most powerful party.

Even in the midst of defensive and dangerous wars with Persia and Macedon, the members never acted in concert, and were, more or fewer of them, eternally the dupes or the hirelings of the common enemy. The intervals of foreign war were filled up by domestic vicissitudes convulsions, and carnage.

After the conclusion of the war with Xerxes, it appears that the Lacedaemonians required that a number of the cities should be turned out of the confederacy for the unfaithful part they had acted. The Athenians, finding that the Lacedaemonians would lose fewer partisans by such a measure than themselves, and would become masters of the public deliberations, vigorously opposed and defeated the attempt. This piece of history proves at once the inefficiency of the union, the ambition and jealousy of its most powerful members, and the dependent and degraded condition of the rest. The smaller members, though entitled by the theory of their system to revolve in equal pride and majesty around the common center, had become, in fact, satellites of the orbs of primary magnitude.

Had the Greeks, says the Abbe Milot, been as wise as they were courageous, they would have been admonished by experience of the necessity of a closer union, and would have availed themselves of the peace which followed their success against the Persian arms, to establish such a reformation. Instead of this obvious policy, Athens and Sparta, inflated with the victories and the glory they had acquired, became first rivals and then enemies; and did each other infinitely more mischief than they had suffered from Xerxes. Their mutual jealousies, fears, hatreds, and injuries ended in the celebrated Peloponnesian war; which itself ended in the ruin and slavery of the Athenians who had begun it.

Documents of Revolution

As a weak government, when not at war, is ever agitated by internal dissentions, so these never fail to bring on fresh calamities from abroad. The Phocians having ploughed up some consecrated ground belonging to the temple of Apollo, the Amphictyonic council, according to the superstition of the age, imposed a fine on the sacrilegious offenders. The Phocians, being abetted by Athens and Sparta, refused to submit to the decree. The Thebans, with others of the cities, undertook to maintain the authority of the Amphictyons, and to avenge the violated god. The latter, being the weaker party, invited the assistance of Philip of Macedon, who had secretly fostered the contest. Philip gladly seized the opportunity of executing the designs he had long planned against the liberties of Greece. By his intrigues and bribes he won over to his interests the popular leaders of several cities; by their influence and votes, gained admission into the Amphictyonic council; and by his arts and his arms, made himself master of the confederacy.

Such were the consequences of the fallacious principle on which this interesting establishment was founded. Had Greece, says a judicious observer on her fate, been united by a stricter confederation, and persevered in her union, she would never have worn the chains of Macedon; and might have proved a barrier to the vast projects of Rome.

The Achaean league, as it is called, was another society of Grecian republics, which supplies us with valuable instruction.

The Union here was far more intimate, and its organization much wiser, than in the preceding instance. It will accordingly appear, that though not exempt from a similar catastrophe, it by no means equally deserved it.

The cities composing this league retained their municipal jurisdiction, appointed their own officers, and enjoyed a perfect equality. The senate, in which they were represented, had the sole and exclusive right of peace and war; of sending and receiving ambassadors; of entering into treaties and alliances; of appointing a chief magistrate or praetor, as he was called, who commanded their armies, and who, with the advice and consent of ten of the senators, not only administered the government in the recess of the senate, but had a great share in its deliberations, when assembled. According to the primitive constitution, there were two praetors associated in the administration; but on trial a single one was preferred.

It appears that the cities had all the same laws and customs, the same weights and measures, and the same money. But how far this effect proceeded from the authority of the federal council is left in uncertainty. It is said only that the cities were in a manner compelled to receive the same laws and usages. When Lacedaemon was brought into the league by Philopoemen, it was attended with an abolition of the institutions and laws of Lycurgus, and an adoption of those of the Achaeans. The Amphictyonic confederacy, of which she had been a member, left her in the full exercise of her government and her legislation. This circumstance alone proves a very material difference in the genius of the two systems.

It is much to be regretted that such imperfect monuments remain of this curious political fabric. Could its interior structure and regular operation be ascertained, it is probable that more light would be thrown by it on the science of federal government, than by any of the like experiments with which we are acquainted.

One important fact seems to be witnessed by all the historians who take notice of Achaean affairs. It is, that as well after the renovation of the league by Aratus, as before its dissolution by the arts of Macedon, there was infinitely more of moderation and justice in the administration of its government, and less of violence and sedition in the people, than were to be found in any of the cities exercising SINGLY all the prerogatives of sovereignty. The Abbe Mably, in his observations on Greece, says that the popular government, which was so tempestuous elsewhere, caused no disorders in the members of the Achaean republic, BECAUSE IT WAS THERE TEMPERED BY THE GENERAL AUTHORITY AND LAWS OF THE CONFEDERACY.

We are not to conclude too hastily, however, that faction did not, in a certain degree, agitate the particular cities; much less that a due subordination and harmony reigned in the general system. The contrary is sufficiently displayed in the vicissitudes and fate of the republic.

Whilst the Amphictyonic confederacy remained, that of the Achaeans, which comprehended the less important cities only, made little figure on the theatre of Greece. When the former became a victim to Macedon, the latter was spared by the policy of Philip and Alexander. Under the successors of these princes, however, a different policy prevailed. The arts of division were practiced among the Achaeans. Each city was seduced into a separate interest; the union was dissolved. Some of the cities fell under the tyranny of Macedonian garrisons; others under that of usurpers springing out of their own confusions. Shame and oppression erelong awaken their love of liberty. A few cities reunited. Their example was followed by others, as opportunities were found of cutting off their tyrants. The league soon embraced almost the whole Peloponnesus. Macedon saw its progress; but was hindered by internal dissensions from stopping it. All Greece caught the enthusiasm and seemed ready to unite in one confederacy, when the jealousy and envy in Sparta and Athens, of the rising glory of the Achaeans, threw a fatal damp on the enterprise. The dread of the Macedonian power induced the league to court the alliance of the Kings of Egypt and Syria, who, as successors of Alexander, were rivals of the king of Macedon. This policy was defeated by Cleomenes, king of Sparta, who was led by his ambition to make an unprovoked attack on his neighbors, the Achaeans, and who, as an enemy to Macedon, had interest enough with the Egyptian and Syrian princes to effect a breach of their engagements with the league.

The Achaeans were now reduced to the dilemma of submitting to Cleomenes, or of supplicating the aid of Macedon, its former oppressor. The latter expedient was adopted. The contests of the Greeks always afforded a pleasing opportunity to that powerful neighbor of intermeddling in their affairs. A Macedonian army quickly appeared. Cleomenes was vanquished. The Achaeans soon experienced, as often happens, that a victorious and powerful ally is but another name for a master. All that their most abject compliances could obtain from him was a toleration of the exercise of their laws. Philip, who was now on the throne of Macedon, soon provoked by his tyrannies, fresh combinations among the Greeks. The Achaeans, though weakened by internal dissensions and by the revolt of Messene, one of its members, being joined by the AEtolians and Athenians, erected the standard of opposition. Finding themselves, though thus supported, unequal to the undertaking, they once more had recourse to the dangerous expedient of introducing the succor of foreign arms. The Romans, to whom the invitation was made, eagerly embraced it. Philip was conquered; Macedon subdued. A new crisis ensued to the league. Dissensions broke out among it members. These the Romans fostered. Callicrates and other popular leaders became mercenary instruments for inveigling their countrymen. The more effectually to nourish discord and disorder the Romans had, to the astonishment of those who confided in their sincerity, already proclaimed universal liberty(1) throughout Greece. With the same insidious views, they now seduced the members from the league, by representing to their pride the violation it committed on their sovereignty. By these arts this union, the last hope of Greece, the last hope of ancient liberty, was torn into pieces; and such imbecility and distraction introduced, that the arms of Rome found little difficulty in completing the ruin which their arts had commenced. The Achaeans were cut to pieces, and Achaia loaded with chains, under which it is groaning at this hour.

I have thought it not superfluous to give the outlines of this important portion of history; both because it teaches more than one lesson, and because, as a supplement to the outlines of the Achaean constitution, it emphatically illustrates the tendency of federal bodies rather to anarchy among the members, than to tyranny in the head.

PUBLIUS

1. This was but another name more specious for the independence of the members on the federal head.

FEDERALIST PAPER NO. 19. THE SAME SUBJECT CONTINUED (THE INSUFFICIENCY OF THE PRESENT CONFEDERATION TO PRESERVE THE UNION)

For the Independent Journal. Saturday, December 8, 1787

MADISON, with HAMILTON

To the People of the State of New York:

THE examples of ancient confederacies, cited in my last paper, have not exhausted the source of experimental instruction on this subject. There are existing institutions, founded on a similar principle, which merit particular consideration. The first which presents itself is the Germanic body.

In the early ages of Christianity, Germany was occupied by seven distinct nations, who had no common chief. The Franks, one of the number, having conquered the Gauls, established the kingdom which has taken its name from them. In the ninth century Charlemagne, its warlike monarch, carried his victorious arms in every direction; and Germany became a part of his vast dominions. On the dismemberment, which took place under his sons, this part was erected into a separate and independent empire. Charlemagne and his immediate descendants possessed the reality, as well as the ensigns and dignity of imperial power. But the principal vassals, whose fiefs had become hereditary, and who composed the national diets which Charlemagne had not abolished, gradually threw off the yoke and advanced to sovereign jurisdiction and independence. The force of imperial sovereignty was insufficient to restrain such powerful dependants; or to preserve the unity and tranquillity of the empire. The most furious private wars, accompanied with every species of calamity, were carried on between the different princes and states. The imperial authority, unable to maintain the public order, declined by degrees till it was almost extinct in the anarchy, which agitated the long interval between the death of the last emperor of the Suabian, and the accession of the first emperor of the Austrian lines. In the eleventh century the emperors enjoyed full sovereignty: In the fifteenth they had little more than the symbols and decorations of power.

Out of this feudal system, which has itself many of the important features of a confederacy, has grown the federal system which constitutes the Germanic empire. Its powers are vested in a diet representing the component members of the confederacy; in the emperor, who is the executive magistrate, with a negative on the decrees of the diet; and in the imperial chamber and the aulic council, two judiciary tribunals having supreme jurisdiction in controversies which concern the empire, or which happen among its members.

The diet possesses the general power of legislating for the empire; of making war and peace; contracting alliances; assessing quotas of troops and money; constructing fortresses; regulating coin; admitting new members; and subjecting disobedient members to the ban of the empire, by which the party is degraded from his sovereign rights and his possessions forfeited. The members of the confederacy are expressly restricted from entering into compacts prejudicial to the empire; from imposing tolls and duties on their mutual intercourse, without the consent of the emperor and diet; from altering the value of money; from doing injustice to one another; or from affording assistance or retreat to disturbers of the public peace. And the ban is denounced against such as shall violate any of these restrictions. The members of the diet, as such, are subject in all cases to be judged by the emperor and diet, and in their private capacities by the aulic council and imperial chamber.

The prerogatives of the emperor are numerous. The most important of them are: his exclusive right to make propositions to the diet; to negative its resolutions; to name ambassadors; to confer dignities and titles; to fill vacant electorates; to found universities; to grant privileges not injurious to the states of the empire; to receive and apply the public revenues; and generally to watch over the public safety. In certain cases, the electors form a council to him. In quality of emperor, he possesses no territory within the empire, nor receives any revenue for his support. But his revenue and dominions, in other qualities, constitute him one of the most powerful princes in Europe.

Documents of Revolution

From such a parade of constitutional powers, in the representatives and head of this confederacy, the natural supposition would be, that it must form an exception to the general character which belongs to its kindred systems. Nothing would be further from the reality. The fundamental principle on which it rests, that the empire is a community of sovereigns, that the diet is a representation of sovereigns and that the laws are addressed to sovereigns, renders the empire a nerveless body, incapable of regulating its own members, insecure against external dangers, and agitated with unceasing fermentations in its own bowels.

The history of Germany is a history of wars between the emperor and the princes and states; of wars among the princes and states themselves; of the licentiousness of the strong, and the oppression of the weak; of foreign intrusions, and foreign intrigues; of requisitions of men and money disregarded, or partially complied with; of attempts to enforce them, altogether abortive, or attended with slaughter and desolation, involving the innocent with the guilty; of general imbecility, confusion, and misery.

In the sixteenth century, the emperor, with one part of the empire on his side, was seen engaged against the other princes and states. In one of the conflicts, the emperor himself was put to flight, and very near being made prisoner by the elector of Saxony. The late king of Prussia was more than once pitted against his imperial sovereign; and commonly proved an overmatch for him. Controversies and wars among the members themselves have been so common, that the German annals are crowded with the bloody pages which describe them. Previous to the peace of Westphalia, Germany was desolated by a war of thirty years, in which the emperor, with one half of the empire, was on one side, and Sweden, with the other half, on the opposite side. Peace was at length negotiated, and dictated by foreign powers; and the articles of it, to which foreign powers are parties, made a fundamental part of the Germanic constitution.

If the nation happens, on any emergency, to be more united by the necessity of self-defense, its situation is still deplorable. Military preparations must be preceded by so many tedious discussions, arising from the jealousies, pride, separate views, and clashing pretensions of sovereign bodies, that before the diet can settle the arrangements, the enemy are in the field; and before the federal troops are ready to take it, are retiring into winter quarters.

The small body of national troops, which has been judged necessary in time of peace, is defectively kept up, badly paid, infected with local prejudices, and supported by irregular and disproportionate contributions to the treasury.

The impossibility of maintaining order and dispensing justice among these sovereign subjects, produced the experiment of dividing the empire into nine or ten circles or districts; of giving them an interior organization, and of charging them with the military execution of the laws against delinquent and contumacious members. This experiment has only served to demonstrate more fully the radical vice of the constitution. Each circle is the miniature picture of the deformities of this political monster. They either fail to execute their commissions, or they do it with all the devastation and carnage of civil war. Sometimes whole circles are defaulters; and then they increase the mischief which they were instituted to remedy.

We may form some judgment of this scheme of military coercion from a sample given by Thuanus. In Donawerth, a free and imperial city of the circle of Suabia, the Abbe de St. Croix enjoyed certain immunities which had been reserved to him. In the exercise of these, on some public occasions, outrages were committed on him by the people of the city. The consequence was that the city was put under the ban of the empire, and the Duke of Bavaria, though director of another circle, obtained an appointment to enforce it. He soon appeared before the city with a corps of ten thousand troops, and finding it a fit occasion, as he had secretly intended from the beginning, to revive an antiquated claim, on the pretext that his ancestors had suffered the place to be dismembered from his territory,(1) he took possession of it in his own name, disarmed, and punished the inhabitants, and reannexed the city to his domains.

It may be asked, perhaps, what has so long kept this disjointed machine from falling entirely to pieces? The answer is obvious: The weakness of most of the members, who are unwilling to expose themselves to the mercy of foreign powers; the weakness of most of the principal members, compared with the formidable powers all around them; the vast weight and influence which the emperor derives from his separate and hereditary dominions; and the interest he feels in preserving a system with which his family pride is connected, and which constitutes him the first prince in Europe;—these causes support a feeble and precarious Union; whilst the repellant quality, incident to the nature of sovereignty, and which time continually strengthens, prevents any reform whatever, founded on a proper consolidation. Nor is it to be imagined, if this obstacle could be surmounted, that the neighboring powers would suffer a revolution to take place which would give to the empire the force and preeminence to which it is entitled. Foreign nations have long considered themselves as interested in the changes made by events in this constitution; and have, on various occasions, betrayed their policy of perpetuating its anarchy and weakness.

If more direct examples were wanting, Poland, as a government over local sovereigns, might not improperly be taken notice of. Nor could any proof more striking be given of the calamities flowing from such institutions. Equally unfit for self-government and self-defense, it has long been at the mercy of its powerful neighbors; who have lately had the mercy to disburden it of one third of its people and territories.

The connection among the Swiss cantons scarcely amounts to a confederacy; though it is sometimes cited as an instance of the stability of such institutions.

They have no common treasury; no common troops even in war; no common coin; no common judicatory; nor any other common mark of sovereignty.

They are kept together by the peculiarity of their topographical position; by their individual weakness and insignificancy; by the fear of powerful neighbors, to one of which they were formerly subject; by the few sources of contention among a people of such simple and homogeneous manners; by their joint interest in their dependent possessions; by the mutual aid they stand in need of, for suppressing insurrections and rebellions, an aid expressly stipulated and often required and afforded; and by the necessity of some regular and permanent provision for accommodating disputes among the cantons. The provision is, that the parties at variance shall each choose four judges out of the neutral cantons, who, in case of disagreement, choose an umpire. This tribunal, under an oath of impartiality, pronounces definitive sentence, which all the cantons are bound to enforce. The competency of this regulation may be estimated by a clause in their treaty of 1683, with Victor Amadeus of Savoy; in which he obliges himself to interpose as mediator in disputes between the cantons, and to employ force, if necessary, against the contumacious party.

So far as the peculiarity of their case will admit of comparison with that of the United States, it serves to confirm the principle intended to be established. Whatever efficacy the union may have had in ordinary cases, it appears that the moment a cause of difference sprang up, capable of trying its strength, it failed. The controversies on the subject of religion, which in three instances have kindled violent and bloody contests, may be said, in fact, to have severed the league. The Protestant and Catholic cantons have since had their separate diets, where all the most important concerns are adjusted, and which have left the general diet little other business than to take care of the common bailages.

That separation had another consequence, which merits attention. It produced opposite alliances with foreign powers: of Berne, at the head of the Protestant association, with the United Provinces; and of Luzerne, at the head of the Catholic association, with France.

PUBLIUS

1. Pfeffel, "Nouvel Abrég. Chronol. de l'Hist., etc., d'Allemagne," says the pretext was to indemnify himself for the expense of the expedition.

FEDERALIST PAPER NO. 20. THE SAME SUBJECT CONTINUED (THE INSUFFICIENCY OF THE PRESENT CONFEDERATION TO PRESERVE THE UNION)

From the New York Packet. Tuesday, December 11, 1787.

MADISON, with HAMILTON

To the People of the State of New York:

THE United Netherlands are a confederacy of republics, or rather of aristocracies of a very remarkable texture, yet confirming all the lessons derived from those which we have already reviewed.

The union is composed of seven coequal and sovereign states, and each state or province is a composition of equal and independent cities. In all important cases, not only the provinces but the cities must be unanimous.

The sovereignty of the Union is represented by the States-General, consisting usually of about fifty deputies appointed by the provinces. They hold their seats, some for life, some for six, three, and one years; from two provinces they continue in appointment during pleasure.

Documents of Revolution

The States-General have authority to enter into treaties and alliances; to make war and peace; to raise armies and equip fleets; to ascertain quotas and demand contributions. In all these cases, however, unanimity and the sanction of their constituents are requisite. They have authority to appoint and receive ambassadors; to execute treaties and alliances already formed; to provide for the collection of duties on imports and exports; to regulate the mint, with a saving to the provincial rights; to govern as sovereigns the dependent territories. The provinces are restrained, unless with the general consent, from entering into foreign treaties; from establishing imposts injurious to others, or charging their neighbors with higher duties than their own subjects. A council of state, a chamber of accounts, with five colleges of admiralty, aid and fortify the federal administration.

The executive magistrate of the union is the stadtholder, who is now an hereditary prince. His principal weight and influence in the republic are derived from this independent title; from his great patrimonial estates; from his family connections with some of the chief potentates of Europe; and, more than all, perhaps, from his being stadtholder in the several provinces, as well as for the union; in which provincial quality he has the appointment of town magistrates under certain regulations, executes provincial decrees, presides when he pleases in the provincial tribunals, and has throughout the power of pardon.

As stadtholder of the union, he has, however, considerable prerogatives.

In his political capacity he has authority to settle disputes between the provinces, when other methods fail; to assist at the deliberations of the States-General, and at their particular conferences; to give audiences to foreign ambassadors, and to keep agents for his particular affairs at foreign courts.

In his military capacity he commands the federal troops, provides for garrisons, and in general regulates military affairs; disposes of all appointments, from colonels to ensigns, and of the governments and posts of fortified towns.

In his marine capacity he is admiral-general, and superintends and directs every thing relative to naval forces and other naval affairs; presides in the admiralties in person or by proxy; appoints lieutenant-admirals and other officers; and establishes councils of war, whose sentences are not executed till he approves them.

His revenue, exclusive of his private income, amounts to three hundred thousand florins. The standing army which he commands consists of about forty thousand men.

Such is the nature of the celebrated Belgic confederacy, as delineated on parchment. What are the characters which practice has stamped upon it? Imbecility in the government; discord among the provinces; foreign influence and indignities; a precarious existence in peace, and peculiar calamities from war.

It was long ago remarked by Grotius, that nothing but the hatred of his countrymen to the house of Austria kept them from being ruined by the vices of their constitution.

The union of Utrecht, says another respectable writer, reposes an authority in the States-General, seemingly sufficient to secure harmony, but the jealousy in each province renders the practice very different from the theory.

The same instrument, says another, obliges each province to levy certain contributions; but this article never could, and probably never will, be executed; because the inland provinces, who have little commerce, cannot pay an equal quota.

In matters of contribution, it is the practice to waive the articles of the constitution. The danger of delay obliges the consenting provinces to furnish their quotas, without waiting for the others; and then to obtain reimbursement from the others, by deputations, which are frequent, or otherwise, as they can. The great wealth and influence of the province of Holland enable her to effect both these purposes.

It has more than once happened, that the deficiencies had to be ultimately collected at the point of the bayonet; a thing practicable, though dreadful, in a confederacy where one of the members exceeds in force all the rest, and where several of them are too small to meditate resistance; but utterly impracticable in one composed of members, several of which are equal to each other in strength and resources, and equal singly to a vigorous and persevering defense.

Foreign ministers, says Sir William Temple, who was himself a foreign minister, elude matters taken ad referendum, by tampering with the provinces and cities. In 1726, the treaty of Hanover was delayed by these means a whole year. Instances of a like nature are numerous and notorious.

In critical emergencies, the States-General are often compelled to overleap their constitutional bounds. In 1688, they concluded a treaty of themselves at the risk of their heads. The treaty of Westphalia, in 1648, by which their independence was formerly and finally recognized, was concluded without the consent of Zealand. Even as recently as the last treaty of peace with Great Britain, the constitutional principle of unanimity was departed from. A weak constitution must necessarily terminate in dissolution, for want of proper powers, or the usurpation of powers requisite for the public safety. Whether the usurpation, when once begun, will stop at the salutary point, or go forward to the dangerous extreme, must depend on the contingencies of the moment. Tyranny has perhaps oftener grown out of the assumptions of power, called for, on pressing exigencies, by a defective constitution, than out of the full exercise of the largest constitutional authorities.

Notwithstanding the calamities produced by the stadtholdership, it has been supposed that without his influence in the individual provinces, the causes of anarchy manifest in the confederacy would long ago have dissolved it. "Under such a government," says the Abbe Mably, "the Union could never have subsisted, if the provinces had not a spring within themselves, capable of quickening their tardiness, and compelling them to the same way of thinking. This spring is the stadtholder." It is remarked by Sir William Temple, "that in the intermissions of the stadtholdership, Holland, by her riches and her authority, which drew the others into a sort of dependence, supplied the place."

These are not the only circumstances which have controlled the tendency to anarchy and dissolution. The surrounding powers impose an absolute necessity of union to a certain degree, at the same time that they nourish by their intrigues the constitutional vices which keep the republic in some degree always at their mercy.

The true patriots have long bewailed the fatal tendency of these vices, and have made no less than four regular experiments by EXTRAORDINARY ASSEMBLIES, convened for the special purpose, to apply a remedy. As many times has their laudable zeal found it impossible to UNITE THE PUBLIC COUNCILS in reforming the known, the acknowledged, the fatal evils of the existing constitution. Let us pause, my fellow-citizens, for one moment, over this melancholy and monitory lesson of history; and with the tear that drops for the calamities brought on mankind by their adverse opinions and selfish passions, let our gratitude mingle an ejaculation to Heaven, for the propitious concord which has distinguished the consultations for our political happiness.

A design was also conceived of establishing a general tax to be administered by the federal authority. This also had its adversaries and failed.

This unhappy people seem to be now suffering from popular convulsions, from dissensions among the states, and from the actual invasion of foreign arms, the crisis of their destiny. All nations have their eyes fixed on the awful spectacle. The first wish prompted by humanity is, that this severe trial may issue in such a revolution of their government as will establish their union, and render it the parent of tranquillity, freedom and happiness: The next, that the asylum under which, we trust, the enjoyment of these blessings will speedily be secured in this country, may receive and console them for the catastrophe of their own.

I make no apology for having dwelt so long on the contemplation of these federal precedents. Experience is the oracle of truth; and where its responses are unequivocal, they ought to be conclusive and sacred. The important truth, which it unequivocally pronounces in the present case, is that a sovereignty over sovereigns, a government over governments, a legislation for communities, as contradistinguished from individuals, as it is a solecism in theory, so in practice it is subversive of the order and ends of civil polity, by substituting VIOLENCE in place of LAW, or the destructive COERCION of the SWORD in place of the mild and salutary COERCION of the MAGISTRACY.

PUBLIUS

FEDERALIST PAPER NO. 21. OTHER DEFECTS OF THE PRESENT CONFEDERATION

For the Independent Journal. Wednesday, December 12, 1787

HAMILTON

To the People of the State of New York:

HAVING in the three last numbers taken a summary review of the principal circumstances and events which have depicted the genius and fate of other confederate governments, I shall now proceed in the enumeration of the most important of those defects which have hitherto disappointed our hopes from the system established among ourselves. To form a safe and satisfactory judgment of the proper remedy, it is absolutely necessary that we should be well acquainted with the extent and malignity of the disease.

The next most palpable defect of the subsisting Confederation, is the total want of a SANCTION to its laws. The United States, as now composed, have no powers to exact obedience, or punish disobedience to their resolutions, either by pecuniary mulcts, by a suspension or divestiture of privileges, or by any other constitutional mode. There is no express delegation of authority to them to use force against delinquent members; and if such a right should be ascribed to the federal head, as resulting from the nature of the social compact between the States, it must be by inference and construction, in the face of that part of the second article, by which it is declared, "that each State shall retain every power, jurisdiction, and right, not EXPRESSLY delegated to the United States in Congress assembled." There is, doubtless, a striking absurdity in supposing that a right of this kind does not exist, but we are reduced to the dilemma either of embracing that supposition, preposterous as it may seem, or of contravening or explaining away a provision, which has been of late a repeated theme of the eulogies of those who oppose the new Constitution; and the want of which, in that plan, has been the subject of much plausible animadversion, and severe criticism. If we are unwilling to impair the force of this applauded provision, we shall be obliged to conclude, that the United States afford the extraordinary spectacle of a government destitute even of the shadow of constitutional power to enforce the execution of its own laws. It will appear, from the specimens which have been cited, that the American Confederacy, in this particular, stands discriminated from every other institution of a similar kind, and exhibits a new and unexampled phenomenon in the political world.

The want of a mutual guaranty of the State governments is another capital imperfection in the federal plan. There is nothing of this kind declared in the articles that compose it; and to imply a tacit guaranty from considerations of utility, would be a still more flagrant departure from the clause which has been mentioned, than to imply a tacit power of coercion from the like considerations. The want of a guaranty, though it might in its consequences endanger the Union, does not so immediately attack its existence as the want of a constitutional sanction to its laws.

Without a guaranty the assistance to be derived from the Union in repelling those domestic dangers which may sometimes threaten the existence of the State constitutions, must be renounced. Usurpation may rear its crest in each State, and trample upon the liberties of the people, while the national government could legally do nothing more than behold its encroachments with indignation and regret. A successful faction may erect a tyranny on the ruins of order and law, while no succor could constitutionally be afforded by the Union to the friends and supporters of the government. The tempestuous situation from which Massachusetts has scarcely emerged, evinces that dangers of this kind are not merely speculative. Who can determine what might have been the issue of her late convulsions, if the malcontents had been headed by a Caesar or by a Cromwell? Who can predict what effect a despotism, established in Massachusetts, would have upon the liberties of New Hampshire or Rhode Island, of Connecticut or New York?

The inordinate pride of State importance has suggested to some minds an objection to the principle of a guaranty in the federal government, as involving an officious interference in the domestic concerns of the members. A scruple of this kind would deprive us of one of the principal advantages to be expected from union, and can only flow from a misapprehension of the nature of the provision itself. It could be no impediment to reforms of the State constitution by a majority of the people in a legal and peaceable mode. This right would remain undiminished. The guaranty could only operate against changes to be effected by violence. Towards the preventions of calamities of this kind, too many checks cannot be provided. The peace of society and the stability of government depend absolutely on the efficacy of the precautions adopted on this head. Where the whole power of the government is in the hands of the people, there is the less pretense for the use of violent remedies in partial or occasional distempers of the State. The natural cure for an ill-administration, in a popular or representative constitution, is a change of men. A guaranty by the national authority would be as much levelled against the usurpations of rulers as against the ferments and outrages of faction and sedition in the community.

The principle of regulating the contributions of the States to the common treasury by QUOTAS is another fundamental error in the Confederation. Its repugnancy to an adequate supply of the national exigencies has been already pointed out, and has sufficiently appeared from the trial which has been made of it. I speak of it now solely with a view to equality among the States. Those who have been accustomed to contemplate the circumstances which produce and constitute national wealth, must be satisfied that there is no common standard or barometer by which the degrees of it can be ascertained. Neither the value of lands, nor the numbers of the people, which have been successively proposed as the rule of State contributions, has any pretension to being a just representative. If we compare the wealth of the United Netherlands with that of Russia or Germany, or even of France, and if we at the same time compare the total value of the lands and the aggregate population of that contracted district with the total value of the lands and the aggregate population of the immense regions of either of the three last-mentioned countries, we shall at once discover that there is no comparison between the proportion of either of these two objects and that of the relative wealth of those nations. If the like parallel were to be run between several of the American States, it would furnish a like result. Let Virginia be contrasted with North Carolina, Pennsylvania with Connecticut, or Maryland with New Jersey, and we shall be convinced that the respective abilities of those States, in relation to revenue, bear little or no analogy to their comparative stock in lands or to their comparative population. The position may be equally illustrated by a similar process between the counties of the same State. No man who is acquainted with the State of New York will doubt that the active wealth of King's County bears a much greater proportion to that of Montgomery than it would appear to be if we should take either the total value of the lands or the total number of the people as a criterion!

The wealth of nations depends upon an infinite variety of causes. Situation, soil, climate, the nature of the productions, the nature of the government, the genius of the citizens, the degree of information they possess, the state of commerce, of arts, of industry, these circumstances and many more, too complex, minute, or adventitious to admit of a particular specification, occasion differences hardly conceivable in the relative opulence and riches of different countries. The consequence clearly is that there can be no common measure of national wealth, and, of course, no general or stationary rule by which the ability of a state to pay taxes can be determined. The attempt, therefore, to regulate the contributions of the members of a confederacy by any such rule, cannot fail to be productive of glaring inequality and extreme oppression.

This inequality would of itself be sufficient in America to work the eventual destruction of the Union, if any mode of enforcing a compliance with its requisitions could be devised. The suffering States would not long consent to remain associated upon a principle which distributes the public burdens with so unequal a hand, and which was calculated to impoverish and oppress the citizens of some States, while those of others would scarcely be conscious of the small proportion of the weight they were required to sustain. This, however, is an evil inseparable from the principle of quotas and requisitions.

There is no method of steering clear of this inconvenience, but by authorizing the national government to raise its own revenues in its own way. Imposts, excises, and, in general, all duties upon articles of consumption, may be compared to a fluid, which will, in time, find its level with the means of paying them. The amount to be contributed by each citizen will in a degree be at his own option, and can be regulated by an attention to his resources. The rich may be extravagant, the poor can be frugal; and private oppression may always be avoided by a judicious selection of objects proper for such impositions. If inequalities should arise in some States from duties on particular objects, these will, in all probability, be counterbalanced by proportional inequalities in other States, from the duties on other objects. In the course of time and things, an equilibrium, as far as it is attainable in so complicated a subject, will be established everywhere. Or, if inequalities should still exist, they would neither be so great in their degree, so uniform in their operation, nor so odious in their appearance, as those which would necessarily spring from quotas, upon any scale that can possibly be devised.

It is a signal advantage of taxes on articles of consumption, that they contain in their own nature a security against excess. They prescribe their own limit; which cannot be exceeded without defeating the end proposed, that is, an extension of the revenue. When applied to this object, the saying is as just as it is witty, that, "in political arithmetic, two and two do not always make four." If duties are too high, they lessen the consumption; the collection is eluded; and the product to the treasury is not so great as when they are confined within proper and moderate bounds. This forms a complete barrier against any material oppression of the citizens by taxes of this class, and is itself a natural limitation of the power of imposing them.

Impositions of this kind usually fall under the denomination of indirect taxes, and must for a long time constitute the chief part of the revenue raised in this country. Those of the direct kind, which principally relate to land and buildings, may admit of a rule of apportionment. Either the value of land, or the number of the people, may serve as a standard. The state of agriculture and the populousness of a country have been considered as nearly connected with each other. And, as a rule, for the purpose intended, numbers, in the view of simplicity and certainty, are entitled to a preference. In every country it is a herculean task to obtain a valuation of the land; in a country imperfectly settled and progressive in improvement, the difficulties are increased almost to impracticability. The expense of an accurate valuation is, in all situations, a formidable objection. In a branch of taxation where no limits to the discretion of the government are to be found in the nature of things, the establishment of a fixed rule, not incompatible with the end, may be attended with fewer inconveniences than to leave that discretion altogether at large.

PUBLIUS

FEDERALIST PAPER NO. 22. THE SAME SUBJECT CONTINUED (OTHER DEFECTS OF THE PRESENT CONFEDERATION)

From the New York Packet. Friday, December 14, 1787.

HAMILTON

To the People of the State of New York:

IN ADDITION to the defects already enumerated in the existing federal system, there are others of not less importance, which concur in rendering it altogether unfit for the administration of the affairs of the Union.

The want of a power to regulate commerce is by all parties allowed to be of the number. The utility of such a power has been anticipated under the first head of our inquiries; and for this reason, as well as from the universal conviction entertained upon the subject, little need be added in this place. It is indeed evident, on the most superficial view, that there is no object, either as it respects the interests of trade or finance, that more strongly demands a federal superintendence. The want of it has already operated as a bar to the formation of beneficial treaties with foreign powers, and has given occasions of dissatisfaction between the States. No nation acquainted with the nature of our political association would be unwise enough to enter into stipulations with the United States, by which they conceded privileges of any importance to them, while they were apprised that the engagements on the part of the Union might at any moment be violated by its members, and while they found from experience that they might enjoy every advantage they desired in our markets, without granting us any return but such as their momentary convenience might suggest. It is not, therefore, to be wondered at that Mr. Jenkinson, in ushering into the House of Commons a bill for regulating the temporary intercourse between the two countries, should preface its introduction by a declaration that similar provisions in former bills had been found to answer every purpose to the commerce of Great Britain, and that it would be prudent to persist in the plan until it should appear whether the American government was likely or not to acquire greater consistency.(1)

Several States have endeavored, by separate prohibitions, restrictions, and exclusions, to influence the conduct of that kingdom in this particular, but the want of concert, arising from the want of a general authority and from clashing and dissimilar views in the State, has hitherto frustrated every experiment of the kind, and will continue to do so as long as the same obstacles to a uniformity of measures continue to exist.

The interfering and unneighborly regulations of some States, contrary to the true spirit of the Union, have, in different instances, given just cause of umbrage and complaint to others, and it is to be feared that examples of this nature, if not restrained by a national control, would be multiplied and extended till they became not less serious sources of animosity and discord than injurious impediments to the intercourse between the different parts of the Confederacy. "The commerce of the German empire(2) is in continual trammels from the multiplicity of the duties which the several princes and states exact upon the merchandises passing through their territories, by means of which the fine streams and navigable rivers with which Germany is so happily watered are rendered almost useless." Though the genius of the people of this country might never permit this description to be strictly applicable to us, yet we may reasonably expect, from the gradual conflicts of State regulations, that the citizens of each would at length come to be considered and treated by the others in no better light than that of foreigners and aliens.

The power of raising armies, by the most obvious construction of the articles of the Confederation, is merely a power of making requisitions upon the States for quotas of men. This practice in the course of the late war, was found replete with obstructions to a vigorous and to an economical system of defense. It gave birth to a competition between the States which created a kind of auction for men. In order to furnish the quotas required of them, they outbid each other till bounties grew to an enormous and insupportable size. The hope of a still further increase afforded an inducement to those who were disposed to serve to procrastinate their enlistment, and disinclined them from engaging for any considerable periods. Hence, slow and scanty levies of men, in the most critical emergencies of our affairs; short enlistments at an unparalleled expense; continual fluctuations in the troops, ruinous to their discipline and subjecting the public safety frequently to the perilous crisis of a disbanded army. Hence, also, those oppressive expedients for raising men which were upon several occasions practiced, and which nothing but the enthusiasm of liberty would have induced the people to endure.

This method of raising troops is not more unfriendly to economy and vigor than it is to an equal distribution of the burden. The States near the seat of war, influenced by motives of self-preservation, made efforts to furnish their quotas, which even exceeded their abilities; while those at a distance from danger were, for the most part, as remiss as the others were diligent, in their exertions. The immediate pressure of this inequality was not in this case, as in that of the contributions of money, alleviated by the hope of a final liquidation. The States which did not pay their proportions of money might at least be charged with their deficiencies; but no account could be formed of the deficiencies in the supplies of men. We shall not, however, see much reason to regret the want of this hope, when we consider how little prospect there is, that the most delinquent States will ever be able to make compensation for their pecuniary failures. The system of quotas and requisitions, whether it be applied to men or money, is, in every view, a system of imbecility in the Union, and of inequality and injustice among the members.

The right of equal suffrage among the States is another exceptionable part of the Confederation. Every idea of proportion and every rule of fair representation conspire to condemn a principle, which gives to Rhode Island an equal weight in the scale of power with Massachusetts, or Connecticut, or New York; and to Delaware an equal voice in the national deliberations with Pennsylvania, or Virginia, or North Carolina. Its operation contradicts the fundamental maxim of republican government, which requires that the sense of the majority should prevail. Sophistry may reply, that sovereigns are equal, and that a majority of the votes of the States will be a majority of confederated America. But this kind of logical legerdemain will never counteract the plain suggestions of justice and common-sense. It may happen that this majority of States is a small minority of the people of America;(3) and two thirds of the people of America could not long be persuaded, upon the credit of artificial distinctions and syllogistic subtleties, to submit their interests to the management and disposal of one third. The larger States would after a while revolt from the idea of receiving the law from the smaller. To acquiesce in such a privation of their due importance in the political scale, would be not merely to be insensible to the love of power, but even to sacrifice the desire of equality. It is neither rational to expect the first, nor just to require the last. The smaller States, considering how peculiarly their safety and welfare depend on union, ought readily to renounce a pretension which, if not relinquished, would prove fatal to its duration.

It may be objected to this, that not seven but nine States, or two thirds of the whole number, must consent to the most important resolutions; and it may be thence inferred that nine States would always comprehend a majority of the Union. But this does not obviate the impropriety of an equal vote between States of the most unequal dimensions and populousness; nor is the inference accurate in point of fact; for we can enumerate nine States which contain less than a majority of the people;(4) and it is constitutionally possible that these nine may give the vote. Besides, there are matters of considerable moment determinable by a bare majority; and there are others, concerning which doubts have been entertained, which, if interpreted in favor of the sufficiency of a vote of seven States, would extend its operation to interests of the first magnitude. In addition to this, it is to be observed that there is a probability of an increase in the number of States, and no provision for a proportional augmentation of the ratio of votes.

But this is not all: what at first sight may seem a remedy, is, in reality, a poison. To give a minority a negative upon the majority (which is always the case where more than a majority is requisite to a decision), is, in its tendency, to subject the sense of the greater number to that of the lesser. Congress, from the nonattendance of a few States, have been frequently in the situation of a Polish diet, where a single VOTE has been sufficient to put a stop to all their movements. A sixtieth part of the Union, which is about the proportion of Delaware and Rhode Island, has several times been able to oppose an entire bar to its operations. This is one of those refinements which, in practice, has an effect the reverse of what is expected from it in theory. The necessity of unanimity in public bodies, or of something approaching towards it, has been founded upon a supposition that it would contribute to security. But its real operation is to embarrass the administration, to destroy the energy of the government, and to substitute the pleasure, caprice, or artifices of an insignificant, turbulent, or corrupt junto, to the regular deliberations and decisions of a respectable majority. In those emergencies of a nation, in which the goodness or badness, the weakness or strength of its government, is of the greatest importance, there is commonly a necessity for action. The public business must, in some way or other, go forward. If a pertinacious minority can control the opinion of a majority, respecting the best mode of conducting it, the majority, in order that something may be done, must conform to the views of the minority; and thus the sense of the smaller number will overrule that of the greater, and give a tone to the national proceedings. Hence, tedious delays; continual negotiation and intrigue; contemptible compromises of the public good. And yet, in such a system, it is even happy when such compromises can take place: for upon some occasions things will not admit of accommodation; and

Documents of Revolution

then the measures of government must be injuriously suspended, or fatally defeated. It is often, by the impracticability of obtaining the concurrence of the necessary number of votes, kept in a state of inaction. Its situation must always savor of weakness, sometimes border upon anarchy.

It is not difficult to discover, that a principle of this kind gives greater scope to foreign corruption, as well as to domestic faction, than that which permits the sense of the majority to decide; though the contrary of this has been presumed. The mistake has proceeded from not attending with due care to the mischiefs that may be occasioned by obstructing the progress of government at certain critical seasons. When the concurrence of a large number is required by the Constitution to the doing of any national act, we are apt to rest satisfied that all is safe, because nothing improper will be likely TO BE DONE, but we forget how much good may be prevented, and how much ill may be produced, by the power of hindering the doing what may be necessary, and of keeping affairs in the same unfavorable posture in which they may happen to stand at particular periods.

Suppose, for instance, we were engaged in a war, in conjunction with one foreign nation, against another. Suppose the necessity of our situation demanded peace, and the interest or ambition of our ally led him to seek the prosecution of the war, with views that might justify us in making separate terms. In such a state of things, this ally of ours would evidently find it much easier, by his bribes and intrigues, to tie up the hands of government from making peace, where two thirds of all the votes were requisite to that object, than where a simple majority would suffice. In the first case, he would have to corrupt a smaller number; in the last, a greater number. Upon the same principle, it would be much easier for a foreign power with which we were at war to perplex our councils and embarrass our exertions. And, in a commercial view, we may be subjected to similar inconveniences. A nation, with which we might have a treaty of commerce, could with much greater facility prevent our forming a connection with her competitor in trade, though such a connection should be ever so beneficial to ourselves.

Evils of this description ought not to be regarded as imaginary. One of the weak sides of republics, among their numerous advantages, is that they afford too easy an inlet to foreign corruption. An hereditary monarch, though often disposed to sacrifice his subjects to his ambition, has so great a personal interest in the government and in the external glory of the nation, that it is not easy for a foreign power to give him an equivalent for what he would sacrifice by treachery to the state. The world has accordingly been witness to few examples of this species of royal prostitution, though there have been abundant specimens of every other kind.

In republics, persons elevated from the mass of the community, by the suffrages of their fellow-citizens, to stations of great pre-eminence and power, may find compensations for betraying their trust, which, to any but minds animated and guided by superior virtue, may appear to exceed the proportion of interest they have in the common stock, and to overbalance the obligations of duty. Hence it is that history furnishes us with so many mortifying examples of the prevalency of foreign corruption in republican governments. How much this contributed to the ruin of the ancient commonwealths has been already delineated. It is well known that the deputies of the United Provinces have, in various instances, been purchased by the emissaries of the neighboring kingdoms. The Earl of Chesterfield (if my memory serves me right), in a letter to his court, intimates that his success in an important negotiation must depend on his obtaining a major's commission for one of those deputies. And in Sweden the parties were alternately bought by France and England in so barefaced and notorious a manner that it excited universal disgust in the nation, and was a principal cause that the most limited monarch in Europe, in a single day, without tumult, violence, or opposition, became one of the most absolute and uncontrolled.

A circumstance which crowns the defects of the Confederation remains yet to be mentioned, the want of a judiciary power. Laws are a dead letter without courts to expound and define their true meaning and operation. The treaties of the United States, to have any force at all, must be considered as part of the law of the land. Their true import, as far as respects individuals, must, like all other laws, be ascertained by judicial determinations. To produce uniformity in these determinations, they ought to be submitted, in the last resort, to one SUPREME TRIBUNAL. And this tribunal ought to be instituted under the same authority which forms the treaties themselves. These ingredients are both indispensable. If there is in each State a court of final jurisdiction, there may be as many different final determinations on the same point as there are courts. There are endless diversities in the opinions of men. We often see not only different courts but the judges of the came court differing from each other. To avoid the confusion which would unavoidably result from the contradictory decisions of a number of independent judicatories, all nations have found it necessary to establish one court paramount to the rest, possessing a general superintendence, and authorized to settle and declare in the last resort a uniform rule of civil justice.

This is the more necessary where the frame of the government is so compounded that the laws of the whole are in danger of being contravened by the laws of the parts. In this case, if the particular tribunals are invested with a right of ultimate jurisdiction, besides the contradictions to be expected from difference of opinion, there will be much to fear from the bias of local views and prejudices, and from the interference of local regulations. As often as such an interference was to happen, there would be reason to apprehend that the provisions of the particular laws might be preferred to those of the general laws; for nothing is more natural to men in office than to look with peculiar deference towards that authority to which they owe their official existence.

The treaties of the United States, under the present Constitution, are liable to the infractions of thirteen different legislatures, and as many different courts of final jurisdiction, acting under the authority of those legislatures. The faith, the reputation, the peace of the whole Union, are thus continually at the mercy of the prejudices, the passions, and the interests of every member of which it is composed. Is it possible that foreign nations can either respect or confide in such a government? Is it possible that the people of America will longer consent to trust their honor, their happiness, their safety, on so precarious a foundation?

In this review of the Confederation, I have confined myself to the exhibition of its most material defects; passing over those imperfections in its details by which even a great part of the power intended to be conferred upon it has been in a great measure rendered abortive. It must be by this time evident to all men of reflection, who can divest themselves of the prepossessions of preconceived opinions, that it is a system so radically vicious and unsound, as to admit not of amendment but by an entire change in its leading features and characters.

The organization of Congress is itself utterly improper for the exercise of those powers which are necessary to be deposited in the Union. A single assembly may be a proper receptacle of those slender, or rather fettered, authorities, which have been heretofore delegated to the federal head; but it would be inconsistent with all the principles of good government, to intrust it with those additional powers which, even the moderate and more rational adversaries of the proposed Constitution admit, ought to reside in the United States. If that plan should not be adopted, and if the necessity of the Union should be able to withstand the ambitious aims of those men who may indulge magnificent schemes of personal aggrandizement from its dissolution, the probability would be, that we should run into the project of conferring supplementary powers upon Congress, as they are now constituted; and either the machine, from the intrinsic feebleness of its structure, will moulder into pieces, in spite of our ill-judged efforts to prop it; or, by successive augmentations of its force an energy, as necessity might prompt, we shall finally accumulate, in a single body, all the most important prerogatives of sovereignty, and thus entail upon our posterity one of the most execrable forms of government that human infatuation ever contrived. Thus, we should create in reality that very tyranny which the adversaries of the new Constitution either are, or affect to be, solicitous to avert.

It has not a little contributed to the infirmities of the existing federal system, that it never had a ratification by the PEOPLE. Resting on no better foundation than the consent of the several legislatures, it has been exposed to frequent and intricate questions concerning the validity of its powers, and has, in some instances, given birth to the enormous doctrine of a right of legislative repeal. Owing its ratification to the law of a State, it has been contended that the same authority might repeal the law by which it was ratified. However gross a heresy it may be to maintain that a PARTY to a COMPACT has a right to revoke that COMPACT, the doctrine itself has had respectable advocates. The possibility of a question of this nature proves the necessity of laying the foundations of our national government deeper than in the mere sanction of delegated authority. The fabric of American empire ought to rest on the solid basis of THE CONSENT OF THE PEOPLE. The streams of national power ought to flow immediately from that pure, original fountain of all legitimate authority.

PUBLIUS

1. This, as nearly as I can recollect, was the sense of his speech on introducing the last bill.

2. Encyclopedia, article "Empire."

3. New Hampshire, Rhode Island, New Jersey, Delaware, Georgia, South Carolina, and Maryland are a majority of the whole number of the States, but they do not contain one third of the people.

4. Add New York and Connecticut to the foregoing seven, and they will be less than a majority.

FEDERALIST PAPER NO. 23. THE NECESSITY OF A GOVERNMENT AS ENERGETIC AS THE ONE PROPOSED TO THE PRESERVATION OF THE UNION

From the New York Packet. Tuesday, December 18, 1787.

HAMILTON

To the People of the State of New York:

THE necessity of a Constitution, at least equally energetic with the one proposed, to the preservation of the Union, is the point at the examination of which we are now arrived.

This inquiry will naturally divide itself into three branches—the objects to be provided for by the federal government, the quantity of power necessary to the accomplishment of those objects, the persons upon whom that power ought to operate. Its distribution and organization will more properly claim our attention under the succeeding head.

The principal purposes to be answered by union are these—the common defense of the members; the preservation of the public peace as well against internal convulsions as external attacks; the regulation of commerce with other nations and between the States; the superintendence of our intercourse, political and commercial, with foreign countries.

The authorities essential to the common defense are these: to raise armies; to build and equip fleets; to prescribe rules for the government of both; to direct their operations; to provide for their support. These powers ought to exist without limitation, BECAUSE IT IS IMPOSSIBLE TO FORESEE OR DEFINE THE EXTENT AND VARIETY OF NATIONAL EXIGENCIES, OR THE CORRESPONDENT EXTENT AND VARIETY OF THE MEANS WHICH MAY BE NECESSARY TO SATISFY THEM. The circumstances that endanger the safety of nations are infinite, and for this reason no constitutional shackles can wisely be imposed on the power to which the care of it is committed. This power ought to be coextensive with all the possible combinations of such circumstances; and ought to be under the direction of the same councils which are appointed to preside over the common defense.

This is one of those truths which, to a correct and unprejudiced mind, carries its own evidence along with it; and may be obscured, but cannot be made plainer by argument or reasoning. It rests upon axioms as simple as they are universal; the MEANS ought to be proportioned to the END; the persons, from whose agency the attainment of any END is expected, ought to possess the MEANS by which it is to be attained.

Whether there ought to be a federal government intrusted with the care of the common defense, is a question in the first instance, open for discussion; but the moment it is decided in the affirmative, it will follow, that that government ought to be clothed with all the powers requisite to complete execution of its trust. And unless it can be shown that the circumstances which may affect the public safety are reducible within certain determinate limits; unless the contrary of this position can be fairly and rationally disputed, it must be admitted, as a necessary consequence, that there can be no limitation of that authority which is to provide for the defense and protection of the community, in any matter essential to its efficacy that is, in any matter essential to the FORMATION, DIRECTION, or SUPPORT of the NATIONAL FORCES.

Defective as the present Confederation has been proved to be, this principle appears to have been fully recognized by the framers of it; though they have not made proper or adequate provision for its exercise. Congress have an unlimited discretion to make requisitions of men and money; to govern the army and navy; to direct their operations. As their requisitions are made constitutionally binding upon the States, who are in fact under the most solemn obligations to furnish the supplies required of them, the intention evidently was that the United States should command whatever resources were by them judged requisite to the "common defense and general welfare." It was presumed that a sense of their true interests, and a regard to the dictates of good faith, would be found sufficient pledges for the punctual performance of the duty of the members to the federal head.

The experiment has, however, demonstrated that this expectation was ill-founded and illusory; and the observations, made under the last head, will, I imagine, have sufficed to convince the impartial and discerning, that there is an absolute necessity for an entire change in the first principles of the system; that if we are in earnest about giving the Union energy and duration, we must abandon the vain project of legislating upon the States in their collective capacities; we must extend the laws of the federal government to the individual citizens of America; we must discard the fallacious scheme of quotas and requisitions, as equally impracticable and unjust. The result from all this is that the Union ought to be invested with full power to levy troops; to build and equip fleets; and to raise the revenues which will be required for the formation and support of an army and navy, in the customary and ordinary modes practiced in other governments.

If the circumstances of our country are such as to demand a compound instead of a simple, a confederate instead of a sole, government, the essential point which will remain to be adjusted will be to discriminate the OBJECTS, as far as it can be done, which shall appertain to the different provinces or departments of power; allowing to each the most ample authority for fulfilling the objects committed to its charge. Shall the Union be constituted the guardian of the common safety? Are fleets and armies and revenues necessary to this purpose? The government of the Union must be empowered to pass all laws, and to make all regulations which have relation to them. The same must be the case in respect to commerce, and to every other matter to which its jurisdiction is permitted to extend. Is the administration of justice between the citizens of the same State the proper department of the local governments? These must possess all the authorities which are connected with this object, and with every other that may be allotted to their particular cognizance and direction. Not to confer in each case a degree of power commensurate to the end, would be to violate the most obvious rules of prudence and propriety, and improvidently to trust the great interests of the nation to hands which are disabled from managing them with vigor and success.

Who is likely to make suitable provisions for the public defense, as that body to which the guardianship of the public safety is confided; which, as the centre of information, will best understand the extent and urgency of the dangers that threaten; as the representative of the WHOLE, will feel itself most deeply interested in the preservation of every part; which, from the responsibility implied in the duty assigned to it, will be most sensibly impressed with the necessity of proper exertions; and which, by the extension of its authority throughout the States, can alone establish uniformity and concert in the plans and measures by which the common safety is to be secured? Is there not a manifest inconsistency in devolving upon the federal government the care of the general defense, and leaving in the State governments the EFFECTIVE powers by which it is to be provided for? Is not a want of co-operation the infallible consequence of such a system? And will not weakness, disorder, an undue distribution of the burdens and calamities of war, an unnecessary and intolerable increase of expense, be its natural and inevitable concomitants? Have we not had unequivocal experience of its effects in the course of the revolution which we have just accomplished?

Every view we may take of the subject, as candid inquirers after truth, will serve to convince us, that it is both unwise and dangerous to deny the federal government an unconfined authority, as to all those objects which are intrusted to its management. It will indeed deserve the most vigilant and careful attention of the people, to see that it be modeled in such a manner as to admit of its being safely vested with the requisite powers. If any plan which has been, or may be, offered to our consideration, should not, upon a dispassionate inspection, be found to answer this description, it ought to be rejected. A government, the constitution of which renders it unfit to be trusted with all the powers which a free people ought to delegate to any government, would be an unsafe and improper depositary of the NATIONAL INTERESTS. Wherever THESE can with propriety be confided, the coincident powers may safely accompany them. This is the true result of all just reasoning upon the subject. And the adversaries of the plan promulgated by the convention ought to have confined themselves to showing, that the internal structure of the proposed government was such as to render it unworthy of the confidence of the people. They ought not to have wandered into inflammatory declamations and unmeaning cavils about the extent of the powers. The POWERS are not too extensive for the OBJECTS of federal administration, or, in other words, for the management of our NATIONAL INTERESTS; nor can any satisfactory argument be framed to show that they are chargeable with such an excess. If it be true, as has been insinuated by some of the writers on the other side, that the difficulty arises from the nature of the thing, and that the extent of the country will not permit us to form a government in which such ample powers can safely be reposed, it would prove that we ought to contract our views, and resort to the expedient of separate confederacies, which will move within more practicable spheres. For the absurdity must continually stare us in the face of confiding to a government the direction of the most essential national interests, without daring to trust it to the authorities which are indispensable to their proper and efficient management. Let us not attempt to reconcile contradictions, but firmly embrace a rational alternative.

I trust, however, that the impracticability of one general system cannot be shown. I am greatly mistaken, if any thing of weight has yet been advanced of this tendency; and I flatter myself, that the observations which have been made in the course of these papers have served to place the reverse of that position in as clear a light as any matter still in the womb of time and experience can be susceptible of. This, at all events, must be evident, that the very difficulty itself, drawn from the extent of the country, is the strongest argument in favor of an energetic government; for any other can certainly never preserve the Union of so large an empire. If we embrace the tenets of those who oppose the adoption of the proposed Constitution, as the standard of our political creed, we cannot fail to verify the gloomy doctrines which predict the impracticability of a national system pervading entire limits of the present Confederacy.

PUBLIUS

FEDERALIST PAPER NO. 24. THE POWERS NECESSARY TO THE COMMON DEFENSE FURTHER CONSIDERED

For the Independent Journal. Wednesday, December 19, 1787

HAMILTON

To the People of the State of New York:

TO THE powers proposed to be conferred upon the federal government, in respect to the creation and direction of the national forces, I have met with but one specific objection, which, if I understand it right, is this, that proper provision has not been made against the existence of standing armies in time of peace; an objection which, I shall now endeavor to show, rests on weak and unsubstantial foundations.

It has indeed been brought forward in the most vague and general form, supported only by bold assertions, without the appearance of argument; without even the sanction of theoretical opinions; in contradiction to the practice of other free nations, and to the general sense of America, as expressed in most of the existing constitutions. The proprietary of this remark will appear, the moment it is recollected that the objection under consideration turns upon a supposed necessity of restraining the LEGISLATIVE authority of the nation, in the article of military establishments; a principle unheard of, except in one or two of our State constitutions, and rejected in all the rest.

A stranger to our politics, who was to read our newspapers at the present juncture, without having previously inspected the plan reported by the convention, would be naturally led to one of two conclusions: either that it contained a positive injunction, that standing armies should be kept up in time of peace; or that it vested in the EXECUTIVE the whole power of levying troops, without subjecting his discretion, in any shape, to the control of the legislature.

If he came afterwards to peruse the plan itself, he would be surprised to discover, that neither the one nor the other was the case; that the whole power of raising armies was lodged in the LEGISLATURE, not in the EXECUTIVE; that this legislature was to be a popular body, consisting of the representatives of the people periodically elected; and that instead of the provision he had supposed in favor of standing armies, there was to be found, in respect to this object, an important qualification even of the legislative discretion, in that clause which forbids the appropriation of money for the support of an army for any longer period than two years a precaution which, upon a nearer view of it, will appear to be a great and real security against the keeping up of troops without evident necessity.

Disappointed in his first surmise, the person I have supposed would be apt to pursue his conjectures a little further. He would naturally say to himself, it is impossible that all this vehement and pathetic declamation can be without some colorable pretext. It must needs be that this people, so jealous of their liberties, have, in all the preceding models of the constitutions which they have established, inserted the most precise and rigid precautions on this point, the omission of which, in the new plan, has given birth to all this apprehension and clamor.

If, under this impression, he proceeded to pass in review the several State constitutions, how great would be his disappointment to find that TWO ONLY of them(1) contained an interdiction of standing armies in time of peace; that the other eleven had either observed a profound silence on the subject, or had in express terms admitted the right of the Legislature to authorize their existence.

Still, however he would be persuaded that there must be some plausible foundation for the cry raised on this head. He would never be able to imagine, while any source of information remained unexplored, that it was nothing more than an experiment upon the public credulity, dictated either by a deliberate intention to deceive, or by the overflowings of a zeal too intemperate to be ingenuous. It would probably occur to him, that he would be likely to find the precautions he was in search of in the primitive compact between the States. Here, at length, he would expect to meet with a solution of the enigma. No doubt, he would observe to himself, the existing Confederation must contain the most explicit provisions against military establishments in time of peace; and a departure from this model, in a favorite point, has occasioned the discontent which appears to influence these political champions.

If he should now apply himself to a careful and critical survey of the articles of Confederation, his astonishment would not only be increased, but would acquire a mixture of indignation, at the unexpected discovery, that these articles, instead of containing the prohibition he looked for, and though they had, with jealous circumspection, restricted the authority of the State legislatures in this particular, had not imposed a single restraint on that of the United States. If he happened to be a man of quick sensibility, or ardent temper, he could now no longer refrain from regarding these clamors as the dishonest artifices of a sinister and unprincipled opposition to a plan which ought at least to receive a fair and candid examination from all sincere lovers of their country! How else, he would say, could the authors of them have been tempted to vent such loud censures upon that plan, about a point in which it seems to have conformed itself to the general sense of America as declared in its different forms of government, and in which it has even superadded a new and powerful guard unknown to any of them? If, on the contrary, he happened to be a man of calm and dispassionate feelings, he would indulge a sigh for the frailty of human nature, and would lament, that in a matter so interesting to the happiness of millions, the true merits of the question should be perplexed and entangled by expedients so unfriendly to an impartial and right determination. Even such a man could hardly forbear remarking, that a conduct of this kind has too much the appearance of an intention to mislead the people by alarming their passions, rather than to convince them by arguments addressed to their understandings.

But however little this objection may be countenanced, even by precedents among ourselves, it may be satisfactory to take a nearer view of its intrinsic merits. From a close examination it will appear that restraints upon the discretion of the legislature in respect to military establishments in time of peace, would be improper to be imposed, and if imposed, from the necessities of society, would be unlikely to be observed.

Though a wide ocean separates the United States from Europe, yet there are various considerations that warn us against an excess of confidence or security. On one side of us, and stretching far into our rear, are growing settlements subject to the dominion of Britain. On the other side, and extending to meet the British settlements, are colonies and establishments subject to the dominion of Spain. This situation and the vicinity of the West India Islands, belonging to these two powers create between them, in respect to their American possessions and in relation to us, a common interest. The savage tribes on our Western frontier ought to be regarded as our natural enemies, their natural allies, because they have most to fear from us, and most to hope from them. The improvements in the art of navigation have, as to the facility of communication, rendered distant nations, in a great measure, neighbors. Britain and Spain are among the principal maritime powers of Europe. A future concert of views between these nations ought not to be regarded as improbable. The increasing remoteness of consanguinity is every day diminishing the force of the family compact between France and Spain. And politicians have ever with great reason considered the ties of blood as feeble and precarious links of political connection. These circumstances combined, admonish us not to be too sanguine in considering ourselves as entirely out of the reach of danger.

Previous to the Revolution, and ever since the peace, there has been a constant necessity for keeping small garrisons on our Western frontier. No person can doubt that these will continue to be indispensable, if it should only be against the ravages and depredations of the Indians. These garrisons must either be furnished by occasional detachments from the militia, or by permanent corps in the pay of the government. The first is impracticable; and if practicable, would be pernicious. The militia would not long, if at all, submit to be dragged from their occupations and families to perform that most disagreeable duty in times of profound peace. And if they could be prevailed upon or compelled to do it, the increased expense of a frequent rotation of service, and the loss of labor and disconcertion of the industrious pursuits of individuals, would form conclusive objections to the scheme. It would be as burdensome and injurious to the public as ruinous to private citizens. The latter resource of permanent corps in the pay of the government amounts to a standing army in time of peace; a small one, indeed, but not the less real for being small. Here is a simple view of the subject, that shows us at once the impropriety of a constitutional interdiction of such establishments, and the necessity of leaving the matter to the discretion and prudence of the legislature.

In proportion to our increase in strength, it is probable, nay, it may be said certain, that Britain and Spain would augment their military establishments in our neighborhood. If we should not be willing to be exposed, in a naked and defenseless condition, to their insults and encroachments, we should find it expedient to increase our frontier garrisons in some ratio to the force by which our Western settlements might be annoyed. There are, and will be, particular posts, the possession of which will include the command of large districts of territory, and facilitate future invasions of the remainder. It may be added that some of those posts will be keys to the trade with the Indian nations. Can any man think it would be wise to leave such posts in a situation to be at any instant seized by one or the other of two neighboring and formidable powers? To act this part would be to desert all the usual maxims of prudence and policy.

Documents of Revolution

If we mean to be a commercial people, or even to be secure on our Atlantic side, we must endeavor, as soon as possible, to have a navy. To this purpose there must be dock-yards and arsenals; and for the defense of these, fortifications, and probably garrisons. When a nation has become so powerful by sea that it can protect its dock-yards by its fleets, this supersedes the necessity of garrisons for that purpose; but where naval establishments are in their infancy, moderate garrisons will, in all likelihood, be found an indispensable security against descents for the destruction of the arsenals and dock-yards, and sometimes of the fleet itself.

PUBLIUS

1 This statement of the matter is taken from the printed collection of State constitutions. Pennsylvania and North Carolina are the two which contain the interdiction in these words: "As standing armies in time of peace are dangerous to liberty, THEY OUGHT NOT to be kept up." This is, in truth, rather a CAUTION than a PROHIBITION. New Hampshire, Massachusetts, Delaware, and Maryland have, in each of their bils of rights, a clause to this effect: "Standing armies are dangerous to liberty, and ought not to be raised or kept up WITHOUT THE CONSENT OF THE LEGISLATURE"; which is a formal admission of the authority of the Legislature. New York has no bills of rights, and her constitution says not a word about the matter. No bills of rights appear annexed to the constitutions of the other States, except the foregoing, and their constitutions are equally silent. I am told, however that one or two States have bills of rights which do not appear in this collection; but that those also recognize the right of the legislative authority in this respect.

FEDERALIST PAPER NO. 25. THE SAME SUBJECT CONTINUED (THE POWERS NECESSARY TO THE COMMON DEFENSE FURTHER CONSIDERED)

From the New York Packet. Friday, December 21, 1787.

HAMILTON

To the People of the State of New York:

IT MAY perhaps be urged that the objects enumerated in the preceding number ought to be provided for by the State governments, under the direction of the Union. But this would be, in reality, an inversion of the primary principle of our political association, as it would in practice transfer the care of the common defense from the federal head to the individual members: a project oppressive to some States, dangerous to all, and baneful to the Confederacy.

The territories of Britain, Spain, and of the Indian nations in our neighborhood do not border on particular States, but encircle the Union from Maine to Georgia. The danger, though in different degrees, is therefore common. And the means of guarding against it ought, in like manner, to be the objects of common councils and of a common treasury. It happens that some States, from local situation, are more directly exposed. New York is of this class. Upon the plan of separate provisions, New York would have to sustain the whole weight of the establishments requisite to her immediate safety, and to the mediate or ultimate protection of her neighbors. This would neither be equitable as it respected New York nor safe as it respected the other States. Various inconveniences would attend such a system. The States, to whose lot it might fall to support the necessary establishments, would be as little able as willing, for a considerable time to come, to bear the burden of competent provisions. The security of all would thus be subjected to the parsimony, improvidence, or inability of a part. If the resources of such part becoming more abundant and extensive, its provisions should be proportionally enlarged, the other States would quickly take the alarm at seeing the whole military force of the Union in the hands of two or three of its members, and those probably amongst the most powerful. They would each choose to have some counterpoise, and pretenses could easily be contrived. In this situation, military establishments, nourished by mutual jealousy, would be apt to swell beyond their natural or proper size; and being at the separate disposal of the members, they would be engines for the abridgment or demolition of the national authority.

Reasons have been already given to induce a supposition that the State governments will too naturally be prone to a rivalship with that of the Union, the foundation of which will be the love of power; and that in any contest between the federal head and one of its members the people will be most apt to unite with their local government. If, in addition to this immense advantage, the ambition of the members should be stimulated by the separate and independent possession of military forces, it would afford too strong a temptation and too great a facility to them to make enterprises upon, and finally to subvert, the constitutional authority of the Union. On the other hand, the liberty of the people would be less safe in this state of things than in that which left the national forces in the hands of the national government. As far as an army may be considered as a dangerous weapon of power, it had better be in those hands of which the people are most likely to be jealous than in those of which they are least likely to be jealous. For it is a truth, which the experience of ages has attested, that the people are always most in danger when the means of injuring their rights are in the possession of those of whom they entertain the least suspicion.

The framers of the existing Confederation, fully aware of the danger to the Union from the separate possession of military forces by the States, have, in express terms, prohibited them from having either ships or troops, unless with the consent of Congress. The truth is, that the existence of a federal government and military establishments under State authority are not less at variance with each other than a due supply of the federal treasury and the system of quotas and requisitions.

There are other lights besides those already taken notice of, in which the impropriety of restraints on the discretion of the national legislature will be equally manifest. The design of the objection, which has been mentioned, is to preclude standing armies in time of peace, though we have never been informed how far it is designed the prohibition should extend; whether to raising armies as well as to KEEPING THEM UP in a season of tranquillity or not. If it be confined to the latter it will have no precise signification, and it will be ineffectual for the purpose intended. When armies are once raised what shall be denominated "keeping them up," contrary to the sense of the Constitution? What time shall be requisite to ascertain the violation? Shall it be a week, a month, a year? Or shall we say they may be continued as long as the danger which occasioned their being raised continues? This would be to admit that they might be kept up IN TIME OF PEACE, against threatening or impending danger, which would be at once to deviate from the literal meaning of the prohibition, and to introduce an extensive latitude of construction. Who shall judge of the continuance of the danger? This must undoubtedly be submitted to the national government, and the matter would then be brought to this issue, that the national government, to provide against apprehended danger, might in the first instance raise troops, and might afterwards keep them on foot as long as they supposed the peace or safety of the community was in any degree of jeopardy. It is easy to perceive that a discretion so latitudinary as this would afford ample room for eluding the force of the provision.

The supposed utility of a provision of this kind can only be founded on the supposed probability, or at least possibility, of a combination between the executive and the legislative, in some scheme of usurpation. Should this at any time happen, how easy would it be to fabricate pretenses of approaching danger! Indian hostilities, instigated by Spain or Britain, would always be at hand. Provocations to produce the desired appearances might even be given to some foreign power, and appeased again by timely concessions. If we can reasonably presume such a combination to have been formed, and that the enterprise is warranted by a sufficient prospect of success, the army, when once raised, from whatever cause, or on whatever pretext, may be applied to the execution of the project.

If, to obviate this consequence, it should be resolved to extend the prohibition to the RAISING of armies in time of peace, the United States would then exhibit the most extraordinary spectacle which the world has yet seen, that of a nation incapacitated by its Constitution to prepare for defense, before it was actually invaded. As the ceremony of a formal denunciation of war has of late fallen into disuse, the presence of an enemy within our territories must be waited for, as the legal warrant to the government to begin its levies of men for the protection of the State. We must receive the blow, before we could even prepare to return it. All that kind of policy by which nations anticipate distant danger, and meet the gathering storm, must be abstained from, as contrary to the genuine maxims of a free government. We must expose our property and liberty to the mercy of foreign invaders, and invite them by our weakness to seize the naked and defenseless prey, because we are afraid that rulers, created by our choice, dependent on our will, might endanger that liberty, by an abuse of the means necessary to its preservation.

Here I expect we shall be told that the militia of the country is its natural bulwark, and would be at all times equal to the national defense. This doctrine, in substance, had like to have lost us our independence. It cost millions to the United States that might have been saved. The facts which, from our own experience, forbid a reliance of this kind, are too recent to permit us to be the dupes of such a suggestion. The steady operations of war against a regular and disciplined army can only be successfully conducted by a force of the same kind. Considerations of economy, not less than of stability and vigor, confirm this position. The American militia, in the course of the late war, have, by their valor on numerous occasions, erected eternal monuments to their fame; but the bravest of them feel and know that the liberty of their country could not have been established by their efforts alone, however great and valuable they were. War, like most other things, is a science to be acquired and perfected by diligence, by perseverance, by time, and by practice.

All violent policy, as it is contrary to the natural and experienced course of human affairs, defeats itself. Pennsylvania, at this instant, affords an example of the truth of this remark. The Bill of Rights of that State declares that standing armies are dangerous to liberty, and ought not to be kept up in time of peace. Pennsylvania, nevertheless, in a time of profound peace, from the existence of partial disorders in one or two of her counties, has resolved to raise a body of troops; and in all probability will keep them up as long as there is any appearance of danger to the public peace. The conduct of Massachusetts affords a lesson on the same subject, though on different ground. That State (without waiting for the sanction of Congress, as the articles of the Confederation require) was compelled to raise troops to quell a domestic insurrection, and still keeps a corps in pay to prevent a revival of the spirit of revolt. The particular constitution of Massachusetts opposed no obstacle to the measure; but the instance is still of use to instruct us that cases are likely to occur under our government, as well as under those of other nations, which will sometimes render a military force in time of peace essential to the security of the society, and that it is therefore improper in this respect to control the legislative discretion. It also teaches us, in its application to the United States, how little the rights of a feeble government are likely to be respected, even by its own constituents. And it teaches us, in addition to the rest, how unequal parchment provisions are to a struggle with public necessity.

Documents of Revolution

It was a fundamental maxim of the Lacedaemonian commonwealth, that the post of admiral should not be conferred twice on the same person. The Peloponnesian confederates, having suffered a severe defeat at sea from the Athenians, demanded Lysander, who had before served with success in that capacity, to command the combined fleets. The Lacedaemonians, to gratify their allies, and yet preserve the semblance of an adherence to their ancient institutions, had recourse to the flimsy subterfuge of investing Lysander with the real power of admiral, under the nominal title of vice-admiral. This instance is selected from among a multitude that might be cited to confirm the truth already advanced and illustrated by domestic examples; which is, that nations pay little regard to rules and maxims calculated in their very nature to run counter to the necessities of society. Wise politicians will be cautious about fettering the government with restrictions that cannot be observed, because they know that every breach of the fundamental laws, though dictated by necessity, impairs that sacred reverence which ought to be maintained in the breast of rulers towards the constitution of a country, and forms a precedent for other breaches where the same plea of necessity does not exist at all, or is less urgent and palpable.
PUBLIUS

FEDERALIST PAPER NO. 26. THE IDEA OF RESTRAINING THE LEGISLATIVE AUTHORITY IN REGARD TO THE COMMON DEFENSE CONSIDERED.

For the Independent Journal. Saturday, December 22, 1788

HAMILTON

To the People of the State of New York:

IT WAS a thing hardly to be expected that in a popular revolution the minds of men should stop at that happy mean which marks the salutary boundary between POWER and PRIVILEGE, and combines the energy of government with the security of private rights. A failure in this delicate and important point is the great source of the inconveniences we experience, and if we are not cautious to avoid a repetition of the error, in our future attempts to rectify and ameliorate our system, we may travel from one chimerical project to another; we may try change after change; but we shall never be likely to make any material change for the better.

The idea of restraining the legislative authority, in the means of providing for the national defense, is one of those refinements which owe their origin to a zeal for liberty more ardent than enlightened. We have seen, however, that it has not had thus far an extensive prevalency; that even in this country, where it made its first appearance, Pennsylvania and North Carolina are the only two States by which it has been in any degree patronized; and that all the others have refused to give it the least countenance; wisely judging that confidence must be placed somewhere; that the necessity of doing it, is implied in the very act of delegating power; and that it is better to hazard the abuse of that confidence than to embarrass the government and endanger the public safety by impolitic restrictions on the legislative authority. The opponents of the proposed Constitution combat, in this respect, the general decision of America; and instead of being taught by experience the propriety of correcting any extremes into which we may have heretofore run, they appear disposed to conduct us into others still more dangerous, and more extravagant. As if the tone of government had been found too high, or too rigid, the doctrines they teach are calculated to induce us to depress or to relax it, by expedients which, upon other occasions, have been condemned or forborne. It may be affirmed without the imputation of invective, that if the principles they inculcate, on various points, could so far obtain as to become the popular creed, they would utterly unfit the people of this country for any species of government whatever. But a danger of this kind is not to be apprehended. The citizens of America have too much discernment to be argued into anarchy. And I am much mistaken, if experience has not wrought a deep and solemn conviction in the public mind, that greater energy of government is essential to the welfare and prosperity of the community.

It may not be amiss in this place concisely to remark the origin and progress of the idea, which aims at the exclusion of military establishments in time of peace. Though in speculative minds it may arise from a contemplation of the nature and tendency of such institutions, fortified by the events that have happened in other ages and countries, yet as a national sentiment, it must be traced to those habits of thinking which we derive from the nation from whom the inhabitants of these States have in general sprung.

In England, for a long time after the Norman Conquest, the authority of the monarch was almost unlimited. Inroads were gradually made upon the prerogative, in favor of liberty, first by the barons, and afterwards by the people, till the greatest part of its most formidable pretensions became extinct. But it was not till the revolution in 1688, which elevated the Prince of Orange to the throne of Great Britain, that English liberty was completely triumphant. As incident to the undefined power of making war, an acknowledged prerogative of the crown, Charles II. had, by his own authority, kept on foot in time of peace a body of 5,000 regular troops. And this number James II. increased to 30,000; who were paid out of his civil list. At the revolution, to abolish the exercise of so dangerous an authority, it became an article of the Bill of Rights then framed, that "the raising or keeping a standing army within the kingdom in time of peace, UNLESS WITH THE CONSENT OF PARLIAMENT, was against law."

Documents of Revolution

In that kingdom, when the pulse of liberty was at its highest pitch, no security against the danger of standing armies was thought requisite, beyond a prohibition of their being raised or kept up by the mere authority of the executive magistrate. The patriots, who effected that memorable revolution, were too temperate, too wellinformed, to think of any restraint on the legislative discretion. They were aware that a certain number of troops for guards and garrisons were indispensable; that no precise bounds could be set to the national exigencies; that a power equal to every possible contingency must exist somewhere in the government: and that when they referred the exercise of that power to the judgment of the legislature, they had arrived at the ultimate point of precaution which was reconcilable with the safety of the community.

From the same source, the people of America may be said to have derived an hereditary impression of danger to liberty, from standing armies in time of peace. The circumstances of a revolution quickened the public sensibility on every point connected with the security of popular rights, and in some instances raise the warmth of our zeal beyond the degree which consisted with the due temperature of the body politic. The attempts of two of the States to restrict the authority of the legislature in the article of military establishments, are of the number of these instances. The principles which had taught us to be jealous of the power of an hereditary monarch were by an injudicious excess extended to the representatives of the people in their popular assemblies. Even in some of the States, where this error was not adopted, we find unnecessary declarations that standing armies ought not to be kept up, in time of peace, WITHOUT THE CONSENT OF THE LEGISLATURE. I call them unnecessary, because the reason which had introduced a similar provision into the English Bill of Rights is not applicable to any of the State constitutions. The power of raising armies at all, under those constitutions, can by no construction be deemed to reside anywhere else, than in the legislatures themselves; and it was superfluous, if not absurd, to declare that a matter should not be done without the consent of a body, which alone had the power of doing it. Accordingly, in some of these constitutions, and among others, in that of this State of New York, which has been justly celebrated, both in Europe and America, as one of the best of the forms of government established in this country, there is a total silence upon the subject.

It is remarkable, that even in the two States which seem to have meditated an interdiction of military establishments in time of peace, the mode of expression made use of is rather cautionary than prohibitory. It is not said, that standing armies SHALL NOT BE kept up, but that they OUGHT NOT to be kept up, in time of peace. This ambiguity of terms appears to have been the result of a conflict between jealousy and conviction; between the desire of excluding such establishments at all events, and the persuasion that an absolute exclusion would be unwise and unsafe.

Can it be doubted that such a provision, whenever the situation of public affairs was understood to require a departure from it, would be interpreted by the legislature into a mere admonition, and would be made to yield to the necessities or supposed necessities of the State? Let the fact already mentioned, with respect to Pennsylvania, decide. What then (it may be asked) is the use of such a provision, if it cease to operate the moment there is an inclination to disregard it?

Let us examine whether there be any comparison, in point of efficacy, between the provision alluded to and that which is contained in the new Constitution, for restraining the appropriations of money for military purposes to the period of two years. The former, by aiming at too much, is calculated to effect nothing; the latter, by steering clear of an imprudent extreme, and by being perfectly compatible with a proper provision for the exigencies of the nation, will have a salutary and powerful operation.

The legislature of the United States will be OBLIGED, by this provision, once at least in every two years, to deliberate upon the propriety of keeping a military force on foot; to come to a new resolution on the point; and to declare their sense of the matter, by a formal vote in the face of their constituents. They are not AT LIBERTY to vest in the executive department permanent funds for the support of an army, if they were even incautious enough to be willing to repose in it so improper a confidence. As the spirit of party, in different degrees, must be expected to infect all political bodies, there will be, no doubt, persons in the national legislature willing enough to arraign the measures and criminate the views of the majority. The provision for the support of a military force will always be a favorable topic for declamation. As often as the question comes forward, the public attention will be roused and attracted to the subject, by the party in opposition; and if the majority should be really disposed to exceed the proper limits, the community will be warned of the danger, and will have an opportunity of taking measures to guard against it. Independent of parties in the national legislature itself, as often as the period of discussion arrived, the State legislatures, who will always be not only vigilant but suspicious and jealous guardians of the rights of the citizens against encroachments from the federal government, will constantly have their attention awake to the conduct of the national rulers, and will be ready enough, if any thing improper appears, to sound the alarm to the people, and not only to be the VOICE, but, if necessary, the ARM of their discontent.

Schemes to subvert the liberties of a great community REQUIRE TIME to mature them for execution. An army, so large as seriously to menace those liberties, could only be formed by progressive augmentations; which would suppose, not merely a temporary combination between the legislature and executive, but a continued conspiracy for a series of time. Is it probable that such a combination would exist at all? Is it probable that it would be persevered in, and transmitted along through all the successive variations in a representative body, which biennial elections would naturally produce in both houses? Is it presumable, that every man, the instant he took his seat in the national Senate or House of Representatives, would commence a traitor to his constituents and to his country? Can it be supposed that there would not be found one man, discerning enough to detect so atrocious a conspiracy, or bold or honest enough to apprise his constituents of their danger? If such presumptions can fairly be made, there ought at once to be an end of all delegated authority. The people should resolve to recall all the powers they have heretofore parted with out of their own hands, and to divide themselves into as many States as there are counties, in order that they may be able to manage their own concerns in person.

If such suppositions could even be reasonably made, still the concealment of the design, for any duration, would be impracticable. It would be announced, by the very circumstance of augmenting the army to so great an extent in time of profound peace. What colorable reason could be assigned, in a country so situated, for such vast augmentations of the military force? It is impossible that the people could be long deceived; and the destruction of the project, and of the projectors, would quickly follow the discovery.

It has been said that the provision which limits the appropriation of money for the support of an army to the period of two years would be unavailing, because the Executive, when once possessed of a force large enough to awe the people into submission, would find resources in that very force sufficient to enable him to dispense with supplies from the acts of the legislature. But the question again recurs, upon what pretense could he be put in possession of a force of that magnitude in time of peace? If we suppose it to have been created in consequence of some domestic insurrection or foreign war, then it becomes a case not within the principles of the objection; for this is levelled against the power of keeping up troops in time of peace. Few persons will be so visionary as seriously to contend that military forces ought not to be raised to quell a rebellion or resist an invasion; and if the defense of the community under such circumstances should make it necessary to have an army so numerous as to hazard its liberty, this is one of those calamities for which there is neither preventative nor cure. It cannot be provided against by any possible form of government; it might even result from a simple league offensive and defensive, if it should ever be necessary for the confederates or allies to form an army for common defense.

But it is an evil infinitely less likely to attend us in a united than in a disunited state; nay, it may be safely asserted that it is an evil altogether unlikely to attend us in the latter situation. It is not easy to conceive a possibility that dangers so formidable can assail the whole Union, as to demand a force considerable enough to place our liberties in the least jeopardy, especially if we take into our view the aid to be derived from the militia, which ought always to be counted upon as a valuable and powerful auxiliary. But in a state of disunion (as has been fully shown in another place), the contrary of this supposition would become not only probable, but almost unavoidable.

PUBLIUS

FEDERALIST PAPER NO. 27. THE SAME SUBJECT CONTINUED (THE IDEA OF RESTRAINING THE LEGISLATIVE AUTHORITY IN REGARD TO THE COMMON DEFENSE CONSIDERED)

From the New York Packet. Tuesday, December 25, 1787.

HAMILTON

To the People of the State of New York:

IT HAS been urged, in different shapes, that a Constitution of the kind proposed by the convention cannot operate without the aid of a military force to execute its laws. This, however, like most other things that have been alleged on that side, rests on mere general assertion, unsupported by any precise or intelligible designation of the reasons upon which it is founded. As far as I have been able to divine the latent meaning of the objectors, it seems to originate in a presupposition that the people will be disinclined to the exercise of federal authority in any matter of an internal nature. Waiving any exception that might be taken to the inaccuracy or inexplicitness of the distinction between internal and external, let us inquire what ground there is to presuppose that disinclination in the people. Unless we presume at the same time that the powers of the general government will be worse administered than those of the State government, there seems to be no room for the presumption of ill-will, disaffection, or opposition in the people. I believe it may be laid down as a general rule that their confidence in and obedience to a government will commonly be proportioned to the goodness or badness of its administration. It must be admitted that there are exceptions to this rule; but these exceptions depend so entirely on accidental causes, that they cannot be considered as having any relation to the intrinsic merits or demerits of a constitution. These can only be judged of by general principles and maxims.

Various reasons have been suggested, in the course of these papers, to induce a probability that the general government will be better administered than the particular governments; the principal of which reasons are that the extension of the spheres of election will present a greater option, or latitude of choice, to the people; that through the medium of the State legislatures which are select bodies of men, and which are to appoint the members of the national Senate there is reason to expect that this branch will generally be composed with peculiar care and judgment; that these circumstances promise greater knowledge and more extensive information in the national councils, and that they will be less apt to be tainted by the spirit of faction, and more out of the reach of those occasional ill-humors, or temporary prejudices and propensities, which, in smaller societies, frequently contaminate the public councils, beget injustice and oppression of a part of the community, and engender schemes which, though they gratify a momentary inclination or desire, terminate in general distress, dissatisfaction, and disgust. Several additional reasons of considerable force, to fortify that probability, will occur when we come to survey, with a more critical eye, the interior structure of the edifice which we are invited to erect. It will be sufficient here to remark, that until satisfactory reasons can be assigned to justify an opinion, that the federal government is likely to be administered in such a manner as to render it odious or contemptible to the people, there can be no reasonable foundation for the supposition that the laws of the Union will meet with any greater obstruction from them, or will stand in need of any other methods to enforce their execution, than the laws of the particular members.

The hope of impunity is a strong incitement to sedition; the dread of punishment, a proportionably strong discouragement to it. Will not the government of the Union, which, if possessed of a due degree of power, can call to its aid the collective resources of the whole Confederacy, be more likely to repress the FORMER sentiment and to inspire the LATTER, than that of a single State, which can only command the resources within itself? A turbulent faction in a State may easily suppose itself able to contend with the friends to the government in that State; but it can hardly be so infatuated as to imagine itself a match for the combined efforts of the Union. If this reflection be just, there is less danger of resistance from irregular combinations of individuals to the authority of the Confederacy than to that of a single member.

I will, in this place, hazard an observation, which will not be the less just because to some it may appear new; which is, that the more the operations of the national authority are intermingled in the ordinary exercise of government, the more the citizens are accustomed to meet with it in the common occurrences of their political life, the more it is familiarized to their sight and to their feelings, the further it enters into those objects which touch the most sensible chords and put in motion the most active springs of the human heart, the greater will be the probability that it will conciliate the respect and attachment of the community. Man is very much a creature of habit. A thing that rarely strikes his senses will generally have but little influence upon his mind. A government continually at a distance and out of sight can hardly be expected to interest the sensations of the people. The inference is, that the authority of the Union, and the affections of the citizens towards it, will be strengthened, rather than weakened, by its extension to what are called matters of internal concern; and will have less occasion to recur to force, in proportion to the familiarity and comprehensiveness of its agency. The more it circulates through those channels and currents in which the passions of mankind naturally flow, the less will it require the aid of the violent and perilous expedients of compulsion.

One thing, at all events, must be evident, that a government like the one proposed would bid much fairer to avoid the necessity of using force, than that species of league contend for by most of its opponents; the authority of which should only operate upon the States in their political or collective capacities. It has been shown that in such a Confederacy there can be no sanction for the laws but force; that frequent delinquencies in the members are the natural offspring of the very frame of the government; and that as often as these happen, they can only be redressed, if at all, by war and violence.

The plan reported by the convention, by extending the authority of the federal head to the individual citizens of the several States, will enable the government to employ the ordinary magistracy of each, in the execution of its laws. It is easy to perceive that this will tend to destroy, in the common apprehension, all distinction between the sources from which they might proceed; and will give the federal government the same advantage for securing a due obedience to its authority which is enjoyed by the government of each State, in addition to the influence on public opinion which will result from the important consideration of its having power to call to its assistance and support the resources of the whole Union. It merits particular attention in this place, that the laws of the Confederacy, as to the ENUMERATED and LEGITIMATE objects of its jurisdiction, will become the SUPREME LAW of the land; to the observance of which all officers, legislative, executive, and judicial, in each State, will be bound by the sanctity of an oath. Thus the legislatures, courts, and magistrates, of the respective members, will be incorporated into the operations of the national government AS FAR AS ITS JUST AND CONSTITUTIONAL AUTHORITY EXTENDS; and will be rendered auxiliary to the enforcement of its laws.(1) Any man who will pursue, by his own reflections, the consequences of this situation, will perceive that there is good ground to calculate upon a regular and peaceable execution of the laws of the Union, if its powers are administered with a common share of prudence. If we will arbitrarily suppose the contrary, we may deduce any inferences we please from the supposition; for it is certainly possible, by an injudicious exercise of the authorities of the best government that ever was, or ever can be instituted, to provoke and precipitate the people into the wildest excesses. But though the adversaries of the proposed Constitution should presume that the national rulers would be insensible to the motives of public good, or to the obligations of duty, I would still ask them how the interests of ambition, or the views of encroachment, can be promoted by such a conduct?

PUBLIUS

1. The sophistry which has been employed to show that this will tend to the destruction of the State governments, will, in its will, in its proper place, be fully detected.

FEDERALIST PAPER NO. 28. THE SAME SUBJECT CONTINUED (THE IDEA OF RESTRAINING THE LEGISLATIVE AUTHORITY IN REGARD TO THE COMMON DEFENSE CONSIDERED)

For the Independent Journal. Wednesday, December 26, 1787

HAMILTON

To the People of the State of New York:

THAT there may happen cases in which the national government may be necessitated to resort to force, cannot be denied. Our own experience has corroborated the lessons taught by the examples of other nations; that emergencies of this sort will sometimes arise in all societies, however constituted; that seditions and insurrections are, unhappily, maladies as inseparable from the body politic as tumors and eruptions from the natural body; that the idea of governing at all times by the simple force of law (which we have been told is the only admissible principle of republican government), has no place but in the reveries of those political doctors whose sagacity disdains the admonitions of experimental instruction.

Should such emergencies at any time happen under the national government, there could be no remedy but force. The means to be employed must be proportioned to the extent of the mischief. If it should be a slight commotion in a small part of a State, the militia of the residue would be adequate to its suppression; and the national presumption is that they would be ready to do their duty. An insurrection, whatever may be its immediate cause, eventually endangers all government. Regard to the public peace, if not to the rights of the Union, would engage the citizens to whom the contagion had not communicated itself to oppose the insurgents; and if the general government should be found in practice conducive to the prosperity and felicity of the people, it were irrational to believe that they would be disinclined to its support.

If, on the contrary, the insurrection should pervade a whole State, or a principal part of it, the employment of a different kind of force might become unavoidable. It appears that Massachusetts found it necessary to raise troops for repressing the disorders within that State; that Pennsylvania, from the mere apprehension of commotions among a part of her citizens, has thought proper to have recourse to the same measure. Suppose the State of New York had been inclined to re-establish her lost jurisdiction over the inhabitants of Vermont, could she have hoped for success in such an enterprise from the efforts of the militia alone? Would she not have been compelled to raise and to maintain a more regular force for the execution of her design? If it must then be admitted that the necessity of recurring to a force different from the militia, in cases of this extraordinary nature, is applicable to the State governments themselves, why should the possibility, that the national government might be under a like necessity, in similar extremities, be made an objection to its existence? Is it not surprising that men who declare an attachment to the Union in the abstract, should urge as an objection to the proposed Constitution what applies with tenfold weight to the plan for which they contend; and what, as far as it has any foundation in truth, is an inevitable consequence of civil society upon an enlarged scale? Who would not prefer that possibility to the unceasing agitations and frequent revolutions which are the continual scourges of petty republics?

Let us pursue this examination in another light. Suppose, in lieu of one general system, two, or three, or even four Confederacies were to be formed, would not the same difficulty oppose itself to the operations of either of these Confederacies? Would not each of them be exposed to the same casualties; and when these happened, be obliged to have recourse to the same expedients for upholding its authority which are objected to in a government for all the States? Would the militia, in this supposition, be more ready or more able to support the federal authority than in the case of a general union? All candid and intelligent men must, upon due consideration, acknowledge that the principle of the objection is equally applicable to either of the two cases; and that whether we have one government for all the States, or different governments for different parcels of them, or even if there should be an entire separation of the States, there might sometimes be a necessity to make use of a force constituted differently from the militia, to preserve the peace of the community and to maintain the just authority of the laws against those violent invasions of them which amount to insurrections and rebellions.

Documents of Revolution

Independent of all other reasonings upon the subject, it is a full answer to those who require a more peremptory provision against military establishments in time of peace, to say that the whole power of the proposed government is to be in the hands of the representatives of the people. This is the essential, and, after all, only efficacious security for the rights and privileges of the people, which is attainable in civil society.(1)

If the representatives of the people betray their constituents, there is then no resource left but in the exertion of that original right of self-defense which is paramount to all positive forms of government, and which against the usurpations of the national rulers, may be exerted with infinitely better prospect of success than against those of the rulers of an individual state. In a single state, if the persons intrusted with supreme power become usurpers, the different parcels, subdivisions, or districts of which it consists, having no distinct government in each, can take no regular measures for defense. The citizens must rush tumultuously to arms, without concert, without system, without resource; except in their courage and despair. The usurpers, clothed with the forms of legal authority, can too often crush the opposition in embryo. The smaller the extent of the territory, the more difficult will it be for the people to form a regular or systematic plan of opposition, and the more easy will it be to defeat their early efforts. Intelligence can be more speedily obtained of their preparations and movements, and the military force in the possession of the usurpers can be more rapidly directed against the part where the opposition has begun. In this situation there must be a peculiar coincidence of circumstances to insure success to the popular resistance.

The obstacles to usurpation and the facilities of resistance increase with the increased extent of the state, provided the citizens understand their rights and are disposed to defend them. The natural strength of the people in a large community, in proportion to the artificial strength of the government, is greater than in a small, and of course more competent to a struggle with the attempts of the government to establish a tyranny. But in a confederacy the people, without exaggeration, may be said to be entirely the masters of their own fate. Power being almost always the rival of power, the general government will at all times stand ready to check the usurpations of the state governments, and these will have the same disposition towards the general government. The people, by throwing themselves into either scale, will infallibly make it preponderate. If their rights are invaded by either, they can make use of the other as the instrument of redress. How wise will it be in them by cherishing the union to preserve to themselves an advantage which can never be too highly prized!

It may safely be received as an axiom in our political system, that the State governments will, in all possible contingencies, afford complete security against invasions of the public liberty by the national authority. Projects of usurpation cannot be masked under pretenses so likely to escape the penetration of select bodies of men, as of the people at large. The legislatures will have better means of information. They can discover the danger at a distance; and possessing all the organs of civil power, and the confidence of the people, they can at once adopt a regular plan of opposition, in which they can combine all the resources of the community. They can readily communicate with each other in the different States, and unite their common forces for the protection of their common liberty.

The great extent of the country is a further security. We have already experienced its utility against the attacks of a foreign power. And it would have precisely the same effect against the enterprises of ambitious rulers in the national councils. If the federal army should be able to quell the resistance of one State, the distant States would have it in their power to make head with fresh forces. The advantages obtained in one place must be abandoned to subdue the opposition in others; and the moment the part which had been reduced to submission was left to itself, its efforts would be renewed, and its resistance revive.

We should recollect that the extent of the military force must, at all events, be regulated by the resources of the country. For a long time to come, it will not be possible to maintain a large army; and as the means of doing this increase, the population and natural strength of the community will proportionably increase. When will the time arrive that the federal government can raise and maintain an army capable of erecting a despotism over the great body of the people of an immense empire, who are in a situation, through the medium of their State governments, to take measures for their own defense, with all the celerity, regularity, and system of independent nations? The apprehension may be considered as a disease, for which there can be found no cure in the resources of argument and reasoning.

PUBLIUS

1. Its full efficacy will be examined hereafter.

FEDERALIST PAPER NO. 29. CONCERNING THE MILITIA

From the New York Packet. Wednesday, January 9, 1788

HAMILTON

To the People of the State of New York:

THE power of regulating the militia, and of commanding its services in times of insurrection and invasion are natural incidents to the duties of superintending the common defense, and of watching over the internal peace of the Confederacy.

It requires no skill in the science of war to discern that uniformity in the organization and discipline of the militia would be attended with the most beneficial effects, whenever they were called into service for the public defense. It would enable them to discharge the duties of the camp and of the field with mutual intelligence and concert an advantage of peculiar moment in the operations of an army; and it would fit them much sooner to acquire the degree of proficiency in military functions which would be essential to their usefulness. This desirable uniformity can only be accomplished by confiding the regulation of the militia to the direction of the national authority. It is, therefore, with the most evident propriety, that the plan of the convention proposes to empower the Union "to provide for organizing, arming, and disciplining the militia, and for governing such part of them as may be employed in the service of the United States, RESERVING TO THE STATES RESPECTIVELY THE APPOINTMENT OF THE OFFICERS, AND THE AUTHORITY OF TRAINING THE MILITIA ACCORDING TO THE DISCIPLINE PRESCRIBED BY CONGRESS."

Of the different grounds which have been taken in opposition to the plan of the convention, there is none that was so little to have been expected, or is so untenable in itself, as the one from which this particular provision has been attacked. If a well-regulated militia be the most natural defense of a free country, it ought certainly to be under the regulation and at the disposal of that body which is constituted the guardian of the national security. If standing armies are dangerous to liberty, an efficacious power over the militia, in the body to whose care the protection of the State is committed, ought, as far as possible, to take away the inducement and the pretext to such unfriendly institutions. If the federal government can command the aid of the militia in those emergencies which call for the military arm in support of the civil magistrate, it can the better dispense with the employment of a different kind of force. If it cannot avail itself of the former, it will be obliged to recur to the latter. To render an army unnecessary, will be a more certain method of preventing its existence than a thousand prohibitions upon paper.

In order to cast an odium upon the power of calling forth the militia to execute the laws of the Union, it has been remarked that there is nowhere any provision in the proposed Constitution for calling out the POSSE COMITATUS, to assist the magistrate in the execution of his duty, whence it has been inferred, that military force was intended to be his only auxiliary. There is a striking incoherence in the objections which have appeared, and sometimes even from the same quarter, not much calculated to inspire a very favorable opinion of the sincerity or fair dealing of their authors. The same persons who tell us in one breath, that the powers of the federal government will be despotic and unlimited, inform us in the next, that it has not authority sufficient even to call out the POSSE COMITATUS. The latter, fortunately, is as much short of the truth as the former exceeds it. It would be as absurd to doubt, that a right to pass all laws NECESSARY AND PROPER to execute its declared powers, would include that of requiring the assistance of the citizens to the officers who may be intrusted with the execution of those laws, as it would be to believe, that a right to enact laws necessary and proper for the imposition and collection of taxes would involve that of varying the rules of descent and of the alienation of landed property, or of abolishing the trial by jury in cases relating to it. It being therefore evident that the supposition of a want of power to require the aid of the POSSE COMITATUS is entirely destitute of color, it will follow, that the conclusion which has been drawn from it, in its application to the authority of the federal government over the militia, is as uncandid as it is illogical. What reason could there be to infer, that force was intended to be the sole instrument of authority, merely because there is a power to make use of it when necessary? What shall we think of the motives which could induce men of sense to reason in this manner? How shall we prevent a conflict between charity and conviction?

By a curious refinement upon the spirit of republican jealousy, we are even taught to apprehend danger from the militia itself, in the hands of the federal government. It is observed that select corps may be formed, composed of the young and ardent, who may be rendered subservient to the views of arbitrary power. What plan for the regulation of the militia may be pursued by the national government, is impossible to be foreseen. But so far from viewing the matter in the same light with those who object to select corps as dangerous, were the Constitution ratified, and were I to deliver my sentiments to a member of the federal legislature from this State on the subject of a militia establishment, I should hold to him, in substance, the following discourse:

"The project of disciplining all the militia of the United States is as futile as it would be injurious, if it were capable of being carried into execution. A tolerable expertness in military movements is a business that requires time and practice. It is not a day, or even a week, that will suffice for the attainment of it. To oblige the great body of the yeomanry, and of the other classes of the citizens, to be under arms for the purpose of going through military exercises and evolutions, as often as might be necessary to acquire the degree of perfection which would entitle them to the character of a well-regulated militia, would be a real grievance to the people, and a serious public inconvenience and loss. It would form an annual deduction from the productive labor of the country, to an amount which, calculating upon the present numbers of the people, would not fall far short of the whole expense of the civil establishments of all the States. To attempt a thing which would abridge the mass of labor and industry to so considerable an extent, would be unwise: and the experiment, if made, could not succeed, because it would not long be endured. Little more can reasonably be aimed at, with respect to the people at large, than to have them properly armed and equipped; and in order to see that this be not neglected, it will be necessary to assemble them once or twice in the course of a year.

"But though the scheme of disciplining the whole nation must be abandoned as mischievous or impracticable; yet it is a matter of the utmost importance that a well-digested plan should, as soon as possible, be adopted for the proper establishment of the militia. The attention of the government ought particularly to be directed to the formation of a select corps of moderate extent, upon such principles as will really fit them for service in case of need. By thus circumscribing the plan, it will be possible to have an excellent body of well-trained militia, ready to take the field whenever the defense of the State shall require it. This will not only lessen the call for military establishments, but if circumstances should at any time oblige the government to form an army of any magnitude that army can never be formidable to the liberties of the people while there is a large body of citizens, little, if at all, inferior to them in discipline and the use of arms, who stand ready to defend their own rights and those of their fellow-citizens. This appears to me the only substitute that can be devised for a standing army, and the best possible security against it, if it should exist."

Thus differently from the adversaries of the proposed Constitution should I reason on the same subject, deducing arguments of safety from the very sources which they represent as fraught with danger and perdition. But how the national legislature may reason on the point, is a thing which neither they nor I can foresee.

There is something so far-fetched and so extravagant in the idea of danger to liberty from the militia, that one is at a loss whether to treat it with gravity or with raillery; whether to consider it as a mere trial of skill, like the paradoxes of rhetoricians; as a disingenuous artifice to instil prejudices at any price; or as the serious offspring of political fanaticism. Where in the name of common-sense, are our fears to end if we may not trust our sons, our brothers, our neighbors, our fellow-citizens? What shadow of danger can there be from men who are daily mingling with the rest of their countrymen and who participate with them in the same feelings, sentiments, habits and interests? What reasonable cause of apprehension can be inferred from a power in the Union to prescribe regulations for the militia, and to command its services when necessary, while the particular States are to have the SOLE AND EXCLUSIVE APPOINTMENT OF THE OFFICERS? If it were possible seriously to indulge a jealousy of the militia upon any conceivable establishment under the federal government, the circumstance of the officers being in the appointment of the States ought at once to extinguish it. There can be no doubt that this circumstance will always secure to them a preponderating influence over the militia.

In reading many of the publications against the Constitution, a man is apt to imagine that he is perusing some ill-written tale or romance, which instead of natural and agreeable images, exhibits to the mind nothing but frightful and distorted shapes—

"Gorgons, hydras, and chimeras dire";

discoloring and disfiguring whatever it represents, and transforming everything it touches into a monster.

A sample of this is to be observed in the exaggerated and improbable suggestions which have taken place respecting the power of calling for the services of the militia. That of New Hampshire is to be marched to Georgia, of Georgia to New Hampshire, of New York to Kentucky, and of Kentucky to Lake Champlain. Nay, the debts due to the French and Dutch are to be paid in militiamen instead of louis d'ors and ducats. At one moment there is to be a large army to lay prostrate the liberties of the people; at another moment the militia of Virginia are to be dragged from their homes five or six hundred miles, to tame the republican contumacy of Massachusetts; and that of Massachusetts is to be transported an equal distance to subdue the refractory haughtiness of the aristocratic Virginians. Do the persons who rave at this rate imagine that their art or their eloquence can impose any conceits or absurdities upon the people of America for infallible truths?

Documents of Revolution

If there should be an army to be made use of as the engine of despotism, what need of the militia? If there should be no army, whither would the militia, irritated by being called upon to undertake a distant and hopeless expedition, for the purpose of riveting the chains of slavery upon a part of their countrymen, direct their course, but to the seat of the tyrants, who had meditated so foolish as well as so wicked a project, to crush them in their imagined intrenchments of power, and to make them an example of the just vengeance of an abused and incensed people? Is this the way in which usurpers stride to dominion over a numerous and enlightened nation? Do they begin by exciting the detestation of the very instruments of their intended usurpations? Do they usually commence their career by wanton and disgustful acts of power, calculated to answer no end, but to draw upon themselves universal hatred and execration? Are suppositions of this sort the sober admonitions of discerning patriots to a discerning people? Or are they the inflammatory ravings of incendiaries or distempered enthusiasts? If we were even to suppose the national rulers actuated by the most ungovernable ambition, it is impossible to believe that they would employ such preposterous means to accomplish their designs.

In times of insurrection, or invasion, it would be natural and proper that the militia of a neighboring State should be marched into another, to resist a common enemy, or to guard the republic against the violence of faction or sedition. This was frequently the case, in respect to the first object, in the course of the late war; and this mutual succor is, indeed, a principal end of our political association. If the power of affording it be placed under the direction of the Union, there will be no danger of a supine and listless inattention to the dangers of a neighbor, till its near approach had superadded the incitements of self-preservation to the too feeble impulses of duty and sympathy.

PUBLIUS

FEDERALIST PAPER NO. 30. CONCERNING THE GENERAL POWER OF TAXATION

From the New York Packet. Friday, December 28, 1787.

HAMILTON

To the People of the State of New York:

IT HAS been already observed that the federal government ought to possess the power of providing for the support of the national forces; in which proposition was intended to be included the expense of raising troops, of building and equipping fleets, and all other expenses in any wise connected with military arrangements and operations. But these are not the only objects to which the jurisdiction of the Union, in respect to revenue, must necessarily be empowered to extend. It must embrace a provision for the support of the national civil list; for the payment of the national debts contracted, or that may be contracted; and, in general, for all those matters which will call for disbursements out of the national treasury. The conclusion is, that there must be interwoven, in the frame of the government, a general power of taxation, in one shape or another.

Money is, with propriety, considered as the vital principle of the body politic; as that which sustains its life and motion, and enables it to perform its most essential functions. A complete power, therefore, to procure a regular and adequate supply of it, as far as the resources of the community will permit, may be regarded as an indispensable ingredient in every constitution. From a deficiency in this particular, one of two evils must ensue; either the people must be subjected to continual plunder, as a substitute for a more eligible mode of supplying the public wants, or the government must sink into a fatal atrophy, and, in a short course of time, perish.

In the Ottoman or Turkish empire, the sovereign, though in other respects absolute master of the lives and fortunes of his subjects, has no right to impose a new tax. The consequence is that he permits the bashaws or governors of provinces to pillage the people without mercy; and, in turn, squeezes out of them the sums of which he stands in need, to satisfy his own exigencies and those of the state. In America, from a like cause, the government of the Union has gradually dwindled into a state of decay, approaching nearly to annihilation. Who can doubt, that the happiness of the people in both countries would be promoted by competent authorities in the proper hands, to provide the revenues which the necessities of the public might require?

The present Confederation, feeble as it is intended to repose in the United States, an unlimited power of providing for the pecuniary wants of the Union. But proceeding upon an erroneous principle, it has been done in such a manner as entirely to have frustrated the intention. Congress, by the articles which compose that compact (as has already been stated), are authorized to ascertain and call for any sums of money necessary, in their judgment, to the service of the United States; and their requisitions, if conformable to the rule of apportionment, are in every constitutional sense obligatory upon the States. These have no right to question the propriety of the demand; no discretion beyond that of devising the ways and means of furnishing the sums demanded. But though this be strictly and truly the case; though the assumption of such a right would be an infringement of the articles of Union; though it may seldom or never have been avowedly claimed, yet in practice it has been constantly exercised, and would continue to be so, as long as the revenues of the Confederacy should remain dependent on the intermediate agency of its members. What the consequences of this system have been, is within the knowledge of every man the least conversant in our public affairs, and has been amply unfolded in different parts of these inquiries. It is this which has chiefly contributed to reduce us to a situation, which affords ample cause both of mortification to ourselves, and of triumph to our enemies.

What remedy can there be for this situation, but in a change of the system which has produced it in a change of the fallacious and delusive system of quotas and requisitions? What substitute can there be imagined for this ignis fatuus in finance, but that of permitting the national government to raise its own revenues by the ordinary methods of taxation authorized in every well-ordered constitution of civil government? Ingenious men may declaim with plausibility on any subject; but no human ingenuity can point out any other expedient to rescue us from the inconveniences and embarrassments naturally resulting from defective supplies of the public treasury.

Documents of Revolution

The more intelligent adversaries of the new Constitution admit the force of this reasoning; but they qualify their admission by a distinction between what they call INTERNAL and EXTERNAL taxation. The former they would reserve to the State governments; the latter, which they explain into commercial imposts, or rather duties on imported articles, they declare themselves willing to concede to the federal head. This distinction, however, would violate the maxim of good sense and sound policy, which dictates that every POWER ought to be in proportion to its OBJECT; and would still leave the general government in a kind of tutelage to the State governments, inconsistent with every idea of vigor or efficiency. Who can pretend that commercial imposts are, or would be, alone equal to the present and future exigencies of the Union? Taking into the account the existing debt, foreign and domestic, upon any plan of extinguishment which a man moderately impressed with the importance of public justice and public credit could approve, in addition to the establishments which all parties will acknowledge to be necessary, we could not reasonably flatter ourselves, that this resource alone, upon the most improved scale, would even suffice for its present necessities. Its future necessities admit not of calculation or limitation; and upon the principle, more than once adverted to, the power of making provision for them as they arise ought to be equally unconfined. I believe it may be regarded as a position warranted by the history of mankind, that, IN THE USUAL PROGRESS OF THINGS, THE NECESSITIES OF A NATION, IN EVERY STAGE OF ITS EXISTENCE, WILL BE FOUND AT LEAST EQUAL TO ITS RESOURCES.

To say that deficiencies may be provided for by requisitions upon the States, is on the one hand to acknowledge that this system cannot be depended upon, and on the other hand to depend upon it for every thing beyond a certain limit. Those who have carefully attended to its vices and deformities as they have been exhibited by experience or delineated in the course of these papers, must feel invincible repugnancy to trusting the national interests in any degree to its operation. Its inevitable tendency, whenever it is brought into activity, must be to enfeeble the Union, and sow the seeds of discord and contention between the federal head and its members, and between the members themselves. Can it be expected that the deficiencies would be better supplied in this mode than the total wants of the Union have heretofore been supplied in the same mode? It ought to be recollected that if less will be required from the States, they will have proportionably less means to answer the demand. If the opinions of those who contend for the distinction which has been mentioned were to be received as evidence of truth, one would be led to conclude that there was some known point in the economy of national affairs at which it would be safe to stop and to say: Thus far the ends of public happiness will be promoted by supplying the wants of government, and all beyond this is unworthy of our care or anxiety. How is it possible that a government half supplied and always necessitous, can fulfill the purposes of its institution, can provide for the security, advance the prosperity, or support the reputation of the commonwealth? How can it ever possess either energy or stability, dignity or credit, confidence at home or respectability abroad? How can its administration be any thing else than a succession of expedients temporizing, impotent, disgraceful? How will it be able to avoid a frequent sacrifice of its engagements to immediate necessity? How can it undertake or execute any liberal or enlarged plans of public good?

Let us attend to what would be the effects of this situation in the very first war in which we should happen to be engaged. We will presume, for argument's sake, that the revenue arising from the impost duties answers the purposes of a provision for the public debt and of a peace establishment for the Union. Thus circumstanced, a war breaks out. What would be the probable conduct of the government in such an emergency? Taught by experience that proper dependence could not be placed on the success of requisitions, unable by its own authority to lay hold of fresh resources, and urged by considerations of national danger, would it not be driven to the expedient of diverting the funds already appropriated from their proper objects to the defense of the State? It is not easy to see how a step of this kind could be avoided; and if it should be taken, it is evident that it would prove the destruction of public credit at the very moment that it was becoming essential to the public safety. To imagine that at such a crisis credit might be dispensed with, would be the extreme of infatuation. In the modern system of war, nations the most wealthy are obliged to have recourse to large loans. A country so little opulent as ours must feel this necessity in a much stronger degree. But who would lend to a government that prefaced its overtures for borrowing by an act which demonstrated that no reliance could be placed on the steadiness of its measures for paying? The loans it might be able to procure would be as limited in their extent as burdensome in their conditions. They would be made upon the same principles that usurers commonly lend to bankrupt and fraudulent debtors, with a sparing hand and at enormous premiums.

It may perhaps be imagined that, from the scantiness of the resources of the country, the necessity of diverting the established funds in the case supposed would exist, though the national government should possess an unrestrained power of taxation. But two considerations will serve to quiet all apprehension on this head: one is, that we are sure the resources of the community, in their full extent, will be brought into activity for the benefit of the Union; the other is, that whatever deficiences there may be, can without difficulty be supplied by loans.

The power of creating new funds upon new objects of taxation, by its own authority, would enable the national government to borrow as far as its necessities might require. Foreigners, as well as the citizens of America, could then reasonably repose confidence in its engagements; but to depend upon a government that must itself depend upon thirteen other governments for the means of fulfilling its contracts, when once its situation is clearly understood, would require a degree of credulity not often to be met with in the pecuniary transactions of mankind, and little reconcilable with the usual sharp-sightedness of avarice.

Reflections of this kind may have trifling weight with men who hope to see realized in America the halcyon scenes of the poetic or fabulous age; but to those who believe we are likely to experience a common portion of the vicissitudes and calamities which have fallen to the lot of other nations, they must appear entitled to serious attention. Such men must behold the actual situation of their country with painful solicitude, and deprecate the evils which ambition or revenge might, with too much facility, inflict upon it.

PUBLIUS

FEDERALIST PAPER NO. 31. THE SAME SUBJECT CONTINUED (CONCERNING THE GENERAL POWER OF TAXATION)

From the New York Packet. Tuesday, January 1, 1788.

HAMILTON

To the People of the State of New York:

IN DISQUISITIONS of every kind, there are certain primary truths, or first principles, upon which all subsequent reasonings must depend. These contain an internal evidence which, antecedent to all reflection or combination, commands the assent of the mind. Where it produces not this effect, it must proceed either from some defect or disorder in the organs of perception, or from the influence of some strong interest, or passion, or prejudice. Of this nature are the maxims in geometry, that "the whole is greater than its part; things equal to the same are equal to one another; two straight lines cannot enclose a space; and all right angles are equal to each other." Of the same nature are these other maxims in ethics and politics, that there cannot be an effect without a cause; that the means ought to be proportioned to the end; that every power ought to be commensurate with its object; that there ought to be no limitation of a power destined to effect a purpose which is itself incapable of limitation. And there are other truths in the two latter sciences which, if they cannot pretend to rank in the class of axioms, are yet such direct inferences from them, and so obvious in themselves, and so agreeable to the natural and unsophisticated dictates of common-sense, that they challenge the assent of a sound and unbiased mind, with a degree of force and conviction almost equally irresistible.

The objects of geometrical inquiry are so entirely abstracted from those pursuits which stir up and put in motion the unruly passions of the human heart, that mankind, without difficulty, adopt not only the more simple theorems of the science, but even those abstruse paradoxes which, however they may appear susceptible of demonstration, are at variance with the natural conceptions which the mind, without the aid of philosophy, would be led to entertain upon the subject. The INFINITE DIVISIBILITY of matter, or, in other words, the INFINITE divisibility of a FINITE thing, extending even to the minutest atom, is a point agreed among geometricians, though not less incomprehensible to common-sense than any of those mysteries in religion, against which the batteries of infidelity have been so industriously leveled.

But in the sciences of morals and politics, men are found far less tractable. To a certain degree, it is right and useful that this should be the case. Caution and investigation are a necessary armor against error and imposition. But this untractableness may be carried too far, and may degenerate into obstinacy, perverseness, or disingenuity. Though it cannot be pretended that the principles of moral and political knowledge have, in general, the same degree of certainty with those of the mathematics, yet they have much better claims in this respect than, to judge from the conduct of men in particular situations, we should be disposed to allow them. The obscurity is much oftener in the passions and prejudices of the reasoner than in the subject. Men, upon too many occasions, do not give their own understandings fair play; but, yielding to some untoward bias, they entangle themselves in words and confound themselves in subtleties.

How else could it happen (if we admit the objectors to be sincere in their opposition), that positions so clear as those which manifest the necessity of a general power of taxation in the government of the Union, should have to encounter any adversaries among men of discernment? Though these positions have been elsewhere fully stated, they will perhaps not be improperly recapitulated in this place, as introductory to an examination of what may have been offered by way of objection to them. They are in substance as follows:

A government ought to contain in itself every power requisite to the full accomplishment of the objects committed to its care, and to the complete execution of the trusts for which it is responsible, free from every other control but a regard to the public good and to the sense of the people.

As the duties of superintending the national defense and of securing the public peace against foreign or domestic violence involve a provision for casualties and dangers to which no possible limits can be assigned, the power of making that provision ought to know no other bounds than the exigencies of the nation and the resources of the community.

As revenue is the essential engine by which the means of answering the national exigencies must be procured, the power of procuring that article in its full extent must necessarily be comprehended in that of providing for those exigencies.

As theory and practice conspire to prove that the power of procuring revenue is unavailing when exercised over the States in their collective capacities, the federal government must of necessity be invested with an unqualified power of taxation in the ordinary modes.

Did not experience evince the contrary, it would be natural to conclude that the propriety of a general power of taxation in the national government might safely be permitted to rest on the evidence of these propositions, unassisted by any additional arguments or illustrations. But we find, in fact, that the antagonists of the proposed Constitution, so far from acquiescing in their justness or truth, seem to make their principal and most zealous effort against this part of the plan. It may therefore be satisfactory to analyze the arguments with which they combat it.

Those of them which have been most labored with that view, seem in substance to amount to this: "It is not true, because the exigencies of the Union may not be susceptible of limitation, that its power of laying taxes ought to be unconfined. Revenue is as requisite to the purposes of the local administrations as to those of the Union; and the former are at least of equal importance with the latter to the happiness of the people. It is, therefore, as necessary that the State governments should be able to command the means of supplying their wants, as that the national government should possess the like faculty in respect to the wants of the Union. But an indefinite power of taxation in the LATTER might, and probably would in time, deprive the FORMER of the means of providing for their own necessities; and would subject them entirely to the mercy of the national legislature. As the laws of the Union are to become the supreme law of the land, as it is to have power to pass all laws that may be NECESSARY for carrying into execution the authorities with which it is proposed to vest it, the national government might at any time abolish the taxes imposed for State objects upon the pretense of an interference with its own. It might allege a necessity of doing this in order to give efficacy to the national revenues. And thus all the resources of taxation might by degrees become the subjects of federal monopoly, to the entire exclusion and destruction of the State governments."

This mode of reasoning appears sometimes to turn upon the supposition of usurpation in the national government; at other times it seems to be designed only as a deduction from the constitutional operation of its intended powers. It is only in the latter light that it can be admitted to have any pretensions to fairness. The moment we launch into conjectures about the usurpations of the federal government, we get into an unfathomable abyss, and fairly put ourselves out of the reach of all reasoning. Imagination may range at pleasure till it gets bewildered amidst the labyrinths of an enchanted castle, and knows not on which side to turn to extricate itself from the perplexities into which it has so rashly adventured. Whatever may be the limits or modifications of the powers of the Union, it is easy to imagine an endless train of possible dangers; and by indulging an excess of jealousy and timidity, we may bring ourselves to a state of absolute scepticism and irresolution. I repeat here what I have observed in substance in another place, that all observations founded upon the danger of usurpation ought to be referred to the composition and structure of the government, not to the nature or extent of its powers. The State governments, by their original constitutions, are invested with complete sovereignty. In what does our security consist against usurpation from that quarter? Doubtless in the manner of their formation, and in a due dependence of those who are to administer them upon the people. If the proposed construction of the federal government be found, upon an impartial examination of it, to be such as to afford, to a proper extent, the same species of security, all apprehensions on the score of usurpation ought to be discarded.

It should not be forgotten that a disposition in the State governments to encroach upon the rights of the Union is quite as probable as a disposition in the Union to encroach upon the rights of the State governments. What side would be likely to prevail in such a conflict, must depend on the means which the contending parties could employ toward insuring success. As in republics strength is always on the side of the people, and as there are weighty reasons to induce a belief that the State governments will commonly possess most influence over them, the natural conclusion is that such contests will be most apt to end to the disadvantage of the Union; and that there is greater probability of encroachments by the members upon the federal head, than by the federal head upon the members. But it is evident that all conjectures of this kind must be extremely vague and fallible: and that it is by far the safest course to lay them altogether aside, and to confine our attention wholly to the nature and extent of the powers as they are delineated in the Constitution. Every thing beyond this must be left to the prudence and firmness of the people; who, as they will hold the scales in their own hands, it is to be hoped, will always take care to preserve the constitutional equilibrium between the general and the State governments. Upon this ground, which is evidently the true one, it will not be difficult to obviate the objections which have been made to an indefinite power of taxation in the United States.

PUBLIUS

FEDERALIST PAPER NO. 32. THE SAME SUBJECT CONTINUED (CONCERNING THE GENERAL POWER OF TAXATION)

From The Independent Journal. Wednesday, January 2, 1788.

HAMILTON

To the People of the State of New York:

ALTHOUGH I am of opinion that there would be no real danger of the consequences which seem to be apprehended to the State governments from a power in the Union to control them in the levies of money, because I am persuaded that the sense of the people, the extreme hazard of provoking the resentments of the State governments, and a conviction of the utility and necessity of local administrations for local purposes, would be a complete barrier against the oppressive use of such a power; yet I am willing here to allow, in its full extent, the justness of the reasoning which requires that the individual States should possess an independent and uncontrollable authority to raise their own revenues for the supply of their own wants. And making this concession, I affirm that (with the sole exception of duties on imports and exports) they would, under the plan of the convention, retain that authority in the most absolute and unqualified sense; and that an attempt on the part of the national government to abridge them in the exercise of it, would be a violent assumption of power, unwarranted by any article or clause of its Constitution.

An entire consolidation of the States into one complete national sovereignty would imply an entire subordination of the parts; and whatever powers might remain in them, would be altogether dependent on the general will. But as the plan of the convention aims only at a partial union or consolidation, the State governments would clearly retain all the rights of sovereignty which they before had, and which were not, by that act, EXCLUSIVELY delegated to the United States. This exclusive delegation, or rather this alienation, of State sovereignty, would only exist in three cases: where the Constitution in express terms granted an exclusive authority to the Union; where it granted in one instance an authority to the Union, and in another prohibited the States from exercising the like authority; and where it granted an authority to the Union, to which a similar authority in the States would be absolutely and totally CONTRADICTORY and REPUGNANT. I use these terms to distinguish this last case from another which might appear to resemble it, but which would, in fact, be essentially different; I mean where the exercise of a concurrent jurisdiction might be productive of occasional interferences in the POLICY of any branch of administration, but would not imply any direct contradiction or repugnancy in point of constitutional authority. These three cases of exclusive jurisdiction in the federal government may be exemplified by the following instances: The last clause but one in the eighth section of the first article provides expressly that Congress shall exercise "EXCLUSIVE LEGISLATION" over the district to be appropriated as the seat of government. This answers to the first case. The first clause of the same section empowers Congress "to lay and collect taxes, duties, imposts and excises"; and the second clause of the tenth section of the same article declares that, "NO STATE SHALL, without the consent of Congress, lay any imposts or duties on imports or exports, except for the purpose of executing its inspection laws." Hence would result an exclusive power in the Union to lay duties on imports and exports, with the particular exception mentioned; but this power is abridged by another clause, which declares that no tax or duty shall be laid on articles exported from any State; in consequence of which qualification, it now only extends to the DUTIES ON IMPORTS. This answers to the second case. The third will be found in that clause which declares that Congress shall have power "to establish an UNIFORM RULE of naturalization throughout the United States." This must necessarily be exclusive; because if each State had power to prescribe a DISTINCT RULE, there could not be a UNIFORM RULE.

A case which may perhaps be thought to resemble the latter, but which is in fact widely different, affects the question immediately under consideration. I mean the power of imposing taxes on all articles other than exports and imports. This, I contend, is manifestly a concurrent and coequal authority in the United States and in the individual States. There is plainly no expression in the granting clause which makes that power EXCLUSIVE in the Union. There is no independent clause or sentence which prohibits the States from exercising it. So far is this from being the case, that a plain and conclusive argument to the contrary is to be deduced from the restraint laid upon the States in relation to duties on imports and exports. This restriction implies an admission that, if it were not inserted, the States would possess the power it excludes; and it implies a further admission, that as to all other taxes, the authority of the States remains undiminished. In any other view it would be both unnecessary and dangerous; it would be unnecessary, because if the grant to the Union of the power of laying such duties implied the exclusion of the States, or even their subordination in this particular, there could be no need of such a restriction; it would be dangerous, because the introduction of it leads directly to the conclusion which has been mentioned, and which, if the reasoning of the objectors be just, could not have been intended; I mean that the States, in all cases to which the restriction did not apply, would have a concurrent power of taxation with the Union. The restriction in question amounts to what lawyers call a NEGATIVE PREGNANT that is, a NEGATION of one thing, and an AFFIRMANCE of another; a negation of the authority of the States to impose taxes on imports and exports, and an affirmance of their authority to impose them on all other articles. It would be mere sophistry to argue that it was meant to exclude them ABSOLUTELY from the imposition of taxes of the former kind, and to leave them at liberty to lay others SUBJECT TO THE CONTROL of the national legislature. The restraining or prohibitory clause only says, that they shall not, WITHOUT THE CONSENT OF CONGRESS, lay such duties; and if we are to understand this in the sense last mentioned, the Constitution would then be made to introduce a formal provision for the sake of a very absurd conclusion; which is, that the States, WITH THE CONSENT of the national legislature, might tax imports and exports; and that they might tax every other article, UNLESS CONTROLLED by the same body. If this was the intention, why not leave it, in the first instance, to what is alleged to be the natural operation of the original clause, conferring a general power of taxation upon the Union? It is evident that this could not have been the intention, and that it will not bear a construction of the kind.

As to a supposition of repugnancy between the power of taxation in the States and in the Union, it cannot be supported in that sense which would be requisite to work an exclusion of the States. It is, indeed, possible that a tax might be laid on a particular article by a State which might render it INEXPEDIENT that thus a further tax should be laid on the same article by the Union; but it would not imply a constitutional inability to impose a further tax. The quantity of the imposition, the expediency or inexpediency of an increase on either side, would be mutually questions of prudence; but there would be involved no direct contradiction of power. The particular policy of the national and of the State systems of finance might now and then not exactly coincide, and might require reciprocal forbearances. It is not, however a mere possibility of inconvenience in the exercise of powers, but an immediate constitutional repugnancy that can by implication alienate and extinguish a pre-existing right of sovereignty.

The necessity of a concurrent jurisdiction in certain cases results from the division of the sovereign power; and the rule that all authorities, of which the States are not explicitly divested in favor of the Union, remain with them in full vigor, is not a theoretical consequence of that division, but is clearly admitted by the whole tenor of the instrument which contains the articles of the proposed Constitution. We there find that, notwithstanding the affirmative grants of general authorities, there has been the most pointed care in those cases where it was deemed improper that the like authorities should reside in the States, to insert negative clauses prohibiting the exercise of them by the States. The tenth section of the first article consists altogether of such provisions. This circumstance is a clear indication of the sense of the convention, and furnishes a rule of interpretation out of the body of the act, which justifies the position I have advanced and refutes every hypothesis to the contrary.

PUBLIUS

FEDERALIST PAPER NO. 33. THE SAME SUBJECT CONTINUED (CONCERNING THE GENERAL POWER OF TAXATION)

From The Independent Journal. Wednesday, January 2, 1788.

HAMILTON

To the People of the State of New York:

THE residue of the argument against the provisions of the Constitution in respect to taxation is ingrafted upon the following clause. The last clause of the eighth section of the first article of the plan under consideration authorizes the national legislature "to make all laws which shall be NECESSARY and PROPER for carrying into execution THE POWERS by that Constitution vested in the government of the United States, or in any department or officer thereof"; and the second clause of the sixth article declares, "that the Constitution and the laws of the United States made IN PURSUANCE THEREOF, and the treaties made by their authority shall be the SUPREME LAW of the land, any thing in the constitution or laws of any State to the contrary notwithstanding."

These two clauses have been the source of much virulent invective and petulant declamation against the proposed Constitution. They have been held up to the people in all the exaggerated colors of misrepresentation as the pernicious engines by which their local governments were to be destroyed and their liberties exterminated; as the hideous monster whose devouring jaws would spare neither sex nor age, nor high nor low, nor sacred nor profane; and yet, strange as it may appear, after all this clamor, to those who may not have happened to contemplate them in the same light, it may be affirmed with perfect confidence that the constitutional operation of the intended government would be precisely the same, if these clauses were entirely obliterated, as if they were repeated in every article. They are only declaratory of a truth which would have resulted by necessary and unavoidable implication from the very act of constituting a federal government, and vesting it with certain specified powers. This is so clear a proposition, that moderation itself can scarcely listen to the railings which have been so copiously vented against this part of the plan, without emotions that disturb its equanimity.

What is a power, but the ability or faculty of doing a thing? What is the ability to do a thing, but the power of employing the MEANS necessary to its execution? What is a LEGISLATIVE power, but a power of making LAWS? What are the MEANS to execute a LEGISLATIVE power but LAWS? What is the power of laying and collecting taxes, but a LEGISLATIVE POWER, or a power of MAKING LAWS, to lay and collect taxes? What are the proper means of executing such a power, but NECESSARY and PROPER laws?

This simple train of inquiry furnishes us at once with a test by which to judge of the true nature of the clause complained of. It conducts us to this palpable truth, that a power to lay and collect taxes must be a power to pass all laws NECESSARY and PROPER for the execution of that power; and what does the unfortunate and calumniated provision in question do more than declare the same truth, to wit, that the national legislature, to whom the power of laying and collecting taxes had been previously given, might, in the execution of that power, pass all laws NECESSARY and PROPER to carry it into effect? I have applied these observations thus particularly to the power of taxation, because it is the immediate subject under consideration, and because it is the most important of the authorities proposed to be conferred upon the Union. But the same process will lead to the same result, in relation to all other powers declared in the Constitution. And it is EXPRESSLY to execute these powers that the sweeping clause, as it has been affectedly called, authorizes the national legislature to pass all NECESSARY and PROPER laws. If there is any thing exceptionable, it must be sought for in the specific powers upon which this general declaration is predicated. The declaration itself, though it may be chargeable with tautology or redundancy, is at least perfectly harmless.

But SUSPICION may ask, Why then was it introduced? The answer is, that it could only have been done for greater caution, and to guard against all cavilling refinements in those who might hereafter feel a disposition to curtail and evade the legitimate authorities of the Union. The Convention probably foresaw, what it has been a principal aim of these papers to inculcate, that the danger which most threatens our political welfare is that the State governments will finally sap the foundations of the Union; and might therefore think it necessary, in so cardinal a point, to leave nothing to construction. Whatever may have been the inducement to it, the wisdom of the precaution is evident from the cry which has been raised against it; as that very cry betrays a disposition to question the great and essential truth which it is manifestly the object of that provision to declare.

But it may be again asked, Who is to judge of the NECESSITY and PROPRIETY of the laws to be passed for executing the powers of the Union? I answer, first, that this question arises as well and as fully upon the simple grant of those powers as upon the declaratory clause; and I answer, in the second place, that the national government, like every other, must judge, in the first instance, of the proper exercise of its powers, and its constituents in the last. If the federal government should overpass the just bounds of its authority and make a tyrannical use of its powers, the people, whose creature it is, must appeal to the standard they have formed, and take such measures to redress the injury done to the Constitution as the exigency may suggest and prudence justify. The propriety of a law, in a constitutional light, must always be determined by the nature of the powers upon which it is founded. Suppose, by some forced constructions of its authority (which, indeed, cannot easily be imagined), the Federal legislature should attempt to vary the law of descent in any State, would it not be evident that, in making such an attempt, it had exceeded its jurisdiction, and infringed upon that of the State? Suppose, again, that upon the pretense of an interference with its revenues, it should undertake to abrogate a landtax imposed by the authority of a State; would it not be equally evident that this was an invasion of that concurrent jurisdiction in respect to this species of tax, which its Constitution plainly supposes to exist in the State governments? If there ever should be a doubt on this head, the credit of it will be entirely due to those reasoners who, in the imprudent zeal of their animosity to the plan of the convention, have labored to envelop it in a cloud calculated to obscure the plainest and simplest truths.

But it is said that the laws of the Union are to be the SUPREME LAW of the land. But what inference can be drawn from this, or what would they amount to, if they were not to be supreme? It is evident they would amount to nothing. A LAW, by the very meaning of the term, includes supremacy. It is a rule which those to whom it is prescribed are bound to observe. This results from every political association. If individuals enter into a state of society, the laws of that society must be the supreme regulator of their conduct. If a number of political societies enter into a larger political society, the laws which the latter may enact, pursuant to the powers intrusted to it by its constitution, must necessarily be supreme over those societies, and the individuals of whom they are composed. It would otherwise be a mere treaty, dependent on the good faith of the parties, and not a government, which is only another word for POLITICAL POWER AND SUPREMACY. But it will not follow from this doctrine that acts of the large society which are NOT PURSUANT to its constitutional powers, but which are invasions of the residuary authorities of the smaller societies, will become the supreme law of the land. These will be merely acts of usurpation, and will deserve to be treated as such. Hence we perceive that the clause which declares the supremacy of the laws of the Union, like the one we have just before considered, only declares a truth, which flows immediately and necessarily from the institution of a federal government. It will not, I presume, have escaped observation, that it EXPRESSLY confines this supremacy to laws made PURSUANT TO THE CONSTITUTION; which I mention merely as an instance of caution in the convention; since that limitation would have been to be understood, though it had not been expressed.

Though a law, therefore, laying a tax for the use of the United States would be supreme in its nature, and could not legally be opposed or controlled, yet a law for abrogating or preventing the collection of a tax laid by the authority of the State, (unless upon imports and exports), would not be the supreme law of the land, but a usurpation of power not granted by the Constitution. As far as an improper accumulation of taxes on the same object might tend to render the collection difficult or precarious, this would be a mutual inconvenience, not arising from a superiority or defect of power on either side, but from an injudicious exercise of power by one or the other, in a manner equally disadvantageous to both. It is to be hoped and presumed, however, that mutual interest would dictate a concert in this respect which would avoid any material inconvenience. The inference from the whole is, that the individual States would, under the proposed Constitution, retain an independent and uncontrollable authority to raise revenue to any extent of which they may stand in need, by every kind of taxation, except duties on imports and exports. It will be shown in the next paper that this CONCURRENT JURISDICTION in the article of taxation was the only admissible substitute for an entire subordination, in respect to this branch of power, of the State authority to that of the Union.

PUBLIUS

FEDERALIST PAPER NO. 34. THE SAME SUBJECT CONTINUED (CONCERNING THE GENERAL POWER OF TAXATION)

From The Independent Journal. Saturday, January 5, 1788.

HAMILTON

To the People of the State of New York:

I FLATTER myself it has been clearly shown in my last number that the particular States, under the proposed Constitution, would have COEQUAL authority with the Union in the article of revenue, except as to duties on imports. As this leaves open to the States far the greatest part of the resources of the community, there can be no color for the assertion that they would not possess means as abundant as could be desired for the supply of their own wants, independent of all external control. That the field is sufficiently wide will more fully appear when we come to advert to the inconsiderable share of the public expenses for which it will fall to the lot of the State governments to provide.

To argue upon abstract principles that this co-ordinate authority cannot exist, is to set up supposition and theory against fact and reality. However proper such reasonings might be to show that a thing OUGHT NOT TO EXIST, they are wholly to be rejected when they are made use of to prove that it does not exist contrary to the evidence of the fact itself. It is well known that in the Roman republic the legislative authority, in the last resort, resided for ages in two different political bodies not as branches of the same legislature, but as distinct and independent legislatures, in each of which an opposite interest prevailed: in one the patrician; in the other, the plebian. Many arguments might have been adduced to prove the unfitness of two such seemingly contradictory authorities, each having power to ANNUL or REPEAL the acts of the other. But a man would have been regarded as frantic who should have attempted at Rome to disprove their existence. It will be readily understood that I allude to the COMITIA CENTURIATA and the COMITIA TRIBUTA. The former, in which the people voted by centuries, was so arranged as to give a superiority to the patrician interest; in the latter, in which numbers prevailed, the plebian interest had an entire predominancy. And yet these two legislatures coexisted for ages, and the Roman republic attained to the utmost height of human greatness.

In the case particularly under consideration, there is no such contradiction as appears in the example cited; there is no power on either side to annul the acts of the other. And in practice there is little reason to apprehend any inconvenience; because, in a short course of time, the wants of the States will naturally reduce themselves within A VERY NARROW COMPASS; and in the interim, the United States will, in all probability, find it convenient to abstain wholly from those objects to which the particular States would be inclined to resort.

To form a more precise judgment of the true merits of this question, it will be well to advert to the proportion between the objects that will require a federal provision in respect to revenue, and those which will require a State provision. We shall discover that the former are altogether unlimited, and that the latter are circumscribed within very moderate bounds. In pursuing this inquiry, we must bear in mind that we are not to confine our view to the present period, but to look forward to remote futurity. Constitutions of civil government are not to be framed upon a calculation of existing exigencies, but upon a combination of these with the probable exigencies of ages, according to the natural and tried course of human affairs. Nothing, therefore, can be more fallacious than to infer the extent of any power, proper to be lodged in the national government, from an estimate of its immediate necessities. There ought to be a CAPACITY to provide for future contingencies as they may happen; and as these are illimitable in their nature, it is impossible safely to limit that capacity. It is true, perhaps, that a computation might be made with sufficient accuracy to answer the purpose of the quantity of revenue requisite to discharge the subsisting engagements of the Union, and to maintain those establishments which, for some time to come, would suffice in time of peace. But would it be wise, or would it not rather be the extreme of folly, to stop at this point, and to leave the government intrusted with the care of the national defense in a state of absolute incapacity to provide for the protection of the community against future invasions of the public peace, by foreign war or domestic convulsions? If, on the contrary, we ought to exceed this point, where can we stop, short of an indefinite power of providing for emergencies as they may arise? Though it is easy to assert, in general terms, the possibility of forming a rational judgment of a due provision against probable dangers, yet we may safely challenge those who make the assertion to bring forward their data, and may affirm that they would be found as vague and uncertain as any that could be produced to establish the probable duration of the world. Observations confined to the mere prospects of internal attacks can deserve no weight; though even these will admit of no satisfactory calculation: but if we mean to be a commercial people, it must form a part of our policy to be able one day to defend that commerce. The support of a navy and of naval wars would involve contingencies that must baffle all the efforts of political arithmetic.

Admitting that we ought to try the novel and absurd experiment in politics of tying up the hands of government from offensive war founded upon reasons of state, yet certainly we ought not to disable it from guarding the community against the ambition or enmity of other nations. A cloud has been for some time hanging over the European world. If it should break forth into a storm, who can insure us that in its progress a part of its fury would not be spent upon us? No reasonable man would hastily pronounce that we are entirely out of its reach. Or if the combustible materials that now seem to be collecting should be dissipated without coming to maturity, or if a flame should be kindled without extending to us, what security can we have that our tranquillity will long remain undisturbed from some other cause or from some other quarter? Let us recollect that peace or war will not always be left to our option; that however moderate or unambitious we may be, we cannot count upon the moderation, or hope to extinguish the ambition of others. Who could have imagined at the conclusion of the last war that France and Britain, wearied and exhausted as they both were, would so soon have looked with so hostile an aspect upon each other? To judge from the history of mankind, we shall be compelled to conclude that the fiery and destructive passions of war reign in the human breast with much more powerful sway than the mild and beneficent sentiments of peace; and that to model our political systems upon speculations of lasting tranquillity, is to calculate on the weaker springs of the human character.

What are the chief sources of expense in every government? What has occasioned that enormous accumulation of debts with which several of the European nations are oppressed? The answers plainly is, wars and rebellions; the support of those institutions which are necessary to guard the body politic against these two most mortal diseases of society. The expenses arising from those institutions which are relative to the mere domestic police of a state, to the support of its legislative, executive, and judicial departments, with their different appendages, and to the encouragement of agriculture and manufactures (which will comprehend almost all the objects of state expenditure), are insignificant in comparison with those which relate to the national defense.

In the kingdom of Great Britain, where all the ostentatious apparatus of monarchy is to be provided for, not above a fifteenth part of the annual income of the nation is appropriated to the class of expenses last mentioned; the other fourteen fifteenths are absorbed in the payment of the interest of debts contracted for carrying on the wars in which that country has been engaged, and in the maintenance of fleets and armies. If, on the one hand, it should be observed that the expenses incurred in the prosecution of the ambitious enterprises and vainglorious pursuits of a monarchy are not a proper standard by which to judge of those which might be necessary in a republic, it ought, on the other hand, to be remarked that there should be as great a disproportion between the profusion and extravagance of a wealthy kingdom in its domestic administration, and the frugality and economy which in that particular become the modest simplicity of republican government. If we balance a proper deduction from one side against that which it is supposed ought to be made from the other, the proportion may still be considered as holding good.

But let us advert to the large debt which we have ourselves contracted in a single war, and let us only calculate on a common share of the events which disturb the peace of nations, and we shall instantly perceive, without the aid of any elaborate illustration, that there must always be an immense disproportion between the objects of federal and state expenditures. It is true that several of the States, separately, are encumbered with considerable debts, which are an excrescence of the late war. But this cannot happen again, if the proposed system be adopted; and when these debts are discharged, the only call for revenue of any consequence, which the State governments will continue to experience, will be for the mere support of their respective civil list; to which, if we add all contingencies, the total amount in every State ought to fall considerably short of two hundred thousand pounds.

In framing a government for posterity as well as ourselves, we ought, in those provisions which are designed to be permanent, to calculate, not on temporary, but on permanent causes of expense. If this principle be a just one our attention would be directed to a provision in favor of the State governments for an annual sum of about two hundred thousand pounds; while the exigencies of the Union could be susceptible of no limits, even in imagination. In this view of the subject, by what logic can it be maintained that the local governments ought to command, in perpetuity, an EXCLUSIVE source of revenue for any sum beyond the extent of two hundred thousand pounds? To extend its power further, in EXCLUSION of the authority of the Union, would be to take the resources of the community out of those hands which stood in need of them for the public welfare, in order to put them into other hands which could have no just or proper occasion for them.

Suppose, then, the convention had been inclined to proceed upon the principle of a repartition of the objects of revenue, between the Union and its members, in PROPORTION to their comparative necessities; what particular fund could have been selected for the use of the States, that would not either have been too much or too little too little for their present, too much for their future wants? As to the line of separation between external and internal taxes, this would leave to the States, at a rough computation, the command of two thirds of the resources of the community to defray from a tenth to a twentieth part of its expenses; and to the Union, one third of the resources of the community, to defray from nine tenths to nineteen twentieths of its expenses. If we desert this boundary and content ourselves with leaving to the States an exclusive power of taxing houses and lands, there would still be a great disproportion between the MEANS and the END; the possession of one third of the resources of the community to supply, at most, one tenth of its wants. If any fund could have been selected and appropriated, equal to and not greater than the object, it would have been inadequate to the discharge of the existing debts of the particular States, and would have left them dependent on the Union for a provision for this purpose.

The preceding train of observation will justify the position which has been elsewhere laid down, that "A CONCURRENT JURISDICTION in the article of taxation was the only admissible substitute for an entire subordination, in respect to this branch of power, of State authority to that of the Union." Any separation of the objects of revenue that could have been fallen upon, would have amounted to a sacrifice of the great INTERESTS of the Union to the POWER of the individual States. The convention thought the concurrent jurisdiction preferable to that subordination; and it is evident that it has at least the merit of reconciling an indefinite constitutional power of taxation in the Federal government with an adequate and independent power in the States to provide for their own necessities. There remain a few other lights, in which this important subject of taxation will claim a further consideration.

PUBLIUS

FEDERALIST PAPER NO. 35. THE SAME SUBJECT CONTINUED (CONCERNING THE GENERAL POWER OF TAXATION)

For the Independent Journal. Saturday, January 5, 1788

HAMILTON

To the People of the State of New York:

BEFORE we proceed to examine any other objections to an indefinite power of taxation in the Union, I shall make one general remark; which is, that if the jurisdiction of the national government, in the article of revenue, should be restricted to particular objects, it would naturally occasion an undue proportion of the public burdens to fall upon those objects. Two evils would spring from this source: the oppression of particular branches of industry; and an unequal distribution of the taxes, as well among the several States as among the citizens of the same State.

Suppose, as has been contended for, the federal power of taxation were to be confined to duties on imports, it is evident that the government, for want of being able to command other resources, would frequently be tempted to extend these duties to an injurious excess. There are persons who imagine that they can never be carried to too great a length; since the higher they are, the more it is alleged they will tend to discourage an extravagant consumption, to produce a favorable balance of trade, and to promote domestic manufactures. But all extremes are pernicious in various ways. Exorbitant duties on imported articles would beget a general spirit of smuggling; which is always prejudicial to the fair trader, and eventually to the revenue itself: they tend to render other classes of the community tributary, in an improper degree, to the manufacturing classes, to whom they give a premature monopoly of the markets; they sometimes force industry out of its more natural channels into others in which it flows with less advantage; and in the last place, they oppress the merchant, who is often obliged to pay them himself without any retribution from the consumer. When the demand is equal to the quantity of goods at market, the consumer generally pays the duty; but when the markets happen to be overstocked, a great proportion falls upon the merchant, and sometimes not only exhausts his profits, but breaks in upon his capital. I am apt to think that a division of the duty, between the seller and the buyer, more often happens than is commonly imagined. It is not always possible to raise the price of a commodity in exact proportion to every additional imposition laid upon it. The merchant, especially in a country of small commercial capital, is often under a necessity of keeping prices down in order to a more expeditious sale.

The maxim that the consumer is the payer, is so much oftener true than the reverse of the proposition, that it is far more equitable that the duties on imports should go into a common stock, than that they should redound to the exclusive benefit of the importing States. But it is not so generally true as to render it equitable, that those duties should form the only national fund. When they are paid by the merchant they operate as an additional tax upon the importing State, whose citizens pay their proportion of them in the character of consumers. In this view they are productive of inequality among the States; which inequality would be increased with the increased extent of the duties. The confinement of the national revenues to this species of imposts would be attended with inequality, from a different cause, between the manufacturing and the non-manufacturing States. The States which can go farthest towards the supply of their own wants, by their own manufactures, will not, according to their numbers or wealth, consume so great a proportion of imported articles as those States which are not in the same favorable situation. They would not, therefore, in this mode alone contribute to the public treasury in a ratio to their abilities. To make them do this it is necessary that recourse be had to excises, the proper objects of which are particular kinds of manufactures. New York is more deeply interested in these considerations than such of her citizens as contend for limiting the power of the Union to external taxation may be aware of. New York is an importing State, and is not likely speedily to be, to any great extent, a manufacturing State. She would, of course, suffer in a double light from restraining the jurisdiction of the Union to commercial imposts.

Documents of Revolution

So far as these observations tend to inculcate a danger of the import duties being extended to an injurious extreme it may be observed, conformably to a remark made in another part of these papers, that the interest of the revenue itself would be a sufficient guard against such an extreme. I readily admit that this would be the case, as long as other resources were open; but if the avenues to them were closed, HOPE, stimulated by necessity, would beget experiments, fortified by rigorous precautions and additional penalties, which, for a time, would have the intended effect, till there had been leisure to contrive expedients to elude these new precautions. The first success would be apt to inspire false opinions, which it might require a long course of subsequent experience to correct. Necessity, especially in politics, often occasions false hopes, false reasonings, and a system of measures correspondingly erroneous. But even if this supposed excess should not be a consequence of the limitation of the federal power of taxation, the inequalities spoken of would still ensue, though not in the same degree, from the other causes that have been noticed. Let us now return to the examination of objections.

One which, if we may judge from the frequency of its repetition, seems most to be relied on, is, that the House of Representatives is not sufficiently numerous for the reception of all the different classes of citizens, in order to combine the interests and feelings of every part of the community, and to produce a due sympathy between the representative body and its constituents. This argument presents itself under a very specious and seducing form; and is well calculated to lay hold of the prejudices of those to whom it is addressed. But when we come to dissect it with attention, it will appear to be made up of nothing but fair-sounding words. The object it seems to aim at is, in the first place, impracticable, and in the sense in which it is contended for, is unnecessary. I reserve for another place the discussion of the question which relates to the sufficiency of the representative body in respect to numbers, and shall content myself with examining here the particular use which has been made of a contrary supposition, in reference to the immediate subject of our inquiries.

The idea of an actual representation of all classes of the people, by persons of each class, is altogether visionary. Unless it were expressly provided in the Constitution, that each different occupation should send one or more members, the thing would never take place in practice. Mechanics and manufacturers will always be inclined, with few exceptions, to give their votes to merchants, in preference to persons of their own professions or trades. Those discerning citizens are well aware that the mechanic and manufacturing arts furnish the materials of mercantile enterprise and industry. Many of them, indeed, are immediately connected with the operations of commerce. They know that the merchant is their natural patron and friend; and they are aware, that however great the confidence they may justly feel in their own good sense, their interests can be more effectually promoted by the merchant than by themselves. They are sensible that their habits in life have not been such as to give them those acquired endowments, without which, in a deliberative assembly, the greatest natural abilities are for the most part useless; and that the influence and weight, and superior acquirements of the merchants render them more equal to a contest with any spirit which might happen to infuse itself into the public councils, unfriendly to the manufacturing and trading interests. These considerations, and many others that might be mentioned prove, and experience confirms it, that artisans and manufacturers will commonly be disposed to bestow their votes upon merchants and those whom they recommend. We must therefore consider merchants as the natural representatives of all these classes of the community.

With regard to the learned professions, little need be observed; they truly form no distinct interest in society, and according to their situation and talents, will be indiscriminately the objects of the confidence and choice of each other, and of other parts of the community.

Nothing remains but the landed interest; and this, in a political view, and particularly in relation to taxes, I take to be perfectly united, from the wealthiest landlord down to the poorest tenant. No tax can be laid on land which will not affect the proprietor of millions of acres as well as the proprietor of a single acre. Every landholder will therefore have a common interest to keep the taxes on land as low as possible; and common interest may always be reckoned upon as the surest bond of sympathy. But if we even could suppose a distinction of interest between the opulent landholder and the middling farmer, what reason is there to conclude, that the first would stand a better chance of being deputed to the national legislature than the last? If we take fact as our guide, and look into our own senate and assembly, we shall find that moderate proprietors of land prevail in both; nor is this less the case in the senate, which consists of a smaller number, than in the assembly, which is composed of a greater number. Where the qualifications of the electors are the same, whether they have to choose a small or a large number, their votes will fall upon those in whom they have most confidence; whether these happen to be men of large fortunes, or of moderate property, or of no property at all.

It is said to be necessary, that all classes of citizens should have some of their own number in the representative body, in order that their feelings and interests may be the better understood and attended to. But we have seen that this will never happen under any arrangement that leaves the votes of the people free. Where this is the case, the representative body, with too few exceptions to have any influence on the spirit of the government, will be composed of landholders, merchants, and men of the learned professions. But where is the danger that the interests and feelings of the different classes of citizens will not be understood or attended to by these three descriptions of men? Will not the landholder know and feel whatever will promote or insure the interest of landed property? And will he not, from his own interest in that species of property, be sufficiently prone to resist every attempt to prejudice or encumber it? Will not the merchant understand and be disposed to cultivate, as far as may be proper, the interests of the mechanic and manufacturing arts, to which his commerce is so nearly allied? Will not the man of the learned profession, who will feel a neutrality to the rivalships between the different branches of industry, be likely to prove an impartial arbiter between them, ready to promote either, so far as it shall appear to him conducive to the general interests of the society?

If we take into the account the momentary humors or dispositions which may happen to prevail in particular parts of the society, and to which a wise administration will never be inattentive, is the man whose situation leads to extensive inquiry and information less likely to be a competent judge of their nature, extent, and foundation than one whose observation does not travel beyond the circle of his neighbors and acquaintances? Is it not natural that a man who is a candidate for the favor of the people, and who is dependent on the suffrages of his fellow-citizens for the continuance of his public honors, should take care to inform himself of their dispositions and inclinations, and should be willing to allow them their proper degree of influence upon his conduct? This dependence, and the necessity of being bound himself, and his posterity, by the laws to which he gives his assent, are the true, and they are the strong chords of sympathy between the representative and the constituent.

There is no part of the administration of government that requires extensive information and a thorough knowledge of the principles of political economy, so much as the business of taxation. The man who understands those principles best will be least likely to resort to oppressive expedients, or sacrifice any particular class of citizens to the procurement of revenue. It might be demonstrated that the most productive system of finance will always be the least burdensome. There can be no doubt that in order to a judicious exercise of the power of taxation, it is necessary that the person in whose hands it should be acquainted with the general genius, habits, and modes of thinking of the people at large, and with the resources of the country. And this is all that can be reasonably meant by a knowledge of the interests and feelings of the people. In any other sense the proposition has either no meaning, or an absurd one. And in that sense let every considerate citizen judge for himself where the requisite qualification is most likely to be found.

PUBLIUS

FEDERALIST PAPER NO. 36. THE SAME SUBJECT CONTINUED (CONCERNING THE GENERAL POWER OF TAXATION)

From the New York Packet. Tuesday, January 8, 1788.

HAMILTON

To the People of the State of New York:

WE HAVE seen that the result of the observations, to which the foregoing number has been principally devoted, is, that from the natural operation of the different interests and views of the various classes of the community, whether the representation of the people be more or less numerous, it will consist almost entirely of proprietors of land, of merchants, and of members of the learned professions, who will truly represent all those different interests and views. If it should be objected that we have seen other descriptions of men in the local legislatures, I answer that it is admitted there are exceptions to the rule, but not in sufficient number to influence the general complexion or character of the government. There are strong minds in every walk of life that will rise superior to the disadvantages of situation, and will command the tribute due to their merit, not only from the classes to which they particularly belong, but from the society in general. The door ought to be equally open to all; and I trust, for the credit of human nature, that we shall see examples of such vigorous plants flourishing in the soil of federal as well as of State legislation; but occasional instances of this sort will not render the reasoning founded upon the general course of things, less conclusive.

The subject might be placed in several other lights that would all lead to the same result; and in particular it might be asked, What greater affinity or relation of interest can be conceived between the carpenter and blacksmith, and the linen manufacturer or stocking weaver, than between the merchant and either of them? It is notorious that there are often as great rivalships between different branches of the mechanic or manufacturing arts as there are between any of the departments of labor and industry; so that, unless the representative body were to be far more numerous than would be consistent with any idea of regularity or wisdom in its deliberations, it is impossible that what seems to be the spirit of the objection we have been considering should ever be realized in practice. But I forbear to dwell any longer on a matter which has hitherto worn too loose a garb to admit even of an accurate inspection of its real shape or tendency.

There is another objection of a somewhat more precise nature that claims our attention. It has been asserted that a power of internal taxation in the national legislature could never be exercised with advantage, as well from the want of a sufficient knowledge of local circumstances, as from an interference between the revenue laws of the Union and of the particular States. The supposition of a want of proper knowledge seems to be entirely destitute of foundation. If any question is depending in a State legislature respecting one of the counties, which demands a knowledge of local details, how is it acquired? No doubt from the information of the members of the county. Cannot the like knowledge be obtained in the national legislature from the representatives of each State? And is it not to be presumed that the men who will generally be sent there will be possessed of the necessary degree of intelligence to be able to communicate that information? Is the knowledge of local circumstances, as applied to taxation, a minute topographical acquaintance with all the mountains, rivers, streams, highways, and bypaths in each State; or is it a general acquaintance with its situation and resources, with the state of its agriculture, commerce, manufactures, with the nature of its products and consumptions, with the different degrees and kinds of its wealth, property, and industry?

Nations in general, even under governments of the more popular kind, usually commit the administration of their finances to single men or to boards composed of a few individuals, who digest and prepare, in the first instance, the plans of taxation, which are afterwards passed into laws by the authority of the sovereign or legislature.

Inquisitive and enlightened statesmen are deemed everywhere best qualified to make a judicious selection of the objects proper for revenue; which is a clear indication, as far as the sense of mankind can have weight in the question, of the species of knowledge of local circumstances requisite to the purposes of taxation.

The taxes intended to be comprised under the general denomination of internal taxes may be subdivided into those of the DIRECT and those of the INDIRECT kind. Though the objection be made to both, yet the reasoning upon it seems to be confined to the former branch. And indeed, as to the latter, by which must be understood duties and excises on articles of consumption, one is at a loss to conceive what can be the nature of the difficulties apprehended. The knowledge relating to them must evidently be of a kind that will either be suggested by the nature of the article itself, or can easily be procured from any well-informed man, especially of the mercantile class. The circumstances that may distinguish its situation in one State from its situation in another must be few, simple, and easy to be comprehended. The principal thing to be attended to, would be to avoid those articles which had been previously appropriated to the use of a particular State; and there could be no difficulty in ascertaining the revenue system of each. This could always be known from the respective codes of laws, as well as from the information of the members from the several States.

The objection, when applied to real property or to houses and lands, appears to have, at first sight, more foundation, but even in this view it will not bear a close examination. Land taxes are commonly laid in one of two modes, either by ACTUAL valuations, permanent or periodical, or by OCCASIONAL assessments, at the discretion, or according to the best judgment, of certain officers whose duty it is to make them. In either case, the EXECUTION of the business, which alone requires the knowledge of local details, must be devolved upon discreet persons in the character of commissioners or assessors, elected by the people or appointed by the government for the purpose. All that the law can do must be to name the persons or to prescribe the manner of their election or appointment, to fix their numbers and qualifications and to draw the general outlines of their powers and duties. And what is there in all this that cannot as well be performed by the national legislature as by a State legislature? The attention of either can only reach to general principles; local details, as already observed, must be referred to those who are to execute the plan.

Documents of Revolution

But there is a simple point of view in which this matter may be placed that must be altogether satisfactory. The national legislature can make use of the SYSTEM OF EACH STATE WITHIN THAT STATE. The method of laying and collecting this species of taxes in each State can, in all its parts, be adopted and employed by the federal government.

Let it be recollected that the proportion of these taxes is not to be left to the discretion of the national legislature, but is to be determined by the numbers of each State, as described in the second section of the first article. An actual census or enumeration of the people must furnish the rule, a circumstance which effectually shuts the door to partiality or oppression. The abuse of this power of taxation seems to have been provided against with guarded circumspection. In addition to the precaution just mentioned, there is a provision that "all duties, imposts, and excises shall be UNIFORM throughout the United States."

It has been very properly observed by different speakers and writers on the side of the Constitution, that if the exercise of the power of internal taxation by the Union should be discovered on experiment to be really inconvenient, the federal government may then forbear the use of it, and have recourse to requisitions in its stead. By way of answer to this, it has been triumphantly asked, Why not in the first instance omit that ambiguous power, and rely upon the latter resource? Two solid answers may be given. The first is, that the exercise of that power, if convenient, will be preferable, because it will be more effectual; and it is impossible to prove in theory, or otherwise than by the experiment, that it cannot be advantageously exercised. The contrary, indeed, appears most probable. The second answer is, that the existence of such a power in the Constitution will have a strong influence in giving efficacy to requisitions. When the States know that the Union can apply itself without their agency, it will be a powerful motive for exertion on their part.

As to the interference of the revenue laws of the Union, and of its members, we have already seen that there can be no clashing or repugnancy of authority. The laws cannot, therefore, in a legal sense, interfere with each other; and it is far from impossible to avoid an interference even in the policy of their different systems. An effectual expedient for this purpose will be, mutually, to abstain from those objects which either side may have first had recourse to. As neither can CONTROL the other, each will have an obvious and sensible interest in this reciprocal forbearance. And where there is an IMMEDIATE common interest, we may safely count upon its operation. When the particular debts of the States are done away, and their expenses come to be limited within their natural compass, the possibility almost of interference will vanish. A small land tax will answer the purpose of the States, and will be their most simple and most fit resource.

Many spectres have been raised out of this power of internal taxation, to excite the apprehensions of the people: double sets of revenue officers, a duplication of their burdens by double taxations, and the frightful forms of odious and oppressive poll-taxes, have been played off with all the ingenious dexterity of political legerdemain.

As to the first point, there are two cases in which there can be no room for double sets of officers: one, where the right of imposing the tax is exclusively vested in the Union, which applies to the duties on imports; the other, where the object has not fallen under any State regulation or provision, which may be applicable to a variety of objects. In other cases, the probability is that the United States will either wholly abstain from the objects preoccupied for local purposes, or will make use of the State officers and State regulations for collecting the additional imposition. This will best answer the views of revenue, because it will save expense in the collection, and will best avoid any occasion of disgust to the State governments and to the people. At all events, here is a practicable expedient for avoiding such an inconvenience; and nothing more can be required than to show that evils predicted to not necessarily result from the plan.

As to any argument derived from a supposed system of influence, it is a sufficient answer to say that it ought not to be presumed; but the supposition is susceptible of a more precise answer. If such a spirit should infest the councils of the Union, the most certain road to the accomplishment of its aim would be to employ the State officers as much as possible, and to attach them to the Union by an accumulation of their emoluments. This would serve to turn the tide of State influence into the channels of the national government, instead of making federal influence flow in an opposite and adverse current. But all suppositions of this kind are invidious, and ought to be banished from the consideration of the great question before the people. They can answer no other end than to cast a mist over the truth.

As to the suggestion of double taxation, the answer is plain. The wants of the Union are to be supplied in one way or another; if to be done by the authority of the federal government, it will not be to be done by that of the State government. The quantity of taxes to be paid by the community must be the same in either case; with this advantage, if the provision is to be made by the Union that the capital resource of commercial imposts, which is the most convenient branch of revenue, can be prudently improved to a much greater extent under federal than under State regulation, and of course will render it less necessary to recur to more inconvenient methods; and with this further advantage, that as far as there may be any real difficulty in the exercise of the power of internal taxation, it will impose a disposition to greater care in the choice and arrangement of the means; and must naturally tend to make it a fixed point of policy in the national administration to go as far as may be practicable in making the luxury of the rich tributary to the public treasury, in order to diminish the necessity of those impositions which might create dissatisfaction in the poorer and most numerous classes of the society. Happy it is when the interest which the government has in the preservation of its own power, coincides with a proper distribution of the public burdens, and tends to guard the least wealthy part of the community from oppression!

As to poll taxes, I, without scruple, confess my disapprobation of them; and though they have prevailed from an early period in those States(1) which have uniformly been the most tenacious of their rights, I should lament to see them introduced into practice under the national government. But does it follow because there is a power to lay them that they will actually be laid? Every State in the Union has power to impose taxes of this kind; and yet in several of them they are unknown in practice. Are the State governments to be stigmatized as tyrannies, because they possess this power? If they are not, with what propriety can the like power justify such a charge against the national government, or even be urged as an obstacle to its adoption? As little friendly as I am to the species of imposition, I still feel a thorough conviction that the power of having recourse to it ought to exist in the federal government. There are certain emergencies of nations, in which expedients, that in the ordinary state of things ought to be forborne, become essential to the public weal. And the government, from the possibility of such emergencies, ought ever to have the option of making use of them. The real scarcity of objects in this country, which may be considered as productive sources of revenue, is a reason peculiar to itself, for not abridging the discretion of the national councils in this respect. There may exist certain critical and tempestuous conjunctures of the State, in which a poll tax may become an inestimable resource. And as I know nothing to exempt this portion of the globe from the common calamities that have befallen other parts of it, I acknowledge my aversion to every project that is calculated to disarm the government of a single weapon, which in any possible contingency might be usefully employed for the general defense and security.

(I have now gone through the examination of such of the powers proposed to be vested in the United States, which may be considered as having an immediate relation to the energy of the government; and have endeavored to answer the principal objections which have been made to them. I have passed over in silence those minor authorities, which are either too inconsiderable to have been thought worthy of the hostilities of the opponents of the Constitution, or of too manifest propriety to admit of controversy. The mass of judiciary power, however, might have claimed an investigation under this head, had it not been for the consideration that its organization and its extent may be more advantageously considered in connection. This has determined me to refer it to the branch of our inquiries upon which we shall next enter.)(E1)

(I have now gone through the examination of those powers proposed to be conferred upon the federal government which relate more peculiarly to its energy, and to its efficiency for answering the great and primary objects of union. There are others which, though omitted here, will, in order to render the view of the subject more complete, be taken notice of under the next head of our inquiries. I flatter myself the progress already made will have sufficed to satisfy the candid and judicious part of the community that some of the objections which have been most strenuously urged against the Constitution, and which were most formidable in their first appearance, are not only destitute of substance, but if they had operated in the formation of the plan, would have rendered it incompetent to the great ends of public happiness and national prosperity. I equally flatter myself that a further and more critical investigation of the system will serve to recommend it still more to every sincere and disinterested advocate for good government and will leave no doubt with men of this character of the propriety and expediency of adopting it. Happy will it be for ourselves, and more honorable for human nature, if we have wisdom and virtue enough to set so glorious an example to mankind!)(E1)

PUBLIUS

1. The New England States.

E1. Two versions of this paragraph appear in different editions.

FEDERALIST PAPER NO. 37. CONCERNING THE DIFFICULTIES OF THE CONVENTION IN DEVISING A PROPER FORM OF GOVERNMENT.

From the Daily Advertiser. Friday, January 11, 1788.

MADISON

To the People of the State of New York:

IN REVIEWING the defects of the existing Confederation, and showing that they cannot be supplied by a government of less energy than that before the public, several of the most important principles of the latter fell of course under consideration. But as the ultimate object of these papers is to determine clearly and fully the merits of this Constitution, and the expediency of adopting it, our plan cannot be complete without taking a more critical and thorough survey of the work of the convention, without examining it on all its sides, comparing it in all its parts, and calculating its probable effects. That this remaining task may be executed under impressions conducive to a just and fair result, some reflections must in this place be indulged, which candor previously suggests.

It is a misfortune, inseparable from human affairs, that public measures are rarely investigated with that spirit of moderation which is essential to a just estimate of their real tendency to advance or obstruct the public good; and that this spirit is more apt to be diminished than promoted, by those occasions which require an unusual exercise of it. To those who have been led by experience to attend to this consideration, it could not appear surprising, that the act of the convention, which recommends so many important changes and innovations, which may be viewed in so many lights and relations, and which touches the springs of so many passions and interests, should find or excite dispositions unfriendly, both on one side and on the other, to a fair discussion and accurate judgment of its merits. In some, it has been too evident from their own publications, that they have scanned the proposed Constitution, not only with a predisposition to censure, but with a predetermination to condemn; as the language held by others betrays an opposite predetermination or bias, which must render their opinions also of little moment in the question. In placing, however, these different characters on a level, with respect to the weight of their opinions, I wish not to insinuate that there may not be a material difference in the purity of their intentions. It is but just to remark in favor of the latter description, that as our situation is universally admitted to be peculiarly critical, and to require indispensably that something should be done for our relief, the predetermined patron of what has been actually done may have taken his bias from the weight of these considerations, as well as from considerations of a sinister nature. The predetermined adversary, on the other hand, can have been governed by no venial motive whatever. The intentions of the first may be upright, as they may on the contrary be culpable. The views of the last cannot be upright, and must be culpable. But the truth is, that these papers are not addressed to persons falling under either of these characters. They solicit the attention of those only, who add to a sincere zeal for the happiness of their country, a temper favorable to a just estimate of the means of promoting it.

Persons of this character will proceed to an examination of the plan submitted by the convention, not only without a disposition to find or to magnify faults; but will see the propriety of reflecting, that a faultless plan was not to be expected. Nor will they barely make allowances for the errors which may be chargeable on the fallibility to which the convention, as a body of men, were liable; but will keep in mind, that they themselves also are but men, and ought not to assume an infallibility in rejudging the fallible opinions of others.

With equal readiness will it be perceived, that besides these inducements to candor, many allowances ought to be made for the difficulties inherent in the very nature of the undertaking referred to the convention.

The novelty of the undertaking immediately strikes us. It has been shown in the course of these papers, that the existing Confederation is founded on principles which are fallacious; that we must consequently change this first foundation, and with it the superstructure resting upon it. It has been shown, that the other confederacies which could be consulted as precedents have been vitiated by the same erroneous principles, and can therefore furnish no other light than that of beacons, which give warning of the course to be shunned, without pointing out that which ought to be pursued. The most that the convention could do in such a situation, was to avoid the errors suggested by the past experience of other countries, as well as of our own; and to provide a convenient mode of rectifying their own errors, as future experiences may unfold them.

Documents of Revolution

Among the difficulties encountered by the convention, a very important one must have lain in combining the requisite stability and energy in government, with the inviolable attention due to liberty and to the republican form. Without substantially accomplishing this part of their undertaking, they would have very imperfectly fulfilled the object of their appointment, or the expectation of the public; yet that it could not be easily accomplished, will be denied by no one who is unwilling to betray his ignorance of the subject. Energy in government is essential to that security against external and internal danger, and to that prompt and salutary execution of the laws which enter into the very definition of good government. Stability in government is essential to national character and to the advantages annexed to it, as well as to that repose and confidence in the minds of the people, which are among the chief blessings of civil society. An irregular and mutable legislation is not more an evil in itself than it is odious to the people; and it may be pronounced with assurance that the people of this country, enlightened as they are with regard to the nature, and interested, as the great body of them are, in the effects of good government, will never be satisfied till some remedy be applied to the vicissitudes and uncertainties which characterize the State administrations. On comparing, however, these valuable ingredients with the vital principles of liberty, we must perceive at once the difficulty of mingling them together in their due proportions. The genius of republican liberty seems to demand on one side, not only that all power should be derived from the people, but that those intrusted with it should be kept in independence on the people, by a short duration of their appointments; and that even during this short period the trust should be placed not in a few, but a number of hands. Stability, on the contrary, requires that the hands in which power is lodged should continue for a length of time the same. A frequent change of men will result from a frequent return of elections; and a frequent change of measures from a frequent change of men: whilst energy in government requires not only a certain duration of power, but the execution of it by a single hand.

How far the convention may have succeeded in this part of their work, will better appear on a more accurate view of it. From the cursory view here taken, it must clearly appear to have been an arduous part.

Not less arduous must have been the task of marking the proper line of partition between the authority of the general and that of the State governments. Every man will be sensible of this difficulty, in proportion as he has been accustomed to contemplate and discriminate objects extensive and complicated in their nature. The faculties of the mind itself have never yet been distinguished and defined, with satisfactory precision, by all the efforts of the most acute and metaphysical philosophers. Sense, perception, judgment, desire, volition, memory, imagination, are found to be separated by such delicate shades and minute gradations that their boundaries have eluded the most subtle investigations, and remain a pregnant source of ingenious disquisition and controversy. The boundaries between the great kingdom of nature, and, still more, between the various provinces, and lesser portions, into which they are subdivided, afford another illustration of the same important truth. The most sagacious and laborious naturalists have never yet succeeded in tracing with certainty the line which separates the district of vegetable life from the neighboring region of unorganized matter, or which marks the termination of the former and the commencement of the animal empire. A still greater obscurity lies in the distinctive characters by which the objects in each of these great departments of nature have been arranged and assorted.

When we pass from the works of nature, in which all the delineations are perfectly accurate, and appear to be otherwise only from the imperfection of the eye which surveys them, to the institutions of man, in which the obscurity arises as well from the object itself as from the organ by which it is contemplated, we must perceive the necessity of moderating still further our expectations and hopes from the efforts of human sagacity. Experience has instructed us that no skill in the science of government has yet been able to discriminate and define, with sufficient certainty, its three great provinces the legislative, executive, and judiciary; or even the privileges and powers of the different legislative branches. Questions daily occur in the course of practice, which prove the obscurity which reins in these subjects, and which puzzle the greatest adepts in political science.

The experience of ages, with the continued and combined labors of the most enlightened legislatures and jurists, has been equally unsuccessful in delineating the several objects and limits of different codes of laws and different tribunals of justice. The precise extent of the common law, and the statute law, the maritime law, the ecclesiastical law, the law of corporations, and other local laws and customs, remains still to be clearly and finally established in Great Britain, where accuracy in such subjects has been more industriously pursued than in any other part of the world. The jurisdiction of her several courts, general and local, of law, of equity, of admiralty, etc., is not less a source of frequent and intricate discussions, sufficiently denoting the indeterminate limits by which they are respectively circumscribed. All new laws, though penned with the greatest technical skill, and passed on the fullest and most mature deliberation, are considered as more or less obscure and equivocal, until their meaning be liquidated and ascertained by a series of particular discussions and adjudications. Besides the obscurity arising from the complexity of objects, and the imperfection of the human faculties, the medium through which the conceptions of men are conveyed to each other adds a fresh embarrassment. The use of words is to express ideas. Perspicuity, therefore, requires not only that the ideas should be distinctly formed, but that they should be expressed by words distinctly and exclusively appropriate to them. But no language is so copious as to supply words and phrases for every complex idea, or so correct as not to include many equivocally denoting different ideas. Hence it must happen that however accurately objects may be discriminated in themselves, and however accurately the discrimination may be considered, the definition of them may be rendered inaccurate by the inaccuracy of the terms in which it is delivered. And this unavoidable inaccuracy must be greater or less, according to the complexity and novelty of the objects defined. When the Almighty himself condescends to address mankind in their own language, his meaning, luminous as it must be, is rendered dim and doubtful by the cloudy medium through which it is communicated.

Here, then, are three sources of vague and incorrect definitions: indistinctness of the object, imperfection of the organ of conception, inadequateness of the vehicle of ideas. Any one of these must produce a certain degree of obscurity. The convention, in delineating the boundary between the federal and State jurisdictions, must have experienced the full effect of them all.

To the difficulties already mentioned may be added the interfering pretensions of the larger and smaller States. We cannot err in supposing that the former would contend for a participation in the government, fully proportioned to their superior wealth and importance; and that the latter would not be less tenacious of the equality at present enjoyed by them. We may well suppose that neither side would entirely yield to the other, and consequently that the struggle could be terminated only by compromise. It is extremely probable, also, that after the ratio of representation had been adjusted, this very compromise must have produced a fresh struggle between the same parties, to give such a turn to the organization of the government, and to the distribution of its powers, as would increase the importance of the branches, in forming which they had respectively obtained the greatest share of influence. There are features in the Constitution which warrant each of these suppositions; and as far as either of them is well founded, it shows that the convention must have been compelled to sacrifice theoretical propriety to the force of extraneous considerations.

Nor could it have been the large and small States only, which would marshal themselves in opposition to each other on various points. Other combinations, resulting from a difference of local position and policy, must have created additional difficulties. As every State may be divided into different districts, and its citizens into different classes, which give birth to contending interests and local jealousies, so the different parts of the United States are distinguished from each other by a variety of circumstances, which produce a like effect on a larger scale. And although this variety of interests, for reasons sufficiently explained in a former paper, may have a salutary influence on the administration of the government when formed, yet every one must be sensible of the contrary influence, which must have been experienced in the task of forming it.

Would it be wonderful if, under the pressure of all these difficulties, the convention should have been forced into some deviations from that artificial structure and regular symmetry which an abstract view of the subject might lead an ingenious theorist to bestow on a Constitution planned in his closet or in his imagination? The real wonder is that so many difficulties should have been surmounted, and surmounted with a unanimity almost as unprecedented as it must have been unexpected. It is impossible for any man of candor to reflect on this circumstance without partaking of the astonishment. It is impossible for the man of pious reflection not to perceive in it a finger of that Almighty hand which has been so frequently and signally extended to our relief in the critical stages of the revolution.

We had occasion, in a former paper, to take notice of the repeated trials which have been unsuccessfully made in the United Netherlands for reforming the baneful and notorious vices of their constitution. The history of almost all the great councils and consultations held among mankind for reconciling their discordant opinions, assuaging their mutual jealousies, and adjusting their respective interests, is a history of factions, contentions, and disappointments, and may be classed among the most dark and degraded pictures which display the infirmities and depravities of the human character. If, in a few scattered instances, a brighter aspect is presented, they serve only as exceptions to admonish us of the general truth; and by their lustre to darken the gloom of the adverse prospect to which they are contrasted. In revolving the causes from which these exceptions result, and applying them to the particular instances before us, we are necessarily led to two important conclusions. The first is, that the convention must have enjoyed, in a very singular degree, an exemption from the pestilential influence of party animosities the disease most incident to deliberative bodies, and most apt to contaminate their proceedings. The second conclusion is that all the deputations composing the convention were satisfactorily accommodated by the final act, or were induced to accede to it by a deep conviction of the necessity of sacrificing private opinions and partial interests to the public good, and by a despair of seeing this necessity diminished by delays or by new experiments.

FEDERALIST PAPER NO. 38. THE SAME SUBJECT CONTINUED, AND THE INCOHERENCE OF THE OBJECTIONS TO THE NEW PLAN EXPOSED.

From The Independent Journal. Saturday, January 12, 1788.

MADISON

To the People of the State of New York:

IT IS not a little remarkable that in every case reported by ancient history, in which government has been established with deliberation and consent, the task of framing it has not been committed to an assembly of men, but has been performed by some individual citizen of preeminent wisdom and approved integrity.

Minos, we learn, was the primitive founder of the government of Crete, as Zaleucus was of that of the Locrians. Theseus first, and after him Draco and Solon, instituted the government of Athens. Lycurgus was the lawgiver of Sparta. The foundation of the original government of Rome was laid by Romulus, and the work completed by two of his elective successors, Numa and Tullius Hostilius. On the abolition of royalty the consular administration was substituted by Brutus, who stepped forward with a project for such a reform, which, he alleged, had been prepared by Tullius Hostilius, and to which his address obtained the assent and ratification of the senate and people. This remark is applicable to confederate governments also. Amphictyon, we are told, was the author of that which bore his name. The Achaean league received its first birth from Achaeus, and its second from Aratus.

What degree of agency these reputed lawgivers might have in their respective establishments, or how far they might be clothed with the legitimate authority of the people, cannot in every instance be ascertained. In some, however, the proceeding was strictly regular. Draco appears to have been intrusted by the people of Athens with indefinite powers to reform its government and laws. And Solon, according to Plutarch, was in a manner compelled, by the universal suffrage of his fellow-citizens, to take upon him the sole and absolute power of new-modeling the constitution. The proceedings under Lycurgus were less regular; but as far as the advocates for a regular reform could prevail, they all turned their eyes towards the single efforts of that celebrated patriot and sage, instead of seeking to bring about a revolution by the intervention of a deliberative body of citizens.

Whence could it have proceeded, that a people, jealous as the Greeks were of their liberty, should so far abandon the rules of caution as to place their destiny in the hands of a single citizen? Whence could it have proceeded, that the Athenians, a people who would not suffer an army to be commanded by fewer than ten generals, and who required no other proof of danger to their liberties than the illustrious merit of a fellow-citizen, should consider one illustrious citizen as a more eligible depositary of the fortunes of themselves and their posterity, than a select body of citizens, from whose common deliberations more wisdom, as well as more safety, might have been expected? These questions cannot be fully answered, without supposing that the fears of discord and disunion among a number of counsellors exceeded the apprehension of treachery or incapacity in a single individual. History informs us, likewise, of the difficulties with which these celebrated reformers had to contend, as well as the expedients which they were obliged to employ in order to carry their reforms into effect. Solon, who seems to have indulged a more temporizing policy, confessed that he had not given to his countrymen the government best suited to their happiness, but most tolerable to their prejudices. And Lycurgus, more true to his object, was under the necessity of mixing a portion of violence with the authority of superstition, and of securing his final success by a voluntary renunciation, first of his country, and then of his life. If these lessons teach us, on one hand, to admire the improvement made by America on the ancient mode of preparing and establishing regular plans of government, they serve not less, on the other, to admonish us of the hazards and difficulties incident to such experiments, and of the great imprudence of unnecessarily multiplying them.

Is it an unreasonable conjecture, that the errors which may be contained in the plan of the convention are such as have resulted rather from the defect of antecedent experience on this complicated and difficult subject, than from a want of accuracy or care in the investigation of it; and, consequently such as will not be ascertained until an actual trial shall have pointed them out? This conjecture is rendered probable, not only by many considerations of a general nature, but by the particular case of the Articles of Confederation. It is observable that among the numerous objections and amendments suggested by the several

States, when these articles were submitted for their ratification, not one is found which alludes to the great and radical error which on actual trial has discovered itself. And if we except the observations which New Jersey was led to make, rather by her local situation, than by her peculiar foresight, it may be questioned whether a single suggestion was of sufficient moment to justify a revision of the system. There is abundant reason, nevertheless, to suppose that immaterial as these objections were, they would have been adhered to with a very dangerous inflexibility, in some States, had not a zeal for their opinions and supposed interests been stifled by the more powerful sentiment of self-preservation. One State, we may remember, persisted for several years in refusing her concurrence, although the enemy remained the whole period at our gates, or rather in the very bowels of our country. Nor was her pliancy in the end effected by a less motive, than the fear of being chargeable with protracting the public calamities, and endangering the event of the contest. Every candid reader will make the proper reflections on these important facts.

A patient who finds his disorder daily growing worse, and that an efficacious remedy can no longer be delayed without extreme danger, after coolly revolving his situation, and the characters of different physicians, selects and calls in such of them as he judges most capable of administering relief, and best entitled to his confidence. The physicians attend; the case of the patient is carefully examined; a consultation is held; they are unanimously agreed that the symptoms are critical, but that the case, with proper and timely relief, is so far from being desperate, that it may be made to issue in an improvement of his constitution. They are equally unanimous in prescribing the remedy, by which this happy effect is to be produced. The prescription is no sooner made known, however, than a number of persons interpose, and, without denying the reality or danger of the disorder, assure the patient that the prescription will be poison to his constitution, and forbid him, under pain of certain death, to make use of it. Might not the patient reasonably demand, before he ventured to follow this advice, that the authors of it should at least agree among themselves on some other remedy to be substituted? And if he found them differing as much from one another as from his first counsellors, would he not act prudently in trying the experiment unanimously recommended by the latter, rather than be hearkening to those who could neither deny the necessity of a speedy remedy, nor agree in proposing one?

Such a patient and in such a situation is America at this moment. She has been sensible of her malady. She has obtained a regular and unanimous advice from men of her own deliberate choice. And she is warned by others against following this advice under pain of the most fatal consequences. Do the monitors deny the reality of her danger? No. Do they deny the necessity of some speedy and powerful remedy? No. Are they agreed, are any two of them agreed, in their objections to the remedy proposed, or in the proper one to be substituted? Let them speak for themselves. This one tells us that the proposed Constitution ought to be rejected, because it is not a confederation of the States, but a government over individuals. Another admits that it ought to be a government over individuals to a certain extent, but by no means to the extent proposed. A third does not object to the government over individuals, or to the extent proposed, but to the want of a bill of rights. A fourth concurs in the absolute necessity of a bill of rights, but contends that it ought to be declaratory, not of the personal rights of individuals, but of the rights reserved to the States in their political capacity. A fifth is of opinion that a bill of rights of any sort would be superfluous and misplaced, and that the plan would be unexceptionable but for the fatal power of regulating the times and places of election. An objector in a large State exclaims loudly against the unreasonable equality of representation in the Senate. An objector in a small State is equally loud against the dangerous inequality in the House of Representatives. From this quarter, we are alarmed with the amazing expense, from the number of persons who are to administer the new government. From another quarter, and sometimes from the same quarter, on another occasion, the cry is that the Congress will be but a shadow of a representation, and that the government would be far less objectionable if the number and the expense were doubled. A patriot in a State that does not import or export, discerns insuperable objections against the power of direct taxation. The patriotic adversary in a State of great exports and imports, is not less dissatisfied that the whole burden of taxes may be thrown on consumption. This politician discovers in the Constitution a direct and irresistible tendency to monarchy; that is equally sure it will end in aristocracy. Another is puzzled to say which of these shapes it will ultimately assume, but sees clearly it must be one or other of them; whilst a fourth is not wanting, who with no less confidence affirms that the Constitution is so far from having a bias towards either of these dangers, that the weight on that side will not be sufficient to keep it upright and firm against its opposite propensities. With another class of adversaries to the Constitution the language is that the legislative, executive, and judiciary departments are intermixed in such a manner as to contradict all the ideas of regular government and all the requisite precautions in favor of liberty. Whilst this objection circulates in vague and general expressions, there are but a few who lend their sanction to it. Let each one come forward with his particular explanation, and scarce any two are exactly agreed upon the subject. In the eyes of one the junction of the Senate with the President in the responsible function of appointing to offices, instead of vesting this executive power in the Executive alone, is the vicious part

Documents of Revolution

of the organization. To another, the exclusion of the House of Representatives, whose numbers alone could be a due security against corruption and partiality in the exercise of such a power, is equally obnoxious. With another, the admission of the President into any share of a power which ever must be a dangerous engine in the hands of the executive magistrate, is an unpardonable violation of the maxims of republican jealousy. No part of the arrangement, according to some, is more inadmissible than the trial of impeachments by the Senate, which is alternately a member both of the legislative and executive departments, when this power so evidently belonged to the judiciary department. "We concur fully," reply others, "in the objection to this part of the plan, but we can never agree that a reference of impeachments to the judiciary authority would be an amendment of the error. Our principal dislike to the organization arises from the extensive powers already lodged in that department." Even among the zealous patrons of a council of state the most irreconcilable variance is discovered concerning the mode in which it ought to be constituted. The demand of one gentleman is, that the council should consist of a small number to be appointed by the most numerous branch of the legislature. Another would prefer a larger number, and considers it as a fundamental condition that the appointment should be made by the President himself.

As it can give no umbrage to the writers against the plan of the federal Constitution, let us suppose, that as they are the most zealous, so they are also the most sagacious, of those who think the late convention were unequal to the task assigned them, and that a wiser and better plan might and ought to be substituted. Let us further suppose that their country should concur, both in this favorable opinion of their merits, and in their unfavorable opinion of the convention; and should accordingly proceed to form them into a second convention, with full powers, and for the express purpose of revising and remoulding the work of the first. Were the experiment to be seriously made, though it required some effort to view it seriously even in fiction, I leave it to be decided by the sample of opinions just exhibited, whether, with all their enmity to their predecessors, they would, in any one point, depart so widely from their example, as in the discord and ferment that would mark their own deliberations; and whether the Constitution, now before the public, would not stand as fair a chance for immortality, as Lycurgus gave to that of Sparta, by making its change to depend on his own return from exile and death, if it were to be immediately adopted, and were to continue in force, not until a BETTER, but until ANOTHER should be agreed upon by this new assembly of lawgivers.

It is a matter both of wonder and regret, that those who raise so many objections against the new Constitution should never call to mind the defects of that which is to be exchanged for it. It is not necessary that the former should be perfect; it is sufficient that the latter is more imperfect. No man would refuse to give brass for silver or gold, because the latter had some alloy in it. No man would refuse to quit a shattered and tottering habitation for a firm and commodious building, because the latter had not a porch to it, or because some of the rooms might be a little larger or smaller, or the ceilings a little higher or lower than his fancy would have planned them. But waiving illustrations of this sort, is it not manifest that most of the capital objections urged against the new system lie with tenfold weight against the existing Confederation? Is an indefinite power to raise money dangerous in the hands of the federal government? The present Congress can make requisitions to any amount they please, and the States are constitutionally bound to furnish them; they can emit bills of credit as long as they will pay for the paper; they can borrow, both abroad and at home, as long as a shilling will be lent. Is an indefinite power to raise troops dangerous? The Confederation gives to Congress that power also; and they have already begun to make use of it. Is it improper and unsafe to intermix the different powers of government in the same body of men? Congress, a single body of men, are the sole depositary of all the federal powers. Is it particularly dangerous to give the keys of the treasury, and the command of the army, into the same hands? The Confederation places them both in the hands of Congress. Is a bill of rights essential to liberty? The Confederation has no bill of rights. Is it an objection against the new Constitution, that it empowers the Senate, with the concurrence of the Executive, to make treaties which are to be the laws of the land? The existing Congress, without any such control, can make treaties which they themselves have declared, and most of the States have recognized, to be the supreme law of the land. Is the importation of slaves permitted by the new Constitution for twenty years? By the old it is permitted forever.

I shall be told, that however dangerous this mixture of powers may be in theory, it is rendered harmless by the dependence of Congress on the State for the means of carrying them into practice; that however large the mass of powers may be, it is in fact a lifeless mass. Then, say I, in the first place, that the Confederation is chargeable with the still greater folly of declaring certain powers in the federal government to be absolutely necessary, and at the same time rendering them absolutely nugatory; and, in the next place, that if the Union is to continue, and no better government be substituted, effective powers must either be granted to, or assumed by, the existing Congress; in either of which events, the contrast just stated will hold good. But this is not all. Out of this lifeless mass has already grown an excrescent power, which tends to realize all the dangers that can be apprehended from a defective construction of the supreme government of the Union. It is now no longer a point of speculation and hope, that the Western territory is a mine of vast wealth to the United States; and although it is not of such a nature as to extricate them from their present distresses, or for some time to come, to yield any regular supplies for the public expenses, yet must it hereafter be able, under proper management, both to effect a gradual discharge of the domestic debt, and to furnish, for a certain period, liberal tributes to the federal treasury. A very large proportion of this fund has been already surrendered by individual States; and it may with reason be expected that the remaining States will not persist in withholding similar proofs of their equity and generosity. We may calculate, therefore, that a rich and fertile country, of an area equal to the inhabited extent of the United States, will soon become a national stock. Congress have assumed the administration of this stock. They have begun to render it productive. Congress have undertaken to do more: they have proceeded to form new States, to erect temporary governments, to appoint officers for them, and to prescribe the conditions on which such States shall be admitted into the Confederacy. All this has been done; and done without the least color of constitutional authority. Yet no blame has been whispered; no alarm has been sounded. A GREAT and INDEPENDENT fund of revenue is passing into the hands of a SINGLE BODY of men, who can RAISE TROOPS to an INDEFINITE NUMBER, and appropriate money to their support for an INDEFINITE PERIOD OF TIME. And yet there are men, who have not only been silent spectators of this prospect, but who are advocates for the system which exhibits it; and, at the same time, urge against the new system the objections which we have heard. Would they not act with more consistency, in urging the establishment of the latter, as no less necessary to guard the Union against the future powers and resources of a body constructed like the existing Congress, than to save it from the dangers threatened by the present impotency of that Assembly?

I mean not, by any thing here said, to throw censure on the measures which have been pursued by Congress. I am sensible they could not have done otherwise. The public interest, the necessity of the case, imposed upon them the task of overleaping their constitutional limits. But is not the fact an alarming proof of the danger resulting from a government which does not possess regular powers commensurate to its objects? A dissolution or usurpation is the dreadful dilemma to which it is continually exposed.

PUBLIUS

FEDERALIST PAPER NO. 39. THE CONFORMITY OF THE PLAN TO REPUBLICAN PRINCIPLES

For the Independent Journal. Wednesday, January 16, 1788

MADISON

To the People of the State of New York:

THE last paper having concluded the observations which were meant to introduce a candid survey of the plan of government reported by the convention, we now proceed to the execution of that part of our undertaking.

The first question that offers itself is, whether the general form and aspect of the government be strictly republican. It is evident that no other form would be reconcilable with the genius of the people of America; with the fundamental principles of the Revolution; or with that honorable determination which animates every votary of freedom, to rest all our political experiments on the capacity of mankind for self-government. If the plan of the convention, therefore, be found to depart from the republican character, its advocates must abandon it as no longer defensible.

What, then, are the distinctive characters of the republican form? Were an answer to this question to be sought, not by recurring to principles, but in the application of the term by political writers, to the constitution of different States, no satisfactory one would ever be found. Holland, in which no particle of the supreme authority is derived from the people, has passed almost universally under the denomination of a republic. The same title has been bestowed on Venice, where absolute power over the great body of the people is exercised, in the most absolute manner, by a small body of hereditary nobles. Poland, which is a mixture of aristocracy and of monarchy in their worst forms, has been dignified with the same appellation. The government of England, which has one republican branch only, combined with an hereditary aristocracy and monarchy, has, with equal impropriety, been frequently placed on the list of republics. These examples, which are nearly as dissimilar to each other as to a genuine republic, show the extreme inaccuracy with which the term has been used in political disquisitions.

If we resort for a criterion to the different principles on which different forms of government are established, we may define a republic to be, or at least may bestow that name on, a government which derives all its powers directly or indirectly from the great body of the people, and is administered by persons holding their offices during pleasure, for a limited period, or during good behavior. It is ESSENTIAL to such a government that it be derived from the great body of the society, not from an inconsiderable proportion, or a favored class of it; otherwise a handful of tyrannical nobles, exercising their oppressions by a delegation of their powers, might aspire to the rank of republicans, and claim for their government the honorable title of republic. It is SUFFICIENT for such a government that the persons administering it be appointed, either directly or indirectly, by the people; and that they hold their appointments by either of the tenures just specified; otherwise every government in the United States, as well as every other popular government that has been or can be well organized or well executed, would be degraded from the republican character. According to the constitution of every State in the Union, some or other of the officers of government are appointed indirectly only by the people. According to most of them, the chief magistrate himself is so appointed. And according to one, this mode of appointment is extended to one of the co-ordinate branches of the legislature. According to all the constitutions, also, the tenure of the highest offices is extended to a definite period, and in many instances, both within the legislative and executive departments, to a period of years. According to the provisions of most of the constitutions, again, as well as according to the most respectable and received opinions on the subject, the members of the judiciary department are to retain their offices by the firm tenure of good behavior.

On comparing the Constitution planned by the convention with the standard here fixed, we perceive at once that it is, in the most rigid sense, conformable to it. The House of Representatives, like that of one branch at least of all the State legislatures, is elected immediately by the great body of the people. The Senate, like the present Congress, and the Senate of Maryland, derives its appointment indirectly from the people. The President is indirectly derived from the choice of the people, according to the example in most of the States. Even the judges, with all other officers of the Union, will, as in the several States, be the choice, though a remote choice, of the people themselves, the duration of the appointments is equally conformable to the republican standard, and to the model of State constitutions The House of Representatives is periodically elective, as in all the States; and for the period of two years, as in the State of South Carolina. The Senate is elective, for the period of six years; which is but one year more than the period of the Senate of Maryland, and but two more than that of the Senates of New York and Virginia. The President is to continue in office for the period of four years; as in New York and Delaware, the chief magistrate is elected for three years, and in South Carolina for two years. In the other States the election is annual. In several of the States, however, no constitutional provision is made for the impeachment of the chief magistrate. And in Delaware and Virginia he is not impeachable till out of office. The President of the United States is impeachable at any time during his continuance in office. The tenure by which the judges are to hold their places, is, as it unquestionably ought to be, that of good behavior. The tenure of the ministerial offices generally, will be a subject of legal regulation, conformably to the reason of the case and the example of the State constitutions.

Could any further proof be required of the republican complexion of this system, the most decisive one might be found in its absolute prohibition of titles of nobility, both under the federal and the State governments; and in its express guaranty of the republican form to each of the latter.

"But it was not sufficient," say the adversaries of the proposed Constitution, "for the convention to adhere to the republican form. They ought, with equal care, to have preserved the FEDERAL form, which regards the Union as a CONFEDERACY of sovereign states; instead of which, they have framed a NATIONAL government, which regards the Union as a CONSOLIDATION of the States." And it is asked by what authority this bold and radical innovation was undertaken? The handle which has been made of this objection requires that it should be examined with some precision.

Without inquiring into the accuracy of the distinction on which the objection is founded, it will be necessary to a just estimate of its force, first, to ascertain the real character of the government in question; secondly, to inquire how far the convention were authorized to propose such a government; and thirdly, how far the duty they owed to their country could supply any defect of regular authority.

First. In order to ascertain the real character of the government, it may be considered in relation to the foundation on which it is to be established; to the sources from which its ordinary powers are to be drawn; to the operation of those powers; to the extent of them; and to the authority by which future changes in the government are to be introduced.

On examining the first relation, it appears, on one hand, that the Constitution is to be founded on the assent and ratification of the people of America, given by deputies elected for the special purpose; but, on the other, that this assent and ratification is to be given by the people, not as individuals composing one entire nation, but as composing the distinct and independent States to which they respectively belong. It is to be the assent and ratification of the several States, derived from the supreme authority in each State, the authority of the people themselves. The act, therefore, establishing the Constitution, will not be a NATIONAL, but a FEDERAL act.

That it will be a federal and not a national act, as these terms are understood by the objectors; the act of the people, as forming so many independent States, not as forming one aggregate nation, is obvious from this single consideration, that it is to result neither from the decision of a MAJORITY of the people of the Union, nor from that of a MAJORITY of the States. It must result from the UNANIMOUS assent of the several States that are parties to it, differing no otherwise from their ordinary assent than in its being expressed, not by the legislative authority, but by that of the people themselves. Were the people regarded in this transaction as forming one nation, the will of the majority of the whole people of the United States would bind the minority, in the same manner as the majority in each State must bind the minority; and the will of the majority must be determined either by a comparison of the individual votes, or by considering the will of the majority of the States as evidence of the will of a majority of the people of the United States. Neither of these rules have been adopted. Each State, in ratifying the Constitution, is considered as a sovereign body, independent of all others, and only to be bound by its own voluntary act. In this relation, then, the new Constitution will, if established, be a FEDERAL, and not a NATIONAL constitution.

The next relation is, to the sources from which the ordinary powers of government are to be derived. The House of Representatives will derive its powers from the people of America; and the people will be represented in the same proportion, and on the same principle, as they are in the legislature of a particular State. So far the government is NATIONAL, not FEDERAL. The Senate, on the other hand, will derive its powers from the States, as political and coequal societies; and these will be represented on the principle of equality in the Senate, as they now are in the existing Congress. So far the government is FEDERAL, not NATIONAL. The executive power will be derived from a very compound source. The immediate election of the President is to be made by the States in their political characters. The votes allotted to them are in a compound ratio, which considers them partly as distinct and coequal societies, partly as unequal members of the same society. The eventual election, again, is to be made by that branch of the legislature which consists of the national representatives; but in this particular act they are to be thrown into the form of individual delegations, from so many distinct and coequal bodies politic. From this aspect of the government it appears to be of a mixed character, presenting at least as many FEDERAL as NATIONAL features.

The difference between a federal and national government, as it relates to the OPERATION OF THE GOVERNMENT, is supposed to consist in this, that in the former the powers operate on the political bodies composing the Confederacy, in their political capacities; in the latter, on the individual citizens composing the nation, in their individual capacities. On trying the Constitution by this criterion, it falls under the NATIONAL, not the FEDERAL character; though perhaps not so completely as has been understood. In several cases, and particularly in the trial of controversies to which States may be parties, they must be viewed and proceeded against in their collective and political capacities only. So far the national countenance of the government on this side seems to be disfigured by a few federal features. But this blemish is perhaps unavoidable in any plan; and the operation of the government on the people, in their individual capacities, in its ordinary and most essential proceedings, may, on the whole, designate it, in this relation, a NATIONAL government.

But if the government be national with regard to the OPERATION of its powers, it changes its aspect again when we contemplate it in relation to the EXTENT of its powers. The idea of a national government involves in it, not only an authority over the individual citizens, but an indefinite supremacy over all persons and things, so far as they are objects of lawful government. Among a people consolidated into one nation, this supremacy is completely vested in the national legislature. Among communities united for particular purposes, it is vested partly in the general and partly in the municipal legislatures. In the former case, all local authorities are subordinate to the supreme; and may be controlled, directed, or abolished by it at pleasure. In the latter, the local or municipal authorities form distinct and independent portions of the supremacy, no more subject, within their respective spheres, to the general authority, than the general authority is subject to them, within its own sphere. In this relation, then, the proposed government cannot be deemed a NATIONAL one; since its jurisdiction extends to certain enumerated objects only, and leaves to the several States a residuary and inviolable sovereignty over all other objects. It is true that in controversies relating to the boundary between the two jurisdictions, the tribunal which is ultimately to decide, is to be established under the general government. But this does not change the principle of the case. The decision is to be impartially made, according to the rules of the Constitution; and all the usual and most effectual precautions are taken to secure this impartiality. Some such tribunal is clearly essential to prevent an appeal to the sword and a dissolution of the compact; and that it ought to be established under the general rather than under the local governments, or, to speak more properly, that it could be safely established under the first alone, is a position not likely to be combated.

If we try the Constitution by its last relation to the authority by which amendments are to be made, we find it neither wholly NATIONAL nor wholly FEDERAL. Were it wholly national, the supreme and ultimate authority would reside in the MAJORITY of the people of the Union; and this authority would be competent at all times, like that of a majority of every national society, to alter or abolish its established government. Were it wholly federal, on the other hand, the concurrence of each State in the Union would be essential to every alteration that would be binding on all. The mode provided by the plan of the convention is not founded on either of these principles. In requiring more than a majority, and principles. In requiring more than a majority, and particularly in computing the proportion by STATES, not by CITIZENS, it departs from the NATIONAL and advances towards the FEDERAL character; in rendering the concurrence of less than the whole number of States sufficient, it loses again the FEDERAL and partakes of the NATIONAL character.

The proposed Constitution, therefore, is, in strictness, neither a national nor a federal Constitution, but a composition of both. In its foundation it is federal, not national; in the sources from which the ordinary powers of the government are drawn, it is partly federal and partly national; in the operation of these powers, it is national, not federal; in the extent of them, again, it is federal, not national; and, finally, in the authoritative mode of introducing amendments, it is neither wholly federal nor wholly national.

PUBLIUS

FEDERALIST PAPER NO. 40. ON THE POWERS OF THE CONVENTION TO FORM A MIXED GOVERNMENT EXAMINED AND SUSTAINED.

For the New York Packet. Friday, January 18, 1788.

MADISON

To the People of the State of New York:

THE SECOND point to be examined is, whether the convention were authorized to frame and propose this mixed Constitution.

The powers of the convention ought, in strictness, to be determined by an inspection of the commissions given to the members by their respective constituents. As all of these, however, had reference, either to the recommendation from the meeting at Annapolis, in September, 1786, or to that from Congress, in February, 1787, it will be sufficient to recur to these particular acts.

The act from Annapolis recommends the "appointment of commissioners to take into consideration the situation of the United States; to devise SUCH FURTHER PROVISIONS as shall appear to them necessary to render the Constitution of the federal government ADEQUATE TO THE EXIGENCIES OF THE UNION; and to report such an act for that purpose, to the United States in Congress assembled, as when agreed to by them, and afterwards confirmed by the legislature of every State, will effectually provide for the same."

The recommendatory act of Congress is in the words following: "WHEREAS, There is provision in the articles of Confederation and perpetual Union, for making alterations therein, by the assent of a Congress of the United States, and of the legislatures of the several States; and whereas experience hath evinced, that there are defects in the present Confederation; as a mean to remedy which, several of the States, and PARTICULARLY THE STATE OF NEW YORK, by express instructions to their delegates in Congress, have suggested a convention for the purposes expressed in the following resolution; and such convention appearing to be the most probable mean of establishing in these States A FIRM NATIONAL GOVERNMENT:

"Resolved, That in the opinion of Congress it is expedient, that on the second Monday of May next a convention of delegates, who shall have been appointed by the several States, be held at Philadelphia, for the sole and express purpose OF REVISING THE ARTICLES OF CONFEDERATION, and reporting to Congress and the several legislatures such ALTERATIONS AND PROVISIONS THEREIN, as shall, when agreed to in Congress, and confirmed by the States, render the federal Constitution ADEQUATE TO THE EXIGENCIES OF GOVERNMENT AND THE PRESERVATION OF THE UNION."

From these two acts, it appears, 1st, that the object of the convention was to establish, in these States, A FIRM NATIONAL GOVERNMENT; 2d, that this government was to be such as would be ADEQUATE TO THE EXIGENCIES OF GOVERNMENT and THE PRESERVATION OF THE UNION; 3d, that these purposes were to be effected by ALTERATIONS AND PROVISIONS IN THE ARTICLES OF CONFEDERATION, as it is expressed in the act of Congress, or by SUCH FURTHER PROVISIONS AS SHOULD APPEAR NECESSARY, as it stands in the recommendatory act from Annapolis; 4th, that the alterations and provisions were to be reported to Congress, and to the States, in order to be agreed to by the former and confirmed by the latter.

From a comparison and fair construction of these several modes of expression, is to be deduced the authority under which the convention acted. They were to frame a NATIONAL GOVERNMENT, adequate to the EXIGENCIES OF GOVERNMENT, and OF THE UNION; and to reduce the articles of Confederation into such form as to accomplish these purposes.

There are two rules of construction, dictated by plain reason, as well as founded on legal axioms. The one is, that every part of the expression ought, if possible, to be allowed some meaning, and be made to conspire to some common end. The other is, that where the several parts cannot be made to coincide, the less important should give way to the more important part; the means should be sacrificed to the end, rather than the end to the means.

Suppose, then, that the expressions defining the authority of the convention were irreconcilably at variance with each other; that a NATIONAL and ADEQUATE GOVERNMENT could not possibly, in the judgment of the convention, be affected by ALTERATIONS and PROVISIONS in the ARTICLES OF CONFEDERATION; which part of the definition ought to have been embraced, and which rejected? Which was the more important, which the less important part? Which the end; which the means? Let the most scrupulous expositors of delegated powers; let the most inveterate objectors against those exercised by the convention, answer these questions. Let them declare, whether it was of most importance to the happiness of the people of America, that the articles of Confederation should be disregarded, and an adequate government be provided, and the Union preserved; or that an adequate government should be omitted, and the articles of Confederation preserved. Let them declare, whether the preservation of these articles was the end, for securing which a reform of the government was to be introduced as the means; or whether the establishment of a government, adequate to the national happiness, was the end at which these articles themselves originally aimed, and to which they ought, as insufficient means, to have been sacrificed.

But is it necessary to suppose that these expressions are absolutely irreconcilable to each other; that no ALTERATIONS or PROVISIONS in the articles of the confederation could possibly mould them into a national and adequate government; into such a government as has been proposed by the convention?

No stress, it is presumed, will, in this case, be laid on the TITLE; a change of that could never be deemed an exercise of ungranted power. ALTERATIONS in the body of the instrument are expressly authorized. NEW PROVISIONS therein are also expressly authorized. Here then is a power to change the title; to insert new articles; to alter old ones. Must it of necessity be admitted that this power is infringed, so long as a part of the old articles remain? Those who maintain the affirmative ought at least to mark the boundary between authorized and usurped innovations; between that degree of change which lies within the compass of ALTERATIONS AND FURTHER PROVISIONS, and that which amounts to a TRANSMUTATION of the government. Will it be said that the alterations ought not to have touched the substance of the Confederation? The States would never have appointed a convention with so much solemnity, nor described its objects with so much latitude, if some SUBSTANTIAL reform had not been in contemplation. Will it be said that the FUNDAMENTAL PRINCIPLES of the Confederation were not within the purview of the convention, and ought not to have been varied? I ask, What are these principles? Do they require that, in the establishment of the Constitution, the States should be regarded as distinct and independent sovereigns? They are so regarded by the Constitution proposed. Do they require that the members of the government should derive their appointment from the legislatures, not from the people of the States? One branch of the new government is to be appointed by these legislatures; and under the Confederation, the delegates to Congress MAY ALL be appointed immediately by the people, and in two States(1) are actually so appointed. Do they require that the powers of the government should act on the States, and not immediately on individuals? In some instances, as has been shown, the powers of the new government will act on the States in their collective characters. In some instances, also, those of the existing government act immediately on individuals. In cases of capture; of piracy; of the post office; of coins, weights, and measures; of trade with the Indians; of claims under grants of land by different States; and, above all, in the case of trials by courts-marshal in the army and navy, by which death may be inflicted without the intervention of a jury, or even of a civil magistrate; in all these cases the powers of the Confederation operate immediately on the persons and interests of individual citizens. Do these fundamental principles require, particularly, that no tax should be levied without the intermediate agency of the States? The Confederation itself authorizes a direct tax, to a certain extent, on the post office. The power of coinage has been so construed by Congress as to levy a tribute immediately from that source also. But pretermitting these instances, was it not an acknowledged object of the convention and the universal expectation of the people, that the regulation of trade should be submitted to the general government in such a form as would render it an immediate source of general revenue? Had not Congress repeatedly recommended this measure as not inconsistent with the fundamental principles of the Confederation? Had not every State but one; had not New York herself, so far complied with the plan of Congress as to recognize the PRINCIPLE of the innovation? Do these principles, in fine, require that the powers of the general government should be limited, and that, beyond this limit, the States should be left in possession of their sovereignty and independence? We have seen that in the new government, as in the old, the general powers are limited; and that the States, in all unenumerated cases, are left in the enjoyment of their sovereign and independent jurisdiction.

The truth is, that the great principles of the Constitution proposed by the convention may be considered less as absolutely new, than as the expansion of principles which are found in the articles of Confederation. The misfortune under the latter system has been, that these principles are so feeble and confined as to justify all the charges of inefficiency which have been urged against it, and to require a degree of enlargement which gives to the new system the aspect of an entire transformation of the old.

In one particular it is admitted that the convention have departed from the tenor of their commission. Instead of reporting a plan requiring the confirmation OF THE LEGISLATURES OF ALL THE STATES, they have reported a plan which is to be confirmed by the PEOPLE, and may be carried into effect by NINE STATES ONLY. It is worthy of remark that this objection, though the most plausible, has been the least urged in the publications which have swarmed against the convention. The forbearance can only have proceeded from an irresistible conviction of the absurdity of subjecting the fate of twelve States to the perverseness or corruption of a thirteenth; from the example of inflexible opposition given by a MAJORITY of one sixtieth of the people of America to a measure approved and called for by the voice of twelve States, comprising fifty-nine sixtieths of the people an example still fresh in the memory and indignation of every citizen who has felt for the wounded honor and prosperity of his country. As this objection, therefore, has been in a manner waived by those who have criticised the powers of the convention, I dismiss it without further observation.

The THIRD point to be inquired into is, how far considerations of duty arising out of the case itself could have supplied any defect of regular authority.

In the preceding inquiries the powers of the convention have been analyzed and tried with the same rigor, and by the same rules, as if they had been real and final powers for the establishment of a Constitution for the United States. We have seen in what manner they have borne the trial even on that supposition. It is time now to recollect that the powers were merely advisory and recommendatory; that they were so meant by the States, and so understood by the convention; and that the latter have accordingly planned and proposed a Constitution which is to be of no more consequence than the paper on which it is written, unless it be stamped with the approbation of those to whom it is addressed. This reflection places the subject in a point of view altogether different, and will enable us to judge with propriety of the course taken by the convention.

Let us view the ground on which the convention stood. It may be collected from their proceedings, that they were deeply and unanimously impressed with the crisis, which had led their country almost with one voice to make so singular and solemn an experiment for correcting the errors of a system by which this crisis had been produced; that they were no less deeply and unanimously convinced that such a reform as they have proposed was absolutely necessary to effect the purposes of their appointment. It could not be unknown to them that the hopes and expectations of the great body of citizens, throughout this great empire, were turned with the keenest anxiety to the event of their deliberations. They had every reason to believe that the contrary sentiments agitated the minds and bosoms of every external and internal foe to the liberty and prosperity of the United States. They had seen in the origin and progress of the experiment, the alacrity with which the PROPOSITION, made by a single State (Virginia), towards a partial amendment of the Confederation, had been attended to and promoted. They had seen the LIBERTY ASSUMED by a VERY FEW deputies from a VERY FEW States, convened at Annapolis, of recommending a great and critical object, wholly foreign to their commission, not only justified by the public opinion, but actually carried into effect by twelve out of the thirteen States. They had seen, in a variety of instances, assumptions by Congress, not only of recommendatory, but of operative, powers, warranted, in the public estimation, by occasions and objects infinitely less urgent than those by which their conduct was to be governed. They must have reflected, that in all great changes of established governments, forms ought to give way to substance; that a rigid adherence in such cases to the former, would render nominal and nugatory the transcendent and precious right of the people to "abolish or alter their governments as to them shall seem most likely to effect their safety and happiness,"(2) since it is impossible for the people spontaneously and universally to move in concert towards their object; and it is therefore essential that such changes be instituted by some INFORMAL AND UNAUTHORIZED PROPOSITIONS, made by some patriotic and respectable citizen or number of citizens. They must have recollected that it was by this irregular and assumed privilege of proposing to the people plans for their safety and happiness, that the States were first united against the danger with which they were threatened by their ancient government; that committees and congresses were formed for concentrating their efforts and defending their rights; and that CONVENTIONS were ELECTED in THE SEVERAL STATES for establishing the constitutions under which they are now governed; nor could it have been forgotten that no little ill-timed scruples, no zeal for adhering to ordinary forms, were anywhere seen, except in those who wished to indulge, under these masks, their secret enmity to the substance contended for. They must have borne in mind, that as the plan to be framed and proposed was to be submitted TO THE PEOPLE THEMSELVES, the disapprobation of this supreme authority would destroy it forever; its approbation blot out antecedent errors and irregularities. It might even have occurred to them, that where a disposition to cavil prevailed, their neglect to execute the degree of power vested in them, and still more their recommendation of any measure whatever, not warranted by their commission, would not less excite animadversion, than a recommendation at once of a measure fully commensurate to the national exigencies.

Had the convention, under all these impressions, and in the midst of all these considerations, instead of exercising a manly confidence in their country, by whose confidence they had been so peculiarly distinguished, and of pointing out a system capable, in their judgment, of securing its happiness, taken the cold and sullen resolution of disappointing its ardent hopes, of sacrificing substance to forms, of committing the dearest interests of their country to the uncertainties of delay and the hazard of events, let me ask the man who can raise his mind to one elevated conception, who can awaken in his bosom one patriotic emotion, what judgment ought to have been pronounced by the impartial world, by the friends of mankind, by every virtuous citizen, on the conduct and character of this assembly? Or if there be a man whose propensity to condemn is susceptible of no control, let me then ask what sentence he has in reserve for the twelve States who USURPED THE POWER of sending deputies to the convention, a body utterly unknown to their constitutions; for Congress, who recommended the appointment of this body, equally unknown to the Confederation; and for the State of New York, in particular, which first urged and then complied with this unauthorized interposition?

But that the objectors may be disarmed of every pretext, it shall be granted for a moment that the convention were neither authorized by their commission, nor justified by circumstances in proposing a Constitution for their country: does it follow that the Constitution ought, for that reason alone, to be rejected? If, according to the noble precept, it be lawful to accept good advice even from an enemy, shall we set the ignoble example of refusing such advice even when it is offered by our friends? The prudent inquiry, in all cases, ought surely to be, not so much FROM WHOM the advice comes, as whether the advice be GOOD.

The sum of what has been here advanced and proved is, that the charge against the convention of exceeding their powers, except in one instance little urged by the objectors, has no foundation to support it; that if they had exceeded their powers, they were not only warranted, but required, as the confidential servants of their country, by the circumstances in which they were placed, to exercise the liberty which they assume; and that finally, if they had violated both their powers and their obligations, in proposing a Constitution, this ought nevertheless to be embraced, if it be calculated to accomplish the views and happiness of the people of America. How far this character is due to the Constitution, is the subject under investigation.

PUBLIUS

1. Connecticut and Rhode Island.
2. Declaration of Independence.

FEDERALIST PAPER NO. 41. GENERAL VIEW OF THE POWERS CONFERRED BY THE CONSTITUTION

For the Independent Journal. Saturday, January 19, 1788

MADISON

To the People of the State of New York:

THE Constitution proposed by the convention may be considered under two general points of view. The FIRST relates to the sum or quantity of power which it vests in the government, including the restraints imposed on the States. The SECOND, to the particular structure of the government, and the distribution of this power among its several branches.

Under the FIRST view of the subject, two important questions arise: 1. Whether any part of the powers transferred to the general government be unnecessary or improper? 2. Whether the entire mass of them be dangerous to the portion of jurisdiction left in the several States?

Is the aggregate power of the general government greater than ought to have been vested in it? This is the FIRST question.

It cannot have escaped those who have attended with candor to the arguments employed against the extensive powers of the government, that the authors of them have very little considered how far these powers were necessary means of attaining a necessary end. They have chosen rather to dwell on the inconveniences which must be unavoidably blended with all political advantages; and on the possible abuses which must be incident to every power or trust, of which a beneficial use can be made. This method of handling the subject cannot impose on the good sense of the people of America. It may display the subtlety of the writer; it may open a boundless field for rhetoric and declamation; it may inflame the passions of the unthinking, and may confirm the prejudices of the misthinking: but cool and candid people will at once reflect, that the purest of human blessings must have a portion of alloy in them; that the choice must always be made, if not of the lesser evil, at least of the GREATER, not the PERFECT, good; and that in every political institution, a power to advance the public happiness involves a discretion which may be misapplied and abused. They will see, therefore, that in all cases where power is to be conferred, the point first to be decided is, whether such a power be necessary to the public good; as the next will be, in case of an affirmative decision, to guard as effectually as possible against a perversion of the power to the public detriment.

That we may form a correct judgment on this subject, it will be proper to review the several powers conferred on the government of the Union; and that this may be the more conveniently done they may be reduced into different classes as they relate to the following different objects: 1. Security against foreign danger; 2. Regulation of the intercourse with foreign nations; 3. Maintenance of harmony and proper intercourse among the States; 4. Certain miscellaneous objects of general utility; 5. Restraint of the States from certain injurious acts; 6. Provisions for giving due efficacy to all these powers.

The powers falling within the FIRST class are those of declaring war and granting letters of marque; of providing armies and fleets; of regulating and calling forth the militia; of levying and borrowing money.

Security against foreign danger is one of the primitive objects of civil society. It is an avowed and essential object of the American Union. The powers requisite for attaining it must be effectually confided to the federal councils.

Is the power of declaring war necessary? No man will answer this question in the negative. It would be superfluous, therefore, to enter into a proof of the affirmative. The existing Confederation establishes this power in the most ample form.

Is the power of raising armies and equipping fleets necessary? This is involved in the foregoing power. It is involved in the power of self-defense.

But was it necessary to give an INDEFINITE POWER of raising TROOPS, as well as providing fleets; and of maintaining both in PEACE, as well as in WAR?

The answer to these questions has been too far anticipated in another place to admit an extensive discussion of them in this place. The answer indeed seems to be so obvious and conclusive as scarcely to justify such a discussion in any place. With what color of propriety could the force necessary for defense be limited by those who cannot limit the force of offense? If a federal Constitution could chain the ambition or set bounds to the exertions of all other nations, then indeed might it prudently chain the discretion of its own government, and set bounds to the exertions for its own safety.

Documents of Revolution

How could a readiness for war in time of peace be safely prohibited, unless we could prohibit, in like manner, the preparations and establishments of every hostile nation? The means of security can only be regulated by the means and the danger of attack. They will, in fact, be ever determined by these rules, and by no others. It is in vain to oppose constitutional barriers to the impulse of self-preservation. It is worse than in vain; because it plants in the Constitution itself necessary usurpations of power, every precedent of which is a germ of unnecessary and multiplied repetitions. If one nation maintains constantly a disciplined army, ready for the service of ambition or revenge, it obliges the most pacific nations who may be within the reach of its enterprises to take corresponding precautions. The fifteenth century was the unhappy epoch of military establishments in the time of peace. They were introduced by Charles VII. of France. All Europe has followed, or been forced into, the example. Had the example not been followed by other nations, all Europe must long ago have worn the chains of a universal monarch. Were every nation except France now to disband its peace establishments, the same event might follow. The veteran legions of Rome were an overmatch for the undisciplined valor of all other nations and rendered her the mistress of the world.

Not the less true is it, that the liberties of Rome proved the final victim to her military triumphs; and that the liberties of Europe, as far as they ever existed, have, with few exceptions, been the price of her military establishments. A standing force, therefore, is a dangerous, at the same time that it may be a necessary, provision. On the smallest scale it has its inconveniences. On an extensive scale its consequences may be fatal. On any scale it is an object of laudable circumspection and precaution. A wise nation will combine all these considerations; and, whilst it does not rashly preclude itself from any resource which may become essential to its safety, will exert all its prudence in diminishing both the necessity and the danger of resorting to one which may be inauspicious to its liberties.

The clearest marks of this prudence are stamped on the proposed Constitution. The Union itself, which it cements and secures, destroys every pretext for a military establishment which could be dangerous. America united, with a handful of troops, or without a single soldier, exhibits a more forbidding posture to foreign ambition than America disunited, with a hundred thousand veterans ready for combat. It was remarked, on a former occasion, that the want of this pretext had saved the liberties of one nation in Europe. Being rendered by her insular situation and her maritime resources impregnable to the armies of her neighbors, the rulers of Great Britain have never been able, by real or artificial dangers, to cheat the public into an extensive peace establishment. The distance of the United States from the powerful nations of the world gives them the same happy security. A dangerous establishment can never be necessary or plausible, so long as they continue a united people. But let it never, for a moment, be forgotten that they are indebted for this advantage to the Union alone. The moment of its dissolution will be the date of a new order of things. The fears of the weaker, or the ambition of the stronger States, or Confederacies, will set the same example in the New, as Charles VII. did in the Old World. The example will be followed here from the same motives which produced universal imitation there. Instead of deriving from our situation the precious advantage which Great Britain has derived from hers, the face of America will be but a copy of that of the continent of Europe. It will present liberty everywhere crushed between standing armies and perpetual taxes. The fortunes of disunited America will be even more disastrous than those of Europe. The sources of evil in the latter are confined to her own limits. No superior powers of another quarter of the globe intrigue among her rival nations, inflame their mutual animosities, and render them the instruments of foreign ambition, jealousy, and revenge. In America the miseries springing from her internal jealousies, contentions, and wars, would form a part only of her lot. A plentiful addition of evils would have their source in that relation in which Europe stands to this quarter of the earth, and which no other quarter of the earth bears to Europe.

This picture of the consequences of disunion cannot be too highly colored, or too often exhibited. Every man who loves peace, every man who loves his country, every man who loves liberty, ought to have it ever before his eyes, that he may cherish in his heart a due attachment to the Union of America, and be able to set a due value on the means of preserving it.

Next to the effectual establishment of the Union, the best possible precaution against danger from standing armies is a limitation of the term for which revenue may be appropriated to their support. This precaution the Constitution has prudently added. I will not repeat here the observations which I flatter myself have placed this subject in a just and satisfactory light. But it may not be improper to take notice of an argument against this part of the Constitution, which has been drawn from the policy and practice of Great Britain. It is said that the continuance of an army in that kingdom requires an annual vote of the legislature; whereas the American Constitution has lengthened this critical period to two years. This is the form in which the comparison is usually stated to the public: but is it a just form? Is it a fair comparison? Does the British Constitution restrain the parliamentary discretion to one year? Does the American impose on the Congress appropriations for two years? On the contrary, it cannot be unknown to the authors of the fallacy themselves, that the British Constitution fixes no limit whatever to the discretion of the legislature, and that the American ties down the legislature to two years, as the longest admissible term.

Documents of Revolution

Had the argument from the British example been truly stated, it would have stood thus: The term for which supplies may be appropriated to the army establishment, though unlimited by the British Constitution, has nevertheless, in practice, been limited by parliamentary discretion to a single year. Now, if in Great Britain, where the House of Commons is elected for seven years; where so great a proportion of the members are elected by so small a proportion of the people; where the electors are so corrupted by the representatives, and the representatives so corrupted by the Crown, the representative body can possess a power to make appropriations to the army for an indefinite term, without desiring, or without daring, to extend the term beyond a single year, ought not suspicion herself to blush, in pretending that the representatives of the United States, elected FREELY by the WHOLE BODY of the people, every SECOND YEAR, cannot be safely intrusted with the discretion over such appropriations, expressly limited to the short period of TWO YEARS?

A bad cause seldom fails to betray itself. Of this truth, the management of the opposition to the federal government is an unvaried exemplification. But among all the blunders which have been committed, none is more striking than the attempt to enlist on that side the prudent jealousy entertained by the people, of standing armies. The attempt has awakened fully the public attention to that important subject; and has led to investigations which must terminate in a thorough and universal conviction, not only that the constitution has provided the most effectual guards against danger from that quarter, but that nothing short of a Constitution fully adequate to the national defense and the preservation of the Union, can save America from as many standing armies as it may be split into States or Confederacies, and from such a progressive augmentation, of these establishments in each, as will render them as burdensome to the properties and ominous to the liberties of the people, as any establishment that can become necessary, under a united and efficient government, must be tolerable to the former and safe to the latter.

The palpable necessity of the power to provide and maintain a navy has protected that part of the Constitution against a spirit of censure, which has spared few other parts. It must, indeed, be numbered among the greatest blessings of America, that as her Union will be the only source of her maritime strength, so this will be a principal source of her security against danger from abroad. In this respect our situation bears another likeness to the insular advantage of Great Britain. The batteries most capable of repelling foreign enterprises on our safety, are happily such as can never be turned by a perfidious government against our liberties.

The inhabitants of the Atlantic frontier are all of them deeply interested in this provision for naval protection, and if they have hitherto been suffered to sleep quietly in their beds; if their property has remained safe against the predatory spirit of licentious adventurers; if their maritime towns have not yet been compelled to ransom themselves from the terrors of a conflagration, by yielding to the exactions of daring and sudden invaders, these instances of good fortune are not to be ascribed to the capacity of the existing government for the protection of those from whom it claims allegiance, but to causes that are fugitive and fallacious. If we except perhaps Virginia and Maryland, which are peculiarly vulnerable on their eastern frontiers, no part of the Union ought to feel more anxiety on this subject than New York. Her seacoast is extensive. A very important district of the State is an island. The State itself is penetrated by a large navigable river for more than fifty leagues. The great emporium of its commerce, the great reservoir of its wealth, lies every moment at the mercy of events, and may almost be regarded as a hostage for ignominious compliances with the dictates of a foreign enemy, or even with the rapacious demands of pirates and barbarians. Should a war be the result of the precarious situation of European affairs, and all the unruly passions attending it be let loose on the ocean, our escape from insults and depredations, not only on that element, but every part of the other bordering on it, will be truly miraculous. In the present condition of America, the States more immediately exposed to these calamities have nothing to hope from the phantom of a general government which now exists; and if their single resources were equal to the task of fortifying themselves against the danger, the object to be protected would be almost consumed by the means of protecting them.

The power of regulating and calling forth the militia has been already sufficiently vindicated and explained.

The power of levying and borrowing money, being the sinew of that which is to be exerted in the national defense, is properly thrown into the same class with it. This power, also, has been examined already with much attention, and has, I trust, been clearly shown to be necessary, both in the extent and form given to it by the Constitution. I will address one additional reflection only to those who contend that the power ought to have been restrained to external—taxation by which they mean, taxes on articles imported from other countries. It cannot be doubted that this will always be a valuable source of revenue; that for a considerable time it must be a principal source; that at this moment it is an essential one. But we may form very mistaken ideas on this subject, if we do not call to mind in our calculations, that the extent of revenue drawn from foreign commerce must vary with the variations, both in the extent and the kind of imports; and that these variations do not correspond with the progress of population, which must be the general measure of the public wants. As long as agriculture continues the sole field of labor, the importation of manufactures must increase as the consumers multiply. As soon as domestic manufactures are begun by the hands not called for by agriculture, the imported manufactures will decrease as the numbers of people increase. In a more remote stage, the imports may consist in a considerable part of raw materials, which will be wrought into articles for exportation, and will, therefore, require rather the encouragement of bounties, than to be loaded with discouraging duties. A system of government, meant for duration, ought to contemplate these revolutions, and be able to accommodate itself to them.

Some, who have not denied the necessity of the power of taxation, have grounded a very fierce attack against the Constitution, on the language in which it is defined. It has been urged and echoed, that the power "to lay and collect taxes, duties, imposts, and excises, to pay the debts, and provide for the common defense and general welfare of the United States," amounts to an unlimited commission to exercise every power which may be alleged to be necessary for the common defense or general welfare. No stronger proof could be given of the distress under which these writers labor for objections, than their stooping to such a misconstruction.

Had no other enumeration or definition of the powers of the Congress been found in the Constitution, than the general expressions just cited, the authors of the objection might have had some color for it; though it would have been difficult to find a reason for so awkward a form of describing an authority to legislate in all possible cases. A power to destroy the freedom of the press, the trial by jury, or even to regulate the course of descents, or the forms of conveyances, must be very singularly expressed by the terms "to raise money for the general welfare."

But what color can the objection have, when a specification of the objects alluded to by these general terms immediately follows, and is not even separated by a longer pause than a semicolon? If the different parts of the same instrument ought to be so expounded, as to give meaning to every part which will bear it, shall one part of the same sentence be excluded altogether from a share in the meaning; and shall the more doubtful and indefinite terms be retained in their full extent, and the clear and precise expressions be denied any signification whatsoever? For what purpose could the enumeration of particular powers be inserted, if these and all others were meant to be included in the preceding general power? Nothing is more natural nor common than first to use a general phrase, and then to explain and qualify it by a recital of particulars. But the idea of an enumeration of particulars which neither explain nor qualify the general meaning, and can have no other effect than to confound and mislead, is an absurdity, which, as we are reduced to the dilemma of charging either on the authors of the objection or on the authors of the Constitution, we must take the liberty of supposing, had not its origin with the latter.

The objection here is the more extraordinary, as it appears that the language used by the convention is a copy from the articles of Confederation. The objects of the Union among the States, as described in article third, are "their common defense, security of their liberties, and mutual and general welfare." The terms of article eighth are still more identical: "All charges of war and all other expenses that shall be incurred for the common defense or general welfare, and allowed by the United States in Congress, shall be defrayed out of a common treasury," etc. A similar language again occurs in article ninth. Construe either of these articles by the rules which would justify the construction put on the new Constitution, and they vest in the existing Congress a power to legislate in all cases whatsoever. But what would have been thought of that assembly, if, attaching themselves to these general expressions, and disregarding the specifications which ascertain and limit their import, they had exercised an unlimited power of providing for the common defense and general welfare? I appeal to the objectors themselves, whether they would in that case have employed the same reasoning in justification of Congress as they now make use of against the convention. How difficult it is for error to escape its own condemnation!

PUBLIUS

FEDERALIST PAPER NO. 42. THE POWERS CONFERRED BY THE CONSTITUTION FURTHER CONSIDERED

From the New York Packet. Tuesday, January 22, 1788.

MADISON

To the People of the State of New York:

THE SECOND class of powers, lodged in the general government, consists of those which regulate the intercourse with foreign nations, to wit: to make treaties; to send and receive ambassadors, other public ministers, and consuls; to define and punish piracies and felonies committed on the high seas, and offenses against the law of nations; to regulate foreign commerce, including a power to prohibit, after the year 1808, the importation of slaves, and to lay an intermediate duty of ten dollars per head, as a discouragement to such importations.

This class of powers forms an obvious and essential branch of the federal administration. If we are to be one nation in any respect, it clearly ought to be in respect to other nations.

The powers to make treaties and to send and receive ambassadors, speak their own propriety. Both of them are comprised in the articles of Confederation, with this difference only, that the former is disembarrassed, by the plan of the convention, of an exception, under which treaties might be substantially frustrated by regulations of the States; and that a power of appointing and receiving "other public ministers and consuls," is expressly and very properly added to the former provision concerning ambassadors. The term ambassador, if taken strictly, as seems to be required by the second of the articles of Confederation, comprehends the highest grade only of public ministers, and excludes the grades which the United States will be most likely to prefer, where foreign embassies may be necessary. And under no latitude of construction will the term comprehend consuls. Yet it has been found expedient, and has been the practice of Congress, to employ the inferior grades of public ministers, and to send and receive consuls.

It is true, that where treaties of commerce stipulate for the mutual appointment of consuls, whose functions are connected with commerce, the admission of foreign consuls may fall within the power of making commercial treaties; and that where no such treaties exist, the mission of American consuls into foreign countries may PERHAPS be covered under the authority, given by the ninth article of the Confederation, to appoint all such civil officers as may be necessary for managing the general affairs of the United States. But the admission of consuls into the United States, where no previous treaty has stipulated it, seems to have been nowhere provided for. A supply of the omission is one of the lesser instances in which the convention have improved on the model before them. But the most minute provisions become important when they tend to obviate the necessity or the pretext for gradual and unobserved usurpations of power. A list of the cases in which Congress have been betrayed, or forced by the defects of the Confederation, into violations of their chartered authorities, would not a little surprise those who have paid no attention to the subject; and would be no inconsiderable argument in favor of the new Constitution, which seems to have provided no less studiously for the lesser, than the more obvious and striking defects of the old.

The power to define and punish piracies and felonies committed on the high seas, and offenses against the law of nations, belongs with equal propriety to the general government, and is a still greater improvement on the articles of Confederation. These articles contain no provision for the case of offenses against the law of nations; and consequently leave it in the power of any indiscreet member to embroil the Confederacy with foreign nations. The provision of the federal articles on the subject of piracies and felonies extends no further than to the establishment of courts for the trial of these offenses. The definition of piracies might, perhaps, without inconveniency, be left to the law of nations; though a legislative definition of them is found in most municipal codes. A definition of felonies on the high seas is evidently requisite. Felony is a term of loose signification, even in the common law of England; and of various import in the statute law of that kingdom. But neither the common nor the statute law of that, or of any other nation, ought to be a standard for the proceedings of this, unless previously made its own by legislative adoption. The meaning of the term, as defined in the codes of the several States, would be as impracticable as the former would be a dishonorable and illegitimate guide. It is not precisely the same in any two of the States; and varies in each with every revision of its criminal laws. For the sake of certainty and uniformity, therefore, the power of defining felonies in this case was in every respect necessary and proper.

Documents of Revolution

The regulation of foreign commerce, having fallen within several views which have been taken of this subject, has been too fully discussed to need additional proofs here of its being properly submitted to the federal administration.

It were doubtless to be wished, that the power of prohibiting the importation of slaves had not been postponed until the year 1808, or rather that it had been suffered to have immediate operation. But it is not difficult to account, either for this restriction on the general government, or for the manner in which the whole clause is expressed. It ought to be considered as a great point gained in favor of humanity, that a period of twenty years may terminate forever, within these States, a traffic which has so long and so loudly upbraided the barbarism of modern policy; that within that period, it will receive a considerable discouragement from the federal government, and may be totally abolished, by a concurrence of the few States which continue the unnatural traffic, in the prohibitory example which has been given by so great a majority of the Union. Happy would it be for the unfortunate Africans, if an equal prospect lay before them of being redeemed from the oppressions of their European brethren!

Attempts have been made to pervert this clause into an objection against the Constitution, by representing it on one side as a criminal toleration of an illicit practice, and on another as calculated to prevent voluntary and beneficial emigrations from Europe to America. I mention these misconstructions, not with a view to give them an answer, for they deserve none, but as specimens of the manner and spirit in which some have thought fit to conduct their opposition to the proposed government.

The powers included in the THIRD class are those which provide for the harmony and proper intercourse among the States.

Under this head might be included the particular restraints imposed on the authority of the States, and certain powers of the judicial department; but the former are reserved for a distinct class, and the latter will be particularly examined when we arrive at the structure and organization of the government. I shall confine myself to a cursory review of the remaining powers comprehended under this third description, to wit: to regulate commerce among the several States and the Indian tribes; to coin money, regulate the value thereof, and of foreign coin; to provide for the punishment of counterfeiting the current coin and securities of the United States; to fix the standard of weights and measures; to establish a uniform rule of naturalization, and uniform laws of bankruptcy, to prescribe the manner in which the public acts, records, and judicial proceedings of each State shall be proved, and the effect they shall have in other States; and to establish post offices and post roads.

The defect of power in the existing Confederacy to regulate the commerce between its several members, is in the number of those which have been clearly pointed out by experience. To the proofs and remarks which former papers have brought into view on this subject, it may be added that without this supplemental provision, the great and essential power of regulating foreign commerce would have been incomplete and ineffectual. A very material object of this power was the relief of the States which import and export through other States, from the improper contributions levied on them by the latter. Were these at liberty to regulate the trade between State and State, it must be foreseen that ways would be found out to load the articles of import and export, during the passage through their jurisdiction, with duties which would fall on the makers of the latter and the consumers of the former. We may be assured by past experience, that such a practice would be introduced by future contrivances; and both by that and a common knowledge of human affairs, that it would nourish unceasing animosities, and not improbably terminate in serious interruptions of the public tranquillity. To those who do not view the question through the medium of passion or of interest, the desire of the commercial States to collect, in any form, an indirect revenue from their uncommercial neighbors, must appear not less impolitic than it is unfair; since it would stimulate the injured party, by resentment as well as interest, to resort to less convenient channels for their foreign trade. But the mild voice of reason, pleading the cause of an enlarged and permanent interest, is but too often drowned, before public bodies as well as individuals, by the clamors of an impatient avidity for immediate and immoderate gain.

The necessity of a superintending authority over the reciprocal trade of confederated States, has been illustrated by other examples as well as our own. In Switzerland, where the Union is so very slight, each canton is obliged to allow to merchandises a passage through its jurisdiction into other cantons, without an augmentation of the tolls. In Germany it is a law of the empire, that the princes and states shall not lay tolls or customs on bridges, rivers, or passages, without the consent of the emperor and the diet; though it appears from a quotation in an antecedent paper, that the practice in this, as in many other instances in that confederacy, has not followed the law, and has produced there the mischiefs which have been foreseen here. Among the restraints imposed by the Union of the Netherlands on its members, one is, that they shall not establish imposts disadvantageous to their neighbors, without the general permission.

The regulation of commerce with the Indian tribes is very properly unfettered from two limitations in the articles of Confederation, which render the provision obscure and contradictory. The power is there restrained to Indians, not members of any of the States, and is not to violate or infringe the legislative right of any State within its own limits. What description of Indians are to be deemed members of a State, is not yet settled, and has been a question of frequent perplexity and contention in the federal councils. And how the trade with Indians, though not members of a State, yet residing within its legislative jurisdiction, can be regulated by an external authority, without so far intruding on the internal rights of legislation, is absolutely incomprehensible. This is not the only case in which the articles of Confederation have inconsiderately endeavored to accomplish impossibilities; to reconcile a partial sovereignty in the Union, with complete sovereignty in the States; to subvert a mathematical axiom, by taking away a part, and letting the whole remain.

All that need be remarked on the power to coin money, regulate the value thereof, and of foreign coin, is, that by providing for this last case, the Constitution has supplied a material omission in the articles of Confederation. The authority of the existing Congress is restrained to the regulation of coin STRUCK by their own authority, or that of the respective States. It must be seen at once that the proposed uniformity in the VALUE of the current coin might be destroyed by subjecting that of foreign coin to the different regulations of the different States.

The punishment of counterfeiting the public securities, as well as the current coin, is submitted of course to that authority which is to secure the value of both.

The regulation of weights and measures is transferred from the articles of Confederation, and is founded on like considerations with the preceding power of regulating coin.

The dissimilarity in the rules of naturalization has long been remarked as a fault in our system, and as laying a foundation for intricate and delicate questions. In the fourth article of the Confederation, it is declared "that the FREE INHABITANTS of each of these States, paupers, vagabonds, and fugitives from justice, excepted, shall be entitled to all privileges and immunities of FREE CITIZENS in the several States; and THE PEOPLE of each State shall, in every other, enjoy all the privileges of trade and commerce," etc. There is a confusion of language here, which is remarkable. Why the terms FREE INHABITANTS are used in one part of the article, FREE CITIZENS in another, and PEOPLE in another; or what was meant by superadding to "all privileges and immunities of free citizens," "all the privileges of trade and commerce," cannot easily be determined. It seems to be a construction scarcely avoidable, however, that those who come under the denomination of FREE INHABITANTS of a State, although not citizens of such State, are entitled, in every other State, to all the privileges of FREE CITIZENS of the latter; that is, to greater privileges than they may be entitled to in their own State: so that it may be in the power of a particular State, or rather every State is laid under a necessity, not only to confer the rights of citizenship in other States upon any whom it may admit to such rights within itself, but upon any whom it may allow to become inhabitants within its jurisdiction. But were an exposition of the term "inhabitants" to be admitted which would confine the stipulated privileges to citizens alone, the difficulty is diminished only, not removed. The very improper power would still be retained by each State, of naturalizing aliens in every other State. In one State, residence for a short term confirms all the rights of citizenship: in another, qualifications of greater importance are required. An alien, therefore, legally incapacitated for certain rights in the latter, may, by previous residence only in the former, elude his incapacity; and thus the law of one State be preposterously rendered paramount to the law of another, within the jurisdiction of the other. We owe it to mere casualty, that very serious embarrassments on this subject have been hitherto escaped. By the laws of several States, certain descriptions of aliens, who had rendered themselves obnoxious, were laid under interdicts inconsistent not only with the rights of citizenship but with the privilege of residence. What would have been the consequence, if such persons, by residence or otherwise, had acquired the character of citizens under the laws of another State, and then asserted their rights as such, both to residence and citizenship, within the State proscribing them? Whatever the legal consequences might have been, other consequences would probably have resulted, of too serious a nature not to be provided against. The new Constitution has accordingly, with great propriety, made provision against them, and all others proceeding from the defect of the Confederation on this head, by authorizing the general government to establish a uniform rule of naturalization throughout the United States.

The power of establishing uniform laws of bankruptcy is so intimately connected with the regulation of commerce, and will prevent so many frauds where the parties or their property may lie or be removed into different States, that the expediency of it seems not likely to be drawn into question.

The power of prescribing by general laws, the manner in which the public acts, records and judicial proceedings of each State shall be proved, and the effect they shall have in other States, is an evident and valuable improvement on the clause relating to this subject in the articles of Confederation. The meaning of the latter is extremely indeterminate, and can be of little importance under any interpretation which it will bear. The power here established may be rendered a very convenient instrument of justice, and be particularly beneficial on the borders of contiguous States, where the effects liable to justice may be suddenly and secretly translated, in any stage of the process, within a foreign jurisdiction.

Documents of Revolution

The power of establishing post roads must, in every view, be a harmless power, and may, perhaps, by judicious management, become productive of great public conveniency. Nothing which tends to facilitate the intercourse between the States can be deemed unworthy of the public care.
PUBLIUS

FEDERALIST PAPER NO. 43. THE SAME SUBJECT CONTINUED (THE POWERS CONFERRED BY THE CONSTITUTION FURTHER CONSIDERED)

For the Independent Journal. Wednesday, January 23, 1788

MADISON

To the People of the State of New York:

THE FOURTH class comprises the following miscellaneous powers:

1. A power "to promote the progress of science and useful arts, by securing, for a limited time, to authors and inventors, the exclusive right to their respective writings and discoveries."

The utility of this power will scarcely be questioned. The copyright of authors has been solemnly adjudged, in Great Britain, to be a right of common law. The right to useful inventions seems with equal reason to belong to the inventors. The public good fully coincides in both cases with the claims of individuals. The States cannot separately make effectual provisions for either of the cases, and most of them have anticipated the decision of this point, by laws passed at the instance of Congress.

2. "To exercise exclusive legislation, in all cases whatsoever, over such district (not exceeding ten miles square) as may, by cession of particular States and the acceptance of Congress, become the seat of the government of the United States; and to exercise like authority over all places purchased by the consent of the legislatures of the States in which the same shall be, for the erection of forts, magazines, arsenals, dockyards, and other needful buildings."

The indispensable necessity of complete authority at the seat of government, carries its own evidence with it. It is a power exercised by every legislature of the Union, I might say of the world, by virtue of its general supremacy. Without it, not only the public authority might be insulted and its proceedings interrupted with impunity; but a dependence of the members of the general government on the State comprehending the seat of the government, for protection in the exercise of their duty, might bring on the national councils an imputation of awe or influence, equally dishonorable to the government and dissatisfactory to the other members of the Confederacy. This consideration has the more weight, as the gradual accumulation of public improvements at the stationary residence of the government would be both too great a public pledge to be left in the hands of a single State, and would create so many obstacles to a removal of the government, as still further to abridge its necessary independence. The extent of this federal district is sufficiently circumscribed to satisfy every jealousy of an opposite nature. And as it is to be appropriated to this use with the consent of the State ceding it; as the State will no doubt provide in the compact for the rights and the consent of the citizens inhabiting it; as the inhabitants will find sufficient inducements of interest to become willing parties to the cession; as they will have had their voice in the election of the government which is to exercise authority over them; as a municipal legislature for local purposes, derived from their own suffrages, will of course be allowed them; and as the authority of the legislature of the State, and of the inhabitants of the ceded part of it, to concur in the cession, will be derived from the whole people of the State in their adoption of the Constitution, every imaginable objection seems to be obviated.

The necessity of a like authority over forts, magazines, etc., established by the general government, is not less evident. The public money expended on such places, and the public property deposited in them, requires that they should be exempt from the authority of the particular State. Nor would it be proper for the places on which the security of the entire Union may depend, to be in any degree dependent on a particular member of it. All objections and scruples are here also obviated, by requiring the concurrence of the States concerned, in every such establishment.

3. "To declare the punishment of treason, but no attainder of treason shall work corruption of blood, or forfeiture, except during the life of the person attained."

As treason may be committed against the United States, the authority of the United States ought to be enabled to punish it. But as new-fangled and artificial treasons have been the great engines by which violent factions, the natural offspring of free government, have usually wreaked their alternate malignity on each other, the convention have, with great judgment, opposed a barrier to this peculiar danger, by inserting a constitutional definition of the crime, fixing the proof necessary for conviction of it, and restraining the Congress, even in punishing it, from extending the consequences of guilt beyond the person of its author.

4. "To admit new States into the Union; but no new State shall be formed or erected within the jurisdiction of any other State; nor any State be formed by the junction of two or more States, or parts of States, without the consent of the legislatures of the States concerned, as well as of the Congress."

In the articles of Confederation, no provision is found on this important subject. Canada was to be admitted of right, on her joining in the measures of the United States; and the other COLONIES, by which were evidently meant the other British colonies, at the discretion of nine States. The eventual establishment of NEW STATES seems to have been overlooked by the compilers of that instrument. We have seen the inconvenience of this omission, and the assumption of power into which Congress have been led by it. With great propriety, therefore, has the new system supplied the defect. The general precaution, that no new States shall be formed, without the concurrence of the federal authority, and that of the States concerned, is consonant to the principles which ought to govern such transactions. The particular precaution against the erection of new States, by the partition of a State without its consent, quiets the jealousy of the larger States; as that of the smaller is quieted by a like precaution, against a junction of States without their consent.

5. "To dispose of and make all needful rules and regulations respecting the territory or other property belonging to the United States," with a proviso, that "nothing in the Constitution shall be so construed as to prejudice any claims of the United States, or of any particular State."

This is a power of very great importance, and required by considerations similar to those which show the propriety of the former. The proviso annexed is proper in itself, and was probably rendered absolutely necessary by jealousies and questions concerning the Western territory sufficiently known to the public.

6. "To guarantee to every State in the Union a republican form of government; to protect each of them against invasion; and on application of the legislature, or of the executive (when the legislature cannot be convened), against domestic violence."

In a confederacy founded on republican principles, and composed of republican members, the superintending government ought clearly to possess authority to defend the system against aristocratic or monarchial innovations. The more intimate the nature of such a union may be, the greater interest have the members in the political institutions of each other; and the greater right to insist that the forms of government under which the compact was entered into should be SUBSTANTIALLY maintained. But a right implies a remedy; and where else could the remedy be deposited, than where it is deposited by the Constitution? Governments of dissimilar principles and forms have been found less adapted to a federal coalition of any sort, than those of a kindred nature. "As the confederate republic of Germany," says Montesquieu, "consists of free cities and petty states, subject to different princes, experience shows us that it is more imperfect than that of Holland and Switzerland." "Greece was undone," he adds, "as soon as the king of Macedon obtained a seat among the Amphictyons." In the latter case, no doubt, the disproportionate force, as well as the monarchical form, of the new confederate, had its share of influence on the events. It may possibly be asked, what need there could be of such a precaution, and whether it may not become a pretext for alterations in the State governments, without the concurrence of the States themselves. These questions admit of ready answers. If the interposition of the general government should not be needed, the provision for such an event will be a harmless superfluity only in the Constitution. But who can say what experiments may be produced by the caprice of particular States, by the ambition of enterprising leaders, or by the intrigues and influence of foreign powers? To the second question it may be answered, that if the general government should interpose by virtue of this constitutional authority, it will be, of course, bound to pursue the authority. But the authority extends no further than to a GUARANTY of a republican form of government, which supposes a pre-existing government of the form which is to be guaranteed. As long, therefore, as the existing republican forms are continued by the States, they are guaranteed by the federal Constitution. Whenever the States may choose to substitute other republican forms, they have a right to do so, and to claim the federal guaranty for the latter. The only restriction imposed on them is, that they shall not exchange republican for antirepublican Constitutions; a restriction which, it is presumed, will hardly be considered as a grievance.

A protection against invasion is due from every society to the parts composing it. The latitude of the expression here used seems to secure each State, not only against foreign hostility, but against ambitious or vindictive enterprises of its more powerful neighbors. The history, both of ancient and modern confederacies, proves that the weaker members of the union ought not to be insensible to the policy of this article.

Protection against domestic violence is added with equal propriety. It has been remarked, that even among the Swiss cantons, which, properly speaking, are not under one government, provision is made for this object; and the history of that league informs us that mutual aid is frequently claimed and afforded; and as well by the most democratic, as the other cantons. A recent and well-known event among ourselves has warned us to be prepared for emergencies of a like nature.

At first view, it might seem not to square with the republican theory, to suppose, either that a majority have not the right, or that a minority will have the force, to subvert a government; and consequently, that the federal interposition can never be required, but when it would be improper. But theoretic reasoning, in this as in most other cases, must be qualified by the lessons of practice. Why may not illicit combinations, for purposes of violence, be formed as well by a majority of a State, especially a small State as by a majority of a county, or a district of the same State; and if the authority of the State ought, in the latter case, to protect the local magistracy, ought not the federal authority, in the former, to support the State authority? Besides, there are certain parts of the State constitutions which are so interwoven with the federal Constitution, that a violent blow cannot be given to the one without communicating the wound to the other. Insurrections in a State will rarely induce a federal interposition, unless the number concerned in them bear some proportion to the friends of government. It will be much better that the violence in such cases should be repressed by the superintending power, than that the majority should be left to maintain their cause by a bloody and obstinate contest. The existence of a right to interpose, will generally prevent the necessity of exerting it.

Is it true that force and right are necessarily on the same side in republican governments? May not the minor party possess such a superiority of pecuniary resources, of military talents and experience, or of secret succors from foreign powers, as will render it superior also in an appeal to the sword? May not a more compact and advantageous position turn the scale on the same side, against a superior number so situated as to be less capable of a prompt and collected exertion of its strength? Nothing can be more chimerical than to imagine that in a trial of actual force, victory may be calculated by the rules which prevail in a census of the inhabitants, or which determine the event of an election! May it not happen, in fine, that the minority of CITIZENS may become a majority of PERSONS, by the accession of alien residents, of a casual concourse of adventurers, or of those whom the constitution of the State has not admitted to the rights of suffrage? I take no notice of an unhappy species of population abounding in some of the States, who, during the calm of regular government, are sunk below the level of men; but who, in the tempestuous scenes of civil violence, may emerge into the human character, and give a superiority of strength to any party with which they may associate themselves.

In cases where it may be doubtful on which side justice lies, what better umpires could be desired by two violent factions, flying to arms, and tearing a State to pieces, than the representatives of confederate States, not heated by the local flame? To the impartiality of judges, they would unite the affection of friends. Happy would it be if such a remedy for its infirmities could be enjoyed by all free governments; if a project equally effectual could be established for the universal peace of mankind!

Should it be asked, what is to be the redress for an insurrection pervading all the States, and comprising a superiority of the entire force, though not a constitutional right? the answer must be, that such a case, as it would be without the compass of human remedies, so it is fortunately not within the compass of human probability; and that it is a sufficient recommendation of the federal Constitution, that it diminishes the risk of a calamity for which no possible constitution can provide a cure.

Among the advantages of a confederate republic enumerated by Montesquieu, an important one is, "that should a popular insurrection happen in one of the States, the others are able to quell it. Should abuses creep into one part, they are reformed by those that remain sound."

7. "To consider all debts contracted, and engagements entered into, before the adoption of this Constitution, as being no less valid against the United States, under this Constitution, than under the Confederation."

This can only be considered as a declaratory proposition; and may have been inserted, among other reasons, for the satisfaction of the foreign creditors of the United States, who cannot be strangers to the pretended doctrine, that a change in the political form of civil society has the magical effect of dissolving its moral obligations.

Among the lesser criticisms which have been exercised on the Constitution, it has been remarked that the validity of engagements ought to have been asserted in favor of the United States, as well as against them; and in the spirit which usually characterizes little critics, the omission has been transformed and magnified into a plot against the national rights. The authors of this discovery may be told, what few others need to be informed of, that as engagements are in their nature reciprocal, an assertion of their validity on one side, necessarily involves a validity on the other side; and that as the article is merely declaratory, the establishment of the principle in one case is sufficient for every case. They may be further told, that every constitution must limit its precautions to dangers that are not altogether imaginary; and that no real danger can exist that the government would DARE, with, or even without, this constitutional declaration before it, to remit the debts justly due to the public, on the pretext here condemned.

8. "To provide for amendments to be ratified by three fourths of the States under two exceptions only."

That useful alterations will be suggested by experience, could not but be foreseen. It was requisite, therefore, that a mode for introducing them should be provided. The mode preferred by the convention seems to be stamped with every mark of propriety. It guards equally against that extreme facility, which would render the Constitution too mutable; and that extreme difficulty, which might perpetuate its discovered faults. It, moreover, equally enables the general and the State governments to originate the amendment of errors, as they may be pointed out by the experience on one side, or on the other. The exception in favor of the equality of suffrage in the Senate, was probably meant as a palladium to the residuary sovereignty of the States, implied and secured by that principle of representation in one branch of the legislature; and was probably insisted on by the States particularly attached to that equality. The other exception must have been admitted on the same considerations which produced the privilege defended by it.

9. "The ratification of the conventions of nine States shall be sufficient for the establishment of this Constitution between the States, ratifying the same."

This article speaks for itself. The express authority of the people alone could give due validity to the Constitution. To have required the unanimous ratification of the thirteen States, would have subjected the essential interests of the whole to the caprice or corruption of a single member. It would have marked a want of foresight in the convention, which our own experience would have rendered inexcusable.

Two questions of a very delicate nature present themselves on this occasion: 1. On what principle the Confederation, which stands in the solemn form of a compact among the States, can be superseded without the unanimous consent of the parties to it? 2. What relation is to subsist between the nine or more States ratifying the Constitution, and the remaining few who do not become parties to it?

The first question is answered at once by recurring to the absolute necessity of the case; to the great principle of self-preservation; to the transcendent law of nature and of nature's God, which declares that the safety and happiness of society are the objects at which all political institutions aim, and to which all such institutions must be sacrificed. PERHAPS, also, an answer may be found without searching beyond the principles of the compact itself. It has been heretofore noted among the defects of the Confederation, that in many of the States it had received no higher sanction than a mere legislative ratification. The principle of reciprocality seems to require that its obligation on the other States should be reduced to the same standard. A compact between independent sovereigns, founded on ordinary acts of legislative authority, can pretend to no higher validity than a league or treaty between the parties. It is an established doctrine on the subject of treaties, that all the articles are mutually conditions of each other; that a breach of any one article is a breach of the whole treaty; and that a breach, committed by either of the parties, absolves the others, and authorizes them, if they please, to pronounce the compact violated and void. Should it unhappily be necessary to appeal to these delicate truths for a justification for dispensing with the consent of particular States to a dissolution of the federal pact, will not the complaining parties find it a difficult task to answer the MULTIPLIED and IMPORTANT infractions with which they may be confronted? The time has been when it was incumbent on us all to veil the ideas which this paragraph exhibits. The scene is now changed, and with it the part which the same motives dictate.

The second question is not less delicate; and the flattering prospect of its being merely hypothetical forbids an overcurious discussion of it. It is one of those cases which must be left to provide for itself. In general, it may be observed, that although no political relation can subsist between the assenting and dissenting States, yet the moral relations will remain uncancelled. The claims of justice, both on one side and on the other, will be in force, and must be fulfilled; the rights of humanity must in all cases be duly and mutually respected; whilst considerations of a common interest, and, above all, the remembrance of the endearing scenes which are past, and the anticipation of a speedy triumph over the obstacles to reunion, will, it is hoped, not urge in vain MODERATION on one side, and PRUDENCE on the other.

PUBLIUS

FEDERALIST PAPER NO. 44. RESTRICTIONS ON THE AUTHORITY OF THE SEVERAL STATES

From the New York Packet. Friday, January 25, 1788.

MADISON

To the People of the State of New York:

A FIFTH class of provisions in favor of the federal authority consists of the following restrictions on the authority of the several States:

1. "No State shall enter into any treaty, alliance, or confederation; grant letters of marque and reprisal; coin money; emit bills of credit; make any thing but gold and silver a legal tender in payment of debts; pass any bill of attainder, ex post facto law, or law impairing the obligation of contracts; or grant any title of nobility."

The prohibition against treaties, alliances, and confederations makes a part of the existing articles of Union; and for reasons which need no explanation, is copied into the new Constitution. The prohibition of letters of marque is another part of the old system, but is somewhat extended in the new. According to the former, letters of marque could be granted by the States after a declaration of war; according to the latter, these licenses must be obtained, as well during war as previous to its declaration, from the government of the United States. This alteration is fully justified by the advantage of uniformity in all points which relate to foreign powers; and of immediate responsibility to the nation in all those for whose conduct the nation itself is to be responsible.

The right of coining money, which is here taken from the States, was left in their hands by the Confederation, as a concurrent right with that of Congress, under an exception in favor of the exclusive right of Congress to regulate the alloy and value. In this instance, also, the new provision is an improvement on the old. Whilst the alloy and value depended on the general authority, a right of coinage in the particular States could have no other effect than to multiply expensive mints and diversify the forms and weights of the circulating pieces. The latter inconveniency defeats one purpose for which the power was originally submitted to the federal head; and as far as the former might prevent an inconvenient remittance of gold and silver to the central mint for recoinage, the end can be as well attained by local mints established under the general authority.

The extension of the prohibition to bills of credit must give pleasure to every citizen, in proportion to his love of justice and his knowledge of the true springs of public prosperity. The loss which America has sustained since the peace, from the pestilent effects of paper money on the necessary confidence between man and man, on the necessary confidence in the public councils, on the industry and morals of the people, and on the character of republican government, constitutes an enormous debt against the States chargeable with this unadvised measure, which must long remain unsatisfied; or rather an accumulation of guilt, which can be expiated no otherwise than by a voluntary sacrifice on the altar of justice, of the power which has been the instrument of it. In addition to these persuasive considerations, it may be observed, that the same reasons which show the necessity of denying to the States the power of regulating coin, prove with equal force that they ought not to be at liberty to substitute a paper medium in the place of coin. Had every State a right to regulate the value of its coin, there might be as many different currencies as States, and thus the intercourse among them would be impeded; retrospective alterations in its value might be made, and thus the citizens of other States be injured, and animosities be kindled among the States themselves. The subjects of foreign powers might suffer from the same cause, and hence the Union be discredited and embroiled by the indiscretion of a single member. No one of these mischiefs is less incident to a power in the States to emit paper money, than to coin gold or silver. The power to make any thing but gold and silver a tender in payment of debts, is withdrawn from the States, on the same principle with that of issuing a paper currency.

Bills of attainder, ex post facto laws, and laws impairing the obligation of contracts, are contrary to the first principles of the social compact, and to every principle of sound legislation. The two former are expressly prohibited by the declarations prefixed to some of the State constitutions, and all of them are prohibited by the spirit and scope of these fundamental charters. Our own experience has taught us, nevertheless, that additional fences against these dangers ought not to be omitted. Very properly, therefore, have the convention added this constitutional bulwark in favor of personal security and private rights; and I am much deceived if they have not, in so doing, as faithfully consulted the genuine sentiments as the undoubted interests of their constituents. The sober people of America are weary of the fluctuating policy which has directed the public councils. They have seen with regret and indignation that sudden changes and legislative interferences, in cases affecting personal rights, become jobs in the hands of enterprising and influential speculators, and snares to the more-industrious and less-informed part of the community. They have seen, too, that one legislative interference is but the first link of a long chain of repetitions, every subsequent interference being naturally produced by the effects of the preceding. They very rightly infer, therefore, that some thorough reform is wanting, which will banish speculations on public measures, inspire a general prudence and industry, and give a regular course to the business of society. The prohibition with respect to titles of nobility is copied from the articles of Confederation and needs no comment.

2. "No State shall, without the consent of the Congress, lay any imposts or duties on imports or exports, except what may be absolutely necessary for executing its inspection laws, and the net produce of all duties and imposts laid by any State on imports or exports, shall be for the use of the treasury of the United States; and all such laws shall be subject to the revision and control of the Congress. No State shall, without the consent of Congress, lay any duty on tonnage, keep troops or ships of war in time of peace, enter into any agreement or compact with another State, or with a foreign power, or engage in war unless actually invaded, or in such imminent danger as will not admit of delay."

The restraint on the power of the States over imports and exports is enforced by all the arguments which prove the necessity of submitting the regulation of trade to the federal councils. It is needless, therefore, to remark further on this head, than that the manner in which the restraint is qualified seems well calculated at once to secure to the States a reasonable discretion in providing for the conveniency of their imports and exports, and to the United States a reasonable check against the abuse of this discretion. The remaining particulars of this clause fall within reasonings which are either so obvious, or have been so fully developed, that they may be passed over without remark.

The SIXTH and last class consists of the several powers and provisions by which efficacy is given to all the rest.

1. Of these the first is, the "power to make all laws which shall be necessary and proper for carrying into execution the foregoing powers, and all other powers vested by this Constitution in the government of the United States, or in any department or officer thereof."

Few parts of the Constitution have been assailed with more intemperance than this; yet on a fair investigation of it, no part can appear more completely invulnerable. Without the SUBSTANCE of this power, the whole Constitution would be a dead letter. Those who object to the article, therefore, as a part of the Constitution, can only mean that the FORM of the provision is improper. But have they considered whether a better form could have been substituted?

There are four other possible methods which the Constitution might have taken on this subject. They might have copied the second article of the existing Confederation, which would have prohibited the exercise of any power not EXPRESSLY delegated; they might have attempted a positive enumeration of the powers comprehended under the general terms "necessary and proper"; they might have attempted a negative enumeration of them, by specifying the powers excepted from the general definition; they might have been altogether silent on the subject, leaving these necessary and proper powers to construction and inference.

Had the convention taken the first method of adopting the second article of Confederation, it is evident that the new Congress would be continually exposed, as their predecessors have been, to the alternative of construing the term "EXPRESSLY" with so much rigor, as to disarm the government of all real authority whatever, or with so much latitude as to destroy altogether the force of the restriction. It would be easy to show, if it were necessary, that no important power, delegated by the articles of Confederation, has been or can be executed by Congress, without recurring more or less to the doctrine of CONSTRUCTION or IMPLICATION. As the powers delegated under the new system are more extensive, the government which is to administer it would find itself still more distressed with the alternative of betraying the public interests by doing nothing, or of violating the Constitution by exercising powers indispensably necessary and proper, but, at the same time, not EXPRESSLY granted.

Had the convention attempted a positive enumeration of the powers necessary and proper for carrying their other powers into effect, the attempt would have involved a complete digest of laws on every subject to which the Constitution relates; accommodated too, not only to the existing state of things, but to all the possible changes which futurity may produce; for in every new application of a general power, the PARTICULAR POWERS, which are the means of attaining the OBJECT of the general power, must always necessarily vary with that object, and be often properly varied whilst the object remains the same.

Had they attempted to enumerate the particular powers or means not necessary or proper for carrying the general powers into execution, the task would have been no less chimerical; and would have been liable to this further objection, that every defect in the enumeration would have been equivalent to a positive grant of authority. If, to avoid this consequence, they had attempted a partial enumeration of the exceptions, and described the residue by the general terms, NOT NECESSARY OR

PROPER, it must have happened that the enumeration would comprehend a few of the excepted powers only; that these would be such as would be least likely to be assumed or tolerated, because the enumeration would of course select such as would be least necessary or proper; and that the unnecessary and improper powers included in the residuum, would be less forcibly excepted, than if no partial enumeration had been made.

Had the Constitution been silent on this head, there can be no doubt that all the particular powers requisite as means of executing the general powers would have resulted to the government, by unavoidable implication. No axiom is more clearly established in law, or in reason, than that wherever the end is required, the means are authorized; wherever a general power to do a thing is given, every particular power necessary for doing it is included. Had this last method, therefore, been pursued by the convention, every objection now urged against their plan would remain in all its plausibility; and the real inconveniency would be incurred of not removing a pretext which may be seized on critical occasions for drawing into question the essential powers of the Union.

If it be asked what is to be the consequence, in case the Congress shall misconstrue this part of the Constitution, and exercise powers not warranted by its true meaning, I answer, the same as if they should misconstrue or enlarge any other power vested in them; as if the general power had been reduced to particulars, and any one of these were to be violated; the same, in short, as if the State legislatures should violate the irrespective constitutional authorities. In the first instance, the success of the usurpation will depend on the executive and judiciary departments, which are to expound and give effect to the legislative acts; and in the last resort a remedy must be obtained from the people who can, by the election of more faithful representatives, annul the acts of the usurpers. The truth is, that this ultimate redress may be more confided in against unconstitutional acts of the federal than of the State legislatures, for this plain reason, that as every such act of the former will be an invasion of the rights of the latter, these will be ever ready to mark the innovation, to sound the alarm to the people, and to exert their local influence in effecting a change of federal representatives. There being no such intermediate body between the State legislatures and the people interested in watching the conduct of the former, violations of the State constitutions are more likely to remain unnoticed and unredressed.

2. "This Constitution and the laws of the United States which shall be made in pursuance thereof, and all treaties made, or which shall be made, under the authority of the United States, shall be the supreme law of the land, and the judges in every State shall be bound thereby, any thing in the constitution or laws of any State to the contrary notwithstanding."

The indiscreet zeal of the adversaries to the Constitution has betrayed them into an attack on this part of it also, without which it would have been evidently and radically defective. To be fully sensible of this, we need only suppose for a moment that the supremacy of the State constitutions had been left complete by a saving clause in their favor.

In the first place, as these constitutions invest the State legislatures with absolute sovereignty, in all cases not excepted by the existing articles of Confederation, all the authorities contained in the proposed Constitution, so far as they exceed those enumerated in the Confederation, would have been annulled, and the new Congress would have been reduced to the same impotent condition with their predecessors.

In the next place, as the constitutions of some of the States do not even expressly and fully recognize the existing powers of the Confederacy, an express saving of the supremacy of the former would, in such States, have brought into question every power contained in the proposed Constitution.

In the third place, as the constitutions of the States differ much from each other, it might happen that a treaty or national law, of great and equal importance to the States, would interfere with some and not with other constitutions, and would consequently be valid in some of the States, at the same time that it would have no effect in others.

In fine, the world would have seen, for the first time, a system of government founded on an inversion of the fundamental principles of all government; it would have seen the authority of the whole society every where subordinate to the authority of the parts; it would have seen a monster, in which the head was under the direction of the members.

3. "The Senators and Representatives, and the members of the several State legislatures, and all executive and judicial officers, both of the United States and the several States, shall be bound by oath or affirmation to support this Constitution."

It has been asked why it was thought necessary, that the State magistracy should be bound to support the federal Constitution, and unnecessary that a like oath should be imposed on the officers of the United States, in favor of the State constitutions.

Several reasons might be assigned for the distinction. I content myself with one, which is obvious and conclusive. The members of the federal government will have no agency in carrying the State constitutions into effect. The members and officers of the State governments, on the contrary, will have an essential agency in giving effect to the federal Constitution. The election of the President and Senate will depend, in all cases, on the legislatures of the several States. And the election of the

House of Representatives will equally depend on the same authority in the first instance; and will, probably, forever be conducted by the officers, and according to the laws, of the States.

4. Among the provisions for giving efficacy to the federal powers might be added those which belong to the executive and judiciary departments: but as these are reserved for particular examination in another place, I pass them over in this.

We have now reviewed, in detail, all the articles composing the sum or quantity of power delegated by the proposed Constitution to the federal government, and are brought to this undeniable conclusion, that no part of the power is unnecessary or improper for accomplishing the necessary objects of the Union. The question, therefore, whether this amount of power shall be granted or not, resolves itself into another question, whether or not a government commensurate to the exigencies of the Union shall be established; or, in other words, whether the Union itself shall be preserved.

PUBLIUS

FEDERALIST PAPER NO. 45. THE ALLEGED DANGER FROM THE POWERS OF THE UNION TO THE STATE GOVERNMENTS.

Considered For the Independent Journal. Saturday, January 26, 1788

MADISON

To the People of the State of New York:

HAVING shown that no one of the powers transferred to the federal government is unnecessary or improper, the next question to be considered is, whether the whole mass of them will be dangerous to the portion of authority left in the several States.

The adversaries to the plan of the convention, instead of considering in the first place what degree of power was absolutely necessary for the purposes of the federal government, have exhausted themselves in a secondary inquiry into the possible consequences of the proposed degree of power to the governments of the particular States. But if the Union, as has been shown, be essential to the security of the people of America against foreign danger; if it be essential to their security against contentions and wars among the different States; if it be essential to guard them against those violent and oppressive factions which embitter the blessings of liberty, and against those military establishments which must gradually poison its very fountain; if, in a word, the Union be essential to the happiness of the people of America, is it not preposterous, to urge as an objection to a government, without which the objects of the Union cannot be attained, that such a government may derogate from the importance of the governments of the individual States? Was, then, the American Revolution effected, was the American Confederacy formed, was the precious blood of thousands spilt, and the hard-earned substance of millions lavished, not that the people of America should enjoy peace, liberty, and safety, but that the government of the individual States, that particular municipal establishments, might enjoy a certain extent of power, and be arrayed with certain dignities and attributes of sovereignty? We have heard of the impious doctrine in the Old World, that the people were made for kings, not kings for the people. Is the same doctrine to be revived in the New, in another shape that the solid happiness of the people is to be sacrificed to the views of political institutions of a different form? It is too early for politicians to presume on our forgetting that the public good, the real welfare of the great body of the people, is the supreme object to be pursued; and that no form of government whatever has any other value than as it may be fitted for the attainment of this object. Were the plan of the convention adverse to the public happiness, my voice would be, Reject the plan. Were the Union itself inconsistent with the public happiness, it would be, Abolish the Union. In like manner, as far as the sovereignty of the States cannot be reconciled to the happiness of the people, the voice of every good citizen must be, Let the former be sacrificed to the latter. How far the sacrifice is necessary, has been shown. How far the unsacrificed residue will be endangered, is the question before us.

Several important considerations have been touched in the course of these papers, which discountenance the supposition that the operation of the federal government will by degrees prove fatal to the State governments. The more I revolve the subject, the more fully I am persuaded that the balance is much more likely to be disturbed by the preponderancy of the last than of the first scale.

We have seen, in all the examples of ancient and modern confederacies, the strongest tendency continually betraying itself in the members, to despoil the general government of its authorities, with a very ineffectual capacity in the latter to defend itself against the encroachments. Although, in most of these examples, the system has been so dissimilar from that under consideration as greatly to weaken any inference concerning the latter from the fate of the former, yet, as the States will retain, under the proposed Constitution, a very extensive portion of active sovereignty, the inference ought not to be wholly disregarded. In the Achaean league it is probable that the federal head had a degree and species of power, which gave it a considerable likeness to the government framed by the convention. The Lycian Confederacy, as far as its principles and form are transmitted, must have borne a still greater analogy to it. Yet history does not inform us that either of them ever degenerated, or tended to degenerate, into one consolidated government. On the contrary, we know that the ruin of one of them proceeded from the incapacity of the federal authority to prevent the dissensions, and finally the disunion, of the subordinate authorities. These cases are the more worthy of our attention, as the external causes by which the component parts were pressed together were much more numerous and powerful than in our case; and consequently less powerful ligaments within would be sufficient to bind the members to the head, and to each other.

In the feudal system, we have seen a similar propensity exemplified. Notwithstanding the want of proper sympathy in every instance between the local sovereigns and the people, and the sympathy in some instances between the general sovereign and the latter, it usually happened that the local sovereigns prevailed in the rivalship for encroachments. Had no external dangers enforced internal harmony and subordination, and particularly, had the local sovereigns possessed the affections of the people, the great kingdoms in Europe would at this time consist of as many independent princes as there were formerly feudatory barons.

The State governments will have the advantage of the Federal government, whether we compare them in respect to the immediate dependence of the one on the other; to the weight of personal influence which each side will possess; to the powers respectively vested in them; to the predilection and probable support of the people; to the disposition and faculty of resisting and frustrating the measures of each other.

The State governments may be regarded as constituent and essential parts of the federal government; whilst the latter is nowise essential to the operation or organization of the former. Without the intervention of the State legislatures, the President of the United States cannot be elected at all. They must in all cases have a great share in his appointment, and will, perhaps, in most cases, of themselves determine it. The Senate will be elected absolutely and exclusively by the State legislatures. Even the House of Representatives, though drawn immediately from the people, will be chosen very much under the influence of that class of men, whose influence over the people obtains for themselves an election into the State legislatures. Thus, each of the principal branches of the federal government will owe its existence more or less to the favor of the State governments, and must consequently feel a dependence, which is much more likely to beget a disposition too obsequious than too overbearing towards them. On the other side, the component parts of the State governments will in no instance be indebted for their appointment to the direct agency of the federal government, and very little, if at all, to the local influence of its members.

The number of individuals employed under the Constitution of the United States will be much smaller than the number employed under the particular States. There will consequently be less of personal influence on the side of the former than of the latter. The members of the legislative, executive, and judiciary departments of thirteen and more States, the justices of peace, officers of militia, ministerial officers of justice, with all the county, corporation, and town officers, for three millions and more of people, intermixed, and having particular acquaintance with every class and circle of people, must exceed, beyond all proportion, both in number and influence, those of every description who will be employed in the administration of the federal system. Compare the members of the three great departments of the thirteen States, excluding from the judiciary department the justices of peace, with the members of the corresponding departments of the single government of the Union; compare the militia officers of three millions of people with the military and marine officers of any establishment which is within the compass of probability, or, I may add, of possibility, and in this view alone, we may pronounce the advantage of the States to be decisive. If the federal government is to have collectors of revenue, the State governments will have theirs also. And as those of the former will be principally on the seacoast, and not very numerous, whilst those of the latter will be spread over the face of the country, and will be very numerous, the advantage in this view also lies on the same side. It is true, that the Confederacy is to possess, and may exercise, the power of collecting internal as well as external taxes throughout the States; but it is probable that this power will not be resorted to, except for supplemental purposes of revenue; that an option will then be given to the States to supply their quotas by previous collections of their own; and that the eventual collection, under the immediate authority of the Union, will generally be made by the officers, and according to the rules, appointed by the several States. Indeed it is extremely probable, that in other instances, particularly in the organization of the judicial power, the officers of the States will be clothed with the correspondent authority of the Union. Should it happen, however, that separate collectors of internal revenue should be appointed under the federal government, the influence of the whole number would not bear a comparison with that of the multitude of State officers in the opposite scale. Within every district to which a federal collector would be allotted, there would not be less than thirty or forty, or even more, officers of different descriptions, and many of them persons of character and weight, whose influence would lie on the side of the State.

The powers delegated by the proposed Constitution to the federal government, are few and defined. Those which are to remain in the State governments are numerous and indefinite. The former will be exercised principally on external objects, as war, peace, negotiation, and foreign commerce; with which last the power of taxation will, for the most part, be connected. The powers reserved to the several States will extend to all the objects which, in the ordinary course of affairs, concern the lives, liberties, and properties of the people, and the internal order, improvement, and prosperity of the State.

The operations of the federal government will be most extensive and important in times of war and danger; those of the State governments, in times of peace and security. As the former periods will probably bear a small proportion to the latter, the State governments will here enjoy another advantage over the federal government. The more adequate, indeed, the federal powers may be rendered to the national defense, the less frequent will be those scenes of danger which might favor their ascendancy over the governments of the particular States.

If the new Constitution be examined with accuracy and candor, it will be found that the change which it proposes consists much less in the addition of NEW POWERS to the Union, than in the invigoration of its ORIGINAL POWERS. The regulation of commerce, it is true, is a new power; but that seems to be an addition which few oppose, and from which no apprehensions are entertained. The powers relating to war and peace, armies and fleets, treaties and finance, with the other more considerable powers, are all vested in the existing Congress by the articles of Confederation. The proposed change does not enlarge these powers; it only substitutes a more effectual mode of administering them. The change relating to taxation may be regarded as the most important; and yet the present Congress have as complete authority to REQUIRE of the States indefinite supplies of money for the common defense and general welfare, as the future Congress will have to require them of individual citizens; and the latter will be no more bound than the States themselves have been, to pay the quotas respectively taxed on them. Had the States complied punctually with the articles of Confederation, or could their compliance have been enforced by as peaceable means as may be used with success towards single persons, our past experience is very far from countenancing an opinion, that the State governments would have lost their constitutional powers, and have gradually undergone an entire consolidation. To maintain that such an event would have ensued, would be to say at once, that the existence of the State governments is incompatible with any system whatever that accomplishes the essential purposes of the Union.

PUBLIUS

Documents of Revolution

FEDERALIST PAPER NO. 46. THE INFLUENCE OF THE STATE AND FEDERAL GOVERNMENTS COMPARED

From the New York Packet. Tuesday, January 29, 1788.

MADISON

To the People of the State of New York:

RESUMING the subject of the last paper, I proceed to inquire whether the federal government or the State governments will have the advantage with regard to the predilection and support of the people. Notwithstanding the different modes in which they are appointed, we must consider both of them as substantially dependent on the great body of the citizens of the United States. I assume this position here as it respects the first, reserving the proofs for another place. The federal and State governments are in fact but different agents and trustees of the people, constituted with different powers, and designed for different purposes. The adversaries of the Constitution seem to have lost sight of the people altogether in their reasonings on this subject; and to have viewed these different establishments, not only as mutual rivals and enemies, but as uncontrolled by any common superior in their efforts to usurp the authorities of each other. These gentlemen must here be reminded of their error. They must be told that the ultimate authority, wherever the derivative may be found, resides in the people alone, and that it will not depend merely on the comparative ambition or address of the different governments, whether either, or which of them, will be able to enlarge its sphere of jurisdiction at the expense of the other. Truth, no less than decency, requires that the event in every case should be supposed to depend on the sentiments and sanction of their common constituents.

Many considerations, besides those suggested on a former occasion, seem to place it beyond doubt that the first and most natural attachment of the people will be to the governments of their respective States. Into the administration of these a greater number of individuals will expect to rise. From the gift of these a greater number of offices and emoluments will flow. By the superintending care of these, all the more domestic and personal interests of the people will be regulated and provided for. With the affairs of these, the people will be more familiarly and minutely conversant. And with the members of these, will a greater proportion of the people have the ties of personal acquaintance and friendship, and of family and party attachments; on the side of these, therefore, the popular bias may well be expected most strongly to incline.

Experience speaks the same language in this case. The federal administration, though hitherto very defective in comparison with what may be hoped under a better system, had, during the war, and particularly whilst the independent fund of paper emissions was in credit, an activity and importance as great as it can well have in any future circumstances whatever. It was engaged, too, in a course of measures which had for their object the protection of everything that was dear, and the acquisition of everything that could be desirable to the people at large. It was, nevertheless, invariably found, after the transient enthusiasm for the early Congresses was over, that the attention and attachment of the people were turned anew to their own particular governments; that the federal council was at no time the idol of popular favor; and that opposition to proposed enlargements of its powers and importance was the side usually taken by the men who wished to build their political consequence on the prepossessions of their fellow-citizens.

If, therefore, as has been elsewhere remarked, the people should in future become more partial to the federal than to the State governments, the change can only result from such manifest and irresistible proofs of a better administration, as will overcome all their antecedent propensities. And in that case, the people ought not surely to be precluded from giving most of their confidence where they may discover it to be most due; but even in that case the State governments could have little to apprehend, because it is only within a certain sphere that the federal power can, in the nature of things, be advantageously administered.

The remaining points on which I propose to compare the federal and State governments, are the disposition and the faculty they may respectively possess, to resist and frustrate the measures of each other.

It has been already proved that the members of the federal will be more dependent on the members of the State governments, than the latter will be on the former. It has appeared also, that the prepossessions of the people, on whom both will depend, will be more on the side of the State governments, than of the federal government. So far as the disposition of each towards the other may be influenced by these causes, the State governments must clearly have the advantage. But in a distinct and very important point of view, the advantage will lie on the same side. The prepossessions, which the members themselves will carry into the federal government, will generally be favorable to the States; whilst it will rarely happen, that the members of the State governments will carry into the public councils a bias in favor of the general government. A local spirit will infallibly prevail much more in the members of Congress, than a national spirit will prevail in the legislatures of the particular States. Every one knows that a great proportion of the errors committed by the State legislatures proceeds from the disposition of the members to sacrifice the comprehensive and permanent interest of the State, to the particular and separate views of the counties or districts in which they reside. And if they do not sufficiently enlarge their policy to embrace the collective welfare of their particular State, how can it be imagined that they will make the aggregate prosperity of the Union, and the dignity and respectability of its government, the objects of their affections and consultations? For the same reason that the members of the State legislatures will be unlikely to attach themselves sufficiently to national objects, the members of the federal legislature will be likely to attach themselves too much to local objects. The States will be to the latter what counties and towns are to the former. Measures will too often be decided according to their probable effect, not on the national prosperity and happiness, but on the prejudices, interests, and pursuits of the governments and people of the individual States. What is the spirit that has in general characterized the proceedings of Congress? A perusal of their journals, as well as the candid acknowledgments of such as have had a seat in that assembly, will inform us, that the members have but too frequently displayed the character, rather of partisans of their respective States, than of impartial guardians of a common interest; that where on one occasion improper sacrifices have been made of local considerations, to the aggrandizement of the federal government, the great interests of the nation have suffered on a hundred, from an undue attention to the local prejudices, interests, and views of the particular States. I mean not by these reflections to insinuate, that the new federal government will not embrace a more enlarged plan of policy than the existing government may have pursued; much less, that its views will be as confined as those of the State legislatures; but only that it will partake sufficiently of the spirit of both, to be disinclined to invade the rights of the individual States, or the prerogatives of their governments. The motives on the part of the State governments, to augment their prerogatives by defalcations from the federal government, will be overruled by no reciprocal predispositions in the members.

Were it admitted, however, that the Federal government may feel an equal disposition with the State governments to extend its power beyond the due limits, the latter would still have the advantage in the means of defeating such encroachments. If an act of a particular State, though unfriendly to the national government, be generally popular in that State and should not too grossly violate the oaths of the State officers, it is executed immediately and, of course, by means on the spot and depending on the State alone. The opposition of the federal government, or the interposition of federal officers, would but inflame the zeal of all parties on the side of the State, and the evil could not be prevented or repaired, if at all, without the employment of means which must always be resorted to with reluctance and difficulty. On the other hand, should an unwarrantable measure of the federal government be unpopular in particular States, which would seldom fail to be the case, or even a warrantable measure be so, which may sometimes be the case, the means of opposition to it are powerful and at hand. The disquietude of the people; their repugnance and, perhaps, refusal to co-operate with the officers of the Union; the frowns of the executive magistracy of the State; the embarrassments created by legislative devices, which would often be added on such occasions, would oppose, in any State, difficulties not to be despised; would form, in a large State, very serious impediments; and where the sentiments of several adjoining States happened to be in unison, would present obstructions which the federal government would hardly be willing to encounter.

But ambitious encroachments of the federal government, on the authority of the State governments, would not excite the opposition of a single State, or of a few States only. They would be signals of general alarm. Every government would espouse the common cause. A correspondence would be opened. Plans of resistance would be concerted. One spirit would animate and conduct the whole. The same combinations, in short, would result from an apprehension of the federal, as was produced by the dread of a foreign, yoke; and unless the projected innovations should be voluntarily renounced, the same appeal to a trial of force would be made in the one case as was made in the other. But what degree of madness could ever drive the federal government to such an extremity. In the contest with Great Britain, one part of the empire was employed against the other. The more numerous part invaded the rights of the less numerous part. The attempt was unjust and unwise; but it was not in speculation absolutely chimerical. But what would be the contest in the case we are supposing? Who would be the parties? A few representatives of the people would be opposed to the people themselves; or rather one set of representatives would be contending against thirteen sets of representatives, with the whole body of their common constituents on the side of the latter.

Documents of Revolution

The only refuge left for those who prophesy the downfall of the State governments is the visionary supposition that the federal government may previously accumulate a military force for the projects of ambition. The reasonings contained in these papers must have been employed to little purpose indeed, if it could be necessary now to disprove the reality of this danger. That the people and the States should, for a sufficient period of time, elect an uninterrupted succession of men ready to betray both; that the traitors should, throughout this period, uniformly and systematically pursue some fixed plan for the extension of the military establishment; that the governments and the people of the States should silently and patiently behold the gathering storm, and continue to supply the materials, until it should be prepared to burst on their own heads, must appear to every one more like the incoherent dreams of a delirious jealousy, or the misjudged exaggerations of a counterfeit zeal, than like the sober apprehensions of genuine patriotism. Extravagant as the supposition is, let it however be made. Let a regular army, fully equal to the resources of the country, be formed; and let it be entirely at the devotion of the federal government; still it would not be going too far to say, that the State governments, with the people on their side, would be able to repel the danger. The highest number to which, according to the best computation, a standing army can be carried in any country, does not exceed one hundredth part of the whole number of souls; or one twenty-fifth part of the number able to bear arms. This proportion would not yield, in the United States, an army of more than twenty-five or thirty thousand men. To these would be opposed a militia amounting to near half a million of citizens with arms in their hands, officered by men chosen from among themselves, fighting for their common liberties, and united and conducted by governments possessing their affections and confidence. It may well be doubted, whether a militia thus circumstanced could ever be conquered by such a proportion of regular troops. Those who are best acquainted with the last successful resistance of this country against the British arms, will be most inclined to deny the possibility of it. Besides the advantage of being armed, which the Americans possess over the people of almost every other nation, the existence of subordinate governments, to which the people are attached, and by which the militia officers are appointed, forms a barrier against the enterprises of ambition, more insurmountable than any which a simple government of any form can admit of. Notwithstanding the military establishments in the several kingdoms of Europe, which are carried as far as the public resources will bear, the governments are afraid to trust the people with arms. And it is not certain, that with this aid alone they would not be able to shake off their yokes. But were the people to possess the additional advantages of local governments chosen by themselves, who could collect the national will and direct the national force, and of officers appointed out of the militia, by these governments, and attached both to them and to the militia, it may be affirmed with the greatest assurance, that the throne of every tyranny in Europe would be speedily overturned in spite of the legions which surround it. Let us not insult the free and gallant citizens of America with the suspicion, that they would be less able to defend the rights of which they would be in actual possession, than the debased subjects of arbitrary power would be to rescue theirs from the hands of their oppressors. Let us rather no longer insult them with the supposition that they can ever reduce themselves to the necessity of making the experiment, by a blind and tame submission to the long train of insidious measures which must precede and produce it.

The argument under the present head may be put into a very concise form, which appears altogether conclusive. Either the mode in which the federal government is to be constructed will render it sufficiently dependent on the people, or it will not. On the first supposition, it will be restrained by that dependence from forming schemes obnoxious to their constituents. On the other supposition, it will not possess the confidence of the people, and its schemes of usurpation will be easily defeated by the State governments, who will be supported by the people.

On summing up the considerations stated in this and the last paper, they seem to amount to the most convincing evidence, that the powers proposed to be lodged in the federal government are as little formidable to those reserved to the individual States, as they are indispensably necessary to accomplish the purposes of the Union; and that all those alarms which have been sounded, of a meditated and consequential annihilation of the State governments, must, on the most favorable interpretation, be ascribed to the chimerical fears of the authors of them.

PUBLIUS

FEDERALIST PAPER NO. 47. THE PARTICULAR STRUCTURE OF THE NEW GOVERNMENT AND THE DISTRIBUTION OF POWER AMONG ITS DIFFERENT PARTS.

For the Independent Journal. Wednesday, January 30, 1788.

MADISON

To the People of the State of New York:

HAVING reviewed the general form of the proposed government and the general mass of power allotted to it, I proceed to examine the particular structure of this government, and the distribution of this mass of power among its constituent parts.

One of the principal objections inculcated by the more respectable adversaries to the Constitution, is its supposed violation of the political maxim, that the legislative, executive, and judiciary departments ought to be separate and distinct. In the structure of the federal government, no regard, it is said, seems to have been paid to this essential precaution in favor of liberty. The several departments of power are distributed and blended in such a manner as at once to destroy all symmetry and beauty of form, and to expose some of the essential parts of the edifice to the danger of being crushed by the disproportionate weight of other parts.

No political truth is certainly of greater intrinsic value, or is stamped with the authority of more enlightened patrons of liberty, than that on which the objection is founded. The accumulation of all powers, legislative, executive, and judiciary, in the same hands, whether of one, a few, or many, and whether hereditary, self-appointed, or elective, may justly be pronounced the very definition of tyranny. Were the federal Constitution, therefore, really chargeable with the accumulation of power, or with a mixture of powers, having a dangerous tendency to such an accumulation, no further arguments would be necessary to inspire a universal reprobation of the system. I persuade myself, however, that it will be made apparent to every one, that the charge cannot be supported, and that the maxim on which it relies has been totally misconceived and misapplied. In order to form correct ideas on this important subject, it will be proper to investigate the sense in which the preservation of liberty requires that the three great departments of power should be separate and distinct.

The oracle who is always consulted and cited on this subject is the celebrated Montesquieu. If he be not the author of this invaluable precept in the science of politics, he has the merit at least of displaying and recommending it most effectually to the attention of mankind. Let us endeavor, in the first place, to ascertain his meaning on this point.

The British Constitution was to Montesquieu what Homer has been to the didactic writers on epic poetry. As the latter have considered the work of the immortal bard as the perfect model from which the principles and rules of the epic art were to be drawn, and by which all similar works were to be judged, so this great political critic appears to have viewed the Constitution of England as the standard, or to use his own expression, as the mirror of political liberty; and to have delivered, in the form of elementary truths, the several characteristic principles of that particular system. That we may be sure, then, not to mistake his meaning in this case, let us recur to the source from which the maxim was drawn.

On the slightest view of the British Constitution, we must perceive that the legislative, executive, and judiciary departments are by no means totally separate and distinct from each other. The executive magistrate forms an integral part of the legislative authority. He alone has the prerogative of making treaties with foreign sovereigns, which, when made, have, under certain limitations, the force of legislative acts. All the members of the judiciary department are appointed by him, can be removed by him on the address of the two Houses of Parliament, and form, when he pleases to consult them, one of his constitutional councils. One branch of the legislative department forms also a great constitutional council to the executive chief, as, on another hand, it is the sole depositary of judicial power in cases of impeachment, and is invested with the supreme appellate jurisdiction in all other cases. The judges, again, are so far connected with the legislative department as often to attend and participate in its deliberations, though not admitted to a legislative vote.

From these facts, by which Montesquieu was guided, it may clearly be inferred that, in saying "There can be no liberty where the legislative and executive powers are united in the same person, or body of magistrates," or, "if the power of judging be not separated from the legislative and executive powers," he did not mean that these departments ought to have no PARTIAL AGENCY in, or no CONTROL over, the acts of each other. His meaning, as his own words import, and still more conclusively as illustrated by the example in his eye, can amount to no more than this, that where the WHOLE power of one department is exercised by the same hands which possess the WHOLE power of another department, the fundamental principles of a free constitution are subverted. This would have been the case in the constitution examined by him, if the king, who is the sole executive magistrate, had possessed also the complete legislative power, or the supreme administration of justice; or if the entire legislative body had possessed the supreme judiciary, or the supreme executive authority. This, however, is not among the vices of that constitution. The magistrate in whom the whole executive power resides cannot of himself make a law, though he can put a negative on every law; nor administer justice in person, though he has the appointment of those who do administer it. The judges can exercise no executive prerogative, though they are shoots from the executive stock; nor any legislative function, though they may be advised with by the legislative councils. The entire legislature can perform no judiciary act, though by the joint act of two of its branches the judges may be removed from their offices, and though one of its branches is possessed of the judicial power in the last resort. The entire legislature, again, can exercise no executive prerogative, though one of its branches constitutes the supreme executive magistracy, and another, on the impeachment of a third, can try and condemn all the subordinate officers in the executive department.

The reasons on which Montesquieu grounds his maxim are a further demonstration of his meaning. "When the legislative and executive powers are united in the same person or body," says he, "there can be no liberty, because apprehensions may arise lest THE SAME monarch or senate should ENACT tyrannical laws to EXECUTE them in a tyrannical manner." Again: "Were the power of judging joined with the legislative, the life and liberty of the subject would be exposed to arbitrary control, for THE JUDGE would then be THE LEGISLATOR. Were it joined to the executive power, THE JUDGE might behave with all the violence of AN OPPRESSOR." Some of these reasons are more fully explained in other passages; but briefly stated as they are here, they sufficiently establish the meaning which we have put on this celebrated maxim of this celebrated author.

If we look into the constitutions of the several States, we find that, notwithstanding the emphatical and, in some instances, the unqualified terms in which this axiom has been laid down, there is not a single instance in which the several departments of power have been kept absolutely separate and distinct. New Hampshire, whose constitution was the last formed, seems to have been fully aware of the impossibility and inexpediency of avoiding any mixture whatever of these departments, and has qualified the doctrine by declaring "that the legislative, executive, and judiciary powers ought to be kept as separate from, and independent of, each other AS THE NATURE OF A FREE GOVERNMENT WILL ADMIT; OR AS IS CONSISTENT WITH THAT CHAIN OF CONNECTION THAT BINDS THE WHOLE FABRIC OF THE CONSTITUTION IN ONE INDISSOLUBLE BOND OF UNITY AND AMITY." Her constitution accordingly mixes these departments in several respects. The Senate, which is a branch of the legislative department, is also a judicial tribunal for the trial of impeachments. The President, who is the head of the executive department, is the presiding member also of the Senate; and, besides an equal vote in all cases, has a casting vote in case of a tie. The executive head is himself eventually elective every year by the legislative department, and his council is every year chosen by and from the members of the same department. Several of the officers of state are also appointed by the legislature. And the members of the judiciary department are appointed by the executive department.

The constitution of Massachusetts has observed a sufficient though less pointed caution, in expressing this fundamental article of liberty. It declares "that the legislative department shall never exercise the executive and judicial powers, or either of them; the executive shall never exercise the legislative and judicial powers, or either of them; the judicial shall never exercise the legislative and executive powers, or either of them." This declaration corresponds precisely with the doctrine of Montesquieu, as it has been explained, and is not in a single point violated by the plan of the convention. It goes no farther than to prohibit any one of the entire departments from exercising the powers of another department. In the very Constitution to which it is prefixed, a partial mixture of powers has been admitted. The executive magistrate has a qualified negative on the legislative body, and the Senate, which is a part of the legislature, is a court of impeachment for members both of the executive and judiciary departments. The members of the judiciary department, again, are appointable by the executive department, and removable by the same authority on the address of the two legislative branches. Lastly, a number of the officers of government are annually appointed by the legislative department. As the appointment to offices, particularly executive offices, is in its nature an executive function, the compilers of the Constitution have, in this last point at least, violated the rule established by themselves.

I pass over the constitutions of Rhode Island and Connecticut, because they were formed prior to the Revolution, and even before the principle under examination had become an object of political attention.

Documents of Revolution

The constitution of New York contains no declaration on this subject; but appears very clearly to have been framed with an eye to the danger of improperly blending the different departments. It gives, nevertheless, to the executive magistrate, a partial control over the legislative department; and, what is more, gives a like control to the judiciary department; and even blends the executive and judiciary departments in the exercise of this control. In its council of appointment members of the legislative are associated with the executive authority, in the appointment of officers, both executive and judiciary. And its court for the trial of impeachments and correction of errors is to consist of one branch of the legislature and the principal members of the judiciary department.

The constitution of New Jersey has blended the different powers of government more than any of the preceding. The governor, who is the executive magistrate, is appointed by the legislature; is chancellor and ordinary, or surrogate of the State; is a member of the Supreme Court of Appeals, and president, with a casting vote, of one of the legislative branches. The same legislative branch acts again as executive council of the governor, and with him constitutes the Court of Appeals. The members of the judiciary department are appointed by the legislative department and removable by one branch of it, on the impeachment of the other.

According to the constitution of Pennsylvania, the president, who is the head of the executive department, is annually elected by a vote in which the legislative department predominates. In conjunction with an executive council, he appoints the members of the judiciary department, and forms a court of impeachment for trial of all officers, judiciary as well as executive. The judges of the Supreme Court and justices of the peace seem also to be removable by the legislature; and the executive power of pardoning in certain cases, to be referred to the same department. The members of the executive council are made EX-OFFICIO justices of peace throughout the State.

In Delaware, the chief executive magistrate is annually elected by the legislative department. The speakers of the two legislative branches are vice-presidents in the executive department. The executive chief, with six others, appointed, three by each of the legislative branches constitutes the Supreme Court of Appeals; he is joined with the legislative department in the appointment of the other judges. Throughout the States, it appears that the members of the legislature may at the same time be justices of the peace; in this State, the members of one branch of it are EX-OFFICIO justices of the peace; as are also the members of the executive council. The principal officers of the executive department are appointed by the legislative; and one branch of the latter forms a court of impeachments. All officers may be removed on address of the legislature.

Maryland has adopted the maxim in the most unqualified terms; declaring that the legislative, executive, and judicial powers of government ought to be forever separate and distinct from each other. Her constitution, notwithstanding, makes the executive magistrate appointable by the legislative department; and the members of the judiciary by the executive department.

The language of Virginia is still more pointed on this subject. Her constitution declares, "that the legislative, executive, and judiciary departments shall be separate and distinct; so that neither exercise the powers properly belonging to the other; nor shall any person exercise the powers of more than one of them at the same time, except that the justices of county courts shall be eligible to either House of Assembly." Yet we find not only this express exception, with respect to the members of the inferior courts, but that the chief magistrate, with his executive council, are appointable by the legislature; that two members of the latter are triennially displaced at the pleasure of the legislature; and that all the principal offices, both executive and judiciary, are filled by the same department. The executive prerogative of pardon, also, is in one case vested in the legislative department.

The constitution of North Carolina, which declares "that the legislative, executive, and supreme judicial powers of government ought to be forever separate and distinct from each other," refers, at the same time, to the legislative department, the appointment not only of the executive chief, but all the principal officers within both that and the judiciary department.

In South Carolina, the constitution makes the executive magistracy eligible by the legislative department. It gives to the latter, also, the appointment of the members of the judiciary department, including even justices of the peace and sheriffs; and the appointment of officers in the executive department, down to captains in the army and navy of the State.

In the constitution of Georgia, where it is declared "that the legislative, executive, and judiciary departments shall be separate and distinct, so that neither exercise the powers properly belonging to the other," we find that the executive department is to be filled by appointments of the legislature; and the executive prerogative of pardon to be finally exercised by the same authority. Even justices of the peace are to be appointed by the legislature.

In citing these cases, in which the legislative, executive, and judiciary departments have not been kept totally separate and distinct, I wish not to be regarded as an advocate for the particular organizations of the several State governments. I am fully aware that among the many excellent principles which they exemplify, they carry strong marks of the haste, and still stronger of the inexperience, under which they were framed. It is but too obvious that in some instances the fundamental principle under consideration has been violated by too great a mixture, and even an actual consolidation, of the different powers; and that in no instance has a competent provision been made for maintaining in practice the separation delineated on paper. What I have wished to evince is, that the charge brought against the proposed Constitution, of violating the sacred maxim of free government, is warranted neither by the real meaning annexed to that maxim by its author, nor by the sense in which it has hitherto been understood in America. This interesting subject will be resumed in the ensuing paper.

PUBLIUS

FEDERALIST PAPER NO. 48. THESE DEPARTMENTS SHOULD NOT BE SO FAR SEPARATED AS TO HAVE NO CONSTITUTIONAL CONTROL OVER EACH OTHER.

From the New York Packet. Friday, February 1, 1788.

MADISON

To the People of the State of New York:

IT WAS shown in the last paper that the political apothegm there examined does not require that the legislative, executive, and judiciary departments should be wholly unconnected with each other. I shall undertake, in the next place, to show that unless these departments be so far connected and blended as to give to each a constitutional control over the others, the degree of separation which the maxim requires, as essential to a free government, can never in practice be duly maintained.

It is agreed on all sides, that the powers properly belonging to one of the departments ought not to be directly and completely administered by either of the other departments. It is equally evident, that none of them ought to possess, directly or indirectly, an overruling influence over the others, in the administration of their respective powers. It will not be denied, that power is of an encroaching nature, and that it ought to be effectually restrained from passing the limits assigned to it. After discriminating, therefore, in theory, the several classes of power, as they may in their nature be legislative, executive, or judiciary, the next and most difficult task is to provide some practical security for each, against the invasion of the others. What this security ought to be, is the great problem to be solved.

Will it be sufficient to mark, with precision, the boundaries of these departments, in the constitution of the government, and to trust to these parchment barriers against the encroaching spirit of power? This is the security which appears to have been principally relied on by the compilers of most of the American constitutions. But experience assures us, that the efficacy of the provision has been greatly overrated; and that some more adequate defense is indispensably necessary for the more feeble, against the more powerful, members of the government. The legislative department is everywhere extending the sphere of its activity, and drawing all power into its impetuous vortex.

The founders of our republics have so much merit for the wisdom which they have displayed, that no task can be less pleasing than that of pointing out the errors into which they have fallen. A respect for truth, however, obliges us to remark, that they seem never for a moment to have turned their eyes from the danger to liberty from the overgrown and all-grasping prerogative of an hereditary magistrate, supported and fortified by an hereditary branch of the legislative authority. They seem never to have recollected the danger from legislative usurpations, which, by assembling all power in the same hands, must lead to the same tyranny as is threatened by executive usurpations.

In a government where numerous and extensive prerogatives are placed in the hands of an hereditary monarch, the executive department is very justly regarded as the source of danger, and watched with all the jealousy which a zeal for liberty ought to inspire. In a democracy, where a multitude of people exercise in person the legislative functions, and are continually exposed, by their incapacity for regular deliberation and concerted measures, to the ambitious intrigues of their executive magistrates, tyranny may well be apprehended, on some favorable emergency, to start up in the same quarter. But in a representative republic, where the executive magistracy is carefully limited; both in the extent and the duration of its power; and where the legislative power is exercised by an assembly, which is inspired, by a supposed influence over the people, with an intrepid confidence in its own strength; which is sufficiently numerous to feel all the passions which actuate a multitude, yet not so numerous as to be incapable of pursuing the objects of its passions, by means which reason prescribes; it is against the enterprising ambition of this department that the people ought to indulge all their jealousy and exhaust all their precautions.

The legislative department derives a superiority in our governments from other circumstances. Its constitutional powers being at once more extensive, and less susceptible of precise limits, it can, with the greater facility, mask, under complicated and indirect measures, the encroachments which it makes on the co-ordinate departments. It is not unfrequently a question of real nicety in legislative bodies, whether the operation of a particular measure will, or will not, extend beyond the legislative sphere. On the other side, the executive power being restrained within a narrower compass, and being more simple in its nature, and the judiciary being described by landmarks still less uncertain, projects of usurpation by either of these departments would immediately betray and defeat themselves. Nor is this all: as the legislative department alone has access to the pockets of the people, and has in some constitutions full discretion, and in all a prevailing influence, over the pecuniary rewards of those who fill the other departments, a dependence is thus created in the latter, which gives still greater facility to encroachments of the former.

I have appealed to our own experience for the truth of what I advance on this subject. Were it necessary to verify this experience by particular proofs, they might be multiplied without end. I might find a witness in every citizen who has shared in, or been attentive to, the course of public administrations. I might collect vouchers in abundance from the records and archives of every State in the Union. But as a more concise, and at the same time equally satisfactory, evidence, I will refer to the example of two States, attested by two unexceptionable authorities.

The first example is that of Virginia, a State which, as we have seen, has expressly declared in its constitution, that the three great departments ought not to be intermixed. The authority in support of it is Mr. Jefferson, who, besides his other advantages for remarking the operation of the government, was himself the chief magistrate of it. In order to convey fully the ideas with which his experience had impressed him on this subject, it will be necessary to quote a passage of some length from his very interesting Notes on the State of Virginia, p. 195. "All the powers of government, legislative, executive, and judiciary, result to the legislative body. The concentrating these in the same hands, is precisely the definition of despotic government. It will be no alleviation, that these powers will be exercised by a plurality of hands, and not by a single one. One hundred and seventy-three despots would surely be as oppressive as one. Let those who doubt it, turn their eyes on the republic of Venice. As little will it avail us, that they are chosen by ourselves. An ELECTIVE DESPOTISM was not the government we fought for; but one which should not only be founded on free principles, but in which the powers of government should be so divided and balanced among several bodies of magistracy, as that no one could transcend their legal limits, without being effectually checked and restrained by the others. For this reason, that convention which passed the ordinance of government, laid its foundation on this basis, that the legislative, executive, and judiciary departments should be separate and distinct, so that no person should exercise the powers of more than one of them at the same time. BUT NO BARRIER WAS PROVIDED BETWEEN THESE SEVERAL POWERS. The judiciary and the executive members were left dependent on the legislative for their subsistence in office, and some of them for their continuance in it. If, therefore, the legislature assumes executive and judiciary powers, no opposition is likely to be made; nor, if made, can be effectual; because in that case they may put their proceedings into the form of acts of Assembly, which will render them obligatory on the other branches. They have accordingly, IN MANY instances, DECIDED RIGHTS which should have been left to JUDICIARY CONTROVERSY, and THE DIRECTION OF THE EXECUTIVE, DURING THE WHOLE TIME OF THEIR SESSION, IS BECOMING HABITUAL AND FAMILIAR."

The other State which I shall take for an example is Pennsylvania; and the other authority, the Council of Censors, which assembled in the years 1783 and 1784. A part of the duty of this body, as marked out by the constitution, was "to inquire whether the constitution had been preserved inviolate in every part; and whether the legislative and executive branches of government had performed their duty as guardians of the people, or assumed to themselves, or exercised, other or greater powers than they are entitled to by the constitution." In the execution of this trust, the council were necessarily led to a comparison of both the legislative and executive proceedings, with the constitutional powers of these departments; and from the facts enumerated, and to the truth of most of which both sides in the council subscribed, it appears that the constitution had been flagrantly violated by the legislature in a variety of important instances.

A great number of laws had been passed, violating, without any apparent necessity, the rule requiring that all bills of a public nature shall be previously printed for the consideration of the people; although this is one of the precautions chiefly relied on by the constitution against improper acts of legislature.

The constitutional trial by jury had been violated, and powers assumed which had not been delegated by the constitution.

Executive powers had been usurped.

The salaries of the judges, which the constitution expressly requires to be fixed, had been occasionally varied; and cases belonging to the judiciary department frequently drawn within legislative cognizance and determination.

Those who wish to see the several particulars falling under each of these heads, may consult the journals of the council, which are in print. Some of them, it will be found, may be imputable to peculiar circumstances connected with the war; but the greater part of them may be considered as the spontaneous shoots of an ill-constituted government.

It appears, also, that the executive department had not been innocent of frequent breaches of the constitution. There are three observations, however, which ought to be made on this head: FIRST, a great proportion of the instances were either immediately produced by the necessities of the war, or recommended by Congress or the commander-in-chief; SECOND, in most of the other instances, they conformed either to the declared or the known sentiments of the legislative department; THIRD, the executive department of Pennsylvania is distinguished from that of the other States by the number of members composing it. In this respect, it has as much affinity to a legislative assembly as to an executive council. And being at once exempt from the restraint of an individual responsibility for the acts of the body, and deriving confidence from mutual example and joint influence, unauthorized measures would, of course, be more freely hazarded, than where the executive department is administered by a single hand, or by a few hands.

The conclusion which I am warranted in drawing from these observations is, that a mere demarcation on parchment of the constitutional limits of the several departments, is not a sufficient guard against those encroachments which lead to a tyrannical concentration of all the powers of government in the same hands.

PUBLIUS

FEDERALIST PAPER NO. 49. METHOD OF GUARDING AGAINST THE ENCROACHMENTS OF ANY ONE DEPARTMENT OF GOVERNMENT BY APPEALING TO THE PEOPLE THROUGH A CONVENTION.

For the Independent Journal. Saturday, February 2, 1788.

MADISON

To the People of the State of New York:

THE author of the "Notes on the State of Virginia," quoted in the last paper, has subjoined to that valuable work the draught of a constitution, which had been prepared in order to be laid before a convention, expected to be called in 1783, by the legislature, for the establishment of a constitution for that commonwealth. The plan, like every thing from the same pen, marks a turn of thinking, original, comprehensive, and accurate; and is the more worthy of attention as it equally displays a fervent attachment to republican government and an enlightened view of the dangerous propensities against which it ought to be guarded. One of the precautions which he proposes, and on which he appears ultimately to rely as a palladium to the weaker departments of power against the invasions of the stronger, is perhaps altogether his own, and as it immediately relates to the subject of our present inquiry, ought not to be overlooked.

His proposition is, "that whenever any two of the three branches of government shall concur in opinion, each by the voices of two thirds of their whole number, that a convention is necessary for altering the constitution, or CORRECTING BREACHES OF IT, a convention shall be called for the purpose."

As the people are the only legitimate fountain of power, and it is from them that the constitutional charter, under which the several branches of government hold their power, is derived, it seems strictly consonant to the republican theory, to recur to the same original authority, not only whenever it may be necessary to enlarge, diminish, or new-model the powers of the government, but also whenever any one of the departments may commit encroachments on the chartered authorities of the others. The several departments being perfectly co-ordinate by the terms of their common commission, none of them, it is evident, can pretend to an exclusive or superior right of settling the boundaries between their respective powers; and how are the encroachments of the stronger to be prevented, or the wrongs of the weaker to be redressed, without an appeal to the people themselves, who, as the grantors of the commissions, can alone declare its true meaning, and enforce its observance?

There is certainly great force in this reasoning, and it must be allowed to prove that a constitutional road to the decision of the people ought to be marked out and kept open, for certain great and extraordinary occasions. But there appear to be insuperable objections against the proposed recurrence to the people, as a provision in all cases for keeping the several departments of power within their constitutional limits.

In the first place, the provision does not reach the case of a combination of two of the departments against the third. If the legislative authority, which possesses so many means of operating on the motives of the other departments, should be able to gain to its interest either of the others, or even one third of its members, the remaining department could derive no advantage from its remedial provision. I do not dwell, however, on this objection, because it may be thought to be rather against the modification of the principle, than against the principle itself.

In the next place, it may be considered as an objection inherent in the principle, that as every appeal to the people would carry an implication of some defect in the government, frequent appeals would, in a great measure, deprive the government of that veneration which time bestows on every thing, and without which perhaps the wisest and freest governments would not possess the requisite stability. If it be true that all governments rest on opinion, it is no less true that the strength of opinion in each individual, and its practical influence on his conduct, depend much on the number which he supposes to have entertained the same opinion. The reason of man, like man himself, is timid and cautious when left alone, and acquires firmness and confidence in proportion to the number with which it is associated. When the examples which fortify opinion are ANCIENT as well as NUMEROUS, they are known to have a double effect. In a nation of philosophers, this consideration ought to be disregarded. A reverence for the laws would be sufficiently inculcated by the voice of an enlightened reason. But a nation of philosophers is as little to be expected as the philosophical race of kings wished for by Plato. And in every other nation, the most rational government will not find it a superfluous advantage to have the prejudices of the community on its side.

The danger of disturbing the public tranquillity by interesting too strongly the public passions, is a still more serious objection against a frequent reference of constitutional questions to the decision of the whole society. Notwithstanding the success which has attended the revisions of our established forms of government, and which does so much honor to the virtue and intelligence of the people of America, it must be confessed that the experiments are of too ticklish a nature to be unnecessarily multiplied. We are to recollect that all the existing constitutions were formed in the midst of a danger which repressed the passions most unfriendly to order and concord; of an enthusiastic confidence of the people in their patriotic leaders, which stifled the ordinary diversity of opinions on great national questions; of a universal ardor for new and opposite forms, produced by a universal resentment and indignation against the ancient government; and whilst no spirit of party connected with the changes to be made, or the abuses to be reformed, could mingle its leaven in the operation. The future situations in which we must expect to be usually placed, do not present any equivalent security against the danger which is apprehended.

But the greatest objection of all is, that the decisions which would probably result from such appeals would not answer the purpose of maintaining the constitutional equilibrium of the government. We have seen that the tendency of republican governments is to an aggrandizement of the legislative at the expense of the other departments. The appeals to the people, therefore, would usually be made by the executive and judiciary departments. But whether made by one side or the other, would each side enjoy equal advantages on the trial? Let us view their different situations. The members of the executive and judiciary departments are few in number, and can be personally known to a small part only of the people. The latter, by the mode of their appointment, as well as by the nature and permanency of it, are too far removed from the people to share much in their prepossessions. The former are generally the objects of jealousy, and their administration is always liable to be discolored and rendered unpopular. The members of the legislative department, on the other hand, are numerous. They are distributed and dwell among the people at large. Their connections of blood, of friendship, and of acquaintance embrace a great proportion of the most influential part of the society. The nature of their public trust implies a personal influence among the people, and that they are more immediately the confidential guardians of the rights and liberties of the people. With these advantages, it can hardly be supposed that the adverse party would have an equal chance for a favorable issue.

But the legislative party would not only be able to plead their cause most successfully with the people. They would probably be constituted themselves the judges. The same influence which had gained them an election into the legislature, would gain them a seat in the convention. If this should not be the case with all, it would probably be the case with many, and pretty certainly with those leading characters, on whom every thing depends in such bodies. The convention, in short, would be composed chiefly of men who had been, who actually were, or who expected to be, members of the department whose conduct was arraigned. They would consequently be parties to the very question to be decided by them.

It might, however, sometimes happen, that appeals would be made under circumstances less adverse to the executive and judiciary departments. The usurpations of the legislature might be so flagrant and so sudden, as to admit of no specious coloring. A strong party among themselves might take side with the other branches. The executive power might be in the hands of a peculiar favorite of the people. In such a posture of things, the public decision might be less swayed by prepossessions in favor of the legislative party. But still it could never be expected to turn on the true merits of the question. It would inevitably be connected with the spirit of pre-existing parties, or of parties springing out of the question itself. It would be connected with persons of distinguished character and extensive influence in the community. It would be pronounced by the very men who had been agents in, or opponents of, the measures to which the decision would relate. The PASSIONS, therefore, not the REASON, of the public would sit in judgment. But it is the reason, alone, of the public, that ought to control and regulate the government. The passions ought to be controlled and regulated by the government.

We found in the last paper, that mere declarations in the written constitution are not sufficient to restrain the several departments within their legal rights. It appears in this, that occasional appeals to the people would be neither a proper nor an effectual provision for that purpose. How far the provisions of a different nature contained in the plan above quoted might be adequate, I do not examine. Some of them are unquestionably founded on sound political principles, and all of them are framed with singular ingenuity and precision.

PUBLIUS

Documents of Revolution

FEDERALIST PAPER NO. 50. PERIODICAL APPEALS TO THE PEOPLE CONSIDERED

From the New York Packet. Tuesday, February 5, 1788.

MADISON

To the People of the State of New York:

IT MAY be contended, perhaps, that instead of OCCASIONAL appeals to the people, which are liable to the objections urged against them, PERIODICAL appeals are the proper and adequate means of PREVENTING AND CORRECTING INFRACTIONS OF THE CONSTITUTION.

It will be attended to, that in the examination of these expedients, I confine myself to their aptitude for ENFORCING the Constitution, by keeping the several departments of power within their due bounds, without particularly considering them as provisions for ALTERING the Constitution itself. In the first view, appeals to the people at fixed periods appear to be nearly as ineligible as appeals on particular occasions as they emerge. If the periods be separated by short intervals, the measures to be reviewed and rectified will have been of recent date, and will be connected with all the circumstances which tend to vitiate and pervert the result of occasional revisions. If the periods be distant from each other, the same remark will be applicable to all recent measures; and in proportion as the remoteness of the others may favor a dispassionate review of them, this advantage is inseparable from inconveniences which seem to counterbalance it. In the first place, a distant prospect of public censure would be a very feeble restraint on power from those excesses to which it might be urged by the force of present motives. Is it to be imagined that a legislative assembly, consisting of a hundred or two hundred members, eagerly bent on some favorite object, and breaking through the restraints of the Constitution in pursuit of it, would be arrested in their career, by considerations drawn from a censorial revision of their conduct at the future distance of ten, fifteen, or twenty years? In the next place, the abuses would often have completed their mischievous effects before the remedial provision would be applied. And in the last place, where this might not be the case, they would be of long standing, would have taken deep root, and would not easily be extirpated.

The scheme of revising the constitution, in order to correct recent breaches of it, as well as for other purposes, has been actually tried in one of the States. One of the objects of the Council of Censors which met in Pennsylvania in 1783 and 1784, was, as we have seen, to inquire, "whether the constitution had been violated, and whether the legislative and executive departments had encroached upon each other." This important and novel experiment in politics merits, in several points of view, very particular attention. In some of them it may, perhaps, as a single experiment, made under circumstances somewhat peculiar, be thought to be not absolutely conclusive. But as applied to the case under consideration, it involves some facts, which I venture to remark, as a complete and satisfactory illustration of the reasoning which I have employed.

First. It appears, from the names of the gentlemen who composed the council, that some, at least, of its most active members had also been active and leading characters in the parties which pre-existed in the State.

Second. It appears that the same active and leading members of the council had been active and influential members of the legislative and executive branches, within the period to be reviewed; and even patrons or opponents of the very measures to be thus brought to the test of the constitution. Two of the members had been vice-presidents of the State, and several other members of the executive council, within the seven preceding years. One of them had been speaker, and a number of others distinguished members, of the legislative assembly within the same period.

Third. Every page of their proceedings witnesses the effect of all these circumstances on the temper of their deliberations. Throughout the continuance of the council, it was split into two fixed and violent parties. The fact is acknowledged and lamented by themselves. Had this not been the case, the face of their proceedings exhibits a proof equally satisfactory. In all questions, however unimportant in themselves, or unconnected with each other, the same names stand invariably contrasted on the opposite columns. Every unbiased observer may infer, without danger of mistake, and at the same time without meaning to reflect on either party, or any individuals of either party, that, unfortunately, PASSION, not REASON, must have presided over their decisions. When men exercise their reason coolly and freely on a variety of distinct questions, they inevitably fall into different opinions on some of them. When they are governed by a common passion, their opinions, if they are so to be called, will be the same.

Fourth. It is at least problematical, whether the decisions of this body do not, in several instances, misconstrue the limits prescribed for the legislative and executive departments, instead of reducing and limiting them within their constitutional places.

Fifth. I have never understood that the decisions of the council on constitutional questions, whether rightly or erroneously formed, have had any effect in varying the practice founded on legislative constructions. It even appears, if I mistake not, that in one instance the contemporary legislature denied the constructions of the council, and actually prevailed in the contest.

This censorial body, therefore, proves at the same time, by its researches, the existence of the disease, and by its example, the inefficacy of the remedy.

This conclusion cannot be invalidated by alleging that the State in which the experiment was made was at that crisis, and had been for a long time before, violently heated and distracted by the rage of party. Is it to be presumed, that at any future septennial epoch the same State will be free from parties? Is it to be presumed that any other State, at the same or any other given period, will be exempt from them? Such an event ought to be neither presumed nor desired; because an extinction of parties necessarily implies either a universal alarm for the public safety, or an absolute extinction of liberty.

Were the precaution taken of excluding from the assemblies elected by the people, to revise the preceding administration of the government, all persons who should have been concerned with the government within the given period, the difficulties would not be obviated. The important task would probably devolve on men, who, with inferior capacities, would in other respects be little better qualified. Although they might not have been personally concerned in the administration, and therefore not immediately agents in the measures to be examined, they would probably have been involved in the parties connected with these measures, and have been elected under their auspices.

PUBLIUS

FEDERALIST PAPER NO. 51. THE STRUCTURE OF THE GOVERNMENT MUST FURNISH THE PROPER CHECKS AND BALANCES BETWEEN THE DIFFERENT DEPARTMENTS.

For the Independent Journal. Wednesday, February 6, 1788.

MADISON

To the People of the State of New York:

TO WHAT expedient, then, shall we finally resort, for maintaining in practice the necessary partition of power among the several departments, as laid down in the Constitution? The only answer that can be given is, that as all these exterior provisions are found to be inadequate, the defect must be supplied, by so contriving the interior structure of the government as that its several constituent parts may, by their mutual relations, be the means of keeping each other in their proper places. Without presuming to undertake a full development of this important idea, I will hazard a few general observations, which may perhaps place it in a clearer light, and enable us to form a more correct judgment of the principles and structure of the government planned by the convention.

In order to lay a due foundation for that separate and distinct exercise of the different powers of government, which to a certain extent is admitted on all hands to be essential to the preservation of liberty, it is evident that each department should have a will of its own; and consequently should be so constituted that the members of each should have as little agency as possible in the appointment of the members of the others. Were this principle rigorously adhered to, it would require that all the appointments for the supreme executive, legislative, and judiciary magistracies should be drawn from the same fountain of authority, the people, through channels having no communication whatever with one another. Perhaps such a plan of constructing the several departments would be less difficult in practice than it may in contemplation appear. Some difficulties, however, and some additional expense would attend the execution of it. Some deviations, therefore, from the principle must be admitted. In the constitution of the judiciary department in particular, it might be inexpedient to insist rigorously on the principle: first, because peculiar qualifications being essential in the members, the primary consideration ought to be to select that mode of choice which best secures these qualifications; secondly, because the permanent tenure by which the appointments are held in that department, must soon destroy all sense of dependence on the authority conferring them.

It is equally evident, that the members of each department should be as little dependent as possible on those of the others, for the emoluments annexed to their offices. Were the executive magistrate, or the judges, not independent of the legislature in this particular, their independence in every other would be merely nominal.

But the great security against a gradual concentration of the several powers in the same department, consists in giving to those who administer each department the necessary constitutional means and personal motives to resist encroachments of the others. The provision for defense must in this, as in all other cases, be made commensurate to the danger of attack. Ambition must be made to counteract ambition. The interest of the man must be connected with the constitutional rights of the place. It may be a reflection on human nature, that such devices should be necessary to control the abuses of government. But what is government itself, but the greatest of all reflections on human nature? If men were angels, no government would be necessary. If angels were to govern men, neither external nor internal controls on government would be necessary. In framing a government which is to be administered by men over men, the great difficulty lies in this: you must first enable the government to control the governed; and in the next place oblige it to control itself. A dependence on the people is, no doubt, the primary control on the government; but experience has taught mankind the necessity of auxiliary precautions.

This policy of supplying, by opposite and rival interests, the defect of better motives, might be traced through the whole system of human affairs, private as well as public. We see it particularly displayed in all the subordinate distributions of power, where the constant aim is to divide and arrange the several offices in such a manner as that each may be a check on the other—that the private interest of every individual may be a sentinel over the public rights. These inventions of prudence cannot be less requisite in the distribution of the supreme powers of the State.

But it is not possible to give to each department an equal power of self-defense. In republican government, the legislative authority necessarily predominates. The remedy for this inconveniency is to divide the legislature into different branches; and to render them, by different modes of election and different principles of action, as little connected with each other as the nature of their common functions and their common dependence on the society will admit. It may even be necessary to guard against dangerous encroachments by still further precautions. As the weight of the legislative authority requires that it should be thus divided, the weakness of the executive may require, on the other hand, that it should be fortified. An absolute negative on the legislature appears, at first view, to be the natural defense with which the executive magistrate should be armed. But perhaps it would be neither altogether safe nor alone sufficient. On ordinary occasions it might not be exerted with the requisite firmness, and on extraordinary occasions it might be perfidiously abused. May not this defect of an absolute negative be supplied by some qualified connection between this weaker department and the weaker branch of the stronger department, by which the latter may be led to support the constitutional rights of the former, without being too much detached from the rights of its own department?

If the principles on which these observations are founded be just, as I persuade myself they are, and they be applied as a criterion to the several State constitutions, and to the federal Constitution it will be found that if the latter does not perfectly correspond with them, the former are infinitely less able to bear such a test.

There are, moreover, two considerations particularly applicable to the federal system of America, which place that system in a very interesting point of view.

First. In a single republic, all the power surrendered by the people is submitted to the administration of a single government; and the usurpations are guarded against by a division of the government into distinct and separate departments. In the compound republic of America, the power surrendered by the people is first divided between two distinct governments, and then the portion allotted to each subdivided among distinct and separate departments. Hence a double security arises to the rights of the people. The different governments will control each other, at the same time that each will be controlled by itself.

Second. It is of great importance in a republic not only to guard the society against the oppression of its rulers, but to guard one part of the society against the injustice of the other part. Different interests necessarily exist in different classes of citizens. If a majority be united by a common interest, the rights of the minority will be insecure. There are but two methods of providing against this evil: the one by creating a will in the community independent of the majority—that is, of the society itself; the other, by comprehending in the society so many separate descriptions of citizens as will render an unjust combination of a majority of the whole very improbable, if not impracticable. The first method prevails in all governments possessing an hereditary or self-appointed authority. This, at best, is but a precarious security; because a power independent of the society may as well espouse the unjust views of the major, as the rightful interests of the minor party, and may possibly be turned against both parties. The second method will be exemplified in the federal republic of the United States. Whilst all authority in it will be derived from and dependent on the society, the society itself will be broken into so many parts, interests, and classes of citizens, that the rights of individuals, or of the minority, will be in little danger from interested combinations of the majority. In a free government the security for civil rights must be the same as that for religious rights. It consists in the one case in the multiplicity of interests, and in the other in the multiplicity of sects. The degree of security in both cases will depend on the number of interests and sects; and this may be presumed to depend on the extent of country and number of people comprehended under the same government. This view of the subject must particularly recommend a proper federal system to all the sincere and considerate friends of republican government, since it shows that in exact proportion as the territory of the Union may be formed into more circumscribed Confederacies, or States oppressive combinations of a majority will be facilitated: the best security, under the republican forms, for the rights of every class of citizens, will be diminished: and consequently the stability and independence of some member of the government, the only other security, must be proportionately increased. Justice is the end of government. It is the end of civil society. It ever has been and ever will be pursued until it be obtained, or until liberty be lost in the pursuit. In a society under the forms of which the stronger faction can readily unite and oppress the weaker, anarchy may as truly be said to reign as in a state of nature, where the weaker individual is not secured against the violence of the stronger; and as, in the latter state, even the stronger individuals are prompted, by the uncertainty of their condition, to submit to a government which may protect the weak as well as themselves; so, in the former state, will the more powerful factions or parties be gradually induced, by a like motive, to wish for a government which will protect all parties, the weaker as well as the more powerful. It can be little doubted that if the State of

Rhode Island was separated from the Confederacy and left to itself, the insecurity of rights under the popular form of government within such narrow limits would be displayed by such reiterated oppressions of factious majorities that some power altogether independent of the people would soon be called for by the voice of the very factions whose misrule had proved the necessity of it. In the extended republic of the United States, and among the great variety of interests, parties, and sects which it embraces, a coalition of a majority of the whole society could seldom take place on any other principles than those of justice and the general good; whilst there being thus less danger to a minor from the will of a major party, there must be less pretext, also, to provide for the security of the former, by introducing into the government a will not dependent on the latter, or, in other words, a will independent of the society itself. It is no less certain than it is important, notwithstanding the contrary opinions which have been entertained, that the larger the society, provided it lie within a practical sphere, the more duly capable it will be of self-government. And happily for the REPUBLICAN CAUSE, the practicable sphere may be carried to a very great extent, by a judicious modification and mixture of the FEDERAL PRINCIPLE.

PUBLIUS

FEDERALIST PAPER NO. 52. THE HOUSE OF REPRESENTATIVES

From the New York Packet. Friday, February 8, 1788.

MADISON

To the People of the State of New York:

FROM the more general inquiries pursued in the four last papers, I pass on to a more particular examination of the several parts of the government. I shall begin with the House of Representatives.

The first view to be taken of this part of the government relates to the qualifications of the electors and the elected. Those of the former are to be the same with those of the electors of the most numerous branch of the State legislatures. The definition of the right of suffrage is very justly regarded as a fundamental article of republican government. It was incumbent on the convention, therefore, to define and establish this right in the Constitution. To have left it open for the occasional regulation of the Congress, would have been improper for the reason just mentioned. To have submitted it to the legislative discretion of the States, would have been improper for the same reason; and for the additional reason that it would have rendered too dependent on the State governments that branch of the federal government which ought to be dependent on the people alone. To have reduced the different qualifications in the different States to one uniform rule, would probably have been as dissatisfactory to some of the States as it would have been difficult to the convention. The provision made by the convention appears, therefore, to be the best that lay within their option. It must be satisfactory to every State, because it is conformable to the standard already established, or which may be established, by the State itself. It will be safe to the United States, because, being fixed by the State constitutions, it is not alterable by the State governments, and it cannot be feared that the people of the States will alter this part of their constitutions in such a manner as to abridge the rights secured to them by the federal Constitution.

The qualifications of the elected, being less carefully and properly defined by the State constitutions, and being at the same time more susceptible of uniformity, have been very properly considered and regulated by the convention. A representative of the United States must be of the age of twenty-five years; must have been seven years a citizen of the United States; must, at the time of his election, be an inhabitant of the State he is to represent; and, during the time of his service, must be in no office under the United States. Under these reasonable limitations, the door of this part of the federal government is open to merit of every description, whether native or adoptive, whether young or old, and without regard to poverty or wealth, or to any particular profession of religious faith.

The term for which the representatives are to be elected falls under a second view which may be taken of this branch. In order to decide on the propriety of this article, two questions must be considered: first, whether biennial elections will, in this case, be safe; secondly, whether they be necessary or useful.

First. As it is essential to liberty that the government in general should have a common interest with the people, so it is particularly essential that the branch of it under consideration should have an immediate dependence on, and an intimate sympathy with, the people. Frequent elections are unquestionably the only policy by which this dependence and sympathy can be effectually secured. But what particular degree of frequency may be absolutely necessary for the purpose, does not appear to be susceptible of any precise calculation, and must depend on a variety of circumstances with which it may be connected. Let us consult experience, the guide that ought always to be followed whenever it can be found.

The scheme of representation, as a substitute for a meeting of the citizens in person, being at most but very imperfectly known to ancient polity, it is in more modern times only that we are to expect instructive examples. And even here, in order to avoid a research too vague and diffusive, it will be proper to confine ourselves to the few examples which are best known, and which bear the greatest analogy to our particular case. The first to which this character ought to be applied, is the House of Commons in Great Britain. The history of this branch of the English Constitution, anterior to the date of Magna Charta, is too obscure to yield instruction. The very existence of it has been made a question among political antiquaries. The earliest records of subsequent date prove that parliaments were to SIT only every year; not that they were to be ELECTED every year. And even these annual sessions were left so much at the discretion of the monarch, that, under various pretexts, very long and dangerous intermissions were often contrived by royal ambition. To remedy this grievance, it was provided by a statute in the reign of Charles II, that the intermissions should not be protracted beyond a period of three years. On the accession of William III, when a revolution took place in the government, the subject was still more seriously resumed, and it was declared to be among the fundamental rights of the people that parliaments ought to be held FREQUENTLY. By another statute, which passed a few years later in the same reign, the term "frequently," which had alluded to the triennial period settled in the time of Charles II, is reduced to a precise meaning, it being expressly enacted that a new parliament shall be called within three years after the termination of the former. The last change, from three to seven years, is well known to have been introduced pretty early in the present century, under on alarm for the Hanoverian succession. From these facts it appears that the greatest frequency of elections which has been deemed necessary in that kingdom, for binding the representatives to their constituents, does not exceed a triennial return of them. And if we may argue from the degree of liberty retained even under septennial elections, and all the other vicious ingredients in the parliamentary constitution, we cannot doubt that a reduction of the period from seven to three years, with the other necessary reforms, would so far extend the influence of the people over their representatives as to satisfy us that biennial elections, under the federal system, cannot possibly be dangerous to the requisite dependence of the House of Representatives on their constituents.

Elections in Ireland, till of late, were regulated entirely by the discretion of the crown, and were seldom repeated, except on the accession of a new prince, or some other contingent event. The parliament which commenced with George II. was continued throughout his whole reign, a period of about thirty-five years. The only dependence of the representatives on the people consisted in the right of the latter to supply occasional vacancies by the election of new members, and in the chance of some event which might produce a general new election. The ability also of the Irish parliament to maintain the rights of their constituents, so far as the disposition might exist, was extremely shackled by the control of the crown over the subjects of their deliberation. Of late these shackles, if I mistake not, have been broken; and octennial parliaments have besides been established. What effect may be produced by this partial reform, must be left to further experience. The example of Ireland, from this view of it, can throw but little light on the subject. As far as we can draw any conclusion from it, it must be that if the people of that country have been able under all these disadvantages to retain any liberty whatever, the advantage of biennial elections would secure to them every degree of liberty, which might depend on a due connection between their representatives and themselves.

Let us bring our inquiries nearer home. The example of these States, when British colonies, claims particular attention, at the same time that it is so well known as to require little to be said on it. The principle of representation, in one branch of the legislature at least, was established in all of them. But the periods of election were different. They varied from one to seven years. Have we any reason to infer, from the spirit and conduct of the representatives of the people, prior to the Revolution, that biennial elections would have been dangerous to the public liberties? The spirit which everywhere displayed itself at the commencement of the struggle, and which vanquished the obstacles to independence, is the best of proofs that a sufficient portion of liberty had been everywhere enjoyed to inspire both a sense of its worth and a zeal for its proper enlargement This remark holds good, as well with regard to the then colonies whose elections were least frequent, as to those whose elections were most frequent Virginia was the colony which stood first in resisting the parliamentary usurpations of Great Britain; it was the first also in espousing, by public act, the resolution of independence. In Virginia, nevertheless, if I have not been misinformed, elections under the former government were septennial. This particular example is brought into view, not as a proof of any peculiar merit, for the priority in those instances was probably accidental; and still less of any advantage in SEPTENNIAL elections, for when compared with a greater frequency they are inadmissible; but merely as a proof, and I conceive it to be a very substantial proof, that the liberties of the people can be in no danger from BIENNIAL elections.

The conclusion resulting from these examples will be not a little strengthened by recollecting three circumstances. The first is, that the federal legislature will possess a part only of that supreme legislative authority which is vested completely in the British Parliament; and which, with a few exceptions, was exercised by the colonial assemblies and the Irish legislature. It is a received and well-founded maxim, that where no other circumstances affect the case, the greater the power is, the shorter ought to be its duration; and, conversely, the smaller the power, the more safely may its duration be protracted. In the second place, it has, on another occasion, been shown that the federal legislature will not only be restrained by its dependence on its people, as other legislative bodies are, but that it will be, moreover, watched and controlled by the several collateral legislatures, which other legislative bodies are not. And in the third place, no comparison can be made between the means that will be possessed by the more permanent branches of the federal government for seducing, if they should be disposed to seduce, the House of Representatives from their duty to the people, and the means of influence over the popular branch possessed by the other branches of the government above cited. With less power, therefore, to abuse, the federal representatives can be less tempted on one side, and will be doubly watched on the other.

PUBLIUS

FEDERALIST PAPER NO. 53. THE SAME SUBJECT CONTINUED (THE HOUSE OF REPRESENTATIVES)

For the Independent Journal. Saturday, February 9, 1788.

MADISON

To the People of the State of New York:

I SHALL here, perhaps, be reminded of a current observation, "that where annual elections end, tyranny begins." If it be true, as has often been remarked, that sayings which become proverbial are generally founded in reason, it is not less true, that when once established, they are often applied to cases to which the reason of them does not extend. I need not look for a proof beyond the case before us. What is the reason on which this proverbial observation is founded? No man will subject himself to the ridicule of pretending that any natural connection subsists between the sun or the seasons, and the period within which human virtue can bear the temptations of power. Happily for mankind, liberty is not, in this respect, confined to any single point of time; but lies within extremes, which afford sufficient latitude for all the variations which may be required by the various situations and circumstances of civil society. The election of magistrates might be, if it were found expedient, as in some instances it actually has been, daily, weekly, or monthly, as well as annual; and if circumstances may require a deviation from the rule on one side, why not also on the other side? Turning our attention to the periods established among ourselves, for the election of the most numerous branches of the State legislatures, we find them by no means coinciding any more in this instance, than in the elections of other civil magistrates. In Connecticut and Rhode Island, the periods are half-yearly. In the other States, South Carolina excepted, they are annual. In South Carolina they are biennial—as is proposed in the federal government. Here is a difference, as four to one, between the longest and shortest periods; and yet it would be not easy to show, that Connecticut or Rhode Island is better governed, or enjoys a greater share of rational liberty, than South Carolina; or that either the one or the other of these States is distinguished in these respects, and by these causes, from the States whose elections are different from both.

In searching for the grounds of this doctrine, I can discover but one, and that is wholly inapplicable to our case. The important distinction so well understood in America, between a Constitution established by the people and unalterable by the government, and a law established by the government and alterable by the government, seems to have been little understood and less observed in any other country. Wherever the supreme power of legislation has resided, has been supposed to reside also a full power to change the form of the government. Even in Great Britain, where the principles of political and civil liberty have been most discussed, and where we hear most of the rights of the Constitution, it is maintained that the authority of the Parliament is transcendent and uncontrollable, as well with regard to the Constitution, as the ordinary objects of legislative provision. They have accordingly, in several instances, actually changed, by legislative acts, some of the most fundamental articles of the government. They have in particular, on several occasions, changed the period of election; and, on the last occasion, not only introduced septennial in place of triennial elections, but by the same act, continued themselves in place four years beyond the term for which they were elected by the people. An attention to these dangerous practices has produced a very natural alarm in the votaries of free government, of which frequency of elections is the corner-stone; and has led them to seek for some security to liberty, against the danger to which it is exposed. Where no Constitution, paramount to the government, either existed or could be obtained, no constitutional security, similar to that established in the United States, was to be attempted. Some other security, therefore, was to be sought for; and what better security would the case admit, than that of selecting and appealing to some simple and familiar portion of time, as a standard for measuring the danger of innovations, for fixing the national sentiment, and for uniting the patriotic exertions? The most simple and familiar portion of time, applicable to the subject was that of a year; and hence the doctrine has been inculcated by a laudable zeal, to erect some barrier against the gradual innovations of an unlimited government, that the advance towards tyranny was to be calculated by the distance of departure from the fixed point of annual elections. But what necessity can there be of applying this expedient to a government limited, as the federal government will be, by the authority of a paramount Constitution? Or who will pretend that the liberties of the people of America will not be more secure under biennial elections, unalterably fixed by such a Constitution, than those of any other nation would be, where elections were annual, or even more frequent, but subject to alterations by the ordinary power of the government?

The second question stated is, whether biennial elections be necessary or useful. The propriety of answering this question in the affirmative will appear from several very obvious considerations.

No man can be a competent legislator who does not add to an upright intention and a sound judgment a certain degree of knowledge of the subjects on which he is to legislate. A part of this knowledge may be acquired by means of information which lie within the compass of men in private as well as public stations. Another part can only be attained, or at least thoroughly attained, by actual experience in the station which requires the use of it. The period of service, ought, therefore, in all such cases, to bear some proportion to the extent of practical knowledge requisite to the due performance of the service. The period of legislative service established in most of the States for the more numerous branch is, as we have seen, one year. The question then may be put into this simple form: does the period of two years bear no greater proportion to the knowledge requisite for federal legislation than one year does to the knowledge requisite for State legislation? The very statement of the question, in this form, suggests the answer that ought to be given to it.

In a single State, the requisite knowledge relates to the existing laws which are uniform throughout the State, and with which all the citizens are more or less conversant; and to the general affairs of the State, which lie within a small compass, are not very diversified, and occupy much of the attention and conversation of every class of people. The great theatre of the United States presents a very different scene. The laws are so far from being uniform, that they vary in every State; whilst the public affairs of the Union are spread throughout a very extensive region, and are extremely diversified by the local affairs connected with them, and can with difficulty be correctly learnt in any other place than in the central councils to which a knowledge of them will be brought by the representatives of every part of the empire. Yet some knowledge of the affairs, and even of the laws, of all the States, ought to be possessed by the members from each of the States. How can foreign trade be properly regulated by uniform laws, without some acquaintance with the commerce, the ports, the usages, and the regulations of the different States? How can the trade between the different States be duly regulated, without some knowledge of their relative situations in these and other respects? How can taxes be judiciously imposed and effectually collected, if they be not accommodated to the different laws and local circumstances relating to these objects in the different States? How can uniform regulations for the militia be duly provided, without a similar knowledge of many internal circumstances by which the States are distinguished from each other? These are the principal objects of federal legislation, and suggest most forcibly the extensive information which the representatives ought to acquire. The other interior objects will require a proportional degree of information with regard to them.

It is true that all these difficulties will, by degrees, be very much diminished. The most laborious task will be the proper inauguration of the government and the primeval formation of a federal code. Improvements on the first draughts will every year become both easier and fewer. Past transactions of the government will be a ready and accurate source of information to new members. The affairs of the Union will become more and more objects of curiosity and conversation among the citizens at large. And the increased intercourse among those of different States will contribute not a little to diffuse a mutual knowledge of their affairs, as this again will contribute to a general assimilation of their manners and laws. But with all these abatements, the business of federal legislation must continue so far to exceed, both in novelty and difficulty, the legislative business of a single State, as to justify the longer period of service assigned to those who are to transact it.

A branch of knowledge which belongs to the acquirements of a federal representative, and which has not been mentioned is that of foreign affairs. In regulating our own commerce he ought to be not only acquainted with the treaties between the United States and other nations, but also with the commercial policy and laws of other nations. He ought not to be altogether ignorant of the law of nations; for that, as far as it is a proper object of municipal legislation, is submitted to the federal government. And although the House of Representatives is not immediately to participate in foreign negotiations and arrangements, yet from the necessary connection between the several branches of public affairs, those particular branches will frequently deserve attention in the ordinary course of legislation, and will sometimes demand particular legislative sanction and co-operation. Some portion of this knowledge may, no doubt, be acquired in a man's closet; but some of it also can only be derived from the public sources of information; and all of it will be acquired to best effect by a practical attention to the subject during the period of actual service in the legislature.

There are other considerations, of less importance, perhaps, but which are not unworthy of notice. The distance which many of the representatives will be obliged to travel, and the arrangements rendered necessary by that circumstance, might be much more serious objections with fit men to this service, if limited to a single year, than if extended to two years. No argument can be drawn on this subject, from the case of the delegates to the existing Congress. They are elected annually, it is true; but their re-election is considered by the legislative assemblies almost as a matter of course. The election of the representatives by the people would not be governed by the same principle.

A few of the members, as happens in all such assemblies, will possess superior talents; will, by frequent reelections, become members of long standing; will be thoroughly masters of the public business, and perhaps not unwilling to avail themselves of those advantages. The greater the proportion of new members, and the less the information of the bulk of the members the more apt will they be to fall into the snares that may be laid for them. This remark is no less applicable to the relation which will subsist between the House of Representatives and the Senate.

It is an inconvenience mingled with the advantages of our frequent elections even in single States, where they are large, and hold but one legislative session in a year, that spurious elections cannot be investigated and annulled in time for the decision to have its due effect. If a return can be obtained, no matter by what unlawful means, the irregular member, who takes his seat of course, is sure of holding it a sufficient time to answer his purposes. Hence, a very pernicious encouragement is given to the use of unlawful means, for obtaining irregular returns. Were elections for the federal legislature to be annual, this practice might become a very serious abuse, particularly in the more distant States. Each house is, as it necessarily must be, the judge of the elections, qualifications, and returns of its members; and whatever improvements may be suggested by experience, for simplifying and accelerating the process in disputed cases, so great a portion of a year would unavoidably elapse, before an illegitimate member could be dispossessed of his seat, that the prospect of such an event would be little check to unfair and illicit means of obtaining a seat.

All these considerations taken together warrant us in affirming, that biennial elections will be as useful to the affairs of the public as we have seen that they will be safe to the liberty of the people.

PUBLIUS

FEDERALIST PAPER NO. 54. THE APPORTIONMENT OF MEMBERS AMONG THE STATES

From the New York Packet. Tuesday, February 12, 1788.

MADISON

To the People of the State of New York:

THE next view which I shall take of the House of Representatives relates to the appointment of its members to the several States which is to be determined by the same rule with that of direct taxes.

It is not contended that the number of people in each State ought not to be the standard for regulating the proportion of those who are to represent the people of each State. The establishment of the same rule for the appointment of taxes, will probably be as little contested; though the rule itself in this case, is by no means founded on the same principle. In the former case, the rule is understood to refer to the personal rights of the people, with which it has a natural and universal connection. In the latter, it has reference to the proportion of wealth, of which it is in no case a precise measure, and in ordinary cases a very unfit one. But notwithstanding the imperfection of the rule as applied to the relative wealth and contributions of the States, it is evidently the least objectionable among the practicable rules, and had too recently obtained the general sanction of America, not to have found a ready preference with the convention.

All this is admitted, it will perhaps be said; but does it follow, from an admission of numbers for the measure of representation, or of slaves combined with free citizens as a ratio of taxation, that slaves ought to be included in the numerical rule of representation? Slaves are considered as property, not as persons. They ought therefore to be comprehended in estimates of taxation which are founded on property, and to be excluded from representation which is regulated by a census of persons. This is the objection, as I understand it, stated in its full force. I shall be equally candid in stating the reasoning which may be offered on the opposite side.

"We subscribe to the doctrine," might one of our Southern brethren observe, "that representation relates more immediately to persons, and taxation more immediately to property, and we join in the application of this distinction to the case of our slaves. But we must deny the fact, that slaves are considered merely as property, and in no respect whatever as persons. The true state of the case is, that they partake of both these qualities: being considered by our laws, in some respects, as persons, and in other respects as property. In being compelled to labor, not for himself, but for a master; in being vendible by one master to another master; and in being subject at all times to be restrained in his liberty and chastised in his body, by the capricious will of another—the slave may appear to be degraded from the human rank, and classed with those irrational animals which fall under the legal denomination of property. In being protected, on the other hand, in his life and in his limbs, against the violence of all others, even the master of his labor and his liberty; and in being punishable himself for all violence committed against others—the slave is no less evidently regarded by the law as a member of the society, not as a part of the irrational creation; as a moral person, not as a mere article of property. The federal Constitution, therefore, decides with great propriety on the case of our slaves, when it views them in the mixed character of persons and of property. This is in fact their true character. It is the character bestowed on them by the laws under which they live; and it will not be denied, that these are the proper criterion; because it is only under the pretext that the laws have transformed the negroes into subjects of property, that a place is disputed them in the computation of numbers; and it is admitted, that if the laws were to restore the rights which have been taken away, the negroes could no longer be refused an equal share of representation with the other inhabitants.

"This question may be placed in another light. It is agreed on all sides, that numbers are the best scale of wealth and taxation, as they are the only proper scale of representation. Would the convention have been impartial or consistent, if they had rejected the slaves from the list of inhabitants, when the shares of representation were to be calculated, and inserted them on the lists when the tariff of contributions was to be adjusted? Could it be reasonably expected, that the Southern States would concur in a system, which considered their slaves in some degree as men, when burdens were to be imposed, but refused to consider them in the same light, when advantages were to be conferred? Might not some surprise also be expressed, that those who reproach the Southern States with the barbarous policy of considering as property a part of their human brethren, should themselves contend, that the government to which all the States are to be parties, ought to consider this unfortunate race more completely in the unnatural light of property, than the very laws of which they complain?

"It may be replied, perhaps, that slaves are not included in the estimate of representatives in any of the States possessing them. They neither vote themselves nor increase the votes of their masters. Upon what principle, then, ought they to be taken into the federal estimate of representation? In rejecting them altogether, the Constitution would, in this respect, have followed the very laws which have been appealed to as the proper guide.

"This objection is repelled by a single observation. It is a fundamental principle of the proposed Constitution, that as the aggregate number of representatives allotted to the several States is to be determined by a federal rule, founded on the aggregate number of inhabitants, so the right of choosing this allotted number in each State is to be exercised by such part of the inhabitants as the State itself may designate. The qualifications on which the right of suffrage depend are not, perhaps, the same in any two States. In some of the States the difference is very material. In every State, a certain proportion of inhabitants are deprived of this right by the constitution of the State, who will be included in the census by which the federal Constitution apportions the representatives. In this point of view the Southern States might retort the complaint, by insisting that the principle laid down by the convention required that no regard should be had to the policy of particular States towards their own inhabitants; and consequently, that the slaves, as inhabitants, should have been admitted into the census according to their full number, in like manner with other inhabitants, who, by the policy of other States, are not admitted to all the rights of citizens. A rigorous adherence, however, to this principle, is waived by those who would be gainers by it. All that they ask is that equal moderation be shown on the other side. Let the case of the slaves be considered, as it is in truth, a peculiar one. Let the compromising expedient of the Constitution be mutually adopted, which regards them as inhabitants, but as debased by servitude below the equal level of free inhabitants, which regards the SLAVE as divested of two fifths of the MAN.

"After all, may not another ground be taken on which this article of the Constitution will admit of a still more ready defense? We have hitherto proceeded on the idea that representation related to persons only, and not at all to property. But is it a just idea? Government is instituted no less for protection of the property, than of the persons, of individuals. The one as well as the other, therefore, may be considered as represented by those who are charged with the government. Upon this principle it is, that in several of the States, and particularly in the State of New York, one branch of the government is intended more especially to be the guardian of property, and is accordingly elected by that part of the society which is most interested in this object of government. In the federal Constitution, this policy does not prevail. The rights of property are committed into the same hands with the personal rights. Some attention ought, therefore, to be paid to property in the choice of those hands.

"For another reason, the votes allowed in the federal legislature to the people of each State, ought to bear some proportion to the comparative wealth of the States. States have not, like individuals, an influence over each other, arising from superior advantages of fortune. If the law allows an opulent citizen but a single vote in the choice of his representative, the respect and consequence which he derives from his fortunate situation very frequently guide the votes of others to the objects of his choice; and through this imperceptible channel the rights of property are conveyed into the public representation. A State possesses no such influence over other States. It is not probable that the richest State in the Confederacy will ever influence the choice of a single representative in any other State. Nor will the representatives of the larger and richer States possess any other advantage in the federal legislature, over the representatives of other States, than what may result from their superior number alone. As far, therefore, as their superior wealth and weight may justly entitle them to any advantage, it ought to be secured to them by a superior share of representation. The new Constitution is, in this respect, materially different from the existing Confederation, as well as from that of the United Netherlands, and other similar confederacies. In each of the latter, the efficacy of the federal resolutions depends on the subsequent and voluntary resolutions of the states composing the union. Hence the states, though possessing an equal vote in the public councils, have an unequal influence, corresponding with the unequal importance of these subsequent and voluntary resolutions. Under the proposed Constitution, the federal acts will take effect without the necessary intervention of the individual States. They will depend merely on the majority of votes in the federal legislature, and consequently each vote, whether proceeding from a larger or smaller State, or a State more or less wealthy or powerful, will have an equal weight and efficacy: in the same manner as the votes individually given in a State legislature, by the representatives of unequal counties or other districts, have each a precise equality of value and effect; or if there be any difference in the case, it proceeds from the difference in the personal character of the individual representative, rather than from any regard to the extent of the district from which he comes."

Such is the reasoning which an advocate for the Southern interests might employ on this subject; and although it may appear to be a little strained in some points, yet, on the whole, I must confess that it fully reconciles me to the scale of representation which the convention have established.

In one respect, the establishment of a common measure for representation and taxation will have a very salutary effect. As the accuracy of the census to be obtained by the Congress will necessarily depend, in a considerable degree on the disposition, if not on the co-operation, of the States, it is of great importance that the States should feel as little bias as possible, to swell or to reduce the amount of their numbers. Were their share of representation alone to be governed by this rule, they would have an interest in exaggerating their inhabitants. Were the rule to decide their share of taxation alone, a contrary temptation would prevail. By extending the rule to both objects, the States will have opposite interests, which will control and balance each other, and produce the requisite impartiality.

PUBLIUS

FEDERALIST PAPER NO. 55. THE TOTAL NUMBER OF THE HOUSE OF REPRESENTATIVES

For the Independent Journal. Wednesday, February 13, 1788.

MADISON

To the People of the State of New York:

THE number of which the House of Representatives is to consist, forms another and a very interesting point of view, under which this branch of the federal legislature may be contemplated. Scarce any article, indeed, in the whole Constitution seems to be rendered more worthy of attention, by the weight of character and the apparent force of argument with which it has been assailed. The charges exhibited against it are, first, that so small a number of representatives will be an unsafe depositary of the public interests; secondly, that they will not possess a proper knowledge of the local circumstances of their numerous constituents; thirdly, that they will be taken from that class of citizens which will sympathize least with the feelings of the mass of the people, and be most likely to aim at a permanent elevation of the few on the depression of the many; fourthly, that defective as the number will be in the first instance, it will be more and more disproportionate, by the increase of the people, and the obstacles which will prevent a correspondent increase of the representatives.

In general it may be remarked on this subject, that no political problem is less susceptible of a precise solution than that which relates to the number most convenient for a representative legislature; nor is there any point on which the policy of the several States is more at variance, whether we compare their legislative assemblies directly with each other, or consider the proportions which they respectively bear to the number of their constituents. Passing over the difference between the smallest and largest States, as Delaware, whose most numerous branch consists of twenty-one representatives, and Massachusetts, where it amounts to between three and four hundred, a very considerable difference is observable among States nearly equal in population. The number of representatives in Pennsylvania is not more than one fifth of that in the State last mentioned. New York, whose population is to that of South Carolina as six to five, has little more than one third of the number of representatives. As great a disparity prevails between the States of Georgia and Delaware or Rhode Island. In Pennsylvania, the representatives do not bear a greater proportion to their constituents than of one for every four or five thousand. In Rhode Island, they bear a proportion of at least one for every thousand. And according to the constitution of Georgia, the proportion may be carried to one to every ten electors; and must unavoidably far exceed the proportion in any of the other States.

Another general remark to be made is, that the ratio between the representatives and the people ought not to be the same where the latter are very numerous as where they are very few. Were the representatives in Virginia to be regulated by the standard in Rhode Island, they would, at this time, amount to between four and five hundred; and twenty or thirty years hence, to a thousand. On the other hand, the ratio of Pennsylvania, if applied to the State of Delaware, would reduce the representative assembly of the latter to seven or eight members. Nothing can be more fallacious than to found our political calculations on arithmetical principles. Sixty or seventy men may be more properly trusted with a given degree of power than six or seven. But it does not follow that six or seven hundred would be proportionably a better depositary. And if we carry on the supposition to six or seven thousand, the whole reasoning ought to be reversed. The truth is, that in all cases a certain number at least seems to be necessary to secure the benefits of free consultation and discussion, and to guard against too easy a combination for improper purposes; as, on the other hand, the number ought at most to be kept within a certain limit, in order to avoid the confusion and intemperance of a multitude. In all very numerous assemblies, of whatever character composed, passion never fails to wrest the sceptre from reason. Had every Athenian citizen been a Socrates, every Athenian assembly would still have been a mob.

It is necessary also to recollect here the observations which were applied to the case of biennial elections. For the same reason that the limited powers of the Congress, and the control of the State legislatures, justify less frequent elections than the public safely might otherwise require, the members of the Congress need be less numerous than if they possessed the whole power of legislation, and were under no other than the ordinary restraints of other legislative bodies.

Documents of Revolution

With these general ideas in our mind, let us weigh the objections which have been stated against the number of members proposed for the House of Representatives. It is said, in the first place, that so small a number cannot be safely trusted with so much power.

The number of which this branch of the legislature is to consist, at the outset of the government, will be sixty-five. Within three years a census is to be taken, when the number may be augmented to one for every thirty thousand inhabitants; and within every successive period of ten years the census is to be renewed, and augmentations may continue to be made under the above limitation. It will not be thought an extravagant conjecture that the first census will, at the rate of one for every thirty thousand, raise the number of representatives to at least one hundred. Estimating the negroes in the proportion of three fifths, it can scarcely be doubted that the population of the United States will by that time, if it does not already, amount to three millions. At the expiration of twenty-five years, according to the computed rate of increase, the number of representatives will amount to two hundred, and of fifty years, to four hundred. This is a number which, I presume, will put an end to all fears arising from the smallness of the body. I take for granted here what I shall, in answering the fourth objection, hereafter show, that the number of representatives will be augmented from time to time in the manner provided by the Constitution. On a contrary supposition, I should admit the objection to have very great weight indeed.

The true question to be decided then is, whether the smallness of the number, as a temporary regulation, be dangerous to the public liberty? Whether sixty-five members for a few years, and a hundred or two hundred for a few more, be a safe depositary for a limited and well-guarded power of legislating for the United States? I must own that I could not give a negative answer to this question, without first obliterating every impression which I have received with regard to the present genius of the people of America, the spirit which actuates the State legislatures, and the principles which are incorporated with the political character of every class of citizens I am unable to conceive that the people of America, in their present temper, or under any circumstances which can speedily happen, will choose, and every second year repeat the choice of, sixty-five or a hundred men who would be disposed to form and pursue a scheme of tyranny or treachery. I am unable to conceive that the State legislatures, which must feel so many motives to watch, and which possess so many means of counteracting, the federal legislature, would fail either to detect or to defeat a conspiracy of the latter against the liberties of their common constituents. I am equally unable to conceive that there are at this time, or can be in any short time, in the United States, any sixty-five or a hundred men capable of recommending themselves to the choice of the people at large, who would either desire or dare, within the short space of two years, to betray the solemn trust committed to them. What change of circumstances, time, and a fuller population of our country may produce, requires a prophetic spirit to declare, which makes no part of my pretensions. But judging from the circumstances now before us, and from the probable state of them within a moderate period of time, I must pronounce that the liberties of America cannot be unsafe in the number of hands proposed by the federal Constitution.

From what quarter can the danger proceed? Are we afraid of foreign gold? If foreign gold could so easily corrupt our federal rulers and enable them to ensnare and betray their constituents, how has it happened that we are at this time a free and independent nation? The Congress which conducted us through the Revolution was a less numerous body than their successors will be; they were not chosen by, nor responsible to, their fellowcitizens at large; though appointed from year to year, and recallable at pleasure, they were generally continued for three years, and prior to the ratification of the federal articles, for a still longer term. They held their consultations always under the veil of secrecy; they had the sole transaction of our affairs with foreign nations; through the whole course of the war they had the fate of their country more in their hands than it is to be hoped will ever be the case with our future representatives; and from the greatness of the prize at stake, and the eagerness of the party which lost it, it may well be supposed that the use of other means than force would not have been scrupled. Yet we know by happy experience that the public trust was not betrayed; nor has the purity of our public councils in this particular ever suffered, even from the whispers of calumny.

Is the danger apprehended from the other branches of the federal government? But where are the means to be found by the President, or the Senate, or both? Their emoluments of office, it is to be presumed, will not, and without a previous corruption of the House of Representatives cannot, more than suffice for very different purposes; their private fortunes, as they must all be American citizens, cannot possibly be sources of danger. The only means, then, which they can possess, will be in the dispensation of appointments. Is it here that suspicion rests her charge? Sometimes we are told that this fund of corruption is to be exhausted by the President in subduing the virtue of the Senate. Now, the fidelity of the other House is to be the victim. The improbability of such a mercenary and perfidious combination of the several members of government, standing on as different foundations as republican principles will well admit, and at the same time accountable to the society over which they are placed, ought alone to quiet this apprehension. But, fortunately, the Constitution has provided a still further safeguard. The members of the Congress are rendered ineligible to any civil offices that may be created, or of which the emoluments may be increased, during the term of their election. No offices therefore can be dealt out to the existing members but such as may become vacant by ordinary casualties: and to suppose that these would be sufficient to purchase the guardians of the people, selected by the people themselves, is to renounce every rule by which events ought to be calculated, and to substitute an indiscriminate and unbounded jealousy, with which all reasoning must be vain. The sincere friends of liberty, who give themselves up to the extravagancies of this passion, are not aware of the injury they do their own cause. As there is a degree of depravity in mankind which requires a certain degree of circumspection and distrust, so there are other qualities in human nature which justify a certain portion of esteem and confidence. Republican government presupposes the existence of these qualities in a higher degree than any other form. Were the pictures which have been drawn by the political jealousy of some among us faithful likenesses of the human character, the inference would be, that there is not sufficient virtue among men for self-government; and that nothing less than the chains of despotism can restrain them from destroying and devouring one another.

PUBLIUS

FEDERALIST PAPER NO. 56. THE SAME SUBJECT CONTINUED (THE TOTAL NUMBER OF THE HOUSE OF REPRESENTATIVES)

For the Independent Journal. Saturday, February 16, 1788.

MADISON

To the People of the State of New York:

THE SECOND charge against the House of Representatives is, that it will be too small to possess a due knowledge of the interests of its constituents.

As this objection evidently proceeds from a comparison of the proposed number of representatives with the great extent of the United States, the number of their inhabitants, and the diversity of their interests, without taking into view at the same time the circumstances which will distinguish the Congress from other legislative bodies, the best answer that can be given to it will be a brief explanation of these peculiarities.

It is a sound and important principle that the representative ought to be acquainted with the interests and circumstances of his constituents. But this principle can extend no further than to those circumstances and interests to which the authority and care of the representative relate. An ignorance of a variety of minute and particular objects, which do not lie within the compass of legislation, is consistent with every attribute necessary to a due performance of the legislative trust. In determining the extent of information required in the exercise of a particular authority, recourse then must be had to the objects within the purview of that authority.

What are to be the objects of federal legislation? Those which are of most importance, and which seem most to require local knowledge, are commerce, taxation, and the militia.

A proper regulation of commerce requires much information, as has been elsewhere remarked; but as far as this information relates to the laws and local situation of each individual State, a very few representatives would be very sufficient vehicles of it to the federal councils.

Taxation will consist, in a great measure, of duties which will be involved in the regulation of commerce. So far the preceding remark is applicable to this object. As far as it may consist of internal collections, a more diffusive knowledge of the circumstances of the State may be necessary. But will not this also be possessed in sufficient degree by a very few intelligent men, diffusively elected within the State? Divide the largest State into ten or twelve districts, and it will be found that there will be no peculiar local interests in either, which will not be within the knowledge of the representative of the district. Besides this source of information, the laws of the State, framed by representatives from every part of it, will be almost of themselves a sufficient guide. In every State there have been made, and must continue to be made, regulations on this subject which will, in many cases, leave little more to be done by the federal legislature, than to review the different laws, and reduce them in one general act. A skillful individual in his closet with all the local codes before him, might compile a law on some subjects of taxation for the whole union, without any aid from oral information, and it may be expected that whenever internal taxes may be necessary, and particularly in cases requiring uniformity throughout the States, the more simple objects will be preferred. To be fully sensible of the facility which will be given to this branch of federal legislation by the assistance of the State codes, we need only suppose for a moment that this or any other State were divided into a number of parts, each having and exercising within itself a power of local legislation. Is it not evident that a degree of local information and preparatory labor would be found in the several volumes of their proceedings, which would very much shorten the labors of the general legislature, and render a much smaller number of members sufficient for it? The federal councils will derive great advantage from another circumstance. The representatives of each State will not only bring with them a considerable knowledge of its laws, and a local knowledge of their respective districts, but will probably in all cases have been members, and may even at the very time be members, of the State legislature, where all the local information and interests of the State are assembled, and from whence they may easily be conveyed by a very few hands into the legislature of the United States.

(The observations made on the subject of taxation apply with greater force to the case of the militia. For however different the rules of discipline may be in different States, they are the same throughout each particular State; and depend on circumstances which can differ but little in different parts of the same State.)(E1)

(With regard to the regulation of the militia, there are scarcely any circumstances in reference to which local knowledge can be said to be necessary. The general face of the country, whether mountainous or level, most fit for the operations of infantry or cavalry, is almost the only consideration of this nature that can occur. The art of war teaches general principles of organization, movement, and discipline, which apply universally.)(E1)

The attentive reader will discern that the reasoning here used, to prove the sufficiency of a moderate number of representatives, does not in any respect contradict what was urged on another occasion with regard to the extensive information which the representatives ought to possess, and the time that might be necessary for acquiring it. This information, so far as it may relate to local objects, is rendered necessary and difficult, not by a difference of laws and local circumstances within a single State, but of those among different States. Taking each State by itself, its laws are the same, and its interests but little diversified. A few men, therefore, will possess all the knowledge requisite for a proper representation of them. Were the interests and affairs of each individual State perfectly simple and uniform, a knowledge of them in one part would involve a knowledge of them in every other, and the whole State might be competently represented by a single member taken from any part of it. On a comparison of the different States together, we find a great dissimilarity in their laws, and in many other circumstances connected with the objects of federal legislation, with all of which the federal representatives ought to have some acquaintance. Whilst a few representatives, therefore, from each State, may bring with them a due knowledge of their own State, every representative will have much information to acquire concerning all the other States. The changes of time, as was formerly remarked, on the comparative situation of the different States, will have an assimilating effect. The effect of time on the internal affairs of the States, taken singly, will be just the contrary. At present some of the States are little more than a society of husbandmen. Few of them have made much progress in those branches of industry which give a variety and complexity to the affairs of a nation. These, however, will in all of them be the fruits of a more advanced population, and will require, on the part of each State, a fuller representation. The foresight of the convention has accordingly taken care that the progress of population may be accompanied with a proper increase of the representative branch of the government.

The experience of Great Britain, which presents to mankind so many political lessons, both of the monitory and exemplary kind, and which has been frequently consulted in the course of these inquiries, corroborates the result of the reflections which we have just made. The number of inhabitants in the two kingdoms of England and Scotland cannot be stated at less than eight millions. The representatives of these eight millions in the House of Commons amount to five hundred and fifty-eight. Of this number, one ninth are elected by three hundred and sixty-four persons, and one half, by five thousand seven hundred and twenty-three persons.(1) It cannot be supposed that the half thus elected, and who do not even reside among the people at large, can add any thing either to the security of the people against the government, or to the knowledge of their circumstances and interests in the legislative councils. On the contrary, it is notorious, that they are more frequently the representatives and instruments of the executive magistrate, than the guardians and advocates of the popular rights. They might therefore, with great propriety, be considered as something more than a mere deduction from the real representatives of the nation. We will, however, consider them in this light alone, and will not extend the deduction to a considerable number of others, who do not reside among their constituents, are very faintly connected with them, and have very little particular knowledge of their affairs. With all these concessions, two hundred and seventy-nine persons only will be the depository of the safety, interest, and happiness of eight millions that is to say, there will be one representative only to maintain the rights and explain the situation of TWENTY-EIGHT THOUSAND SIX HUNDRED AND SEVENTY constitutents, in an assembly exposed to the whole force of executive influence, and extending its authority to every object of legislation within a nation whose affairs are in the highest degree diversified and complicated. Yet it is very certain, not only that a valuable portion of freedom has been preserved under all these circumstances, but that the defects in the British code are chargeable, in a very small proportion, on the ignorance of the legislature concerning the circumstances of the people. Allowing to this case the weight which is due to it, and comparing it with that of the House of Representatives as above explained it seems to give the fullest assurance, that a representative for every THIRTY THOUSAND INHABITANTS will render the latter both a safe and competent guardian of the interests which will be confided to it.

PUBLIUS

1. Burgh's "Political Disquisitions."
E1. Two versions of this paragraph appear in different editions.

FEDERALIST PAPER NO. 57. THE ALLEGED TENDENCY OF THE NEW PLAN TO ELEVATE THE FEW AT THE EXPENSE OF THE MANY CONSIDERED IN CONNECTION WITH REPRESENTATION.

From the New York Packet. Tuesday, February 19, 1788.

MADISON

To the People of the State of New York:

THE THIRD charge against the House of Representatives is, that it will be taken from that class of citizens which will have least sympathy with the mass of the people, and be most likely to aim at an ambitious sacrifice of the many to the aggrandizement of the few.

Of all the objections which have been framed against the federal Constitution, this is perhaps the most extraordinary. Whilst the objection itself is levelled against a pretended oligarchy, the principle of it strikes at the very root of republican government.

The aim of every political constitution is, or ought to be, first to obtain for rulers men who possess most wisdom to discern, and most virtue to pursue, the common good of the society; and in the next place, to take the most effectual precautions for keeping them virtuous whilst they continue to hold their public trust. The elective mode of obtaining rulers is the characteristic policy of republican government. The means relied on in this form of government for preventing their degeneracy are numerous and various. The most effectual one, is such a limitation of the term of appointments as will maintain a proper responsibility to the people.

Let me now ask what circumstance there is in the constitution of the House of Representatives that violates the principles of republican government, or favors the elevation of the few on the ruins of the many? Let me ask whether every circumstance is not, on the contrary, strictly conformable to these principles, and scrupulously impartial to the rights and pretensions of every class and description of citizens?

Documents of Revolution

Who are to be the electors of the federal representatives? Not the rich, more than the poor; not the learned, more than the ignorant; not the haughty heirs of distinguished names, more than the humble sons of obscurity and unpropitious fortune. The electors are to be the great body of the people of the United States. They are to be the same who exercise the right in every State of electing the corresponding branch of the legislature of the State.

Who are to be the objects of popular choice? Every citizen whose merit may recommend him to the esteem and confidence of his country. No qualification of wealth, of birth, of religious faith, or of civil profession is permitted to fetter the judgement or disappoint the inclination of the people.

If we consider the situation of the men on whom the free suffrages of their fellow-citizens may confer the representative trust, we shall find it involving every security which can be devised or desired for their fidelity to their constituents.

In the first place, as they will have been distinguished by the preference of their fellow-citizens, we are to presume that in general they will be somewhat distinguished also by those qualities which entitle them to it, and which promise a sincere and scrupulous regard to the nature of their engagements.

In the second place, they will enter into the public service under circumstances which cannot fail to produce a temporary affection at least to their constituents. There is in every breast a sensibility to marks of honor, of favor, of esteem, and of confidence, which, apart from all considerations of interest, is some pledge for grateful and benevolent returns. Ingratitude is a common topic of declamation against human nature; and it must be confessed that instances of it are but too frequent and flagrant, both in public and in private life. But the universal and extreme indignation which it inspires is itself a proof of the energy and prevalence of the contrary sentiment.

In the third place, those ties which bind the representative to his constituents are strengthened by motives of a more selfish nature. His pride and vanity attach him to a form of government which favors his pretensions and gives him a share in its honors and distinctions. Whatever hopes or projects might be entertained by a few aspiring characters, it must generally happen that a great proportion of the men deriving their advancement from their influence with the people, would have more to hope from a preservation of the favor, than from innovations in the government subversive of the authority of the people.

All these securities, however, would be found very insufficient without the restraint of frequent elections. Hence, in the fourth place, the House of Representatives is so constituted as to support in the members an habitual recollection of their dependence on the people. Before the sentiments impressed on their minds by the mode of their elevation can be effaced by the exercise of power, they will be compelled to anticipate the moment when their power is to cease, when their exercise of it is to be reviewed, and when they must descend to the level from which they were raised; there forever to remain unless a faithful discharge of their trust shall have established their title to a renewal of it.

I will add, as a fifth circumstance in the situation of the House of Representatives, restraining them from oppressive measures, that they can make no law which will not have its full operation on themselves and their friends, as well as on the great mass of the society. This has always been deemed one of the strongest bonds by which human policy can connect the rulers and the people together. It creates between them that communion of interests and sympathy of sentiments, of which few governments have furnished examples; but without which every government degenerates into tyranny. If it be asked, what is to restrain the House of Representatives from making legal discriminations in favor of themselves and a particular class of the society? I answer: the genius of the whole system; the nature of just and constitutional laws; and above all, the vigilant and manly spirit which actuates the people of America—a spirit which nourishes freedom, and in return is nourished by it.

If this spirit shall ever be so far debased as to tolerate a law not obligatory on the legislature, as well as on the people, the people will be prepared to tolerate any thing but liberty.

Such will be the relation between the House of Representatives and their constituents. Duty, gratitude, interest, ambition itself, are the chords by which they will be bound to fidelity and sympathy with the great mass of the people. It is possible that these may all be insufficient to control the caprice and wickedness of man. But are they not all that government will admit, and that human prudence can devise? Are they not the genuine and the characteristic means by which republican government provides for the liberty and happiness of the people? Are they not the identical means on which every State government in the Union relies for the attainment of these important ends? What then are we to understand by the objection which this paper has combated? What are we to say to the men who profess the most flaming zeal for republican government, yet boldly impeach the fundamental principle of it; who pretend to be champions for the right and the capacity of the people to choose their own rulers, yet maintain that they will prefer those only who will immediately and infallibly betray the trust committed to them?

Were the objection to be read by one who had not seen the mode prescribed by the Constitution for the choice of representatives, he could suppose nothing less than that some unreasonable qualification of property was annexed to the right of suffrage; or that the right of eligibility was limited to persons of particular families or fortunes; or at least that the mode prescribed by the State constitutions was in some respect or other, very grossly departed from. We have seen how far such a supposition would err, as to the two first points. Nor would it, in fact, be less erroneous as to the last. The only difference discoverable between the two cases is, that each representative of the United States will be elected by five or six thousand citizens; whilst in the individual States, the election of a representative is left to about as many hundreds. Will it be pretended that this difference is sufficient to justify an attachment to the State governments, and an abhorrence to the federal government? If this be the point on which the objection turns, it deserves to be examined.

Is it supported by REASON? This cannot be said, without maintaining that five or six thousand citizens are less capable of choosing a fit representative, or more liable to be corrupted by an unfit one, than five or six hundred. Reason, on the contrary, assures us, that as in so great a number a fit representative would be most likely to be found, so the choice would be less likely to be diverted from him by the intrigues of the ambitious or the ambitious or the bribes of the rich.

Is the CONSEQUENCE from this doctrine admissible? If we say that five or six hundred citizens are as many as can jointly exercise their right of suffrage, must we not deprive the people of the immediate choice of their public servants, in every instance where the administration of the government does not require as many of them as will amount to one for that number of citizens?

Is the doctrine warranted by FACTS? It was shown in the last paper, that the real representation in the British House of Commons very little exceeds the proportion of one for every thirty thousand inhabitants. Besides a variety of powerful causes not existing here, and which favor in that country the pretensions of rank and wealth, no person is eligible as a representative of a county, unless he possess real estate of the clear value of six hundred pounds sterling per year; nor of a city or borough, unless he possess a like estate of half that annual value. To this qualification on the part of the county representatives is added another on the part of the county electors, which restrains the right of suffrage to persons having a freehold estate of the annual value of more than twenty pounds sterling, according to the present rate of money. Notwithstanding these unfavorable circumstances, and notwithstanding some very unequal laws in the British code, it cannot be said that the representatives of the nation have elevated the few on the ruins of the many.

But we need not resort to foreign experience on this subject. Our own is explicit and decisive. The districts in New Hampshire in which the senators are chosen immediately by the people, are nearly as large as will be necessary for her representatives in the Congress. Those of Massachusetts are larger than will be necessary for that purpose; and those of New York still more so. In the last State the members of Assembly for the cities and counties of New York and Albany are elected by very nearly as many voters as will be entitled to a representative in the Congress, calculating on the number of sixty-five representatives only. It makes no difference that in these senatorial districts and counties a number of representatives are voted for by each elector at the same time. If the same electors at the same time are capable of choosing four or five representatives, they cannot be incapable of choosing one. Pennsylvania is an additional example. Some of her counties, which elect her State representatives, are almost as large as her districts will be by which her federal representatives will be elected. The city of Philadelphia is supposed to contain between fifty and sixty thousand souls. It will therefore form nearly two districts for the choice of federal representatives. It forms, however, but one county, in which every elector votes for each of its representatives in the State legislature. And what may appear to be still more directly to our purpose, the whole city actually elects a SINGLE MEMBER for the executive council. This is the case in all the other counties of the State.

Are not these facts the most satisfactory proofs of the fallacy which has been employed against the branch of the federal government under consideration? Has it appeared on trial that the senators of New Hampshire, Massachusetts, and New York, or the executive council of Pennsylvania, or the members of the Assembly in the two last States, have betrayed any peculiar disposition to sacrifice the many to the few, or are in any respect less worthy of their places than the representatives and magistrates appointed in other States by very small divisions of the people?

But there are cases of a stronger complexion than any which I have yet quoted. One branch of the legislature of Connecticut is so constituted that each member of it is elected by the whole State. So is the governor of that State, of Massachusetts, and of this State, and the president of New Hampshire. I leave every man to decide whether the result of any one of these experiments can be said to countenance a suspicion, that a diffusive mode of choosing representatives of the people tends to elevate traitors and to undermine the public liberty.

PUBLIUS

FEDERALIST PAPER NO. 58. OBJECTION THAT THE NUMBER OF MEMBERS WILL NOT BE AUGMENTED AS THE PROGRESS OF POPULATION DEMANDS.

Considered For the Independent Journal Wednesday, February 20, 1788.

MADISON

To the People of the State of New York:

THE remaining charge against the House of Representatives, which I am to examine, is grounded on a supposition that the number of members will not be augmented from time to time, as the progress of population may demand.

It has been admitted, that this objection, if well supported, would have great weight. The following observations will show that, like most other objections against the Constitution, it can only proceed from a partial view of the subject, or from a jealousy which discolors and disfigures every object which is beheld.

1. Those who urge the objection seem not to have recollected that the federal Constitution will not suffer by a comparison with the State constitutions, in the security provided for a gradual augmentation of the number of representatives. The number which is to prevail in the first instance is declared to be temporary. Its duration is limited to the short term of three years.

Within every successive term of ten years a census of inhabitants is to be repeated. The unequivocal objects of these regulations are, first, to readjust, from time to time, the apportionment of representatives to the number of inhabitants, under the single exception that each State shall have one representative at least; secondly, to augment the number of representatives at the same periods, under the sole limitation that the whole number shall not exceed one for every thirty thousand inhabitants. If we review the constitutions of the several States, we shall find that some of them contain no determinate regulations on this subject, that others correspond pretty much on this point with the federal Constitution, and that the most effectual security in any of them is resolvable into a mere directory provision.

2. As far as experience has taken place on this subject, a gradual increase of representatives under the State constitutions has at least kept pace with that of the constituents, and it appears that the former have been as ready to concur in such measures as the latter have been to call for them.

3. There is a peculiarity in the federal Constitution which insures a watchful attention in a majority both of the people and of their representatives to a constitutional augmentation of the latter. The peculiarity lies in this, that one branch of the legislature is a representation of citizens, the other of the States: in the former, consequently, the larger States will have most weight; in the latter, the advantage will be in favor of the smaller States. From this circumstance it may with certainty be inferred that the larger States will be strenuous advocates for increasing the number and weight of that part of the legislature in which their influence predominates. And it so happens that four only of the largest will have a majority of the whole votes in the House of Representatives. Should the representatives or people, therefore, of the smaller States oppose at any time a reasonable addition of members, a coalition of a very few States will be sufficient to overrule the opposition; a coalition which, notwithstanding the rivalship and local prejudices which might prevent it on ordinary occasions, would not fail to take place, when not merely prompted by common interest, but justified by equity and the principles of the Constitution.

It may be alleged, perhaps, that the Senate would be prompted by like motives to an adverse coalition; and as their concurrence would be indispensable, the just and constitutional views of the other branch might be defeated. This is the difficulty which has probably created the most serious apprehensions in the jealous friends of a numerous representation. Fortunately it is among the difficulties which, existing only in appearance, vanish on a close and accurate inspection. The following reflections will, if I mistake not, be admitted to be conclusive and satisfactory on this point.

Notwithstanding the equal authority which will subsist between the two houses on all legislative subjects, except the originating of money bills, it cannot be doubted that the House, composed of the greater number of members, when supported by the more powerful States, and speaking the known and determined sense of a majority of the people, will have no small advantage in a question depending on the comparative firmness of the two houses.

Documents of Revolution

This advantage must be increased by the consciousness, felt by the same side of being supported in its demands by right, by reason, and by the Constitution; and the consciousness, on the opposite side, of contending against the force of all these solemn considerations.

It is farther to be considered, that in the gradation between the smallest and largest States, there are several, which, though most likely in general to arrange themselves among the former are too little removed in extent and population from the latter, to second an opposition to their just and legitimate pretensions. Hence it is by no means certain that a majority of votes, even in the Senate, would be unfriendly to proper augmentations in the number of representatives.

It will not be looking too far to add, that the senators from all the new States may be gained over to the just views of the House of Representatives, by an expedient too obvious to be overlooked. As these States will, for a great length of time, advance in population with peculiar rapidity, they will be interested in frequent reapportionments of the representatives to the number of inhabitants. The large States, therefore, who will prevail in the House of Representatives, will have nothing to do but to make reapportionments and augmentations mutually conditions of each other; and the senators from all the most growing States will be bound to contend for the latter, by the interest which their States will feel in the former.

These considerations seem to afford ample security on this subject, and ought alone to satisfy all the doubts and fears which have been indulged with regard to it. Admitting, however, that they should all be insufficient to subdue the unjust policy of the smaller States, or their predominant influence in the councils of the Senate, a constitutional and infallible resource still remains with the larger States, by which they will be able at all times to accomplish their just purposes. The House of Representatives cannot only refuse, but they alone can propose, the supplies requisite for the support of government. They, in a word, hold the purse—that powerful instrument by which we behold, in the history of the British Constitution, an infant and humble representation of the people gradually enlarging the sphere of its activity and importance, and finally reducing, as far as it seems to have wished, all the overgrown prerogatives of the other branches of the government. This power over the purse may, in fact, be regarded as the most complete and effectual weapon with which any constitution can arm the immediate representatives of the people, for obtaining a redress of every grievance, and for carrying into effect every just and salutary measure.

But will not the House of Representatives be as much interested as the Senate in maintaining the government in its proper functions, and will they not therefore be unwilling to stake its existence or its reputation on the pliancy of the Senate? Or, if such a trial of firmness between the two branches were hazarded, would not the one be as likely first to yield as the other? These questions will create no difficulty with those who reflect that in all cases the smaller the number, and the more permanent and conspicuous the station, of men in power, the stronger must be the interest which they will individually feel in whatever concerns the government. Those who represent the dignity of their country in the eyes of other nations, will be particularly sensible to every prospect of public danger, or of dishonorable stagnation in public affairs. To those causes we are to ascribe the continual triumph of the British House of Commons over the other branches of the government, whenever the engine of a money bill has been employed. An absolute inflexibility on the side of the latter, although it could not have failed to involve every department of the state in the general confusion, has neither been apprehended nor experienced. The utmost degree of firmness that can be displayed by the federal Senate or President, will not be more than equal to a resistance in which they will be supported by constitutional and patriotic principles.

In this review of the Constitution of the House of Representatives, I have passed over the circumstances of economy, which, in the present state of affairs, might have had some effect in lessening the temporary number of representatives, and a disregard of which would probably have been as rich a theme of declamation against the Constitution as has been shown by the smallness of the number proposed. I omit also any remarks on the difficulty which might be found, under present circumstances, in engaging in the federal service a large number of such characters as the people will probably elect. One observation, however, I must be permitted to add on this subject as claiming, in my judgment, a very serious attention. It is, that in all legislative assemblies the greater the number composing them may be, the fewer will be the men who will in fact direct their proceedings. In the first place, the more numerous an assembly may be, of whatever characters composed, the greater is known to be the ascendency of passion over reason. In the next place, the larger the number, the greater will be the proportion of members of limited information and of weak capacities. Now, it is precisely on characters of this description that the eloquence and address of the few are known to act with all their force. In the ancient republics, where the whole body of the people assembled in person, a single orator, or an artful statesman, was generally seen to rule with as complete a sway as if a sceptre had been placed in his single hand. On the same principle, the more multitudinous a representative assembly may be rendered, the more it will partake of the infirmities incident to collective meetings of the people. Ignorance will be the dupe of cunning, and passion the slave of sophistry and declamation. The people can never err more than in supposing that by multiplying their representatives beyond a certain limit, they strengthen the barrier against the government of a few. Experience will forever admonish them that, on the contrary, AFTER SECURING A SUFFICIENT NUMBER FOR THE PURPOSES OF SAFETY, OF LOCAL INFORMATION, AND OF DIFFUSIVE SYMPATHY WITH THE WHOLE SOCIETY, they will counteract their own views by every addition to their representatives. The countenance of the government may become more democratic, but the soul that animates it will be more oligarchic. The machine will be enlarged, but the fewer, and often the more secret, will be the springs by which its motions are directed.

As connected with the objection against the number of representatives, may properly be here noticed, that which has been suggested against the number made competent for legislative business. It has been said that more than a majority ought to have been required for a quorum; and in particular cases, if not in all, more than a majority of a quorum for a decision. That some advantages might have resulted from such a precaution, cannot be denied. It might have been an additional shield to some particular interests, and another obstacle generally to hasty and partial measures. But these considerations are outweighed by the inconveniences in the opposite scale. In all cases where justice or the general good might require new laws to be passed, or active measures to be pursued, the fundamental principle of free government would be reversed. It would be no longer the majority that would rule: the power would be transferred to the minority. Were the defensive privilege limited to particular cases, an interested minority might take advantage of it to screen themselves from equitable sacrifices to the general weal, or, in particular emergencies, to extort unreasonable indulgences. Lastly, it would facilitate and foster the baneful practice of secessions; a practice which has shown itself even in States where a majority only is required; a practice subversive of all the principles of order and regular government; a practice which leads more directly to public convulsions, and the ruin of popular governments, than any other which has yet been displayed among us.

PUBLIUS

FEDERALIST PAPER NO. 59. CONCERNING THE POWER OF CONGRESS TO REGULATE THE ELECTION OF MEMBERS

From the New York Packet. Friday, February 22, 1788.

HAMILTON

To the People of the State of New York:

THE natural order of the subject leads us to consider, in this place, that provision of the Constitution which authorizes the national legislature to regulate, in the last resort, the election of its own members. It is in these words: "The TIMES, PLACES, and MANNER of holding elections for senators and representatives shall be prescribed in each State by the legislature thereof; but the Congress may, at any time, by law, make or alter SUCH REGULATIONS, except as to the PLACES of choosing senators."(1) This provision has not only been declaimed against by those who condemn the Constitution in the gross, but it has been censured by those who have objected with less latitude and greater moderation; and, in one instance it has been thought exceptionable by a gentleman who has declared himself the advocate of every other part of the system.

I am greatly mistaken, notwithstanding, if there be any article in the whole plan more completely defensible than this. Its propriety rests upon the evidence of this plain proposition, that EVERY GOVERNMENT OUGHT TO CONTAIN IN ITSELF THE MEANS OF ITS OWN PRESERVATION. Every just reasoner will, at first sight, approve an adherence to this rule, in the work of the convention; and will disapprove every deviation from it which may not appear to have been dictated by the necessity of incorporating into the work some particular ingredient, with which a rigid conformity to the rule was incompatible. Even in this case, though he may acquiesce in the necessity, yet he will not cease to regard and to regret a departure from so fundamental a principle, as a portion of imperfection in the system which may prove the seed of future weakness, and perhaps anarchy.

It will not be alleged, that an election law could have been framed and inserted in the Constitution, which would have been always applicable to every probable change in the situation of the country; and it will therefore not be denied, that a discretionary power over elections ought to exist somewhere. It will, I presume, be as readily conceded, that there were only three ways in which this power could have been reasonably modified and disposed: that it must either have been lodged wholly in the national legislature, or wholly in the State legislatures, or primarily in the latter and ultimately in the former. The last mode has, with reason, been preferred by the convention. They have submitted the regulation of elections for the federal government, in the first instance, to the local administrations; which, in ordinary cases, and when no improper views prevail, may be both more convenient and more satisfactory; but they have reserved to the national authority a right to interpose, whenever extraordinary circumstances might render that interposition necessary to its safety.

Nothing can be more evident, than that an exclusive power of regulating elections for the national government, in the hands of the State legislatures, would leave the existence of the Union entirely at their mercy. They could at any moment annihilate it, by neglecting to provide for the choice of persons to administer its affairs. It is to little purpose to say, that a neglect or omission of this kind would not be likely to take place. The constitutional possibility of the thing, without an equivalent for the risk, is an unanswerable objection. Nor has any satisfactory reason been yet assigned for incurring that risk. The extravagant surmises of a distempered jealousy can never be dignified with that character. If we are in a humor to presume abuses of power, it is as fair to presume them on the part of the State governments as on the part of the general government. And as it is more consonant to the rules of a just theory, to trust the Union with the care of its own existence, than to transfer that care to any other hands, if abuses of power are to be hazarded on the one side or on the other, it is more rational to hazard them where the power would naturally be placed, than where it would unnaturally be placed.

Suppose an article had been introduced into the Constitution, empowering the United States to regulate the elections for the particular States, would any man have hesitated to condemn it, both as an unwarrantable transposition of power, and as a premeditated engine for the destruction of the State governments? The violation of principle, in this case, would have required no comment; and, to an unbiased observer, it will not be less apparent in the project of subjecting the existence of the national government, in a similar respect, to the pleasure of the State governments. An impartial view of the matter cannot fail to result in a conviction, that each, as far as possible, ought to depend on itself for its own preservation.

As an objection to this position, it may be remarked that the constitution of the national Senate would involve, in its full extent, the danger which it is suggested might flow from an exclusive power in the State legislatures to regulate the federal elections. It may be alleged, that by declining the appointment of Senators, they might at any time give a fatal blow to the Union; and from this it may be inferred, that as its existence would be thus rendered dependent upon them in so essential a point, there can be no objection to intrusting them with it in the particular case under consideration. The interest of each State, it may be added, to maintain its representation in the national councils, would be a complete security against an abuse of the trust.

This argument, though specious, will not, upon examination, be found solid. It is certainly true that the State legislatures, by forbearing the appointment of senators, may destroy the national government. But it will not follow that, because they have a power to do this in one instance, they ought to have it in every other. There are cases in which the pernicious tendency of such a power may be far more decisive, without any motive equally cogent with that which must have regulated the conduct of the convention in respect to the formation of the Senate, to recommend their admission into the system. So far as that construction may expose the Union to the possibility of injury from the State legislatures, it is an evil; but it is an evil which could not have been avoided without excluding the States, in their political capacities, wholly from a place in the organization of the national government. If this had been done, it would doubtless have been interpreted into an entire dereliction of the federal principle; and would certainly have deprived the State governments of that absolute safeguard which they will enjoy under this provision. But however wise it may have been to have submitted in this instance to an inconvenience, for the attainment of a necessary advantage or a greater good, no inference can be drawn from thence to favor an accumulation of the evil, where no necessity urges, nor any greater good invites.

It may be easily discerned also that the national government would run a much greater risk from a power in the State legislatures over the elections of its House of Representatives, than from their power of appointing the members of its Senate. The senators are to be chosen for the period of six years; there is to be a rotation, by which the seats of a third part of them are to be vacated and replenished every two years; and no State is to be entitled to more than two senators; a quorum of the body is to consist of sixteen members. The joint result of these circumstances would be, that a temporary combination of a few States to intermit the appointment of senators, could neither annul the existence nor impair the activity of the body; and it is not from a general and permanent combination of the States that we can have any thing to fear. The first might proceed from sinister designs in the leading members of a few of the State legislatures; the last would suppose a fixed and rooted disaffection in the great body of the people, which will either never exist at all, or will, in all probability, proceed from an experience of the inaptitude of the general government to the advancement of their happiness in which event no good citizen could desire its continuance.

But with regard to the federal House of Representatives, there is intended to be a general election of members once in two years. If the State legislatures were to be invested with an exclusive power of regulating these elections, every period of making them would be a delicate crisis in the national situation, which might issue in a dissolution of the Union, if the leaders of a few of the most important States should have entered into a previous conspiracy to prevent an election.

I shall not deny, that there is a degree of weight in the observation, that the interests of each State, to be represented in the federal councils, will be a security against the abuse of a power over its elections in the hands of the State legislatures. But the security will not be considered as complete, by those who attend to the force of an obvious distinction between the interest of the people in the public felicity, and the interest of their local rulers in the power and consequence of their offices. The people of America may be warmly attached to the government of the Union, at times when the particular rulers of particular States, stimulated by the natural rivalship of power, and by the hopes of personal aggrandizement, and supported by a strong faction in each of those States, may be in a very opposite temper. This diversity of sentiment between a majority of the people, and the individuals who have the greatest credit in their councils, is exemplified in some of the States at the present moment, on the present question. The scheme of separate confederacies, which will always multiply the chances of ambition, will be a never failing bait to all such influential characters in the State administrations as are capable of preferring their own emolument and advancement to the public weal. With so effectual a weapon in their hands as the exclusive power of regulating elections for the national government, a combination of a few such men, in a few of the most considerable States, where the temptation will always be the strongest, might accomplish the destruction of the Union, by seizing the opportunity of some casual dissatisfaction among the people (and which perhaps they may themselves have excited), to discontinue the choice of members for the federal House of Representatives. It ought never to be forgotten, that a firm union of this country, under an efficient government, will probably be an increasing object of jealousy to more than one nation of Europe; and that enterprises to subvert it will sometimes originate in the intrigues of foreign powers, and will seldom fail to be patronized and abetted by some of them. Its preservation, therefore ought in no case that can be avoided, to be committed to the guardianship of any but those whose situation will uniformly beget an immediate interest in the faithful and vigilant performance of the trust.

PUBLIUS

1. 1st clause, 4th section, of the 1st article.

FEDERALIST PAPER NO. 60. THE SAME SUBJECT CONTINUED (CONCERNING THE POWER OF CONGRESS TO REGULATE THE ELECTION OF MEMBERS)

From The Independent Journal. Saturday, February 23, 1788.

HAMILTON

To the People of the State of New York:

WE HAVE seen, that an uncontrollable power over the elections to the federal government could not, without hazard, be committed to the State legislatures. Let us now see, what would be the danger on the other side; that is, from confiding the ultimate right of regulating its own elections to the Union itself. It is not pretended, that this right would ever be used for the exclusion of any State from its share in the representation. The interest of all would, in this respect at least, be the security of all. But it is alleged, that it might be employed in such a manner as to promote the election of some favorite class of men in exclusion of others, by confining the places of election to particular districts, and rendering it impracticable to the citizens at large to partake in the choice. Of all chimerical suppositions, this seems to be the most chimerical. On the one hand, no rational calculation of probabilities would lead us to imagine that the disposition which a conduct so violent and extraordinary would imply, could ever find its way into the national councils; and on the other, it may be concluded with certainty, that if so improper a spirit should ever gain admittance into them, it would display itself in a form altogether different and far more decisive.

The improbability of the attempt may be satisfactorily inferred from this single reflection, that it could never be made without causing an immediate revolt of the great body of the people, headed and directed by the State governments. It is not difficult to conceive that this characteristic right of freedom may, in certain turbulent and factious seasons, be violated, in respect to a particular class of citizens, by a victorious and overbearing majority; but that so fundamental a privilege, in a country so situated and enlightened, should be invaded to the prejudice of the great mass of the people, by the deliberate policy of the government, without occasioning a popular revolution, is altogether inconceivable and incredible.

In addition to this general reflection, there are considerations of a more precise nature, which forbid all apprehension on the subject. The dissimilarity in the ingredients which will compose the national government, and still more in the manner in which they will be brought into action in its various branches, must form a powerful obstacle to a concert of views in any partial scheme of elections. There is sufficient diversity in the state of property, in the genius, manners, and habits of the people of the different parts of the Union, to occasion a material diversity of disposition in their representatives towards the different ranks and conditions in society. And though an intimate intercourse under the same government will promote a gradual assimilation in some of these respects, yet there are causes, as well physical as moral, which may, in a greater or less degree, permanently nourish different propensities and inclinations in this respect. But the circumstance which will be likely to have the greatest influence in the matter, will be the dissimilar modes of constituting the several component parts of the government. The House of Representatives being to be elected immediately by the people, the Senate by the State legislatures, the President by electors chosen for that purpose by the people, there would be little probability of a common interest to cement these different branches in a predilection for any particular class of electors.

As to the Senate, it is impossible that any regulation of "time and manner," which is all that is proposed to be submitted to the national government in respect to that body, can affect the spirit which will direct the choice of its members. The collective sense of the State legislatures can never be influenced by extraneous circumstances of that sort; a consideration which alone ought to satisfy us that the discrimination apprehended would never be attempted. For what inducement could the Senate have to concur in a preference in which itself would not be included? Or to what purpose would it be established, in reference to one branch of the legislature, if it could not be extended to the other? The composition of the one would in this case counteract that of the other. And we can never suppose that it would embrace the appointments to the Senate, unless we can at the same time suppose the voluntary co-operation of the State legislatures. If we make the latter supposition, it then becomes immaterial where the power in question is placed—whether in their hands or in those of the Union.

But what is to be the object of this capricious partiality in the national councils? Is it to be exercised in a discrimination between the different departments of industry, or between the different kinds of property, or between the different degrees of property? Will it lean in favor of the landed interest, or the moneyed interest, or the mercantile interest, or the manufacturing interest? Or, to speak in the fashionable language of the adversaries to the Constitution, will it court the elevation of "the wealthy and the well-born," to the exclusion and debasement of all the rest of the society?

If this partiality is to be exerted in favor of those who are concerned in any particular description of industry or property, I presume it will readily be admitted, that the competition for it will lie between landed men and merchants. And I scruple not to affirm, that it is infinitely less likely that either of them should gain an ascendant in the national councils, than that the one or the other of them should predominate in all the local councils. The inference will be, that a conduct tending to give an undue preference to either is much less to be dreaded from the former than from the latter.

The several States are in various degrees addicted to agriculture and commerce. In most, if not all of them, agriculture is predominant. In a few of them, however, commerce nearly divides its empire, and in most of them has a considerable share of influence. In proportion as either prevails, it will be conveyed into the national representation; and for the very reason, that this will be an emanation from a greater variety of interests, and in much more various proportions, than are to be found in any single State, it will be much less apt to espouse either of them with a decided partiality, than the representation of any single State.

In a country consisting chiefly of the cultivators of land, where the rules of an equal representation obtain, the landed interest must, upon the whole, preponderate in the government. As long as this interest prevails in most of the State legislatures, so long it must maintain a correspondent superiority in the national Senate, which will generally be a faithful copy of the majorities of those assemblies. It cannot therefore be presumed, that a sacrifice of the landed to the mercantile class will ever be a favorite object of this branch of the federal legislature. In applying thus particularly to the Senate a general observation suggested by the situation of the country, I am governed by the consideration, that the credulous votaries of State power cannot, upon their own principles, suspect, that the State legislatures would be warped from their duty by any external influence. But in reality the same situation must have the same effect, in the primitive composition at least of the federal House of Representatives: an improper bias towards the mercantile class is as little to be expected from this quarter as from the other.

In order, perhaps, to give countenance to the objection at any rate, it may be asked, is there not danger of an opposite bias in the national government, which may dispose it to endeavor to secure a monopoly of the federal administration to the landed class? As there is little likelihood that the supposition of such a bias will have any terrors for those who would be immediately injured by it, a labored answer to this question will be dispensed with. It will be sufficient to remark, first, that for the reasons elsewhere assigned, it is less likely that any decided partiality should prevail in the councils of the Union than in those of any of its members. Secondly, that there would be no temptation to violate the Constitution in favor of the landed class, because that class would, in the natural course of things, enjoy as great a preponderancy as itself could desire. And thirdly, that men accustomed to investigate the sources of public prosperity upon a large scale, must be too well convinced of the utility of commerce, to be inclined to inflict upon it so deep a wound as would result from the entire exclusion of those who would best understand its interest from a share in the management of them. The importance of commerce, in the view of revenue alone, must effectually guard it against the enmity of a body which would be continually importuned in its favor, by the urgent calls of public necessity.

I the rather consult brevity in discussing the probability of a preference founded upon a discrimination between the different kinds of industry and property, because, as far as I understand the meaning of the objectors, they contemplate a discrimination of another kind. They appear to have in view, as the objects of the preference with which they endeavor to alarm us, those whom they designate by the description of "the wealthy and the well-born." These, it seems, are to be exalted to an odious pre-eminence over the rest of their fellow-citizens. At one time, however, their elevation is to be a necessary consequence of the smallness of the representative body; at another time it is to be effected by depriving the people at large of the opportunity of exercising their right of suffrage in the choice of that body.

But upon what principle is the discrimination of the places of election to be made, in order to answer the purpose of the meditated preference? Are "the wealthy and the well-born," as they are called, confined to particular spots in the several States? Have they, by some miraculous instinct or foresight, set apart in each of them a common place of residence? Are they only to be met with in the towns or cities? Or are they, on the contrary, scattered over the face of the country as avarice or chance may have happened to cast their own lot or that of their predecessors? If the latter is the case, (as every intelligent man knows it to be,(1)) is it not evident that the policy of confining the places of election to particular districts would be as subversive of its own aim as it would be exceptionable on every other account? The truth is, that there is no method of securing to the rich the preference apprehended, but by prescribing qualifications of property either for those who may elect or be elected. But this forms no part of the power to be conferred upon the national government. Its authority would be expressly restricted to the regulation of the TIMES, the PLACES, the MANNER of elections. The qualifications of the persons who may choose or be chosen, as has been remarked upon other occasions, are defined and fixed in the Constitution, and are unalterable by the legislature.

Let it, however, be admitted, for argument sake, that the expedient suggested might be successful; and let it at the same time be equally taken for granted that all the scruples which a sense of duty or an apprehension of the danger of the experiment might inspire, were overcome in the breasts of the national rulers, still I imagine it will hardly be pretended that they could ever hope to carry such an enterprise into execution without the aid of a military force sufficient to subdue the resistance of the great body of the people. The improbability of the existence of a force equal to that object has been discussed and demonstrated in different parts of these papers; but that the futility of the objection under consideration may appear in the strongest light, it shall be conceded for a moment that such a force might exist, and the national government shall be supposed to be in the actual possession of it. What will be the conclusion? With a disposition to invade the essential rights of the community, and with the means of gratifying that disposition, is it presumable that the persons who were actuated by it would amuse themselves in the ridiculous task of fabricating election laws for securing a preference to a favorite class of men? Would they not be likely to prefer a conduct better adapted to their own immediate aggrandizement? Would they not rather boldly resolve to perpetuate themselves in office by one decisive act of usurpation, than to trust to precarious expedients which, in spite of all the precautions that might accompany them, might terminate in the dismission, disgrace, and ruin of their authors? Would they not fear that citizens, not less tenacious than conscious of their rights, would flock from the remote extremes of their respective States to the places of election, to overthrow their tyrants, and to substitute men who would be disposed to avenge the violated majesty of the people?

PUBLIUS

1. Particularly in the Southern States and in this State.

FEDERALIST PAPER NO. 61. THE SAME SUBJECT CONTINUED (CONCERNING THE POWER OF CONGRESS TO REGULATE THE ELECTION OF MEMBERS)

From the New York Packet. Tuesday, February 26, 1788.

HAMILTON

To the People of the State of New York:

THE more candid opposers of the provision respecting elections, contained in the plan of the convention, when pressed in argument, will sometimes concede the propriety of that provision; with this qualification, however, that it ought to have been accompanied with a declaration, that all elections should be had in the counties where the electors resided. This, say they, was a necessary precaution against an abuse of the power. A declaration of this nature would certainly have been harmless; so far as it would have had the effect of quieting apprehensions, it might not have been undesirable. But it would, in fact, have afforded little or no additional security against the danger apprehended; and the want of it will never be considered, by an impartial and judicious examiner, as a serious, still less as an insuperable, objection to the plan. The different views taken of the subject in the two preceding papers must be sufficient to satisfy all dispassionate and discerning men, that if the public liberty should ever be the victim of the ambition of the national rulers, the power under examination, at least, will be guiltless of the sacrifice.

If those who are inclined to consult their jealousy only, would exercise it in a careful inspection of the several State constitutions, they would find little less room for disquietude and alarm, from the latitude which most of them allow in respect to elections, than from the latitude which is proposed to be allowed to the national government in the same respect. A review of their situation, in this particular, would tend greatly to remove any ill impressions which may remain in regard to this matter. But as that view would lead into long and tedious details, I shall content myself with the single example of the State in which I write. The constitution of New York makes no other provision for LOCALITY of elections, than that the members of the Assembly shall be elected in the COUNTIES; those of the Senate, in the great districts into which the State is or may be divided: these at present are four in number, and comprehend each from two to six counties. It may readily be perceived that it would not be more difficult to the legislature of New York to defeat the suffrages of the citizens of New York, by confining elections to particular places, than for the legislature of the United States to defeat the suffrages of the citizens of the Union, by the like expedient. Suppose, for instance, the city of Albany was to be appointed the sole place of election for the county and district of which it is a part, would not the inhabitants of that city speedily become the only electors of the members both of the Senate and Assembly for that county and district? Can we imagine that the electors who reside in the remote subdivisions of the counties of Albany, Saratoga, Cambridge, etc., or in any part of the county of Montgomery, would take the trouble to come to the city of Albany, to give their votes for members of the Assembly or Senate, sooner than they would repair to the city of New York, to participate in the choice of the members of the federal House of Representatives? The alarming indifference discoverable in the exercise of so invaluable a privilege under the existing laws, which afford every facility to it, furnishes a ready answer to this question. And, abstracted from any experience on the subject, we can be at no loss to determine, that when the place of election is at an INCONVENIENT DISTANCE from the elector, the effect upon his conduct will be the same whether that distance be twenty miles or twenty thousand miles. Hence it must appear, that objections to the particular modification of the federal power of regulating elections will, in substance, apply with equal force to the modification of the like power in the constitution of this State; and for this reason it will be impossible to acquit the one, and to condemn the other. A similar comparison would lead to the same conclusion in respect to the constitutions of most of the other States.

If it should be said that defects in the State constitutions furnish no apology for those which are to be found in the plan proposed, I answer, that as the former have never been thought chargeable with inattention to the security of liberty, where the imputations thrown on the latter can be shown to be applicable to them also, the presumption is that they are rather the cavilling refinements of a predetermined opposition, than the well-founded inferences of a candid research after truth. To those who are disposed to consider, as innocent omissions in the State constitutions, what they regard as unpardonable blemishes in the plan of the convention, nothing can be said; or at most, they can only be asked to assign some substantial reason why the representatives of the people in a single State should be more impregnable to the lust of power, or other sinister motives, than the representatives of the people of the United States? If they cannot do this, they ought at least to prove to us that it is easier to subvert the liberties of three millions of people, with the advantage of local governments to head their opposition, than of two hundred thousand people who are destitute of that advantage. And in relation to the point immediately under consideration, they ought to convince us that it is less probable that a predominant faction in a single State should, in order to maintain its superiority, incline to a preference of a particular class of electors, than that a similar spirit should take possession of the representatives of thirteen States, spread over a vast region, and in several respects distinguishable from each other by a diversity of local circumstances, prejudices, and interests.

Hitherto my observations have only aimed at a vindication of the provision in question, on the ground of theoretic propriety, on that of the danger of placing the power elsewhere, and on that of the safety of placing it in the manner proposed. But there remains to be mentioned a positive advantage which will result from this disposition, and which could not as well have been obtained from any other: I allude to the circumstance of uniformity in the time of elections for the federal House of Representatives. It is more than possible that this uniformity may be found by experience to be of great importance to the public welfare, both as a security against the perpetuation of the same spirit in the body, and as a cure for the diseases of faction. If each State may choose its own time of election, it is possible there may be at least as many different periods as there are months in the year. The times of election in the several States, as they are now established for local purposes, vary between extremes as wide as March and November. The consequence of this diversity would be that there could never happen a total dissolution or renovation of the body at one time. If an improper spirit of any kind should happen to prevail in it, that spirit would be apt to infuse itself into the new members, as they come forward in succession. The mass would be likely to remain nearly the same, assimilating constantly to itself its gradual accretions. There is a contagion in example which few men have sufficient force of mind to resist. I am inclined to think that treble the duration in office, with the condition of a total dissolution of the body at the same time, might be less formidable to liberty than one third of that duration subject to gradual and successive alterations.

Uniformity in the time of elections seems not less requisite for executing the idea of a regular rotation in the Senate, and for conveniently assembling the legislature at a stated period in each year.

It may be asked, Why, then, could not a time have been fixed in the Constitution? As the most zealous adversaries of the plan of the convention in this State are, in general, not less zealous admirers of the constitution of the State, the question may be retorted, and it may be asked, Why was not a time for the like purpose fixed in the constitution of this State? No better answer can be given than that it was a matter which might safely be entrusted to legislative discretion; and that if a time had been appointed, it might, upon experiment, have been found less convenient than some other time. The same answer may be given to the question put on the other side. And it may be added that the supposed danger of a gradual change being merely speculative, it would have been hardly advisable upon that speculation to establish, as a fundamental point, what would deprive several States of the convenience of having the elections for their own governments and for the national government at the same epochs.

PUBLIUS

FEDERALIST PAPER NO. 62. THE SENATE

For the Independent Journal. Wednesday, February 27, 1788

MADISON

To the People of the State of New York:

HAVING examined the constitution of the House of Representatives, and answered such of the objections against it as seemed to merit notice, I enter next on the examination of the Senate. The heads into which this member of the government may be considered are: I. The qualification of senators; II. The appointment of them by the State legislatures; III. The equality of representation in the Senate; IV. The number of senators, and the term for which they are to be elected; V. The powers vested in the Senate.

I. The qualifications proposed for senators, as distinguished from those of representatives, consist in a more advanced age and a longer period of citizenship. A senator must be thirty years of age at least; as a representative must be twenty-five. And the former must have been a citizen nine years; as seven years are required for the latter. The propriety of these distinctions is explained by the nature of the senatorial trust, which, requiring greater extent of information and stability of character, requires at the same time that the senator should have reached a period of life most likely to supply these advantages; and which, participating immediately in transactions with foreign nations, ought to be exercised by none who are not thoroughly weaned from the prepossessions and habits incident to foreign birth and education. The term of nine years appears to be a prudent mediocrity between a total exclusion of adopted citizens, whose merits and talents may claim a share in the public confidence, and an indiscriminate and hasty admission of them, which might create a channel for foreign influence on the national councils.

II. It is equally unnecessary to dilate on the appointment of senators by the State legislatures. Among the various modes which might have been devised for constituting this branch of the government, that which has been proposed by the convention is probably the most congenial with the public opinion. It is recommended by the double advantage of favoring a select appointment, and of giving to the State governments such an agency in the formation of the federal government as must secure the authority of the former, and may form a convenient link between the two systems.

III. The equality of representation in the Senate is another point, which, being evidently the result of compromise between the opposite pretensions of the large and the small States, does not call for much discussion. If indeed it be right, that among a people thoroughly incorporated into one nation, every district ought to have a PROPORTIONAL share in the government, and that among independent and sovereign States, bound together by a simple league, the parties, however unequal in size, ought to have an EQUAL share in the common councils, it does not appear to be without some reason that in a compound republic, partaking both of the national and federal character, the government ought to be founded on a mixture of the principles of proportional and equal representation. But it is superfluous to try, by the standard of theory, a part of the Constitution which is allowed on all hands to be the result, not of theory, but "of a spirit of amity, and that mutual deference and concession which the peculiarity of our political situation rendered indispensable." A common government, with powers equal to its objects, is called for by the voice, and still more loudly by the political situation, of America. A government founded on principles more consonant to the wishes of the larger States, is not likely to be obtained from the smaller States. The only option, then, for the former, lies between the proposed government and a government still more objectionable. Under this alternative, the advice of prudence must be to embrace the lesser evil; and, instead of indulging a fruitless anticipation of the possible mischiefs which may ensue, to contemplate rather the advantageous consequences which may qualify the sacrifice.

In this spirit it may be remarked, that the equal vote allowed to each State is at once a constitutional recognition of the portion of sovereignty remaining in the individual States, and an instrument for preserving that residuary sovereignty. So far the equality ought to be no less acceptable to the large than to the small States; since they are not less solicitous to guard, by every possible expedient, against an improper consolidation of the States into one simple republic.

Another advantage accruing from this ingredient in the constitution of the Senate is, the additional impediment it must prove against improper acts of legislation. No law or resolution can now be passed without the concurrence, first, of a majority of the people, and then, of a majority of the States. It must be acknowledged that this complicated check on legislation may in some instances be injurious as well as beneficial; and that the peculiar defense which it involves in favor of the smaller States, would be more rational, if any interests common to them, and distinct from those of the other States, would otherwise be exposed to peculiar danger. But as the larger States will always be able, by their power over the supplies, to defeat unreasonable exertions of this prerogative of the lesser States, and as the faculty and excess of law-making seem to be the diseases to which our governments are most liable, it is not impossible that this part of the Constitution may be more convenient in practice than it appears to many in contemplation.

IV. The number of senators, and the duration of their appointment, come next to be considered. In order to form an accurate judgment on both of these points, it will be proper to inquire into the purposes which are to be answered by a senate; and in order to ascertain these, it will be necessary to review the inconveniences which a republic must suffer from the want of such an institution.

First. It is a misfortune incident to republican government, though in a less degree than to other governments, that those who administer it may forget their obligations to their constituents, and prove unfaithful to their important trust. In this point of view, a senate, as a second branch of the legislative assembly, distinct from, and dividing the power with, a first, must be in all cases a salutary check on the government. It doubles the security to the people, by requiring the concurrence of two distinct bodies in schemes of usurpation or perfidy, where the ambition or corruption of one would otherwise be sufficient. This is a precaution founded on such clear principles, and now so well understood in the United States, that it would be more than superfluous to enlarge on it. I will barely remark, that as the improbability of sinister combinations will be in proportion to the dissimilarity in the genius of the two bodies, it must be politic to distinguish them from each other by every circumstance which will consist with a due harmony in all proper measures, and with the genuine principles of republican government.

Second. The necessity of a senate is not less indicated by the propensity of all single and numerous assemblies to yield to the impulse of sudden and violent passions, and to be seduced by factious leaders into intemperate and pernicious resolutions. Examples on this subject might be cited without number; and from proceedings within the United States, as well as from the history of other nations. But a position that will not be contradicted, need not be proved. All that need be remarked is, that a body which is to correct this infirmity ought itself to be free from it, and consequently ought to be less numerous. It ought, moreover, to possess great firmness, and consequently ought to hold its authority by a tenure of considerable duration.

Third. Another defect to be supplied by a senate lies in a want of due acquaintance with the objects and principles of legislation. It is not possible that an assembly of men called for the most part from pursuits of a private nature, continued in appointment for a short time, and led by no permanent motive to devote the intervals of public occupation to a study of the laws, the affairs, and the comprehensive interests of their country, should, if left wholly to themselves, escape a variety of important errors in the exercise of their legislative trust. It may be affirmed, on the best grounds, that no small share of the present embarrassments of America is to be charged on the blunders of our governments; and that these have proceeded from the heads rather than the hearts of most of the authors of them. What indeed are all the repealing, explaining, and amending laws, which fill and disgrace our voluminous codes, but so many monuments of deficient wisdom; so many impeachments exhibited by each succeeding against each preceding session; so many admonitions to the people, of the value of those aids which may be expected from a well-constituted senate?

A good government implies two things: first, fidelity to the object of government, which is the happiness of the people; secondly, a knowledge of the means by which that object can be best attained. Some governments are deficient in both these qualities; most governments are deficient in the first. I scruple not to assert, that in American governments too little attention has been paid to the last. The federal Constitution avoids this error; and what merits particular notice, it provides for the last in a mode which increases the security for the first.

Fourth. The mutability in the public councils arising from a rapid succession of new members, however qualified they may be, points out, in the strongest manner, the necessity of some stable institution in the government. Every new election in the States is found to change one half of the representatives. From this change of men must proceed a change of opinions; and from a change of opinions, a change of measures. But a continual change even of good measures is inconsistent with every rule of prudence and every prospect of success. The remark is verified in private life, and becomes more just, as well as more important, in national transactions.

To trace the mischievous effects of a mutable government would fill a volume. I will hint a few only, each of which will be perceived to be a source of innumerable others.

In the first place, it forfeits the respect and confidence of other nations, and all the advantages connected with national character. An individual who is observed to be inconstant to his plans, or perhaps to carry on his affairs without any plan at all, is marked at once, by all prudent people, as a speedy victim to his own unsteadiness and folly. His more friendly neighbors may pity him, but all will decline to connect their fortunes with his; and not a few will seize the opportunity of making their fortunes out of his. One nation is to another what one individual is to another; with this melancholy distinction perhaps, that the former, with fewer of the benevolent emotions than the latter, are under fewer restraints also from taking undue advantage from the indiscretions of each other. Every nation, consequently, whose affairs betray a want of wisdom and stability, may calculate on every loss which can be sustained from the more systematic policy of their wiser neighbors. But the best instruction on this subject is unhappily conveyed to America by the example of her own situation. She finds that she is held in no respect by her friends; that she is the derision of her enemies; and that she is a prey to every nation which has an interest in speculating on her fluctuating councils and embarrassed affairs.

The internal effects of a mutable policy are still more calamitous. It poisons the blessing of liberty itself. It will be of little avail to the people, that the laws are made by men of their own choice, if the laws be so voluminous that they cannot be read, or so incoherent that they cannot be understood; if they be repealed or revised before they are promulgated, or undergo such incessant changes that no man, who knows what the law is to-day, can guess what it will be to-morrow. Law is defined to be a rule of action; but how can that be a rule, which is little known, and less fixed?

Another effect of public instability is the unreasonable advantage it gives to the sagacious, the enterprising, and the moneyed few over the industrious and uninformed mass of the people. Every new regulation concerning commerce or revenue, or in any way affecting the value of the different species of property, presents a new harvest to those who watch the change, and can trace its consequences; a harvest, reared not by themselves, but by the toils and cares of the great body of their fellow-citizens. This is a state of things in which it may be said with some truth that laws are made for the FEW, not for the MANY.

In another point of view, great injury results from an unstable government. The want of confidence in the public councils damps every useful undertaking, the success and profit of which may depend on a continuance of existing arrangements. What prudent merchant will hazard his fortunes in any new branch of commerce when he knows not but that his plans may be rendered unlawful before they can be executed? What farmer or manufacturer will lay himself out for the encouragement given to any particular cultivation or establishment, when he can have no assurance that his preparatory labors and advances will not render him a victim to an inconstant government? In a word, no great improvement or laudable enterprise can go forward which requires the auspices of a steady system of national policy.

But the most deplorable effect of all is that diminution of attachment and reverence which steals into the hearts of the people, towards a political system which betrays so many marks of infirmity, and disappoints so many of their flattering hopes. No government, any more than an individual, will long be respected without being truly respectable; nor be truly respectable, without possessing a certain portion of order and stability.

PUBLIUS

FEDERALIST PAPER NO. 63. THE SENATE CONTINUED

For the Independent Journal. Saturday, March 1, 1788

MADISON

To the People of the State of New York:

A FIFTH desideratum, illustrating the utility of a senate, is the want of a due sense of national character. Without a select and stable member of the government, the esteem of foreign powers will not only be forfeited by an unenlightened and variable policy, proceeding from the causes already mentioned, but the national councils will not possess that sensibility to the opinion of the world, which is perhaps not less necessary in order to merit, than it is to obtain, its respect and confidence.

An attention to the judgment of other nations is important to every government for two reasons: the one is, that, independently of the merits of any particular plan or measure, it is desirable, on various accounts, that it should appear to other nations as the offspring of a wise and honorable policy; the second is, that in doubtful cases, particularly where the national councils may be warped by some strong passion or momentary interest, the presumed or known opinion of the impartial world may be the best guide that can be followed. What has not America lost by her want of character with foreign nations; and how many errors and follies would she not have avoided, if the justice and propriety of her measures had, in every instance, been previously tried by the light in which they would probably appear to the unbiased part of mankind?

Yet however requisite a sense of national character may be, it is evident that it can never be sufficiently possessed by a numerous and changeable body. It can only be found in a number so small that a sensible degree of the praise and blame of public measures may be the portion of each individual; or in an assembly so durably invested with public trust, that the pride and consequence of its members may be sensibly incorporated with the reputation and prosperity of the community. The half-yearly representatives of Rhode Island would probably have been little affected in their deliberations on the iniquitous measures of that State, by arguments drawn from the light in which such measures would be viewed by foreign nations, or even by the sister States; whilst it can scarcely be doubted that if the concurrence of a select and stable body had been necessary, a regard to national character alone would have prevented the calamities under which that misguided people is now laboring.

I add, as a SIXTH defect the want, in some important cases, of a due responsibility in the government to the people, arising from that frequency of elections which in other cases produces this responsibility. This remark will, perhaps, appear not only new, but paradoxical. It must nevertheless be acknowledged, when explained, to be as undeniable as it is important.

Responsibility, in order to be reasonable, must be limited to objects within the power of the responsible party, and in order to be effectual, must relate to operations of that power, of which a ready and proper judgment can be formed by the constituents. The objects of government may be divided into two general classes: the one depending on measures which have singly an immediate and sensible operation; the other depending on a succession of well-chosen and well-connected measures, which have a gradual and perhaps unobserved operation. The importance of the latter description to the collective and permanent welfare of every country, needs no explanation. And yet it is evident that an assembly elected for so short a term as to be unable to provide more than one or two links in a chain of measures, on which the general welfare may essentially depend, ought not to be answerable for the final result, any more than a steward or tenant, engaged for one year, could be justly made to answer for places or improvements which could not be accomplished in less than half a dozen years. Nor is it possible for the people to estimate the SHARE of influence which their annual assemblies may respectively have on events resulting from the mixed transactions of several years. It is sufficiently difficult to preserve a personal responsibility in the members of a NUMEROUS body, for such acts of the body as have an immediate, detached, and palpable operation on its constituents.

The proper remedy for this defect must be an additional body in the legislative department, which, having sufficient permanency to provide for such objects as require a continued attention, and a train of measures, may be justly and effectually answerable for the attainment of those objects.

Thus far I have considered the circumstances which point out the necessity of a well-constructed Senate only as they relate to the representatives of the people. To a people as little blinded by prejudice or corrupted by flattery as those whom I address, I shall not scruple to add, that such an institution may be sometimes necessary as a defense to the people against their own temporary errors and delusions. As the cool and deliberate sense of the community ought, in all governments, and actually will, in all free governments, ultimately prevail over the views of its rulers; so there are particular moments in public affairs when the people, stimulated by some irregular passion, or some illicit advantage, or misled by the artful misrepresentations of interested men, may call for measures which they themselves will afterwards be the most ready to lament and condemn. In these critical moments, how salutary will be the interference of some temperate and respectable body of citizens, in order to check the misguided career, and to suspend the blow meditated by the people against themselves, until reason, justice, and truth can regain their authority over the public mind? What bitter anguish would not the people of Athens have often escaped if their government had contained so provident a safeguard against the tyranny of their own passions? Popular liberty might then have escaped the indelible reproach of decreeing to the same citizens the hemlock on one day and statues on the next.

It may be suggested, that a people spread over an extensive region cannot, like the crowded inhabitants of a small district, be subject to the infection of violent passions, or to the danger of combining in pursuit of unjust measures. I am far from denying that this is a distinction of peculiar importance. I have, on the contrary, endeavored in a former paper to show, that it is one of the principal recommendations of a confederated republic. At the same time, this advantage ought not to be considered as superseding the use of auxiliary precautions. It may even be remarked, that the same extended situation, which will exempt the people of America from some of the dangers incident to lesser republics, will expose them to the inconveniency of remaining for a longer time under the influence of those misrepresentations which the combined industry of interested men may succeed in distributing among them.

Documents of Revolution

It adds no small weight to all these considerations, to recollect that history informs us of no long-lived republic which had not a senate. Sparta, Rome, and Carthage are, in fact, the only states to whom that character can be applied. In each of the two first there was a senate for life. The constitution of the senate in the last is less known. Circumstantial evidence makes it probable that it was not different in this particular from the two others. It is at least certain, that it had some quality or other which rendered it an anchor against popular fluctuations; and that a smaller council, drawn out of the senate, was appointed not only for life, but filled up vacancies itself. These examples, though as unfit for the imitation, as they are repugnant to the genius, of America, are, notwithstanding, when compared with the fugitive and turbulent existence of other ancient republics, very instructive proofs of the necessity of some institution that will blend stability with liberty. I am not unaware of the circumstances which distinguish the American from other popular governments, as well ancient as modern; and which render extreme circumspection necessary, in reasoning from the one case to the other. But after allowing due weight to this consideration, it may still be maintained, that there are many points of similitude which render these examples not unworthy of our attention. Many of the defects, as we have seen, which can only be supplied by a senatorial institution, are common to a numerous assembly frequently elected by the people, and to the people themselves. There are others peculiar to the former, which require the control of such an institution. The people can never wilfully betray their own interests; but they may possibly be betrayed by the representatives of the people; and the danger will be evidently greater where the whole legislative trust is lodged in the hands of one body of men, than where the concurrence of separate and dissimilar bodies is required in every public act.

The difference most relied on, between the American and other republics, consists in the principle of representation; which is the pivot on which the former move, and which is supposed to have been unknown to the latter, or at least to the ancient part of them. The use which has been made of this difference, in reasonings contained in former papers, will have shown that I am disposed neither to deny its existence nor to undervalue its importance. I feel the less restraint, therefore, in observing, that the position concerning the ignorance of the ancient governments on the subject of representation, is by no means precisely true in the latitude commonly given to it. Without entering into a disquisition which here would be misplaced, I will refer to a few known facts, in support of what I advance.

In the most pure democracies of Greece, many of the executive functions were performed, not by the people themselves, but by officers elected by the people, and REPRESENTING the people in their EXECUTIVE capacity.

Prior to the reform of Solon, Athens was governed by nine Archons, annually ELECTED BY THE PEOPLE AT LARGE. The degree of power delegated to them seems to be left in great obscurity. Subsequent to that period, we find an assembly, first of four, and afterwards of six hundred members, annually ELECTED BY THE PEOPLE; and PARTIALLY representing them in their LEGISLATIVE capacity, since they were not only associated with the people in the function of making laws, but had the exclusive right of originating legislative propositions to the people. The senate of Carthage, also, whatever might be its power, or the duration of its appointment, appears to have been ELECTIVE by the suffrages of the people. Similar instances might be traced in most, if not all the popular governments of antiquity.

Lastly, in Sparta we meet with the Ephori, and in Rome with the Tribunes; two bodies, small indeed in numbers, but annually ELECTED BY THE WHOLE BODY OF THE PEOPLE, and considered as the REPRESENTATIVES of the people, almost in their PLENIPOTENTIARY capacity. The Cosmi of Crete were also annually ELECTED BY THE PEOPLE, and have been considered by some authors as an institution analogous to those of Sparta and Rome, with this difference only, that in the election of that representative body the right of suffrage was communicated to a part only of the people.

From these facts, to which many others might be added, it is clear that the principle of representation was neither unknown to the ancients nor wholly overlooked in their political constitutions. The true distinction between these and the American governments, lies IN THE TOTAL EXCLUSION OF THE PEOPLE, IN THEIR COLLECTIVE CAPACITY, from any share in the LATTER, and not in the TOTAL EXCLUSION OF THE REPRESENTATIVES OF THE PEOPLE from the administration of the FORMER. The distinction, however, thus qualified, must be admitted to leave a most advantageous superiority in favor of the United States. But to insure to this advantage its full effect, we must be careful not to separate it from the other advantage, of an extensive territory. For it cannot be believed, that any form of representative government could have succeeded within the narrow limits occupied by the democracies of Greece.

In answer to all these arguments, suggested by reason, illustrated by examples, and enforced by our own experience, the jealous adversary of the Constitution will probably content himself with repeating, that a senate appointed not immediately by the people, and for the term of six years, must gradually acquire a dangerous pre-eminence in the government, and finally transform it into a tyrannical aristocracy.

Documents of Revolution

To this general answer, the general reply ought to be sufficient, that liberty may be endangered by the abuses of liberty as well as by the abuses of power; that there are numerous instances of the former as well as of the latter; and that the former, rather than the latter, are apparently most to be apprehended by the United States. But a more particular reply may be given.

Before such a revolution can be effected, the Senate, it is to be observed, must in the first place corrupt itself; must next corrupt the State legislatures; must then corrupt the House of Representatives; and must finally corrupt the people at large. It is evident that the Senate must be first corrupted before it can attempt an establishment of tyranny. Without corrupting the State legislatures, it cannot prosecute the attempt, because the periodical change of members would otherwise regenerate the whole body. Without exerting the means of corruption with equal success on the House of Representatives, the opposition of that coequal branch of the government would inevitably defeat the attempt; and without corrupting the people themselves, a succession of new representatives would speedily restore all things to their pristine order. Is there any man who can seriously persuade himself that the proposed Senate can, by any possible means within the compass of human address, arrive at the object of a lawless ambition, through all these obstructions?

If reason condemns the suspicion, the same sentence is pronounced by experience. The constitution of Maryland furnishes the most apposite example. The Senate of that State is elected, as the federal Senate will be, indirectly by the people, and for a term less by one year only than the federal Senate. It is distinguished, also, by the remarkable prerogative of filling up its own vacancies within the term of its appointment, and, at the same time, is not under the control of any such rotation as is provided for the federal Senate. There are some other lesser distinctions, which would expose the former to colorable objections, that do not lie against the latter. If the federal Senate, therefore, really contained the danger which has been so loudly proclaimed, some symptoms at least of a like danger ought by this time to have been betrayed by the Senate of Maryland, but no such symptoms have appeared. On the contrary, the jealousies at first entertained by men of the same description with those who view with terror the correspondent part of the federal Constitution, have been gradually extinguished by the progress of the experiment; and the Maryland constitution is daily deriving, from the salutary operation of this part of it, a reputation in which it will probably not be rivalled by that of any State in the Union.

But if anything could silence the jealousies on this subject, it ought to be the British example. The Senate there instead of being elected for a term of six years, and of being unconfined to particular families or fortunes, is an hereditary assembly of opulent nobles. The House of Representatives, instead of being elected for two years, and by the whole body of the people, is elected for seven years, and, in very great proportion, by a very small proportion of the people. Here, unquestionably, ought to be seen in full display the aristocratic usurpations and tyranny which are at some future period to be exemplified in the United States. Unfortunately, however, for the anti-federal argument, the British history informs us that this hereditary assembly has not been able to defend itself against the continual encroachments of the House of Representatives; and that it no sooner lost the support of the monarch, than it was actually crushed by the weight of the popular branch.

As far as antiquity can instruct us on this subject, its examples support the reasoning which we have employed. In Sparta, the Ephori, the annual representatives of the people, were found an overmatch for the senate for life, continually gained on its authority and finally drew all power into their own hands. The Tribunes of Rome, who were the representatives of the people, prevailed, it is well known, in almost every contest with the senate for life, and in the end gained the most complete triumph over it. The fact is the more remarkable, as unanimity was required in every act of the Tribunes, even after their number was augmented to ten. It proves the irresistible force possessed by that branch of a free government, which has the people on its side. To these examples might be added that of Carthage, whose senate, according to the testimony of Polybius, instead of drawing all power into its vortex, had, at the commencement of the second Punic War, lost almost the whole of its original portion.

Besides the conclusive evidence resulting from this assemblage of facts, that the federal Senate will never be able to transform itself, by gradual usurpations, into an independent and aristocratic body, we are warranted in believing, that if such a revolution should ever happen from causes which the foresight of man cannot guard against, the House of Representatives, with the people on their side, will at all times be able to bring back the Constitution to its primitive form and principles. Against the force of the immediate representatives of the people, nothing will be able to maintain even the constitutional authority of the Senate, but such a display of enlightened policy, and attachment to the public good, as will divide with that branch of the legislature the affections and support of the entire body of the people themselves.

PUBLIUS

FEDERALIST PAPER NO. 64. THE POWERS OF THE SENATE

From The Independent Journal. Wednesday, March 5, 1788.

JAY

To the People of the State of New York:

IT IS a just and not a new observation, that enemies to particular persons, and opponents to particular measures, seldom confine their censures to such things only in either as are worthy of blame. Unless on this principle, it is difficult to explain the motives of their conduct, who condemn the proposed Constitution in the aggregate, and treat with severity some of the most unexceptionable articles in it.

The second section gives power to the President, "BY AND WITH THE ADVICE AND CONSENT OF THE SENATE, TO MAKE TREATIES, PROVIDED TWO THIRDS OF THE SENATORS PRESENT CONCUR."

The power of making treaties is an important one, especially as it relates to war, peace, and commerce; and it should not be delegated but in such a mode, and with such precautions, as will afford the highest security that it will be exercised by men the best qualified for the purpose, and in the manner most conducive to the public good. The convention appears to have been attentive to both these points: they have directed the President to be chosen by select bodies of electors, to be deputed by the people for that express purpose; and they have committed the appointment of senators to the State legislatures. This mode has, in such cases, vastly the advantage of elections by the people in their collective capacity, where the activity of party zeal, taking the advantage of the supineness, the ignorance, and the hopes and fears of the unwary and interested, often places men in office by the votes of a small proportion of the electors.

As the select assemblies for choosing the President, as well as the State legislatures who appoint the senators, will in general be composed of the most enlightened and respectable citizens, there is reason to presume that their attention and their votes will be directed to those men only who have become the most distinguished by their abilities and virtue, and in whom the people perceive just grounds for confidence. The Constitution manifests very particular attention to this object. By excluding men under thirty-five from the first office, and those under thirty from the second, it confines the electors to men of whom the people have had time to form a judgment, and with respect to whom they will not be liable to be deceived by those brilliant appearances of genius and patriotism, which, like transient meteors, sometimes mislead as well as dazzle. If the observation be well founded, that wise kings will always be served by able ministers, it is fair to argue, that as an assembly of select electors possess, in a greater degree than kings, the means of extensive and accurate information relative to men and characters, so will their appointments bear at least equal marks of discretion and discernment. The inference which naturally results from these considerations is this, that the President and senators so chosen will always be of the number of those who best understand our national interests, whether considered in relation to the several States or to foreign nations, who are best able to promote those interests, and whose reputation for integrity inspires and merits confidence. With such men the power of making treaties may be safely lodged.

Although the absolute necessity of system, in the conduct of any business, is universally known and acknowledged, yet the high importance of it in national affairs has not yet become sufficiently impressed on the public mind. They who wish to commit the power under consideration to a popular assembly, composed of members constantly coming and going in quick succession, seem not to recollect that such a body must necessarily be inadequate to the attainment of those great objects, which require to be steadily contemplated in all their relations and circumstances, and which can only be approached and achieved by measures which not only talents, but also exact information, and often much time, are necessary to concert and to execute. It was wise, therefore, in the convention to provide, not only that the power of making treaties should be committed to able and honest men, but also that they should continue in place a sufficient time to become perfectly acquainted with our national concerns, and to form and introduce a a system for the management of them. The duration prescribed is such as will give them an opportunity of greatly extending their political information, and of rendering their accumulating experience more and more beneficial to their country. Nor has the convention discovered less prudence in providing for the frequent elections of senators in such a way as to obviate the inconvenience of periodically transferring those great affairs entirely to new men; for by leaving a considerable residue of the old ones in place, uniformity and order, as well as a constant succession of official information will be preserved.

There are a few who will not admit that the affairs of trade and navigation should be regulated by a system cautiously formed and steadily pursued; and that both our treaties and our laws should correspond with and be made to promote it. It is of much consequence that this correspondence and conformity be carefully maintained; and they who assent to the truth of this position will see and confess that it is well provided for by making concurrence of the Senate necessary both to treaties and to laws.

It seldom happens in the negotiation of treaties, of whatever nature, but that perfect SECRECY and immediate DESPATCH are sometimes requisite. These are cases where the most useful intelligence may be obtained, if the persons possessing it can be relieved from apprehensions of discovery. Those apprehensions will operate on those persons whether they are actuated by mercenary or friendly motives; and there doubtless are many of both descriptions, who would rely on the secrecy of the President, but who would not confide in that of the Senate, and still less in that of a large popular Assembly. The convention have done well, therefore, in so disposing of the power of making treaties, that although the President must, in forming them, act by the advice and consent of the Senate, yet he will be able to manage the business of intelligence in such a manner as prudence may suggest.

They who have turned their attention to the affairs of men, must have perceived that there are tides in them; tides very irregular in their duration, strength, and direction, and seldom found to run twice exactly in the same manner or measure. To discern and to profit by these tides in national affairs is the business of those who preside over them; and they who have had much experience on this head inform us, that there frequently are occasions when days, nay, even when hours, are precious. The loss of a battle, the death of a prince, the removal of a minister, or other circumstances intervening to change the present posture and aspect of affairs, may turn the most favorable tide into a course opposite to our wishes. As in the field, so in the cabinet, there are moments to be seized as they pass, and they who preside in either should be left in capacity to improve them. So often and so essentially have we heretofore suffered from the want of secrecy and despatch, that the Constitution would have been inexcusably defective, if no attention had been paid to those objects. Those matters which in negotiations usually require the most secrecy and the most despatch, are those preparatory and auxiliary measures which are not otherwise important in a national view, than as they tend to facilitate the attainment of the objects of the negotiation. For these, the President will find no difficulty to provide; and should any circumstance occur which requires the advice and consent of the Senate, he may at any time convene them. Thus we see that the Constitution provides that our negotiations for treaties shall have every advantage which can be derived from talents, information, integrity, and deliberate investigations, on the one hand, and from secrecy and despatch on the other.

But to this plan, as to most others that have ever appeared, objections are contrived and urged.

Some are displeased with it, not on account of any errors or defects in it, but because, as the treaties, when made, are to have the force of laws, they should be made only by men invested with legislative authority. These gentlemen seem not to consider that the judgments of our courts, and the commissions constitutionally given by our governor, are as valid and as binding on all persons whom they concern, as the laws passed by our legislature. All constitutional acts of power, whether in the executive or in the judicial department, have as much legal validity and obligation as if they proceeded from the legislature; and therefore, whatever name be given to the power of making treaties, or however obligatory they may be when made, certain it is, that the people may, with much propriety, commit the power to a distinct body from the legislature, the executive, or the judicial. It surely does not follow, that because they have given the power of making laws to the legislature, that therefore they should likewise give them the power to do every other act of sovereignty by which the citizens are to be bound and affected.

Others, though content that treaties should be made in the mode proposed, are averse to their being the SUPREME laws of the land. They insist, and profess to believe, that treaties like acts of assembly, should be repealable at pleasure. This idea seems to be new and peculiar to this country, but new errors, as well as new truths, often appear. These gentlemen would do well to reflect that a treaty is only another name for a bargain, and that it would be impossible to find a nation who would make any bargain with us, which should be binding on them ABSOLUTELY, but on us only so long and so far as we may think proper to be bound by it. They who make laws may, without doubt, amend or repeal them; and it will not be disputed that they who make treaties may alter or cancel them; but still let us not forget that treaties are made, not by only one of the contracting parties, but by both; and consequently, that as the consent of both was essential to their formation at first, so must it ever afterwards be to alter or cancel them. The proposed Constitution, therefore, has not in the least extended the obligation of treaties. They are just as binding, and just as far beyond the lawful reach of legislative acts now, as they will be at any future period, or under any form of government.

However useful jealousy may be in republics, yet when like bile in the natural, it abounds too much in the body politic, the eyes of both become very liable to be deceived by the delusive appearances which that malady casts on surrounding objects. From this cause, probably, proceed the fears and apprehensions of some, that the President and Senate may make treaties without an equal eye to the interests of all the States. Others suspect that two thirds will oppress the remaining third, and ask whether those gentlemen are made sufficiently responsible for their conduct; whether, if they act corruptly, they can be punished; and if they make disadvantageous treaties, how are we to get rid of those treaties?

As all the States are equally represented in the Senate, and by men the most able and the most willing to promote the interests of their constituents, they will all have an equal degree of influence in that body, especially while they continue to be careful in appointing proper persons, and to insist on their punctual attendance. In proportion as the United States assume a national form and a national character, so will the good of the whole be more and more an object of attention, and the government must be a weak one indeed, if it should forget that the good of the whole can only be promoted by advancing the good of each of the parts or members which compose the whole. It will not be in the power of the President and Senate to make any treaties by which they and their families and estates will not be equally bound and affected with the rest of the community; and, having no private interests distinct from that of the nation, they will be under no temptations to neglect the latter.

As to corruption, the case is not supposable. He must either have been very unfortunate in his intercourse with the world, or possess a heart very susceptible of such impressions, who can think it probable that the President and two thirds of the Senate will ever be capable of such unworthy conduct. The idea is too gross and too invidious to be entertained. But in such a case, if it should ever happen, the treaty so obtained from us would, like all other fraudulent contracts, be null and void by the law of nations.

With respect to their responsibility, it is difficult to conceive how it could be increased. Every consideration that can influence the human mind, such as honor, oaths, reputations, conscience, the love of country, and family affections and attachments, afford security for their fidelity. In short, as the Constitution has taken the utmost care that they shall be men of talents and integrity, we have reason to be persuaded that the treaties they make will be as advantageous as, all circumstances considered, could be made; and so far as the fear of punishment and disgrace can operate, that motive to good behavior is amply afforded by the article on the subject of impeachments.

PUBLIUS

FEDERALIST PAPER NO. 65. THE POWERS OF THE SENATE CONTINUED

From the New York Packet. Friday, March 7, 1788.

HAMILTON

To the People of the State of New York:

THE remaining powers which the plan of the convention allots to the Senate, in a distinct capacity, are comprised in their participation with the executive in the appointment to offices, and in their judicial character as a court for the trial of impeachments. As in the business of appointments the executive will be the principal agent, the provisions relating to it will most properly be discussed in the examination of that department. We will, therefore, conclude this head with a view of the judicial character of the Senate.

A well-constituted court for the trial of impeachments is an object not more to be desired than difficult to be obtained in a government wholly elective. The subjects of its jurisdiction are those offenses which proceed from the misconduct of public men, or, in other words, from the abuse or violation of some public trust. They are of a nature which may with peculiar propriety be denominated POLITICAL, as they relate chiefly to injuries done immediately to the society itself. The prosecution of them, for this reason, will seldom fail to agitate the passions of the whole community, and to divide it into parties more or less friendly or inimical to the accused. In many cases it will connect itself with the pre-existing factions, and will enlist all their animosities, partialities, influence, and interest on one side or on the other; and in such cases there will always be the greatest danger that the decision will be regulated more by the comparative strength of parties, than by the real demonstrations of innocence or guilt.

The delicacy and magnitude of a trust which so deeply concerns the political reputation and existence of every man engaged in the administration of public affairs, speak for themselves. The difficulty of placing it rightly, in a government resting entirely on the basis of periodical elections, will as readily be perceived, when it is considered that the most conspicuous characters in it will, from that circumstance, be too often the leaders or the tools of the most cunning or the most numerous faction, and on this account, can hardly be expected to possess the requisite neutrality towards those whose conduct may be the subject of scrutiny.

The convention, it appears, thought the Senate the most fit depositary of this important trust. Those who can best discern the intrinsic difficulty of the thing, will be least hasty in condemning that opinion, and will be most inclined to allow due weight to the arguments which may be supposed to have produced it.

What, it may be asked, is the true spirit of the institution itself? Is it not designed as a method of NATIONAL INQUEST into the conduct of public men? If this be the design of it, who can so properly be the inquisitors for the nation as the representatives of the nation themselves? It is not disputed that the power of originating the inquiry, or, in other words, of preferring the impeachment, ought to be lodged in the hands of one branch of the legislative body. Will not the reasons which indicate the propriety of this arrangement strongly plead for an admission of the other branch of that body to a share of the inquiry? The model from which the idea of this institution has been borrowed, pointed out that course to the convention. In Great Britain it is the province of the House of Commons to prefer the impeachment, and of the House of Lords to decide upon it. Several of the State constitutions have followed the example. As well the latter, as the former, seem to have regarded the practice of impeachments as a bridle in the hands of the legislative body upon the executive servants of the government. Is not this the true light in which it ought to be regarded?

Where else than in the Senate could have been found a tribunal sufficiently dignified, or sufficiently independent? What other body would be likely to feel CONFIDENCE ENOUGH IN ITS OWN SITUATION, to preserve, unawed and uninfluenced, the necessary impartiality between an INDIVIDUAL accused, and the REPRESENTATIVES OF THE PEOPLE, HIS ACCUSERS?

Could the Supreme Court have been relied upon as answering this description? It is much to be doubted, whether the members of that tribunal would at all times be endowed with so eminent a portion of fortitude, as would be called for in the execution of so difficult a task; and it is still more to be doubted, whether they would possess the degree of credit and authority, which might, on certain occasions, be indispensable towards reconciling the people to a decision that should happen to clash with an accusation brought by their immediate representatives. A deficiency in the first, would be fatal to the accused; in the last, dangerous to the public tranquillity. The hazard in both these respects, could only be avoided, if at all, by rendering that tribunal more numerous than would consist with a reasonable attention to economy. The necessity of a numerous court for the trial of impeachments, is equally dictated by the nature of the proceeding. This can never be tied down by such strict rules, either in the delineation of the offense by the prosecutors, or in the construction of it by the judges, as in common cases serve to limit the discretion of courts in favor of personal security. There will be no jury to stand between the judges who are to pronounce the sentence of the law, and the party who is to receive or suffer it. The awful discretion which a court of impeachments must necessarily have, to doom to honor or to infamy the most confidential and the most distinguished characters of the community, forbids the commitment of the trust to a small number of persons.

These considerations seem alone sufficient to authorize a conclusion, that the Supreme Court would have been an improper substitute for the Senate, as a court of impeachments. There remains a further consideration, which will not a little strengthen this conclusion. It is this: The punishment which may be the consequence of conviction upon impeachment, is not to terminate the chastisement of the offender. After having been sentenced to a perpetual ostracism from the esteem and confidence, and honors and emoluments of his country, he will still be liable to prosecution and punishment in the ordinary course of law. Would it be proper that the persons who had disposed of his fame, and his most valuable rights as a citizen in one trial, should, in another trial, for the same offense, be also the disposers of his life and his fortune? Would there not be the greatest reason to apprehend, that error, in the first sentence, would be the parent of error in the second sentence? That the strong bias of one decision would be apt to overrule the influence of any new lights which might be brought to vary the complexion of another decision? Those who know anything of human nature, will not hesitate to answer these questions in the affirmative; and will be at no loss to perceive, that by making the same persons judges in both cases, those who might happen to be the objects of prosecution would, in a great measure, be deprived of the double security intended them by a double trial. The loss of life and estate would often be virtually included in a sentence which, in its terms, imported nothing more than dismission from a present, and disqualification for a future, office. It may be said, that the intervention of a jury, in the second instance, would obviate the danger. But juries are frequently influenced by the opinions of judges. They are sometimes induced to find special verdicts, which refer the main question to the decision of the court. Who would be willing to stake his life and his estate upon the verdict of a jury acting under the auspices of judges who had predetermined his guilt?

Would it have been an improvement of the plan, to have united the Supreme Court with the Senate, in the formation of the court of impeachments? This union would certainly have been attended with several advantages; but would they not have been overbalanced by the signal disadvantage, already stated, arising from the agency of the same judges in the double prosecution to which the offender would be liable? To a certain extent, the benefits of that union will be obtained from making the chief justice of the Supreme Court the president of the court of impeachments, as is proposed to be done in the plan of the convention; while the inconveniences of an entire incorporation of the former into the latter will be substantially avoided. This was perhaps the prudent mean. I forbear to remark upon the additional pretext for clamor against the judiciary, which so considerable an augmentation of its authority would have afforded.

Would it have been desirable to have composed the court for the trial of impeachments, of persons wholly distinct from the other departments of the government? There are weighty arguments, as well against, as in favor of, such a plan. To some minds it will not appear a trivial objection, that it could tend to increase the complexity of the political machine, and to add a new spring to the government, the utility of which would at best be questionable. But an objection which will not be thought by any unworthy of attention, is this: a court formed upon such a plan, would either be attended with a heavy expense, or might in practice be subject to a variety of casualties and inconveniences. It must either consist of permanent officers, stationary at the seat of government, and of course entitled to fixed and regular stipends, or of certain officers of the State governments to be called upon whenever an impeachment was actually depending. It will not be easy to imagine any third mode materially different, which could rationally be proposed. As the court, for reasons already given, ought to be numerous, the first scheme will be reprobated by every man who can compare the extent of the public wants with the means of supplying them. The second will be espoused with caution by those who will seriously consider the difficulty of collecting men dispersed over the whole Union; the injury to the innocent, from the procrastinated determination of the charges which might be brought against them; the advantage to the guilty, from the opportunities which delay would afford to intrigue and corruption; and in some cases the detriment to the State, from the prolonged inaction of men whose firm and faithful execution of their duty might have exposed them to the persecution of an intemperate or designing majority in the House of Representatives. Though this latter supposition may seem harsh, and might not be likely often to be verified, yet it ought not to be forgotten that the demon of faction will, at certain seasons, extend his sceptre over all numerous bodies of men.

But though one or the other of the substitutes which have been examined, or some other that might be devised, should be thought preferable to the plan in this respect, reported by the convention, it will not follow that the Constitution ought for this reason to be rejected. If mankind were to resolve to agree in no institution of government, until every part of it had been adjusted to the most exact standard of perfection, society would soon become a general scene of anarchy, and the world a desert. Where is the standard of perfection to be found? Who will undertake to unite the discordant opinions of a whole community, in the same judgment of it; and to prevail upon one conceited projector to renounce his INFALLIBLE criterion for the FALLIBLE criterion of his more CONCEITED NEIGHBOR? To answer the purpose of the adversaries of the Constitution, they ought to prove, not merely that particular provisions in it are not the best which might have been imagined, but that the plan upon the whole is bad and pernicious.

PUBLIUS

FEDERALIST PAPER NO. 66. OBJECTIONS TO THE POWER OF THE SENATE TO SET AS A COURT FOR IMPEACHMENTS FURTHER CONSIDERED.

From The Independent Journal. Saturday, March 8, 1788.

HAMILTON

To the People of the State of New York:

A REVIEW of the principal objections that have appeared against the proposed court for the trial of impeachments, will not improbably eradicate the remains of any unfavorable impressions which may still exist in regard to this matter.

The FIRST of these objections is, that the provision in question confounds legislative and judiciary authorities in the same body, in violation of that important and well-established maxim which requires a separation between the different departments of power. The true meaning of this maxim has been discussed and ascertained in another place, and has been shown to be entirely compatible with a partial intermixture of those departments for special purposes, preserving them, in the main, distinct and unconnected. This partial intermixture is even, in some cases, not only proper but necessary to the mutual defense of the several members of the government against each other. An absolute or qualified negative in the executive upon the acts of the legislative body, is admitted, by the ablest adepts in political science, to be an indispensable barrier against the encroachments of the latter upon the former. And it may, perhaps, with no less reason be contended, that the powers relating to impeachments are, as before intimated, an essential check in the hands of that body upon the encroachments of the executive. The division of them between the two branches of the legislature, assigning to one the right of accusing, to the other the right of judging, avoids the inconvenience of making the same persons both accusers and judges; and guards against the danger of persecution, from the prevalency of a factious spirit in either of those branches. As the concurrence of two thirds of the Senate will be requisite to a condemnation, the security to innocence, from this additional circumstance, will be as complete as itself can desire.

It is curious to observe, with what vehemence this part of the plan is assailed, on the principle here taken notice of, by men who profess to admire, without exception, the constitution of this State; while that constitution makes the Senate, together with the chancellor and judges of the Supreme Court, not only a court of impeachments, but the highest judicatory in the State, in all causes, civil and criminal. The proportion, in point of numbers, of the chancellor and judges to the senators, is so inconsiderable, that the judiciary authority of New York, in the last resort, may, with truth, be said to reside in its Senate. If the plan of the convention be, in this respect, chargeable with a departure from the celebrated maxim which has been so often mentioned, and seems to be so little understood, how much more culpable must be the constitution of New York?(1)

A SECOND objection to the Senate, as a court of impeachments, is, that it contributes to an undue accumulation of power in that body, tending to give to the government a countenance too aristocratic. The Senate, it is observed, is to have concurrent authority with the Executive in the formation of treaties and in the appointment to offices: if, say the objectors, to these prerogatives is added that of deciding in all cases of impeachment, it will give a decided predominancy to senatorial influence. To an objection so little precise in itself, it is not easy to find a very precise answer. Where is the measure or criterion to which we can appeal, for determining what will give the Senate too much, too little, or barely the proper degree of influence? Will it not be more safe, as well as more simple, to dismiss such vague and uncertain calculations, to examine each power by itself, and to decide, on general principles, where it may be deposited with most advantage and least inconvenience?

If we take this course, it will lead to a more intelligible, if not to a more certain result. The disposition of the power of making treaties, which has obtained in the plan of the convention, will, then, if I mistake not, appear to be fully justified by the considerations stated in a former number, and by others which will occur under the next head of our inquiries. The expediency of the junction of the Senate with the Executive, in the power of appointing to offices, will, I trust, be placed in a light not less satisfactory, in the disquisitions under the same head. And I flatter myself the observations in my last paper must have gone no inconsiderable way towards proving that it was not easy, if practicable, to find a more fit receptacle for the power of determining impeachments, than that which has been chosen. If this be truly the case, the hypothetical dread of the too great weight of the Senate ought to be discarded from our reasonings.

But this hypothesis, such as it is, has already been refuted in the remarks applied to the duration in office prescribed for the senators. It was by them shown, as well on the credit of historical examples, as from the reason of the thing, that the most POPULAR branch of every government, partaking of the republican genius, by being generally the favorite of the people, will be as generally a full match, if not an overmatch, for every other member of the Government.

But independent of this most active and operative principle, to secure the equilibrium of the national House of Representatives, the plan of the convention has provided in its favor several important counterpoises to the additional authorities to be conferred upon the Senate. The exclusive privilege of originating money bills will belong to the House of Representatives. The same house will possess the sole right of instituting impeachments: is not this a complete counterbalance to that of determining them? The same house will be the umpire in all elections of the President, which do not unite the suffrages of a majority of the whole number of electors; a case which it cannot be doubted will sometimes, if not frequently, happen. The constant possibility of the thing must be a fruitful source of influence to that body. The more it is contemplated, the more important will appear this ultimate though contingent power, of deciding the competitions of the most illustrious citizens of the Union, for the first office in it. It would not perhaps be rash to predict, that as a mean of influence it will be found to outweigh all the peculiar attributes of the Senate.

A THIRD objection to the Senate as a court of impeachments, is drawn from the agency they are to have in the appointments to office. It is imagined that they would be too indulgent judges of the conduct of men, in whose official creation they had participated. The principle of this objection would condemn a practice, which is to be seen in all the State governments, if not in all the governments with which we are acquainted: I mean that of rendering those who hold offices during pleasure, dependent on the pleasure of those who appoint them. With equal plausibility might it be alleged in this case, that the favoritism of the latter would always be an asylum for the misbehavior of the former. But that practice, in contradiction to this principle, proceeds upon the presumption, that the responsibility of those who appoint, for the fitness and competency of the persons on whom they bestow their choice, and the interest they will have in the respectable and prosperous administration of affairs, will inspire a sufficient disposition to dismiss from a share in it all such who, by their conduct, shall have proved themselves unworthy of the confidence reposed in them. Though facts may not always correspond with this presumption, yet if it be, in the main, just, it must destroy the supposition that the Senate, who will merely sanction the choice of the Executive, should feel a bias, towards the objects of that choice, strong enough to blind them to the evidences of guilt so extraordinary, as to have induced the representatives of the nation to become its accusers.

If any further arguments were necessary to evince the improbability of such a bias, it might be found in the nature of the agency of the Senate in the business of appointments. It will be the office of the President to NOMINATE, and, with the advice and consent of the Senate, to APPOINT. There will, of course, be no exertion of CHOICE on the part of the Senate. They may defeat one choice of the Executive, and oblige him to make another; but they cannot themselves CHOOSE—they can only ratify or reject the choice of the President. They might even entertain a preference to some other person, at the very moment they were assenting to the one proposed, because there might be no positive ground of opposition to him; and they could not be sure, if they withheld their assent, that the subsequent nomination would fall upon their own favorite, or upon any other person in their estimation more meritorious than the one rejected. Thus it could hardly happen, that the majority of the Senate would feel any other complacency towards the object of an appointment than such as the appearances of merit might inspire, and the proofs of the want of it destroy.

A FOURTH objection to the Senate in the capacity of a court of impeachments, is derived from its union with the Executive in the power of making treaties. This, it has been said, would constitute the senators their own judges, in every case of a corrupt or perfidious execution of that trust. After having combined with the Executive in betraying the interests of the nation in a ruinous treaty, what prospect, it is asked, would there be of their being made to suffer the punishment they would deserve, when they were themselves to decide upon the accusation brought against them for the treachery of which they have been guilty?

This objection has been circulated with more earnestness and with greater show of reason than any other which has appeared against this part of the plan; and yet I am deceived if it does not rest upon an erroneous foundation.

The security essentially intended by the Constitution against corruption and treachery in the formation of treaties, is to be sought for in the numbers and characters of those who are to make them. The JOINT AGENCY of the Chief Magistrate of the Union, and of two thirds of the members of a body selected by the collective wisdom of the legislatures of the several States, is designed to be the pledge for the fidelity of the national councils in this particular. The convention might with propriety have meditated the punishment of the Executive, for a deviation from the instructions of the Senate, or a want of integrity in the conduct of the negotiations committed to him; they might also have had in view the punishment of a few leading individuals in the Senate, who should have prostituted their influence in that body as the mercenary instruments of foreign corruption: but they could not, with more or with equal propriety, have contemplated the impeachment and punishment of two thirds of the Senate, consenting to an improper treaty, than of a majority of that or of the other branch of the national legislature, consenting to a pernicious or unconstitutional law—a principle which, I believe, has never been admitted into any government. How, in fact, could a majority in the House of Representatives impeach themselves? Not better, it is evident, than two thirds of the Senate might try themselves. And yet what reason is there, that a majority of the House of Representatives, sacrificing the interests of the society by an unjust and tyrannical act of legislation, should escape with impunity, more than two thirds of the Senate, sacrificing the same interests in an injurious treaty with a foreign power? The truth is, that in all such cases it is essential to the freedom and to the necessary independence of the deliberations of the body, that the members of it should be exempt from punishment for acts done in a collective capacity; and the security to the society must depend on the care which is taken to confide the trust to proper hands, to make it their interest to execute it with fidelity, and to make it as difficult as possible for them to combine in any interest opposite to that of the public good.

So far as might concern the misbehavior of the Executive in perverting the instructions or contravening the views of the Senate, we need not be apprehensive of the want of a disposition in that body to punish the abuse of their confidence or to vindicate their own authority. We may thus far count upon their pride, if not upon their virtue. And so far even as might concern the corruption of leading members, by whose arts and influence the majority may have been inveigled into measures odious to the community, if the proofs of that corruption should be satisfactory, the usual propensity of human nature will warrant us in concluding that there would be commonly no defect of inclination in the body to divert the public resentment from themselves by a ready sacrifice of the authors of their mismanagement and disgrace.

PUBLIUS

1. In that of New Jersey, also, the final judiciary authority is in a branch of the legislature. In New Hampshire, Massachusetts, Pennsylvania, and South Carolina, one branch of the legislature is the court for the trial of impeachments.

FEDERALIST PAPER NO. 67. THE EXECUTIVE DEPARTMENT

From the New York Packet. Tuesday, March 11, 1788.

HAMILTON

To the People of the State of New York:

THE constitution of the executive department of the proposed government, claims next our attention.

There is hardly any part of the system which could have been attended with greater difficulty in the arrangement of it than this; and there is, perhaps, none which has been inveighed against with less candor or criticised with less judgment.

Here the writers against the Constitution seem to have taken pains to signalize their talent of misrepresentation. Calculating upon the aversion of the people to monarchy, they have endeavored to enlist all their jealousies and apprehensions in opposition to the intended President of the United States; not merely as the embryo, but as the full-grown progeny, of that detested parent. To establish the pretended affinity, they have not scrupled to draw resources even from the regions of fiction. The authorities of a magistrate, in few instances greater, in some instances less, than those of a governor of New York, have been magnified into more than royal prerogatives. He has been decorated with attributes superior in dignity and splendor to those of a king of Great Britain. He has been shown to us with the diadem sparkling on his brow and the imperial purple flowing in his train. He has been seated on a throne surrounded with minions and mistresses, giving audience to the envoys of foreign potentates, in all the supercilious pomp of majesty. The images of Asiatic despotism and voluptuousness have scarcely been wanting to crown the exaggerated scene. We have been taught to tremble at the terrific visages of murdering janizaries, and to blush at the unveiled mysteries of a future seraglio.

Attempts so extravagant as these to disfigure or, it might rather be said, to metamorphose the object, render it necessary to take an accurate view of its real nature and form: in order as well to ascertain its true aspect and genuine appearance, as to unmask the disingenuity and expose the fallacy of the counterfeit resemblances which have been so insidiously, as well as industriously, propagated.

In the execution of this task, there is no man who would not find it an arduous effort either to behold with moderation, or to treat with seriousness, the devices, not less weak than wicked, which have been contrived to pervert the public opinion in relation to the subject. They so far exceed the usual though unjustifiable licenses of party artifice, that even in a disposition the most candid and tolerant, they must force the sentiments which favor an indulgent construction of the conduct of political adversaries to give place to a voluntary and unreserved indignation. It is impossible not to bestow the imputation of deliberate imposture and deception upon the gross pretense of a similitude between a king of Great Britain and a magistrate of the character marked out for that of the President of the United States. It is still more impossible to withhold that imputation from the rash and barefaced expedients which have been employed to give success to the attempted imposition.

In one instance, which I cite as a sample of the general spirit, the temerity has proceeded so far as to ascribe to the President of the United States a power which by the instrument reported is EXPRESSLY allotted to the Executives of the individual States. I mean the power of filling casual vacancies in the Senate.

This bold experiment upon the discernment of his countrymen has been hazarded by a writer who (whatever may be his real merit) has had no inconsiderable share in the applauses of his party(1); and who, upon this false and unfounded suggestion, has built a series of observations equally false and unfounded. Let him now be confronted with the evidence of the fact, and let him, if he be able, justify or extenuate the shameful outrage he has offered to the dictates of truth and to the rules of fair dealing.

The second clause of the second section of the second article empowers the President of the United States "to nominate, and by and with the advice and consent of the Senate, to appoint ambassadors, other public ministers and consuls, judges of the Supreme Court, and all other OFFICERS of United States whose appointments are NOT in the Constitution OTHERWISE PROVIDED FOR, and WHICH SHALL BE ESTABLISHED BY LAW." Immediately after this clause follows another in these words: "The President shall have power to fill up all VACANCIES that may happen DURING THE RECESS OF THE SENATE, by granting commissions which shall EXPIRE AT THE END OF THEIR NEXT SESSION." It is from this last provision that the pretended power of the President to fill vacancies in the Senate has been deduced. A slight attention to the connection of the clauses, and to the obvious meaning of the terms, will satisfy us that the deduction is not even colorable.

The first of these two clauses, it is clear, only provides a mode for appointing such officers, "whose appointments are NOT OTHERWISE PROVIDED FOR in the Constitution, and which SHALL BE ESTABLISHED BY LAW"; of course it cannot extend to the appointments of senators, whose appointments are OTHERWISE PROVIDED FOR in the Constitution(2), and who are ESTABLISHED BY THE CONSTITUTION, and will not require a future establishment by law. This position will hardly be contested.

The last of these two clauses, it is equally clear, cannot be understood to comprehend the power of filling vacancies in the Senate, for the following reasons: First. The relation in which that clause stands to the other, which declares the general mode of appointing officers of the United States, denotes it to be nothing more than a supplement to the other, for the purpose of establishing an auxiliary method of appointment, in cases to which the general method was inadequate. The ordinary power of appointment is confined to the President and Senate JOINTLY, and can therefore only be exercised during the session of the Senate; but as it would have been improper to oblige this body to be continually in session for the appointment of officers and as vacancies might happen IN THEIR RECESS, which it might be necessary for the public service to fill without delay, the succeeding clause is evidently intended to authorize the President, SINGLY, to make temporary appointments "during the recess of the Senate, by granting commissions which shall expire at the end of their next session." Second. If this clause is to be considered as supplementary to the one which precedes, the VACANCIES of which it speaks must be construed to relate to the "officers" described in the preceding one; and this, we have seen, excludes from its description the members of the Senate. Third. The time within which the power is to operate, "during the recess of the Senate," and the duration of the appointments, "to the end of the next session" of that body, conspire to elucidate the sense of the provision, which, if it had been intended to comprehend senators, would naturally have referred the temporary power of filling vacancies to the recess of the State legislatures, who are to make the permanent appointments, and not to the recess of the national Senate, who are to have no concern in those appointments; and would have extended the duration in office of the temporary senators to the next session of the legislature of the State, in whose representation the vacancies had happened, instead of making it to expire at the end of the ensuing session of the national Senate. The circumstances of the body authorized to make the permanent appointments would, of course, have governed the modification of a power which related to the temporary appointments; and as the national Senate is the body, whose situation is alone contemplated in the clause upon which the suggestion under examination has been founded, the vacancies to which it alludes can only be deemed to respect those officers in whose appointment that body has a concurrent agency with the President. But last, the first and second clauses of the third section of the first article, not only obviate all possibility of doubt, but destroy the pretext of misconception. The former provides, that "the Senate of the United States shall be composed of two Senators from each State, chosen BY THE LEGISLATURE THEREOF for six years"; and the latter directs, that, "if vacancies in that body should happen by resignation or otherwise, DURING THE RECESS OF THE LEGISLATURE OF ANY STATE, the Executive THEREOF may make temporary appointments until the NEXT MEETING OF THE LEGISLATURE, which shall then fill such vacancies." Here is an express power given, in clear and unambiguous terms, to the State Executives, to fill casual vacancies in the Senate, by temporary appointments; which not only invalidates the supposition, that the clause before considered could have been intended to confer that power upon the President of the United States, but proves that this supposition, destitute as it is even of the merit of plausibility, must have originated in an intention to deceive the people, too palpable to be obscured by sophistry, too atrocious to be palliated by hypocrisy.

I have taken the pains to select this instance of misrepresentation, and to place it in a clear and strong light, as an unequivocal proof of the unwarrantable arts which are practiced to prevent a fair and impartial judgment of the real merits of the Constitution submitted to the consideration of the people. Nor have I scrupled, in so flagrant a case, to allow myself a severity of animadversion little congenial with the general spirit of these papers. I hesitate not to submit it to the decision of any candid and honest adversary of the proposed government, whether language can furnish epithets of too much asperity, for so shameless and so prostitute an attempt to impose on the citizens of America.

PUBLIUS

1. See CATO, No. V.
2. Article I, section 3, clause 1.

FEDERALIST PAPER NO. 68. THE MODE OF ELECTING THE PRESIDENT

From The Independent Journal. Wednesday, March 12, 1788.

HAMILTON

To the People of the State of New York:

THE mode of appointment of the Chief Magistrate of the United States is almost the only part of the system, of any consequence, which has escaped without severe censure, or which has received the slightest mark of approbation from its opponents. The most plausible of these, who has appeared in print, has even deigned to admit that the election of the President is pretty well guarded.(1) I venture somewhat further, and hesitate not to affirm, that if the manner of it be not perfect, it is at least excellent. It unites in an eminent degree all the advantages, the union of which was to be wished for.(E1)

It was desirable that the sense of the people should operate in the choice of the person to whom so important a trust was to be confided. This end will be answered by committing the right of making it, not to any preestablished body, but to men chosen by the people for the special purpose, and at the particular conjuncture.

It was equally desirable, that the immediate election should be made by men most capable of analyzing the qualities adapted to the station, and acting under circumstances favorable to deliberation, and to a judicious combination of all the reasons and inducements which were proper to govern their choice. A small number of persons, selected by their fellow-citizens from the general mass, will be most likely to possess the information and discernment requisite to such complicated investigations.

It was also peculiarly desirable to afford as little opportunity as possible to tumult and disorder. This evil was not least to be dreaded in the election of a magistrate, who was to have so important an agency in the administration of the government as the President of the United States. But the precautions which have been so happily concerted in the system under consideration, promise an effectual security against this mischief. The choice of SEVERAL, to form an intermediate body of electors, will be much less apt to convulse the community with any extraordinary or violent movements, than the choice of ONE who was himself to be the final object of the public wishes. And as the electors, chosen in each State, are to assemble and vote in the State in which they are chosen, this detached and divided situation will expose them much less to heats and ferments, which might be communicated from them to the people, than if they were all to be convened at one time, in one place.

Nothing was more to be desired than that every practicable obstacle should be opposed to cabal, intrigue, and corruption. These most deadly adversaries of republican government might naturally have been expected to make their approaches from more than one quarter, but chiefly from the desire in foreign powers to gain an improper ascendant in our councils. How could they better gratify this, than by raising a creature of their own to the chief magistracy of the Union? But the convention have guarded against all danger of this sort, with the most provident and judicious attention. They have not made the appointment of the President to depend on any preexisting bodies of men, who might be tampered with beforehand to prostitute their votes; but they have referred it in the first instance to an immediate act of the people of America, to be exerted in the choice of persons for the temporary and sole purpose of making the appointment. And they have excluded from eligibility to this trust, all those who from situation might be suspected of too great devotion to the President in office. No senator, representative, or other person holding a place of trust or profit under the United States, can be of the numbers of the electors. Thus without corrupting the body of the people, the immediate agents in the election will at least enter upon the task free from any sinister bias. Their transient existence, and their detached situation, already taken notice of, afford a satisfactory prospect of their continuing so, to the conclusion of it. The business of corruption, when it is to embrace so considerable a number of men, requires time as well as means. Nor would it be found easy suddenly to embark them, dispersed as they would be over thirteen

States, in any combinations founded upon motives, which though they could not properly be denominated corrupt, might yet be of a nature to mislead them from their duty.

Another and no less important desideratum was, that the Executive should be independent for his continuance in office on all but the people themselves. He might otherwise be tempted to sacrifice his duty to his complaisance for those whose favor was necessary to the duration of his official consequence. This advantage will also be secured, by making his re-election to depend on a special body of representatives, deputed by the society for the single purpose of making the important choice.

All these advantages will happily combine in the plan devised by the convention; which is, that the people of each State shall choose a number of persons as electors, equal to the number of senators and representatives of such State in the national government, who shall assemble within the State, and vote for some fit person as President. Their votes, thus given, are to be transmitted to the seat of the national government, and the person who may happen to have a majority of the whole number of votes will be the President. But as a majority of the votes might not always happen to centre in one man, and as it might be unsafe to permit less than a majority to be conclusive, it is provided that, in such a contingency, the House of Representatives shall select out of the candidates who shall have the five highest number of votes, the man who in their opinion may be best qualified for the office.

The process of election affords a moral certainty, that the office of President will never fall to the lot of any man who is not in an eminent degree endowed with the requisite qualifications. Talents for low intrigue, and the little arts of popularity, may alone suffice to elevate a man to the first honors in a single State; but it will require other talents, and a different kind of merit, to establish him in the esteem and confidence of the whole Union, or of so considerable a portion of it as would be necessary to make him a successful candidate for the distinguished office of President of the United States. It will not be too strong to say, that there will be a constant probability of seeing the station filled by characters pre-eminent for ability and virtue. And this will be thought no inconsiderable recommendation of the Constitution, by those who are able to estimate the share which the executive in every government must necessarily have in its good or ill administration. Though we cannot acquiesce in the political heresy of the poet who says:

"For forms of government let fools contest—That which is best administered is best,"—yet we may safely pronounce, that the true test of a good government is its aptitude and tendency to produce a good administration.

The Vice-President is to be chosen in the same manner with the President; with this difference, that the Senate is to do, in respect to the former, what is to be done by the House of Representatives, in respect to the latter.

The appointment of an extraordinary person, as Vice-President, has been objected to as superfluous, if not mischievous. It has been alleged, that it would have been preferable to have authorized the Senate to elect out of their own body an officer answering that description. But two considerations seem to justify the ideas of the convention in this respect. One is, that to secure at all times the possibility of a definite resolution of the body, it is necessary that the President should have only a casting vote. And to take the senator of any State from his seat as senator, to place him in that of President of the Senate, would be to exchange, in regard to the State from which he came, a constant for a contingent vote. The other consideration is, that as the Vice-President may occasionally become a substitute for the President, in the supreme executive magistracy, all the reasons which recommend the mode of election prescribed for the one, apply with great if not with equal force to the manner of appointing the other. It is remarkable that in this, as in most other instances, the objection which is made would lie against the constitution of this State. We have a Lieutenant-Governor, chosen by the people at large, who presides in the Senate, and is the constitutional substitute for the Governor, in casualties similar to those which would authorize the Vice-President to exercise the authorities and discharge the duties of the President.

PUBLIUS

1. Vide federal farmer.
E1. Some editions substitute "desired" for "wished for".

FEDERALIST PAPER NO. 69. THE REAL CHARACTER OF THE EXECUTIVE

From the New York Packet. Friday, March 14, 1788.

HAMILTON

To the People of the State of New York:

I PROCEED now to trace the real characters of the proposed Executive, as they are marked out in the plan of the convention. This will serve to place in a strong light the unfairness of the representations which have been made in regard to it.

The first thing which strikes our attention is, that the executive authority, with few exceptions, is to be vested in a single magistrate. This will scarcely, however, be considered as a point upon which any comparison can be grounded; for if, in this particular, there be a resemblance to the king of Great Britain, there is not less a resemblance to the Grand Seignior, to the khan of Tartary, to the Man of the Seven Mountains, or to the governor of New York.

That magistrate is to be elected for four years; and is to be re-eligible as often as the people of the United States shall think him worthy of their confidence. In these circumstances there is a total dissimilitude between him and a king of Great Britain, who is an hereditary monarch, possessing the crown as a patrimony descendible to his heirs forever; but there is a close analogy between him and a governor of New York, who is elected for three years, and is re-eligible without limitation or intermission. If we consider how much less time would be requisite for establishing a dangerous influence in a single State, than for establishing a like influence throughout the United States, we must conclude that a duration of four years for the Chief Magistrate of the Union is a degree of permanency far less to be dreaded in that office, than a duration of three years for a corresponding office in a single State.

The President of the United States would be liable to be impeached, tried, and, upon conviction of treason, bribery, or other high crimes or misdemeanors, removed from office; and would afterwards be liable to prosecution and punishment in the ordinary course of law. The person of the king of Great Britain is sacred and inviolable; there is no constitutional tribunal to which he is amenable; no punishment to which he can be subjected without involving the crisis of a national revolution. In this delicate and important circumstance of personal responsibility, the President of Confederated America would stand upon no better ground than a governor of New York, and upon worse ground than the governors of Maryland and Delaware.

The President of the United States is to have power to return a bill, which shall have passed the two branches of the legislature, for reconsideration; and the bill so returned is to become a law, if, upon that reconsideration, it be approved by two thirds of both houses. The king of Great Britain, on his part, has an absolute negative upon the acts of the two houses of Parliament. The disuse of that power for a considerable time past does not affect the reality of its existence; and is to be ascribed wholly to the crown's having found the means of substituting influence to authority, or the art of gaining a majority in one or the other of the two houses, to the necessity of exerting a prerogative which could seldom be exerted without hazarding some degree of national agitation. The qualified negative of the President differs widely from this absolute negative of the British sovereign; and tallies exactly with the revisionary authority of the council of revision of this State, of which the governor is a constituent part. In this respect the power of the President would exceed that of the governor of New York, because the former would possess, singly, what the latter shares with the chancellor and judges; but it would be precisely the same with that of the governor of Massachusetts, whose constitution, as to this article, seems to have been the original from which the convention have copied.

The President is to be the "commander-in-chief of the army and navy of the United States, and of the militia of the several States, when called into the actual service of the United States. He is to have power to grant reprieves and pardons for offenses against the United States, except in cases of impeachment; to recommend to the consideration of Congress such measures as he shall judge necessary and expedient; to convene, on extraordinary occasions, both houses of the legislature, or either of them, and, in case of disagreement between them with respect to the time of adjournment, to adjourn them to such time as he shall think proper; to take care that the laws be faithfully executed; and to commission all officers of the United States." In most of these particulars, the power of the President will resemble equally that of the king of Great Britain and of the governor of New

Documents of Revolution

York. The most material points of difference are these:—First. The President will have only the occasional command of such part of the militia of the nation as by legislative provision may be called into the actual service of the Union. The king of Great Britain and the governor of New York have at all times the entire command of all the militia within their several jurisdictions. In this article, therefore, the power of the President would be inferior to that of either the monarch or the governor. Second. The President is to be commander-in-chief of the army and navy of the United States. In this respect his authority would be nominally the same with that of the king of Great Britain, but in substance much inferior to it. It would amount to nothing more than the supreme command and direction of the military and naval forces, as first General and admiral of the Confederacy; while that of the British king extends to the declaring of war and to the raising and regulating of fleets and armies—all which, by the Constitution under consideration, would appertain to the legislature.(1) The governor of New York, on the other hand, is by the constitution of the State vested only with the command of its militia and navy. But the constitutions of several of the States expressly declare their governors to be commanders-in-chief, as well of the army as navy; and it may well be a question, whether those of New Hampshire and Massachusetts, in particular, do not, in this instance, confer larger powers upon their respective governors, than could be claimed by a President of the United States. Third. The power of the President, in respect to pardons, would extend to all cases, except those of impeachment. The governor of New York may pardon in all cases, even in those of impeachment, except for treason and murder. Is not the power of the governor, in this article, on a calculation of political consequences, greater than that of the President? All conspiracies and plots against the government, which have not been matured into actual treason, may be screened from punishment of every kind, by the interposition of the prerogative of pardoning. If a governor of New York, therefore, should be at the head of any such conspiracy, until the design had been ripened into actual hostility he could insure his accomplices and adherents an entire impunity. A President of the Union, on the other hand, though he may even pardon treason, when prosecuted in the ordinary course of law, could shelter no offender, in any degree, from the effects of impeachment and conviction. Would not the prospect of a total indemnity for all the preliminary steps be a greater temptation to undertake and persevere in an enterprise against the public liberty, than the mere prospect of an exemption from death and confiscation, if the final execution of the design, upon an actual appeal to arms, should miscarry? Would this last expectation have any influence at all, when the probability was computed, that the person who was to afford that exemption might himself be involved in the consequences of the measure, and might be incapacitated by his agency in it from affording the desired impunity? The better to judge of this matter, it will be necessary to recollect, that, by the proposed Constitution, the offense of treason is limited "to levying war upon the United States, and adhering to their enemies, giving them aid and comfort"; and that by the laws of New York it is confined within similar bounds. Fourth. The President can only adjourn the national legislature in the single case of disagreement about the time of adjournment. The British monarch may prorogue or even dissolve the Parliament. The governor of New York may also prorogue the legislature of this State for a limited time; a power which, in certain situations, may be employed to very important purposes.

The President is to have power, with the advice and consent of the Senate, to make treaties, provided two thirds of the senators present concur. The king of Great Britain is the sole and absolute representative of the nation in all foreign transactions. He can of his own accord make treaties of peace, commerce, alliance, and of every other description. It has been insinuated, that his authority in this respect is not conclusive, and that his conventions with foreign powers are subject to the revision, and stand in need of the ratification, of Parliament. But I believe this doctrine was never heard of, until it was broached upon the present occasion. Every jurist(2) of that kingdom, and every other man acquainted with its Constitution, knows, as an established fact, that the prerogative of making treaties exists in the crown in its utmost plentitude; and that the compacts entered into by the royal authority have the most complete legal validity and perfection, independent of any other sanction. The Parliament, it is true, is sometimes seen employing itself in altering the existing laws to conform them to the stipulations in a new treaty; and this may have possibly given birth to the imagination, that its co-operation was necessary to the obligatory efficacy of the treaty. But this parliamentary interposition proceeds from a different cause: from the necessity of adjusting a most artificial and intricate system of revenue and commercial laws, to the changes made in them by the operation of the treaty; and of adapting new provisions and precautions to the new state of things, to keep the machine from running into disorder. In this respect, therefore, there is no comparison between the intended power of the President and the actual power of the British sovereign. The one can perform alone what the other can do only with the concurrence of a branch of the legislature. It must be admitted, that, in this instance, the power of the federal Executive would exceed that of any State Executive. But this arises naturally from the sovereign power which relates to treaties. If the Confederacy were to be dissolved, it would become a question, whether the Executives of the several States were not solely invested with that delicate and important prerogative.

Documents of Revolution

The President is also to be authorized to receive ambassadors and other public ministers. This, though it has been a rich theme of declamation, is more a matter of dignity than of authority. It is a circumstance which will be without consequence in the administration of the government; and it was far more convenient that it should be arranged in this manner, than that there should be a necessity of convening the legislature, or one of its branches, upon every arrival of a foreign minister, though it were merely to take the place of a departed predecessor.

The President is to nominate, and, with the advice and consent of the Senate, to appoint ambassadors and other public ministers, judges of the Supreme Court, and in general all officers of the United States established by law, and whose appointments are not otherwise provided for by the Constitution. The king of Great Britain is emphatically and truly styled the fountain of honor. He not only appoints to all offices, but can create offices. He can confer titles of nobility at pleasure; and has the disposal of an immense number of church preferments. There is evidently a great inferiority in the power of the President, in this particular, to that of the British king; nor is it equal to that of the governor of New York, if we are to interpret the meaning of the constitution of the State by the practice which has obtained under it. The power of appointment is with us lodged in a council, composed of the governor and four members of the Senate, chosen by the Assembly. The governor claims, and has frequently exercised, the right of nomination, and is entitled to a casting vote in the appointment. If he really has the right of nominating, his authority is in this respect equal to that of the President, and exceeds it in the article of the casting vote. In the national government, if the Senate should be divided, no appointment could be made; in the government of New York, if the council should be divided, the governor can turn the scale, and confirm his own nomination.(3) If we compare the publicity which must necessarily attend the mode of appointment by the President and an entire branch of the national legislature, with the privacy in the mode of appointment by the governor of New York, closeted in a secret apartment with at most four, and frequently with only two persons; and if we at the same time consider how much more easy it must be to influence the small number of which a council of appointment consists, than the considerable number of which the national Senate would consist, we cannot hesitate to pronounce that the power of the chief magistrate of this State, in the disposition of offices, must, in practice, be greatly superior to that of the Chief Magistrate of the Union.

Hence it appears that, except as to the concurrent authority of the President in the article of treaties, it would be difficult to determine whether that magistrate would, in the aggregate, possess more or less power than the Governor of New York. And it appears yet more unequivocally, that there is no pretense for the parallel which has been attempted between him and the king of Great Britain. But to render the contrast in this respect still more striking, it may be of use to throw the principal circumstances of dissimilitude into a closer group.

The President of the United States would be an officer elected by the people for four years; the king of Great Britain is a perpetual and hereditary prince. The one would be amenable to personal punishment and disgrace; the person of the other is sacred and inviolable. The one would have a qualified negative upon the acts of the legislative body; the other has an absolute negative. The one would have a right to command the military and naval forces of the nation; the other, in addition to this right, possesses that of declaring war, and of raising and regulating fleets and armies by his own authority. The one would have a concurrent power with a branch of the legislature in the formation of treaties; the other is the sole possessor of the power of making treaties. The one would have a like concurrent authority in appointing to offices; the other is the sole author of all appointments. The one can confer no privileges whatever; the other can make denizens of aliens, noblemen of commoners; can erect corporations with all the rights incident to corporate bodies. The one can prescribe no rules concerning the commerce or currency of the nation; the other is in several respects the arbiter of commerce, and in this capacity can establish markets and fairs, can regulate weights and measures, can lay embargoes for a limited time, can coin money, can authorize or prohibit the circulation of foreign coin. The one has no particle of spiritual jurisdiction; the other is the supreme head and governor of the national church! What answer shall we give to those who would persuade us that things so unlike resemble each other? The same that ought to be given to those who tell us that a government, the whole power of which would be in the hands of the elective and periodical servants of the people, is an aristocracy, a monarchy, and a despotism.

PUBLIUS

1. A writer in a Pennsylvania paper, under the signature of TAMONY, has asserted that the king of Great Britain owes his prerogative as commander-in-chief to an annual mutiny bill. The truth is, on the contrary, that his prerogative, in this respect, is immemorial, and was only disputed, "contrary to all reason and precedent," as Blackstone vol. i., page 262, expresses it, by the Long Parliament of Charles I. but by the statute the 13th of Charles II., chap. 6, it was declared to be in the king alone, for that the sole supreme government and command of the militia within his Majesty's realms and dominions, and of all forces by sea and land, and of all forts and places of strength, EVER WAS AND IS the undoubted right of his Majesty and his royal

predecessors, kings and queens of England, and that both or either house of Parliament cannot nor ought to pretend to the same.

2. Vide Blackstone's Commentaries, Vol I., p. 257.

3. Candor, however, demands an acknowledgment that I do not think the claim of the governor to a right of nomination well founded. Yet it is always justifiable to reason from the practice of a government, till its propriety has been constitutionally questioned. And independent of this claim, when we take into view the other considerations, and pursue them through all their consequences, we shall be inclined to draw much the same conclusion.

FEDERALIST PAPER NO. 70. THE EXECUTIVE DEPARTMENT FURTHER CONSIDERED

From The Independent Journal. Saturday, March 15, 1788.

HAMILTON

To the People of the State of New York:

THERE is an idea, which is not without its advocates, that a vigorous Executive is inconsistent with the genius of republican government. The enlightened well-wishers to this species of government must at least hope that the supposition is destitute of foundation; since they can never admit its truth, without at the same time admitting the condemnation of their own principles. Energy in the Executive is a leading character in the definition of good government. It is essential to the protection of the community against foreign attacks; it is not less essential to the steady administration of the laws; to the protection of property against those irregular and high-handed combinations which sometimes interrupt the ordinary course of justice; to the security of liberty against the enterprises and assaults of ambition, of faction, and of anarchy. Every man the least conversant in Roman story, knows how often that republic was obliged to take refuge in the absolute power of a single man, under the formidable title of Dictator, as well against the intrigues of ambitious individuals who aspired to the tyranny, and the seditions of whole classes of the community whose conduct threatened the existence of all government, as against the invasions of external enemies who menaced the conquest and destruction of Rome.

There can be no need, however, to multiply arguments or examples on this head. A feeble Executive implies a feeble execution of the government. A feeble execution is but another phrase for a bad execution; and a government ill executed, whatever it may be in theory, must be, in practice, a bad government.

Taking it for granted, therefore, that all men of sense will agree in the necessity of an energetic Executive, it will only remain to inquire, what are the ingredients which constitute this energy? How far can they be combined with those other ingredients which constitute safety in the republican sense? And how far does this combination characterize the plan which has been reported by the convention?

The ingredients which constitute energy in the Executive are, first, unity; secondly, duration; thirdly, an adequate provision for its support; fourthly, competent powers.

The ingredients which constitute safety in the republican sense are, first, a due dependence on the people, secondly, a due responsibility.

Those politicians and statesmen who have been the most celebrated for the soundness of their principles and for the justice of their views, have declared in favor of a single Executive and a numerous legislature. They have with great propriety, considered energy as the most necessary qualification of the former, and have regarded this as most applicable to power in a single hand, while they have, with equal propriety, considered the latter as best adapted to deliberation and wisdom, and best calculated to conciliate the confidence of the people and to secure their privileges and interests.

That unity is conducive to energy will not be disputed. Decision, activity, secrecy, and despatch will generally characterize the proceedings of one man in a much more eminent degree than the proceedings of any greater number; and in proportion as the number is increased, these qualities will be diminished.

Documents of Revolution

This unity may be destroyed in two ways: either by vesting the power in two or more magistrates of equal dignity and authority; or by vesting it ostensibly in one man, subject, in whole or in part, to the control and co-operation of others, in the capacity of counsellors to him. Of the first, the two Consuls of Rome may serve as an example; of the last, we shall find examples in the constitutions of several of the States. New York and New Jersey, if I recollect right, are the only States which have intrusted the executive authority wholly to single men.(1) Both these methods of destroying the unity of the Executive have their partisans; but the votaries of an executive council are the most numerous. They are both liable, if not to equal, to similar objections, and may in most lights be examined in conjunction.

The experience of other nations will afford little instruction on this head. As far, however, as it teaches any thing, it teaches us not to be enamoured of plurality in the Executive. We have seen that the Achaeans, on an experiment of two Praetors, were induced to abolish one. The Roman history records many instances of mischiefs to the republic from the dissensions between the Consuls, and between the military Tribunes, who were at times substituted for the Consuls. But it gives us no specimens of any peculiar advantages derived to the state from the circumstance of the plurality of those magistrates. That the dissensions between them were not more frequent or more fatal, is a matter of astonishment, until we advert to the singular position in which the republic was almost continually placed, and to the prudent policy pointed out by the circumstances of the state, and pursued by the Consuls, of making a division of the government between them. The patricians engaged in a perpetual struggle with the plebeians for the preservation of their ancient authorities and dignities; the Consuls, who were generally chosen out of the former body, were commonly united by the personal interest they had in the defense of the privileges of their order. In addition to this motive of union, after the arms of the republic had considerably expanded the bounds of its empire, it became an established custom with the Consuls to divide the administration between themselves by lot—one of them remaining at Rome to govern the city and its environs, the other taking the command in the more distant provinces. This expedient must, no doubt, have had great influence in preventing those collisions and rivalships which might otherwise have embroiled the peace of the republic.

But quitting the dim light of historical research, attaching ourselves purely to the dictates of reason and good sense, we shall discover much greater cause to reject than to approve the idea of plurality in the Executive, under any modification whatever.

Wherever two or more persons are engaged in any common enterprise or pursuit, there is always danger of difference of opinion. If it be a public trust or office, in which they are clothed with equal dignity and authority, there is peculiar danger of personal emulation and even animosity. From either, and especially from all these causes, the most bitter dissensions are apt to spring. Whenever these happen, they lessen the respectability, weaken the authority, and distract the plans and operation of those whom they divide. If they should unfortunately assail the supreme executive magistracy of a country, consisting of a plurality of persons, they might impede or frustrate the most important measures of the government, in the most critical emergencies of the state. And what is still worse, they might split the community into the most violent and irreconcilable factions, adhering differently to the different individuals who composed the magistracy.

Men often oppose a thing, merely because they have had no agency in planning it, or because it may have been planned by those whom they dislike. But if they have been consulted, and have happened to disapprove, opposition then becomes, in their estimation, an indispensable duty of self-love. They seem to think themselves bound in honor, and by all the motives of personal infallibility, to defeat the success of what has been resolved upon contrary to their sentiments. Men of upright, benevolent tempers have too many opportunities of remarking, with horror, to what desperate lengths this disposition is sometimes carried, and how often the great interests of society are sacrificed to the vanity, to the conceit, and to the obstinacy of individuals, who have credit enough to make their passions and their caprices interesting to mankind. Perhaps the question now before the public may, in its consequences, afford melancholy proofs of the effects of this despicable frailty, or rather detestable vice, in the human character.

Upon the principles of a free government, inconveniences from the source just mentioned must necessarily be submitted to in the formation of the legislature; but it is unnecessary, and therefore unwise, to introduce them into the constitution of the Executive. It is here too that they may be most pernicious. In the legislature, promptitude of decision is oftener an evil than a benefit. The differences of opinion, and the jarrings of parties in that department of the government, though they may sometimes obstruct salutary plans, yet often promote deliberation and circumspection, and serve to check excesses in the majority. When a resolution too is once taken, the opposition must be at an end. That resolution is a law, and resistance to it punishable. But no favorable circumstances palliate or atone for the disadvantages of dissension in the executive department. Here, they are pure and unmixed. There is no point at which they cease to operate. They serve to embarrass and weaken the execution of the plan or measure to which they relate, from the first step to the final conclusion of it. They constantly counteract those qualities in the Executive which are the most necessary ingredients in its composition—vigor and expedition, and this without any counterbalancing good. In the conduct of war, in which the energy of the Executive is the bulwark of the national security, every thing would be to be apprehended from its plurality.

It must be confessed that these observations apply with principal weight to the first case supposed—that is, to a plurality of magistrates of equal dignity and authority a scheme, the advocates for which are not likely to form a numerous sect; but they apply, though not with equal, yet with considerable weight to the project of a council, whose concurrence is made constitutionally necessary to the operations of the ostensible Executive. An artful cabal in that council would be able to distract and to enervate the whole system of administration. If no such cabal should exist, the mere diversity of views and opinions would alone be sufficient to tincture the exercise of the executive authority with a spirit of habitual feebleness and dilatoriness.

(But one of the weightiest objections to a plurality in the Executive, and which lies as much against the last as the first plan, is, that it tends to conceal faults and destroy responsibility. Responsibility is of two kinds—to censure and to punishment. The first is the more important of the two, especially in an elective office. Man, in public trust, will much oftener act in such a manner as to render him unworthy of being any longer trusted, than in such a manner as to make him obnoxious to legal punishment. But the multiplication of the Executive adds to the difficulty of detection in either case. It often becomes impossible, amidst mutual accusations, to determine on whom the blame or the punishment of a pernicious measure, or series of pernicious measures, ought really to fall. It is shifted from one to another with so much dexterity, and under such plausible appearances, that the public opinion is left in suspense about the real author. The circumstances which may have led to any national miscarriage or misfortune are sometimes so complicated that, where there are a number of actors who may have had different degrees and kinds of agency, though we may clearly see upon the whole that there has been mismanagement, yet it may be impracticable to pronounce to whose account the evil which may have been incurred is truly chargeable.)(E1)

(But one of the weightiest objections to a plurality in the Executive, and which lies as much against the last as the first plan, is, that it tends to conceal faults and destroy responsibility.

Responsibility is of two kinds—to censure and to punishment. The first is the more important of the two, especially in an elective office. Man, in public trust, will much oftener act in such a manner as to render him unworthy of being any longer trusted, than in such a manner as to make him obnoxious to legal punishment. But the multiplication of the Executive adds to the difficulty of detection in either case. It often becomes impossible, amidst mutual accusations, to determine on whom the blame or the punishment of a pernicious measure, or series of pernicious measures, ought really to fall. It is shifted from one to another with so much dexterity, and under such plausible appearances, that the public opinion is left in suspense about the real author. The circumstances which may have led to any national miscarriage or misfortune are sometimes so complicated that, where there are a number of actors who may have had different degrees and kinds of agency, though we may clearly see upon the whole that there has been mismanagement, yet it may be impracticable to pronounce to whose account the evil which may have been incurred is truly chargeable.)(E1)

"I was overruled by my council. The council were so divided in their opinions that it was impossible to obtain any better resolution on the point." These and similar pretexts are constantly at hand, whether true or false. And who is there that will either take the trouble or incur the odium, of a strict scrutiny into the secret springs of the transaction? Should there be found a citizen zealous enough to undertake the unpromising task, if there happen to be collusion between the parties concerned, how easy it is to clothe the circumstances with so much ambiguity, as to render it uncertain what was the precise conduct of any of those parties?

In the single instance in which the governor of this State is coupled with a council—that is, in the appointment to offices, we have seen the mischiefs of it in the view now under consideration. Scandalous appointments to important offices have been made. Some cases, indeed, have been so flagrant that ALL PARTIES have agreed in the impropriety of the thing. When inquiry has been made, the blame has been laid by the governor on the members of the council, who, on their part, have charged it upon his nomination; while the people remain altogether at a loss to determine, by whose influence their interests have been committed to hands so unqualified and so manifestly improper. In tenderness to individuals, I forbear to descend to particulars.

It is evident from these considerations, that the plurality of the Executive tends to deprive the people of the two greatest securities they can have for the faithful exercise of any delegated power, first, the restraints of public opinion, which lose their efficacy, as well on account of the division of the censure attendant on bad measures among a number, as on account of the uncertainty on whom it ought to fall; and, second, the opportunity of discovering with facility and clearness the misconduct of the persons they trust, in order either to their removal from office or to their actual punishment in cases which admit of it.

In England, the king is a perpetual magistrate; and it is a maxim which has obtained for the sake of the public peace, that he is unaccountable for his administration, and his person sacred. Nothing, therefore, can be wiser in that kingdom, than to annex to the king a constitutional council, who may be responsible to the nation for the advice they give. Without this, there would be no responsibility whatever in the executive department an idea inadmissible in a free government. But even there the king is not bound by the resolutions of his council, though they are answerable for the advice they give. He is the absolute master of his own conduct in the exercise of his office, and may observe or disregard the counsel given to him at his sole discretion.

But in a republic, where every magistrate ought to be personally responsible for his behavior in office the reason which in the British Constitution dictates the propriety of a council, not only ceases to apply, but turns against the institution. In the monarchy of Great Britain, it furnishes a substitute for the prohibited responsibility of the chief magistrate, which serves in some degree as a hostage to the national justice for his good behavior. In the American republic, it would serve to destroy, or would greatly diminish, the intended and necessary responsibility of the Chief Magistrate himself.

The idea of a council to the Executive, which has so generally obtained in the State constitutions, has been derived from that maxim of republican jealousy which considers power as safer in the hands of a number of men than of a single man. If the maxim should be admitted to be applicable to the case, I should contend that the advantage on that side would not counterbalance the numerous disadvantages on the opposite side. But I do not think the rule at all applicable to the executive power. I clearly concur in opinion, in this particular, with a writer whom the celebrated Junius pronounces to be "deep, solid, and ingenious," that "the executive power is more easily confined when it is ONE";(2) that it is far more safe there should be a single object for the jealousy and watchfulness of the people; and, in a word, that all multiplication of the Executive is rather dangerous than friendly to liberty.

A little consideration will satisfy us, that the species of security sought for in the multiplication of the Executive, is unattainable. Numbers must be so great as to render combination difficult, or they are rather a source of danger than of security. The united credit and influence of several individuals must be more formidable to liberty, than the credit and influence of either of them separately. When power, therefore, is placed in the hands of so small a number of men, as to admit of their interests and views being easily combined in a common enterprise, by an artful leader, it becomes more liable to abuse, and more dangerous when abused, than if it be lodged in the hands of one man; who, from the very circumstance of his being alone, will be more narrowly watched and more readily suspected, and who cannot unite so great a mass of influence as when he is associated with others. The Decemvirs of Rome, whose name denotes their number,(3) were more to be dreaded in their usurpation than any ONE of them would have been. No person would think of proposing an Executive much more numerous than that body; from six to a dozen have been suggested for the number of the council. The extreme of these numbers, is not too great for an easy combination; and from such a combination America would have more to fear, than from the ambition of any single individual. A council to a magistrate, who is himself responsible for what he does, are generally nothing better than a clog upon his good intentions, are often the instruments and accomplices of his bad and are almost always a cloak to his faults.

I forbear to dwell upon the subject of expense; though it be evident that if the council should be numerous enough to answer the principal end aimed at by the institution, the salaries of the members, who must be drawn from their homes to reside at the seat of government, would form an item in the catalogue of public expenditures too serious to be incurred for an object of equivocal utility. I will only add that, prior to the appearance of the Constitution, I rarely met with an intelligent man from any of the States, who did not admit, as the result of experience, that the UNITY of the executive of this State was one of the best of the distinguishing features of our constitution.

PUBLIUS

1. New York has no council except for the single purpose of appointing to offices; New Jersey has a council whom the governor may consult. But I think, from the terms of the constitution, their resolutions do not bind him.

2. De Lolme.

3. Ten.

E1. Two versions of these paragraphs appear in different editions.

FEDERALIST PAPER NO. 71. THE DURATION IN OFFICE OF THE EXECUTIVE

From the New York Packet. Tuesday, March 18, 1788.

HAMILTON

To the People of the State of New York:

DURATION in office has been mentioned as the second requisite to the energy of the Executive authority. This has relation to two objects: to the personal firmness of the executive magistrate, in the employment of his constitutional powers; and to the stability of the system of administration which may have been adopted under his auspices. With regard to the first, it must be evident, that the longer the duration in office, the greater will be the probability of obtaining so important an advantage. It is a general principle of human nature, that a man will be interested in whatever he possesses, in proportion to the firmness or precariousness of the tenure by which he holds it; will be less attached to what he holds by a momentary or uncertain title, than to what he enjoys by a durable or certain title; and, of course, will be willing to risk more for the sake of the one, than for the sake of the other. This remark is not less applicable to a political privilege, or honor, or trust, than to any article of ordinary property. The inference from it is, that a man acting in the capacity of chief magistrate, under a consciousness that in a very short time he MUST lay down his office, will be apt to feel himself too little interested in it to hazard any material censure or perplexity, from the independent exertion of his powers, or from encountering the ill-humors, however transient, which may happen to prevail, either in a considerable part of the society itself, or even in a predominant faction in the legislative body. If the case should only be, that he MIGHT lay it down, unless continued by a new choice, and if he should be desirous of being continued, his wishes, conspiring with his fears, would tend still more powerfully to corrupt his integrity, or debase his fortitude. In either case, feebleness and irresolution must be the characteristics of the station.

There are some who would be inclined to regard the servile pliancy of the Executive to a prevailing current, either in the community or in the legislature, as its best recommendation. But such men entertain very crude notions, as well of the purposes for which government was instituted, as of the true means by which the public happiness may be promoted. The republican principle demands that the deliberate sense of the community should govern the conduct of those to whom they intrust the management of their affairs; but it does not require an unqualified complaisance to every sudden breeze of passion, or to every transient impulse which the people may receive from the arts of men, who flatter their prejudices to betray their interests. It is a just observation, that the people commonly INTEND the PUBLIC GOOD. This often applies to their very errors. But their good sense would despise the adulator who should pretend that they always REASON RIGHT about the MEANS of promoting it. They know from experience that they sometimes err; and the wonder is that they so seldom err as they do, beset, as they continually are, by the wiles of parasites and sycophants, by the snares of the ambitious, the avaricious, the desperate, by the artifices of men who possess their confidence more than they deserve it, and of those who seek to possess rather than to deserve it. When occasions present themselves, in which the interests of the people are at variance with their inclinations, it is the duty of the persons whom they have appointed to be the guardians of those interests, to withstand the temporary delusion, in order to give them time and opportunity for more cool and sedate reflection. Instances might be cited in which a conduct of this kind has saved the people from very fatal consequences of their own mistakes, and has procured lasting monuments of their gratitude to the men who had courage and magnanimity enough to serve them at the peril of their displeasure.

But however inclined we might be to insist upon an unbounded complaisance in the Executive to the inclinations of the people, we can with no propriety contend for a like complaisance to the humors of the legislature. The latter may sometimes stand in opposition to the former, and at other times the people may be entirely neutral. In either supposition, it is certainly desirable that the Executive should be in a situation to dare to act his own opinion with vigor and decision.

The same rule which teaches the propriety of a partition between the various branches of power, teaches us likewise that this partition ought to be so contrived as to render the one independent of the other. To what purpose separate the executive or the judiciary from the legislative, if both the executive and the judiciary are so constituted as to be at the absolute devotion of the legislative? Such a separation must be merely nominal, and incapable of producing the ends for which it was established. It is one thing to be subordinate to the laws, and another to be dependent on the legislative body. The first comports with, the last violates, the fundamental principles of good government; and, whatever may be the forms of the Constitution, unites all power in the same hands. The tendency of the legislative authority to absorb every other, has been fully displayed and illustrated by examples in some preceding numbers. In governments purely republican, this tendency is almost irresistible. The representatives of the people, in a popular assembly, seem sometimes to fancy that they are the people themselves, and betray strong symptoms of impatience and disgust at the least sign of opposition from any other quarter; as if the exercise of its rights, by either the executive or judiciary, were a breach of their privilege and an outrage to their dignity. They often appear disposed to exert an imperious control over the other departments; and as they commonly have the people on their side, they always act with such momentum as to make it very difficult for the other members of the government to maintain the balance of the Constitution.

It may perhaps be asked, how the shortness of the duration in office can affect the independence of the Executive on the legislature, unless the one were possessed of the power of appointing or displacing the other. One answer to this inquiry may be drawn from the principle already remarked that is, from the slender interest a man is apt to take in a short-lived advantage, and the little inducement it affords him to expose himself, on account of it, to any considerable inconvenience or hazard. Another answer, perhaps more obvious, though not more conclusive, will result from the consideration of the influence of the legislative body over the people; which might be employed to prevent the re-election of a man who, by an upright resistance to any sinister project of that body, should have made himself obnoxious to its resentment.

It may be asked also, whether a duration of four years would answer the end proposed; and if it would not, whether a less period, which would at least be recommended by greater security against ambitious designs, would not, for that reason, be preferable to a longer period, which was, at the same time, too short for the purpose of inspiring the desired firmness and independence of the magistrate.

It cannot be affirmed, that a duration of four years, or any other limited duration, would completely answer the end proposed; but it would contribute towards it in a degree which would have a material influence upon the spirit and character of the government. Between the commencement and termination of such a period, there would always be a considerable interval, in which the prospect of annihilation would be sufficiently remote, not to have an improper effect upon the conduct of a man indued with a tolerable portion of fortitude; and in which he might reasonably promise himself, that there would be time enough before it arrived, to make the community sensible of the propriety of the measures he might incline to pursue. Though it be probable that, as he approached the moment when the public were, by a new election, to signify their sense of his conduct, his confidence, and with it his firmness, would decline; yet both the one and the other would derive support from the opportunities which his previous continuance in the station had afforded him, of establishing himself in the esteem and good-will of his constituents. He might, then, hazard with safety, in proportion to the proofs he had given of his wisdom and integrity, and to the title he had acquired to the respect and attachment of his fellow-citizens. As, on the one hand, a duration of four years will contribute to the firmness of the Executive in a sufficient degree to render it a very valuable ingredient in the composition; so, on the other, it is not enough to justify any alarm for the public liberty. If a British House of Commons, from the most feeble beginnings, FROM THE MERE POWER OF ASSENTING OR DISAGREEING TO THE IMPOSITION OF A NEW TAX, have, by rapid strides, reduced the prerogatives of the crown and the privileges of the nobility within the limits they conceived to be compatible with the principles of a free government, while they raised themselves to the rank and consequence of a coequal branch of the legislature; if they have been able, in one instance, to abolish both the royalty and the aristocracy, and to overturn all the ancient establishments, as well in the Church as State; if they have been able, on a recent occasion, to make the monarch tremble at the prospect of an innovation(1) attempted by them, what would be to be feared from an elective magistrate of four years' duration, with the confined authorities of a President of the United States? What, but that he might be unequal to the task which the Constitution assigns him? I shall only add, that if his duration be such as to leave a doubt of his firmness, that doubt is inconsistent with a jealousy of his encroachments.

PUBLIUS

1. This was the case with respect to Mr. Fox's India bill, which was carried in the House of Commons, and rejected in the House of Lords, to the entire satisfaction, as it is said, of the people.

FEDERALIST PAPER NO. 72. THE SAME SUBJECT CONTINUED, AND RE-ELIGIBILITY OF THE EXECUTIVE CONSIDERED.

From The Independent Journal. Wednesday, March 19, 1788.

HAMILTON

To the People of the State of New York:

THE administration of government, in its largest sense, comprehends all the operations of the body politic, whether legislative, executive, or judiciary; but in its most usual, and perhaps its most precise signification. it is limited to executive details, and falls peculiarly within the province of the executive department. The actual conduct of foreign negotiations, the preparatory plans of finance, the application and disbursement of the public moneys in conformity to the general appropriations of the legislature, the arrangement of the army and navy, the directions of the operations of war—these, and other matters of a like nature, constitute what seems to be most properly understood by the administration of government. The persons, therefore, to whose immediate management these different matters are committed, ought to be considered as the assistants or deputies of the chief magistrate, and on this account, they ought to derive their offices from his appointment, at least from his nomination, and ought to be subject to his superintendence. This view of the subject will at once suggest to us the intimate connection between the duration of the executive magistrate in office and the stability of the system of administration. To reverse and undo what has been done by a predecessor, is very often considered by a successor as the best proof he can give of his own capacity and desert; and in addition to this propensity, where the alteration has been the result of public choice, the person substituted is warranted in supposing that the dismission of his predecessor has proceeded from a dislike to his measures; and that the less he resembles him, the more he will recommend himself to the favor of his constituents. These considerations, and the influence of personal confidences and attachments, would be likely to induce every new President to promote a change of men to fill the subordinate stations; and these causes together could not fail to occasion a disgraceful and ruinous mutability in the administration of the government.

With a positive duration of considerable extent, I connect the circumstance of re-eligibility. The first is necessary to give to the officer himself the inclination and the resolution to act his part well, and to the community time and leisure to observe the tendency of his measures, and thence to form an experimental estimate of their merits. The last is necessary to enable the people, when they see reason to approve of his conduct, to continue him in his station, in order to prolong the utility of his talents and virtues, and to secure to the government the advantage of permanency in a wise system of administration.

Nothing appears more plausible at first sight, nor more ill-founded upon close inspection, than a scheme which in relation to the present point has had some respectable advocates—I mean that of continuing the chief magistrate in office for a certain time, and then excluding him from it, either for a limited period or forever after. This exclusion, whether temporary or perpetual, would have nearly the same effects, and these effects would be for the most part rather pernicious than salutary.

One ill effect of the exclusion would be a diminution of the inducements to good behavior. There are few men who would not feel much less zeal in the discharge of a duty when they were conscious that the advantages of the station with which it was connected must be relinquished at a determinate period, than when they were permitted to entertain a hope of obtaining, by meriting, a continuance of them. This position will not be disputed so long as it is admitted that the desire of reward is one of the strongest incentives of human conduct; or that the best security for the fidelity of mankind is to make their interests coincide with their duty. Even the love of fame, the ruling passion of the noblest minds, which would prompt a man to plan and undertake extensive and arduous enterprises for the public benefit, requiring considerable time to mature and perfect them, if he could flatter himself with the prospect of being allowed to finish what he had begun, would, on the contrary, deter him from the undertaking, when he foresaw that he must quit the scene before he could accomplish the work, and must commit that, together with his own reputation, to hands which might be unequal or unfriendly to the task. The most to be expected from the generality of men, in such a situation, is the negative merit of not doing harm, instead of the positive merit of doing good.

Another ill effect of the exclusion would be the temptation to sordid views, to peculation, and, in some instances, to usurpation. An avaricious man, who might happen to fill the office, looking forward to a time when he must at all events yield up the emoluments he enjoyed, would feel a propensity, not easy to be resisted by such a man, to make the best use of the opportunity he enjoyed while it lasted, and might not scruple to have recourse to the most corrupt expedients to make the harvest as abundant as it was transitory; though the same man, probably, with a different prospect before him, might content himself with the regular perquisites of his situation, and might even be unwilling to risk the consequences of an abuse of his opportunities. His avarice might be a guard upon his avarice. Add to this that the same man might be vain or ambitious, as well as avaricious. And if he could expect to prolong his honors by his good conduct, he might hesitate to sacrifice his appetite for them to his appetite for gain. But with the prospect before him of approaching an inevitable annihilation, his avarice would be likely to get the victory over his caution, his vanity, or his ambition.

An ambitious man, too, when he found himself seated on the summit of his country's honors, when he looked forward to the time at which he must descend from the exalted eminence for ever, and reflected that no exertion of merit on his part could save him from the unwelcome reverse; such a man, in such a situation, would be much more violently tempted to embrace a favorable conjuncture for attempting the prolongation of his power, at every personal hazard, than if he had the probability of answering the same end by doing his duty.

Would it promote the peace of the community, or the stability of the government to have half a dozen men who had had credit enough to be raised to the seat of the supreme magistracy, wandering among the people like discontented ghosts, and sighing for a place which they were destined never more to possess?

A third ill effect of the exclusion would be, the depriving the community of the advantage of the experience gained by the chief magistrate in the exercise of his office. That experience is the parent of wisdom, is an adage the truth of which is recognized by the wisest as well as the simplest of mankind. What more desirable or more essential than this quality in the governors of nations? Where more desirable or more essential than in the first magistrate of a nation? Can it be wise to put this desirable and essential quality under the ban of the Constitution, and to declare that the moment it is acquired, its possessor shall be compelled to abandon the station in which it was acquired, and to which it is adapted? This, nevertheless, is the precise import of all those regulations which exclude men from serving their country, by the choice of their fellowcitizens, after they have by a course of service fitted themselves for doing it with a greater degree of utility.

A fourth ill effect of the exclusion would be the banishing men from stations in which, in certain emergencies of the state, their presence might be of the greatest moment to the public interest or safety. There is no nation which has not, at one period or another, experienced an absolute necessity of the services of particular men in particular situations; perhaps it would not be too strong to say, to the preservation of its political existence. How unwise, therefore, must be every such self-denying ordinance as serves to prohibit a nation from making use of its own citizens in the manner best suited to its exigencies and circumstances! Without supposing the personal essentiality of the man, it is evident that a change of the chief magistrate, at the breaking out of a war, or at any similar crisis, for another, even of equal merit, would at all times be detrimental to the community, inasmuch as it would substitute inexperience to experience, and would tend to unhinge and set afloat the already settled train of the administration.

A fifth ill effect of the exclusion would be, that it would operate as a constitutional interdiction of stability in the administration. By necessitating a change of men, in the first office of the nation, it would necessitate a mutability of measures. It is not generally to be expected, that men will vary and measures remain uniform. The contrary is the usual course of things. And we need not be apprehensive that there will be too much stability, while there is even the option of changing; nor need we desire to prohibit the people from continuing their confidence where they think it may be safely placed, and where, by constancy on their part, they may obviate the fatal inconveniences of fluctuating councils and a variable policy.

These are some of the disadvantages which would flow from the principle of exclusion. They apply most forcibly to the scheme of a perpetual exclusion; but when we consider that even a partial exclusion would always render the readmission of the person a remote and precarious object, the observations which have been made will apply nearly as fully to one case as to the other.

What are the advantages promised to counterbalance these disadvantages? They are represented to be: 1st, greater independence in the magistrate; 2d, greater security to the people. Unless the exclusion be perpetual, there will be no pretense to infer the first advantage. But even in that case, may he have no object beyond his present station, to which he may sacrifice his independence? May he have no connections, no friends, for whom he may sacrifice it? May he not be less willing by a firm conduct, to make personal enemies, when he acts under the impression that a time is fast approaching, on the arrival of which he not only MAY, but MUST, be exposed to their resentments, upon an equal, perhaps upon an inferior, footing? It is not an easy point to determine whether his independence would be most promoted or impaired by such an arrangement.

As to the second supposed advantage, there is still greater reason to entertain doubts concerning it. If the exclusion were to be perpetual, a man of irregular ambition, of whom alone there could be reason in any case to entertain apprehension, would, with infinite reluctance, yield to the necessity of taking his leave forever of a post in which his passion for power and pre-eminence had acquired the force of habit. And if he had been fortunate or adroit enough to conciliate the good-will of the people, he might induce them to consider as a very odious and unjustifiable restraint upon themselves, a provision which was calculated to debar them of the right of giving a fresh proof of their attachment to a favorite. There may be conceived circumstances in which this disgust of the people, seconding the thwarted ambition of such a favorite, might occasion greater danger to liberty, than could ever reasonably be dreaded from the possibility of a perpetuation in office, by the voluntary suffrages of the community, exercising a constitutional privilege.

There is an excess of refinement in the idea of disabling the people to continue in office men who had entitled themselves, in their opinion, to approbation and confidence; the advantages of which are at best speculative and equivocal, and are overbalanced by disadvantages far more certain and decisive.

PUBLIUS

FEDERALIST PAPER NO. 73. THE PROVISION FOR THE SUPPORT OF THE EXECUTIVE, AND THE VETO POWER

From the New York Packet. Friday, March 21, 1788.

HAMILTON

To the People of the State of New York:

THE third ingredient towards constituting the vigor of the executive authority, is an adequate provision for its support. It is evident that, without proper attention to this article, the separation of the executive from the legislative department would be merely nominal and nugatory. The legislature, with a discretionary power over the salary and emoluments of the Chief Magistrate, could render him as obsequious to their will as they might think proper to make him. They might, in most cases, either reduce him by famine, or tempt him by largesses, to surrender at discretion his judgment to their inclinations. These expressions, taken in all the latitude of the terms, would no doubt convey more than is intended. There are men who could neither be distressed nor won into a sacrifice of their duty; but this stern virtue is the growth of few soils; and in the main it will be found that a power over a man's support is a power over his will. If it were necessary to confirm so plain a truth by facts, examples would not be wanting, even in this country, of the intimidation or seduction of the Executive by the terrors or allurements of the pecuniary arrangements of the legislative body.

It is not easy, therefore, to commend too highly the judicious attention which has been paid to this subject in the proposed Constitution. It is there provided that "The President of the United States shall, at stated times, receive for his services a compensation which shall neither be increased nor diminished during the period for which he shall have been elected; and he shall not receive within that period any other emolument from the United States, or any of them." It is impossible to imagine any provision which would have been more eligible than this. The legislature, on the appointment of a President, is once for all to declare what shall be the compensation for his services during the time for which he shall have been elected. This done, they will have no power to alter it, either by increase or diminution, till a new period of service by a new election commences. They can neither weaken his fortitude by operating on his necessities, nor corrupt his integrity by appealing to his avarice. Neither the Union, nor any of its members, will be at liberty to give, nor will he be at liberty to receive, any other emolument than that which may have been determined by the first act. He can, of course, have no pecuniary inducement to renounce or desert the independence intended for him by the Constitution.

Documents of Revolution

The last of the requisites to energy, which have been enumerated, are competent powers. Let us proceed to consider those which are proposed to be vested in the President of the United States.

The first thing that offers itself to our observation, is the qualified negative of the President upon the acts or resolutions of the two houses of the legislature; or, in other words, his power of returning all bills with objections, to have the effect of preventing their becoming laws, unless they should afterwards be ratified by two thirds of each of the component members of the legislative body.

The propensity of the legislative department to intrude upon the rights, and to absorb the powers, of the other departments, has been already suggested and repeated; the insufficiency of a mere parchment delineation of the boundaries of each, has also been remarked upon; and the necessity of furnishing each with constitutional arms for its own defense, has been inferred and proved. From these clear and indubitable principles results the propriety of a negative, either absolute or qualified, in the Executive, upon the acts of the legislative branches. Without the one or the other, the former would be absolutely unable to defend himself against the depredations of the latter. He might gradually be stripped of his authorities by successive resolutions, or annihilated by a single vote. And in the one mode or the other, the legislative and executive powers might speedily come to be blended in the same hands. If even no propensity had ever discovered itself in the legislative body to invade the rights of the Executive, the rules of just reasoning and theoretic propriety would of themselves teach us, that the one ought not to be left to the mercy of the other, but ought to possess a constitutional and effectual power of self-defense.

But the power in question has a further use. It not only serves as a shield to the Executive, but it furnishes an additional security against the enaction of improper laws. It establishes a salutary check upon the legislative body, calculated to guard the community against the effects of faction, precipitancy, or of any impulse unfriendly to the public good, which may happen to influence a majority of that body.

The propriety of a negative has, upon some occasions, been combated by an observation, that it was not to be presumed a single man would possess more virtue and wisdom than a number of men; and that unless this presumption should be entertained, it would be improper to give the executive magistrate any species of control over the legislative body.

But this observation, when examined, will appear rather specious than solid. The propriety of the thing does not turn upon the supposition of superior wisdom or virtue in the Executive, but upon the supposition that the legislature will not be infallible; that the love of power may sometimes betray it into a disposition to encroach upon the rights of other members of the government; that a spirit of faction may sometimes pervert its deliberations; that impressions of the moment may sometimes hurry it into measures which itself, on maturer reflexion, would condemn. The primary inducement to conferring the power in question upon the Executive is, to enable him to defend himself; the secondary one is to increase the chances in favor of the community against the passing of bad laws, through haste, inadvertence, or design. The oftener the measure is brought under examination, the greater the diversity in the situations of those who are to examine it, the less must be the danger of those errors which flow from want of due deliberation, or of those missteps which proceed from the contagion of some common passion or interest. It is far less probable, that culpable views of any kind should infect all the parts of the government at the same moment and in relation to the same object, than that they should by turns govern and mislead every one of them.

It may perhaps be said that the power of preventing bad laws includes that of preventing good ones; and may be used to the one purpose as well as to the other. But this objection will have little weight with those who can properly estimate the mischiefs of that inconstancy and mutability in the laws, which form the greatest blemish in the character and genius of our governments. They will consider every institution calculated to restrain the excess of law-making, and to keep things in the same state in which they happen to be at any given period, as much more likely to do good than harm; because it is favorable to greater stability in the system of legislation. The injury which may possibly be done by defeating a few good laws, will be amply compensated by the advantage of preventing a number of bad ones.

Nor is this all. The superior weight and influence of the legislative body in a free government, and the hazard to the Executive in a trial of strength with that body, afford a satisfactory security that the negative would generally be employed with great caution; and there would oftener be room for a charge of timidity than of rashness in the exercise of it. A king of Great Britain, with all his train of sovereign attributes, and with all the influence he draws from a thousand sources, would, at this day, hesitate to put a negative upon the joint resolutions of the two houses of Parliament. He would not fail to exert the utmost resources of that influence to strangle a measure disagreeable to him, in its progress to the throne, to avoid being reduced to the dilemma of permitting it to take effect, or of risking the displeasure of the nation by an opposition to the sense of the legislative body. Nor is it probable, that he would ultimately venture to exert his prerogatives, but in a case of manifest propriety, or extreme necessity. All well-informed men in that kingdom will accede to the justness of this remark. A very considerable period has elapsed since the negative of the crown has been exercised.

If a magistrate so powerful and so well fortified as a British monarch, would have scruples about the exercise of the power under consideration, how much greater caution may be reasonably expected in a President of the United States, clothed for the short period of four years with the executive authority of a government wholly and purely republican?

It is evident that there would be greater danger of his not using his power when necessary, than of his using it too often, or too much. An argument, indeed, against its expediency, has been drawn from this very source. It has been represented, on this account, as a power odious in appearance, useless in practice. But it will not follow, that because it might be rarely exercised, it would never be exercised. In the case for which it is chiefly designed, that of an immediate attack upon the constitutional rights of the Executive, or in a case in which the public good was evidently and palpably sacrificed, a man of tolerable firmness would avail himself of his constitutional means of defense, and would listen to the admonitions of duty and responsibility. In the former supposition, his fortitude would be stimulated by his immediate interest in the power of his office; in the latter, by the probability of the sanction of his constituents, who, though they would naturally incline to the legislative body in a doubtful case, would hardly suffer their partiality to delude them in a very plain case. I speak now with an eye to a magistrate possessing only a common share of firmness. There are men who, under any circumstances, will have the courage to do their duty at every hazard.

But the convention have pursued a mean in this business, which will both facilitate the exercise of the power vested in this respect in the executive magistrate, and make its efficacy to depend on the sense of a considerable part of the legislative body. Instead of an absolute negative, it is proposed to give the Executive the qualified negative already described. This is a power which would be much more readily exercised than the other. A man who might be afraid to defeat a law by his single VETO, might not scruple to return it for reconsideration; subject to being finally rejected only in the event of more than one third of each house concurring in the sufficiency of his objections. He would be encouraged by the reflection, that if his opposition should prevail, it would embark in it a very respectable proportion of the legislative body, whose influence would be united with his in supporting the propriety of his conduct in the public opinion. A direct and categorical negative has something in the appearance of it more harsh, and more apt to irritate, than the mere suggestion of argumentative objections to be approved or disapproved by those to whom they are addressed. In proportion as it would be less apt to offend, it would be more apt to be exercised; and for this very reason, it may in practice be found more effectual. It is to be hoped that it will not often happen that improper views will govern so large a proportion as two thirds of both branches of the legislature at the same time; and this, too, in spite of the counterposing weight of the Executive. It is at any rate far less probable that this should be the case, than that such views should taint the resolutions and conduct of a bare majority. A power of this nature in the Executive, will often have a silent and unperceived, though forcible, operation. When men, engaged in unjustifiable pursuits, are aware that obstructions may come from a quarter which they cannot control, they will often be restrained by the bare apprehension of opposition, from doing what they would with eagerness rush into, if no such external impediments were to be feared.

This qualified negative, as has been elsewhere remarked, is in this State vested in a council, consisting of the governor, with the chancellor and judges of the Supreme Court, or any two of them. It has been freely employed upon a variety of occasions, and frequently with success. And its utility has become so apparent, that persons who, in compiling the Constitution, were violent opposers of it, have from experience become its declared admirers.(1)

I have in another place remarked, that the convention, in the formation of this part of their plan, had departed from the model of the constitution of this State, in favor of that of Massachusetts. Two strong reasons may be imagined for this preference. One is that the judges, who are to be the interpreters of the law, might receive an improper bias, from having given a previous opinion in their revisionary capacities; the other is that by being often associated with the Executive, they might be induced to embark too far in the political views of that magistrate, and thus a dangerous combination might by degrees be cemented between the executive and judiciary departments. It is impossible to keep the judges too distinct from every other avocation than that of expounding the laws. It is peculiarly dangerous to place them in a situation to be either corrupted or influenced by the Executive.

PUBLIUS

1. Mr. Abraham Yates, a warm opponent of the plan of the convention is of this number.

FEDERALIST PAPER NO. 74. THE COMMAND OF THE MILITARY AND NAVAL FORCES, AND THE PARDONING POWER OF THE EXECUTIVE.

From the New York Packet. Tuesday, March 25, 1788.

HAMILTON

To the People of the State of New York:

THE President of the United States is to be "commander-in-chief of the army and navy of the United States, and of the militia of the several States when called into the actual service of the United States." The propriety of this provision is so evident in itself, and it is, at the same time, so consonant to the precedents of the State constitutions in general, that little need be said to explain or enforce it. Even those of them which have, in other respects, coupled the chief magistrate with a council, have for the most part concentrated the military authority in him alone. Of all the cares or concerns of government, the direction of war most peculiarly demands those qualities which distinguish the exercise of power by a single hand. The direction of war implies the direction of the common strength; and the power of directing and employing the common strength, forms a usual and essential part in the definition of the executive authority.

"The President may require the opinion, in writing, of the principal officer in each of the executive departments, upon any subject relating to the duties of their respective officers." This I consider as a mere redundancy in the plan, as the right for which it provides would result of itself from the office.

He is also to be authorized to grant "reprieves and pardons for offenses against the United States, except in cases of impeachment." Humanity and good policy conspire to dictate, that the benign prerogative of pardoning should be as little as possible fettered or embarrassed. The criminal code of every country partakes so much of necessary severity, that without an easy access to exceptions in favor of unfortunate guilt, justice would wear a countenance too sanguinary and cruel. As the sense of responsibility is always strongest, in proportion as it is undivided, it may be inferred that a single man would be most ready to attend to the force of those motives which might plead for a mitigation of the rigor of the law, and least apt to yield to considerations which were calculated to shelter a fit object of its vengeance. The reflection that the fate of a fellow-creature depended on his sole fiat, would naturally inspire scrupulousness and caution; the dread of being accused of weakness or connivance, would beget equal circumspection, though of a different kind. On the other hand, as men generally derive confidence from their numbers, they might often encourage each other in an act of obduracy, and might be less sensible to the apprehension of suspicion or censure for an injudicious or affected clemency. On these accounts, one man appears to be a more eligible dispenser of the mercy of government, than a body of men.

The expediency of vesting the power of pardoning in the President has, if I mistake not, been only contested in relation to the crime of treason. This, it has been urged, ought to have depended upon the assent of one, or both, of the branches of the legislative body. I shall not deny that there are strong reasons to be assigned for requiring in this particular the concurrence of that body, or of a part of it. As treason is a crime levelled at the immediate being of the society, when the laws have once ascertained the guilt of the offender, there seems a fitness in referring the expediency of an act of mercy towards him to the judgment of the legislature. And this ought the rather to be the case, as the supposition of the connivance of the Chief Magistrate ought not to be entirely excluded. But there are also strong objections to such a plan. It is not to be doubted, that a single man of prudence and good sense is better fitted, in delicate conjunctures, to balance the motives which may plead for and against the remission of the punishment, than any numerous body whatever. It deserves particular attention, that treason will often be connected with seditions which embrace a large proportion of the community; as lately happened in Massachusetts. In every such case, we might expect to see the representation of the people tainted with the same spirit which had given birth to the offense. And when parties were pretty equally matched, the secret sympathy of the friends and favorers of the condemned person, availing itself of the good-nature and weakness of others, might frequently bestow impunity where the terror of an example was necessary. On the other hand, when the sedition had proceeded from causes which had inflamed the resentments of the major party, they might often be found obstinate and inexorable, when policy demanded a conduct of forbearance and clemency. But the principal argument for reposing the power of pardoning in this case to the Chief Magistrate is this: in seasons of insurrection or rebellion, there are often critical moments, when a well-timed offer of pardon to the insurgents or rebels may restore the tranquillity of the commonwealth; and which, if suffered to pass unimproved, it may never be possible afterwards to recall. The dilatory process of convening the legislature, or one of its branches, for the purpose of obtaining its sanction to the measure, would frequently be the occasion of letting slip the golden opportunity. The loss of a week, a day, an hour, may sometimes be fatal. If it should be observed, that a discretionary power, with a view to such contingencies, might be occasionally conferred upon the President, it may be answered in the first place, that it is questionable, whether, in a limited Constitution, that power could be delegated by law; and in the second place, that it would generally be impolitic beforehand to take any step which might hold out the prospect of impunity. A proceeding of this kind, out of the usual course, would be likely to be construed into an argument of timidity or of weakness, and would have a tendency to embolden guilt.

PUBLIUS

FEDERALIST PAPER NO. 75. THE TREATY-MAKING POWER OF THE EXECUTIVE

For the Independent Journal. Wednesday, March 26, 1788

HAMILTON

To the People of the State of New York:

THE President is to have power, "by and with the advice and consent of the Senate, to make treaties, provided two thirds of the senators present concur." Though this provision has been assailed, on different grounds, with no small degree of vehemence, I scruple not to declare my firm persuasion, that it is one of the best digested and most unexceptionable parts of the plan. One ground of objection is the trite topic of the intermixture of powers; some contending that the President ought alone to possess the power of making treaties; others, that it ought to have been exclusively deposited in the Senate. Another source of objection is derived from the small number of persons by whom a treaty may be made. Of those who espouse this objection, a part are of opinion that the House of Representatives ought to have been associated in the business, while another part seem to think that nothing more was necessary than to have substituted two thirds of all the members of the Senate, to two thirds of the members present. As I flatter myself the observations made in a preceding number upon this part of the plan must have sufficed to place it, to a discerning eye, in a very favorable light, I shall here content myself with offering only some supplementary remarks, principally with a view to the objections which have been just stated.

With regard to the intermixture of powers, I shall rely upon the explanations already given in other places, of the true sense of the rule upon which that objection is founded; and shall take it for granted, as an inference from them, that the union of the Executive with the Senate, in the article of treaties, is no infringement of that rule. I venture to add, that the particular nature of the power of making treaties indicates a peculiar propriety in that union. Though several writers on the subject of government place that power in the class of executive authorities, yet this is evidently an arbitrary disposition; for if we attend carefully to its operation, it will be found to partake more of the legislative than of the executive character, though it does not seem strictly to fall within the definition of either of them. The essence of the legislative authority is to enact laws, or, in other words, to prescribe rules for the regulation of the society; while the execution of the laws, and the employment of the common strength, either for this purpose or for the common defense, seem to comprise all the functions of the executive magistrate. The power of making treaties is, plainly, neither the one nor the other. It relates neither to the execution of the subsisting laws, nor to the enaction of new ones; and still less to an exertion of the common strength. Its objects are CONTRACTS with foreign nations, which have the force of law, but derive it from the obligations of good faith. They are not rules prescribed by the sovereign to the subject, but agreements between sovereign and sovereign. The power in question seems therefore to form a distinct department, and to belong, properly, neither to the legislative nor to the executive. The qualities elsewhere detailed as indispensable in the management of foreign negotiations, point out the Executive as the most fit agent in those transactions; while the vast importance of the trust, and the operation of treaties as laws, plead strongly for the participation of the whole or a portion of the legislative body in the office of making them.

However proper or safe it may be in governments where the executive magistrate is an hereditary monarch, to commit to him the entire power of making treaties, it would be utterly unsafe and improper to intrust that power to an elective magistrate of four years' duration. It has been remarked, upon another occasion, and the remark is unquestionably just, that an hereditary monarch, though often the oppressor of his people, has personally too much stake in the government to be in any material danger of being corrupted by foreign powers. But a man raised from the station of a private citizen to the rank of chief magistrate, possessed of a moderate or slender fortune, and looking forward to a period not very remote when he may probably be obliged to return to the station from which he was taken, might sometimes be under temptations to sacrifice his duty to his interest, which it would require superlative virtue to withstand. An avaricious man might be tempted to betray the interests of the state to the acquisition of wealth. An ambitious man might make his own aggrandizement, by the aid of a foreign power, the price of his treachery to his constituents. The history of human conduct does not warrant that exalted opinion of human virtue which would make it wise in a nation to commit interests of so delicate and momentous a kind, as those which concern its intercourse with the rest of the world, to the sole disposal of a magistrate created and circumstanced as would be a President of the United States.

To have intrusted the power of making treaties to the Senate alone, would have been to relinquish the benefits of the constitutional agency of the President in the conduct of foreign negotiations. It is true that the Senate would, in that case, have the option of employing him in this capacity, but they would also have the option of letting it alone, and pique or cabal might induce the latter rather than the former. Besides this, the ministerial servant of the Senate could not be expected to enjoy the confidence and respect of foreign powers in the same degree with the constitutional representatives of the nation, and, of course, would not be able to act with an equal degree of weight or efficacy. While the Union would, from this cause, lose a considerable advantage in the management of its external concerns, the people would lose the additional security which would result from the co-operation of the Executive. Though it would be imprudent to confide in him solely so important a trust, yet it cannot be doubted that his participation would materially add to the safety of the society. It must indeed be clear to a demonstration that the joint possession of the power in question, by the President and Senate, would afford a greater prospect of security, than the separate possession of it by either of them. And whoever has maturely weighed the circumstances which must concur in the appointment of a President, will be satisfied that the office will always bid fair to be filled by men of such characters as to render their concurrence in the formation of treaties peculiarly desirable, as well on the score of wisdom, as on that of integrity.

The remarks made in a former number, which have been alluded to in another part of this paper, will apply with conclusive force against the admission of the House of Representatives to a share in the formation of treaties. The fluctuating and, taking its future increase into the account, the multitudinous composition of that body, forbid us to expect in it those qualities which are essential to the proper execution of such a trust. Accurate and comprehensive knowledge of foreign politics; a steady and systematic adherence to the same views; a nice and uniform sensibility to national character; decision, secrecy, and despatch, are incompatible with the genius of a body so variable and so numerous. The very complication of the business, by introducing a necessity of the concurrence of so many different bodies, would of itself afford a solid objection. The greater frequency of the calls upon the House of Representatives, and the greater length of time which it would often be necessary to keep them together when convened, to obtain their sanction in the progressive stages of a treaty, would be a source of so great inconvenience and expense as alone ought to condemn the project.

The only objection which remains to be canvassed, is that which would substitute the proportion of two thirds of all the members composing the senatorial body, to that of two thirds of the members present. It has been shown, under the second head of our inquiries, that all provisions which require more than the majority of any body to its resolutions, have a direct tendency to embarrass the operations of the government, and an indirect one to subject the sense of the majority to that of the minority. This consideration seems sufficient to determine our opinion, that the convention have gone as far in the endeavor to secure the advantage of numbers in the formation of treaties as could have been reconciled either with the activity of the public councils or with a reasonable regard to the major sense of the community. If two thirds of the whole number of members had been required, it would, in many cases, from the non-attendance of a part, amount in practice to a necessity of unanimity. And the history of every political establishment in which this principle has prevailed, is a history of impotence, perplexity, and disorder. Proofs of this position might be adduced from the examples of the Roman Tribuneship, the Polish Diet, and the States-General of the Netherlands, did not an example at home render foreign precedents unnecessary.

To require a fixed proportion of the whole body would not, in all probability, contribute to the advantages of a numerous agency, better then merely to require a proportion of the attending members. The former, by making a determinate number at all times requisite to a resolution, diminishes the motives to punctual attendance. The latter, by making the capacity of the body to depend on a proportion which may be varied by the absence or presence of a single member, has the contrary effect. And as, by promoting punctuality, it tends to keep the body complete, there is great likelihood that its resolutions would generally be dictated by as great a number in this case as in the other; while there would be much fewer occasions of delay. It ought not to be forgotten that, under the existing Confederation, two members may, and usually do, represent a State; whence it happens that Congress, who now are solely invested with all the powers of the Union, rarely consist of a greater number of persons than would compose the intended Senate. If we add to this, that as the members vote by States, and that where there is only a single member present from a State, his vote is lost, it will justify a supposition that the active voices in the Senate, where the members are to vote individually, would rarely fall short in number of the active voices in the existing Congress. When, in addition to these considerations, we take into view the co-operation of the President, we shall not hesitate to infer that the people of America would have greater security against an improper use of the power of making treaties, under the new Constitution, than they now enjoy under the Confederation. And when we proceed still one step further, and look forward to the probable augmentation of the Senate, by the erection of new States, we shall not only perceive ample ground of confidence in the sufficiency of the members to whose agency that power will be intrusted, but we shall probably be led to conclude that a body more numerous than the Senate would be likely to become, would be very little fit for the proper discharge of the trust.

PUBLIUS

FEDERALIST PAPER NO. 76. THE APPOINTING POWER OF THE EXECUTIVE

From the New York Packet. Tuesday, April 1, 1788.

HAMILTON

To the People of the State of New York:

THE President is "to nominate, and, by and with the advice and consent of the Senate, to appoint ambassadors, other public ministers and consuls, judges of the Supreme Court, and all other officers of the United States whose appointments are not otherwise provided for in the Constitution. But the Congress may by law vest the appointment of such inferior officers as they think proper, in the President alone, or in the courts of law, or in the heads of departments. The President shall have power to fill up all vacancies which may happen during the recess of the Senate, by granting commissions which shall expire at the end of their next session."

It has been observed in a former paper, that "the true test of a good government is its aptitude and tendency to produce a good administration." If the justness of this observation be admitted, the mode of appointing the officers of the United States contained in the foregoing clauses, must, when examined, be allowed to be entitled to particular commendation. It is not easy to conceive a plan better calculated than this to promote a judicious choice of men for filling the offices of the Union; and it will not need proof, that on this point must essentially depend the character of its administration.

It will be agreed on all hands, that the power of appointment, in ordinary cases, ought to be modified in one of three ways. It ought either to be vested in a single man, or in a select assembly of a moderate number; or in a single man, with the concurrence of such an assembly. The exercise of it by the people at large will be readily admitted to be impracticable; as waiving every other consideration, it would leave them little time to do anything else. When, therefore, mention is made in the subsequent reasonings of an assembly or body of men, what is said must be understood to relate to a select body or assembly, of the description already given. The people collectively, from their number and from their dispersed situation, cannot be regulated in their movements by that systematic spirit of cabal and intrigue, which will be urged as the chief objections to reposing the power in question in a body of men.

Those who have themselves reflected upon the subject, or who have attended to the observations made in other parts of these papers, in relation to the appointment of the President, will, I presume, agree to the position, that there would always be great probability of having the place supplied by a man of abilities, at least respectable. Premising this, I proceed to lay it down as a rule, that one man of discernment is better fitted to analyze and estimate the peculiar qualities adapted to particular offices, than a body of men of equal or perhaps even of superior discernment.

The sole and undivided responsibility of one man will naturally beget a livelier sense of duty and a more exact regard to reputation. He will, on this account, feel himself under stronger obligations, and more interested to investigate with care the qualities requisite to the stations to be filled, and to prefer with impartiality the persons who may have the fairest pretensions to them. He will have fewer personal attachments to gratify, than a body of men who may each be supposed to have an equal number; and will be so much the less liable to be misled by the sentiments of friendship and of affection. A single well-directed man, by a single understanding, cannot be distracted and warped by that diversity of views, feelings, and interests, which frequently distract and warp the resolutions of a collective body. There is nothing so apt to agitate the passions of mankind as personal considerations whether they relate to ourselves or to others, who are to be the objects of our choice or preference. Hence, in every exercise of the power of appointing to offices, by an assembly of men, we must expect to see a full display of all the private and party likings and dislikes, partialities and antipathies, attachments and animosities, which are felt by those who compose the assembly. The choice which may at any time happen to be made under such circumstances, will of course be the result either of a victory gained by one party over the other, or of a compromise between the parties. In either case, the intrinsic merit of the candidate will be too often out of sight. In the first, the qualifications best adapted to uniting the suffrages of the party, will be more considered than those which fit the person for the station. In the last, the coalition will commonly turn upon some interested equivalent: "Give us the man we wish for this office, and you shall have the one you wish for that." This will be the usual condition of the bargain. And it will rarely happen that the advancement of the public service will be the primary object either of party victories or of party negotiations.

The truth of the principles here advanced seems to have been felt by the most intelligent of those who have found fault with the provision made, in this respect, by the convention. They contend that the President ought solely to have been authorized to make the appointments under the federal government. But it is easy to show, that every advantage to be expected from such an arrangement would, in substance, be derived from the power of nomination, which is proposed to be conferred upon him; while several disadvantages which might attend the absolute power of appointment in the hands of that officer would be avoided. In the act of nomination, his judgment alone would be exercised; and as it would be his sole duty to point out the man who, with the approbation of the Senate, should fill an office, his responsibility would be as complete as if he were to make the final appointment. There can, in this view, be no difference between nominating and appointing. The same motives which would influence a proper discharge of his duty in one case, would exist in the other. And as no man could be appointed but on his previous nomination, every man who might be appointed would be, in fact, his choice.

But might not his nomination be overruled? I grant it might, yet this could only be to make place for another nomination by himself. The person ultimately appointed must be the object of his preference, though perhaps not in the first degree. It is also not very probable that his nomination would often be overruled. The Senate could not be tempted, by the preference they might feel to another, to reject the one proposed; because they could not assure themselves, that the person they might wish would be brought forward by a second or by any subsequent nomination. They could not even be certain, that a future nomination would present a candidate in any degree more acceptable to them; and as their dissent might cast a kind of stigma upon the individual rejected, and might have the appearance of a reflection upon the judgment of the chief magistrate, it is not likely that their sanction would often be refused, where there were not special and strong reasons for the refusal.

To what purpose then require the co-operation of the Senate? I answer, that the necessity of their concurrence would have a powerful, though, in general, a silent operation. It would be an excellent check upon a spirit of favoritism in the President, and would tend greatly to prevent the appointment of unfit characters from State prejudice, from family connection, from personal attachment, or from a view to popularity. In addition to this, it would be an efficacious source of stability in the administration.

It will readily be comprehended, that a man who had himself the sole disposition of offices, would be governed much more by his private inclinations and interests, than when he was bound to submit the propriety of his choice to the discussion and determination of a different and independent body, and that body an entire branch of the legislature. The possibility of rejection would be a strong motive to care in proposing. The danger to his own reputation, and, in the case of an elective magistrate, to his political existence, from betraying a spirit of favoritism, or an unbecoming pursuit of popularity, to the observation of a body whose opinion would have great weight in forming that of the public, could not fail to operate as a barrier to the one and to the other. He would be both ashamed and afraid to bring forward, for the most distinguished or lucrative stations, candidates who had no other merit than that of coming from the same State to which he particularly belonged, or of being in some way or other personally allied to him, or of possessing the necessary insignificance and pliancy to render them the obsequious instruments of his pleasure.

To this reasoning it has been objected that the President, by the influence of the power of nomination, may secure the complaisance of the Senate to his views. This supposition of universal venalty in human nature is little less an error in political reasoning, than the supposition of universal rectitude. The institution of delegated power implies, that there is a portion of virtue and honor among mankind, which may be a reasonable foundation of confidence; and experience justifies the theory. It has been found to exist in the most corrupt periods of the most corrupt governments. The venalty of the British House of Commons has been long a topic of accusation against that body, in the country to which they belong as well as in this; and it cannot be doubted that the charge is, to a considerable extent, well founded. But it is as little to be doubted, that there is always a large proportion of the body, which consists of independent and public-spirited men, who have an influential weight in the councils of the nation. Hence it is (the present reign not excepted) that the sense of that body is often seen to control the inclinations of the monarch, both with regard to men and to measures. Though it might therefore be allowable to suppose that the Executive might occasionally influence some individuals in the Senate, yet the supposition, that he could in general purchase the integrity of the whole body, would be forced and improbable. A man disposed to view human nature as it is, without either flattering its virtues or exaggerating its vices, will see sufficient ground of confidence in the probity of the Senate, to rest satisfied, not only that it will be impracticable to the Executive to corrupt or seduce a majority of its members, but that the necessity of its co-operation, in the business of appointments, will be a considerable and salutary restraint upon the conduct of that magistrate. Nor is the integrity of the Senate the only reliance. The Constitution has provided some important guards against the danger of executive influence upon the legislative body: it declares that "No senator or representative shall during the time for which he was elected, be appointed to any civil office under the United States, which shall have been created, or the emoluments whereof shall have been increased, during such time; and no person, holding any office under the United States, shall be a member of either house during his continuance in office."

PUBLIUS

FEDERALIST PAPER NO. 77. THE APPOINTING POWER CONTINUED AND OTHER POWERS OF THE EXECUTIVE CONSIDERED.

From The Independent Journal. Wednesday, April 2, 1788.

HAMILTON

To the People of the State of New York:

IT HAS been mentioned as one of the advantages to be expected from the co-operation of the Senate, in the business of appointments, that it would contribute to the stability of the administration. The consent of that body would be necessary to displace as well as to appoint. A change of the Chief Magistrate, therefore, would not occasion so violent or so general a revolution in the officers of the government as might be expected, if he were the sole disposer of offices. Where a man in any station had given satisfactory evidence of his fitness for it, a new President would be restrained from attempting a change in favor of a person more agreeable to him, by the apprehension that a discountenance of the Senate might frustrate the attempt, and bring some degree of discredit upon himself. Those who can best estimate the value of a steady administration, will be most disposed to prize a provision which connects the official existence of public men with the approbation or disapprobation of that body which, from the greater permanency of its own composition, will in all probability be less subject to inconstancy than any other member of the government.

To this union of the Senate with the President, in the article of appointments, it has in some cases been suggested that it would serve to give the President an undue influence over the Senate, and in others that it would have an opposite tendency—a strong proof that neither suggestion is true.

To state the first in its proper form, is to refute it. It amounts to this: the President would have an improper influence over the Senate, because the Senate would have the power of restraining him. This is an absurdity in terms. It cannot admit of a doubt that the entire power of appointment would enable him much more effectually to establish a dangerous empire over that body, than a mere power of nomination subject to their control.

Let us take a view of the converse of the proposition: "the Senate would influence the Executive." As I have had occasion to remark in several other instances, the indistinctness of the objection forbids a precise answer. In what manner is this influence to be exerted? In relation to what objects? The power of influencing a person, in the sense in which it is here used, must imply a power of conferring a benefit upon him. How could the Senate confer a benefit upon the President by the manner of employing their right of negative upon his nominations? If it be said they might sometimes gratify him by an acquiescence in a favorite choice, when public motives might dictate a different conduct, I answer, that the instances in which the President could be personally interested in the result, would be too few to admit of his being materially affected by the compliances of the Senate. The POWER which can originate the disposition of honors and emoluments, is more likely to attract than to be attracted by the POWER which can merely obstruct their course. If by influencing the President be meant restraining him, this is precisely what must have been intended. And it has been shown that the restraint would be salutary, at the same time that it would not be such as to destroy a single advantage to be looked for from the uncontrolled agency of that Magistrate. The right of nomination would produce all the (good, without the ill.)(E1) (good of that of appointment, and would in a great measure avoid its evils.)(E1)

Upon a comparison of the plan for the appointment of the officers of the proposed government with that which is established by the constitution of this State, a decided preference must be given to the former. In that plan the power of nomination is unequivocally vested in the Executive. And as there would be a necessity for submitting each nomination to the judgment of an entire branch of the legislature, the circumstances attending an appointment, from the mode of conducting it, would naturally become matters of notoriety; and the public would be at no loss to determine what part had been performed by the different actors. The blame of a bad nomination would fall upon the President singly and absolutely. The censure of rejecting a good one would lie entirely at the door of the Senate; aggravated by the consideration of their having counteracted the good intentions of the Executive. If an ill appointment should be made, the Executive for nominating, and the Senate for approving, would participate, though in different degrees, in the opprobrium and disgrace.

The reverse of all this characterizes the manner of appointment in this State. The council of appointment consists of from three to five persons, of whom the governor is always one. This small body, shut up in a private apartment, impenetrable to the public eye, proceed to the execution of the trust committed to them. It is known that the governor claims the right of nomination, upon the strength of some ambiguous expressions in the constitution; but it is not known to what extent, or in what manner he exercises it; nor upon what occasions he is contradicted or opposed. The censure of a bad appointment, on account of the uncertainty of its author, and for want of a determinate object, has neither poignancy nor duration. And while an unbounded field for cabal and intrigue lies open, all idea of responsibility is lost. The most that the public can know, is that the governor claims the right of nomination; that two out of the inconsiderable number of four men can too often be managed without much difficulty; that if some of the members of a particular council should happen to be of an uncomplying character, it is frequently not impossible to get rid of their opposition by regulating the times of meeting in such a manner as to render their attendance inconvenient; and that from whatever cause it may proceed, a great number of very improper appointments are from time to time made. Whether a governor of this State avails himself of the ascendant he must necessarily have, in this delicate and important part of the administration, to prefer to offices men who are best qualified for them, or whether he prostitutes that advantage to the advancement of persons whose chief merit is their implicit devotion to his will, and to the support of a despicable and dangerous system of personal influence, are questions which, unfortunately for the community, can only be the subjects of speculation and conjecture.

Every mere council of appointment, however constituted, will be a conclave, in which cabal and intrigue will have their full scope. Their number, without an unwarrantable increase of expense, cannot be large enough to preclude a facility of combination. And as each member will have his friends and connections to provide for, the desire of mutual gratification will beget a scandalous bartering of votes and bargaining for places. The private attachments of one man might easily be satisfied; but to satisfy the private attachments of a dozen, or of twenty men, would occasion a monopoly of all the principal employments of the government in a few families, and would lead more directly to an aristocracy or an oligarchy than any measure that could be contrived. If, to avoid an accumulation of offices, there was to be a frequent change in the persons who were to compose the council, this would involve the mischiefs of a mutable administration in their full extent. Such a council would also be more liable to executive influence than the Senate, because they would be fewer in number, and would act less immediately under the public inspection. Such a council, in fine, as a substitute for the plan of the convention, would be productive of an increase of expense, a multiplication of the evils which spring from favoritism and intrigue in the distribution of public honors, a decrease of stability in the administration of the government, and a diminution of the security against an undue influence of the Executive. And yet such a council has been warmly contended for as an essential amendment in the proposed Constitution.

I could not with propriety conclude my observations on the subject of appointments without taking notice of a scheme for which there have appeared some, though but few advocates; I mean that of uniting the House of Representatives in the power of making them. I shall, however, do little more than mention it, as I cannot imagine that it is likely to gain the countenance of any considerable part of the community. A body so fluctuating and at the same time so numerous, can never be deemed proper for the exercise of that power. Its unfitness will appear manifest to all, when it is recollected that in half a century it may consist of three or four hundred persons. All the advantages of the stability, both of the Executive and of the Senate, would be defeated by this union, and infinite delays and embarrassments would be occasioned. The example of most of the States in their local constitutions encourages us to reprobate the idea.

The only remaining powers of the Executive are comprehended in giving information to Congress of the state of the Union; in recommending to their consideration such measures as he shall judge expedient; in convening them, or either branch, upon extraordinary occasions; in adjourning them when they cannot themselves agree upon the time of adjournment; in receiving ambassadors and other public ministers; in faithfully executing the laws; and in commissioning all the officers of the United States.

Except some cavils about the power of convening either house of the legislature, and that of receiving ambassadors, no objection has been made to this class of authorities; nor could they possibly admit of any. It required, indeed, an insatiable avidity for censure to invent exceptions to the parts which have been excepted to. In regard to the power of convening either house of the legislature, I shall barely remark, that in respect to the Senate at least, we can readily discover a good reason for it. AS this body has a concurrent power with the Executive in the article of treaties, it might often be necessary to call it together with a view to this object, when it would be unnecessary and improper to convene the House of Representatives. As to the reception of ambassadors, what I have said in a former paper will furnish a sufficient answer.

We have now completed a survey of the structure and powers of the executive department, which, I have endeavored to show, combines, as far as republican principles will admit, all the requisites to energy. The remaining inquiry is: Does it also combine the requisites to safety, in a republican sense—a due dependence on the people, a due responsibility? The answer to this question has been anticipated in the investigation of its other characteristics, and is satisfactorily deducible from these circumstances; from the election of the President once in four years by persons immediately chosen by the people for that purpose; and from his being at all times liable to impeachment, trial, dismission from office, incapacity to serve in any other, and to forfeiture of life and estate by subsequent prosecution in the common course of law. But these precautions, great as they are, are not the only ones which the plan of the convention has provided in favor of the public security. In the only instances in which the abuse of the executive authority was materially to be feared, the Chief Magistrate of the United States would, by that plan, be subjected to the control of a branch of the legislative body. What more could be desired by an enlightened and reasonable people?

PUBLIUS

E1. These two alternate endings of this sentence appear in different editions.

FEDERALIST PAPER NO. 78. THE JUDICIARY DEPARTMENT

From McLEAN'S Edition, New York. Wednesday, May 28, 1788

HAMILTON

To the People of the State of New York:

WE PROCEED now to an examination of the judiciary department of the proposed government.

In unfolding the defects of the existing Confederation, the utility and necessity of a federal judicature have been clearly pointed out. It is the less necessary to recapitulate the considerations there urged, as the propriety of the institution in the abstract is not disputed; the only questions which have been raised being relative to the manner of constituting it, and to its extent. To these points, therefore, our observations shall be confined.

The manner of constituting it seems to embrace these several objects: 1st. The mode of appointing the judges. 2d. The tenure by which they are to hold their places. 3d. The partition of the judiciary authority between different courts, and their relations to each other.

First. As to the mode of appointing the judges; this is the same with that of appointing the officers of the Union in general, and has been so fully discussed in the two last numbers, that nothing can be said here which would not be useless repetition.

Second. As to the tenure by which the judges are to hold their places; this chiefly concerns their duration in office; the provisions for their support; the precautions for their responsibility.

According to the plan of the convention, all judges who may be appointed by the United States are to hold their offices during good behavior; which is conformable to the most approved of the State constitutions and among the rest, to that of this State. Its propriety having been drawn into question by the adversaries of that plan, is no light symptom of the rage for objection, which disorders their imaginations and judgments. The standard of good behavior for the continuance in office of the judicial magistracy, is certainly one of the most valuable of the modern improvements in the practice of government. In a monarchy it is an excellent barrier to the despotism of the prince; in a republic it is a no less excellent barrier to the encroachments and oppressions of the representative body. And it is the best expedient which can be devised in any government, to secure a steady, upright, and impartial administration of the laws.

Whoever attentively considers the different departments of power must perceive, that, in a government in which they are separated from each other, the judiciary, from the nature of its functions, will always be the least dangerous to the political rights of the Constitution; because it will be least in a capacity to annoy or injure them. The Executive not only dispenses the honors, but holds the sword of the community. The legislature not only commands the purse, but prescribes the rules by which the duties and rights of every citizen are to be regulated. The judiciary, on the contrary, has no influence over either the sword or the purse; no direction either of the strength or of the wealth of the society; and can take no active resolution whatever. It may truly be said to have neither FORCE nor WILL, but merely judgment; and must ultimately depend upon the aid of the executive arm even for the efficacy of its judgments.

This simple view of the matter suggests several important consequences. It proves incontestably, that the judiciary is beyond comparison the weakest of the three departments of power(1); that it can never attack with success either of the other two; and that all possible care is requisite to enable it to defend itself against their attacks. It equally proves, that though individual oppression may now and then proceed from the courts of justice, the general liberty of the people can never be endangered from that quarter; I mean so long as the judiciary remains truly distinct from both the legislature and the Executive. For I agree, that "there is no liberty, if the power of judging be not separated from the legislative and executive powers."(2) And it proves, in the last place, that as liberty can have nothing to fear from the judiciary alone, but would have every thing to fear from its union with either of the other departments; that as all the effects of such a union must ensue from a dependence of the former on the latter, notwithstanding a nominal and apparent separation; that as, from the natural feebleness of the judiciary, it is in continual jeopardy of being overpowered, awed, or influenced by its co-ordinate branches; and that as nothing can contribute so much to its firmness and independence as permanency in office, this quality may therefore be justly regarded as an indispensable ingredient in its constitution, and, in a great measure, as the citadel of the public justice and the public security.

The complete independence of the courts of justice is peculiarly essential in a limited Constitution. By a limited Constitution, I understand one which contains certain specified exceptions to the legislative authority; such, for instance, as that it shall pass no bills of attainder, no ex post facto laws, and the like. Limitations of this kind can be preserved in practice no other way than through the medium of courts of justice, whose duty it must be to declare all acts contrary to the manifest tenor of the Constitution void. Without this, all the reservations of particular rights or privileges would amount to nothing.

Some perplexity respecting the rights of the courts to pronounce legislative acts void, because contrary to the Constitution, has arisen from an imagination that the doctrine would imply a superiority of the judiciary to the legislative power. It is urged that the authority which can declare the acts of another void, must necessarily be superior to the one whose acts may be declared void. As this doctrine is of great importance in all the American constitutions, a brief discussion of the ground on which it rests cannot be unacceptable.

There is no position which depends on clearer principles, than that every act of a delegated authority, contrary to the tenor of the commission under which it is exercised, is void. No legislative act, therefore, contrary to the Constitution, can be valid. To deny this, would be to affirm, that the deputy is greater than his principal; that the servant is above his master; that the representatives of the people are superior to the people themselves; that men acting by virtue of powers, may do not only what their powers do not authorize, but what they forbid.

If it be said that the legislative body are themselves the constitutional judges of their own powers, and that the construction they put upon them is conclusive upon the other departments, it may be answered, that this cannot be the natural presumption, where it is not to be collected from any particular provisions in the Constitution. It is not otherwise to be supposed, that the Constitution could intend to enable the representatives of the people to substitute their will to that of their constituents. It is far more rational to suppose, that the courts were designed to be an intermediate body between the people and the legislature, in order, among other things, to keep the latter within the limits assigned to their authority. The interpretation of the laws is the proper and peculiar province of the courts. A constitution is, in fact, and must be regarded by the judges, as a fundamental law. It therefore belongs to them to ascertain its meaning, as well as the meaning of any particular act proceeding from the legislative body. If there should happen to be an irreconcilable variance between the two, that which has the superior obligation and validity ought, of course, to be preferred; or, in other words, the Constitution ought to be preferred to the statute, the intention of the people to the intention of their agents.

Nor does this conclusion by any means suppose a superiority of the judicial to the legislative power. It only supposes that the power of the people is superior to both; and that where the will of the legislature, declared in its statutes, stands in opposition to that of the people, declared in the Constitution, the judges ought to be governed by the latter rather than the former. They ought to regulate their decisions by the fundamental laws, rather than by those which are not fundamental.

This exercise of judicial discretion, in determining between two contradictory laws, is exemplified in a familiar instance. It not uncommonly happens, that there are two statutes existing at one time, clashing in whole or in part with each other, and neither of them containing any repealing clause or expression. In such a case, it is the province of the courts to liquidate and fix their meaning and operation. So far as they can, by any fair construction, be reconciled to each other, reason and law conspire to dictate that this should be done; where this is impracticable, it becomes a matter of necessity to give effect to one, in exclusion of the other. The rule which has obtained in the courts for determining their relative validity is, that the last in order of time shall be preferred to the first. But this is a mere rule of construction, not derived from any positive law, but from the nature and reason of the thing. It is a rule not enjoined upon the courts by legislative provision, but adopted by themselves, as consonant to truth and propriety, for the direction of their conduct as interpreters of the law. They thought it reasonable, that between the interfering acts of an EQUAL authority, that which was the last indication of its will should have the preference.

But in regard to the interfering acts of a superior and subordinate authority, of an original and derivative power, the nature and reason of the thing indicate the converse of that rule as proper to be followed. They teach us that the prior act of a superior ought to be preferred to the subsequent act of an inferior and subordinate authority; and that accordingly, whenever a particular statute contravenes the Constitution, it will be the duty of the judicial tribunals to adhere to the latter and disregard the former.

It can be of no weight to say that the courts, on the pretense of a repugnancy, may substitute their own pleasure to the constitutional intentions of the legislature. This might as well happen in the case of two contradictory statutes; or it might as well happen in every adjudication upon any single statute. The courts must declare the sense of the law; and if they should be disposed to exercise WILL instead of JUDGMENT, the consequence would equally be the substitution of their pleasure to that of the legislative body. The observation, if it prove any thing, would prove that there ought to be no judges distinct from that body.

If, then, the courts of justice are to be considered as the bulwarks of a limited Constitution against legislative encroachments, this consideration will afford a strong argument for the permanent tenure of judicial offices, since nothing will contribute so much as this to that independent spirit in the judges which must be essential to the faithful performance of so arduous a duty.

This independence of the judges is equally requisite to guard the Constitution and the rights of individuals from the effects of those ill humors, which the arts of designing men, or the influence of particular conjunctures, sometimes disseminate among the people themselves, and which, though they speedily give place to better information, and more deliberate reflection, have a tendency, in the meantime, to occasion dangerous innovations in the government, and serious oppressions of the minor party in the community. Though I trust the friends of the proposed Constitution will never concur with its enemies,(3) in questioning that fundamental principle of republican government, which admits the right of the people to alter or abolish the established Constitution, whenever they find it inconsistent with their happiness, yet it is not to be inferred from this principle, that the representatives of the people, whenever a momentary inclination happens to lay hold of a majority of their constituents, incompatible with the provisions in the existing Constitution, would, on that account, be justifiable in a violation of those provisions; or that the courts would be under a greater obligation to connive at infractions in this shape, than when they had proceeded wholly from the cabals of the representative body. Until the people have, by some solemn and authoritative act, annulled or changed the established form, it is binding upon themselves collectively, as well as individually; and no presumption, or even knowledge, of their sentiments, can warrant their representatives in a departure from it, prior to such an act. But it is easy to see, that it would require an uncommon portion of fortitude in the judges to do their duty as faithful guardians of the Constitution, where legislative invasions of it had been instigated by the major voice of the community.

But it is not with a view to infractions of the Constitution only, that the independence of the judges may be an essential safeguard against the effects of occasional ill humors in the society. These sometimes extend no farther than to the injury of the private rights of particular classes of citizens, by unjust and partial laws. Here also the firmness of the judicial magistracy is of vast importance in mitigating the severity and confining the operation of such laws. It not only serves to moderate the immediate mischiefs of those which may have been passed, but it operates as a check upon the legislative body in passing them; who, perceiving that obstacles to the success of iniquitous intention are to be expected from the scruples of the courts, are in a manner compelled, by the very motives of the injustice they meditate, to qualify their attempts. This is a circumstance calculated to have more influence upon the character of our governments, than but few may be aware of. The benefits of the integrity and moderation of the judiciary have already been felt in more States than one; and though they may have displeased those whose sinister expectations they may have disappointed, they must have commanded the esteem and applause of all the virtuous and disinterested. Considerate men, of every description, ought to prize whatever will tend to beget or fortify that temper in the courts: as no man can be sure that he may not be to-morrow the victim of a spirit of injustice, by which he may be a gainer to-day. And every man must now feel, that the inevitable tendency of such a spirit is to sap the foundations of public and private confidence, and to introduce in its stead universal distrust and distress.

That inflexible and uniform adherence to the rights of the Constitution, and of individuals, which we perceive to be indispensable in the courts of justice, can certainly not be expected from judges who hold their offices by a temporary commission. Periodical appointments, however regulated, or by whomsoever made, would, in some way or other, be fatal to their necessary independence. If the power of making them was committed either to the Executive or legislature, there would be danger of an improper complaisance to the branch which possessed it; if to both, there would be an unwillingness to hazard the displeasure of either; if to the people, or to persons chosen by them for the special purpose, there would be too great a disposition to consult popularity, to justify a reliance that nothing would be consulted but the Constitution and the laws.

There is yet a further and a weightier reason for the permanency of the judicial offices, which is deducible from the nature of the qualifications they require. It has been frequently remarked, with great propriety, that a voluminous code of laws is one of the inconveniences necessarily connected with the advantages of a free government. To avoid an arbitrary discretion in the courts, it is indispensable that they should be bound down by strict rules and precedents, which serve to define and point out their duty in every particular case that comes before them; and it will readily be conceived from the variety of controversies which grow out of the folly and wickedness of mankind, that the records of those precedents must unavoidably swell to a very considerable bulk, and must demand long and laborious study to acquire a competent knowledge of them. Hence it is, that there can be but few men in the society who will have sufficient skill in the laws to qualify them for the stations of judges. And making the proper deductions for the ordinary depravity of human nature, the number must be still smaller of those who unite the requisite integrity with the requisite knowledge. These considerations apprise us, that the government can have no great option between fit character; and that a temporary duration in office, which would naturally discourage such characters from quitting a lucrative line of practice to accept a seat on the bench, would have a tendency to throw the administration of justice into hands less able, and less well qualified, to conduct it with utility and dignity. In the present circumstances of this country, and in those in which it is likely to be for a long time to come, the disadvantages on this score would be greater than they may at first sight appear; but it must be confessed, that they are far inferior to those which present themselves under the other aspects of the subject.

Upon the whole, there can be no room to doubt that the convention acted wisely in copying from the models of those constitutions which have established good behavior as the tenure of their judicial offices, in point of duration; and that so far from being blamable on this account, their plan would have been inexcusably defective, if it had wanted this important feature of good government. The experience of Great Britain affords an illustrious comment on the excellence of the institution.

PUBLIUS

1. The celebrated Montesquieu, speaking of them, says: "Of the three powers above mentioned, the judiciary is next to nothing."—Spirit of Laws. Vol. I, page 186.
2. Idem, page 181.
3. Vide Protest of the Minority of the Convention of Pennsylvania, Martin's Speech, etc.

FEDERALIST PAPER NO. 79. THE JUDICIARY CONTINUED

From MCLEAN's Edition, New York. Wednesday, May 28, 1788

HAMILTON

To the People of the State of New York:

NEXT to permanency in office, nothing can contribute more to the independence of the judges than a fixed provision for their support. The remark made in relation to the President is equally applicable here. In the general course of human nature, a power over a man's subsistence amounts to a power over his will. And we can never hope to see realized in practice, the complete separation of the judicial from the legislative power, in any system which leaves the former dependent for pecuniary resources on the occasional grants of the latter. The enlightened friends to good government in every State, have seen cause to lament the want of precise and explicit precautions in the State constitutions on this head. Some of these indeed have declared that permanent(1) salaries should be established for the judges; but the experiment has in some instances shown that such expressions are not sufficiently definite to preclude legislative evasions. Something still more positive and unequivocal has been evinced to be requisite. The plan of the convention accordingly has provided that the judges of the United States "shall at stated times receive for their services a compensation which shall not be diminished during their continuance in office."

This, all circumstances considered, is the most eligible provision that could have been devised. It will readily be understood that the fluctuations in the value of money and in the state of society rendered a fixed rate of compensation in the Constitution inadmissible. What might be extravagant to-day, might in half a century become penurious and inadequate. It was therefore necessary to leave it to the discretion of the legislature to vary its provisions in conformity to the variations in circumstances, yet under such restrictions as to put it out of the power of that body to change the condition of the individual for the worse. A man may then be sure of the ground upon which he stands, and can never be deterred from his duty by the apprehension of being placed in a less eligible situation. The clause which has been quoted combines both advantages. The salaries of judicial officers may from time to time be altered, as occasion shall require, yet so as never to lessen the allowance with which any particular judge comes into office, in respect to him. It will be observed that a difference has been made by the convention between the compensation of the President and of the judges, That of the former can neither be increased nor diminished; that of the latter can only not be diminished. This probably arose from the difference in the duration of the respective offices. As the President is to be elected for no more than four years, it can rarely happen that an adequate salary, fixed at the commencement of that period, will not continue to be such to its end. But with regard to the judges, who, if they behave properly, will be secured in their places for life, it may well happen, especially in the early stages of the government, that a stipend, which would be very sufficient at their first appointment, would become too small in the progress of their service.

This provision for the support of the judges bears every mark of prudence and efficacy; and it may be safely affirmed that, together with the permanent tenure of their offices, it affords a better prospect of their independence than is discoverable in the constitutions of any of the States in regard to their own judges.

The precautions for their responsibility are comprised in the article respecting impeachments. They are liable to be impeached for malconduct by the House of Representatives, and tried by the Senate; and, if convicted, may be dismissed from office, and disqualified for holding any other. This is the only provision on the point which is consistent with the necessary independence of the judicial character, and is the only one which we find in our own Constitution in respect to our own judges.

The want of a provision for removing the judges on account of inability has been a subject of complaint. But all considerate men will be sensible that such a provision would either not be practiced upon or would be more liable to abuse than calculated to answer any good purpose. The mensuration of the faculties of the mind has, I believe, no place in the catalogue of known arts. An attempt to fix the boundary between the regions of ability and inability, would much oftener give scope to personal and party attachments and enmities than advance the interests of justice or the public good. The result, except in the case of insanity, must for the most part be arbitrary; and insanity, without any formal or express provision, may be safely pronounced to be a virtual disqualification.

The constitution of New York, to avoid investigations that must forever be vague and dangerous, has taken a particular age as the criterion of inability. No man can be a judge beyond sixty. I believe there are few at present who do not disapprove of this provision. There is no station, in relation to which it is less proper than to that of a judge. The deliberating and comparing faculties generally preserve their strength much beyond that period in men who survive it; and when, in addition to this circumstance, we consider how few there are who outlive the season of intellectual vigor, and how improbable it is that any considerable portion of the bench, whether more or less numerous, should be in such a situation at the same time, we shall be ready to conclude that limitations of this sort have little to recommend them. In a republic, where fortunes are not affluent, and pensions not expedient, the dismission of men from stations in which they have served their country long and usefully, on which they depend for subsistence, and from which it will be too late to resort to any other occupation for a livelihood, ought to have some better apology to humanity than is to be found in the imaginary danger of a superannuated bench.

PUBLIUS

1. Vide Constitution of Massachusetts, Chapter 2, Section 1, Article 13.

FEDERALIST PAPER NO. 80. THE POWERS OF THE JUDICIARY

From McLEAN's Edition, New York. Wednesday, May 28, 1788.

HAMILTON

To the People of the State of New York:

TO JUDGE with accuracy of the proper extent of the federal judicature, it will be necessary to consider, in the first place, what are its proper objects.

It seems scarcely to admit of controversy, that the judiciary authority of the Union ought to extend to these several descriptions of cases: 1st, to all those which arise out of the laws of the United States, passed in pursuance of their just and constitutional powers of legislation; 2d, to all those which concern the execution of the provisions expressly contained in the articles of Union; 3d, to all those in which the United States are a party; 4th, to all those which involve the PEACE of the CONFEDERACY, whether they relate to the intercourse between the United States and foreign nations, or to that between the States themselves; 5th, to all those which originate on the high seas, and are of admiralty or maritime jurisdiction; and, lastly, to all those in which the State tribunals cannot be supposed to be impartial and unbiased.

The first point depends upon this obvious consideration, that there ought always to be a constitutional method of giving efficacy to constitutional provisions. What, for instance, would avail restrictions on the authority of the State legislatures, without some constitutional mode of enforcing the observance of them? The States, by the plan of the convention, are prohibited from doing a variety of things, some of which are incompatible with the interests of the Union, and others with the principles of good government. The imposition of duties on imported articles, and the emission of paper money, are specimens of each kind. No man of sense will believe, that such prohibitions would be scrupulously regarded, without some effectual power in the government to restrain or correct the infractions of them. This power must either be a direct negative on the State laws, or an authority in the federal courts to overrule such as might be in manifest contravention of the articles of Union. There is no third course that I can imagine. The latter appears to have been thought by the convention preferable to the former, and, I presume, will be most agreeable to the States.

As to the second point, it is impossible, by any argument or comment, to make it clearer than it is in itself. If there are such things as political axioms, the propriety of the judicial power of a government being coextensive with its legislative, may be ranked among the number. The mere necessity of uniformity in the interpretation of the national laws, decides the question. Thirteen independent courts of final jurisdiction over the same causes, arising upon the same laws, is a hydra in government, from which nothing but contradiction and confusion can proceed.

Still less need be said in regard to the third point. Controversies between the nation and its members or citizens, can only be properly referred to the national tribunals. Any other plan would be contrary to reason, to precedent, and to decorum.

The fourth point rests on this plain proposition, that the peace of the WHOLE ought not to be left at the disposal of a PART. The Union will undoubtedly be answerable to foreign powers for the conduct of its members. And the responsibility for an injury ought ever to be accompanied with the faculty of preventing it. As the denial or perversion of justice by the sentences of courts, as well as in any other manner, is with reason classed among the just causes of war, it will follow that the federal judiciary ought to have cognizance of all causes in which the citizens of other countries are concerned. This is not less essential to the preservation of the public faith, than to the security of the public tranquillity. A distinction may perhaps be imagined between cases arising upon treaties and the laws of nations and those which may stand merely on the footing of the municipal law. The former kind may be supposed proper for the federal jurisdiction, the latter for that of the States. But it is at least problematical, whether an unjust sentence against a foreigner, where the subject of controversy was wholly relative to the lex loci, would not, if unredressed, be an aggression upon his sovereign, as well as one which violated the stipulations of a treaty or the general law of nations. And a still greater objection to the distinction would result from the immense difficulty, if not impossibility, of a practical discrimination between the cases of one complexion and those of the other. So great a proportion of the cases in which foreigners are parties, involve national questions, that it is by far most safe and most expedient to refer all those in which they are concerned to the national tribunals.

The power of determining causes between two States, between one State and the citizens of another, and between the citizens of different States, is perhaps not less essential to the peace of the Union than that which has been just examined. History gives us a horrid picture of the dissensions and private wars which distracted and desolated Germany prior to the institution of the Imperial Chamber by Maximilian, towards the close of the fifteenth century; and informs us, at the same time, of the vast influence of that institution in appeasing the disorders and establishing the tranquillity of the empire. This was a court invested with authority to decide finally all differences among the members of the Germanic body.

A method of terminating territorial disputes between the States, under the authority of the federal head, was not unattended to, even in the imperfect system by which they have been hitherto held together. But there are many other sources, besides interfering claims of boundary, from which bickerings and animosities may spring up among the members of the Union. To some of these we have been witnesses in the course of our past experience. It will readily be conjectured that I allude to the fraudulent laws which have been passed in too many of the States. And though the proposed Constitution establishes particular guards against the repetition of those instances which have heretofore made their appearance, yet it is warrantable to apprehend that the spirit which produced them will assume new shapes, that could not be foreseen nor specifically provided against. Whatever practices may have a tendency to disturb the harmony between the States, are proper objects of federal superintendence and control.

Documents of Revolution

It may be esteemed the basis of the Union, that "the citizens of each State shall be entitled to all the privileges and immunities of citizens of the several States." And if it be a just principle that every government ought to possess the means of executing its own provisions by its own authority, it will follow, that in order to the inviolable maintenance of that equality of privileges and immunities to which the citizens of the Union will be entitled, the national judiciary ought to preside in all cases in which one State or its citizens are opposed to another State or its citizens. To secure the full effect of so fundamental a provision against all evasion and subterfuge, it is necessary that its construction should be committed to that tribunal which, having no local attachments, will be likely to be impartial between the different States and their citizens, and which, owing its official existence to the Union, will never be likely to feel any bias inauspicious to the principles on which it is founded.

The fifth point will demand little animadversion. The most bigoted idolizers of State authority have not thus far shown a disposition to deny the national judiciary the cognizances of maritime causes. These so generally depend on the laws of nations, and so commonly affect the rights of foreigners, that they fall within the considerations which are relative to the public peace. The most important part of them are, by the present Confederation, submitted to federal jurisdiction.

The reasonableness of the agency of the national courts in cases in which the State tribunals cannot be supposed to be impartial, speaks for itself. No man ought certainly to be a judge in his own cause, or in any cause in respect to which he has the least interest or bias. This principle has no inconsiderable weight in designating the federal courts as the proper tribunals for the determination of controversies between different States and their citizens. And it ought to have the same operation in regard to some cases between citizens of the same State. Claims to land under grants of different States, founded upon adverse pretensions of boundary, are of this description. The courts of neither of the granting States could be expected to be unbiased. The laws may have even prejudged the question, and tied the courts down to decisions in favor of the grants of the State to which they belonged. And even where this had not been done, it would be natural that the judges, as men, should feel a strong predilection to the claims of their own government.

Having thus laid down and discussed the principles which ought to regulate the constitution of the federal judiciary, we will proceed to test, by these principles, the particular powers of which, according to the plan of the convention, it is to be composed. It is to comprehend "all cases in law and equity arising under the Constitution, the laws of the United States, and treaties made, or which shall be made, under their authority; to all cases affecting ambassadors, other public ministers, and consuls; to all cases of admiralty and maritime jurisdiction; to controversies to which the United States shall be a party; to controversies between two or more States; between a State and citizens of another State; between citizens of different States; between citizens of the same State claiming lands and grants of different States; and between a State or the citizens thereof and foreign states, citizens, and subjects." This constitutes the entire mass of the judicial authority of the Union. Let us now review it in detail. It is, then, to extend:

First. To all cases in law and equity, arising under the Constitution and the laws of the United States. This corresponds with the two first classes of causes, which have been enumerated, as proper for the jurisdiction of the United States. It has been asked, what is meant by "cases arising under the Constitution," in contradiction from those "arising under the laws of the United States"? The difference has been already explained. All the restrictions upon the authority of the State legislatures furnish examples of it. They are not, for instance, to emit paper money; but the interdiction results from the Constitution, and will have no connection with any law of the United States. Should paper money, notwithstanding, be emited, the controversies concerning it would be cases arising under the Constitution and not the laws of the United States, in the ordinary signification of the terms. This may serve as a sample of the whole.

It has also been asked, what need of the word "equity". What equitable causes can grow out of the Constitution and laws of the United States? There is hardly a subject of litigation between individuals, which may not involve those ingredients of fraud, accident, trust, or hardship, which would render the matter an object of equitable rather than of legal jurisdiction, as the distinction is known and established in several of the States. It is the peculiar province, for instance, of a court of equity to relieve against what are called hard bargains: these are contracts in which, though there may have been no direct fraud or deceit, sufficient to invalidate them in a court of law, yet there may have been some undue and unconscionable advantage taken of the necessities or misfortunes of one of the parties, which a court of equity would not tolerate. In such cases, where foreigners were concerned on either side, it would be impossible for the federal judicatories to do justice without an equitable as well as a legal jurisdiction. Agreements to convey lands claimed under the grants of different States, may afford another example of the necessity of an equitable jurisdiction in the federal courts. This reasoning may not be so palpable in those States where the formal and technical distinction between LAW and EQUITY is not maintained, as in this State, where it is exemplified by every day's practice.

The judiciary authority of the Union is to extend:

Second. To treaties made, or which shall be made, under the authority of the United States, and to all cases affecting ambassadors, other public ministers, and consuls. These belong to the fourth class of the enumerated cases, as they have an evident connection with the preservation of the national peace.

Third. To cases of admiralty and maritime jurisdiction. These form, altogether, the fifth of the enumerated classes of causes proper for the cognizance of the national courts.

Fourth. To controversies to which the United States shall be a party. These constitute the third of those classes.

Fifth. To controversies between two or more States; between a State and citizens of another State; between citizens of different States. These belong to the fourth of those classes, and partake, in some measure, of the nature of the last.

Sixth. To cases between the citizens of the same State, claiming lands under grants of different States. These fall within the last class, and are the only instances in which the proposed Constitution directly contemplates the cognizance of disputes between the citizens of the same State.

Seventh. To cases between a State and the citizens thereof, and foreign States, citizens, or subjects. These have been already explained to belong to the fourth of the enumerated classes, and have been shown to be, in a peculiar manner, the proper subjects of the national judicature.

From this review of the particular powers of the federal judiciary, as marked out in the Constitution, it appears that they are all conformable to the principles which ought to have governed the structure of that department, and which were necessary to the perfection of the system. If some partial inconveniences should appear to be connected with the incorporation of any of them into the plan, it ought to be recollected that the national legislature will have ample authority to make such exceptions, and to prescribe such regulations as will be calculated to obviate or remove these inconveniences. The possibility of particular mischiefs can never be viewed, by a wellinformed mind, as a solid objection to a general principle, which is calculated to avoid general mischiefs and to obtain general advantages.

PUBLIUS

FEDERALIST PAPER NO. 81. THE JUDICIARY CONTINUED, AND THE DISTRIBUTION OF THE JUDICIAL AUTHORITY.

From McLEAN's Edition, New York. Wednesday, May 28, 1788.

HAMILTON

To the People of the State of New York:

LET US now return to the partition of the judiciary authority between different courts, and their relations to each other.

"The judicial power of the United States is" (by the plan of the convention) "to be vested in one Supreme Court, and in such inferior courts as the Congress may, from time to time, ordain and establish."(1)

That there ought to be one court of supreme and final jurisdiction, is a proposition which is not likely to be contested. The reasons for it have been assigned in another place, and are too obvious to need repetition. The only question that seems to have been raised concerning it, is, whether it ought to be a distinct body or a branch of the legislature. The same contradiction is observable in regard to this matter which has been remarked in several other cases. The very men who object to the Senate as a court of impeachments, on the ground of an improper intermixture of powers, advocate, by implication at least, the propriety of vesting the ultimate decision of all causes, in the whole or in a part of the legislative body.

Documents of Revolution

The arguments, or rather suggestions, upon which this charge is founded, are to this effect: "The authority of the proposed Supreme Court of the United States, which is to be a separate and independent body, will be superior to that of the legislature. The power of construing the laws according to the spirit of the Constitution, will enable that court to mould them into whatever shape it may think proper; especially as its decisions will not be in any manner subject to the revision or correction of the legislative body. This is as unprecedented as it is dangerous. In Britain, the judicial power, in the last resort, resides in the House of Lords, which is a branch of the legislature; and this part of the British government has been imitated in the State constitutions in general. The Parliament of Great Britain, and the legislatures of the several States, can at any time rectify, by law, the exceptionable decisions of their respective courts. But the errors and usurpations of the Supreme Court of the United States will be uncontrollable and remediless." This, upon examination, will be found to be made up altogether of false reasoning upon misconceived fact.

In the first place, there is not a syllable in the plan under consideration which directly empowers the national courts to construe the laws according to the spirit of the Constitution, or which gives them any greater latitude in this respect than may be claimed by the courts of every State. I admit, however, that the Constitution ought to be the standard of construction for the laws, and that wherever there is an evident opposition, the laws ought to give place to the Constitution. But this doctrine is not deducible from any circumstance peculiar to the plan of the convention, but from the general theory of a limited Constitution; and as far as it is true, is equally applicable to most, if not to all the State governments. There can be no objection, therefore, on this account, to the federal judicature which will not lie against the local judicatures in general, and which will not serve to condemn every constitution that attempts to set bounds to legislative discretion.

But perhaps the force of the objection may be thought to consist in the particular organization of the Supreme Court; in its being composed of a distinct body of magistrates, instead of being one of the branches of the legislature, as in the government of Great Britain and that of the State. To insist upon this point, the authors of the objection must renounce the meaning they have labored to annex to the celebrated maxim, requiring a separation of the departments of power. It shall, nevertheless, be conceded to them, agreeably to the interpretation given to that maxim in the course of these papers, that it is not violated by vesting the ultimate power of judging in a PART of the legislative body. But though this be not an absolute violation of that excellent rule, yet it verges so nearly upon it, as on this account alone to be less eligible than the mode preferred by the convention. From a body which had even a partial agency in passing bad laws, we could rarely expect a disposition to temper and moderate them in the application. The same spirit which had operated in making them, would be too apt in interpreting them; still less could it be expected that men who had infringed the Constitution in the character of legislators, would be disposed to repair the breach in the character of judges. Nor is this all. Every reason which recommends the tenure of good behavior for judicial offices, militates against placing the judiciary power, in the last resort, in a body composed of men chosen for a limited period. There is an absurdity in referring the determination of causes, in the first instance, to judges of permanent standing; in the last, to those of a temporary and mutable constitution. And there is a still greater absurdity in subjecting the decisions of men, selected for their knowledge of the laws, acquired by long and laborious study, to the revision and control of men who, for want of the same advantage, cannot but be deficient in that knowledge. The members of the legislature will rarely be chosen with a view to those qualifications which fit men for the stations of judges; and as, on this account, there will be great reason to apprehend all the ill consequences of defective information, so, on account of the natural propensity of such bodies to party divisions, there will be no less reason to fear that the pestilential breath of faction may poison the fountains of justice. The habit of being continually marshalled on opposite sides will be too apt to stifle the voice both of law and of equity.

These considerations teach us to applaud the wisdom of those States who have committed the judicial power, in the last resort, not to a part of the legislature, but to distinct and independent bodies of men. Contrary to the supposition of those who have represented the plan of the convention, in this respect, as novel and unprecedented, it is but a copy of the constitutions of New Hampshire, Massachusetts, Pennsylvania, Delaware, Maryland, Virginia, North Carolina, South Carolina, and Georgia; and the preference which has been given to those models is highly to be commended.

It is not true, in the second place, that the Parliament of Great Britain, or the legislatures of the particular States, can rectify the exceptionable decisions of their respective courts, in any other sense than might be done by a future legislature of the United States. The theory, neither of the British, nor the State constitutions, authorizes the revisal of a judicial sentence by a legislative act. Nor is there any thing in the proposed Constitution, more than in either of them, by which it is forbidden. In the former, as well as in the latter, the impropriety of the thing, on the general principles of law and reason, is the sole obstacle. A legislature, without exceeding its province, cannot reverse a determination once made in a particular case; though it may prescribe a new rule for future cases. This is the principle, and it applies in all its consequences, exactly in the same manner and extent, to the State governments, as to the national government now under consideration. Not the least difference can be pointed out in any view of the subject.

It may in the last place be observed that the supposed danger of judiciary encroachments on the legislative authority, which has been upon many occasions reiterated, is in reality a phantom. Particular misconstructions and contraventions of the will of the legislature may now and then happen; but they can never be so extensive as to amount to an inconvenience, or in any sensible degree to affect the order of the political system. This may be inferred with certainty, from the general nature of the judicial power, from the objects to which it relates, from the manner in which it is exercised, from its comparative weakness, and from its total incapacity to support its usurpations by force. And the inference is greatly fortified by the consideration of the important constitutional check which the power of instituting impeachments in one part of the legislative body, and of determining upon them in the other, would give to that body upon the members of the judicial department. This is alone a complete security. There never can be danger that the judges, by a series of deliberate usurpations on the authority of the legislature, would hazard the united resentment of the body intrusted with it, while this body was possessed of the means of punishing their presumption, by degrading them from their stations. While this ought to remove all apprehensions on the subject, it affords, at the same time, a cogent argument for constituting the Senate a court for the trial of impeachments.

Having now examined, and, I trust, removed the objections to the distinct and independent organization of the Supreme Court, I proceed to consider the propriety of the power of constituting inferior courts,(2) and the relations which will subsist between these and the former.

The power of constituting inferior courts is evidently calculated to obviate the necessity of having recourse to the Supreme Court in every case of federal cognizance. It is intended to enable the national government to institute or authorize, in each State or district of the United States, a tribunal competent to the determination of matters of national jurisdiction within its limits.

But why, it is asked, might not the same purpose have been accomplished by the instrumentality of the State courts? This admits of different answers. Though the fitness and competency of those courts should be allowed in the utmost latitude, yet the substance of the power in question may still be regarded as a necessary part of the plan, if it were only to empower the national legislature to commit to them the cognizance of causes arising out of the national Constitution. To confer the power of determining such causes upon the existing courts of the several States, would perhaps be as much "to constitute tribunals," as to create new courts with the like power. But ought not a more direct and explicit provision to have been made in favor of the State courts? There are, in my opinion, substantial reasons against such a provision: the most discerning cannot foresee how far the prevalency of a local spirit may be found to disqualify the local tribunals for the jurisdiction of national causes; whilst every man may discover, that courts constituted like those of some of the States would be improper channels of the judicial authority of the Union. State judges, holding their offices during pleasure, or from year to year, will be too little independent to be relied upon for an inflexible execution of the national laws. And if there was a necessity for confiding the original cognizance of causes arising under those laws to them there would be a correspondent necessity for leaving the door of appeal as wide as possible. In proportion to the grounds of confidence in, or distrust of, the subordinate tribunals, ought to be the facility or difficulty of appeals. And well satisfied as I am of the propriety of the appellate jurisdiction, in the several classes of causes to which it is extended by the plan of the convention. I should consider every thing calculated to give, in practice, an unrestrained course to appeals, as a source of public and private inconvenience.

I am not sure, but that it will be found highly expedient and useful, to divide the United States into four or five or half a dozen districts; and to institute a federal court in each district, in lieu of one in every State. The judges of these courts, with the aid of the State judges, may hold circuits for the trial of causes in the several parts of the respective districts. Justice through them may be administered with ease and despatch; and appeals may be safely circumscribed within a narrow compass. This plan appears to me at present the most eligible of any that could be adopted; and in order to it, it is necessary that the power of constituting inferior courts should exist in the full extent in which it is to be found in the proposed Constitution.

These reasons seem sufficient to satisfy a candid mind, that the want of such a power would have been a great defect in the plan. Let us now examine in what manner the judicial authority is to be distributed between the supreme and the inferior courts of the Union.

The Supreme Court is to be invested with original jurisdiction, only "in cases affecting ambassadors, other public ministers, and consuls, and those in which A STATE shall be a party." Public ministers of every class are the immediate representatives of their sovereigns. All questions in which they are concerned are so directly connected with the public peace, that, as well for the preservation of this, as out of respect to the sovereignties they represent, it is both expedient and proper that such questions should be submitted in the first instance to the highest judicatory of the nation. Though consuls have not in strictness a diplomatic character, yet as they are the public agents of the nations to which they belong, the same observation is in a great measure applicable to them. In cases in which a State might happen to be a party, it would ill suit its dignity to be turned over to an inferior tribunal.

Though it may rather be a digression from the immediate subject of this paper, I shall take occasion to mention here a supposition which has excited some alarm upon very mistaken grounds. It has been suggested that an assignment of the public securities of one State to the citizens of another, would enable them to prosecute that State in the federal courts for the amount of those securities; a suggestion which the following considerations prove to be without foundation.

It is inherent in the nature of sovereignty not to be amenable to the suit of an individual without its consent. This is the general sense, and the general practice of mankind; and the exemption, as one of the attributes of sovereignty, is now enjoyed by the government of every State in the Union. Unless, therefore, there is a surrender of this immunity in the plan of the convention, it will remain with the States, and the danger intimated must be merely ideal. The circumstances which are necessary to produce an alienation of State sovereignty were discussed in considering the article of taxation, and need not be repeated here. A recurrence to the principles there established will satisfy us, that there is no color to pretend that the State governments would, by the adoption of that plan, be divested of the privilege of paying their own debts in their own way, free from every constraint but that which flows from the obligations of good faith. The contracts between a nation and individuals are only binding on the conscience of the sovereign, and have no pretensions to a compulsive force. They confer no right of action, independent of the sovereign will. To what purpose would it be to authorize suits against States for the debts they owe? How could recoveries be enforced? It is evident, it could not be done without waging war against the contracting State; and to ascribe to the federal courts, by mere implication, and in destruction of a pre-existing right of the State governments, a power which would involve such a consequence, would be altogether forced and unwarrantable.

Let us resume the train of our observations. We have seen that the original jurisdiction of the Supreme Court would be confined to two classes of causes, and those of a nature rarely to occur. In all other cases of federal cognizance, the original jurisdiction would appertain to the inferior tribunals; and the Supreme Court would have nothing more than an appellate jurisdiction, "with such exceptions and under such regulations as the Congress shall make."

The propriety of this appellate jurisdiction has been scarcely called in question in regard to matters of law; but the clamors have been loud against it as applied to matters of fact. Some well-intentioned men in this State, deriving their notions from the language and forms which obtain in our courts, have been induced to consider it as an implied supersedure of the trial by jury, in favor of the civil-law mode of trial, which prevails in our courts of admiralty, probate, and chancery. A technical sense has been affixed to the term "appellate," which, in our law parlance, is commonly used in reference to appeals in the course of the civil law. But if I am not misinformed, the same meaning would not be given to it in any part of New England. There an appeal from one jury to another, is familiar both in language and practice, and is even a matter of course, until there have been two verdicts on one side. The word "appellate," therefore, will not be understood in the same sense in New England as in New York, which shows the impropriety of a technical interpretation derived from the jurisprudence of any particular State. The expression, taken in the abstract, denotes nothing more than the power of one tribunal to review the proceedings of another, either as to the law or fact, or both. The mode of doing it may depend on ancient custom or legislative provision (in a new government it must depend on the latter), and may be with or without the aid of a jury, as may be judged advisable. If, therefore, the re-examination of a fact once determined by a jury, should in any case be admitted under the proposed Constitution, it may be so regulated as to be done by a second jury, either by remanding the cause to the court below for a second trial of the fact, or by directing an issue immediately out of the Supreme Court.

But it does not follow that the re-examination of a fact once ascertained by a jury, will be permitted in the Supreme Court. Why may not it be said, with the strictest propriety, when a writ of error is brought from an inferior to a superior court of law in this State, that the latter has jurisdiction of the fact as well as the law? It is true it cannot institute a new inquiry concerning the fact, but it takes cognizance of it as it appears upon the record, and pronounces the law arising upon it.(3) This is jurisdiction of both fact and law; nor is it even possible to separate them. Though the common-law courts of this State ascertain disputed facts by a jury, yet they unquestionably have jurisdiction of both fact and law; and accordingly when the former is agreed in the pleadings, they have no recourse to a jury, but proceed at once to judgment. I contend, therefore, on this ground, that the expressions, "appellate jurisdiction, both as to law and fact," do not necessarily imply a re-examination in the Supreme Court of facts decided by juries in the inferior courts.

The following train of ideas may well be imagined to have influenced the convention, in relation to this particular provision. The appellate jurisdiction of the Supreme Court (it may have been argued) will extend to causes determinable in different modes, some in the course of the COMMON LAW, others in the course of the CIVIL LAW. In the former, the revision of the law only will be, generally speaking, the proper province of the Supreme Court; in the latter, the re-examination of the fact is agreeable to usage, and in some cases, of which prize causes are an example, might be essential to the preservation of the public peace. It is therefore necessary that the appellate jurisdiction should, in certain cases, extend in the broadest sense to matters of fact. It will not answer to make an express exception of cases which shall have been originally tried by a jury, because in the courts of some of the States all causes are tried in this mode(4); and such an exception would preclude the revision of matters of fact, as well where it might be proper, as where it might be improper. To avoid all inconveniencies, it will be safest to declare generally, that the Supreme Court shall possess appellate jurisdiction both as to law and fact, and that this jurisdiction shall be subject to such exceptions and regulations as the national legislature may prescribe. This will enable the government to modify it in such a manner as will best answer the ends of public justice and security.

This view of the matter, at any rate, puts it out of all doubt that the supposed abolition of the trial by jury, by the operation of this provision, is fallacious and untrue. The legislature of the United States would certainly have full power to provide, that in appeals to the Supreme Court there should be no re-examination of facts where they had been tried in the original causes by juries. This would certainly be an authorized exception; but if, for the reason already intimated, it should be thought too extensive, it might be qualified with a limitation to such causes only as are determinable at common law in that mode of trial.

The amount of the observations hitherto made on the authority of the judicial department is this: that it has been carefully restricted to those causes which are manifestly proper for the cognizance of the national judicature; that in the partition of this authority a very small portion of original jurisdiction has been preserved to the Supreme Court, and the rest consigned to the subordinate tribunals; that the Supreme Court will possess an appellate jurisdiction, both as to law and fact, in all the cases referred to them, both subject to any exceptions and regulations which may be thought advisable; that this appellate jurisdiction does, in no case, abolish the trial by jury; and that an ordinary degree of prudence and integrity in the national councils will insure us solid advantages from the establishment of the proposed judiciary, without exposing us to any of the inconveniences which have been predicted from that source.

PUBLIUS

1. Article 3, Sec. 1.

2. This power has been absurdly represented as intended to abolish all the county courts in the several States, which are commonly called inferior courts. But the expressions of the Constitution are, to constitute "tribunals INFERIOR TO THE SUPREME COURT"; and the evident design of the provision is to enable the institution of local courts, subordinate to the Supreme, either in States or larger districts. It is ridiculous to imagine that county courts were in contemplation.

3. This word is composed of JUS and DICTIO, juris dictio or a speaking and pronouncing of the law.

4. I hold that the States will have concurrent jurisdiction with the subordinate federal judicatories, in many cases of federal cognizance, as will be explained in my next paper.

FEDERALIST PAPER NO. 82. THE JUDICIARY CONTINUED.

From McLEAN's Edition, New York. Wednesday, May 28, 1788

HAMILTON
To the People of the State of New York:

THE erection of a new government, whatever care or wisdom may distinguish the work, cannot fail to originate questions of intricacy and nicety; and these may, in a particular manner, be expected to flow from the establishment of a constitution founded upon the total or partial incorporation of a number of distinct sovereignties. 'Tis time only that can mature and perfect so compound a system, can liquidate the meaning of all the parts, and can adjust them to each other in a harmonious and consistent WHOLE.

Such questions, accordingly, have arisen upon the plan proposed by the convention, and particularly concerning the judiciary department. The principal of these respect the situation of the State courts in regard to those causes which are to be submitted to federal jurisdiction. Is this to be exclusive, or are those courts to possess a concurrent jurisdiction? If the latter, in what relation will they stand to the national tribunals? These are inquiries which we meet with in the mouths of men of sense, and which are certainly entitled to attention.

The principles established in a former paper(1) teach us that the States will retain all pre-existing authorities which may not be exclusively delegated to the federal head; and that this exclusive delegation can only exist in one of three cases: where an exclusive authority is, in express terms, granted to the Union; or where a particular authority is granted to the Union, and the exercise of a like authority is prohibited to the States; or where an authority is granted to the Union, with which a similar authority in the States would be utterly incompatible. Though these principles may not apply with the same force to the judiciary as to the legislative power, yet I am inclined to think that they are, in the main, just with respect to the former, as well as the latter. And under this impression, I shall lay it down as a rule, that the State courts will retain the jurisdiction they now have, unless it appears to be taken away in one of the enumerated modes.

The only thing in the proposed Constitution, which wears the appearance of confining the causes of federal cognizance to the federal courts, is contained in this passage: "THE JUDICIAL POWER of the United States shall be vested in one Supreme Court, and in such inferior courts as the Congress shall from time to time ordain and establish." This might either be construed to signify, that the supreme and subordinate courts of the Union should alone have the power of deciding those causes to which their authority is to extend; or simply to denote, that the organs of the national judiciary should be one Supreme Court, and as many subordinate courts as Congress should think proper to appoint; or in other words, that the United States should exercise the judicial power with which they are to be invested, through one supreme tribunal, and a certain number of inferior ones, to be instituted by them. The first excludes, the last admits, the concurrent jurisdiction of the State tribunals; and as the first would amount to an alienation of State power by implication, the last appears to me the most natural and the most defensible construction.

But this doctrine of concurrent jurisdiction is only clearly applicable to those descriptions of causes of which the State courts have previous cognizance. It is not equally evident in relation to cases which may grow out of, and be peculiar to, the Constitution to be established; for not to allow the State courts a right of jurisdiction in such cases, can hardly be considered as the abridgment of a pre-existing authority. I mean not therefore to contend that the United States, in the course of legislation upon the objects intrusted to their direction, may not commit the decision of causes arising upon a particular regulation to the federal courts solely, if such a measure should be deemed expedient; but I hold that the State courts will be divested of no part of their primitive jurisdiction, further than may relate to an appeal; and I am even of opinion that in every case in which they were not expressly excluded by the future acts of the national legislature, they will of course take cognizance of the causes to which those acts may give birth. This I infer from the nature of judiciary power, and from the general genius of the system. The judiciary power of every government looks beyond its own local or municipal laws, and in civil cases lays hold of all subjects of litigation between parties within its jurisdiction, though the causes of dispute are relative to the laws of the most distant part of the globe. Those of Japan, not less than of New York, may furnish the objects of legal discussion to our courts. When in addition to this we consider the State governments and the national governments, as they truly are, in the light of kindred systems, and as parts of ONE WHOLE, the inference seems to be conclusive, that the State courts would have a concurrent jurisdiction in all cases arising under the laws of the Union, where it was not expressly prohibited.

Here another question occurs: What relation would subsist between the national and State courts in these instances of concurrent jurisdiction? I answer, that an appeal would certainly lie from the latter, to the Supreme Court of the United States. The Constitution in direct terms gives an appellate jurisdiction to the Supreme Court in all the enumerated cases of federal cognizance in which it is not to have an original one, without a single expression to confine its operation to the inferior federal courts. The objects of appeal, not the tribunals from which it is to be made, are alone contemplated. From this circumstance, and from the reason of the thing, it ought to be construed to extend to the State tribunals. Either this must be the case, or the local courts must be excluded from a concurrent jurisdiction in matters of national concern, else the judiciary authority of the Union may be eluded at the pleasure of every plaintiff or prosecutor. Neither of these consequences ought, without evident necessity, to be involved; the latter would be entirely inadmissible, as it would defeat some of the most important and avowed purposes of the proposed government, and would essentially embarrass its measures. Nor do I perceive any foundation for such a supposition. Agreeably to the remark already made, the national and State systems are to be regarded as ONE WHOLE. The courts of the latter will of course be natural auxiliaries to the execution of the laws of the Union, and an appeal from them will as naturally lie to that tribunal which is destined to unite and assimilate the principles of national justice and the rules of national decisions. The evident aim of the plan of the convention is, that all the causes of the specified classes shall, for weighty public reasons, receive their original or final determination in the courts of the Union. To confine, therefore, the general expressions giving appellate jurisdiction to the Supreme Court, to appeals from the subordinate federal courts, instead of allowing their extension to the State courts, would be to abridge the latitude of the terms, in subversion of the intent, contrary to every sound rule of interpretation.

But could an appeal be made to lie from the State courts to the subordinate federal judicatories? This is another of the questions which have been raised, and of greater difficulty than the former. The following considerations countenance the affirmative. The plan of the convention, in the first place, authorizes the national legislature "to constitute tribunals inferior to the Supreme Court."(2) It declares, in the next place, that "the JUDICIAL POWER of the United States shall be vested in one Supreme Court, and in such inferior courts as Congress shall ordain and establish"; and it then proceeds to enumerate the cases to which this judicial power shall extend. It afterwards divides the jurisdiction of the Supreme Court into original and appellate, but gives no definition of that of the subordinate courts. The only outlines described for them, are that they shall be "inferior to the Supreme Court," and that they shall not exceed the specified limits of the federal judiciary. Whether their authority shall be original or appellate, or both, is not declared. All this seems to be left to the discretion of the legislature. And this being the case, I perceive at present no impediment to the establishment of an appeal from the State courts to the subordinate national tribunals; and many advantages attending the power of doing it may be imagined. It would diminish the motives to the multiplication of federal courts, and would admit of arrangements calculated to contract the appellate jurisdiction of the Supreme Court. The State tribunals may then be left with a more entire charge of federal causes; and appeals, in most cases in which they may be deemed proper, instead of being carried to the Supreme Court, may be made to lie from the State courts to district courts of the Union.

PUBLIUS

1. No. 31.
2. Sec. 8, Art. 1.

FEDERALIST PAPER NO. 83. THE JUDICIARY CONTINUED IN RELATION TO TRIAL BY JURY

From MCLEAN's Edition, New York. Wednesday, May 28, 1788

HAMILTON

To the People of the State of New York:

THE objection to the plan of the convention, which has met with most success in this State, and perhaps in several of the other States, is that relative to the want of a constitutional provision for the trial by jury in civil cases. The disingenuous form in which this objection is usually stated has been repeatedly adverted to and exposed, but continues to be pursued in all the conversations and writings of the opponents of the plan. The mere silence of the Constitution in regard to civil causes, is represented as an abolition of the trial by jury, and the declamations to which it has afforded a pretext are artfully calculated to induce a persuasion that this pretended abolition is complete and universal, extending not only to every species of civil, but even to criminal causes. To argue with respect to the latter would, however, be as vain and fruitless as to attempt the serious proof of the existence of matter, or to demonstrate any of those propositions which, by their own internal evidence, force conviction, when expressed in language adapted to convey their meaning.

With regard to civil causes, subtleties almost too contemptible for refutation have been employed to countenance the surmise that a thing which is only not provided for, is entirely abolished. Every man of discernment must at once perceive the wide difference between silence and abolition. But as the inventors of this fallacy have attempted to support it by certain legal maxims of interpretation, which they have perverted from their true meaning, it may not be wholly useless to explore the ground they have taken.

The maxims on which they rely are of this nature: "A specification of particulars is an exclusion of generals"; or, "The expression of one thing is the exclusion of another." Hence, say they, as the Constitution has established the trial by jury in criminal cases, and is silent in respect to civil, this silence is an implied prohibition of trial by jury in regard to the latter.

The rules of legal interpretation are rules of common sense, adopted by the courts in the construction of the laws. The true test, therefore, of a just application of them is its conformity to the source from which they are derived. This being the case, let me ask if it is consistent with common-sense to suppose that a provision obliging the legislative power to commit the trial of criminal causes to juries, is a privation of its right to authorize or permit that mode of trial in other cases? Is it natural to suppose, that a command to do one thing is a prohibition to the doing of another, which there was a previous power to do, and which is not incompatible with the thing commanded to be done? If such a supposition would be unnatural and unreasonable, it cannot be rational to maintain that an injunction of the trial by jury in certain cases is an interdiction of it in others.

A power to constitute courts is a power to prescribe the mode of trial; and consequently, if nothing was said in the Constitution on the subject of juries, the legislature would be at liberty either to adopt that institution or to let it alone. This discretion, in regard to criminal causes, is abridged by the express injunction of trial by jury in all such cases; but it is, of course, left at large in relation to civil causes, there being a total silence on this head. The specification of an obligation to try all criminal causes in a particular mode, excludes indeed the obligation or necessity of employing the same mode in civil causes, but does not abridge the power of the legislature to exercise that mode if it should be thought proper. The pretense, therefore, that the national legislature would not be at full liberty to submit all the civil causes of federal cognizance to the determination of juries, is a pretense destitute of all just foundation.

From these observations this conclusion results: that the trial by jury in civil cases would not be abolished; and that the use attempted to be made of the maxims which have been quoted, is contrary to reason and common-sense, and therefore not admissible. Even if these maxims had a precise technical sense, corresponding with the idea of those who employ them upon the present occasion, which, however, is not the case, they would still be inapplicable to a constitution of government. In relation to such a subject, the natural and obvious sense of its provisions, apart from any technical rules, is the true criterion of construction.

Documents of Revolution

Having now seen that the maxims relied upon will not bear the use made of them, let us endeavor to ascertain their proper use and true meaning. This will be best done by examples. The plan of the convention declares that the power of Congress, or, in other words, of the national legislature, shall extend to certain enumerated cases. This specification of particulars evidently excludes all pretension to a general legislative authority, because an affirmative grant of special powers would be absurd, as well as useless, if a general authority was intended.

In like manner the judicial authority of the federal judicatures is declared by the Constitution to comprehend certain cases particularly specified. The expression of those cases marks the precise limits, beyond which the federal courts cannot extend their jurisdiction, because the objects of their cognizance being enumerated, the specification would be nugatory if it did not exclude all ideas of more extensive authority.

These examples are sufficient to elucidate the maxims which have been mentioned, and to designate the manner in which they should be used. But that there may be no misapprehensions upon this subject, I shall add one case more, to demonstrate the proper use of these maxims, and the abuse which has been made of them.

Let us suppose that by the laws of this State a married woman was incapable of conveying her estate, and that the legislature, considering this as an evil, should enact that she might dispose of her property by deed executed in the presence of a magistrate. In such a case there can be no doubt but the specification would amount to an exclusion of any other mode of conveyance, because the woman having no previous power to alienate her property, the specification determines the particular mode which she is, for that purpose, to avail herself of. But let us further suppose that in a subsequent part of the same act it should be declared that no woman should dispose of any estate of a determinate value without the consent of three of her nearest relations, signified by their signing the deed; could it be inferred from this regulation that a married woman might not procure the approbation of her relations to a deed for conveying property of inferior value? The position is too absurd to merit a refutation, and yet this is precisely the position which those must establish who contend that the trial by juries in civil cases is abolished, because it is expressly provided for in cases of a criminal nature.

From these observations it must appear unquestionably true, that trial by jury is in no case abolished by the proposed Constitution, and it is equally true, that in those controversies between individuals in which the great body of the people are likely to be interested, that institution will remain precisely in the same situation in which it is placed by the State constitutions, and will be in no degree altered or influenced by the adoption of the plan under consideration. The foundation of this assertion is, that the national judiciary will have no cognizance of them, and of course they will remain determinable as heretofore by the State courts only, and in the manner which the State constitutions and laws prescribe. All land causes, except where claims under the grants of different States come into question, and all other controversies between the citizens of the same State, unless where they depend upon positive violations of the articles of union, by acts of the State legislatures, will belong exclusively to the jurisdiction of the State tribunals. Add to this, that admiralty causes, and almost all those which are of equity jurisdiction, are determinable under our own government without the intervention of a jury, and the inference from the whole will be, that this institution, as it exists with us at present, cannot possibly be affected to any great extent by the proposed alteration in our system of government.

The friends and adversaries of the plan of the convention, if they agree in nothing else, concur at least in the value they set upon the trial by jury; or if there is any difference between them it consists in this: the former regard it as a valuable safeguard to liberty; the latter represent it as the very palladium of free government. For my own part, the more the operation of the institution has fallen under my observation, the more reason I have discovered for holding it in high estimation; and it would be altogether superfluous to examine to what extent it deserves to be esteemed useful or essential in a representative republic, or how much more merit it may be entitled to, as a defense against the oppressions of an hereditary monarch, than as a barrier to the tyranny of popular magistrates in a popular government. Discussions of this kind would be more curious than beneficial, as all are satisfied of the utility of the institution, and of its friendly aspect to liberty. But I must acknowledge that I cannot readily discern the inseparable connection between the existence of liberty, and the trial by jury in civil cases. Arbitrary impeachments, arbitrary methods of prosecuting pretended offenses, and arbitrary punishments upon arbitrary convictions, have ever appeared to me to be the great engines of judicial despotism; and these have all relation to criminal proceedings. The trial by jury in criminal cases, aided by the habeas corpus act, seems therefore to be alone concerned in the question. And both of these are provided for, in the most ample manner, in the plan of the convention.

It has been observed, that trial by jury is a safeguard against an oppressive exercise of the power of taxation. This observation deserves to be canvassed.

Documents of Revolution

It is evident that it can have no influence upon the legislature, in regard to the amount of taxes to be laid, to the objects upon which they are to be imposed, or to the rule by which they are to be apportioned. If it can have any influence, therefore, it must be upon the mode of collection, and the conduct of the officers intrusted with the execution of the revenue laws.

As to the mode of collection in this State, under our own Constitution, the trial by jury is in most cases out of use. The taxes are usually levied by the more summary proceeding of distress and sale, as in cases of rent. And it is acknowledged on all hands, that this is essential to the efficacy of the revenue laws. The dilatory course of a trial at law to recover the taxes imposed on individuals, would neither suit the exigencies of the public nor promote the convenience of the citizens. It would often occasion an accumulation of costs, more burdensome than the original sum of the tax to be levied.

And as to the conduct of the officers of the revenue, the provision in favor of trial by jury in criminal cases, will afford the security aimed at. Wilful abuses of a public authority, to the oppression of the subject, and every species of official extortion, are offenses against the government, for which the persons who commit them may be indicted and punished according to the circumstances of the case.

The excellence of the trial by jury in civil cases appears to depend on circumstances foreign to the preservation of liberty. The strongest argument in its favor is, that it is a security against corruption. As there is always more time and better opportunity to tamper with a standing body of magistrates than with a jury summoned for the occasion, there is room to suppose that a corrupt influence would more easily find its way to the former than to the latter. The force of this consideration is, however, diminished by others. The sheriff, who is the summoner of ordinary juries, and the clerks of courts, who have the nomination of special juries, are themselves standing officers, and, acting individually, may be supposed more accessible to the touch of corruption than the judges, who are a collective body. It is not difficult to see, that it would be in the power of those officers to select jurors who would serve the purpose of the party as well as a corrupted bench. In the next place, it may fairly be supposed, that there would be less difficulty in gaining some of the jurors promiscuously taken from the public mass, than in gaining men who had been chosen by the government for their probity and good character. But making every deduction for these considerations, the trial by jury must still be a valuable check upon corruption. It greatly multiplies the impediments to its success. As matters now stand, it would be necessary to corrupt both court and jury; for where the jury have gone evidently wrong, the court will generally grant a new trial, and it would be in most cases of little use to practice upon the jury, unless the court could be likewise gained. Here then is a double security; and it will readily be perceived that this complicated agency tends to preserve the purity of both institutions. By increasing the obstacles to success, it discourages attempts to seduce the integrity of either. The temptations to prostitution which the judges might have to surmount, must certainly be much fewer, while the co-operation of a jury is necessary, than they might be, if they had themselves the exclusive determination of all causes.

Notwithstanding, therefore, the doubts I have expressed, as to the essentiality of trial by jury in civil cases to liberty, I admit that it is in most cases, under proper regulations, an excellent method of determining questions of property; and that on this account alone it would be entitled to a constitutional provision in its favor if it were possible to fix the limits within which it ought to be comprehended. There is, however, in all cases, great difficulty in this; and men not blinded by enthusiasm must be sensible that in a federal government, which is a composition of societies whose ideas and institutions in relation to the matter materially vary from each other, that difficulty must be not a little augmented. For my own part, at every new view I take of the subject, I become more convinced of the reality of the obstacles which, we are authoritatively informed, prevented the insertion of a provision on this head in the plan of the convention.

The great difference between the limits of the jury trial in different States is not generally understood; and as it must have considerable influence on the sentence we ought to pass upon the omission complained of in regard to this point, an explanation of it is necessary. In this State, our judicial establishments resemble, more nearly than in any other, those of Great Britain. We have courts of common law, courts of probates (analogous in certain matters to the spiritual courts in England), a court of admiralty and a court of chancery. In the courts of common law only, the trial by jury prevails, and this with some exceptions. In all the others a single judge presides, and proceeds in general either according to the course of the canon or civil law, without the aid of a jury.(1) In New Jersey, there is a court of chancery which proceeds like ours, but neither courts of admiralty nor of probates, in the sense in which these last are established with us. In that State the courts of common law have the cognizance of those causes which with us are determinable in the courts of admiralty and of probates, and of course the jury trial is more extensive in New Jersey than in New York. In Pennsylvania, this is perhaps still more the case, for there is no court of chancery in that State, and its common-law courts have equity jurisdiction. It has a court of admiralty, but none of probates, at least on the plan of ours. Delaware has in these respects imitated Pennsylvania. Maryland approaches more nearly to New York, as does also Virginia, except that the latter has a plurality of chancellors. North Carolina bears most affinity to

Pennsylvania; South Carolina to Virginia. I believe, however, that in some of those States which have distinct courts of admiralty, the causes depending in them are triable by juries. In Georgia there are none but common-law courts, and an appeal of course lies from the verdict of one jury to another, which is called a special jury, and for which a particular mode of appointment is marked out. In Connecticut, they have no distinct courts either of chancery or of admiralty, and their courts of probates have no jurisdiction of causes. Their common-law courts have admiralty and, to a certain extent, equity jurisdiction. In cases of importance, their General Assembly is the only court of chancery. In Connecticut, therefore, the trial by jury extends in practice further than in any other State yet mentioned. Rhode Island is, I believe, in this particular, pretty much in the situation of Connecticut. Massachusetts and New Hampshire, in regard to the blending of law, equity, and admiralty jurisdictions, are in a similar predicament. In the four Eastern States, the trial by jury not only stands upon a broader foundation than in the other States, but it is attended with a peculiarity unknown, in its full extent, to any of them. There is an appeal of course from one jury to another, till there have been two verdicts out of three on one side.

From this sketch it appears that there is a material diversity, as well in the modification as in the extent of the institution of trial by jury in civil cases, in the several States; and from this fact these obvious reflections flow: first, that no general rule could have been fixed upon by the convention which would have corresponded with the circumstances of all the States; and secondly, that more or at least as much might have been hazarded by taking the system of any one State for a standard, as by omitting a provision altogether and leaving the matter, as has been done, to legislative regulation.

The propositions which have been made for supplying the omission have rather served to illustrate than to obviate the difficulty of the thing. The minority of Pennsylvania have proposed this mode of expression for the purpose—"Trial by jury shall be as heretofore"—and this I maintain would be senseless and nugatory. The United States, in their united or collective capacity, are the OBJECT to which all general provisions in the Constitution must necessarily be construed to refer. Now it is evident that though trial by jury, with various limitations, is known in each State individually, yet in the United States, as such, it is at this time altogether unknown, because the present federal government has no judiciary power whatever; and consequently there is no proper antecedent or previous establishment to which the term heretofore could relate. It would therefore be destitute of a precise meaning, and inoperative from its uncertainty.

As, on the one hand, the form of the provision would not fulfil the intent of its proposers, so, on the other, if I apprehend that intent rightly, it would be in itself inexpedient. I presume it to be, that causes in the federal courts should be tried by jury, if, in the State where the courts sat, that mode of trial would obtain in a similar case in the State courts; that is to say, admiralty causes should be tried in Connecticut by a jury, in New York without one. The capricious operation of so dissimilar a method of trial in the same cases, under the same government, is of itself sufficient to indispose every wellregulated judgment towards it. Whether the cause should be tried with or without a jury, would depend, in a great number of cases, on the accidental situation of the court and parties.

But this is not, in my estimation, the greatest objection. I feel a deep and deliberate conviction that there are many cases in which the trial by jury is an ineligible one. I think it so particularly in cases which concern the public peace with foreign nations—that is, in most cases where the question turns wholly on the laws of nations. Of this nature, among others, are all prize causes. Juries cannot be supposed competent to investigations that require a thorough knowledge of the laws and usages of nations; and they will sometimes be under the influence of impressions which will not suffer them to pay sufficient regard to those considerations of public policy which ought to guide their inquiries. There would of course be always danger that the rights of other nations might be infringed by their decisions, so as to afford occasions of reprisal and war. Though the proper province of juries be to determine matters of fact, yet in most cases legal consequences are complicated with fact in such a manner as to render a separation impracticable.

It will add great weight to this remark, in relation to prize causes, to mention that the method of determining them has been thought worthy of particular regulation in various treaties between different powers of Europe, and that, pursuant to such treaties, they are determinable in Great Britain, in the last resort, before the king himself, in his privy council, where the fact, as well as the law, undergoes a re-examination. This alone demonstrates the impolicy of inserting a fundamental provision in the Constitution which would make the State systems a standard for the national government in the article under consideration, and the danger of encumbering the government with any constitutional provisions the propriety of which is not indisputable.

My convictions are equally strong that great advantages result from the separation of the equity from the law jurisdiction, and that the causes which belong to the former would be improperly committed to juries. The great and primary use of a court of equity is to give relief in extraordinary cases, which are exceptions(2) to general rules. To unite the jurisdiction of such cases with the ordinary jurisdiction, must have a tendency to unsettle the general rules, and to subject every case that arises to a special determination; while a separation of the one from the other has the contrary effect of rendering one a sentinel over the other, and of keeping each within the expedient limits. Besides this, the circumstances that constitute cases proper for courts of equity are in many instances so nice and intricate, that they are incompatible with the genius of trials by jury. They require often such long, deliberate, and critical investigation as would be impracticable to men called from their occupations, and obliged to decide before they were permitted to return to them. The simplicity and expedition which form the distinguishing characters of this mode of trial require that the matter to be decided should be reduced to some single and obvious point; while the litigations usual in chancery frequently comprehend a long train of minute and independent particulars.

It is true that the separation of the equity from the legal jurisdiction is peculiar to the English system of jurisprudence: which is the model that has been followed in several of the States. But it is equally true that the trial by jury has been unknown in every case in which they have been united. And the separation is essential to the preservation of that institution in its pristine purity. The nature of a court of equity will readily permit the extension of its jurisdiction to matters of law; but it is not a little to be suspected, that the attempt to extend the jurisdiction of the courts of law to matters of equity will not only be unproductive of the advantages which may be derived from courts of chancery, on the plan upon which they are established in this State, but will tend gradually to change the nature of the courts of law, and to undermine the trial by jury, by introducing questions too complicated for a decision in that mode.

These appeared to be conclusive reasons against incorporating the systems of all the States, in the formation of the national judiciary, according to what may be conjectured to have been the attempt of the Pennsylvania minority. Let us now examine how far the proposition of Massachusetts is calculated to remedy the supposed defect.

It is in this form: "In civil actions between citizens of different States, every issue of fact, arising in actions at common law, may be tried by a jury if the parties, or either of them request it."

This, at best, is a proposition confined to one description of causes; and the inference is fair, either that the Massachusetts convention considered that as the only class of federal causes, in which the trial by jury would be proper; or that if desirous of a more extensive provision, they found it impracticable to devise one which would properly answer the end. If the first, the omission of a regulation respecting so partial an object can never be considered as a material imperfection in the system. If the last, it affords a strong corroboration of the extreme difficulty of the thing.

But this is not all: if we advert to the observations already made respecting the courts that subsist in the several States of the Union, and the different powers exercised by them, it will appear that there are no expressions more vague and indeterminate than those which have been employed to characterize that species of causes which it is intended shall be entitled to a trial by jury. In this State, the boundaries between actions at common law and actions of equitable jurisdiction, are ascertained in conformity to the rules which prevail in England upon that subject. In many of the other States the boundaries are less precise. In some of them every cause is to be tried in a court of common law, and upon that foundation every action may be considered as an action at common law, to be determined by a jury, if the parties, or either of them, choose it. Hence the same irregularity and confusion would be introduced by a compliance with this proposition, that I have already noticed as resulting from the regulation proposed by the Pennsylvania minority. In one State a cause would receive its determination from a jury, if the parties, or either of them, requested it; but in another State, a cause exactly similar to the other, must be decided without the intervention of a jury, because the State judicatories varied as to common-law jurisdiction.

It is obvious, therefore, that the Massachusetts proposition, upon this subject cannot operate as a general regulation, until some uniform plan, with respect to the limits of common-law and equitable jurisdictions, shall be adopted by the different States. To devise a plan of that kind is a task arduous in itself, and which it would require much time and reflection to mature. It would be extremely difficult, if not impossible, to suggest any general regulation that would be acceptable to all the States in the Union, or that would perfectly quadrate with the several State institutions.

It may be asked, Why could not a reference have been made to the constitution of this State, taking that, which is allowed by me to be a good one, as a standard for the United States? I answer that it is not very probable the other States would entertain the same opinion of our institutions as we do ourselves. It is natural to suppose that they are hitherto more attached to their own, and that each would struggle for the preference. If the plan of taking one State as a model for the whole had been thought of in the convention, it is to be presumed that the adoption of it in that body would have been rendered difficult by the predilection of each representation in favor of its own government; and it must be uncertain which of the States would have been taken as the model. It has been shown that many of them would be improper ones. And I leave it to conjecture, whether, under all circumstances, it is most likely that New York, or some other State, would have been preferred. But admit that a judicious selection could have been effected in the convention, still there would have been great danger of jealousy and disgust in the other States, at the partiality which had been shown to the institutions of one. The enemies of the plan would have been furnished with a fine pretext for raising a host of local prejudices against it, which perhaps might have hazarded, in no inconsiderable degree, its final establishment.

To avoid the embarrassments of a definition of the cases which the trial by jury ought to embrace, it is sometimes suggested by men of enthusiastic tempers, that a provision might have been inserted for establishing it in all cases whatsoever. For this I believe, no precedent is to be found in any member of the Union; and the considerations which have been stated in discussing the proposition of the minority of Pennsylvania, must satisfy every sober mind that the establishment of the trial by jury in all cases would have been an unpardonable error in the plan.

In short, the more it is considered the more arduous will appear the task of fashioning a provision in such a form as not to express too little to answer the purpose, or too much to be advisable; or which might not have opened other sources of opposition to the great and essential object of introducing a firm national government.

I cannot but persuade myself, on the other hand, that the different lights in which the subject has been placed in the course of these observations, will go far towards removing in candid minds the apprehensions they may have entertained on the point. They have tended to show that the security of liberty is materially concerned only in the trial by jury in criminal cases, which is provided for in the most ample manner in the plan of the convention; that even in far the greatest proportion of civil cases, and those in which the great body of the community is interested, that mode of trial will remain in its full force, as established in the State constitutions, untouched and unaffected by the plan of the convention; that it is in no case abolished(3) by that plan; and that there are great if not insurmountable difficulties in the way of making any precise and proper provision for it in a Constitution for the United States.

The best judges of the matter will be the least anxious for a constitutional establishment of the trial by jury in civil cases, and will be the most ready to admit that the changes which are continually happening in the affairs of society may render a different mode of determining questions of property preferable in many cases in which that mode of trial now prevails. For my part, I acknowledge myself to be convinced that even in this State it might be advantageously extended to some cases to which it does not at present apply, and might as advantageously be abridged in others. It is conceded by all reasonable men that it ought not to obtain in all cases. The examples of innovations which contract its ancient limits, as well in these States as in Great Britain, afford a strong presumption that its former extent has been found inconvenient, and give room to suppose that future experience may discover the propriety and utility of other exceptions. I suspect it to be impossible in the nature of the thing to fix the salutary point at which the operation of the institution ought to stop, and this is with me a strong argument for leaving the matter to the discretion of the legislature.

This is now clearly understood to be the case in Great Britain, and it is equally so in the State of Connecticut; and yet it may be safely affirmed that more numerous encroachments have been made upon the trial by jury in this State since the Revolution, though provided for by a positive article of our constitution, than has happened in the same time either in Connecticut or Great Britain. It may be added that these encroachments have generally originated with the men who endeavor to persuade the people they are the warmest defenders of popular liberty, but who have rarely suffered constitutional obstacles to arrest them in a favorite career. The truth is that the general GENIUS of a government is all that can be substantially relied upon for permanent effects. Particular provisions, though not altogether useless, have far less virtue and efficacy than are commonly ascribed to them; and the want of them will never be, with men of sound discernment, a decisive objection to any plan which exhibits the leading characters of a good government.

It certainly sounds not a little harsh and extraordinary to affirm that there is no security for liberty in a Constitution which expressly establishes the trial by jury in criminal cases, because it does not do it in civil also; while it is a notorious fact that Connecticut, which has been always regarded as the most popular State in the Union, can boast of no constitutional provision for either.

PUBLIUS

1. It has been erroneously insinuated with regard to the court of chancery, that this court generally tries disputed facts by a jury. The truth is, that references to a jury in that court rarely happen, and are in no case necessary but where the validity of a devise of land comes into question.

2. It is true that the principles by which that relief is governed are now reduced to a regular system; but it is not the less true that they are in the main applicable to SPECIAL circumstances, which form exceptions to general rules.

3. Vide No. 81, in which the supposition of its being abolished by the appellate jurisdiction in matters of fact being vested in the Supreme Court, is examined and refuted.

FEDERALIST PAPER NO. 84. CERTAIN GENERAL AND MISCELLANEOUS OBJECTIONS TO THE CONSTITUTION CONSIDERED AND ANSWERED.

From McLEAN's Edition, New York. Wednesday, May 28, 1788

HAMILTON

To the People of the State of New York:

IN THE course of the foregoing review of the Constitution, I have taken notice of, and endeavored to answer most of the objections which have appeared against it. There, however, remain a few which either did not fall naturally under any particular head or were forgotten in their proper places. These shall now be discussed; but as the subject has been drawn into great length, I shall so far consult brevity as to comprise all my observations on these miscellaneous points in a single paper.

The most considerable of the remaining objections is that the plan of the convention contains no bill of rights. Among other answers given to this, it has been upon different occasions remarked that the constitutions of several of the States are in a similar predicament. I add that New York is of the number. And yet the opposers of the new system, in this State, who profess an unlimited admiration for its constitution, are among the most intemperate partisans of a bill of rights. To justify their zeal in this matter, they allege two things: one is that, though the constitution of New York has no bill of rights prefixed to it, yet it contains, in the body of it, various provisions in favor of particular privileges and rights, which, in substance amount to the same thing; the other is, that the Constitution adopts, in their full extent, the common and statute law of Great Britain, by which many other rights, not expressed in it, are equally secured.

To the first I answer, that the Constitution proposed by the convention contains, as well as the constitution of this State, a number of such provisions.

Independent of those which relate to the structure of the government, we find the following: Article 1, section 3, clause 7—"Judgment in cases of impeachment shall not extend further than to removal from office, and disqualification to hold and enjoy any office of honor, trust, or profit under the United States; but the party convicted shall, nevertheless, be liable and subject to indictment, trial, judgment, and punishment according to law." Section 9, of the same article, clause 2—"The privilege of the writ of habeas corpus shall not be suspended, unless when in cases of rebellion or invasion the public safety may require it." Clause 3—"No bill of attainder or ex-post-facto law shall be passed." Clause 7—"No title of nobility shall be granted by the United States; and no person holding any office of profit or trust under them, shall, without the consent of the Congress, accept of any present, emolument, office, or title of any kind whatever, from any king, prince, or foreign state." Article 3, section 2, clause 3—"The trial of all crimes, except in cases of impeachment, shall be by jury; and such trial shall be held in the State where the said crimes shall have been committed; but when not committed within any State, the trial shall be at such place or places as the Congress may by law have directed." Section 3, of the same article—"Treason against the United States shall consist only in levying war against them, or in adhering to their enemies, giving them aid and comfort. No person shall be convicted of treason, unless on the testimony of two witnesses to the same overt act, or on confession in open court." And clause 3, of the same section—"The Congress shall have power to declare the punishment of treason; but no attainder of treason shall work corruption of blood, or forfeiture, except during the life of the person attainted."

It may well be a question, whether these are not, upon the whole, of equal importance with any which are to be found in the constitution of this State. The establishment of the writ of habeas corpus, the prohibition of ex post facto laws, and of TITLES OF NOBILITY, to which we have no corresponding provision in our Constitution, are perhaps greater securities to liberty and republicanism than any it contains. The creation of crimes after the commission of the fact, or, in other words, the subjecting of men to punishment for things which, when they were done, were breaches of no law, and the practice of arbitrary imprisonments, have been, in all ages, the favorite and most formidable instruments of tyranny. The observations of the judicious Blackstone,(1) in reference to the latter, are well worthy of recital: "To bereave a man of life, (says he) or by violence to confiscate his estate, without accusation or trial, would be so gross and notorious an act of despotism, as must at once convey the alarm of tyranny throughout the whole nation; but confinement of the person, by secretly hurrying him to jail, where his sufferings are unknown or forgotten, is a less public, a less striking, and therefore a more dangerous engine of arbitrary government." And as a remedy for this fatal evil he is everywhere peculiarly emphatical in his encomiums on the habeas corpus act, which in one place he calls "the BULWARK of the British Constitution."(2)

Nothing need be said to illustrate the importance of the prohibition of titles of nobility. This may truly be denominated the corner-stone of republican government; for so long as they are excluded, there can never be serious danger that the government will be any other than that of the people.

To the second that is, to the pretended establishment of the common and state law by the Constitution, I answer, that they are expressly made subject "to such alterations and provisions as the legislature shall from time to time make concerning the same." They are therefore at any moment liable to repeal by the ordinary legislative power, and of course have no constitutional sanction. The only use of the declaration was to recognize the ancient law and to remove doubts which might have been occasioned by the Revolution. This consequently can be considered as no part of a declaration of rights, which under our constitutions must be intended as limitations of the power of the government itself.

It has been several times truly remarked that bills of rights are, in their origin, stipulations between kings and their subjects, abridgements of prerogative in favor of privilege, reservations of rights not surrendered to the prince. Such was MAGNA CHARTA, obtained by the barons, sword in hand, from King John. Such were the subsequent confirmations of that charter by succeeding princes. Such was the Petition of Right assented to by Charles I., in the beginning of his reign. Such, also, was the Declaration of Right presented by the Lords and Commons to the Prince of Orange in 1688, and afterwards thrown into the form of an act of parliament called the Bill of Rights. It is evident, therefore, that, according to their primitive signification, they have no application to constitutions professedly founded upon the power of the people, and executed by their immediate representatives and servants. Here, in strictness, the people surrender nothing; and as they retain every thing they have no need of particular reservations. "WE, THE PEOPLE of the United States, to secure the blessings of liberty to ourselves and our posterity, do ordain and establish this Constitution for the United States of America." Here is a better recognition of popular rights, than volumes of those aphorisms which make the principal figure in several of our State bills of rights, and which would sound much better in a treatise of ethics than in a constitution of government.

But a minute detail of particular rights is certainly far less applicable to a Constitution like that under consideration, which is merely intended to regulate the general political interests of the nation, than to a constitution which has the regulation of every species of personal and private concerns. If, therefore, the loud clamors against the plan of the convention, on this score, are well founded, no epithets of reprobation will be too strong for the constitution of this State. But the truth is, that both of them contain all which, in relation to their objects, is reasonably to be desired.

I go further, and affirm that bills of rights, in the sense and to the extent in which they are contended for, are not only unnecessary in the proposed Constitution, but would even be dangerous. They would contain various exceptions to powers not granted; and, on this very account, would afford a colorable pretext to claim more than were granted. For why declare that things shall not be done which there is no power to do? Why, for instance, should it be said that the liberty of the press shall not be restrained, when no power is given by which restrictions may be imposed? I will not contend that such a provision would confer a regulating power; but it is evident that it would furnish, to men disposed to usurp, a plausible pretense for claiming that power. They might urge with a semblance of reason, that the Constitution ought not to be charged with the absurdity of providing against the abuse of an authority which was not given, and that the provision against restraining the liberty of the press afforded a clear implication, that a power to prescribe proper regulations concerning it was intended to be vested in the national government. This may serve as a specimen of the numerous handles which would be given to the doctrine of constructive powers, by the indulgence of an injudicious zeal for bills of rights.

On the subject of the liberty of the press, as much as has been said, I cannot forbear adding a remark or two: in the first place, I observe, that there is not a syllable concerning it in the constitution of this State; in the next, I contend, that whatever has been said about it in that of any other State, amounts to nothing. What signifies a declaration, that "the liberty of the press shall be inviolably preserved"? What is the liberty of the press? Who can give it any definition which would not leave the utmost latitude for evasion? I hold it to be impracticable; and from this I infer, that its security, whatever fine declarations may be inserted in any constitution respecting it, must altogether depend on public opinion, and on the general spirit of the people and of the government.(3) And here, after all, as is intimated upon another occasion, must we seek for the only solid basis of all our rights.

There remains but one other view of this matter to conclude the point. The truth is, after all the declamations we have heard, that the Constitution is itself, in every rational sense, and to every useful purpose, A BILL OF RIGHTS. The several bills of rights in Great Britain form its Constitution, and conversely the constitution of each State is its bill of rights. And the proposed Constitution, if adopted, will be the bill of rights of the Union. Is it one object of a bill of rights to declare and specify the political privileges of the citizens in the structure and administration of the government? This is done in the most ample and precise manner in the plan of the convention; comprehending various precautions for the public security, which are not to be found in any of the State constitutions. Is another object of a bill of rights to define certain immunities and modes of proceeding, which are relative to personal and private concerns? This we have seen has also been attended to, in a variety of cases, in the same plan. Adverting therefore to the substantial meaning of a bill of rights, it is absurd to allege that it is not to be found in the work of the convention. It may be said that it does not go far enough, though it will not be easy to make this appear; but it can with no propriety be contended that there is no such thing. It certainly must be immaterial what mode is observed as to the order of declaring the rights of the citizens, if they are to be found in any part of the instrument which establishes the government. And hence it must be apparent, that much of what has been said on this subject rests merely on verbal and nominal distinctions, entirely foreign from the substance of the thing.

Another objection which has been made, and which, from the frequency of its repetition, it is to be presumed is relied on, is of this nature: "It is improper (say the objectors) to confer such large powers, as are proposed, upon the national government, because the seat of that government must of necessity be too remote from many of the States to admit of a proper knowledge on the part of the constituent, of the conduct of the representative body." This argument, if it proves any thing, proves that there ought to be no general government whatever. For the powers which, it seems to be agreed on all hands, ought to be vested in the Union, cannot be safely intrusted to a body which is not under every requisite control. But there are satisfactory reasons to show that the objection is in reality not well founded. There is in most of the arguments which relate to distance a palpable illusion of the imagination. What are the sources of information by which the people in Montgomery County must regulate their judgment of the conduct of their representatives in the State legislature? Of personal observation they can have no benefit. This is confined to the citizens on the spot. They must therefore depend on the information of intelligent men, in whom they confide; and how must these men obtain their information? Evidently from the complexion of public measures, from the public prints, from correspondences with their representatives, and with other persons who reside at the place of their deliberations. This does not apply to Montgomery County only, but to all the counties at any considerable distance from the seat of government.

It is equally evident that the same sources of information would be open to the people in relation to the conduct of their representatives in the general government, and the impediments to a prompt communication which distance may be supposed to create, will be overbalanced by the effects of the vigilance of the State governments. The executive and legislative bodies of each State will be so many sentinels over the persons employed in every department of the national administration; and as it will be in their power to adopt and pursue a regular and effectual system of intelligence, they can never be at a loss to know the behavior of those who represent their constituents in the national councils, and can readily communicate the same knowledge to the people. Their disposition to apprise the community of whatever may prejudice its interests from another quarter, may be relied upon, if it were only from the rivalship of power. And we may conclude with the fullest assurance that the people, through that channel, will be better informed of the conduct of their national representatives, than they can be by any means they now possess of that of their State representatives.

It ought also to be remembered that the citizens who inhabit the country at and near the seat of government will, in all questions that affect the general liberty and prosperity, have the same interest with those who are at a distance, and that they will stand ready to sound the alarm when necessary, and to point out the actors in any pernicious project. The public papers will be expeditious messengers of intelligence to the most remote inhabitants of the Union.

Among the many curious objections which have appeared against the proposed Constitution, the most extraordinary and the least colorable is derived from the want of some provision respecting the debts due to the United States. This has been represented as a tacit relinquishment of those debts, and as a wicked contrivance to screen public defaulters. The newspapers have teemed with the most inflammatory railings on this head; yet there is nothing clearer than that the suggestion is entirely void of foundation, the offspring of extreme ignorance or extreme dishonesty. In addition to the remarks I have made upon the subject in another place, I shall only observe that as it is a plain dictate of common-sense, so it is also an established doctrine of political law, that "States neither lose any of their rights, nor are discharged from any of their obligations, by a change in the form of their civil government."(4)

The last objection of any consequence, which I at present recollect, turns upon the article of expense. If it were even true, that the adoption of the proposed government would occasion a considerable increase of expense, it would be an objection that ought to have no weight against the plan.

The great bulk of the citizens of America are with reason convinced, that Union is the basis of their political happiness. Men of sense of all parties now, with few exceptions, agree that it cannot be preserved under the present system, nor without radical alterations; that new and extensive powers ought to be granted to the national head, and that these require a different organization of the federal government—a single body being an unsafe depositary of such ample authorities. In conceding all this, the question of expense must be given up; for it is impossible, with any degree of safety, to narrow the foundation upon which the system is to stand. The two branches of the legislature are, in the first instance, to consist of only sixty-five persons, which is the same number of which Congress, under the existing Confederation, may be composed. It is true that this number is intended to be increased; but this is to keep pace with the progress of the population and resources of the country. It is evident that a less number would, even in the first instance, have been unsafe, and that a continuance of the present number would, in a more advanced stage of population, be a very inadequate representation of the people.

Whence is the dreaded augmentation of expense to spring? One source indicated, is the multiplication of offices under the new government. Let us examine this a little.

It is evident that the principal departments of the administration under the present government, are the same which will be required under the new. There are now a Secretary of War, a Secretary of Foreign Affairs, a Secretary for Domestic Affairs, a Board of Treasury, consisting of three persons, a Treasurer, assistants, clerks, etc. These officers are indispensable under any system, and will suffice under the new as well as the old. As to ambassadors and other ministers and agents in foreign countries, the proposed Constitution can make no other difference than to render their characters, where they reside, more respectable, and their services more useful. As to persons to be employed in the collection of the revenues, it is unquestionably true that these will form a very considerable addition to the number of federal officers; but it will not follow that this will occasion an increase of public expense. It will be in most cases nothing more than an exchange of State for national officers. In the collection of all duties, for instance, the persons employed will be wholly of the latter description. The States individually will stand in no need of any for this purpose. What difference can it make in point of expense to pay officers of the customs appointed by the State or by the United States? There is no good reason to suppose that either the number or the salaries of the latter will be greater than those of the former.

Where then are we to seek for those additional articles of expense which are to swell the account to the enormous size that has been represented to us? The chief item which occurs to me respects the support of the judges of the United States. I do not add the President, because there is now a president of Congress, whose expenses may not be far, if any thing, short of those which will be incurred on account of the President of the United States. The support of the judges will clearly be an extra expense, but to what extent will depend on the particular plan which may be adopted in regard to this matter. But upon no reasonable plan can it amount to a sum which will be an object of material consequence.

Let us now see what there is to counterbalance any extra expense that may attend the establishment of the proposed government. The first thing which presents itself is that a great part of the business which now keeps Congress sitting through the year will be transacted by the President. Even the management of foreign negotiations will naturally devolve upon him, according to general principles concerted with the Senate, and subject to their final concurrence. Hence it is evident that a portion of the year will suffice for the session of both the Senate and the House of Representatives; we may suppose about a fourth for the latter and a third, or perhaps half, for the former. The extra business of treaties and appointments may give this extra occupation to the Senate. From this circumstance we may infer that, until the House of Representatives shall be increased greatly beyond its present number, there will be a considerable saving of expense from the difference between the constant session of the present and the temporary session of the future Congress.

But there is another circumstance of great importance in the view of economy. The business of the United States has hitherto occupied the State legislatures, as well as Congress. The latter has made requisitions which the former have had to provide for. Hence it has happened that the sessions of the State legislatures have been protracted greatly beyond what was necessary for the execution of the mere local business of the States. More than half their time has been frequently employed in matters which related to the United States. Now the members who compose the legislatures of the several States amount to two thousand and upwards, which number has hitherto performed what under the new system will be done in the first instance by sixty-five persons, and probably at no future period by above a fourth or fifth of that number. The Congress under the proposed government will do all the business of the United States themselves, without the intervention of the State legislatures, who thenceforth will have only to attend to the affairs of their particular States, and will not have to sit in any proportion as long as they have heretofore done. This difference in the time of the sessions of the State legislatures will be clear gain, and will alone form an article of saving, which may be regarded as an equivalent for any additional objects of expense that may be occasioned by the adoption of the new system.

The result from these observations is that the sources of additional expense from the establishment of the proposed Constitution are much fewer than may have been imagined; that they are counterbalanced by considerable objects of saving;

and that while it is questionable on which side the scale will preponderate, it is certain that a government less expensive would be incompetent to the purposes of the Union.

PUBLIUS

1. Vide Blackstone's Commentaries, Vol. 1, p. 136.

2. Idem, Vol. 4, p. 438.

3. To show that there is a power in the Constitution by which the liberty of the press may be affected, recourse has been had to the power of taxation. It is said that duties may be laid upon the publications so high as to amount to a prohibition. I know not by what logic it could be maintained, that the declarations in the State constitutions, in favor of the freedom of the press, would be a constitutional impediment to the imposition of duties upon publications by the State legislatures. It cannot certainly be pretended that any degree of duties, however low, would be an abridgment of the liberty of the press. We know that newspapers are taxed in Great Britain, and yet it is notorious that the press nowhere enjoys greater liberty than in that country. And if duties of any kind may be laid without a violation of that liberty, it is evident that the extent must depend on legislative discretion, respecting the liberty of the press, will give it no greater security than it will have without them. The same invasions of it may be effected under the State constitutions which contain those declarations through the means of taxation, as under the proposed Constitution, which has nothing of the kind. It would be quite as significant to declare that government ought to be free, that taxes ought not to be excessive, etc., as that the liberty of the press ought not to be restrained.

4. Vide Rutherford's Institutes, Vol. 2, Book II, Chapter X, Sections XIV and XV. Vide also Grotius, Book II, Chapter IX, Sections VIII and IX.

FEDERALIST PAPER NO. 85. CONCLUDING REMARKS

From MCLEAN's Edition, New York. Wednesday, May 28, 1788

HAMILTON

To the People of the State of New York:

ACCORDING to the formal division of the subject of these papers, announced in my first number, there would appear still to remain for discussion two points: "the analogy of the proposed government to your own State constitution," and "the additional security which its adoption will afford to republican government, to liberty, and to property." But these heads have been so fully anticipated and exhausted in the progress of the work, that it would now scarcely be possible to do any thing more than repeat, in a more dilated form, what has been heretofore said, which the advanced stage of the question, and the time already spent upon it, conspire to forbid.

It is remarkable, that the resemblance of the plan of the convention to the act which organizes the government of this State holds, not less with regard to many of the supposed defects, than to the real excellences of the former. Among the pretended defects are the re-eligibility of the Executive, the want of a council, the omission of a formal bill of rights, the omission of a provision respecting the liberty of the press. These and several others which have been noted in the course of our inquiries are as much chargeable on the existing constitution of this State, as on the one proposed for the Union; and a man must have slender pretensions to consistency, who can rail at the latter for imperfections which he finds no difficulty in excusing in the former. Nor indeed can there be a better proof of the insincerity and affectation of some of the zealous adversaries of the plan of the convention among us, who profess to be the devoted admirers of the government under which they live, than the fury with which they have attacked that plan, for matters in regard to which our own constitution is equally or perhaps more vulnerable.

The additional securities to republican government, to liberty and to property, to be derived from the adoption of the plan under consideration, consist chiefly in the restraints which the preservation of the Union will impose on local factions and insurrections, and on the ambition of powerful individuals in single States, who may acquire credit and influence enough, from leaders and favorites, to become the despots of the people; in the diminution of the opportunities to foreign intrigue, which the dissolution of the Confederacy would invite and facilitate; in the prevention of extensive military establishments, which could not fail to grow out of wars between the States in a disunited situation; in the express guaranty of a republican form of government to each; in the absolute and universal exclusion of titles of nobility; and in the precautions against the repetition of those practices on the part of the State governments which have undermined the foundations of property and credit, have planted mutual distrust in the breasts of all classes of citizens, and have occasioned an almost universal prostration of morals.

Thus have I, fellow-citizens, executed the task I had assigned to myself; with what success, your conduct must determine. I trust at least you will admit that I have not failed in the assurance I gave you respecting the spirit with which my endeavors should be conducted. I have addressed myself purely to your judgments, and have studiously avoided those asperities which are too apt to disgrace political disputants of all parties, and which have been not a little provoked by the language and conduct of the opponents of the Constitution. The charge of a conspiracy against the liberties of the people, which has been indiscriminately brought against the advocates of the plan, has something in it too wanton and too malignant, not to excite the indignation of every man who feels in his own bosom a refutation of the calumny. The perpetual changes which have been rung upon the wealthy, the well-born, and the great, have been such as to inspire the disgust of all sensible men. And the unwarrantable concealments and misrepresentations which have been in various ways practiced to keep the truth from the public eye, have been of a nature to demand the reprobation of all honest men. It is not impossible that these circumstances may have occasionally betrayed me into intemperances of expression which I did not intend; it is certain that I have frequently felt a struggle between sensibility and moderation; and if the former has in some instances prevailed, it must be my excuse that it has been neither often nor much.

Let us now pause and ask ourselves whether, in the course of these papers, the proposed Constitution has not been satisfactorily vindicated from the aspersions thrown upon it; and whether it has not been shown to be worthy of the public approbation, and necessary to the public safety and prosperity. Every man is bound to answer these questions to himself, according to the best of his conscience and understanding, and to act agreeably to the genuine and sober dictates of his judgment. This is a duty from which nothing can give him a dispensation. 'T is one that he is called upon, nay, constrained by all the obligations that form the bands of society, to discharge sincerely and honestly. No partial motive, no particular interest, no pride of opinion, no temporary passion or prejudice, will justify to himself, to his country, or to his posterity, an improper election of the part he is to act. Let him beware of an obstinate adherence to party; let him reflect that the object upon which he is to decide is not a particular interest of the community, but the very existence of the nation; and let him remember that a majority of America has already given its sanction to the plan which he is to approve or reject.

I shall not dissemble that I feel an entire confidence in the arguments which recommend the proposed system to your adoption, and that I am unable to discern any real force in those by which it has been opposed. I am persuaded that it is the best which our political situation, habits, and opinions will admit, and superior to any the revolution has produced.

Concessions on the part of the friends of the plan, that it has not a claim to absolute perfection, have afforded matter of no small triumph to its enemies. "Why," say they, "should we adopt an imperfect thing? Why not amend it and make it perfect before it is irrevocably established?" This may be plausible enough, but it is only plausible. In the first place I remark, that the extent of these concessions has been greatly exaggerated. They have been stated as amounting to an admission that the plan is radically defective, and that without material alterations the rights and the interests of the community cannot be safely confided to it. This, as far as I have understood the meaning of those who make the concessions, is an entire perversion of their sense. No advocate of the measure can be found, who will not declare as his sentiment, that the system, though it may not be perfect in every part, is, upon the whole, a good one; is the best that the present views and circumstances of the country will permit; and is such an one as promises every species of security which a reasonable people can desire.

I answer in the next place, that I should esteem it the extreme of imprudence to prolong the precarious state of our national affairs, and to expose the Union to the jeopardy of successive experiments, in the chimerical pursuit of a perfect plan. I never expect to see a perfect work from imperfect man. The result of the deliberations of all collective bodies must necessarily be a compound, as well of the errors and prejudices, as of the good sense and wisdom, of the individuals of whom they are composed. The compacts which are to embrace thirteen distinct States in a common bond of amity and union, must as necessarily be a compromise of as many dissimilar interests and inclinations. How can perfection spring from such materials?

The reasons assigned in an excellent little pamphlet lately published in this city,(1) are unanswerable to show the utter improbability of assembling a new convention, under circumstances in any degree so favorable to a happy issue, as those in which the late convention met, deliberated, and concluded. I will not repeat the arguments there used, as I presume the production itself has had an extensive circulation. It is certainly well worthy the perusal of every friend to his country. There is, however, one point of light in which the subject of amendments still remains to be considered, and in which it has not yet been exhibited to public view. I cannot resolve to conclude without first taking a survey of it in this aspect.

It appears to me susceptible of absolute demonstration, that it will be far more easy to obtain subsequent than previous amendments to the Constitution. The moment an alteration is made in the present plan, it becomes, to the purpose of adoption, a new one, and must undergo a new decision of each State. To its complete establishment throughout the Union, it will therefore require the concurrence of thirteen States. If, on the contrary, the Constitution proposed should once be ratified by all the States as it stands, alterations in it may at any time be effected by nine States. Here, then, the chances are as thirteen to nine(2) in favor of subsequent amendment, rather than of the original adoption of an entire system.

This is not all. Every Constitution for the United States must inevitably consist of a great variety of particulars, in which thirteen independent States are to be accommodated in their interests or opinions of interest. We may of course expect to see, in any body of men charged with its original formation, very different combinations of the parts upon different points. Many of those who form a majority on one question, may become the minority on a second, and an association dissimilar to either may constitute the majority on a third. Hence the necessity of moulding and arranging all the particulars which are to compose the whole, in such a manner as to satisfy all the parties to the compact; and hence, also, an immense multiplication of difficulties and casualties in obtaining the collective assent to a final act. The degree of that multiplication must evidently be in a ratio to the number of particulars and the number of parties.

But every amendment to the Constitution, if once established, would be a single proposition, and might be brought forward singly. There would then be no necessity for management or compromise, in relation to any other point—no giving nor taking. The will of the requisite number would at once bring the matter to a decisive issue. And consequently, whenever nine, or rather ten States, were united in the desire of a particular amendment, that amendment must infallibly take place. There can, therefore, be no comparison between the facility of affecting an amendment, and that of establishing in the first instance a complete Constitution.

Documents of Revolution

In opposition to the probability of subsequent amendments, it has been urged that the persons delegated to the administration of the national government will always be disinclined to yield up any portion of the authority of which they were once possessed. For my own part I acknowledge a thorough conviction that any amendments which may, upon mature consideration, be thought useful, will be applicable to the organization of the government, not to the mass of its powers; and on this account alone, I think there is no weight in the observation just stated. I also think there is little weight in it on another account. The intrinsic difficulty of governing THIRTEEN STATES at any rate, independent of calculations upon an ordinary degree of public spirit and integrity, will, in my opinion constantly impose on the national rulers the necessity of a spirit of accommodation to the reasonable expectations of their constituents. But there is yet a further consideration, which proves beyond the possibility of a doubt, that the observation is futile. It is this that the national rulers, whenever nine States concur, will have no option upon the subject. By the fifth article of the plan, the Congress will be obliged "on the application of the legislatures of two thirds of the States (which at present amount to nine), to call a convention for proposing amendments, which shall be valid, to all intents and purposes, as part of the Constitution, when ratified by the legislatures of three fourths of the States, or by conventions in three fourths thereof." The words of this article are peremptory. The Congress "shall call a convention." Nothing in this particular is left to the discretion of that body. And of consequence, all the declamation about the disinclination to a change vanishes in air. Nor however difficult it may be supposed to unite two thirds or three fourths of the State legislatures, in amendments which may affect local interests, can there be any room to apprehend any such difficulty in a union on points which are merely relative to the general liberty or security of the people. We may safely rely on the disposition of the State legislatures to erect barriers against the encroachments of the national authority.

If the foregoing argument is a fallacy, certain it is that I am myself deceived by it, for it is, in my conception, one of those rare instances in which a political truth can be brought to the test of a mathematical demonstration. Those who see the matter in the same light with me, however zealous they may be for amendments, must agree in the propriety of a previous adoption, as the most direct road to their own object.

The zeal for attempts to amend, prior to the establishment of the Constitution, must abate in every man who is ready to accede to the truth of the following observations of a writer equally solid and ingenious: "To balance a large state or society (says he), whether monarchical or republican, on general laws, is a work of so great difficulty, that no human genius, however comprehensive, is able, by the mere dint of reason and reflection, to effect it. The judgments of many must unite in the work; EXPERIENCE must guide their labor; TIME must bring it to perfection, and the FEELING of inconveniences must correct the mistakes which they inevitably fall into in their first trials and experiments."(3) These judicious reflections contain a lesson of moderation to all the sincere lovers of the Union, and ought to put them upon their guard against hazarding anarchy, civil war, a perpetual alienation of the States from each other, and perhaps the military despotism of a victorious demagogue, in the pursuit of what they are not likely to obtain, but from TIME and EXPERIENCE. It may be in me a defect of political fortitude, but I acknowledge that I cannot entertain an equal tranquillity with those who affect to treat the dangers of a longer continuance in our present situation as imaginary. A NATION, without a NATIONAL GOVERNMENT, is, in my view, an awful spectacle. The establishment of a Constitution, in time of profound peace, by the voluntary consent of a whole people, is a PRODIGY, to the completion of which I look forward with trembling anxiety. I can reconcile it to no rules of prudence to let go the hold we now have, in so arduous an enterprise, upon seven out of the thirteen States, and after having passed over so considerable a part of the ground, to recommence the course. I dread the more the consequences of new attempts, because I know that POWERFUL INDIVIDUALS, in this and in other States, are enemies to a general national government in every possible shape.

PUBLIUS

1. Entitled "An Address to the People of the State of New York."
2. It may rather be said TEN, for though two thirds may set on foot the measure, three fourths must ratify.
3. Hume's Essays, Vol. I, p. 128: "The Rise of Arts and Sciences."

* * *

THE ANTI-FEDERALIST PAPERS

Documents of Revolution

THE ANTI-FEDERALIST PAPERS

Anti-Federalist Papers is the collective name given to works written by the Founding Fathers who were opposed to or concerned with the merits of the United States Constitution of 1787. Starting on 25 September 1787 (8 days after the final draft of the US Constitution) and running through the early 1790s, these anti-Federalists published a series of essays arguing against a stronger and more energetic union as embodied in the new Constitution. Although less influential than their counterparts, The Federalist Papers, these works nonetheless played an important role in shaping the early American political landscape and in the passage of the US Bill of Rights.

Anti-Federalism was a late-18th century movement that opposed the creation of a stronger U.S. federal government and which later opposed the ratification of the 1787 Constitution. The previous constitution, called the Articles of Confederation, gave state governments more authority. Led by Patrick Henry of Virginia, Anti-Federalists worried, among other things, that the position of president, then a novelty, might evolve into a monarchy. Though the Constitution was ratified and supplanted the Articles of Confederation, Anti-Federalist influence helped lead to the passage of the United States Bill of Rights.

Major Points

- They believed the Constitution needed a Bill of Rights.
- They believed the Constitution created a presidency so powerful that it would become a monarchy.
- They believed the Constitution did too little with the courts and would create an out-of-control judiciary.
- They believed that the national government would be too far away from the people and thus unresponsive to the needs of localities.

Notable Anti-Federalists

- Patrick Henry
- Samuel Adams
- George Mason
- Richard Henry Lee
- Robert Yates
- James Monroe
- Amos Singletary
- Mercy Otis Warren
- George Clinton
- Melancton Smith
- Arthur Fenner
- James Winthrop
- Luther Martin

ANTI-FEDERALIST PAPER NO. 1

GENERAL INTRODUCTION: A DANGEROUS PLAN OF BENEFIT ONLY TO THE "ARISTOCRATICK COMBINATION"

From The Boston Gazette and Country Journal, November 26, 1787.

I am pleased to see a spirit of inquiry burst the band of constraint upon the subject of the NEW PLAN for consolidating the governments of the United States, as recommended by the late Convention. If it is suitable to the GENIUS and HABITS of the citizens of these states, it will bear the strictest scrutiny. The PEOPLE are the grand inquest who have a RIGHT to judge of its merits. The hideous daemon of Aristocracy has hitherto had so much influence as to bar the channels of investigation, preclude the people from inquiry and extinguish every spark of liberal information of its qualities. At length the luminary of intelligence begins to beam its effulgent rays upon this important production; the deceptive mists cast before the eyes of the people by the delusive machinations of its INTERESTED advocates begins to dissipate, as darkness flies before the burning taper; and I dare venture to predict, that in spite of those mercenary dectaimers, the plan will have a candid and complete examination. Those furious zealots who are for cramming it down the throats of the people, without allowing them either time or opportunity to scan or weigh it in the balance of their understandings, bear the same marks in their features as those who have been long wishing to erect an aristocracy in THIS COMMONWEALTH [of Massachusetts]. Their menacing cry is for a RIGID government, it matters little to them of what kind, provided it answers THAT description. As the plan now offered comes something near their wishes, and is the most consonant to their views of any they can hope for, they come boldly forward and DEMAND its adoption. They brand with infamy every man who is not as determined and zealous in its favor as themselves. They cry aloud the whole must be swallowed or none at all, thinking thereby to preclude any amendment; they are afraid of having it abated of its present RIGID aspect. They have strived to overawe or seduce printers to stifle and obstruct a free discussion, and have endeavored to hasten it to a decision before the people can duty reflect upon its properties. In order to deceive them, they incessantly declare that none can discover any defect in the system but bankrupts who wish no government, and officers of the present government who fear to lose a part of their power. These zealous partisans may injure their own cause, and endanger the public tranquility by impeding a proper inquiry; the people may suspect the WHOLE to be a dangerous plan, from such COVERED and DESIGNING schemes to enforce it upon them. Compulsive or treacherous measures to establish any government whatever, will always excite jealousy among a free people: better remain single and alone, than blindly adopt whatever a few individuals shall demand, be they ever so wise. I had rather be a free citizen of the small republic of Massachusetts, than an oppressed subject of the great American empire. Let all act understandingly or not at all. If we can confederate upon terms that wilt secure to us our liberties, it is an object highly desirable, because of its additional security to the whole. If the proposed plan proves such an one, I hope it will be adopted, but if it will endanger our liberties as it stands, let it be amended; in order to which it must and ought to be open to inspection and free inquiry. The inundation of abuse that has been thrown out upon the heads of those who have had any doubts of its universal good qualities, have been so redundant, that it may not be improper to scan the characters of its most strenuous advocates. It will first be allowed that many undesigning citizens may wish its adoption from the best motives, but these are modest and silent, when compared to the greater number, who endeavor to suppress all attempts for investigation. These violent partisans are for having the people gulp down the gilded pill blindfolded, whole, and without any qualification whatever. These consist generally, of the NOBLE order of C[incinnatu]s, holders of public securities, men of great wealth and expectations of public office, B[an]k[er]s and L[aw]y[er]s: these with their train of dependents form the Aristocratick combination. The Lawyers in particular, keep up an incessant declamation for its adoption; like greedy gudgeons they long to satiate their voracious stomachs with the golden bait. The numerous tribunals to be erected by the new plan of consolidated empire, will find employment for ten times their present numbers; these are the LOAVES AND FISHES for which they hunger. They will probably find it suited to THEIR HABITS, if not to the HABITS

OF THE PEOPLE. There may be reasons for having but few of them in the State Convention, lest THEIR '0@' INTEREST should be too strongly considered. The time draws near for the choice of Delegates. I hope my fellow-citizens will look well to the characters of their preference, and remember the Old Patriots of 75; they have never led them astray, nor need they fear to try them on this momentous occasion.

A FEDERALIST

ANTI-FEDERALIST PAPER NO. 2

"we Have Been Told Of Phantoms"

This essay is an excerpted from a speech of William Grayson, June 11, 1788, in Jonathan Elliot (ed.), The Debates in the Several State Conventions on the Adoption of the Federal Constitution.......
(Philadelphia, 1876) 5 vols., III, 274-79.

The adoption of this government will not meliorate our own particular system. I beg leave to consider the circumstances of the Union antecedent to the meeting of the Convention at Philadelphia. We have been told of phantoms and ideal dangers to lead us into measures which will, in my opinion, be the ruin of our country. If the existence of those dangers cannot be proved, if there be no apprehension of wars, if there be no rumors of wars, it will place the subject in a different light, and plainly evince to the world that there cannot be any reason for adopting measures which we apprehend to be ruinous and destructive. When this state [Virginia]

proposed that the general government should be improved, Massachusetts was just recovered from a rebellion which had brought the republic to the brink of destruction from a rebellion which was crushed by that federal government which is now so much contemned and abhorred.

A vote of that august body for fifteen hundred men, aided by the exertions of the state, silenced all opposition, and shortly restored the public tranquility. Massachusetts was satisfied that these internal commotions were so happily settled, and was unwilling to risk any similar distresses by theoretic experiments. Were the Eastern States willing to enter into this measure? Were they willing to accede to the proposal of Virginia? In what manner was it received? Connecticut revolted at the idea. The Eastern States, sir, were unwilling to recommend a meeting of a convention. They were well aware of the dangers of revolutions and changes. Why was every effort used, and such uncommon pains taken, to bring it about? This would have been unnecessary, had it been approved of by the people. Was Pennsylvania disposed for the reception of this project of reformation? No, sir. She was even unwilling to amend her revenue laws, so as to make the five per centum operative. She was satisfied with things as they were. There was no complaint, that ever I heard of, from any other part of the Union, except Virginia. This being the case among ourselves, what dangers were there to be apprehended from foreign nations? It will be easily shown that dangers from that quarter were absolutely imaginary. Was not France friendly? Unequivocally so. She was devising new regulations of commerce for our advantage.

Did she harass us with applications for her money? Is it likely that France will quarrel with us? Is it not reasonable to suppose that she will be more desirous than ever to cling, after losing the Dutch republic, to her best ally? How are the Dutch? We owe them money, it is true; and are they not willing that we should owe them more? Mr. [John] Adams applied to them for a new loan to the poor, despised Confederation. They readily granted it. The Dutch have a fellow-feeling for us. They were in the same situation with ourselves.

I believe that the money which the Dutch borrowed of Henry IV is not yet paid. How did they pass Queen Elizabeth's loan? At a very considerable discount. They took advantage of the weakness and necessities of James I, and made their own terms with that contemptible monarch.

Loans from nations are not like loans from private men. Nations lend money, and grant assistance, to one another, from views of national interest-France was willing to pluck the fairest

feather out of the British crown. This was her object in aiding us. She will not quarrel with us on pecuniary considerations. Congress considered it in this point of view; for when a proposition was made to make it a debt of private persons, it was rejected without hesitation. That respectable body wisely considered, that, while we remained their debtors in so considerable a degree, they would not be inattentive to our interest.

With respect to Spain, she is friendly in a high degree. I wish to know by whose interposition was the treaty with Morocco made. Was it not by that of the king of Spain? Several predatory nations disturbed us, on going into the Mediterranean. The influence of Charles III at the Barbary court, and four thousand pounds, procured as good a treaty with Morocco as could be expected.

But I acknowledge it is not of any consequence, since the Algerines and people of Tunis have not entered into similar measures. We have nothing to fear from Spain; and, were she hostile, she could never be formidable to this country. Her strength is so scattered, that she never can be dangerous to us either in peace or war. As to Portugal, we have a treaty with her, which may be very advantageous, though it be not yet ratified.

Documents of Revolution

The domestic debt is diminished by considerable sales of western lands to Cutler, Sergeant, and Company; to Simms; and to Royal, Flint, and Company. The board of treasury is authorized to sell in Europe, or any where else, the residue of those lands. An act of Congress has passed, to adjust the public debts between the individual states and the United States.

Was our trade in a despicable situation? I shall say nothing of what did not come under my own observation. When I was in Congress, sixteen vessels had had sea letters in the East India trade, and two hundred vessels entered and cleared out, in the French West India Islands, in one year.

I must confess that public credit has suffered, and that our public creditors have been ill used.

This was owing to a fault at the head-quarters-to Congress themselves-in not selling the western lands at an earlier period. If requisitions have not been complied with, it must be owing to Congress, who might have put the unpopular debts on the back lands. Commutation is abhorrent to New England ideas. Speculation is abhorrent to the Eastern States. Those inconveniences have resulted from the bad policy of Congress.

There are certain modes of governing the people which will succeed. There are others which will not. The idea of consolidation is abhorrent to the people of this country. How were the sentiments of the people before the meeting of the Convention at Philadelphia? They had only one object in view. Their ideas reached no farther than to give the general government the five per centum impost, and the regulation of trade. When it was agitated in Congress, in a committee of the whole, this was all that was asked, or was deemed necessary. Since that period, their views have extended much farther. Horrors have been greatly magnified since the rising of the Convention.

We are now told by the honorable gentleman (Governor Randolph) that we shall have wars and rumors of wars, that every calamity is to attend us, and that we shall be ruined and disunited forever, unless we adopt this Constitution. Pennsylvania and Maryland are to fall upon us from

the north, like the Goths and Vandals of old; the Algerines, whose flat-sided vessels never came farther than Madeira, are to fill the Chesapeake with mighty fleets, and to attack us on our front; the Indians are to invade us with numerous armies on our rear, in order to convert our cleared lands into hunting- grounds; and the Carolinians, from the south, (mounted on alligators, I presume,) are to come and destroy our cornfields, and eat up our little children! These, sir, are the mighty dangers which await us if we reject dangers which are merely imaginary, and ludicrous in the extreme! Are we to be destroyed by Maryland and Pennsylvania? What will democratic states make war for, and how long since have they imbibed a hostile spirit?

But the generality are to attack us. Will they attack us after violating their faith in the first Union? Will they not violate their faith if they do not take us into their confederacy? Have they not agreed, by the old Confederation, that the Union shall be perpetual, and that no alteration should take place without the consent of Congress, and the confirmation of the legislatures of every state? I cannot think that there is such depravity in mankind as that, after violating public faith so flagrantly, they should make war upon us, also, for not following their example.

The large states have divided the back lands among themselves, and have given as much as they thought proper to the generality. For the fear of disunion, we are told that we ought to take measures which we otherwise should not. Disunion is impossible. The Eastern States hold the fisheries, which are their cornfields, by a hair. They have a dispute with the British government about their limits at this moment. Is not a general and strong government necessary for their interest? If ever nations had inducements to peace, the Eastern States now have. New York and Pennsylvania anxiously look forward for the fur trade. How can they obtain it but by union? Can the western posts be got or retained without union? How are the little states inclined? They are not likely to disunite. Their weakness will prevent them from quarrelling. Little men are seldom fond of quarrelling among giants. Is there not a strong inducement to union, while the British are on one side and the Spaniards on the other? Thank Heaven, we have a Carthage of our own . . .

But what would I do on the present occasion to remedy the existing defects of the present Confederation? There are two opinions prevailing in the world-the one, that mankind can only be governed by force; the other, that they are capable of freedom and a good government. Under a supposition that mankind can govern themselves, I would recommend that the present Confederation should be amended. Give Congress the regulation of commerce. Infuse new strength and spirit into the state governments; for, when the component parts are strong, it will give energy to the government, although it be otherwise weak....

Apportion the public debts in such a manner as to throw the unpopular ones on the back lands.

Call only for requisitions for the foreign interest and aid them by loans. Keep on so till the American character be marked with some certain features. We are yet too young to know what we are fit for. The continual migration of people from Europe, and the settlement of new countries on our western frontiers, are strong arguments against making new experiments now in government. When these things are removed, we can with greater prospect of success, devise changes. We ought to consider, as

Montesquieu says, whether the construction of the government be suitable to the genius and disposition of the people, as well as a variety of other circumstances.

ANTI-FEDERALIST PAPER NO. 3

New Constitution Creates A National Government : Will Not Abate Foreign Influence; Dangers Of Civil War And Despotism

Like the nome de plume "Publius" used by pro Constitution writers in the Federalist Papers, several Antifederalists signed their writings "A FARMER." While the occupation of the writers may not have coincided with the name given, the arguments against consolodating power in the hands of a central government were widely read. The following was published in the Maryland Gazette and Baltimore Advertiser, March 7, 1788. The true identity of the author is unknown.

There are but two modes by which men are connected in society, the one which operates on individuals, this always has been, and ought still to be called, national government; the other which binds States and governments together (not corporations, for there is no considerable nation on earth, despotic, monarchical, or republican, that does not contain many subordinate corporations with various constitutions) this last has heretofore been denominated a league or confederacy. The term federalists is therefore improperly applied to themselves, by the friends and supporters of the proposed constitution. This abuse of language does not help the cause; every degree of imposition serves only to irritate, but can never convince. They are national men, and their opponents, or at least a great majority of them, are federal, in the only true and strict sense of the word.

Whether any form of national government is preferable for the Americans, to a league or confederacy, is a previous question we must first make up our minds upon....

That a national government will add to the dignity and increase the splendor of the United States abroad, can admit of no doubt: it is essentially requisite for both. That it will render government, and officers of government, more dignified at home is equally certain. That these objects are more suited to the manners, if not [the] genius and disposition of our people is, I fear, also true.

That it is requisite in order to keep us at peace among ourselves, is doubtful. That it is necessary, to prevent foreigners from dividing us, or interfering in our government, I deny positively; and, after all, I have strong doubts whether all its advantages are not more specious than solid. We are vain, like other nations. We wish to make a noise in the world; and feel hurt that Europeans are not so attentive to America in peace, as they were to America in war. We are also, no doubt, desirous of cutting a figure in history. Should we not reflect, that quiet is happiness? That content and pomp are incompatible? I have either read or heard this truth, which the Americans should never forget: That the silence of historians is the surest record of the happiness of a people. The Swiss have been four hundred years the envy of mankind, and there is yet scarcely an history of their nation. What is history, but a disgusting and painful detail of the butcheries of conquerors, and the woeful calamities of the conquered? Many of us are proud, and are frequently disappointed that office confers neither respect or difference. No man of merit can ever be disgraced by office. A rogue in office may be feared in some governments-he will be respected in none. After all, what we call respect and difference only arise from contrast of situation, as most of our ideas come by comparison and relation. Where the people are free there can be no great contrast or distinction among honest citizens in or out of office. In proportion as the people

lose their freedom, every gradation of distinction, between the Governors and governed obtains, until the former become masters, and the latter become slaves. In all governments virtue will command reverence. The divine Cato knew every Roman citizen by name, and never assumed any preeminence; yet Cato found, and his memory will find, respect and reverence in the bosoms of mankind, until this world returns into that nothing, from whence Omnipotence called it. That the people are not at present disposed for, and are actually incapable of, governments of simplicity and equal rights, I can no longer doubt. But whose fault is it? We make them bad, by bad governments, and then abuse and despise them for being so. Our people are capable of being made anything that human nature was or is capable of, if we would only have a little patience and give them good and wholesome institutions; but I see none such and very little prospect of such. Alas! I see nothing in my fellow-citizens, that will permit my still fostering the delusion, that they are now capable of sustaining the weight of SELF-GOVERNMENT: a burden to which Greek and Roman shoulders proved unequal. The honor of supporting the dignity of the human character, seems reserved to the hardy Helvetians alone. If the body of the people will not govern themselves, and govern themselves well too, the consequence is unavoidable-a FEW will, and must govern them. Then it is that government becomes truly a government by force only, where men relinquish part of their natural rights to secure the rest, instead of an union of will and force, to protect all their natural rights, which ought to be the foundation of every rightful social compact.

Whether national government will be productive of internal peace, is too uncertain to admit of decided opinion. I only hazard a conjecture when I say, that our state disputes, in a confederacy, would be disputes of levity and passion, which would subside before injury. The people being free, government having no right to them, but they to government, they would separate and divide as interest or inclination prompted-as they do at this day, and always have done, in Switzerland. In a national government, unless cautiously and fortunately administered, the disputes will be the deep-rooted differences of interest, where part of the empire must be injured by the operation of general law; and then should the sword of government be once drawn (which Heaven avert) I fear it will not be sheathed, until we have waded through that series of desolation, which France, Spain, and the other great kingdoms of the world have suffered, in order to bring so many separate States into uniformity, of government and law; in which event the legislative power can only be entrusted to one man (as it is with them) who can have no local attachments, partial interests, or private views to gratify.

That a national government will prevent the influence or danger of foreign intrigue, or secure us from invasion, is in my judgment directly the reverse of the truth. The only foreign, or at least evil foreign influence, must be obtained through corruption. Where the government is lodged in the body of the people, as in Switzerland, they can never be corrupted; for no prince, or people, can have resources enough to corrupt the majority of a nation; and if they could, the play is not worth the candle. The facility of corruption is increased in proportion as power tends by representation or delegation, to a concentration in the hands of a few. . . .

As to any nation attacking a number of confederated independent republics ... it is not to be expected, more especially as the wealth of the empire is there universally diffused, and will not be collected into any one overgrown, luxurious and effeminate capital to become a lure to the enterprizing ambitious. That extensive empire is a misfortune to be deprecated, will not now be disputed. The balance of power has long engaged the attention of all the European world, in order to avoid the horrid evils of a general government. The same government pervading a vast extent of territory, terrifies the minds of individuals into meanness and submission. All human authority, however organized, must have confined limits, or insolence and oppression will prove the offspring of its grandeur, and the difficulty or rather impossibility of escape prevents resistance. Gibbon relates that some Roman Knights who had offended government in Rome were taken up in Asia, in a very few days after. It was the extensive territory of the Roman republic that produced a Sylla, a Marius, a Caligula, a Nero, and an Elagabalus. In small independent States contiguous to each other, the people run away and leave despotism to reek its vengeance on itself; and thus it is that moderation becomes with them, the law of self-preservation. These and such reasons founded on the eternal and immutable nature of things have long caused and will continue to cause much difference of sentiment throughout our wide extensive territories. From our divided and dispersed situation, and from the natural moderation of the American character, it has hitherto proved a warfare of argument and reason.

A FARMER

ANTI-FEDERALIST PAPER NO. 4

Foreign Wars, Civil Wars, And Indian Wars - Three Bugbears

Patrick Henry was a somewhat the antithesis to James Madison of Federalist note. While every bit as emotional a writer, Henry (who penned the well remembered "Give Me Liberty of Give Me Death" phrase) opposed the new Constitution for many reasons. He delivered long speeches to the Virginia Ratification convention June 5, 7, and 9, 1788. The following is taken from Elliot's Debates, 111, 46, 48, 141-42, 150-56.

If we recollect, on last Saturday, I made some observations on some of those dangers which these gentlemen would fain persuade us hang over the citizens of this commonwealth [Virginia] to induce us to change the government, and adopt the new plan. Unless there be great and awful dangers, the change is dangerous, and the experiment ought not to be made. In estimating the magnitude of these dangers, we are obliged to take a most serious view of them--to see them, to handle them, and to be familiar with them. It is not sufficient to feign mere imaginary dangers; there must be a dreadful reality. The great question between us is: Does that reality exist? These dangers are partially attributed to bad laws, execrated by the community at large. It is said the people wish to change the government. I should be happy to meet them on that ground. Should the people wish to change it, we should be innocent of the dangers. It is a fact that the people do not wish to change their government. How am I to prove it? It will rest on my bare assertion, unless supported by an internal conviction in men's breasts. My poor say-so is a mere nonentity.

But, sir, I am persuaded that four fifths of the people of Virginia must have amendments to the new plan, to reconcile them to a change of their government. It is a slippery foundation for the people to rest their political salvation on my or their assertions. No government can flourish unless it be founded on the affection of the people. Unless gentlemen can be sure that this new system is founded on that ground, they ought to stop their career.

I will not repeat what the gentlemen say-I will mention one thing. There is a dispute between us and the Spaniards about the right of navigating the Mississippi ... Seven states wished to relinquish this river to them. The six Southern states opposed it. Seven states not being sufficient to convey it away, it remains now ours....

There is no danger of a dismemberment of our country, unless a Constitution be adopted which will enable the government to plant enemies on our backs. By the Confederation, the rights of territory are secured. No treaty can be made without the consent of nine states. While the consent of nine states is necessary to the cession of territory, you are safe. If it be put in the power of a less number, you will most infallibly lose the Mississippi. As long as we can preserve our unalienable rights, we are in safety. This new Constitution will involve in its operation the loss of the navigation of that valuable river.

The honorable gentleman [either James Madison or Edmund Randolph], cannot be ignorant of the Spanish transactions [the Jay-Gardoqui negotiations]. A treaty had been nearly entered into with Spain, to relinquish that navigation. That relinquishment would absolutely have taken place,

had the consent of seven states been sufficient ... This new government, I conceive, will enable those states who have already discovered their inclination that way, to give away this river....

We are threatened with danger [according to some,] for the non-payment of our debt due to France. We have information come from an illustrious citizen of Virginia, who is now in Paris, which disproves the suggestions of such danger. This citizen has not been in the airy regions of theoretic speculation-our ambassador [Thomas Jefferson] is this worthy citizen. The ambassador of the United States of America is not so despised as the honorable gentleman would make us believe. A servant of a republic is as much respected as that of a monarch. The honorable gentleman tells us that hostile fleets are to be sent to make reprisals upon us. Our ambassador tells you that the king of France has taken into consideration to enter into commercial regulations, on reciprocal terms, with us, which will be of peculiar advantage to us. Does this look like hostility? I might go farther. I might say, not from public authority, but good information, that his opinion is, that you reject this government. His character and abilities are in the highest estimation; he is well acquainted, in every respect, with this country; equally so with the policy of the European nations. Let us follow the sage advice of this common friend of our happiness.

It is little usual for nations to send armies to collect debts. The house of Bourbon, that great friend of America, will never attack her for her unwilling delay of payment. Give me leave to say, that Europe is too much engaged about objects of greater importance, to attend to us. On that great theatre of the world, the little American matters vanish. Do you believe that the mighty monarch of France, beholding the greatest scenes that ever engaged the attention of a prince of that country, will divert himself from those important objects, and now call for a settlement of accounts with America? This proceeding is not warranted by good sense. The friendly disposition to us, and the actual situation of France, render the idea of danger from that quarter absurd. Would this countryman of ours be fond of advising us to a measure which he knew to be dangerous? And can it be reasonably supposed that he can be ignorant of any premeditated hostility against this country? The honorable gentleman may suspect the account; but I will do our friend the justice to say, that he would warn us of any danger from France.

Do you suppose the Spanish monarch will risk a contest with the United States, when his feeble colonies are exposed to them? Every advance the people make to the westward, makes them tremble for Mexico and Peru. Despised as we are among ourselves, under our present government, we are terrible to that monarchy. If this be not a fact, it is generally said so.

We are, in the next place, frightened by dangers from Holland. We must change our government to escape the wrath of that republic. Holland groans under a government like this new one. A stadtholder, sir, a Dutch president, has brought on that country miseries which will not permit them to collect debts with fleets or armies ... This President will bring miseries on us like those of Holland. Such is the condition of European affairs, that it would be unsafe for them to send fleets or armies to collect debts.

But here, sir, they make a transition to objects of another kind. We are presented with dangers of a very uncommon nature. I am not acquainted with the arts of painting. Some gentlemen have a peculiar talent for them. They are practised with great ingenuity on this occasion. As a

counterpart to what we have already been intimidated with, we are told that some lands have been sold, which cannot be found; and that this will bring war on this country. Here the picture will not stand examination. Can it be supposed, if a few land speculators and jobbers have violated the principles of probity, that it will involve this country in war? Is there no redress to be otherwise obtained, even admitting the delinquents and sufferers to be numerous? When gentlemen are thus driven to produce imaginary dangers, to induce this Convention to assent to this change, I am sure it will not be uncandid to say that the change itself is really dangerous.

Then the Maryland compact is broken, and will produce perilous consequences. I see nothing very terrible in this. The adoption of the new system will not remove the evil. Will they forfeit good neighborhood with us, because the compact is broken? Then the disputes concerning the Carolina line are to involve us in dangers. A strip of land running from the westward of the Alleghany to the Mississippi, is the subject of this pretended dispute. I do not know the length or breadth of this disputed spot. Have they not regularly confirmed our right to it, and relinquished all claims to it? I can venture to pledge that the people of Carolina will never disturb us....

Then, sir, comes Pennsylvania, in terrible array. Pennsylvania is to go in conflict with Virginia.

Pennsylvania has been a good neighbor heretofore. She is federal--something terrible--Virginia cannot look her in the face. If we sufficiently attend to the actual situation of things, we shall conclude that Pennsylvania will do what we do. A number of that country are strongly opposed to it. Many of them have lately been convinced of its fatal tendency. They are disgorged of their federalism.... Place yourselves in their situation; would you fight your neighbors for considering this great and awful matter?... Whatever may be the disposition of the aristocratical politicians of that country, I know there are friends of human nature in that state. If so, they will never make war on those who make professions of what they are attached to themselves.

As to the danger arising from borderers, it is mutual and reciprocal. If it be dangerous for Virginia, it is equally so for them. It will be their true interest to be united with us. The danger of our being their enemies will be a prevailing argument in our favor. It will be as powerful to admit us into the Union, as a vote of adoption, without previous amendments, could possibly be.

Then the savage Indians are to destroy us. We cannot look them in the face. The danger is here divided; they are as terrible to the other states as to us. But, sir, it is well known that we have nothing to fear from them. Our back settlers are considerably stronger than they. Their superiority increases daily. Suppose the states to be confederated all around us; what we want in numbers, we shall make up otherwise. Our compact situation and natural strength will secure us.

But, to avoid all dangers, we must take shelter under the federal government. Nothing gives a decided importance but this federal government. You will sip sorrow, according to the vulgar phrase, if you want any other security than the laws of Virginia....

Where is the danger? If, sir, there was any, I would recur to the American spirit to defend us; that spirit which has enabled us to surmount the greatest difficulties--to that illustrious spirit I address my most fervent prayer to prevent our adopting a system destructive to liberty. Let not gentlemen be told that it is not safe to reject this government. Wherefore is it not safe? We are told there are dangers, but those dangers are ideal; they cannot be demonstrated....

The Confederation, this despised government, merits, in my opinion, the highest encomium--it carried us through a long and dangerous war; it rendered us victorious in that bloody conflict

with a powerful nation; it has secured us a territory greater than any European monarch possesses--and shall a government which has been thus strong and vigorous, be accused of imbecility, and abandoned for want of energy? Consider what you are about to do before you part with the government. Take longer time in reckoning things; revolutions like this have happened in almost every country in Europe; similar examples are to be found in ancient Greece and ancient Rome--instances of the people losing their liberty by their own carelessness and the ambition of a few. We are cautioned... against faction and turbulence. I acknowledge that licentiousness is dangerous, and that it ought to be provided against. I acknowledge, also, the new form of government may effectually prevent it. Yet there is another thing it will as effectually do--it will oppress and ruin the people.

ANTI-FEDERALIST PAPER NO. 5

Scotland And England – A Case in Point

The ongoing Federalist essays appeared from October of 1787 to May of 1788. Rebuttals (Antifederalist in nature) to Federalist writers seldom were published. This selection was an answer to Publius [John Jay] Federalist No. 5. This article by "AN OBSERVER," was printed in The New-York Journal and was reprinted in the [Boston] American Herald on December 3, 1787.

A writer, under the signature Publius or The Federalist, No. V, in the Daily Advertiser, and in the New York Packet, with a view of proving the advantages which, he says, will be derived by the states if the new constitution is adopted, has given extracts of a letter from Queen Anne to the Scotch parliament, on the subject of a union between Scotland and England.

I would beg leave to remark, that Publius has been very unfortunate in selecting these extracts as a case in point, to convince the people of America of the benefits they would derive from a union, under such a government as would be effected by the new system. It is a certainty, that when the union was the subject of debate in the Scottish legislature, some of their most sensible and disinterested nobles, as well as commoners! (who were not corrupted by English gold), violently opposed the union, and predicted that the people of Scotland would, in fact, derive no advantages from a consolidation of government with England; but, on the contrary, they would bear a great proportion of her debt, and furnish large bodies of men to assist in her wars with France, with whom, before the union, Scotland was at all times on terms of the most cordial amity. It was also predicted that the representation in the parliament of Great Britain, particularly in the house of commons, was too small; forty-five members being very far from the proportion of Scotland, when its extent and numbers were duly considered; and that even they, being so few, might (or at least a majority of them might) at all times be immediately under the influence of the English ministry; and, of course, very little of their attention would be given to the true interest of their constituents, especially if they came in competition with the prospects of views of the ministry. How far these predictions have been verified I believe it will not require much trouble to prove. It must be obvious to everyone, the least acquainted with English history, that since the union of the two nations the great body of the people in Scotland are in a much worse situation now, than they would be, were they a separate nation. This will be fully illustrated by attending to the great emigrations which are made to America. For if the people could have but a common support at home, it is unreasonable to suppose that such large numbers would quit their country, break from the tender ties of kindred and friendship and trust themselves on a dangerous voyage across a vast ocean, to a country of which they can know but very little except by common report. I will only further remark, that it is not about two or three years since a member of the British parliament (I believe Mr. Dempster) gave a most pathetic description of the sufferings of the commonalty of Scotland, particularly on the sea coast, and endeavored to call the attention of parliament to their distresses, and afford them some relief by encouraging their fisheries. It deserves also to be remembered, that the people of Scotland, in the late war between France and Great Britain, petitioned to have arms and ammunition supplied them by their general government, for their defense, alleging that they were incapable of defending themselves and their property from an invasion unless they were assisted by government. It is a truth that their

petitions were disregarded, and reasons were assigned, that it would be dangerous to entrust them with the means of defense, as they would then have it in their power to break the union. From this representation of the situation of Scotland, surely no one can draw any conclusion that this country would derive happiness or security from a government which would, in reality, give the people but the mere name of being free. For if the representation, stipulated by the constitution, framed by the late convention, be attentively and dispassionately considered, it must be obvious to every disinterested observer (besides many other weighty objections which will present themselves to view), that the number is not, by any means, adequate to the present inhabitants of this extensive continent, much less to those it will contain at a future period.

I observe that the writer above mentioned, takes great pains to show the disadvantages which would result from three or four distinct confederacies of these states. I must confess that I have not seen, in any of the pieces published against the proposed constitution, any thing which gives the most distant idea that their writers are in favor of such governments; but it is clear these objections arise from a consolidation not affording security for the liberties of their country, and from hence it must evidently appear, that the design of Publius, in artfully holding up to public view [the bugbear of] such confederacies, can be with no other intention than wilfully to deceive his fellow citizens. I am confident it must be, and that it is, the sincere wish of every true friend to the United States, that there should be a confederated national government, but that it should be one which would have a control over national and external matters only, and not interfere with the internal regulations and police of the

different states in the union. Such a government, while it would give us respectability abroad, would not encroach upon, or subvert our liberties at home.
AN OBSERVER

ANTI-FEDERALIST PAPER NO. 6

The Hobgoblins Of Anarchy And Dissensions Among The States

One of largest series of Antifederalist essays was penned under the pseudonym "CENTINEL."
The Philadelphia Independent Gazetteer ran this 24 essay series between October 5, 1787 and November 24, 1788.
Some historians feel most of the "Centinel" letters were written by Samuel Bryan, and a few by Eleazer Oswald, owner of the Independent Gazetteer. A more recent study by Charles Page Smith, James Wilson, Founding Father (Chapel Hill, 1956), refrains from making such theory This selection is from the eleventh letter of "Centinel," appearing in the Independent Gazetteer on January 16, 1788.

The evils of anarchy have been portrayed with all the imagery of language in the growing colors of eloquence; the affrighted mind is thence led to clasp the new Constitution as the instrument of deliverance, as the only avenue to safety and happiness. To avoid the possible and transitory evils of one extreme, it is seduced into the certain and permanent misery necessarily attendant on the other. A state of anarchy from its very nature can never be of long continuance; the greater its violence the shorter the duration. Order and security are immediately sought by the distracted people beneath the shelter of equal laws and the salutary restraints of regular government; and if this be not attainable, absolute power is assumed by the one, or a few, who shall be the most enterprising and successful. If anarchy, therefore, were the inevitable consequence of rejecting the new Constitution, it would be infinitely better to incur it, for even then there would be at least the chance of a good government rising out of licentiousness. But to rush at once into despotism because there is a bare possibility of anarchy ensuing from the rejection, or from what is yet more visionary, the small delay that would be occasioned by a revision and correction of the proposed system of government is so superlatively weak, so fatally blind, that it is astonishing any person of common understanding should suffer such an imposition to have the least influence on his judgment; still more astonishing that so flimsy and deceptive a doctrine should make converts among the enlightened freemen of America, who have so long enjoyed the blessings of liberty. But when I view among such converts men otherwise pre-eminent it raises a blush for the weakness of humanity that these, her brightest ornaments, should be so dimsighted to what is self-evident to most men, that such imbecility of judgment should appear where so much perfection was looked for. This ought to teach us to depend more on our own judgment and the nature of the case than upon the opinions of the greatest and best of men, who, from constitutional infirmities or particular situations, may sometimes view an object through a delusive medium; but the opinions of great men are more frequently the dictates of ambition or private interest.

The source of the apprehensions of this so much dreaded anarchy would upon investigation be found to arise from the artful suggestions of designing men, and not from a rational probability grounded on the actual state of affairs. The least reflection is sufficient to detect the fallacy to show that there is no one circumstance to justify the prediction of such an event. On the contrary
a short time will evince, to the utter dismay and confusion of the conspirators, that a perseverance in cramming down their scheme of power upon the freemen of this State
[Pennsylvania] will inevitably produce an anarchy destructive of their darling domination, and may kindle a flame prejudicial to their safety. They should be cautious not to trespass too far on the forbearance of freemen when wresting their dearest concerns, but prudently retreat from the gathering storm.

The other specter that has been raised to terrify and alarm the people out of the exercise of their judgment on this great occasion, is the dread of our splitting into separate confederacies or republics, that might become rival powers and consequently liable to mutual wars from the usual motives of contention. This is an event still more improbable than the foregoing. It is a presumption unwarranted, either by the situation of affairs, or the sentiments of the people; no disposition leading to it exists; the advocates of the new constitution seem to view such a separation with horror, and its opponents are strenuously contending for a confederation that shall embrace all America under its comprehensive and salutary protection.

This hobgoblin appears to have sprung from the deranged brain of Publius, [The Federalist] a New York writer, who, mistaking sound for argument, has with Herculean labor accumulated myriads of unmeaning sentences, and mechanically endeavored to force conviction by a torrent of misplaced words. He might have spared his readers the fatigue of wading through his long-winded disquisitions on the direful effects of the contentions of inimical states, as totally inapplicable to the subject he was professedly treating; this writer has devoted much time, and wasted more paper in combating chimeras of his own creation. However, for the sake of argument, I will admit that the necessary consequence of rejecting or delaying the establishment of the new constitution would be the dissolution of the union, and the institution of even rival and inimical republics; yet ought such an apprehension, if well founded, to drive us into the fangs of despotism? Infinitely preferable would be occasional wars to such an event. The former, although a severe scourge, is transient in its continuance, and in its operation partial, but a small proportion of the community are exposed to its greatest horrors, and yet fewer experience its greatest evils; the latter is permanent and universal misery, without remission or exemption. As passing clouds obscure for a time the splendor of the sun, so do wars interrupt the welfare of mankind; but despotism is a settled gloom that totally extinguishes happiness. Not a ray of comfort can penetrate to cheer the dejected mind; the goad of power with unabating rigor insists upon the utmost exaction; like a merciless taskmaster, [it] is continually inflicting the lash, and is never satiated with the feast of unfeeling domination, or the most abject servility.

The celebrated Lord Kaims, whose disquisitions of human nature evidence extraordinary strength of judgment and depth of investigation, says that a continual civil war, which is the most destructive and horrible scene of human discord, is preferable to the uniformity of wretchedness and misery attendant upon despotism; of all possible evils, as I observed in my first number, this is the worst and the most to be dreaded.

I congratulate my fellow citizens that a good government, the greatest earthly blessing, may be so easily obtained, that our circumstances are so favorable, that nothing but the folly of the conspirators can produce anarchy or civil war, which would presently terminate in their destruction and the permanent harmony of the state, alone interrupted by their ambitious machinations.

CENTINEL

ANTI-FEDERALIST PAPER NO. 7

Adoption Of The Constitution Will Lead To Civil War

"PHILANTHROPOS," (an anonymous Virginia Antifederalist) appeared in The Virginia Journal and Alexandria Advertiser, December 6, 1787, writing his version of history under the proposed new Constitution.

The time in which the constitution or government of a nation undergoes any particular change, is always interesting and critical. Enemies are vigilant, allies are in suspense, friends hesitating between hope and fear; and all men are in eager expectation to see what such a change may produce. But the state of our affairs at present, is of such moment, as even to arouse the dead ...

[A certain defender of the Constitution has stated that objections to it] are more calculated to alarm the fears of the people than to answer any valuable end. Was that the case, as it is not, will any man in his sober senses say, that the least infringement or appearance of infringement on our liberty -that liberty which has lately cost so much blood and treasure, together with anxious days and sleepless nights-ought not both to rouse our fears and awaken our jealousy? ... The new constitution in its present form is calculated to produce despotism, thraldom and confusion, and if the United States do swallow it, they will find it a bolus, that will create convulsions to their utmost extremities. Were they mine enemies, the worst imprecation I could devise would be, may they adopt it. For tyranny, where it has been chained (as for a few years past) is always more cursed, and sticks its teeth in deeper than before. Were Col. [George] Mason's objections obviated, the improvement would be very considerable, though even then, not so complete as might be. The Congress's having power without control-to borrow money on the credit of the United States; their having power to appoint their own salaries, and their being paid out of the treasury of the United States, thereby, in some measure, rendering them independent of the individual states; their being judges of the qualification and election of their own members, by which means they can get men to suit any purpose; together with Col. Mason's wise and judicious objections-are grievances, the very idea of which is enough to make every honest citizen exclaim in the language of

Documents of Revolution

Cato, 0 Liberty, 0 my country! Our present constitution, with a few additional powers to Congress, seems better calculated to preserve the rights and defend the liberties of our citizens, than the one proposed, without proper amendments. Let us therefore, for once, show our judgment and solidity by continuing it, and prove the opinion to be erroneous, that levity and fickleness are not only the foibles of our tempers, but the reigning principles in these states. There are men amongst us, of such dissatisfied tempers, that place them in Heaven, they would find something to blame; and so restless and self- sufficient, that they must be eternally reforming the state. But the misfortune is, they always leave affairs worse than they find them. A change of government is at all times dangerous, but at present may be fatal, without the utmost caution, just after emerging out of a tedious and expensive war. Feeble in our nature, and complicated in our form, we are little able to bear the rough Posting of civil dissensions which are likely to ensue. Even now, discontent and opposition distract our councils. Division and despondency affect our people. Is it then a time to alter our government, that government which even now totters on its foundation, and will, without tender care, produce ruin by its fall?

Beware my countrymen! Our enemies- -uncontrolled as they are in their ambitious schemes, fretted with losses, and perplexed with disappointments-will exert their whole power and policy to increase and continue our confusion. And while we are destroying one another, they will be repairing their losses, and ruining our trade.

Of all the plagues that infest a nation, a civil war is the worst. Famine is severe, pestilence is dreadful; but in these, though men die, they die in peace. The father expires without the guilt of the son; and the son, if he survives, enjoys the inheritance of his father. Cities may be thinned, but they neither plundered nor burnt. But when a civil war is kindled, there is then forth no security of property nor protection from any law. Life and fortune become precarious. And all that is dear to men is at the discretion of profligate soldiery, doubly licentious on such an occasion. Cities are exhausted by heavy contributions, or sacked because they cannot answer exorbitant demand. Countries are eaten up by the parties they favor, and ravaged by the one they oppose. Fathers and sons, sheath their swords in anothers bowels in the field, and their wives and daughters are exposed to rudeness and lust of ruffians at home. And when the sword has decided quarrel, the scene is closed with banishments, forfeitures, and barbarous executions that entail distress on children then unborn. May Heaven avert the dreadful catastrophe! In the most limited governments, what wranglings, animosities, factions, partiality, and all other evils that tend to embroil a nation and weaken a state, are constantly practised by legislators. What then may we expect if the new constitution be adopted as it now stands? The great will struggle for power, honor and wealth; the poor become a prey to avarice, insolence and oppression. And while some are studying to supplant their neighbors, and others striving to keep their stations, one villain will wink at the oppression of another, the people be fleeced, and the public business neglected. From despotism and tyranny good Lord deliver us.

ANTI-FEDERALIST PAPER NO. 8

"The Power Vested In Congress Of Sending Troops For Suppressing Insurrections Will Always Enable Them To Stifle The First Struggles Of Freedom"

"A FEDERAL REPUBLICAN" (from Virginia) had his `letter to the editor' appear in The Norfolk and Portsmouth Register March 5, 1788.

.... By the Articles of Confederation, the congress of the United State was vested with powers for conducting the common concerns of the continent. They had the sole and exclusive right and power of determining on peace and war; of sending and receiving ambassadors; of entering into treaties and alliances; and of pointing out the respective quotas of men and men which each state should furnish. But it was expressly provided that the money to be supplied by each state should be raised by the authority and direction of the legislature thereof-- thus reserving to the states the important privilege of levying taxes upon their citizens in such manner as might be most conformable to their peculiar circumstances and form of government. With powers thus constituted was congress enabled to unite the general exertions of the continent in the cause of liberty and to carry us triumphantly through a long and bloody war. It was not until sometime after peace and a glorious independence had been established that defects were discovered in that system of federal government which had procured to us those blessings. It was then perceived that the Articles of Confederation were inadequate to the purposes of the union; and it was particularly suggested as necessary to vest in congress the further power of exclusively regulating the commerce of the United States, as well to enable us, by a system more uniform, to counteract the policy of foreign nations, as for other important reasons. Upon this principle, a general convention of the United States was proposed to be held, and deputies were accordingly appointed by twelve of the states charged with power to revise, alter, and amend the Articles of Confederation. When these deputies met, instead of confining themselves to the powers with which they were entrusted, they pronounced all amendments to the Articles of Confederation wholly impracticable; and with a spirit of amity and concession truly remarkable proceeded to form a government entirely new, and totally different in its principles and its organization.

Instead of a congress whose members could serve but three years out of six-and then to return to a level with their fellow citizens; and who were liable at all times, whenever the states might deem it necessary, to be recalled-- Congress, by this new constitution, will be composed of a body whose members during the time they are appointed to serve, can receive no check from their constituents. Instead of the powers formerly granted to congress of ascertaining each state's quota of men and money-to be raised by the legislatures of the different states in such a mode as they might think proper- -congress, by this new government, will be invested with the formidable powers of raising armies, and lending money, totally independent of the different states. They will moreover, have the power of leading troops among you in order to suppress those struggles which may sometimes happen among a free people, and which tyranny will impiously brand with the name of sedition. On one day the state collector will call on you for your proportion of those taxes which have been laid on you by the general assembly, where you are fully and adequately represented; on the next will come the Continental collector to demand from you those taxes which shall be levied by the continental congress, where the whole state of Virginia

will be represented by only ten men! Thus shall we imprudently confer on so small a number the very important power of taking our money out of our pockets, and of levying taxes without control-a right which the wisdom of our state constitution will, in vain, have confided to the most numerous branch of the legislature. Should the sheriff or state collector in any manner aggrieve you either in person or property, these sacred rights are amply secured by the most solemn compact. Beside, the arm of government is always at hand to shield you from his injustice and oppression. But if a Continental collector, in the execution of his office, should invade your freedom (according to this new government, which has expressly declared itself paramount to all state laws and constitutions) the state of which you are a citizen will have no authority to afford you relief. A continental court may, indeed, be established in the state, and it may be urged that you will find a remedy here; but, my fellow citizens, let me ask, what protection this will afford you against the insults or rapacity of a continental officer, when he will have it in his power to appeal to the seat of congress perhaps at several hundred miles distance, and by this means oblige you to expend hundreds of pounds in obtaining redress for twenty shillings unjustly extorted? Thus will you be necessarily compelled either to make a bold effort to extricate yourselves from these grievous and oppressive extortions, or you will be fatigued by fruitless attempts into the quiet and peaceable surrender of those rights, for which the blood of your fellow citizens has been shed in vain. But the latter will, no doubt, be the melancholy fate of a people once inspired with the love of liberty, as the power vested in congress of sending troops for suppressing insurrections will always enable them to stifle the first struggles of freedom.
A FEDERAL REPUBLICAN

ANTI-FEDERALIST PAPER NO. 9

A Consolidated Government Is A Tyranny

"MONTEZUMA," regarded as a Pennsylvanian, wrote this essay which showed up in the Independent Gazetteer on October 17, 1787.

We the Aristocratic party of the United States, lamenting the many inconveniences to which the late confederation subjected the well-born, the better kind of people, bringing them down to the level of the rabble-and holding in utter detestation that frontispiece to every bill of rights, "that all men are born equal"-beg leave (for the purpose of drawing a line between such as we think were ordained to govern, and such as were made to bear the weight of government without having any share in its administration) to submit to our Friends in the first class for their inspection, the following defense of our monarchical, aristocratical democracy.

lst. As a majority of all societies consist of men who (though totally incapable of thinking or acting in governmental matters) are more readily led than driven, we have thought meet to indulge them in something like a democracy in the new constitution,

Documents of Revolution

which part we have designated by the popular name of the House of Representatives. But to guard against every possible danger from this lower house, we have subjected every bill they bring forward, to the double negative of our upper house and president. Nor have we allowed the populace the right to elect their representatives annually... lest this body should be too much under the influence and control of their constituents, and thereby prove the "weatherboard of our grand edifice, to show the shiftings of every fashionable gale,"-for we have not yet to learn that little else is wanting to aristocratize the most democratical representative than to make him somewhat independent of his political creators. We have taken away that rotation of appointment which has so long perplexed us-that grand engine of popular influence. Every man is eligible into our government from time to time for life. This will have a two-fold good effect. First, it prevents the representatives from mixing with the lower class, and imbibing their foolish sentiments, with which they would have come charged on re-election.

2d. They will from the perpetuality of office be under our eye, and in a short time will think and act like us, independently of popular whims and prejudices. For the assertion "that evil communications corrupt good manners," is not more true than its reverse. We have allowed this house the power to impeach, but we have tenaciously reserved the right to try. We hope gentlemen, you will see the policy of this clause-for what matters it who accuses, if the accused is tried by his friends. In fine, this plebian house will have little power, and that little be rightly shaped by our house of gentlemen, who will have a very extensive influence-from their being chosen out of the genteeler class ... It is true, every third senatorial seat is to be vacated duennually, but two-thirds of this influential body will remain in office, and be ready to direct or (if necessary) bring over to the good old way, the young members, if the old ones should not be returned. And whereas many of our brethren, from a laudable desire to support their rank in life above the commonalty, have not only deranged their finances, but subjected their persons to indecent treatment (as being arrested for debt, etc.) we have framed a privilege clause, by which they may laugh at the fools who trusted them. But we have given out, that this clause was

provided, only that the members might be able without interruption, to deliberate on the important business of their country. We have frequently endeavored to effect in our respective states, the happy discrimination which pervades this system; but finding we could not bring the states into it individually, we have determined ... and have taken pains to leave the legislature of each free and independent state, as they now call themselves, in such a situation that they will eventually be absorbed by our grand continental vortex, or dwindle into petty corporations, and have power over little else than yoaking hogs or determining the width of cart wheels. But (aware that an intention to annihilate state legislatures, would be objected to our favorite scheme) we have made their existence (as a board of electors) necessary to ours. This furnishes us and our advocates with a fine answer to any clamors that may be raised on this subject. We have so interwoven continental and state legislatures that they cannot exist separately; whereas we in truth only leave them the power of electing us, for what can a provincial legislature do when we possess the exclusive regulation of external and internal commerce, excise, duties, imposts, post-offices and roads; when we and we alone, have the power to wage war, make peace, coin money (if we can get bullion) if not, borrow money, organize the militia and call them forth to execute our decrees, and crush insurrections assisted by a noble body of veterans subject to our nod, which we have the power of raising and keeping even in the time of peace. What have we to fear from state legislatures or even from states, when we are armed with such powers, with a president at our head? (A name we thought proper to adopt in conformity to the prejudices of a silly people who are so foolishly fond of a Republican government, that we were obliged to accommodate in names and forms to them, in order more effectually to secure the substance of our proposed plan; but we all know that Cromwell was a King, with the title of Protector). I repeat it, what have we to fear armed with such powers, with a president at our head who is captain--general of the army, navy and militia of the United States, who can make and unmake treaties, appoint and commission ambassadors and other ministers, who can grant or refuse reprieves or pardons, who can make judges of the supreme and other continental courts-in short, who will be the source, the fountain of honor, profit and power, whose influence like the rays of the sun, will diffuse itself far and wide, will exhale all democratical vapors and break the clouds of popular insurrection? But again gentlemen, our judicial power is a strong work, a masked battery, few people see the guns we can and will ere long play off from it. For the judicial power embraces every question which can arise in law or equity, under this constitution and under the laws of "the United States" (which laws will be, you know, the supreme laws of the land). This power extends to all cases, affecting ambassadors or other public ministers, "and consuls; to all cases of admiralty and maritime jurisdiction; to controversies to which the United States shall be a party; to controversies between two or more States; between a State and citizens of another State; between citizens of different States; between citizens of the same State, claiming lands under grants of different States; and between a State or the citizens thereof, and foreign States, citizens or subjects."

Now, can a question arise in the colonial courts, which the ingenuity or sophistry of an able lawyer may not bring within one or other of the above cases? Certainly not. Then our court will have original or appellate jurisdiction in all cases-and if so, how fallen are state judicatures-and must not every provincial law yield to our supreme flat? Our constitution answers yes.... And finally we shall entrench ourselves so as to laugh at the cabals of the commonalty. A few regiments will do at first; it must be spread abroad that they are absolutely necessary to defend

the frontiers. Now a regiment and then a legion must be added quietly; by and by a frigate or two must be built, still taking care to intimate that they are essential to the support of our revenue laws and to prevent smuggling. We have said nothing about a bill of rights, for we viewed it as an eternal clog upon our designs, as a lock chain to the wheels of government-though, by the way, as we have not insisted on rotation in our offices, the simile of a wheel is ill. We have for some time considered the freedom of the press as a great evil-it spreads information, and begets a licentiousness in the people which needs the rein more than the spur; besides, a daring printer may expose the plans of government and lessen the consequence of our president and senate-for these and many other reasons we have said nothing with respect to the "right of the people to speak and publish their sentiments" or about their "palladiums of liberty" and such stuff. We do not much like that sturdy privilege of the people-the right to demand the writ of habeas corpus.

We have therefore reserved the power of refusing it in cases of rebellion, and you know we are the judges of what is rebellion.... Our friends we find have been assiduous in representing our federal calamities, until at length the people at large-frightened by the gloomy picture on one side, and allured by the prophecies of some of our fanciful and visionary adherents on the other- are ready to accept and confirm our proposed government without the delay or forms of examination--which was the more to be wished, as they are wholly unfit to investigate the principles or pronounce on the merit of so exquisite a system. Impressed with a conviction that this constitution is calculated to restrain the influence and power of the LOWER CLASS-to draw that discrimination we have so long sought after; to secure to our friends privileges and offices, which were not to be ... [obtained] under the former government, because they were in common; to take the burden of legislation and attendance on public business off the commonalty, who will be much better able thereby to prosecute with effect their private business; to destroy that political thirteen headed monster, the state sovereignties; to check the licentiousness of the people by making it dangerous to speak or publish daring or tumultuary sentiments; to enforce obedience to laws by a strong executive, aided by military pensioners; and finally to promote the public and private interests of the better kind of people-we submit it to your judgment to take such measures for its adoption as you in your wisdom may think fit.

Signed by unanimous order of the lords spiritual and temporal.

MONTEZUMA

ANTI-FEDERALIST PAPER NO. 10

On The Preservation Of Parties, Public Liberty Depends

This essay follows a theme similar to Federalist No. 10, and appeared in the Maryland Gazette and Baltimore Advertiser, March 18, 1788.

The opposite qualities of the first confederation were rather caused by than the cause of two parties, which from its first existence began and have continued their operations, I believe, unknown to their country and almost unknown to themselves-as really but few men have the capacity or resolution to develop the secret causes which influence their daily conduct. The old Congress was a national government and an union of States, both brought into one political body, as these opposite powers-I do not mean parties were so exactly blended and very nearly balanced, like every artificial, operative machine where action is equal to reaction. It stood perfectly still. It would not move at all. Those who were merely confederal in their views, were for dividing the public debt. Those who were for national government, were for increasing of it.

Those who thought any national government would be destructive to the liberties of America . . .

assisted those who thought it our only safety-to put everything as wrong as possible. Requisitions were made, which every body knew it was impossible to comply with. Either in 82 or 83, ten millions of hard dollars, if not thirteen, were called into the continental treasury, when there could not be half that sum in the whole tract of territory between Nova-Scotia and Florida. The States neglected them in despair. The public honor was tarnished, and our governments abused by their servants and best friends. In fine, it became a cant word things are not yet bad enough to mend. However, as [a] great part of the important objects of society were entrusted to this mongrel species of general government, the sentiment of pushing it forward became general throughout America, and the late Convention met at Philadelphia under the uniform impression, that such was the desire of their constituents. But even then the advantages and disadvantages of national government operated so strongly, although silently, on each individual, that the conflict was nearly equal. A third or middle opinion, which always arises in such cases, broke off and took the lead-the national party [thus] assisted, pursued steadily their object- the federal party dropped off, one by one, and finally, when the middle party came to view the offspring which they had given birth to, and in a great measure reared, several of them immediately disowned the child. Such has been hitherto the progress of party; or rather of the human mind dispassionately contemplating our separate and relative situation, and aiming at that perfect completion of social happiness and grandeur, which perhaps can be combined only in ideas. Every description of men entertain the same wishes (excepting perhaps a few very bad men of each)-they forever will differ about the mode of accomplishment-and some must be permitted to doubt the practicability.

As our citizens are now apprized of the progress of parties or political opinions on the continent, it is fit they should also be informed of the present state, force and designs of each, in order that they may form their decisions with safety to the public and themselves-this shall be given with all the precision and impartiality the author is capable of.

America is at present divided into three classes or descriptions of men, and in a few years there will be but two.

[First]. The first class comprehends all those men of fortune and reputation who stepped forward in the late revolution, from opposition to the administration, rather than the government of Great Britain. All those aristocrats whose pride disdains equal law. Many men of very large fortune, who entertain real or imaginary fears for the security of property. Those young men, who have sacrificed their time and their talents to public service, without any prospect of an adequate pecuniary or honorary reward. All your people of fashion and pleasure who are corrupted by the dissipation of the French, English and American armies; and a love of European manners and luxury. The public creditors of the continent, whose interest has been heretofore sacrificed by their friends, in order to retain their services on this occasion. A large majority of the mercantile people, which is at present a very unformed and consequently dangerous interest. Our old native merchants have been almost universally ruined by the receipt of their debts in paper during the war, and the payment in hard money of what they owed their British correspondents since peace.

Those who are not bankrupts, have generally retired and given place to a set of young men, who conducting themselves as rashly as ignorantly, have embarrassed their affairs and lay the blame on the government, and who are really unacquainted with the true mercantile interest of the country-which is perplexed from circumstances rather temporary than permanent. The foreign merchants are generally not to be trusted with influence in our government-- they are most of them birds of passage. Some, perhaps British emissaries increasing and rejoicing in our political mistakes, and even those who have settled among us with an intention to fix themselves and their posterity in our soil, have brought with them more foreign prejudices than wealth. Time must elapse before the mercantile interest will be so organized as to govern themselves, much less others, with propriety. And lastly, to this class I suppose we may ultimately add the tory interest, with the exception of very many respectable characters, who reflect with a gratification mixed with disdain, that those principles are now become fashionable for which they have been persecuted and hunted down-which, although by no means so formidable as is generally imagined, is still considerable. They are at present wavering. They are generally, though with very many exceptions, openly for the proposed, but secretly against any American government.

A burnt child dreads the fire. But should they see any fair prospect of confusion arise, these gentry will be off at any moment for these five and twenty years to come. Ultimately, should the administration promise stability to the new government, they may be counted on as the Janizaries of power, ready to efface all suspicion by the violence of their zeal.

In general, all these various people would prefer a government, as nearly copied after that of Great Britain, as our circumstances will permit. Some would strain these circumstances. Others still retain a deep rooted jealousy of the executive branch and strong republican prejudices as they are called. Finally, this class contains more aggregate wisdom and moral virtue than both the other two together. It commands nearly two thirds of the property and almost one half the numbers of America, and has at present, become almost irresistible from the name of the truly great and amiable man who it has been said, is disposed to patronize it, and from the influence which it has over the second class. This [first] class is nearly at the height of their power; they must decline or moderate, or another revolution will ensue, for the opinion of America is becoming daily more unfavorable to those radical changes which high-toned government requires. A conflict would terminate in the destruction of this class, or the liberties of their country. May the Guardian Angel of America prevent both!

[Second]. The second class is composed of those descriptions of men who are certainly more numerous with us than in any other part of the globe. First, those men who are so wise as to discover that their ancestors and indeed all the rest of mankind were and are fools. We have a vast overproportion of these great men, who, when you tell them that from the earliest period at which mankind devoted their attention to social happiness, it has been their uniform judgment, that a government over governments cannot exist- -that is two governments operating on the same individual-assume the smile of confidence, and tell you of two people travelling the same road-of a perfect and precise division of the duties of the individual. Still, however, the political apothegm is as old as the proverb-That no man can serve two masters-and whoever will run their noddles against old proverbs will be sure to break them, however hard they may be. And if they broke only their own, all would be right; but it is very horrible to reflect that all our numskulls must be cracked in concert. Second. The trimmers, who from sympathetic indecision are always united with, and when not regularly employed, always fight under the banners of these great men, These people are forever at market, and when parties are nearly equally divided, they get very well paid for their services. Thirdly. The indolent, that is almost every second man of independent fortune you meet with in America-these are quite easy, and can live under any government. If men can be said to live, who scarcely breathe; and if breathing was attended with any bodily exertion, would give up their small portion of life in despair. These men do not swim with the stream as the trimmers do, but are dragged like mud at the bottom. As they have no other weight than their tat flesh, they are hardly worth mentioning when we speak of the sentiments and opinions of America. As this second class never can include any of the yeomanry of the union, who never affect superior wisdom, and can have no interests but the public good, it can be only said to exist at the birth of government, and as soon as the first and third classes become more decided in their views, this will divide with each and dissipate like a mist, or sink down into what are called moderate men, and become the tools and instruments of others. These people are prevented by a cloud from having any view; and if they are not virtuous, they at least preserve the appearance, which in this world amounts to the same thing.

[Third]. At the head of the third class appear the old rigid republicans, who although few in number, are still formidable. Reverence will follow these men in spite of detraction, as long as wisdom and virtue are esteemed among mankind. They are joined by the true democrats, who are in general fanatics and enthusiasts, and some few sensible, charming madmen. A decided majority of the yeomanry of America will, for a length of years, be ready to support these two descriptions of men. But as this last class is forced to act as a residuary legatee, and receive all the trash and filth, it is in some measure disgraced and its influence weakened. 3dly. The freebooters and plunderers, who infest all countries and ours perhaps as little as any other whatever. These men have that natural antipathy to any kind or sort of government, that a rogue has to a halter. In number they are few indeed such characters are the offspring of dissipation and want, and there is not that country in the world where so much real property is shared so equally among so few citizens, for where property is as easily acquired by fair means, very

few indeed will resort to foul. Lastly, by the poor mob, infoelix pecus!1 The property of whoever will feed them and take care of them-let them be spared. Let the burden of taxation sit lightly on their shoulders. But alas! This is not their fate. It is here that government forever falls with all its weight. It is here that the proposed government will press where it should scarcely be felt.
. . .

In this [third] class may be counted men of the greatest mental powers and of as sublime virtue as any in America. They at present command nearly one-third of the property and above half the numbers of the United States, and in either event they must continue to increase in influence by great desertions from both the other classes. . . . If the [proposed] government is not adopted, theirs will be the prevalent opinion. The object of this class either is or will be purely federal-an union of independent States, not a government of individuals. And should the proposed federal plan fail, from the obstinacy of those who will listen to no conditional amendments, although such as they cannot disapprove; or should it ultimately in its execution upon a fair trial, disappoint the wishes and expectations of our country-[then] an union purely federal is what the reasonable and dispassionate patriots of America must bend their views to. My countrymen, preserve your jealousy-reject suspicion, it is the fiend that destroys public and private happiness.

I know some weak, but very few if any wicked men in public confidence. And learn this most difficult and necessary lesson: That on the preservation of parties, public liberty depends.

Whenever men are unanimous on great public questions, whenever there is but one party, freedom ceases and despotism commences. The object of a free and wise people should be so to balance parties, that from the weakness of all you may be governed by the moderation of the combined judgments of the whole, not tyrannized over by the blind passions of a few individuals.

A FARMER

ANTI-FEDERALIST PAPER NO. 11

Unrestricted Power Over Commerce Should Not Be Given Thenational Government

Scholars regard James Winthrop of Cambridge, Mass. to be the "Agrippa" who contributed the series to The Massachusetts Gazette from November 23, 1787 to February 5, 1788. This is a compilation of excerpts from "Agrippa's" letters of December 14, 18, 25, and 28, 1787, taken from Ford, Essays, pp. 70-73, 76-77, 79-81.

It has been proved, by indisputable evidence, that power is not the grand principle of union among the parts of a very extensive empire; and that when this principle is pushed beyond the degree necessary for rendering justice between man and man, it debases the character of individuals, and renders them less secure in their persons and property. Civil liberty consists in the consciousness of that security, and is best guarded by political liberty, which is the share that every citizen has in the government. Accordingly all our accounts agree, that in those empires which are commonly called despotic, and which comprehend by far the greatest part of the world, the government is most fluctuating, and property least secure. In those countries insults are borne by the sovereign, which, if offered to one of our governors, would fill us with horror, and we should think the government dissolving.

The common conclusion from this reasoning is an exceedingly unfair one, that we must then separate, and form distinct confederacies. This would be true if there was no principle to substitute in the room of power. Fortunately there is one. This is commerce. All the states have local advantages, and in a considerable degree separate interests. They are, therefore, in a situation to supply each other's wants. Carolina, for instance, is inhabited by planters, while Massachusetts is more engaged in commerce and manufactures. Congress has the power of deciding their differences. The most friendly intercourse may therefore be established between them. A diversity of produce, wants and interests, produces commerce; and commerce, where there is a common, equal and moderate authority to preside, produces friendship.

The same principles apply to the connection with the new settlers in the west. Many supplies they want, for which they must look to the older settlements, and the greatness of their crops enables them to make payments. Here, then, we have a bond of - union which applies to all parts of the empire, and would continue to operate if the empire comprehended all America.

We are now, in the strictest sense of the terms, a federal republic. Each part has within its own limits the sovereignty over its citizens, while some of the general concerns are committed to Congress. The complaints of the deficiency of the Congressional powers are confined to two articles. They are not able to raise a revenue by taxation, and they have not a complete regulation of the intercourse between us and foreigners. For each of these complaints there is some foundation, but not enough to justify the clamor which has been raised....

The second article of complaint against the present confederation . . . is that Congress has not the sole power to regulate the intercourse between us and foreigners. Such a power extends not only to war and peace, but to trade and naturalization. This last article ought never to be given them; for though most of the states may be willing for certain reasons to receive foreigners as citizens, yet reasons of equal weight may induce other states, differently circumstanced, to keep their blood pure. Pennsylvania has chosen to receive all that would come there. Let any indifferent person judge whether that state in point of morals, education, [or] energy, is equal to any of the eastern states; the small state of Rhode Island only excepted. Pennsylvania in the course of a century has acquired her present extent and population at the expense of religion and good morals. The eastern states have, by keeping separate from the foreign mixtures, acquired their present greatness in the course of a century and an half, and have preserved their religion and morals. They have also preserved that manly virtue which is equally fitted for rendering them respectable in war, and industrious in peace.

The remaining power for peace and trade might perhaps be safely lodged with Congress under some limitations. Three restrictions appear to me to be essentially necessary to preserve that equality of rights to the states, which it is the object of the state governments to secure to each citizen. 1st. It ought not to be in the power of Congress, either by treaty or otherwise, to alienate part of any state without the consent of the legislature. 2nd. They ought not to be able, by treaty or other law, to give any legal preference to one part above another. 3rd. They ought to be restrained from creating any monopolies....

The idea of consolidation is further kept up in the right given to regulate trade. Though this power under certain limitations would be a proper one for the department of Congress, it is in this system carried much too far, and much farther than is necessary. This is, without exception, the most commercial state upon the continent. Our extensive coasts, cold climate, small estates, and equality of rights, with a variety of subordinate and concurring circumstances, place us in this respect at the head of the Union. We must, therefore, be indulged if a point which so nearly relates to our welfare be rigidly examined. The new constitution not only prohibits vessels, bound from one state to another, from paying any duties, but even from entering and clearing.

The only use of such a regulation is, to keep each state in complete ignorance of its own resources. It certainly is no hardship to enter and clear at the custom house, and the expense is too small to be an object.

The unlimited right to regulate trade, includes the right of granting exclusive charters. This, in all old countries, is considered as one principal branch of prerogative. We find hardly a country in Europe which has not felt the ill effects of such a power. Holland has carried the exercise of it farther than any other state, and the reason why that country has felt less evil from it is, that the territory is very small, and they have drawn large revenues from their colonies in the East and West Indies. In this respect, the whole country is to be considered as a trading company, having exclusive privileges. The colonies are large in proportion to the parent state; so that, upon the whole, the latter may gain by such a system. We are also to take into consideration the industry which the genius of a free government inspires. But in the British islands all these circumstances together have not prevented them from being injured by the monopolies created there.

Individuals have been enriched, but the country at large has been hurt. Some valuable branches of trade being granted to companies, who transact their business in London, that city is, perhaps,

the place of the greatest trade in the world. But Ireland, under such influence, suffers exceedingly, and is impoverished; and Scotland is a mere by-word. Bristol, the second city in England, ranks not much above this town [Boston] in population. These things must be accounted for by the incorporation of trading companies; and if they are felt so severely in countries of small extent, they will operate with tenfold severity upon us, who inhabit an immense tract; and living towards one extreme of an extensive empire, shall feel the evil, without retaining that influence in government, which may enable us to procure redress. There ought, then, to have been inserted a restraining clause which might prevent the Congress from making any such grant, because they consequentially defeat the trade of the out-ports, and are also injurious to the general commerce, by enhancing prices and destroying that rivalship which is the great stimulus to industry....

There cannot be a doubt, that, while the trade of this continent remains free, the activity of our countrymen will secure their full share. AR the estimates for the present year, let them be made by what party they may, suppose the balance of trade to be largely in our favor. The credit of our merchants is, therefore, fully established in foreign countries. This is a sufficient proof, that when business is unshackled, it will find out that channel which is most friendly to its course.

We ought, therefore, to be exceedingly cautious about diverting or restraining it. Every day produces fresh proofs, that people, under the immediate pressure of difficulties, do not, at first glance, discover the proper relief. The last year, a desire to get rid

of embarrassments induced many honest people to agree to a tender act, and many others, of a different description, to obstruct the courts of justice. Both these methods only increased the evil they were intended to cure. Experience has since shown that, instead of trying to lessen an evil by altering the present course of things, that every endeavor should have been applied to facilitate the course of law, and thus to encourage a mutual confidence among the citizens, which increases the resources of them all, and renders easy the payment of debts. By this means one does not grow rich at the expense of another, but all are benefited. The case is the same with the States. Pennsylvania, with one port and a large territory, is less favorably situated for trade than Massachusetts, which has an extensive coast in proportion to its limits of jurisdiction. Accordingly a much larger proportion of our people are engaged in maritime affairs. We ought therefore to be particularly attentive to securing so great an interest. It is vain to tell us that we ought to overlook local interests. It is only by protecting local concerns that the interest of the whole is preserved. No man when he enters into society does it from a view to promote the good of others, but he does it for his own good. All men having the same view are bound equally to promote the welfare of the whole. To recur then to such a principle as that local interests must be disregarded, is requiring of one man to do more than another, and is subverting the foundation of a free government. The Philadelphians would be shocked with a proposition to place the seat of general government and the unlimited right to regulate trade in Massachusetts. There can be no greater reason for our surrendering the preference to them. Such sacrifices, however we may delude ourselves with the form of words, always originate in folly, and not in generosity.
AGRIPPA

ANTI-FEDERALIST PAPER NO. 12

How Will The New Government Raise Money?

"CINCINNATUS" is an Antifederalist writer. In this essay, from an Address to a Meeting of the Citizens of Philadelphia, the writer responds to James Wilson's statements about Congress'
powers to tax under the Constitution. It appeared in the November 29 and December 6, 1787, New-York Journal, as reprinted from a Philadelphia newspaper.
On the subject of taxation, in which powers are to be given so largely by the new constitution, you [James Wilson of Pennsylvania] lull our fears of abuse by venturing to predict "that the great revenue of the United States must, and always will, be raised by impost"-and you elevate our hopes by holding out, "the reviving and supporting the national credit." If you have any other plan for this, than by raising money upon the people to pay the interest of the national debt, your ingenuity will deserve our thanks. Supposing however, that raising money is necessary to payment of the interest, and such a payment [is] requisite to support the credit of the union-let us see how much will be necessary for that end, and how far the impost will supply what we want.
The arrearages of French and Spanish interest amount now to--1,500,000 dollars; Interest and installments of do. for 1788--850,227; Support of government; and its departments, for 1788--
500,000; Arrears and anticipations of 1787-- 300,000; Interest of domestic debt-- 500,000 {total} 4,650,227 [3,650,227]
The new Congress then, supposing it to get into operation towards October, 1788, will have to provide for this sum, and for the additional sum of 3,000,000 at least for the ensuing year; which together will make the sum of 7,650,227 [6,650,227].
Now let us see how the impost will answer this. Congress have furnished us with their estimate of the produce of the whole imports of America at five per cent and that is 800,000 dollars. There will remain to provide for, by other taxes, 6,850,227 [5,850,227].
We know too, that our imports diminish yearly, and from the nature of things must continue to diminish; and consequently that the above estimate of the produce of the impost, will in all probability fall much short of the supposed sum. But even without this, it must appear that you
[were] either intentionally misleading your hearers, or [were] very little acquainted with the subject when you ventured to predict that the great revenue of the United States would always flow from the impost. The estimate above is from the publications of Congress, and I presume is right. But the sum stated, necessary to be raised by the new government, in order to

answer the expectations they have raised, is not all. The state debts, independent of what each owes to the United States, amount to about 30,000,000 dollars; the annual interest of this is 1,000,000.

It will be expected that the new government will provide for this also; and such expectation is founded, not only on the promise you hold forth, of its reviving and supporting public credit among us, but also on this unavoidable principle of justice-that is, the new government takes away the impost, and other substantial taxes, from the produce of which the several states paid the interest of their debt, or funded the paper with which they paid it. The new government must

find ways and means of supplying that deficiency, . . . in hard money, for . . . paper . . . cannot

[be used] without a violation of the principles it boasts. The sum then which it must annually raise in specie, after the first year, cannot be less than 4,800,000. At present there is not one half of this sum in specie raised in all the states. And yet the complaints of intolerable taxes has produced one rebellion and will be mainly operative in the adoption of your constitution. How you will get this sum is inconceivable and yet get it you must, or lose all credit. With magnificent promises you have bought golden opinions of all sorts of people, and with gold you must answer them, . . .

To satisfy [our fellow citizens] more fully on the subject of the revenue, that is to be raised upon them, in order to give enormous fortunes to the jobbers in public securities, I shall lay before them a proposition to Congress, from Mr. Robert Morris, when superintendent of finance. It is dated, I think,' the 29th of June, 1782, and is in these words:

[1 say, I think, because by accident the month is erased in the note I have, and I have not access to public papers which would enable me to supply the defect.]

"The requisition of a five per cent impost, made on the 3d of February, 1781, has not yet been complied with by the state of Rhode Island, but as there is reason to believe, that their compliance is not far off, this revenue may be considered as already granted. It will, however, be very inadequate to the purposes intended. If goods be imported, and prizes introduced to the amount of twelve millions annually, the five per cent would be six hundred thousand, from which at least one sixth must be deducted, as well for the cost of collection as for the various defalcations which will necessarily happen, and which it is unnecessary to enumerate. It is not safe therefore, to estimate this revenue at more than half a million of dollars; for though it may produce more, yet probably it will not produce so much. It was in consequence of this, that on the 27th day of February last, I took the liberty to submit the propriety of asking the states for a land tax of one dollar for every hundred acres of land-a poll-tax of one dollar on all freemen, and all male slaves, between sixteen and sixty, excepting such as are in the federal army, or by wounds or otherwise rendered unfit for service-and an excise of one eighth of a dollar, on all distilled spiritous liquors. Each of these may be estimated at half a million; and should the product be equal to the estimation, the sum total of revenues for funding the public debts, would be equal to two millions."

You will readily perceive, Mr. Wilson, that there is a vast difference between your prediction and your friend's proposition. Give me leave to say, sir, that it was not discreet, in you, to speak upon finance without instructions from this great financier. Since, independent of its delusive effect upon your audience, it may excite his jealousy, lest you should have a secret design of rivalling him in the expected office of superintendent under the new constitution. It is true, there is no real foundation for it; but then you know jealousy makes the food it feeds on. A quarrel between two such able and honest friends to the United States, would, I am persuaded, be felt as a public calamity. I beseech you then to be very tender upon this point in your next harangue. And if four months' study will not furnish you with sufficient discretion, we will indulge you with six.

It may be said, that let the government be what it may, the sums I have stated must be raised, and the same difficulties exist. This is not altogether true. For first, we are now in the way of paying

the interest of the domestic debt, with paper, which under the new system is utterly reprobated.

This makes a difference between the specie to be raised of 1,800,000 dollars per annum. If the new government raises this sum in specie on the people, it will certainly support public credit, but it will overwhelm the people. It will give immense fortunes to the speculators; but it will grind the poor to dust. Besides, the present government is now redeeming the principal of the domestic debt by the sale of western lands. But let the full interest be paid in specie, and who will part with the principal for those lands? A principal, which having been generally purchased for two shillings and six pence on the pound, will yield to the holders two hundred and forty per cent. This paper system therefore, though in general an evil, is in this instance attended with the great benefit of enabling the public to cancel a debt upon easy terms, which has been swelled to its enormous size, by as enormous impositions. And the new government, by promising too much, will involve itself in a disreputable breach of faith. . . .

The present government promises nothing; the intended government, everything. From the present government little is expected; from the intended one, much. Because it is conceived that to the latter much is given; to the former, little. And yet

the inability of the people to pay what is required in specie, remaining the same, the funds of the one will not much exceed those of the other. The public creditors are easy with the present government from a conviction of its inability [to pay]. They will be urgent with the new one from an opinion, that as is promised, so it can and will perform every thing. Whether the change will be for our prosperity and honor, is yet to be tried. Perhaps it will be found, that the supposed want of power in Congress to levy taxes is, at present a veil happily thrown over the inability of the people; and that the large powers given to the new government will, to every one, expose the nakedness of our land. Certain it is, that if the expectations which are grafted on the gift of those plenary powers, are not answered, our credit will be irretrievably ruined.
CINCINNATUS

ANTI-FEDERALIST PAPER NO. 13

The Expense Of The New Government

Part 1: From The Feeeman's Oracle and New Hampshire Advertiser, January 11, 1788, by "A FARMER"
Part 2: An unsigned essay from The Connecticut Journal, October 17, 1787.

.... Great complaint has been made, that Congress [under the Articles] has been too liberal in their grants of salaries to individuals, and I think not without just cause. For if I am rightly informed, there have been men whose salaries have been fifteen hundred dollars per year, and some of them did not do business at any rate, that the sum they negotiated would amount to their yearly salary. And some men [are] now in office, at twenty five hundred dollars per year, who I think would have been glad to have set down at one hundred pounds a year before the war, and would have done as much or more business. The truth is, when you carry a man's salary beyond what decency requires, he immediately becomes a man of consequence, and does little or no business at all. Let us cast our eyes around us, in the other departments-the judges of the superior court have but about one hundred pounds salary a year. The judges of the courts of common pleas, on an average, not more than sixty dollars per year. The ministers of the gospel-a very valuable set of men, who have done honor to themselves, and rendered great service to their country, in completing the revolution-have salaries but from sixty to an hundred pounds a year in general. The contrast is striking. I heartily wish that all ranks of men among us, ministers of the gospel as well as others, would turn their attention toward the Constitution they may be more concerned in the event than they at present think of.

Rouse up, my friends, a matter of infinite importance is before you on the carpet, soon to be decided in your convention: The New Constitution. Seize the happy moment. Secure to yourselves and your posterity the jewel Liberty, which has cost you so much blood and treasure, by a well regulated Bill of Rights, from the encroachments of men in power. For if Congress will do these things in the dry tree when their power is small, what won't they do when they have all the resources of the United States at their command? They are the servants of the public. You have an undoubted right to set their wages, or at least to say, thus far you and those under you may go and no further. This would in the end ease Congress of a great deal of trouble, as it would put a stop to the impertinence of individuals in asking large salaries. I would say that the wages of a Representative in Congress do not exceed five dollars per day; a Senator not to exceed six; and the President seven per day, with an allowance for his table. And that the wages of no person employed in the United States exceed the daily pay of a Representative in Congress, but be paid according to their service, not exceeding that sum. Perhaps it may be said that money may depreciate, or appreciate. Let a price current be taken when this Constitution is completed, of the produce of each state, and let that be the general standard.

My friends and countrymen, let us pause for a moment and consider. We are not driven to such great straits as to be obliged to swallow down every potion offered us by wholesale, or else die immediately by our disease. We can form a Constitution at our leisure; and guard and secure it on all sides. We are paying off our state debt, and the interest on the domestic, as fast as Congress call upon us for it. As to the foreign debt, they have the promise of more interest from us than they can get anywhere else, and we shall be able to pay them both interest and principal shortly. But it is said they win declare war against us if we don't pay them immediately.

Common sense will teach them better. We live at too great a distance, and are too hardy and robust a people, for them to make money out of us in that way.

Documents of Revolution

But it is said, the trading towns are fond of this Constitution. Let us consider how they stand, including their interest.

1st. The merchant wishes to have it adopted, that trade might be regulated. 2dly. Another set of men wishes to have it adopted, that the idea of paper money might be annihilated. 3dly. Another class of men wish to have it take place, that the public might be enabled to pay off the foreign debt, and appear respectable abroad among the nations. So do I, with all my heart. But in neither of these cases do I wish to see it adopted without being guarded on all sides with a Magna Charta, or a Bill of Rights, as a bulwark to our liberties. Again, another class of men wish to have it adopted, so that the public chest might be furnished with money to pay the interest on their securities, which they purchased of the poor soldiers at two shillings on the pound. I wish the soldiers were now the holders of those securites they fought so hard for. However, as the public finances were such that they could not be paid off as they became due, and they have carried them to market, and sold them as the boy did his top-we must pay them to the holders.

But we need not be in a hurry about it; certificates will do for that. Consider, my friends, you are the persons who must live and die by this Constitution. A merchant or mechanic may dispose of his goods, or pack them up in trunks and remove to another clime in the course of a few months.

But you cannot shoulder your lands, or dispose of them when you please. It therefore behooves you to rouse up, and turn your most serious and critical attention to this Constitution. . . .

A FARMER

. . A large representation has ever been esteemed by the best whigs in Great Britain the best barrier against bribery and corruption. And yet we find a British king, having the disposition of all places, civil and military, and an immense revenue SQUEEZED out of the very mouths of his wretched subjects, is able to corrupt the parliament, to vote him any supplies he demands, to support armies, to defend the prerogatives of his crown, and carry fire and sword by his fleets and armies; to desolate whole provinces in the eastern world, to aggrandize himself, and satisfy the avarice of his tyrannical subjects.

No wonder our American ambassador, struck with the brilliancy of the British court [John Adams], where everything around St. James's wears the appearance of wealth, ease and plenty, should imagine a three branched legislature only can produce these effects, and make the subjects happy, should write a book in favor of such a government, and send it over for the illumination of this western world. If this is the sole fruit of his embassy, America will not canonize him for a saint on account of his services, when they have experienced the consequences of such a kind of government as be has planned out. In order to have formed a right judgment, he should have looked into the ditches which serve for graves for many of the human race-under hedges which serve as dreary habitations for the living; into the cottages of the poor and miserable, and critically examine with how much parsimony the mechanics, the day

laborers, cottagers and villagers live in order to support their high pampered lords-before he had wrote a book to persuade his country to pursue the same road to greatness, splendor and glory, and have reflected in his own mind, whether he could wish to see that country which gave him birth reduced to the same situation....

Now I submit it to the good sense of the people of these states, whether it is prudent we should make so liberal and extensive a grant of power and property to any body of men in these United States, before they have ever informed the public, the amount of the public debt, or what the annual expenses of the federal government is, or will be. It is now almost five years since the peace. Congress has employed thirteen commissioners, at 1500 dollars per annum, as I am informed, to settle the public accounts, and we know now no more what the national debt is, than at the first moment of their appointment. Nor do we know any more what is the amount of the annual expenses of the federal government, than we do of the empire of China. To grant therefore such an ample power of taxation, and the right of soil, to the amount of millions, upon the recommendation of this honorable Convention, without either knowing the amount of the national debt, or the annual expenses of government, would not argue, in my opinion, the highest degree of prudence.

ANTI-FEDERALIST PAPER NO. 14

Extent Of Territory Under Consolidated Government Too Large To Preserve Liberty Or Protect Property

George Clinton, Governor of New York, was an adversary of the Constitution. He composed several letters under the nome de plume "CATO." This essay is from the third letter of "Cato,"
The New-York Journal of October 25, 1787.

... The recital, or premises on which the new form of government is erected, declares a consolidation or union of all the thirteen parts, or states, into one great whole, under the form of the United States, for all the various and important purposes therein set forth. But whoever seriously considers the immense extent of territory comprehended within the limits of the United States, together with the variety of its climates, productions, and commerce, the difference of extent, and number of inhabitants in all; the dissimilitude of interest, morals, and politics, in almost every one, will receive it as an intuitive truth, that a consolidated republican form of government therein, can never form a perfect union, establish justice, insure domestic tranquility, promote the general welfare, and secure the blessings of liberty to you and your posterity, for to these objects it must be directed. This unkindred legislature therefore, composed of interests opposite and dissimilar in their nature, will in its exercise, emphatically be like a house divided against itself.

The governments of Europe have taken their limits and form from adventitious circumstances, and nothing can be argued on the motive of agreement from them; but these adventitious political principles have nevertheless produced effects that have attracted the attention of philosophy, which have established axioms in the science of politics therefrom, as irrefragable as any in Euclid. It is natural, says Montesquieu, to a republic to have only a small territory, otherwise it cannot long subsist: in a large one, there are men of large fortunes, and consequently of less moderation; there are too great deposits to trust in the hands of a single subject, an ambitious person soon becomes sensible that he may be happy, great, and glorious by oppressing his fellow citizens, and that he might raise himself to grandeur, on the ruins of his country. In large republics, the public good is sacrificed to a thousand views, in a small one, the interest of the public is easily perceived, better understood, and more within the reach of every citizen; abuses have a less extent, and of course are less protected. He also shows you, that the duration of the republic of Sparta was owing to its having continued with the same extent of territory after all its wars; and that the ambition of Athens and Lacedemon to command and direct the union, lost them their liberties, and gave them a monarchy.

From this picture, what can you promise yourselves, on the score of consolidation of the United States into one government? Impracticability in the just exercise of it, your freedom insecure, even this form of government limited in its continuance, the employments of your country disposed of to the opulent, to whose contumely you will continually be an object. You must risk much, by indispensably placing trusts of the greatest magnitude, into the hands of individuals whose ambition for power, and aggrandizement, will oppress and grind you. Where, from the vast extent of your territory, and the complication of interests, the science of government will

become intricate and perplexed, and too mysterious for you to understand and observe; and by which you are to be conducted into a monarchy, either limited or despotic; the latter, Mr. Locke remarks, is a government derived from neither nature nor compact.

Political liberty, the great Montesquieu again observes, consists in security, or at least in the opinion we have of security; and this security, therefore, or the opinion, is best obtained in moderate governments, where the mildness of the laws, and the equality of the manners, beget a confidence in the people, which produces this security, or the opinion. This moderation in governments depends in a great measure on their limits, connected with their political distribution.

The extent of many of the states of the Union, is at this time almost too great for the superintendence of a republican form of government, and must one day or other revolve into more vigorous ones, or by separation be reduced into smaller and more useful, as well as moderate ones. You have already observed the feeble efforts of Massachusetts against their insurgents; with what difficulty did they quell that insurrection; and is not the province of Maine at this moment on the eve of separation from her? The reason of these things is, that for the security of the property of the community-in which expressive term Mr. Locke makes life, liberty, and estate, to consist the wheels of a republic are necessarily slow in their operation.

Hence, in large free republics, the evil sometimes is not only begun, but almost completed, before they are in a situation to turn the current into a contrary progression. The extremes are also too remote from the usual seat of government, and the laws, therefore, too feeble to afford protection to all its parts, and insure domestic tranquility without the aid of another principle. If, therefore, this state [New York], and that of North Carolina, had an army under their control, they never would have lost Vermont, and Frankland, nor the state of Massachusetts suffered an insurrection, or the dismemberment of her fairest district; but the exercise of a principle which would have prevented these things, if we may believe the experience of ages, would have ended in the destruction of their liberties.

Will this consolidated republic, if established, in its exercise beget such confidence and compliance, among the citizens of these states, as to do without the aid of a standing army? I deny that it will. The malcontents in each state, who will not be a few, nor the least important, will be exciting factions against it. The fear of a dismemberment of some of its parts, and the necessity to enforce the execution Of revenue laws (a fruitful source of oppression) on the extremes and in the other districts of the government, will incidentally and necessarily require a permanent force, to be kept on foot. Will not political security, and even the opinion of it, be extinguished? Can mildness and moderation exist in a government where the primary incident in its exercise must be force? Will not violence destroy confidence, and can equality subsist where the extent, policy, and practice of it will naturally lead to make odious distinctions among citizens?

The people who may compose this national legislature from the southern states, in which, from the mildness of the climate, the fertility of the soil, and the value of its productions, wealth is rapidly acquired, and where the same causes naturally lead to luxury, dissipation, and a passion for aristocratic distinction; where slavery is encouraged, and liberty of course less respected and protected; who know not what it is to acquire property by their own toil, nor to economize with

the savings of industry-will these men, therefore, be as tenacious of the liberties and interests of the more northern states, where freedom, independence, industry, equality and frugality are natural to the climate and soil, as men who are your own citizens, legislating in your own state, under your inspection, and whose manners and fortunes bear a more equal resemblance to your own?

It may be suggested, in answer to this, that whoever is a citizen of one state is a citizen of each, and that therefore he will be as interested in the happiness and interest of all, as the one he is delegated from. But the argument is fallacious, and, whoever has attended to the history of mankind, and the principles which bind them together as parents, citizens, or men, will readily perceive it. These principles are, in their exercise, like a pebble cast on the calm surface of a river-the circles begin in the center, and are small, active and forcible, but as they depart from that point, they lose their force, and vanish into calmness. The strongest principle of union resides within our domestic walls. The ties of the parent exceed that of any other. As we depart from home, the next general principle of union is amongst citizens of the same state, where acquaintance, habits, and fortunes, nourish affection, and attachment. Enlarge the circle still further, and, as citizens of different states, though we acknowledge the same national denomination, we lose in the ties of acquaintance, habits, and fortunes, and thus by degrees we lessen in our attachments, till, at length, we no more than acknowledge a sameness of species. Is it, therefore, from certainty like this, reasonable to believe, that inhabitants of Georgia, or New Hampshire, will have the same obligations towards you as your own, and preside over your lives, liberties, and property, with the same care and attachment? Intuitive reason answers in the negative.

CATO

ANTI-FEDERALIST PAPER NO. 15

Rhode Island Is Right!

This essay appeared in The Massachusetts Gazette, December 7, 1787, as reprinted From The Freeman's Journal; (Or, The North-American Intelligencer?)

The abuse which has been thrown upon the state of Rhode Island seems to be greatly unmerited.

Popular favor is variable, and those who are now despised and insulted may soon change situations with the present idols of the people. Rhode Island has out done even Pennsylvania in the glorious work of freeing the Negroes in this country, without which the patriotism of some states appears ridiculous. The General Assembly of the state of Rhode Island has prevented the further importation of Negroes, and have made a law by which all blacks born in that state after March, 1784, are absolutely and at once free.

They have fully complied with the recommendations of Congress in regard to the late treaty of peace with Great Britain, and have passed an act declaring it to be the law of the land. They have never refused their quota of taxes demanded by Congress, excepting the five per cent impost, which they considered as a dangerous tax, and for which at present there is perhaps no great necessity, as the western territory, of which a part has very lately been sold at a considerable price, may soon produce an immense revenue; and, in the interim, Congress may raise in the old manner the taxes which shall be found necessary for the support of the government.

The state of Rhode Island refused to send delegates to the Federal Convention, and the event has manifested that their refusal was a happy one as the new constitution, which the Convention has proposed to us, is an elective monarchy, which is proverbially the worst government. This new government would have been supported at a vast expense, by which our taxes-the right of which is solely vested in Congress, (a circumstance which manifests that the various states of the union will be merely corporations) -- would be doubled or trebled. The liberty of the press is not stipulated for, and therefore may be invaded at pleasure. The supreme continental court is to have, almost in every case, "appellate jurisdiction, both as to law and fact," which signifies, if there is any meaning in words, the setting aside the trial by jury. Congress will have the power of guaranteeing to every state a right to import Negroes for twenty one years, by which some of the states, who have now declined that iniquitous traffic, may re-enter into it-for the private laws of every state are to submit to the superior jurisdiction of Congress. A standing army is to be kept on foot, by which the vicious, the sycophantick, and the time- serving will be exalted, and the brave, the patriotic, and the virtuous will be depressed.

The writer, therefore, thinks it the part of wisdom to abide, like the state of Rhode Island, by the old articles of confederation, which, if re-examined with attention, we shall find worthy of great regard; that we should give high praise to the manly and public spirited sixteen members, who lately seceded from our house of Assembly [in Pennsylvania]; and that we should all impress with great care, this truth on our minds-That it is very easy to change a free government into an arbitrary one, but that it is very difficult to convert tyranny into freedom.

ANTI-FEDERALIST PAPER NO. 16

Europeans Admire And Federalists Decry The Present System

"ALFRED" defended the Articles of Confederation, taken from The New-York Journal, December 25, 1787 as reprinted from the [Philadelphia] Independent Gazetteer.

To the real PATRIOTS of America: . . . America is now free. She now enjoys a greater portion of political liberty than any other country under heaven. How long she may continue so depends entirely upon her own caution and wisdom. If she would look to herself more, and to Europe less, I am persuaded it would tend to promote her felicity. She possesses all the advantages which characterize a rich country-rich within herself, she ought less to regard the politics, the manufactures, and the interests of distant nations.

When I look to our situation-climate, extent, soil, and its productions, rivers, ports; when I find I can at this time purchase grain, bread, meat, and other necessaries of life at as reasonable a rate as in any country; when I see we are sending great quantities of tobacco, wheat and flour to England and other parts of the globe beyond the Atlantic; when I get on the other side of the western mountains, and see an extensive country, which for its multitude of rivers and fertility of soil is equal, if not superior, to any other whatever when I see these things, I cannot be brought to believe that America is in that deplorable ruined condition which some designing politicians represent; or that we are in a state of anarchy beyond redemption, unless we adopt, without any addition or amendment, the new constitution proposed by the late convention; a constitution which, in my humble opinion, contains the seeds and scions of slavery and despotism. When the volume of American constitutions [by John Adams] first made its appearance in Europe, we find some of the most eminent political writers of the present age, and the reviewers of literature, full of admiration and declaring they had never before seen so much good sense, freedom, and real wisdom in one publication. Our good friend Dr. [Richard] Price was charmed, and almost prophesied the near approach of the happy days of the millennium. We have lived under these constitutions; and, after the experience of a few years, some among us are ready to trample them under their feet, though they have been esteemed, even by our enemies, as "pearls of great price."

Let us not, ye lovers of freedom, be rash and hasty. Perhaps the real evils we labor under do not arise from these systems. There may be other causes to which our misfortunes may be properly attributed. Read the American constitutions, and you will find our essential rights and privileges well guarded and secured. May not our manners be the source of our national evils? May not our attachment to foreign trade increase them? Have we not acted imprudently in exporting almost all our gold and silver for foreign luxuries? It is now acknowledged that we have not a sufficient quantity of the precious metals to answer the various purposes of government and commerce; and without a breach of charity, it may be said, that this deficiency arises from the want of public virtue, in preferring private interest to every other consideration.

If the states had in any tolerable degree been able to answer the requisitions of Congress-if the continental treasury had been so far assisted, as to have enabled us to pay the interest of our foreign debt-possibly we should have heard little, very little about a new system of government.

It is a just observation that in modern times money does everything. If a government can command this unum necessarium from a certain revenue, it may be considered as wealthy and respectable; if not, it will lose its dignity, become inefficient and contemptible. But cannot we regulate our finances and lay the foundations for a permanent and certain revenue, without undoing all that we have done, without making an entire new government? The most wise and philosophic characters have bestowed on our old systems the highest encomiums. Are we sure this new political phenomenon will not fail? If it should fail, is there not a great probability, that our last state will be worse than the first? Orators may declaim on the badness of the times as long as they please, but I must tell them that the want of public virtue, and the want of money, are two of the principal sources of our grievances; and if we are -under the pressure of these wants, it ought to teach us frugality-to adopt a frugal administration of public affairs....

ALFRED

ANTI-FEDERALIST PAPER NO. 17

Federalist Power Will Ultimately Subvert State Authority

The "necessary and proper" clause has, from the beginning, been a thorn in the side of those seeking to reduce federal power, but its attack by Brutus served to call attention to it, leaving a paper trail of intent verifying its purpose was not to give Congress anything the Constitution
"forgot," but rather to show two additional tests for any legislation Congress should attempt: to wit--that the intended actions would be both necessary AND proper to executing powers given under clauses 1-17 of Article I Section 8. This is the famous BRUTUS.

This [new] government is to possess absolute and uncontrollable powers, legislative, executive and judicial, with respect to every object to which it extends, for by the last clause of section eighth, article first, it is declared, that the Congress shall have power "to make all laws which shall be necessary and proper for carrying into execution the foregoing powers, and all other powers vested by this Constitution in the government of the United States, or in any department or office thereof." And by the sixth article, it is declared, "that this Constitution, and the laws of the United States, which shall be made in pursuance thereof, and the treaties made, or which shall be made, under the authority of the United States, shall be the supreme law of the land; and the judges in every State shall be bound thereby, any thing in the Constitution or law of any State to the contrary notwithstanding." It appears from these articles, that there is no need of any intervention of the State governments, between the Congress and the people, to execute any one power vested in the general government, and that the Constitution and laws of every State are nullified and declared void, so far as they are or shall be inconsistent with this Constitution, or the laws made in pursuance of it, or with treaties made under the authority of the United States.

The government, then, so far as it extends, is a complete one, and not a confederation. It is as much one complete government as that of New York or Massachusetts; has as absolute and perfect powers to make and execute all laws, to appoint officers, institute courts, declare offenses, and annex penalties, with respect to every object to which it extends, as any other in the world. So far, therefore, as its powers reach, all ideas of confederation are given up and lost. It is true this government is limited to certain objects, or to speak more properly, some small degree of power is still left to the States; but a little attention to the powers vested in the general government, will convince every candid man, that if it is capable of being executed, all that is reserved for the individual States must very soon be annihilated, except so far as they are barely necessary to the organization of the general government. The powers of the general legislature extend to every case that is of the least importance-there is nothing valuable to human nature, nothing dear to freemen, but what is within its power. It has the authority to make laws which will affect the lives, the liberty, and property of every man in the United States; nor can the Constitution or laws of any State, in any way prevent or impede the full and complete execution of every power given. The legislative power is competent to lay taxes, duties, imposts, and excises;-there is no limitation to this power, unless it be said that the clause which directs the use to which those taxes and duties shall be applied, may be said to be a limitation. But this is no restriction of the power at all, for by this clause they are to be applied to pay the debts and provide for the common defense and general welfare of the United States; but the legislature have authority to contract debts at their discretion; they are the sole judges of what is necessary
to provide for the common defense, and they only are to determine what is for the general welfare. This power, therefore, is neither more nor less than a power to lay and collect taxes, imposts, and excises, at their pleasure; not only the power to lay taxes unlimited as to the amount they may require, but it is perfect and absolute to raise ;hem in any mode they please. No State legislature, or any power in the State governments, have any more to do in carrying this into effect than the authority of one State has to do with that of another. In the business, therefore, of laying and collecting taxes, the idea of confederation is totally lost, and that of one entire republic is embraced. It is proper here to remark, that the authority to lay and collect taxes is the most important of any power that can be granted; it connects with it almost all other powers, or at least will in process of time draw all others after it; it is the great mean of protection, security, and defense, in a good government, and the great engine of oppression and tyranny in a bad one.

Documents of Revolution

This cannot fail of being the case, if we consider the contracted limits which are set by this Constitution, to the State governments, on this article of raising money. No State can emit paper money, lay any duties or imposts, on imports, or exports, but by consent of the Congress; and then the net produce shall be for the benefit of the United States. The only means, therefore, left for any State to support its government and discharge its debts, is by direct taxation; and the United States have also power to lay and collect taxes, in any way they please. Everyone who has thought on the subject, must be convinced that but small sums of money can he collected in any country, by direct tax; when the federal government begins to exercise the right of taxation in all its parts, the legislatures of the several states will find it impossible to raise monies to support their governments. Without money they cannot be supported, and they must dwindle away, and, as before observed, their powers be absorbed in that of the general government.

It might be here shown, that the power in the federal legislature, to raise and support armies at pleasure, as well in peace as in war, and their control over the militia, tend not only to a consolidation of the government, but the destruction of liberty. I shall not, however, dwell upon these, as a few observations upon the judicial power of this government, in addition to the preceding, will fully evince the truth of the position.

The judicial power of the United States is to be vested in a supreme court, and in such inferior courts as Congress may, from time to time, ordain and establish. The powers of these courts are very extensive; their jurisdiction comprehends all civil causes, except such as arise between citizens of the same State; and it extends to all cases in law and equity arising under the Constitution. One inferior court must be established, I presume, in each State, at least, with the necessary executive officers appendant thereto. It is easy to see, that in the common course of things, these courts will eclipse the dignity, and take away from the respectability, of the State courts. These courts will be, in themselves, totally independent of the States, deriving their authority from the United States, and receiving from them fixed salaries; and in the course of human events it is to be expected that they will swallow up all the powers of the courts in the respective States.

How far the clause in the eighth section of the first article may operate to do away with all idea of confederated States, and to effect an entire consolidation of the whole into one general government, it is impossible to say. The powers given by this article are very general and comprehensive, and it may receive a construction to justify the passing almost any law. A power to make all laws, which shall be necessary and proper, for carrying into execution all powers

vested by the Constitution in the government of the United States, or any department or officer thereof, is a power very comprehensive and definite, and may, for aught I know, be exercised in such manner as entirely to abolish the State legislatures. Suppose the legislature of a State should pass a law to raise money to support their government and pay the State debt; may the Congress repeal this law, because it may prevent the collection of a tax which they may think proper and necessary to lay, to provide for the general welfare of the United States? For all laws made, in pursuance of this Constitution, are the supreme law of the land, and the judges in every State shall be bound thereby, anything in the Constitution or laws of the different States to the contrary notwithstanding. By such a law, the government of a particular State might be overturned at one stroke, and thereby be deprived of every means of its support.

It is not meant, by stating this case, to insinuate that the Constitution would warrant a law of this kind! Or unnecessarily to alarm the fears of the people, by suggesting that the Federal legislature would be more likely to pass the limits assigned them by the Constitution, than that of an individual State, further than they are less responsible to the people. But what is meant is, that the legislature of the United States are vested with the great and uncontrollable powers of laying and collecting taxes, duties, imposts, and excises; of regulating trade, raising and supporting armies, organizing, arming, and disciplining the militia, instituting courts, and other general powers; and are by this clause invested with the power of making all laws, proper and necessary, for carrying all these into execution; and they may so exercise this power as entirely to annihilate all the State governments, and reduce this country to one single government. And if they may do it, it is pretty certain they will; for it will be found that the power retained by individual States, small as it is, will be a clog upon the wheels of the government of the United States; the latter, therefore, will be naturally inclined to remove it out of the way. Besides, it is a truth confirmed by the unerring experience of ages, that every man, and every body of men, invested with power, are ever disposed to increase it, and to acquire a superiority over everything that stands in their way. This disposition, which is implanted in human nature, will operate in the Federal legislature to lessen and ultimately to subvert the State authority, and having such advantages, will most certainly succeed, if the Federal government succeeds at all. It must be very evident, then, that what this Constitution wants of being a complete consolidation of the several parts of the union into one complete government, possessed of perfect legislative, judicial, and executive powers, to all intents and purposes, it will necessarily acquire in its exercise in operation.

BRUTUS

ANTI-FEDERALIST PAPER NO. 18-20

(PART 1) What Does History Teach?

"AN OLD WHIG," taken from The Massachusetts Gazette, November 27, 1787, as reprinted from the [Philadelphia] Independent Gazetteer.

.... By the proposed constitution, every law, before it passes, is to undergo repeated revisions; and the constitution of every state in the union provide for the revision of the most trifling laws, either by their passing through different houses of assembly and senate, or by requiring them to be published for the consideration of the people. Why then is a constitution which affects all the inhabitants of the United States-which is to be the foundation of all laws and the source of misery or happiness to one- quarter of the globe-why is this to be so hastily adopted or rejected, that it cannot admit of a revision? If a law to regulate highways requires to be leisurely considered and undergo the examination of different bodies of men, one after another, before it be passed, why is it that the framing of a constitution for the government of a great people-a work which has been justly considered as the greatest effort of human genius, and which from the beginning of the world has so often baffled the skill of the wisest men in every age-shall be considered as a thing to be thrown out, in the first shape which it may happen to assume? Where is the impracticability of a revision? Cannot the same power which called the late convention call another? Are not the people still their own masters? If, when the several state conventions come to consider this constitution, they should not approve of it, in its present form, they may easily apply to congress and state their objections. Congress may as easily direct the calling another convention, as they did the calling the last. The plan may then be reconsidered, deliberately received and corrected, so as to meet the approbation of every friend to his country. A few months only will be necessary for this purpose; and if we consider the magnitude of the object, we shall deem it well worth a little time and attention. It is Much better to pause and reflect before hand, than to repent when it is too late; when no peaceable remedy will be left us, and unanimity will be forever banished. The struggles of the people against a bad government, when it is once fixed, afford but a gloomy picture in the annals of mankind, They are often unfortunate; they are always destructive of private and public happiness; but the peaceable consent of a people to establish a free and effective government is one of the most glorious objects that is ever exhibited on the theater of human affairs. Some, I know, have objected that another convention will not be likely to agree upon anything-I am far however from being of that opinion. The public voice calls so loudly for a new constitution that I have no doubt we shall have one of some sort. My only fear is that the impatience of the people will lead them to accept the first that is offered them without examining whether it is right or wrong. And after all, if a new convention cannot agree upon any amendments in the constitution, which is at present proposed, we can still adopt this in its present form; and all further opposition being vain, it is to be hoped we shall be unanimous in endeavouring to make the best of it. The experiment is at least worth trying, and I shall be much astonished, if a new convention called together for the purpose of revising the proposed constitution, do not greatly reform it ...

It is beyond a doubt that the new federal constitution, if adopted, will in a great measure destroy, if it does not totally annihilate, the separate governments of the several states. We shall, in effect,

become one great republic. Every measure of any importance will be continental. What will be the consequence of this? One thing is evident-that no republic of so great magnitude ever did or ever can exist. But a few years elapsed, from the time in which ancient Rome extended her dominions beyond the bounds of Italy, until the downfall of her republic. And all political writers agree, that a republican government can exist only in a narrow territory. But a confederacy of different republics has, in many instances, existed and flourished for a long time together. The celebrated Helvetian league, which exists at this moment in full vigor, and with unimpaired strength, while its origin may be traced to the confines of antiquity, is one among many examples on this head; and at the same time furnishes an eminent proof of how much less importance it is, that the constituent parts of a confederacy of republics may be rightly framed, than it is that the confederacy itself should be rightly organized. For hardly any two of the Swiss cantons have the same form of government, and they are almost equally divided in their religious principles, which have so often rent asunder the firmest establishments. A confederacy of republics must be the establishment in America, or we must cease altogether to retain the republican form of government. From the moment we become one great republic, either in form or substance, the period is very shortly removed when we shall sink first into monarchy, and then into despotism. .

. . If the men who at different times have been entrusted to form plans of government for the world, had been really actuated by no other motives than the public good, the condition of human nature in all ages would have been widely different from that which has been exhibited to us in history. In this country perhaps we are possessed of more than our share of political virtue. If we will exercise a little patience and bestow our best endeavors on the business, I do not think it impossible, that we may yet form a federal constitution much superior to any form of government which has ever existed in the world. But whenever this important work shall be accomplished, I venture to pronounce that it will not be done without a careful attention to the Framing of a bill of rights. . . .

In different nations, we find different grants or reservations of privileges appealed to in the struggles between the rulers and the people; many of which, in the different nations of Europe, have long since been swallowed up and lost by time, or destroyed by the arbitrary hand of power.

In England, we find the people, with the barons at their head, exacting a solemn resignation of their rights from King John, in their celebrated magna charta, which was many times renewed in Parliament during the reigns of his successors. The petition of rights was afterwards consented to by Charles I and contained a declaration of the liberties of the people. The habeas corpus act, after the restoration of Charles 11, the bill of rights, which was obtained of the Prince and Princess of Orange, on their accession to the throne, and the act of settlement, at the accession of the Hanover family-are other instances to show the care and watchfulness of that nation to improve every Opportunity, of the reign of a weak prince or the revolution in their government, to obtain the most explicit declarations in favor of their liberties. In like manner the people of this country, at the revolution, having all power in their own hands, in forming the constitutions of the several states, took care to secure themselves, by bills of rights, so as to prevent as far as possible the encroachments of their future rulers upon the rights of the people. Some of these rights are said to be unalienable, such as the rights of conscience. Yet even these have been often invaded, where they have not been carefully secured, by express and solemn bills and declarations in their favor.

Before we establish a government, whose acts will be the supreme law of the land, and whose power will extend to almost every case without exception, we ought carefully to guard ourselves by a bill of rights, against the invasion of those liberties which it is essential for us to retain, which it is of no real use for government to deprive us of; but which, in the course of human events, have been too often insulted with all the wantonness of an idle barbarity.

AN OLD WHIG

ANTI-FEDERALIST PAPER NO. 18-20 (PART II)

what Does History Teach?

"A NEWPORT MAN," wrote this wit which appeared in The Newport Mercury, March 17, 1788.

. . . - I perceive in your last [issue a] piece signed "A Rhode-Island Man," it seems wrote with an air of confidence and triumph; he speaks of reason and reasoning-I wish he had known or practised some of that reasoning he so much pretends to; his essay had been much shorter. We are told in this piece, as well as others on the same side, that an ability given to British subjects to recover their debts in this country will be one of the blessings of a new government, by inducing the British to abandon the frontiers, or be left without excuse. But the British have no other reason for holding the posts, after the time named in the treaty for their evacuation, than the last reason of Kings, that is, their guns. And giving them the treasure of the United States is a very unlikely means of removing that. If the British subject met with legal impediments to the recovery of his debts in this country, for [the] British government to have put the same stop on our citizens would have been a proper, an ample retaliation. But there is nothing within the compass of possibility of which I am not perfectly sure, that I am more fully persuaded of than I am, that the British will never relinquish the posts in question until compelled by force; because no nation pays less regard to the faith of treaties than the British. Witness their conduct to the French in 1755, when they took a very great number of men of war and merchant ships before war was declared, because the French had built some forts on the south side of an imaginary line in the wilds of America; and again, the violation of the articles by which the people of Boston resigned their arms; and the violation of the capitulation of Charles Town. Again we are told that Congress has no credit with foreigners, because they have no power to fulfill their engagements.

And this we are told, with a boldness exceeded by nothing but its falsehood, perhaps in the same paper that announces to the world the loan of a million of Holland gilders-if I mistake not the sum; a sum equal to 250,000 Spanish Dollars-and all this done by the procurement of that very Congress whose insignificancy and want of power had been constantly proclaimed for two or three years before. The Dutch are the most cautious people on earth, and it is reasonable to suppose they were abundantly persuaded of the permanency and efficacy of our government by their risking so much money on it.

We are told that so long as we withhold this power from Congress we shall be a weak, despised people. We were long contending for Independence, and now we are in a passion to be rid of it.

But let us attempt to reason on this subject, and see to which side that will lead us. Reason is truly defined, in all cases short of mathematical demonstration, to be a supposing that the like causes will produce the like effects. Let us proceed by this rule. The Swiss Cantons for a hundred years have remained separate Independent States, consequently without any controlling power.

Even the little Republic of St. Marino, containing perhaps but little more ground than the town of Newport, and about five thousand inhabitants, surrounded by powerful and ambitious neighbors, has kept its freedom and independence these thirteen hundred years, and is mentioned by travellers as a very enlightened and happy people. If these small republics, in the neighborhood of the warlike and intriguing Courts of Paris, Vienna, and Berlin, have kept their freedom and original form of government, is it not reasonable to suppose that the same good sense and love of freedom, on this side the Atlantic, will secure us from all attempt within and without. And the only internal discord that has happened in Switzerland was on a religious account, and a supreme controlling power is no security against this, as appears by what happened in Ireland in the time of Charles the First, and in France in the time of Henry the Fourth. It seems rational in a case of this importance to consult the opinion of the ablest men, and to whom can we better appeal than to J. J. Rousseau, a republican by birth and education-one of the most exalted geniuses and one of the greatest writers of his age, or perhaps any age; a man the most disinterested and benevolent towards mankind; a man the most industrious in the acquisition of knowledge and information, by travel, conversation, reading, and thinking; and one who has wrote a Volume on Government entitled the Social Contract, wherein he inculcates, that the people should examine and determine every public act themselves. His words are, that "every law that the people have not ratified in person, is void; it is no law. The people of England think they are free. They are much mistaken. They are never so but during the election of members of Parliament. As soon as they are elected, they are slaves, they are nothing. And by the use they make of their liberty during the short moments they possess it, they well deserve to lose it." This is far from advising that thirty thousand souls should resign their judgments and wishes entirely to one man for two years-to a man, who, perhaps, may go from home sincere and patriotic but by the time he has dined in pomp for a week with the wealthy citizens of New York or Philadelphia, will have lost all his rigid ideas of economy and equality. He becomes fascinated with the elegancies and luxuries of wealth. . . . Objects and intimations like these soon change the champion for the people to an advocate for power; and the people, finding themselves thus basely betrayed, cry that virtue is but a name. We are not sure that men have more virtue at this time and place than they had in England in the time of George the Second. Let anyone look into the history of those times, and see with what boldness men changed sides and deserted the people in pursuit of profit and power. If to take up the cross and renounce the pomps and vanities of this sinful world is a hard lesson for divines, 'tis much harder for politicians. A Cincinnatus, a Cato, a Fabricius, and a Washington, are rarely to be found. We are told that the Trustees of our powers and freedom, being mostly married men, and all of them inhabitants and proprietors of the country, is an ample security against an abuse of power. Whether human nature be less corrupt than formerly I will not determine-but this I know: that Julius Caesar, Oliver Cromwell, and the nobles of Venice, were natives and inhabitants of the countries whose power they usurped and drenched in blood.

Again, our country is compared to a ship of which we are all passengers, and, from thence 'tis gravely concluded that no officer can ever betray or abuse his trust. But that men will sacrifice the public to their private interest, is a saying too well known to need repeating. And the instances of designed shipwrecks, and ships run away with by a combination of masters, supercargoes, and part owners, is so great that nothing can equal them but those instances in which pretended patriots and politicians have raised themselves and families to power and greatness, by destroying that freedom and those laws they were chosen to defend. If it were necessary to cite more precedents to prove that the people ought not to trust or remove their power any further from them, the little Republic of Lucca may be mentioned-which, surrounded by the Dukedom of Tuscany, has existed under its present constitution about five hundred years, and as Mr. Addison says, is for the extent of its dominion the richest and best peopled of all the States of Italy. And he says further that "the whole administration of the government passes into different hands every two months." This is very far from confirming the doctrine of choosing those officers for two years who were before chosen for one. The want of a decisive, efficient power is much talked of by the discontented, and that we are in danger of being conquered by the intrigues of European powers. But it has already been shown that we have delegated a more decisive power to our Congress than is granted by the Republic Swiss Cantons to their General Diet. These Republics have enjoyed peace some hundreds of years; while those governments which possess this decisive, efficient power, so much aimed at, are as often as twenty or thirty years, drawing their men from the plough and loom to be shot at and cut each other's throats for the honor of their respective nations. And by how much further we are from Europe than the Swiss Cantons with their allies, and Lucca and St. Marino are from France, Prussia, and Austria, by so much less are we in danger of being conquered than those republics which have existed, some earlier than others, but the youngest of them one hundred and thirty years, without being conquered. As for the United Provinces of Holland, they are but nominal Republics; their Stadtholder, very much like our intended President, making them in reality a monarchy, and subject to all its calamities. But supposing that the present constitution, penned by the ablest men, four or five years in completion, and its adoption considered as the happiest event-supposing, I say, the present Constitution destroyed, can a new one be ratified with more solemnity, agreed to in stronger or more binding terms? What security can be given that in seven years hence, another Convention shall not be called to frame a third Constitution? And as ancient Greece counted by olympiads, and monarchies by their Kings' reigns, we shall date in the first, second, or third year, of the seventh, eighth, or ninth Constitution.

In treating this subject I have not presumed to advise, and have intruded but few comments. I have mentioned the state of those countries which most resemble our own and leave to the natural sense of the reader to make his own conclusions. The malcontents, the lovers of novelty, delight much in allegory. Should I be indulged a few words in that way, I should not compare the new Constitution to a house. I should fetch my simile from the country and compare it to Siberian Wheat (otherwise called Siberian cheat) which is known to have been the most praised, the most dear, the most worthless, and most short-lived thing that was ever adopted. But if the free men of this continent are weary of that power and freedom they have so dearly bought and so shortly enjoyed- the power of judging and determining what laws are most wholesome; what taxes are requisite and sufficient-I say, if the people are tired of these privileges, now is the time to part with them forever. Much more might be said to show the bitterness and mischief contained in this gilded pill, but being fond of brevity, I shall rely on the good sense of the public to keep themselves out of the trap, and sign myself in plain English.

A NEWPORT MAN

ANTI-FEDERALIST PAPER NO. 21

Why The Articles Failed

This essay is composed of excerpts from "CENTINEL" letters appearing in the (Philadelphia) Independent Gazetteer, October 5 and November 30, 1787.

That the present confederation is inadequate to the objects of the union, seems to be universally allowed. The only question is, what additional powers are wanting to give due energy to the federal government? We should, however, be careful, in forming our opinion on this subject, not to impute the temporary and extraordinary difficulties that have hitherto impeded the execution of the confederation, to defects in the system itself. For years past, the harpies of power have been industriously inculcating the idea that all our difficulties proceed from the impotency of Congress, and have at length succeeded to give to this sentiment almost universal currency and belief. The devastations, losses and burdens occasioned by the late war; the excessive importations of foreign merchandise and luxuries, which have drained the country of its specie and involved it in debt, are all overlooked, and the inadequacy of the powers of the present confederation is erroneously supposed to be the only cause of our difficulties. Hence persons of every description are revelling in the anticipation of the halcyon days consequent on the establishment of the new constitution. What gross deception and fatal delusion! Although very considerable benefit might be derived from strengthening the hands of Congress, so as to enable them to regulate commerce, and counteract the adverse restrictions of other nations, which would meet with the concurrence of all persons; yet this benefit is accompanied in the new constitution with the scourge of despotic power....

Taxation is in every government a very delicate and difficult subject. Hence it has been the policy of all wise statesmen, as far as circumstances permitted, to lead the people by small beginnings and almost imperceptible degrees, into the habits of taxation. Where the contrary conduct has been pursued, it has ever failed of full success, not unfrequently proving the ruin of the projectors. The imposing of a burdensome tax at once on a people, without the usual gradations, is the severest test that any government can be put to; despotism itself has often proved unequal to the attempt. Under this conviction, let us take a review of our situation before and since the revolution. From the first settlement of this country until the commencement of the late war, the taxes were so light and trivial as to be scarcely felt by the people. When we engaged in the expensive contest with Great Britain, the Congress, sensible of the difficulty of levying the monies necessary to its support, by direct taxation, had resource to an anticipation of the public resources, by emitting bills of credit, and thus postponed the necessity of taxation for several years. This means was pursued to a most ruinous length. But about the year 80 or 81, it was wholly exhausted, the bills of credit had suffered such a depreciation from the excessive quantities in circulation, that they ceased to be useful as a medium. The country at this period was very much impoverished and exhausted; commerce had been suspended for near six years; the husbandman, for want of a market, limited his crops to his own subsistence; the frequent calls of the militia and long continuance in actual service, the devastations of the enemy, the subsistence of our own armies, the evils of the depreciation of the paper money, which fell chiefly upon the patriotic and virtuous part of the community, had all concurred to produce great distress throughout America. In this situation of affairs, we still had the same powerful enemy to contend with, who had even more numerous and better appointed armies in the field than at any former time. Our allies were applied to in this exigency, but the pecuniary assistance that we could procure from them was soon exhausted. The only resource now remaining was to obtain by direct taxation, the moneys necessary for our defense. The history of mankind does not furnish a similar instance of an attempt to levy such enormous taxes at once, nor of a people so wholly unprepared and uninured to them-the lamp of sacred liberty must indeed have burned with unsullied lustre, every sordid principle of the mind must have been then extinct, when the people not only submitted to the grievous impositions, but cheerfully exerted themselves to comply with the calls of their country. Their abilities, however, were not equal to furnish the necessary sums-indeed, the requisition of the year 1782, amounted to the whole income of their farms and other property, including the means of their subsistence. Perhaps the strained exertions of two years would not have sufficed to the discharge of this requisition. How then can we impute the difficulties of the people to a due compliance with the requisitions of Congress, to a defect in the confederation? Any government, however energetic, in similar circumstances, would have experienced the same fate. If we review the proceedings of the States, we shall find that they gave every sanction and authority to the requisitions of Congress that their laws could confer, that they attempted to collect the sums called for in the same manner as is proposed to be done in future by the general government, instead of the State legislatures....

The wheels of the general government having been thus clogged, and the arrearages of taxes still accumulating, it may be asked what prospect is there of the government resuming its proper tone,

-unless more compulsory powers are granted? To this it may be answered, that the produce of imposts on commerce, which all agree to vest in Congress, together with the immense tracts of land at their disposal, will rapidly lessen and eventually discharge the present encumbrances.

When this takes place, the mode by requisition will be found perfectly adequate to the extraordinary exigencies of the union. Congress have lately sold land to the amount of eight millions of dollars, which is a considerable portion of the whole debt.

It is to be lamented that the interested and designing have availed themselves so successfully of the present crisis, and under the specious pretence of having discovered a panacea for all the ills of the people, they are about establishing a system of government, that will prove more destructive to them than the wooden horse filled with soldiers did in ancient times to the city of Troy. This horse was introduced by their hostile enemy the Grecians, by a prostitution of the sacred rites of their religion; in like manner, my fellow citizens, are aspiring despots among yourselves prostituting the name of a Washington to cloak their designs upon your liberties.

I would ask how was the proposed Constitution to have showered down those treasures upon every class of citizens, as has been so industriously inculcated and so fondly believed by some?

Would it have been by the addition of numerous and expensive establishments? By doubling our judiciaries, instituting federal courts in every county of every state? By a superb presidential court? By a large standing army? In short, by putting it in the power of the future government to levy money at pleasure, and placing this government so independent of the people as to enable the administration to gratify every corrupt passion of the mind, to riot on your spoils, without check or control?

A transfer to Congress of the power of imposing imposts on commerce, the unlimited regulation of trade, and to make treaties, I believe is all that is wanting to render America as prosperous as it is in the power of any form of government to render her; this properly understood would meet the views of all the honest and well meaning.

What gave birth to the late continental Convention? Was it not the situation of our commerce, which lay at the mercy of every foreign power, who, from motives of interest or enmity, could restrict and control it without risking a retaliation on the part of America, as Congress was impotent on this subject? Such indeed was the case with respect to Britain, whose hostile regulations gave such a stab to our navigation as to threaten its annihilation, it became the interest of even the American merchant to give a preference to foreign bottoms; hence the distress of our seamen, shipwrights, and every mechanic art dependent on navigation.

By these regulations too, we were limited in markets for our produce; our vessels were excluded from their West India islands; many of our staple commodities were denied entrance in Britain.

Hence the husbandman were distressed by the demand for their crops being lessened and their prices reduced. This is the source to which may be traced every evil we experience, that can be relieved by a more energetic government. Recollect the language of complaint for years past; compare the recommendations of Congress, founded on such complaints, pointing out the remedy; examine the reasons assigned by the different states for appointing delegates to the late Convention; view the powers vested in that body-they all harmonize in the sentiment, that the due regulation of trade and navigation was the anxious wish of every class of citizens, was the great object of calling the Convention.

This object being provided for by the Constitution proposed by the general Convention, people overlooked and were not sensible of the needless sacrifice they were making for it. Allowing for a moment that it would be possible for trade to flourish under a despotic government, of what avail would be a prosperous state of commerce, when the produce of it would be at the absolute disposal of an arbitrary unchecked general government, who may levy at pleasure the most oppressive taxes; who may destroy every principle of freedom; who may even destroy the privilege of complaining....

After so recent a triumph over British despots, after such torrents of blood and treasure have been spent, after involving ourselves in the distresses of an arduous war, and incurring such a debt, for the express purpose of asserting the rights of humanity, it is truly astonishing that a set of men among ourselves should have had the effrontery to attempt the destruction of our liberties. But in this enlightened age, to dupe the people by the arts they are practising, is still more extraordinary...

CENTINEL

ANTI-FEDERALIST PAPER NO. 22

Articles Of Confederation Simply Requires Amendments, Particularly For Commercial Power And Judicial Power: Constitution Goes Too Far

Benjamin Austin of Massachusetts, used the pen-name "CANDIDUS." Taken from two letters by "Candidus" which appeared in the [Boston] Independent Chronicle, December 6 and 20, 1787.

.... Many people are sanguine for the Constitution, because they apprehend our commerce will be benefited. I would advise those persons to distinguish between the evils that arise from extraneous causes and our private imprudencies, and those that arise from our government. It does not appear that the embarrassments of our trade will be removed by the adoption of this Constitution. The powers of Europe do not lay any extraordinary duties on our oil, fish, or tobacco, because of our government; neither do they discourage our ship building on this account. I would ask what motive would induce Britain to repeal the duties on our oil, or France on our fish, if we should adopt the proposed Constitution? Those nations laid these duties to promote their own fishery, etc., and let us adopt what mode of government we please, they will pursue their own politics respecting our imports and exports, unless we can check them by some commercial regulations.

But it may be said, that such commercial regulations will take place after we have adopted the Constitution, and that the northern states would then become carriers for the southern. The great question then is, whether it is necessary in order to obtain these purposes, for every state to give up their whole power of legislation and taxation, and become an unwieldy republic, when it is probable the important object of our commerce could be effected by a uniform navigation act, giving Congress full power to regulate the whole commerce of the States? This power Congress have often said was sufficient to answer all their purposes. The circular letter from the Boston merchants and others, was urgent on this subject. Also the navigation act of this state

[Massachusetts], was adopted upon similar principles, and . . . was declared by our Minister in England, to be the most effectual plan to promote our navigation, provided it had been adopted by the whole confederacy.

But it may be said, this regulation of commerce, without energy to enforce a compliance, is quite ideal. Coercion with some persons seems the principal object, but I believe we have more to expect from the affections of the people, than from an armed body of men. Provided a uniform commercial system was adopted, and each State felt its agreeable operations, we should have but little occasion to exercise force. But however, as power is thought necessary to raise an army, if required, to carry into effect any federal measure, I am willing to place it, where it is likely to be used with the utmost caution. This power I am willing to place among the confederated States, to be exercised when two thirds of them in their legislative capacities shall say the common good requires it. But to trust this power in the hands of a few men delegated for two, four and six years, is complimenting the ambition of human nature too highly, to risk the tranquility of these

States on their absolute determination. Certain characters now on the stage, we have reason to venerate, but though this country is now blessed with a Washington, Franklin, Hancock and Adams, yet posterity may have reason to rue the day when their political welfare depends on the decision of men who may fill the places of these worthies....

The advocates for the Constitution, have always assumed an advantage by saying, that their opposers have never offered any plan as a substitute; the following outlines are therefore submitted, not as originating from an individual, but as copied from former resolutions of Congress, and united with some parts of the Constitution proposed by the respectable convention. This being the case, I presume it will not be invalidated by the cant term of antifederalism.

1st. That the Legislature of each state, empower Congress to frame a navigation act, to operate uniformly throughout the states; receiving to Congress all necessary powers to regulate our commerce with foreign nations, and among the several states, and with the Indian tribes. The revenue arising from the impost to be subject to their appropriations, "to enable them to fulfill their public engagements with foreign creditors."

2nd. That the Legislature of each state, instruct their delegates in Congress, to frame a treaty of AMITY for the purposes of discharging each state's proportion of the public debt, either foreign or domestic, and to enforce (if necessary) their immediate payment. Each state obligating themselves in the treaty of amity, to furnish (whenever required by Congress) a proportionate number of the Militia who are ever to be well organized and disciplined, for the purposes of repelling any invasion; suppressing any insurrection; or reducing any delinquent state within the confederacy, to a compliance with the federal treaty of commerce and amity. Such assistance to be furnished by the Supreme Executive of each state, on the application of Congress. The troops in cases of invasion to be under the command of the Supreme Executive of the state immediately in danger; but in cases of insurrection, and when employed against any delinquent state in the confederacy, the troops to be under the command of Congress.

3d. That such states as did not join the confederacy of commerce and amity, should be considered as aliens; and any goods brought from such state into any of the confederated states, together with their vessels, should be subject to heavy extra duties.

4th. The treaty of amity, agreed to by the several states, should expressly declare that no State (without the consent of Congress) should enter into any treaty, alliances, or confederacy; grant letters of marque and reprisal; make anything but gold and silver coin a tender in payment of debts; pass any bill of attainder or ex post facto law, or impair the obligations of contracts; engage in war, or declare peace.

5th. A Supreme Judicial Court to be constituted for the following federal purposes-to extend to all treaties made previous to, or which shall be made under the authority of the confederacy; all cases affecting Ambassadors, and other public Ministers and Consuls; controversies between two or more states; and between citizens of the same state claiming lands under grants of different states; to define and punish piracies, and felonies committed on the high seas, and offenses against the law of nations.

6th. That it be recommended to Congress, that the said navigation act, and treaty of amity, be sent to the Legislatures (or people) of the several states, for their assenting to, and ratifying the same.

7th. A regular statement and account of the receipts and expenditures, of all public monies, should be published from time to time.

The above plan it is humbly conceived-secures the internal government of the several states; promotes the commerce of the whole union; preserves a due degree of energy; lays restraints on aliens; secures the several states against invasions and insurrection by a MILITIA, rather than a STANDING ARMY; checks all ex post facto laws; cements the states by certain federal restrictions; confines the judiciary powers to national matters; and provides for the public information of receipts and expenditures. In a word, it places us in a complete federal state.

The resolves of Congress, 18th April, 1783, "recommends to the several States, to invest them with powers to levy for the use of the United States, certain duties upon goods, imported from any foreign port, island or plantation;" which measures is declared by them, "to be a system more free, from well founded exception, and is better calculated to receive the approbation of the several States, than any other, that the wisdom of Congress could devise; and if adopted, would enable them to fulfill their public engagements with their foreign creditors.". . . .

Should we adopt this plan, no extraordinary expenses would arise, and Congress having but one object to attend, every commercial regulation would be uniformly adopted; the duties of impost and excise, would operate equally throughout the states; our ship building and carrying trade, would claim their immediate attention; and in consequence thereof, our agriculture, trade and manufactures would revive and flourish. No acts of legislation, independent of this great business, would disaffect one State against the other; but the whole, . . . in one Federal System of commerce, would serve to remove all local attachments, and establish our navigation upon a most extensive basis. The powers of Europe, would be alarmed at our Union, and would fear lest we should retaliate on them by laying restrictions on their trade....

These states, by the blessing of Heaven, are now in a very tranquil state. This government, in particular, has produced an instance of ENERGY, in suppressing a late rebellion, which no absolute monarchy can boast. And notwithstanding the insinuations of a "small party," who are ever branding the PEOPLE with the most opprobrious epithets-representing them as aiming to level all distinctions; emit paper money; encourage the rebellion-yet the present General Court, the voice of that body, whom they have endeavored to stigmatize, have steadily pursued measures foreign from the suggestions of such revilers. And the public credit has been constantly appreciating since the present Administration.

Let us then be cautious how we disturb this general harmony. Every exertion is now making, by the people, to discharge their taxes. Industry and frugality prevail. Our commerce is every day increasing by the enterprise of our merchants. And above all, the PEOPLE of the several states are convinced of the necessity of adopting some Federal Commercial Plan....

CANDIDUS

ANTI-FEDERALIST PAPER NO. 23

Certain Powers Necessary For The Common Defense, Can And Should Be Limited

In Federalist No. 23, Alexander Hamilton spoke of the necessity for an energetic government.
"BRUTUS" replied.
Taken from the 7th and 8th essays of "Brutus" in The New-York Journal, January 3 and 10, 1788.
In a confederated government, where the powers are divided between the general and the state government, it is essential . . . that the revenues of the country, without which no government can exist, should be divided between them, and so apportioned to each, as to answer their respective exigencies, as far as human wisdom can effect such a division and apportionment....
No such allotment is made in this constitution, but every source of revenue is under the control of Congress; it therefore follows, that if this system is intended to be a complex and not a simple, a confederate and not an entire consolidated government, it contains in it the sure seeds of its own dissolution. One of two things must happen. Either the new constitution will become a mere nudum pactum, and all the authority of the rulers under it be cried down, as has happened to the present confederacy. Or the authority of the individual states will be totally supplanted, and they will retain the mere form without any of the powers of government. To one or the other of these issues, I think, this new government, if it is adopted, will advance with great celerity.
It is said, I know, that such a separation of the sources of revenue, cannot be made without endangering the public safety- "unless (says a writer) [Alexander Hamilton] it can be shown that the circumstances which may affect the public safety are reducible within certain determinate limits; unless the contrary of this position can be fairly and rationally disputed, it must be admitted, as a necessary consequence, that there can be no limitation of that authority which is to provide for the defense and protection of the community, etc."(1)

(1 Federalist, No. 23.)
The pretended demonstration of this writer will instantly vanish, when it is considered, that the protection and defense of the community is not intended to be entrusted solely into the hands of the general government, and by his own confession it ought not to be. It is true this system commits to the general government the protection and defense of the community against foreign force and invasion, against piracies and felonies on the high seas, and against insurrection among ourselves. They are also authorized to provide for the administration of justice in certain matters of a general concern, and in some that I think are not so. But it ought to be left to the state governments to provide for the protection and defense of the citizen against the hand of private violence, and the wrongs done or attempted by individuals to each other. Protection and defense against the murderer, the robber, the thief, the cheat, and the unjust person, is to be derived from the respective state governments. The just way of reasoning therefore on this subject is this, the general government is to provide for the protection and defense of the community against foreign attacks, etc. They therefore ought to have authority sufficient to effect this, so far as is consistent with the providing for our internal protection and defense. The state governments are entrusted
with the care of administering justice among its citizens, and the management of other internal concerns; they ought therefore to retain power adequate to that end. The preservation of internal peace and good order, and the due administration of law and justice, ought to be the first care of every government. The happiness of a people depends infinitely more on this than it does upon all that glory and respect which nations acquire by the most brilliant martial achievements. And I believe history will furnish but few examples of nations who have duly attended to these, who have been subdued by foreign invaders. If a proper respect and submission to the laws prevailed over all orders of men in our country; and if a spirit of public and private justice, economy, and industry influenced the people, we need not be under any apprehensions but what they would be ready to repel any invasion that might be made on the country. And more than this, I would not wish from them. A defensive war is the only one I think justifiable. I do not make these observations to prove, that a government ought not to be authorised to provide for the protection and defense of a country against external enemies, but to show that this is not the most important, much less the only object of their care.

Documents of Revolution

The European governments are almost all of them framed, and administered with a view to arms, and war, as that in which their chief glory consists. They mistake the end of government. It was designed to save men's lives, not to destroy them. We ought to furnish the world with an example of a great people, who in their civil institutions hold chiefly in view, the attainment of virtue, and happiness among ourselves. Let the monarchs in Europe share among them the glory of depopulating countries, and butchering thousands of their innocent citizens, to revenge private quarrels, or to punish an insult offered to a wife, a mistress, or a favorite. I envy them not the honor, and I pray heaven this country may never be ambitious of it. The czar Peter the great, acquired great glory by his arms; but all this was nothing, compared with the true glory which he obtained, by civilizing his rude and barbarous subjects, diffusing among them knowledge, and establishing and cultivating the arts of life. By the former he desolated countries, and drenched the earth with human blood; by the latter he softened the ferocious nature of his people, and pointed them to the means of human happiness. The most important end of government then, is the proper direction of its internal police, and economy; this is the province of the state governments, and it is evident, and is indeed admitted, that these ought to be under their control.

Is it not then preposterous, and in the highest degree absurd, when the state governments are vested with powers so essential to the peace and good order of society, to take from them the means of their own preservation?

The idea that the powers of congress in respect to revenue ought to be unlimited, because 'the circumstances which may affect the public safety are not reducible to certain determinate limits'

is novel, as it relates to the government of the United States. The inconveniencies which resulted from the feebleness of the present confederation was discerned, and felt soon after its adoption. It was soon discovered, that a power to require money, without either the authority or means to enforce a collection of it, could not be relied upon either to provide for the common defense, discharge the national debt, or for support of government. Congress therefore, as early as February 1781, recommended to the states to invest them with a power to levy an impost of :five per cent ad valorem, on all imported goods, as a fund to be appropriated to discharge the debts already contracted, or which should hereafter be contracted for the support of the war, to be continued until the debts should be fully and finally discharged. There is not the most distant idea held out in this act, that an unlimited power to collect taxes, duties and excises was

necessary to be vested in the United States, and yet this was a time of the most pressing danger and distress. The idea then was, that if certain definite funds were assigned to the union, which were certain in their natures, productive, and easy of collection, it would enable them to answer their engagements, and provide for their defense, and the impost of five per cent was fixed upon for the purpose.

This same subject was revived in the winter and spring of 1783, and after a long consideration of the subject, many schemes were proposed. The result was, a recommendation of the revenue system of April 1783; this system does not suggest an idea that it was necessary to grant the United States unlimited authority in matters of revenue. A variety of amendments were proposed to this system, some of which are upon the journals of Congress, but it does not appear that any of them proposed to invest the general government with discretionary power to raise money. On the contrary, all of them limit them to certain definite objects, and fix the bounds over which they could not pass. This recommendation was passed at the conclusion of the war, and was founded on an estimate of the whole national debt. It was computed, that one million and an half of dollars, in addition to the impost, was a sufficient sum to pay the annual interest of the debt, and gradually to abolish the principal. Events have proved that their estimate was sufficiently liberal, as the domestic debt appears upon its being adjusted to be less than it was computed; and since this period a considerable portion of the principal of the domestic debt has been discharged by the sale of the western lands. It has been constantly urged by Congress, and by individuals, ever since, until lately, that had this revenue been appropriated by the states, as it was recommended, it would have been adequate to every exigency of the union. Now indeed it is insisted, that all the treasures of the country are to be under the control of that body, whom we are to appoint to provide for our protection and defense against foreign enemies. The debts of the several states, and the support of the governments of them are to trust to fortune and accident. If the union should not have occasion for all the money they can raise, they will leave a portion for the state, but this must be a matter of mere grace and favor. Doctrines like these would not have been listened to by any state in the union, at a time when we were pressed on every side by a powerful enemy, and were called upon to make greater exertions than we have any reason to expect we shall ever be again. . . .

I may be asked to point out the sources, from which the general government could derive a sufficient revenue, to answer the demands of the union. ... There is one source of revenue, which it is agreed, the general government ought to have the sole control of. This is an impost upon all goods imported from foreign countries. This would, of itself, be very productive, and would be collected with ease and certainty. It will be a fund too, constantly increasing, for our commerce will grow with the productions of the country. And these, together with our consumption of foreign goods, wilt increase with our population. It is said, that the impost will not produce a sufficient sum to satisfy the demands of the general government; perhaps it would not.... My own opinion is, that the objects from which the general government should have authority to raise a revenue, should be of such a nature, that the tax should be raised by simple laws, with few officers, with certainty and expedition, and with the least interference with the internal police of the states. Of this nature is the impost on imported goods. And it appears to me that a duty on exports, would also be of this nature. Therefore, for ought I can discover, this would be the best source of revenue to grant the general government. I know neither the Congress nor the state legislatures will have authority under the new constitution to raise a revenue in this way. But I

cannot perceive the reason of the restriction. It appears to me evident, that a tax on articles exported, would be as nearly equal as any that we can expect to lay, and it certainly would be collected with more ease and less expense than any direct tax. I do not however, contend for this mode; it may be liable to well founded objections that have not occurred to me. But this I do contend for, that some mode is practicable, and that limits must be marked between the general government, and the states on this head, or if they be not, either the Congress in the exercise of this power, will deprive the state legislatures of the means of their existence, or the states by resisting the constitutional authority of the general government, will render it nugatory....

The next powers vested by this Constitution in the general government, which we shall consider, are those which authorize them to "borrow money on the credit of the United States, and to raise and support armies." I take these two together and connect them with the power to lay and collect taxes, duties, imposts and excises, because their extent, and the danger that will arise from the exercise of these powers, cannot be fully understood, unless they are viewed in relation to each other.

The power to borrow money is general and unlimited, and the clause so often before referred to, authorizes the passing [of] any laws proper and necessary to carry this into execution. Under this authority, Congress may mortgage any or all the revenues of the union, as a fund to loan money upon; and it is probable, in this way, they may borrow of foreign nations, a principal sum, the interest of which will be equal to the annual revenues of the country. By this means, they may create a national debt, so large, as to exceed the ability of the country ever to sink. I can scarcely contemplate a greater calamity that could befall this country, than to be loaded with a debt exceeding their ability ever to discharge. If this be a just remark, it is unwise and improvident to vest in the general government a power to borrow at discretion, without any limitation or restriction.

It may possibly happen that the safety and welfare of the country may require, that money be borrowed, and it is proper when such a necessity arises that the power should be exercised by the general government. But it certainly ought never to be exercised, but on the most urgent occasions, and then we should not borrow of foreigners if we could possibly avoid it.

The constitution should therefore have so restricted the exercise of this power as to have rendered it very difficult for the government to practice it. The present confederation requires the assent of nine states to exercise this, and a number of other important powers of the confederacy.

It would certainly have been a wise provision in this constitution, to have made it necessary that two thirds of the members should assent to borrowing money. When the necessity was indispensable, this assent would always be given, and in no other cause ought it to be.

The power to raise armies is indefinite and unlimited, and authorises the raising [of] forces, as well in peace as in war. Whether the clause which empowers the Congress to pass all laws which are proper and necessary, to carry this into execution, will not authorise them to impress men for the army, is a question well worthy [of] consideration. If the general legislature deem it for the general welfare to raise a body of troops, and they cannot be procured by voluntary enlistments, it seems evident, that it will be proper and necessary to effect it, that men be impressed from the militia to make up the deficiency.

These powers taken in connection, amount to this: that the general government have unlimited authority and control over all the wealth and all the force of the union. The advocates for this scheme, would favor the world with a new discovery, if they would show, what kind of freedom or independency is left to the state governments, when they cannot command any part of the property or of the force of the country, but at the will of the Congress. It seems to me as absurd, as it would be to say, that I was free and independent, when I had conveyed all my property to another, and was tenant to him, and had beside, given an indenture of myself to serve him during life....

ANTI-FEDERALIST PAPER NO. 24

(part I)objections To A Standing Army

BRUTUS
The first essay is taken from the ninth letter of "BRUTUS" which appeared in The New-York Journal, January 17, 1788.
.... Standing armies are dangerous to the liberties of a people.... [If] necessary, the truth of the position might be confirmed by the history of almost every nation in the world. A cloud of the most illustrious patriots of every age and country, where freedom has been enjoyed, might be adduced as witnesses in support of the sentiment. But I presume it would be useless, to enter into a labored argument, to prove to the people of America, a position which has so long and so generally been received by them as a kind of axiom.
Some of the advocates for this new system controvert this sentiment, as they do almost every other that has been maintained by the best writers on free government. Others, though they will not expressly deny, that standing armies in times of peace are dangerous, yet join with these in maintaining, that it is proper the general government should be vested with the power to do it. I shall now proceed to examine the arguments they adduce in support of their opinions.
A writer, in favor of this system, treats this objection as a ridiculous one. He supposes it would be as proper to provide against the introduction of Turkish Janizaries, or against making the Alcoran a rule of faith.'
{1 A citizen of America [Noah Webster], An Examination Into the Leading Principles of the Federal Constitution proposed by the late Convention held at Philadelphia. With Answers to the Principal Objections Raised Against the System (Philadelphia, 1787), reprinted in Ford (ed.), Pamphlets pp. 29-65.}
From the positive, and dogmatic manner, in which this author delivers his opinions, and answers objections made to his sentiments-one would conclude, that he was some pedantic pedagogue who had been accustomed to deliver his dogmas to pupils, who always placed implicit faith in what he delivered.
But, why is this provision so ridiculous? Because, says this author, it is unnecessary. But, why is it unnecessary? Because, "the principles and habits, as well as the power of the Americans are directly opposed to standing armies; and there is as little necessity to guard against them by positive constitutions, as to prohibit the establishment of the Mahometan religion." It is admitted then, that a standing army in time of peace is an evil. I ask then, why should this government be authorised to do evil? If the principles and habits of the people of this country are opposed to standing armies in time of peace, if they do not contribute to the public good, but would endanger the public liberty and happiness, why should the government be vested with the power?
No reason can be given, why rulers should be authorised to do, what, if done, would oppose the principles and habits of the people, and endanger the public safety; but there is every reason in
the world, that they should be prohibited from the exercise of such a power. But this author supposes, that no danger is to be apprehended from the exercise of this power, because if armies are kept up, it will be by the people themselves, and therefore, to provide against it would be as absurd as for a man to "pass a law in his family, that no troops should be quartered in his family by his consent." This reasoning supposes, that the general government is to be exercised by the people of America themselves. But such an idea is groundless and absurd. There is surely a distinction between the people and their rulers, even when the latter are representatives of the former. They certainly are not identically the same, and it cannot be disputed, but it may and often does happen, that they do not possess the same sentiments or pursue the same interests. I think I have shown [in a previous paper] that as this government is constructed, there is little reason to expect, that the interest of the people and their rulers will be the same.
Besides, if the habits and sentiments of the people of America are to be relied upon, as the sole security against the encroachment of their rulers, all restrictions in constitutions are unnecessary; nothing more is requisite, than to declare who shall be authorized to exercise the powers of government, and about this we need not be very careful-for the habits and principles of the people will oppose every abuse of power. This I suppose to be the sentiments of this author, as it seems to be

of many of the advocates of this new system. An opinion like this, is as directly opposed to the principles and habits of the people of America, as it is to the sentiments of every writer of reputation on the science of government, and repugnant to the principles of reason and common sense.

The idea that there is no danger of the establishment of a standing army, under the new constitution, is without foundation. It is a well known fact, that a number of those who had an agency in producing this system, and many of those who it is probable will have a principal share in the administration of the government under it, if it is adopted, are avowedly in favor of standing armies. It is a language common among them, "That no people can be kept in order, unless the government have an army to awe them into obedience; it is necessary to support the dignity of government, to have a military establishment. And there will not be wanting a variety of plausible reasons to justify the raising one, drawn from the danger we are in from the Indians on our frontiers, or from the European provinces in our neighborhood. If to this we add, that an army will afford a decent support, and agreeable employment to the young men of many families, who are too indolent to follow occupations that will require care and industry, and too poor to live without doing any business, we can have little reason to doubt but that we shall have a large standing army as soon as this government can find money to pay them, and perhaps sooner.

A writer, who is the boast of the advocates of this new constitution, has taken great pains to show, that this power was proper and necessary to be vested in the general government.

He sets out with calling in question the candor and integrity of those who advance the objection; and with insinuating, that it is their intention to mislead the people, by alarming their passions, rather than to convince them by arguments addressed to their understandings.

The man who reproves another for a fault, should be careful that he himself be not guilty of it.

How far this writer has manifested a spirit of candor, and has pursued fair reasoning on this subject, the impartial public will judge, when his arguments pass before them in review.

He first attempts to show, that this objection is futile and disingenuous, because the power to keep up standing armies, in time of peace, is vested, under the present government, in the legislature of every state in the union, except two. Now this is so far from being true, that it is expressly declared by the present articles of confederation, that no body of forces "Shall be kept up by any state, in time of peace, except such number only, as in the judgment of the United States in Congress assembled, shall be deemed requisite to garrison the forts necessary for the defence of such state." Now, was it candid and ingenuous to endeavour to persuade the public, that the general government had no other power than your own legislature have on this head; when the truth is, your legislature have no authority to raise and keep up any forces?

He next tells us, that the power given by this constitution, on this head, is similar to that which Congress possess under the present confederation. As little ingenuity is manifested in this representation as in that of the former.

I shall not undertake to inquire whether or not Congress are vested with a power to keep up a standing army in time of peace; it has been a subject warmly debated in Congress, more than once, since the peace; and one of the most respectable states in the union, were so fully convinced that they had no such power, that they expressly instructed their delegates to enter a solemn protest against it on the journals of Congress, should they attempt to exercise it.

But should it be admitted that they have the power, there is such a striking dissimilarity between the restrictions under which the present Congress can exercise it, and that of the proposed government, that the comparison will serve rather to show the impropriety of vesting the proposed government with the power, than of justifying it.

It is acknowledged by this writer, that the powers of Congress, under the present confederation, amount to little more than that of recommending. If they determine to raise troops, they are obliged to effect it through the authority of the state legislatures. This will, in the first instance, be a most powerful restraint upon them, against ordering troops to be raised. But if they should vote an army, contrary to the opinion and wishes of the people, the legislatures of the respective states would not raise them. Besides, the present Congress hold their places at the wilt and pleasure of the legislatures of the states who send them, and no troops can be raised, but by the assent of nine states out of the thirteen. Compare the power proposed to be lodged in the legislature on this head, under this constitution, with that vested in the present Congress, and every person of the least discernment, whose understanding is not totally blinded by prejudice, will perceive, that they bear no analogy to each other. Under the present confederation, the representatives of nine states, out of thirteen, must assent to the raising of troops, or they cannot be levied. Under the proposed constitution, a less number than the representatives of two states, in the house of representatives, and the representatives of three states and an half in the senate, with the assent of the president, may raise any number of troops they please. The present Congress are restrained from an undue exercise of this power; from this consideration, they know the state legislatures, through whose authority it must be carried into effect, would not comply with the requisition for the purpose, [if] it was evidently opposed to the public good. The proposed constitution authorizes the legislature to carry their determinations into execution, without intervention of any other body between them and the people. The Congress under the present form are amenable to, and removable by, the legislatures of the respective states, and are chosen for one year only. The proposed constitution does not make the members of the legislature accountable to, or removable by the state legislatures at all; and they are chosen, the one house for six, and the other for two years; and cannot be removed until their time of service is expired, let them conduct ever so badly. The public will judge, from the above comparison, how just a claim this writer has to that candor he asserts to possess. In the mean time, to convince him, and the advocates for this system, that I possess some share of candor, I pledge myself to give up all opposition to it, on the head of standing armies, if the power to raise them be restricted as it is in the present confederation; and I believe I may safely answer, not only for myself, but for all who make the objection, that they will [not] be satisfied with less.

ANTI-FEDERALIST PAPER NO. 25 (PART II)

objections To A Standing Army

From the tenth letter of "BRUTUS" appearing in The New-York Journal, January 24, 1788.
The liberties of a people are in danger from a large standing army, not only because the rulers may employ them for the purposes of supporting themselves in any usurpations of power, which they may see proper to exercise; but there is great hazard, that an army will subvert the forms of the government, under whose authority they are raised, and establish one [rule] according to the pleasure of their leaders.
We are informed, in the faithful pages of history, of such events frequently happening. Two instances have been mentioned in a former paper. They are so remarkable, that they are worthy of the most careful attention of every lover of freedom. They are taken from the history of the two most powerful nations that have ever existed in the world; and who are the most renowned, for the freedom they enjoyed, and the excellency of their constitutions-I mean Rome and Britain.
In the first, the liberties of the commonwealth were destroyed, and the constitution over-turned, by an army, led by Julius Caesar, who was appointed to the command by the constitutional authority of that commonwealth. He changed it from a free republic, whose fame ... is still celebrated by all the world, into that of the most absolute despotism. A standing army effected this change, and a standing army supported it through a succession of ages, which are marked in the annals of history with the most horrid cruelties, bloodshed, and carnage-the most devilish, beastly, and unnatural vices, that ever punished or disgraced human nature.
The same army, that in Britain, vindicated the liberties of that people from the encroachments and despotism of a tyrant king, assisted Cromwell, their General, in wresting from the people that liberty they had so dearly earned.
You may be told, these instances will not apply to our case. But those who would persuade you to believe this, either mean to deceive you, or have not themselves considered the subject.
I firmly believe, no country in the world had ever a more patriotic army, than the one which so ably served this country in the late war. But had the General who commanded them been possessed of the spirit of a Julius Caesar or a Cromwell, the liberties of this country . - . [might have] in all probability terminated with the war. Or bad they been maintained, [they] might have cost more blood and treasure than was expended in the conflict with Great Britain. When an anonymous writer addressed the officers of the army at the close of the war, advising them not to part with their arms, until justice was done them-the effect it had is well known. It affected them like an electric shock. He wrote like Caesar; and had the commander in chief, and a few more officers of rank, countenanced the measure, the desperate resolution. . . [might have] been taken, to refuse to disband. What the consequences of such a determination would have been, heaven only knows. The army were in the full vigor of health and spirits, in the habit of discipline, and possessed of all our military stores and apparatus. They would have acquired great accessions of strength from the country. Those who were disgusted at our republican forms of government (for
such there then were, of high rank among us) would have lent them all their aid. We should in all probability have seen a constitution and laws dictated to us, at the head of an army, and at the point of a bayonet, and the liberties for which we had so

severely struggled, snatched from us in a moment. It remains a secret, yet to be revealed, whether this measure was not suggested, or at least countenanced, by some, who have bad great influence in producing the present system.

Fortunately indeed for this country, it had at the head of the army, a patriot as well as a general; and many of our principal officers had not abandoned the characters of citizens, by assuming that of soldiers; and therefore, the scheme proved abortive. But are we to expect, that this will always be the case? Are we so much better than the people of other ages and of other countries, that the same allurements of power and greatness, which led them aside from their duty, will have no influence upon men in our country? Such an idea is wild and extravagant. Had we indulged such a delusion, enough has appeared in a little time past, to convince the most credulous, that the passion for pomp, power, and greatness, works as powerfully in the hearts of many of our better sort, as it ever did in any country under heaven. Were the same opportunity again to offer, we should very probably be grossly disappointed, if we made dependence, that all who then rejected the overture, would do it again.

From these remarks, it appears, that the evils to be feared from a large standing army in time of peace, do not arise solely from the apprehension, that the rulers may employ them for the purpose of promoting their own ambitious views; but that equal, and perhaps greater danger, is to be apprehended from their overturning the constitutional powers of the government, and assuming the power to dictate any form they please.

The advocates for power, in support of this right in the proposed government, urge that a restraint upon the discretion of the legislatures, in respect to military establishments in time of peace, would be improper to be imposed, because they say, it will be necessary to maintain small garrisons on the frontiers, to guard against the depredations of the Indians, and to be prepared to repel any encroachments or invasions that may be made by Spain or Britain.

The amount of this argument stripped of the abundant verbiages with which the author has dressed it, is this:

It will probably be necessary to keep up a small body of troops to garrison a few posts, which it will be necessary to maintain, in order to guard against the sudden encroachments of the Indians, or of the Spaniards and British; and therefore, the general government ought to be invested with power to raise and keep up a standing army in time of peace, without restraint, at their discretion.

I confess, I cannot perceive that the conclusion follows from the premises. Logicians say, it is not good reasoning to infer a general conclusion from particular premises. Though I am not much of a logician, it seems to me, this argument is very like that species of reasoning.

When the patriots in the parliament in Great Britain, contended with such force of argument, and all the powers of eloquence, against keeping up standing armies in time of peace, it is obvious they never entertained an idea, that small garrisons on their frontiers, or in the neighborhood of powers from whom they were in danger of encroachments, or guards to take care of public arsenals, would thereby be prohibited.

The advocates for this power further urge that it is necessary, because it may, and probably will happen, that circumstances will render it requisite to raise an army to be prepared to repel attacks of an enemy, before a formal declaration of war, which in modern times has fallen into disuse. If the constitution prohibited the raising an army, until a war actually commenced, it would deprive the government of the power of providing for the defense of the country, until the enemy were within our territory. If the restriction is not to extend to the raising armies in cases of emergency, but only to the keeping them up, this would leave the matter to the discretion of the legislature, and they might, under the pretence that there was danger of an invasion, keep up the army as long as they judged proper-and hence it is inferred, that the legislature should have authority to raise and keep up an army without any restriction. But from these premises nothing more will follow than this: that the legislature should not be so restrained, as to put it out of their power to raise an army, when such exigencies as are instanced shall arise. But it does not thence follow, that the government should be empowered to raise and maintain standing armies at their discretion as well in peace as in war. If indeed, it is impossible to vest the general government with the power of raising troops to garrison the frontier posts, to guard arsenals, or to be prepared to repel an attack, when we saw a power preparing to make one, without giving them a general and indefinite authority to raise and keep up armies, without any restriction or qualification, then this reasoning might have weight; but this has not been proved nor can it be.

It is admitted that to prohibit the general government from keeping up standing armies, while yet they were authorised to raise them in case of exigency, would be an insufficient guard against the danger. A discretion of such latitude would give room to elude the force of the provision.

It is also admitted that an absolute prohibition against raising troops, except in cases of actual war, would be improper; because it will be requisite to raise and support a small number of troops to garrison the important frontier posts, and to guard arsenals; and it may happen, that the danger of an attack from a foreign power may be so imminent, as to render it highly proper we should raise an army, in order to be prepared to resist them. But to raise and keep up forces for such purposes and on such occasions, is not included in the idea of keeping up standing armies in times of peace.

It is a thing very practicable to give the government sufficient authority to provide for these cases, and at the same time to provide a reasonable and competent security against the evil of a standing army-a clause to the following purpose would answer the end:

As standing armies in time of peace are dangerous to liberty, and have often been the means of overturning the best constitutions of government, no standing army, or troops of any description whatsoever, shall be raised or kept up by the legislature, except so many as shall be necessary for guards to the arsenals of the United States, or for garrisons to such posts on the frontiers, as it shall be deemed absolutely necessary to hold, to secure the inhabitants, and facilitate the trade with the Indians: unless when the United States are threatened with an attack or invasion from some foreign power, in which case the legislature shall be authorised to raise an army to be prepared to repel the attack; provided that no troops whatsoever shall be raised in time of peace, without the assent of two thirds of the members, composing both houses of the legislature.

A clause similar to this would afford sufficient latitude to the legislature to raise troops in all cases that were really necessary, and at the same time competent security against the establishment of that dangerous engine of despotism, a standing army. The same writer who advances the arguments I have noticed, makes a number of other observations with a view to prove that the power to raise and keep up armies ought to be discretionary in the general legislature. Some of them are curious. He instances the raising of troops in Massachusetts and Pennsylvania, to show the necessity of keeping a standing army in time of peace; the least reflection must convince every candid mind that both these cases are totally foreign to his purpose. Massachusetts raised a body of troops for six months, at the expiration of which they were to disband ... ; this looks very little like a standing army. But beside, was that commonwealth in a state of peace at that time? So far from it, that they were in the most violent commotions and contests, and their legislature had formally declared that an unnatural rebellion existed within the state. The situation of Pennsylvania was similar; a number of armed men had levied war against the authority of the state and openly avowed their intention of withdrawing their allegiance from it. To what purpose examples are brought, of states raising troops for short periods in times of war or insurrections, on a question concerning the propriety of keeping up standing armies in times of peace, the public must judge.

It is further said, that no danger can arise from this power being lodged in the hands of the general government, because the legislatures will be a check upon them, to prevent their abusing it.

This is offered, as what force there is in it will hereafter receive a more particular examination.

At present, I shall only remark, that it is difficult to conceive how the state legislatures can, in any case, hold a check over the general legislature, in a constitutional way. The latter has, in every instance to which their powers extend, complete control over the former. The state legislatures can, in no case-by law, resolution, or otherwise of right, prevent or impede the general government, from enacting any law, or executing it, which this constitution authorizes them to enact or execute. If then the state legislatures check the general legislature, it must be by exciting the people to resist constitutional laws. In this way every individual, or every body of men, may check any government, in proportion to the influence they may have over the body of the people. But such kinds of checks as these, though they sometimes correct the abuses of government, [more] often destroy all government.

It is further said, that no danger is to be apprehended from the exercise of this power, because it is lodged in the hands of representatives of the people. If they abuse it, it is in the power of the people to remove them, and choose others who will pursue their interests.... That it is unwise in any people, to authorize their rulers to do, what, if done, would prove injurious-I have, in some former numbers, shown. . . . The representation in the proposed government will be a mere shadow without the substance. I am so confident that I am well founded in this opinion, that I am persuaded if it was to be adopted or rejected, upon a fair discussion of its merits without taking into contemplation circumstances extraneous to it, as reasons for its adoption, nineteen-twentieths of the sensible men in the union would reject it on this account alone; unless its powers were confined to much fewer objects than it embraces.

BRUTUS

ANTI-FEDERALIST PAPER NO. 26

(PART I) The Use Of Coercion By The New Government

"A FARMER AND PLANTER" had his work printed in The Maryland Journal, and Baltimore Advertiser, April 1, 1788.

The time is nearly at hand, when you are called upon to render up that glorious liberty you obtained, by resisting the tyranny and oppression of George the Third, King of England, and his ministers. The first Monday in April is the day appointed by our assembly, for you to meet and choose delegates in each county, to take into consideration the new Federal Government, and either adopt or refuse it. Let me entreat you, my fellows, to consider well what you are about.

Read the said constitution, and consider it well before you act. I have done so, and can find that we are to receive but little good, and a great deal of evil. Aristocracy, or government in the hands of a very few nobles, or RICH MEN, is therein concealed in the most artful wrote plan that ever was formed to entrap a free people. The contrivers of it have so completely entrapped you, and laid their plans so sure and secretly, that they have only left you to do one of two things-that is either to receive or refuse it. And in order to bring you into their snare, you may daily read new pieces published in the newspapers, in favor of this new government; and should a writer dare to publish any piece against it, he is immediately abused and vilified.

Look round you and observe well the RICH MEN, who are to be your only rulers, lords and masters in future! Are they not all for it? Yes! Ought not this to put you on your guard? Does not riches beget power, and power, oppression and tyranny?

I am told that four of the richest men in Ann-Arundel County [Maryland], have offered themselves candidates to serve in the convention, who are all in favor of the new Federal Government. Let me beg of you to reflect a moment on the danger you run. If you choose these men, or others like them, they certainly will do everything in their power to adopt the new government. Should they succeed, your liberty is gone forever; and you will then be nothing better than a strong ass crouching down between two burdens. The new form of government gives Congress liberty at any time, by their laws, to alter the state laws, and the time, places and manner of holding elections for representatives. By this clause they may command, by their laws, the people of Maryland to go to Georgia, and the people of Georgia to go to Boston, to choose their representatives. Congress, or our future lords and masters, are to have power to lay and collect taxes, duties, imposts, and excises. Excise is a new thing in America, and few country farmers and planters know the meaning of it. But it is not so in Old England, where I have seen the effects of it, and felt the smart. It is there a duty, or tax, laid upon almost every necessary of life and convenience, and a great number of other articles. The excise on salt in the year 1762, to the best of my recollection, in England, was 4s. sterling per bushel, for all that was made use of in families; and the price of salt per bushel about 6s. sterling, and the excise 4s.6d. on every gallon of rum made use of. If a private family make their own soap, candles, beer, cider, etc., they pay an excise duty on them. And if they neglect calling in an excise officer at the time of making these things, they are liable to grievous fines and forfeitures, besides a long train of evils and inconveniences attending this detestable excise-to enumerate particularly would fill a

volume. The excise officers have power to enter your houses at all times, by night or day, and if you refuse them entrance, they can, under pretense of searching for exciseable goods, that the duty has not been paid on, break open your doors, chests, trunks, desks, boxes, and rummage your houses from bottom to top. Nay, they often search the clothes, petticoats and pockets of ladies or gentlemen (particularly when they are coming from on board an East-India ship), and if they find any the least article that you cannot prove the duty to be paid on, seize it and carry it away with them; who are the very scum and refuse of mankind, who value not their oaths, and will break them for a shilling. This is their true character in England, and I speak from experience, for I have had the opportunity of putting their virtue to the test, and saw two of them break their oath for one guinea, and a third for one shilling's worth of punch. What do you think of a law to let loose such a set of vile officers among you! Do you expect the Congress excise-officers will be any better-if God, in his anger, should think it proper to punish us for our ignorance, and sins of ingratitude to him, after carrying us through the late war, and giving us liberty, and now so tamely to give it up by adopting this aristocratical government?

Representatives and direct taxes shall be apportioned among the several states which may be included within this union according to their respective numbers. This seems to imply, that we shall be taxed by the poll again, which is contrary to our Bill of Rights. But it is possible that the rich men, who are the great land holders, will tax us in this manner, which will exempt them from paying assessments on their great bodies of land in the old and new parts of the United States; many of them having but few taxable by the poll. Our great Lords and Masters are to lay taxes, raise and support armies, provide a navy, and may appropriate money for two years, call forth the militia to execute their laws, suppress insurrections, and the President is to have the command of the militia. Now, my countrymen, I would ask you, why are all these things directed and put into their power? Why, I conceive, they are to keep you in a good humor; and if you should, at any time, think you are imposed upon by Congress and your great Lords and Masters, and refuse or delay to pay your taxes, or do anything that they shall think proper to order you to do, they can, and I have not a doubt but they will, send the militia of Pennsylvania, Boston, or any other state or place, to cut your throats, ravage and destroy your plantations, drive away your cattle and horses, abuse your wives, kill your infants, and ravish your daughters, and live in free quarters, until you get into a good humor, and pay all that they may think proper to ask of you, and you become good and faithful servants and slaves.[1] Such things have been done, and I have no doubt will be done again, if you consent to the adoption of this new Federal Government. You labored under many hardships while the British tyrannized over you! You fought, conquered and gained your liberty-then keep it, I pray you, as a precious jewel. Trust it not out of your own hands; be assured, if you do, you will never more regain it. The train is laid, the match is on fire, and they only wait for yourselves to put it to the train, to blow up all your liberty and commonwealth governments, and introduce aristocracy and monarchy, and despotism will follow of course in a few years. Four-years President will be in time a King for life; and after him, his son, or he that has the greatest power among them, will be King also. View your danger, and find out good men to represent you in convention-men of your own profession and station in life; men who will not adopt this destructive and diabolical form of a federal government. There are many among you that will not be led by the nose by rich men, and would scorn a bribe. Rich men can live easy under any government, be it ever so tyrannical. They come in for a great share of the tyranny, because they are the ministers of tyrants, and always engross the places of honor and profit, while the greater part of the common people are led by the nose, and played about by

these very men, for the destruction of themselves and their class. Be wise, be virtuous, and catch the precious moment as it passes, to refuse this newfangled federal government, and extricate yourselves and posterity from tyranny, oppression, aristocratical or monarchical government. . . .

A FARMER AND PLANTER

[1] See the history of the confederate Grecian states-also the history of England, for the massacre of the people in the valley of Glenco, in the time of William the Third. [Note by "A Farmer and Planter".]

ANTI-FEDERALIST PAPER NO. 27

(PART II) The Use Of Coercion By The New Government

"JOHN HUMBLE's," following piece was published in the Independent Gazetteer, October 29, 1787.

The humble address of the low-born of the United States of America, to their fellow slaves scattered throughout the world-greeting:

Whereas it hath been represented unto us that a most dreadful disease hath for these five years last past infected, preyed upon and almost ruined the government and people of this our country; and of this malady we ourselves have had perfect demonstration, not mentally, but bodily, through every one of the five senses. For although our sensations in regard to the mind be not just so nice as those of the well born, yet our feeling, through the medium of the plow, the hoe and the grubbing ax, is as acute as any nobleman's in the world. And, whereas, a number of skillful physicians having met together at Philadelphia last summer, for the purpose of exploring, and, if possible, removing the cause of this direful disease, have, through the assistance of John Adams, Esq., in the profundity of their great political knowledge, found out and discovered that nothing but a new government, consisting of three different branches, namely, king, lords, and commons or, in the American language, President, Senate and Representatives-can save this, our country, from inevitable destruction. And, whereas, it has been reported that several of our low-born brethren have had the horrid audacity to think for themselves in regard to this new system of government, and, dreadful thought! have wickedly begun to doubt concerning the perfection of this evangelical constitution, which our political doctors have declared to be a panacea, which (by inspiration) they know will infallibly heal every distemper in the confederation, and finally terminate in the salvation of America.

Now we the low born, that is, all the people of the United States, except 600 thereabouts, well born, do by this our humble address, declare and most solemnly engage, that we will allow and admit the said 600 well born, immediately to establish and confirm this most noble, most excellent and truly divine constitution. And we further declare that without any equivocation or mental reservation whatever we will support and maintain the same according to the best of our power, and after the manner and custom of all other slaves in foreign countries, namely by the sweat and toil of our body. Nor will we at any future period of time ever attempt to complain of this our royal government, let the consequences be what they may.

And although it appears to us that a standing army, composed of the purgings of the jails of Great Britain, Ireland and Germany, shall be employed in collecting the revenues of this our king and government, yet, we again in the most solemn manner declare, that we will abide by our present determination of non- resistance and passive obedience-so that we shall not dare to molest or disturb those military gentlemen in the service of our royal government. And (which is not improbable) should any one of those soldiers when employed on duty in collecting the taxes, strike off the arm (with his sword) of one of our fellow slaves, we will conceive our case remarkably fortunate if he leaves the other arm on. And moreover, because we are aware that many of our fellow slaves shall be unable to pay their taxes, and this incapacity of theirs is a just

cause of impeachment of treason; wherefore in such cases we will use our utmost endeavors, in conjunction with the standing army, to bring such atrocious offenders before our federal judges, who shall have power, without jury or trial, to order the said miscreants for immediate execution; nor will we think their sentence severe unless after being hanged they are also to be both beheaded and quartered. And finally we shall henceforth and forever leave all power, authority and dominion over our persons and properties in the hands of the well born, who were designed by Providence to govern. And in regard to the liberty of the press, we renounce all claim to it forever more, Amen; and we shall in future be perfectly contented if our tongues be left us to lick the feet of our well born masters.

Done on behalf of three millions of low-born American slaves.

JOHN HUMBLE, Secretary

ANTI-FEDERALIST PAPER NO. 28

The Use Of Coercion By The New Government (part III)

This essay was published in either the (Philadelphia) Freeman's Journal; or, The North-American Intelligencer, January 16, 1788.

The Congress under the new Constitution have the power "of organizing, arming and disciplining the militia, and of governing them when in the service of the United States, giving to the separate States the appointment of the officers and the authority of training the militia according to the discipline prescribed by Congress." Let us inquire why they have assumed this great power. Was it to strengthen the power which is now lodged in your hands, and relying upon you and you solely for aid and support to the civil power in the execution of all the laws of the new Congress? Is this probable? Does the complexion of this new plan countenance such a supposition? When they unprecedently claim the power of raising and supporting armies, do they tell you for what purposes they are to be raised? How they are to be employed? How many they are to consist of, and where to be stationed? Is this power fettered with any one of those restrictions, which will show they depend upon the militia, and not upon this infernal engine of oppression to execute their civil laws? The nature of the demand in itself contradicts such a supposition, and forces you to believe that it is for none of these causes-but rather for the purpose of consolidating and finally destroying your strength, as your respective governments are to be destroyed. They well know the impolicy of putting or keeping arms in the hands of a nervous people, at a distance from the seat of a government, upon whom they mean to exercise the powers granted in that government. They have no idea of calling upon or trusting to the party aggrieved to support and enforce their own grievances, (notwithstanding they may select and subject them to as strict subordination as regular troops) unless they have a standing army to back and compel the execution of their orders. It is asserted by the most respectable writers upon government, that a well regulated militia, composed of the yeomanry of the country, have ever been considered as the bulwark of a free people. Tyrants have never placed any confidence on a militia composed of freemen. Experience has taught them that a standing body of regular forces, whenever they can be completely introduced, are always efficacious in enforcing their edicts, however arbitrary; and slaves by profession themselves, are "nothing loth" to break down the barriers of freedom with a gout. No, my fellow citizens, this plainly shows they do not mean to depend upon the citizens of the States alone to enforce their powers. They mean to lean upon something more substantial and summary. They have left the appointment of officers in the breasts of the several States; but this appears to me an insult rather than a privilege, for what avails this right if they at their pleasure may arm or disarm all or any part of the freemen of the United States, so that when their army is sufficiently numerous, they may put it out of the power of the freemen militia of America to assert and defend their liberties, however they might be encroached upon by Congress. Does any, after reading this provision for a regular standing army, suppose that they intended to apply to the militia in all cases, and to pay particular attention to making them the bulwark of this continent? And would they not be equal to such an undertaking? Are they not abundantly able to give security and stability to your government as long as it is free? Are they not the only proper persons to do it? Are they not the most respectable body of yeomanry in that character upon earth? Have they not been engaged in some of the most brilliant actions in America, and more than once decided the fate of princes? In short, do they not preclude the necessity of any standing army whatsoever, unless in case of invasion? And in that case it would be time enough to raise them, for no free government under heaven, with a well disciplined militia, was ever yet subdued by mercenary troops.

The advocates at the present day, for a standing army in the new Congress, pretend it is necessary for the respectability of government. I defy them to produce an instance in any country, in the Old or New World, where they have not finally done away the liberties of the people. Every writer upon government-- Locke, Sidney, Hampden, and a list of others have uniformly asserted, that standing armies are a solecism in any government; that no nation ever supported them, that did not resort to, rely upon, and finally become a prey to them. No western historians have yet been hardy enough to advance principles that look a different way. What historians have asserted, all the Grecian republics have verified. They are brought up to obedience and unconditional submission; with arms in their bands, they are taught to feel the weight of rigid discipline; they are excluded from the enjoyments which liberty gives to its votaries; they, in consequence, hate and envy the rest of the community in which they are placed, and indulge a malignant pleasure in destroying those privileges to which they never can be admitted.

Documents of Revolution

"Without a standing army," (says the Marquis of Beccaria), "in every society there is an effort constantly tending to confer on one part the height and to reduce the other to the extreme of weakness, and this is of itself sufficient to employ the people's attention." There is no instance of any government being reduced to a confirmed tyranny without military oppression.

And the first policy of tyrants has been to annihilate all other means of national activity and defense, when they feared opposition, and to rely solely upon standing troops. Repeated were the trials, before the sovereigns of Europe dared to introduce them upon any pretext whatever; and the whole record of the transactions of mankind cannot furnish an instance, (unless the proposed constitution may be called part of that record) where the motives which caused that establishment were not completely disguised. Peisistratus in Greece, and Dionysius in Syracuse, Charles in France, and Henry in England, all cloaked their villainous intentions under an idea of raising a small body as a guard for their persons; and Spain could not succeed in the same nefarious plan, until thro' the influence of an ambitious priest (who have in all countries and in all ages, even at this day, encouraged and preached up arbitrary power) they obtained it. "Caesar, who first attacked the commonwealth with mines, very soon opened his batteries."

Notwithstanding all these objections to this engine of oppression, which are made by the most experienced men, and confirmed by every country where the rays of freedom ever extended-yet in America, which has hitherto been her favorite abode; in this civilized territory, where property is so valuable, and men are found with feelings that win not patiently submit to arbitrary control; in this western region, where, my fellow countrymen, it is confessedly proper that you should associate and dwell in society from choice and reflection, and not be kept together by force and fear-you are modestly requested to engraft into the component parts of your constitution a Standing Army, without any qualifying restraints whatever, certainly to exist somewhere in the bowels of your country in time of peace. It is very true that Lawyer [James] Wilson-member of the Federal Convention, and who we may suppose breathes in some measure the spirit of that body-tells you it is for the purpose of forming cantonments upon your frontiers, and for the dignity and safety of your country, as it respects foreign nations. No man that loves his country could object to their being raised for the first of these causes, but for the last it cannot be necessary. God has so separated us by an extensive ocean from the rest of mankind; he hath so

liberally endowed us with privileges, and so abundantly taught us to esteem them precious, it would be impossible while we retain our integrity, and advert to first principles, for any nation whatever to subdue us. We have succeeded in our opposition to the most powerful people upon the globe; and the wound that America received in the struggle, where is it? As speedily healed as the track in the ocean is buried by the succeeding wave. It has scarcely stopped her progress, and our private dissensions only, at this moment, tarnish the lustre of the most illustrious infant nation under heaven.

You cannot help suspecting this gentleman [James Wilson], when he goes on to tell you "that standing armies in time of peace have always been a topic of popular declamation, but Europe hath found them necessary to maintain the appearance of strength in a season of the most profound tranquility." This shows you his opinion-and that he, as one of the Convention, was for unequivocally establishing them in time of peace; and to object to them, is a mere popular declamation. But I will not, my countrymen-I cannot believe you to be of the same sentiment.

Where is the standing army in the world that, like the musket they make use of, hath been in time of peace brightened and burnished for the sake only of maintaining an appearance of strength, without being put to a different use-without having had a pernicious influence upon the morals, the habits, and the sentiments of society, and finally, taking a chief part in executing its laws? . . .

If tyranny is at all feared, the tyranny of the many is to be guarded against MORE than that of a single person. The Athenians found by sad experience, that 30 tyrants were thirty times worse than one. A bad aristocracy is thirty times worse than a bad monarchy, allowing each to have a standing army as unrestricted as in the proposed constitution.

If the people are not in general disposed to execute the powers of government, it is time to suspect there is something wrong in that government; and rather than employ a standing army, they had better have another. For, in my humble opinion, it is yet much too early to set it down for a fact, that mankind cannot be governed but by force.

ANTI-FEDERALIST PAPER NO. 29

Objections To National Control Of The Militia

"A DEMOCRATIC FEDERALIST," appeared in "the Pennsylvania Packet," October 23, 1787; following #29, #30 is excerpted from THE ADDRESS AND REASONS OF DISSENT OF THE
MINORITY OF THE CONVENTION OF THE STATE OF PENNSYLVANIA TO THEIR
CONSTITUENTS, December 12, 1787.

Hume, an aristocratical writer, has candidly confessed that an army is a moral distemper in a government, of which it must at last inevitably perish (2d Burgh, 349); and the Earl of Oxford (Oxford the friend of France and the Pretender, the attainted Oxford), said in the British parliament, in a speech on the mutiny bill, that, "While he had breath he would speak for the liberties of his country, and against courts martial and a standing army in peace, as dangerous to the Constitution." (Ibid., page 455.) Such were the speeches even of the enemies of liberty when Britain had yet a right to be called free. But, says Mr. [James] Wilson, "It is necessary to maintain the appearance of strength even in times of the most profound tranquillity." And what is this more than a threadbare hackneyed argument, which has been answered over and over in different ages, and does not deserve even the smallest consideration? Had we a standing army when the British invaded our peaceful shores? Was it a standing army that gained the battles of Lexington and Bunker Hill, and took the ill-fated Burgoyne? Is not a well- regulated militia sufficient for every purpose of internal defense? And which of you, my fellow citizens, is afraid of any invasion from foreign powers that our brave militia would not be able immediately to repel?

Mr. Wilson says, that he does not know of any nation in the world which has not found it necessary to maintain the appearance of strength in a season of the most profound tranquillity. If by this equivocal assertion he has meant to say that there is no nation in the world without a standing army in time of peace, he has been mistaken. I need only adduce the example of Switzerland, which, like us, is a republic, whose thirteen cantons, like our thirteen States, are under a federal government, and which besides is surrounded by the most powerful nations in Europe, all jealous of its liberty and prosperity. And yet that nation has preserved its freedom for many ages, with the sole help of a militia, and has never been known to have a standing army, except when in actual war. Why should we not follow so glorious an example; and are we less able to defend our liberty without an army, than that brave but small nation which, with its militia alone has hitherto defied all Europe?

A DEMOCRATIC FEDERALIST

The framers of this constitution appear to have been . . . sensible that no dependence could be placed on the people for their support; but on the contrary, that the government must be executed by force. They have therefore made a provision for this purpose in a permanent standing army and a militia that may be objected to as strict discipline and government.

A standing army in the hands of a government placed so independent of the people, may be made a fatal instrument to overturn the public liberties; it may be employed to enforce the collection of
the most oppressive taxes; and to carry into execution the most arbitrary measures. An ambitious man who may have the army at his devotion, may step up into the throne, and seize upon absolute power.

The absolute unqualified command that Congress have over the militia may be made instrumental to the destruction of all liberty both public and private; whether of a personal, civil or religious nature.

First, the personal liberty of every man, probably from sixteen to sixty years of age, may be destroyed by the power Congress have in organizing and governing of the militia. As militia they may be subjected to fines to any amount, levied in a military manner; they may be subjected to corporal punishments of the most disgraceful and humiliating kind; and to death itself, by the sentence of a court martial. To this our young men will be more immediately subjected, as a select militia, composed of them, will best answer the purposes of government.

Secondly, the rights of conscience may be violated, as there is no exemption of those persons who are conscientiously scrupulous of hearing arms. These compose a respectable proportion of the community in the State [Pennsylvania]. This is the more remarkable, because even when the distresses of the late war and the evident disaffection of many citizens of that description inflamed our passions, and when every person who was obliged to risk his own life must have been exasperated against such as on any account kept back from the common danger, yet even then, when outrage and violence might have been expected, the rights of conscience were held sacred.

At this momentous crisis, the framers of our State Constitution made the most express and decided declaration and stipulations in favor of the rights of conscience; but now, when no necessity exists, those dearest rights of men are left insecure.

Thirdly, the absolute command of Congress over the militia may be destructive of public liberty; for under the guidance of an arbitrary government, they may be made the unwilling instruments of tyranny. The militia of Pennsylvania may be marched to New England or Virginia to quell an insurrection occasioned by the most galling oppression, and aided by the standing army, they will no doubt be successful in subduing their liberty and independency. But in so doing, although the magnanimity of their minds will be extinguished, yet the meaner passions of resentment and revenge will be increased, and these in turn will be the ready and obedient instruments of despotism to enslave the others; and that with an irritated vengeance. Thus may the militia be made the instruments of crushing the last efforts of expiring liberty, of riveting the chains of despotism on their fellow-citizens, and on one another. This power can be exercised not only without violating the Constitution, but in strict conformity with it; it is calculated for this express purpose, and will doubtless be executed accordingly.

As this government will not enjoy the confidence of the people, but be executed by force, it will be a very expensive and burdensome government. The standing army must be numerous, and as a further support, it wilt be the policy of this government to multiply officers in every department; judges, collectors, tax-gatherers, excisemen and the whole host of revenue officers,

will swarm over the land, devouring the hard earnings of the industrious like the locusts of old, impoverishing and desolating all before them. . .

ANTI-FEDERALIST PAPER NO. 30-31

A Virginia Antifederalist On The Issue Of Taxation

From The Freeman's Journal; or, The North-American Intelligencer, October 31, 1787.

.... It has been the language, since the peace, of the most virtuous and discerning men in America, that the powers vested in Congress were inadequate to the procuring of the benefits that should result from the union. It was found that our national character was sinking in the opinion of foreign nations, and that the selfish views of some of the states were likely to become the source of dangerous jealousy. The requisitions of Congress were set at naught; the government, that represented the union, had not a shilling in its treasury to enable it to pay off the federal debts, nor had it any method within its power to alter its situation. It could make treaties of commerce, but could not enforce the observance of them; and it was felt that we were suffering from the restrictions of foreign nations, who seeing the want of energy in our federal constitution, and the unlikelihood of cooperation in thirteen separate legislatures, had shackled our commerce, without any dread of recrimination on our part. To obviate these grievances, it was I believe the general opinion, that new powers should be vested in Congress to enable it, in the amplest manner, to regulate the commerce, to lay and collect duties on the imports of the United States. Delegates were appointed by most of them, for those purposes, to a convention to be held at Annapolis in the September before last. A few of them met, and without waiting for the others, who were coming on, they dissolved the convention-after resolving among themselves, that the powers vested in them were not sufficiently extensive; and that they would apply to the legislatures of the several states, which they represented, to appoint members to another convention, with powers to new model the federal constitution. This, indeed, it has now done in the most unequivocal manner; nor has it stopped here, for it has fairly annihilated the constitution of each individual state. It has proposed to you a high prerogative government, which, like Aaron's serpent, is to swallow up the rest. This is what the thinking people in America were apprehensive of. They knew how difficult it is to hit the golden mean, how natural the transition is from one extreme to another-from anarchy to tyranny, from the inconvenient laxity of thirteen separate governments to the too sharp and grinding one, before which our sovereignty, as a state, was to vanish.

In Art. I, Sect. 8, of the proposed constitution, it is said, "Congress shall have power to lay and collect taxes, duties, imposts, and excises." Are you then, Virginians, about to abandon your country to the depredations of excisemen, and the pressure of excise laws? Did it ever enter the mind of any one of you, that you could live to see the day, that any other government but the General Assembly of Virginia should have power of direct taxation in this state? How few of you ever expected to see excise laws, those instruments of tyranny, in force in your country? But who could imagine, that any man but a Virginian, were they found to be necessary, would ever have a voice towards enacting them? That any tribunal, but the courts of Virginia, would be allowed to take cognizance of disputes between her citizens and their tax gatherers and excisemen? And that, if ever it should be found necessary to curse this land with these hateful excisemen, any one, but a fellow citizen, should be entrusted with that office?

For my part, I cannot discover the necessity there was of allowing Congress to subject us to excise laws, unless-that considering the extensiveness of the single republic into which this constitution would collect all the others, and the well known difficulty of governing large republics with harmony and ease-it was thought expedient to bit our mouths with massive curbs, to break us, bridled with excise laws and managed by excisemen, into an uniform, sober pace, and thus, gradually, tame the troublesome mettle of freemen. This necessity could not, surely, arise from the desire of furnishing Congress with a sufficient revenue to enable it to exercise the prerogatives which every friend to America would wish to see vested in it. As it would, by unanimous consent, have the management of the impost, it could increase it to any amount, and this would fall sufficiently uniform on every one, according to his ability. Or, were this not found sufficient, could not the deficiency be made up by requisitions to the states? Could it not have been made an article of the federal constitution, that, if any of them refused their quota, Congress may be allowed to make it up by an increase of the impost on that particular state so refusing?

This would, surely, be a sufficient security to Congress, that their requisitions would be punctually complied with.

In any dispute between you and the revenue officers and excisemen of Congress, it is true that it is provided the trial shall be in the first instance within the state, though before a federal tribunal.

It is said in par. 3, sect. 2, art. 3, "The trial of all crimes except in cases of impeachments shall be by jury; and such trial shall be held in the state where the crime shall be committed." But what does this avail, when an appeal will lie against you to the supreme federal court. In the paragraph preceding the one just now quoted, it is said, "In all cases affecting ambassadors, other public ministers and consuls, and those in which a state shall be a party, the Supreme Court shall have original jurisdiction. In all the other cases before mentioned, the Supreme Court shall have appellate jurisdiction, both as to law and fact, with such exceptions and under such regulations as the Congress shall make." But where is this Supreme Court to sit? Will it not be where Congress shall fix its residence? Thither then you will be carried for trial. Who are to be your jury? Is there any provision made that you shall have a Venire from your county, or even from your state, as they please to call it? Not You are to be tried within the territory of Congress, and Congress itself is to be a party. You are to be deprived of the benefit of a jury from your vicinage, that boast and birthright of a freeman.

Should it not at least have been provided, that those revenue officers and excisemen-against whom free governments have always justly entertained a jealousy-should be citizens of the state?

Was it inadmissible that they should be endued with the bowels of fellow citizens? Are we not to expect that New England will now send us revenue officers instead of onions and apples? When you observe that the few places already under Congress in this state are in the hands of strangers, you will own that my suspicion is not without some foundation. And if the first cause of it be required, those who have served in Congress can tell you that the New England delegates to that assembly have always stood by each other, and have formed a firm phalanx, which the southern delegates have not; that, on the contrary, the maneuvers of the former have been commonly engaged, with success, in dividing the latter against each other.

CATO UTICENSIS

ANTI-FEDERALIST PAPER NO. 32

(PART I)Federal Taxation And The Doctrine Of Implied Powers

A powerful rebuttal of Hamilton, the logic of Brutus can be found in a supreme Court decision of 1819, McCulloch v. Maryland. Taken from "Brutus" fifth essay, The New-York Journal of December 13, 1787.

This constitution considers the people of the several states as one body corporate, and is intended as an original compact; it will therefore dissolve all contracts which may be inconsistent with it.

This not only results from its nature, but is expressly declared in the 6th article of it. The design of the constitution is expressed in the preamble, to be, "in order to form a more perfect union, to establish justice, insure domestic tranquility, provide for the common defense, promote the general welfare, and secure the blessings of liberty to ourselves and posterity." These are the ends this government is to accomplish, and for which it is invested with certain powers; among these is the power "to make all laws which are necessary and proper for carrying into execution the foregoing powers and all other powers vested by this constitution in the government of the United States, or in any department or officer thereof." It is a rule in construing a law to consider the objects the legislature had in view in passing it, and to give it such an explanation as to promote their intention. The same rule will apply in explaining a constitution. The great objects then are declared in this preamble in general and indefinite terms to be to provide for the common welfare, and an express power being vested in the legislature to make all laws which shall be necessary and proper for carrying into execution all the powers vested in the general government. The inference is natural that the legislature will have an authority to make all laws which they shall judge necessary for the common safety, and to promote the general welfare.

This amounts to a power to make laws at discretion. No terms can be found more indefinite than these, and it is obvious, that the legislature alone must judge what laws are proper and necessary for the purpose. It may be said, that this way of explaining the constitution, is torturing and making it speak what it never intended. This is far from my intention, and I shall not even insist upon this implied power, but join issue with those who say we are to collect the idea of the powers given from the express words of the clauses granting them; and it will not be difficult to show that the same authority is expressly given which is supposed to be implied in the foregoing paragraphs.

Documents of Revolution

In the 1st article, 8th section, it is declared, "that Congress shall have power to lay and collect taxes, duties, imposts, and excises, to pay the debts, and provide for the common defense, and general welfare of the United States." In the preamble, the intent of the constitution, among other things, is declared to be to provide for the common defense, and promote the general welfare, and in this clause the power is in express words given to Congress "to provide for the common defense, and general welfare." And in the last paragraph of the same section there is an express authority to make all laws which shall be necessary and proper for carrying into execution this power. It is therefore evident, that the legislature under this constitution may pass any law which they may think proper. It is true the 9th section restrains their power with respect to certain subjects. But these restrictions are very limited, some of them improper, some unimportant, and others not easily understood, as I shall hereafter show. It has been urged that the meaning I give

to this part of the constitution is not the true one, that the intent of it is to confer on the legislature the power to lay and collect taxes, etc., in order to provide for the common defense and general welfare. To this I would reply, that the meaning and intent of the constitution is to be collected from the words of it, and I submit to the public, whether the construction I have given it is not the most natural and easy. But admitting the contrary opinion to prevail, I shall nevertheless, be able to show, that the same powers are substantially vested in the general government, by several other articles in the constitution'. It invests the legislature with authority to lay and collect taxes, duties, imposts and excises, in order to provide for the common defense, and promote the general welfare, and to pass all laws which may be necessary and proper for carrying this power into effect. To comprehend the extent of this authority, it will be requisite to examine 1st. What is included in this power to lay and collect taxes, duties, imposts and excises.

2nd. What is implied in the authority, to pass all laws which shall be necessary and proper for carrying this power into execution.

3rd. What limitation, if any, is set to the exercise of this power by the constitution.

First. To detail the particulars comprehended in the general terms, taxes, duties, imposts and excises, would require a volume, instead of a single piece in a newspaper. Indeed it would be a task far beyond my ability, and to which no one can be competent, unless possessed of a mind capable of comprehending every possible source of revenue; for they extend to every possible way of raising money, whether by direct or indirect taxation. Under this clause may be imposed a poll tax, a land tax, a tax on houses and buildings, on windows and fireplaces, on cattle and on all kinds of personal property. It extends to duties on all kinds of goods to any amount, to tonnage and poundage on vessels, to duties on written instruments, newspapers, almanacks, and books. It comprehends an excise on all kinds of liquors, spirits, wines, cider, beer, etc., and indeed takes in duty or excise on every necessary or conveniency of life, whether of foreign or home growth or manufactory. In short, we can have no conception of any way in which a government can raise money from the people, but what is included in one or other of these general terms. We may say then that this clause commits to the hands of the general legislature every conceivable source of revenue within the United States, Not only are these terms very comprehensive, and extend to a vast number of objects, but the power to lay and collect has great latitude; it will lead to the passing a vast number of laws, which may affect the personal rights of the citizens of the states, expose their property to fines and confiscation, and put their lives in jeopardy. It opens a door to the appointment of a swarm of revenue and excise collectors to prey upon the honest and industrious part of the community, [and] eat up their substance. . . .

Second. We will next inquire into what is implied in the authority to pass all laws which shall be necessary and proper to carry this power into execution.

It is, perhaps, utterly impossible fully to define this power. The authority granted in the first clause can only be understood in its full extent, by descending to all the particular cases in which a revenue can be raised; the number and variety of these cases are so endless, and as it were infinite, that no man living has, as yet, been able to reckon them up. The greatest geniuses in the world have been for ages employed in the research, and when mankind had supposed that the

subject was exhausted they have been astonished with the refined improvements that have been made in modern times ' and especially in the English nation on the subject. If then the objects of this power cannot be comprehended, how is it possible to understand the extent of that power which can pass all laws which shall be necessary and proper for carrying it into executions It is truly incomprehensible. A case cannot be conceived of, which is not included in this power. It is well known that the subject of revenue is the most difficult and extensive in the science of government. It requires the greatest talents of a statesman, and the most numerous and exact provisions of the legislature. The command of the revenues 'Of a state gives the command of every thing in it. He that has the purse will have the sword, and they that have both, have everything; so that the legislature having every source from which money can be drawn under their direction, with a right to make all laws necessary and proper for drawing forth all the resource of the country, would have, in fact, all power.

Documents of Revolution

Were I to enter into the detail, it would be easy to show how this power in its operation, would totally destroy all the powers of the individual states. But this is not necessary for those who will think for themselves, and it will be useless to such as take things upon trust; nothing will awaken them to reflection, until the iron hand of oppression compel them to it.

I shall only remark, that this power, given to the federal legislature, directly annihilates all the powers of the state legislatures. There cannot be a greater solecism in politics than to talk of power in a government, without the command of any revenue. It is as absurd as to talk of an animal without blood, or the subsistence of one without food. Now the general government having in their control every possible source of revenue, and authority to pass any law they may deem necessary to draw them forth, or to facilitate their collection, no source of revenue is therefore left in the hands 'Of any state. Should any state attempt to raise money by law, the general government may repeal or arrest it in the execution, for all their laws will be the supreme law of the land. If then any one can be weak enough to believe that a government can exist without having the authority to raise money to pay a door-keeper to their assembly, he may believe that the state government can exist, should this new constitution take place.

It is agreed by most of the advocates of this new system, that the government which is proper for the United States should be a confederated one; that the respective states ought to retain a portion of their sovereignty, and that they should preserve not only the forms of their legislatures, but also the power to conduct certain internal concerns. How far the powers to be retained by the states are to extend, is the question; we need not spend much time on this subject, as it respects this constitution, for a government without power to raise money is one only in name. It is clear that the legislatures of the respective states must be altogether dependent on the will of the general legislature, for the means of supporting their government. The legislature of the United States will have a right to exhaust every source of revenue in every state, and to annul all laws of the states which may stand in the way of effecting it; unless therefore we can suppose the state governments can exist without money to support the officers who execute them, we must conclude they will exist no longer than the general legislatures choose they should. Indeed the idea of any government existing, in any respect, as an independent one, without any means of support in their own hands, is an absurdity. If therefore, this constitution has in view, what many of its framers and advocates say it has, to secure and guarantee to the separate states the exercise of certain powers of government, it certainly ought to have left in their hands some sources of

revenue. It should have marked the line in which the general government should have raised money, and set bounds over which they should not pass, leaving to the separate states other means to raise supplies for the support of their governments, and to discharge their respective debts. To this it is objected, that the general government ought to have power competent to the purposes of the union; they are to provide for the common defense, to pay the debts of the United States, support foreign ministers, and the civil establishment of the union, and to do these they ought to have authority to raise money adequate to the purpose. On this I observe, that the state governments have also contracted debts; they require money to support their civil officers; . . . if they give to the general government a power to raise money in every way in which it can possibly be raised, with . . . a control over the state legislatures as to prohibit them, whenever the general legislature may think proper, from raising any money, (the states will fail]. It is again objected that it is very difficult, if not impossible, to draw the line of distinction between the powers of the general and state governments on this subject. The first, it is said, must have the power to raise the money necessary for the purposes of the union; if they are limited to certain objects the revenue may fall short of a sufficiency for the public exigencies; they must therefore have discretionary power. The line may be easily and accurately drawn between the powers of the two governments on this head. The distinction between external and internal taxes, is not a novel one in this country. It is a plain one, and easily understood. The first includes impost duties on all imported goods; this species of taxes it is proper should be laid by the general government; many reasons might be urged to show that no danger is to be apprehended from their exercise of it. They may be collected in few places, and from few hands with certainty and expedition. But few officers are necessary to be employed in collecting them, and there is no danger of oppression in laying them, because if they are laid higher than trade will bear, the merchants will cease importing, or smuggle their goods. We have therefore sufficient security, arising from the nature of the thing, against burdensome, and intolerable impositions from this kind of tax. The case is far otherwise with regard to direct taxes; these include poll taxes, land taxes, excises, duties on written instruments, on everything we eat, drink, or wear; they take hold of every species of property, and come home to every man's house and pocket. These are often so oppressive, as to grind the face of the poor, and render the lives of the common people a burden to them. The great and only security the people can have against oppression from this kind of taxes, must rest in their representatives. If they are sufficiently numerous to be well informed of the circumstances, . . . and have a proper regard for the people, they will be secure. The general legislature, as I have shown in a former paper, will not be thus qualified,' and therefore, on this account, ought not to exercise the power of direct taxation. If the power of laying imposts will not be sufficient, some other

specific mode of raising a revenue should have been assigned the general government; many may be suggested in which their power may be accurately defined and limited, and it would be much better to give them authority to lay and collect a duty on exports, not to exceed a certain rate per cent, than to have surrendered every kind of resource that the country has, to the complete abolition of the state governments, and which will introduce such an infinite number of laws and ordinances, fines and penalties, courts, and judges, collectors, and excisemen, that when a man can number them, he may enumerate the stars of Heaven.
BRUTUS

ANTI-FEDERALIST PAPER NO. 33

(Part II)Federal Taxation And The doctrine Of Implied Powers

The Federalist writers apparently never responded to "BRUTUS." The following "Brutus" article was extracted from his sixth essay, The New-York Journal of December 27, 1787.

.... The general government is to be vested with authority to levy and collect taxes, duties, and excises; the separate states have also power to impose taxes, duties, and excises, except that they cannot lay duties on exports and imports without the consent of Congress. Here then the two governments have concurrent jurisdiction; both may lay impositions of this kind. But then the general government have superadded to this power, authority to make all laws which shall be necessary and proper for carrying the foregoing power into execution. Suppose then that both governments should lay taxes, duties, and excises, and it should fall so heavy on the people that they would be unable, or be so burdensome that they would refuse to pay them both would it not be necessary that the general legislature should suspend the collection of the state tax? It certainly would. For, if the people could not, or would not pay both, they must be discharged from the tax to the state, or the tax to the general government could not be collected. The conclusion therefore is inevitable, that the respective state governments will not have the power to raise one shilling in any way, but by the permission of the Congress. I presume no one will pretend that the states can exercise legislative authority, or administer justice among their citizens for any length of time, without being able to raise a sufficiency to pay those who administer their governments.

If this be true, and if the states can raise money only by permission of the general government, it follows that the state governments will be dependent on the will of the general government for their existence.

What will render this power in Congress effectual and sure in its operation is that the government will have complete judicial and executive authority to carry all their laws into effect, which will be paramount to the judicial and executive authority of the individual states: in vain therefore will be all interference of the legislatures, courts, or magistrates of any of the states on the subject; for they will be subordinate to the general government, and engaged by oath to support it, and will be constitutionally bound to submit to their decisions.

The general legislature will be empowered to lay any tax they choose, to annex any penalties they please to the breach of their revenue laws; and to appoint as many officers as they may think proper to collect the taxes. They will have authority to farm the revenues and to vest the farmer general, with his subalterns, with plenary powers to collect them, in any way which to them may appear eligible, And the courts of law which they will be authorized to institute, will have cognizance of every case arising under the revenue laws, [and] the conduct of all the officers employed in collecting them; and the officers of these courts will execute their judgments. There is no way, therefore, of avoiding the destruction of the state governments, whenever the Congress please to do it, unless the people rise up, and, with a strong hand, resist and prevent the execution of constitutional laws. The fear of this will, it is presumed, restrain the general
government for some time, within proper bounds; but it will not be many years before they will have a revenue, and force, at their command, which will place them above any apprehensions on that score.

How far the power to lay and collect duties and excises, may operate to dissolve the state governments, and oppress the people, it is impossible to say. It would assist us much in forming a just opinion on this head, to consider the various objects to which this kind of taxes extend, in European nations, and the infinity of laws they have passed respecting them. Perhaps, it leisure will permit, this may be essayed in some future paper.

Documents of Revolution

It was observed in my last number, that the power to lay and collect duties and excises, would invest the Congress with authority to impose a duty and excise on every necessary and convenience of life. As the principal object of the government, in laying a duty or excise, will be, to raise money, it is obvious, that they will fix on such articles as are of the most general use and consumption; because, unless great quantities of the article, on which the duty is laid, is used, the revenue cannot be considerable. We may therefore presume, that the articles which will be the object of this species of taxes will be either the real necessaries of life; or if not those, such as from custom and habit are esteemed so. I will single out a few of the productions of our own country, which may, and probably will, be of the number.

Cider is an article that most probably will be one of those on which an excise will be laid, because it is one, which this country produces in great abundance, which is in very general use, is consumed in great quantities, and which may be said not to be a real necessary of life. An excise on this would raise a large sum of money in the United States. How would the power, to lay and collect an excise on cider, and to pass all laws proper and necessary to carry it into execution, operate in its exercise? It might be necessary, in order to collect the excise on cider, to grant to one man, in each county, an exclusive right of building and keeping cider-mills, and oblige him to give bonds and security for payment of the excise; or, if this was not done, it might be necessary to license the mills, which are to make this liquor, and to take from them security, to account for the excise, or, if otherwise, a great number of officers must be employed, to take account of the cider made, and to collect the duties on it. Porter, ale, and all kinds of malt-liquors, are articles that would probably be subject also to an excise. It would be necessary, in order to collect such an excise, to regulate the manufactory of these, that the quantity made might be ascertained, or other wise security could not be had for the payment of the excise, Every brewery must then be licensed, and officers appointed, to take account of its product, and to secure the payment of the duty, or excise, before it is sold. Many other articles might be named, which would be objects of this species of taxation, but I refrain from enumerating them. It will probably be said, by those who advocate this system, that the observations already made on this head, are calculated only to inflame the minds of the people, with the apprehension of dangers merely imaginary; that there is not the least reason to apprehend the general legislature will exercise their power in this manner. To this I would only say, that these kinds of taxes exist in Great Britain, and are severely felt. The excise on cider and perry, was imposed in that nation a few years ago, and it is in the memory of everyone, who read the history of the transaction, what great tumults it occasioned.

This power, exercised without limitation, will introduce itself into every corner of the city, and country-it will wait upon the ladies at their toilet, and will not leave them in any of their domestic concerns; it will accompany them to the ball, the play, and assembly; it will go with them when they visit, and will, on all occasions, sit beside them in their carriages, nor will it desert them even at church; it will enter the house of every gentleman, watch over his cellar, wait upon his cook in the kitchen, follow the servants into the parlor, preside over the table, and note down all he eats or drinks; it will attend him to his bedchamber, and watch him while he sleeps; it will take cognizance of the professional man in his office, or his study; it will watch the merchant in the counting-house, or in his store; it will follow the mechanic to his shop, and in his work, and will haunt him in his family, and in his bed; it will be a constant companion of the industrious farmer in all his labor, it will be with him in the house, and in the field, observe the toil of his hands, and the sweat of his brow; it will penetrate into the most obscure cottage; and finally, it will light upon the head of every person in the United States. To all these different classes of people, and in all these circumstances, in which it will attend them, the language in which it will address them, will be GIVE! GIVE! A power that has such latitude, which reaches every person in the community in every conceivable circumstance, and lays hold of every species of property they possess, and which has no bounds set to it, but the discretion of those who exercise it-I say, such a power must necessarily, from its very nature, swallow up all the power of the state governments. I shall add but one other observation on this head, which is this: It appears to me a solecism, for two men, or bodies of men, to have unlimited power respecting the same object. It contradicts the ... maxim, which saith, "no man can serve two masters," the one power or the other must prevail, or else they will destroy each other, and neither of them effect their purpose. It may be compared to two mechanic powers, acting upon the same body in opposite directions, the consequence would be, if the powers were equal, the body would remain in a state of rest, or if the force of the one was superior to that of the other, the stronger would prevail, and overcome the resistance of the weaker. But it is said, by some of the advocates of this system, that "the idea that Congress can levy taxes at pleasure is false, and the suggestion wholly unsupported. The preamble to the constitution is declaratory of the purposes of the [our]

union, and the assumption of any power not necessary to establish justice, etc., provide for the common defense, etc., will be unconstitutional.

... Besides, in the very clause which gives the power of levying duties and taxes, the purposes to which the money shall be appropriated are specified, viz., to pay the debts and provide for the common defense and general welfare."' I would ask those,

Documents of Revolution

who reason thus, to define what ideas are included under the terms, to provide for the common defense and general welfare? Are these terms definite, and will they be understood in the same manner, and to apply to the same cases by everyone? No one will pretend they will. It will then be matter of opinion, what tends to the general welfare; and the Congress will be the only judges in the matter. To provide for the general welfare, is an abstract proposition, which mankind differ in the explanation of, as much as they do on any political or moral proposition that can be proposed; the most opposite measures may be pursued by different parties, and both may profess, that they have in view the general welfare and both sides may be honest in their professions, or both may have sinister views. Those who advocate this new constitution declare, they are influenced by a regard to the general welfare; those who oppose it, declare they are moved by the same principle; and I have no doubt but a number on both sides are honest in their professions; and yet nothing is more

certain than this, that to adopt this constitution, and not to adopt it, cannot both of them be promotive of the general welfare. It is absurd to say, that the power of Congress is limited by these general expressions "to provide for the common safety, and general welfare," as it would be to say, that it would be limited, had the constitution said they should have power to lay taxes, etc. at will and pleasure. Were this authority given, it might be said, that under it the legislature could not do injustice, or pursue any measures, but such as were calculated to promote the public good, and happiness. For every man, rulers as well as others, are bound by the immutable laws of God and reason, always to will what is right. It is certainly right and fit, that the governors of every people should provide for the common defense and general welfare; every government, therefore, in the world, even the greatest despot, is limited in the exercise of his power. But however just this reasoning may be, it would be found, in practice, a most pitiful restriction. The government would always say, their measures were designed and calculated to promote the public good; and there being no judge between them and the people, the rulers themselves must, and would always, judge for themselves.

There are others of the favorers of this system, who admit, that the power of the Congress under it, with respect to revenue, will exist without limitation, and contend, that so it ought to be.

It is said, the power "to raise armies; to build and equip fleets; . . . [and] to provide for their support, . . . ought to exist without limitation, because it is impossible to foresee or define the extent and variety of national exigencies, or the correspondent extent and variety of the means which may be necessary to satisfy them."

This, it is said, "is one of those truths which, to a correct and unprejudiced mind, carries its own evidence along with it.... It rests upon axioms as simple as they are universal; the means ought to be proportioned to the end; the persons, from whose agency the attainment of any end is expected, ought to possess the means by which it is to be attained."

This same writer insinuates, that the opponents to the plan promulgated by the convention, manifests a want of candor, in objecting to the extent of the powers proposed to be vested in this government; because he asserts, with an air of confidence, that the powers ought to be unlimited as to the object to which they extend; and that this position, if not self-evident, is at least clearly demonstrated by the foregoing mode of reasoning. But with submission to this author's better judgment, I humbly conceive his reasoning will appear, upon examination, more specious than solid. The means, says the gentleman, ought to be proportioned to the end. Admit the proposition to be true, it is then necessary to inquire, what is the end of the government of the United States, in order to draw any just conclusions from it. Is this end simply to preserve the general government, and to provide for the common defense and general welfare of the union only?

Certainly not. For beside this, the state governments are to be supported, and provision made for the managing such of their internal concerns as are allotted to them. It is admitted "that the circumstances of our country are such as to demand a compound instead of a simple, a confederate instead of a sole, government," that the objects of each ought to be pointed out, and that each ought to possess ample authority to execute the powers committed to them. The government then, being complex in its nature, the end it has in view is so also; and it is as

necessary that the state governments should possess the means to attain the end expected from them, as for the general government. Neither the general government nor the state governments ought to be vested with all the powers proper to be exercised for promoting the ends of government. The powers are divided between them—certain ends are to be attained by the one, and certain ends by the other; and these, taken together, include all the ends of good government.

This being the case, the conclusion follows, that each should be furnished with the means, to attain the ends, to which they are designed.

To apply this reasoning to the case of revenue, the general government is charged with the care of providing for the payment of the debts of the United States, supporting the general government, and providing for the defense of the union. To obtain these ends, they should be furnished with means. But does it thence follow, that they should command all the revenues of the United States? Most certainly it does not. For if so, it will follow, that no means will be left to attain other ends, as necessary to the happiness of the country, as those committed to their care. The individual states have debts to discharge; their legislatures and executives are to be supported, and provision is to be made for the administration of justice in the respective states.

For these objects the general government has no authority to provide; nor is it proper it should. It is clear then, that the states should have the command of such revenues, as to answer the ends they have to obtain. To say, that "the circumstances that endanger the safety of nations are infinite,"" and from hence to infer, that all the sources of revenue in the states should be yielded to the general government, is not conclusive reasoning: for the Congress are authorized only to control in general concerns, and not regulate local and internal ones. . . The peace and happiness of a community is as intimately connected with the prudent direction of their domestic affairs, and the due administration of justice among themselves, as with a competent provision for their defense against foreign invaders, and indeed more so.

Upon the whole, I conceive, that there cannot be a clearer position than this, that the state governments ought to have an uncontrollable power to raise a revenue, adequate to the exigencies of their governments; and, I presume, no such power is left them by this constitution.

BRUTUS

ANTI-FEDERALIST PAPER NO. 34

The Problem Of Concurrent Taxation

The following speech by Patrick Henry was delivered to the Virginia ratifying convention, June 5, 1788.

I never will give up the power of direct taxation but for a scourge. I am willing to give it conditionally; that is, after non-compliance with requisitions. I will do more, sir, and what I hope will convince the most skeptical man that I am a lover of the American Union-that, in case Virginia shall not make punctual payment, the control of our custom-houses, and the whole regulation of trade, shall be given to Congress, and that Virginia shall depend on Congress even for passports, till Virginia shall have paid the last farthing, and furnished the last soldier. Nay, sir, there is another alternative to which I would consent; even that they should strike us out of the Union, and take away from us all federal privileges, till we comply with federal requisitions: but let it depend upon our own pleasure to pay our money in the most easy manner for our people. Were all the states, more terrible than the mother country, to join against us, I hope Virginia could defend herself; but, sir, the dissolution of the Union is most abhorrent to my mind. The first thing I have at heart is American liberty; the second thing is American union; and I hope the people of Virginia will endeavor to preserve that union. The increasing population of the Southern States is far greater than that of New England; consequently, in a short time, they will be far more numerous than the people of that country. Consider this, and you will find this state more particularly interested to support American liberty, and not bind our posterity by an improvident relinquishment of our rights. I would give the best security for a punctual compliance with requisitions; but I beseech gentlemen, at all hazards, not to give up this unlimited power of taxation. . . .

In this scheme of energetic government, the people will find two sets of taxgatherers-the state and the federal sheriffs. This, it seems to me, will produce such dreadful oppression as the people cannot possibly bear. The federal sheriff may commit what oppression, make what distresses, he pleases, and ruin you with impunity; for how are you to tie his hands? Have you any sufficiently decided means of preventing him from sucking your blood by speculations, commissions, and fees? Thus thousands of your people will be most shamefully robbed: our state sheriffs, those unfeeling blood-suckers, have, under the watchful eye of our legislature, committed the most horrid and barbarous ravages on our people. It has required the most constant vigilance of the legislature to keep them from totally ruining the people; a repeated succession of laws has been made to suppress their iniquitous speculations and cruel extortions; and as often has their nefarious ingenuity devised methods of evading the force of those laws: in the struggle they have generally triumphed over the legislature. It is a fact that lands have been sold for five shillings, which were worth one hundred pounds: if sheriffs, thus immediately under the eye of our state legislature and judiciary, have dared to commit these outrages, what would they not have done if their masters had been at Philadelphia or New York? If they perpetrate the most unwarrantable outrage on your person or property, you cannot get redress on this side of Philadelphia or New York; and how can you get it there? If your domestic avocations could permit you to go thither, there you must appeal to judges sworn to support this Constitution, in opposition to that of any state, and who may also be inclined to favor their own officers. When these harpies are aided by excisemen, who may search, at any time, your houses, and most secret recesses, will the people bear it? If you think so, you differ from me. Where I thought there was a possibility of such mischiefs, I would grant power with a niggardly hand; and here there is a strong probability that these oppressions shall actually happen. I may be told that it is safe to err on that side, because such regulations may be made by Congress as shall restrain these officers, and because laws are made by our representatives, and judged by righteous judges: but, Sir, as these regulations may be made, so they may not; and many reasons there are to induce a belief that they will not, I shall therefore be an infidel on that point till the day of my death.

ANTI-FEDERALIST PAPER NO. 35

Federal Taxing Power Must Be Restrained

George Mason of Virginia opposed the Constitution because it lacked a Bill of Rights, and centralized powers further than he felt it necessary. Mason delivered the following speech before the Virginia ratifying convention, June 4, 1788.

Mr. Chairman, whether the Constitution be good or bad, the present clause [Article 1, Section 2]
clearly discovers that it is a national government, and no longer a Confederation. I mean that clause which gives the first hint of the general government laying direct taxes. The assumption of this power of laying direct taxes does, of itself, entirely change the confederation of the states into one consolidated government. This power, being at discretion, unconfined, and without any kind of control, must carry every thing before it. The very idea of converting what was formerly a confederation to a consolidated government is totally subversive of every principle which has hitherto governed us. This power is calculated to annihilate totally the state governments. Will the people of this great community [Virginia] submit to be individually taxed by two different and distinct powers? Will they suffer themselves to be doubly harassed? These two concurrent powers cannot exist long together; the one will destroy the other. The general government being paramount to, and in every respect more powerful than the state governments, the latter must give way to the former....

Requisitions [under the Articles of Confederation] have been often refused, sometimes from an impossibility of complying with them; often from that great variety of circumstances which retards the collection of moneys; and perhaps sometimes from a wilful design of procrastinating.

But why shall we give up to the national government this power, so dangerous in its nature, and for which its members will not have sufficient information? Is it not well known that what would be a proper tax in one state would be grievous in another? The gentleman who has favored us with a eulogium in favor of this system [Wilson C. Nicholas], must, after all the encomiums he has been pleased to bestow upon it, acknowledge that our federal representatives must be unacquainted with the situation of their constituents. Sixty-five members cannot possibly know the situation and circumstances of all the inhabitants of this immense continent. When a certain sum comes to be taxed, and the mode of levying to be fixed, they will lay the tax on that article which will be most productive and easiest in the collection, without consulting the real circumstances or convenience of a country, with which, in fact, they cannot be sufficiently acquainted.

The mode of levying taxes is of the utmost consequence; and yet here it is to be determined by those who have neither knowledge of our situation, nor a common interest with us, nor a fellow-feeling for us. The subject of taxation differs in three fourths, nay, I might say with truth, in four fifths of the states. If we trust the national government with an effectual way of raising the necessary sums, it is sufficient: everything we do further is trusting the happiness and rights of the people. Why, then, should we give up this dangerous power of individual taxation? Why leave the manner of laying taxes to those who, in the nature of things, cannot be acquainted with the situation of those on whom they are to impose them, when it can be done by those who are well acquainted with it? If, instead of giving this oppressive power, we give them such an
effectual alternative as will answer the purpose, without encountering the evil and danger that might arise from it, then I would cheerfully acquiesce; and would it not be far more eligible? I candidly acknowledge the inefficacy of the Confederation; but requisitions have been made which were impossible to be complied with- requisitions for more gold and silver than were in the United States. If we give the general government the power of demanding their quotas of the states, with an alternative of laying direct taxes in case of non-compliance, then the mischief would be avoided. And the certainty of this conditional power would, in all human probability, prevent the application, and the sums necessary for the Union would be then laid by the states,

by those who know how it can best be raised, by those who have a fellow-feeling for us. Give me leave to say, that the sum raised one way with convenience and ease, would be very oppressive another way. Why, then, not leave this power to be exercised by those who know the mode most convenient for the inhabitants, and not by those who must necessarily apportion it in such manner as shall be oppressive? ... An indispensable amendment ... is, that Congress shall not exercise the power of raising direct taxes till the states shall have refused to comply with the requisitions of Congress. On this condition it may be granted; but I see no reason to grant it unconditionally, as the states can raise the taxes with more ease, and lay them on the inhabitants with more propriety, than it is possible for the general government to do. If Congress hath this power without control, the taxes will be laid by those who have no fellow- feeling or acquaintance with the people. This is my objection to the article now under consideration. It is a very great and important one. I therefore beg gentlemen to consider it. Should this power be restrained, I shall withdraw my objections to this part of the Constitution; but as it stands, it is an objection so strong in my mind, that its amendment is with me a sine qua non of its adoption. I wish for such amendments, and such only, as are necessary to secure the dearest rights of the people....

ANTI-FEDERALIST PAPER NO. 36

Representation And Internal Taxation

Richard Henry Lee was arguably the best known Antifederalist writer. His pamphlets were widely distributed and reprinted in newspapers. Antifederalist Papers # 36/37 are excerpts from his first pamphlet. Anti-Federalist Paper No.s. 41, 42, 43, 55, 56, 57, 58, 61, 63, 69, 76-77 are taken from his second pamphlet.

A power to lay and collect taxes at discretion, is, in itself, of very great importance. By means of taxes, the government may command the whole or any part of the subject's property. Taxes may be of various kinds; but there is a strong distinction between external and internal taxes. External taxes are import duties, which are laid on imported goods; they may usually be collected in a few seaport towns, and of a few individuals, though ultimately paid by the consumer; a few officers can collect them, and they can be carried no higher than trade will bear, or smuggling permit-that in the very nature of commerce, bounds are set to them. But internal taxes, as poll and land taxes, excises, duties on all written instruments, etc., may fix themselves on every person and species of property in the community; they may be carried to any lengths, and in proportion as they are extended, numerous officers must be employed to assess them, and to enforce the collection of them. In the United Netherlands the general government has complete powers, as to external taxation; but as to internal taxes, it makes requisitions on the provinces. Internal taxation in this country is more important, as the country is so very extensive As many assessors and collectors of federal taxes will be above three hundred miles from the seat of the federal government, as will be less. Besides, to lay and collect taxes, in this extensive country, must require a great number of congressional ordinances, immediately operating upon the body of the people; these must continually interfere with the state laws, and thereby produce disorder and general dissatisfaction, till the one system of laws or the other, operating on the same subjects, shall be abolished. These ordinances alone, to say nothing of those respecting the militia, coin, commerce, federal judiciary, etc., will probably soon defeat the operations of the state laws and governments.

Should the general government think it politic, as some administration (if not all) probably will, to look for a support in a system of influence, the government will take every occasion to multiply laws, and officers to execute them, considering these as so many necessary props for its own support. Should this system of policy be adopted, taxes more productive than the impost duties will, probably, be wanted to support the government, and to discharge foreign demands, without leaving anything for the domestic creditors. The internal sources of taxation then must be called into operation, and internal tax laws and federal assessors and collectors spread over this immense country. All these circumstances considered, is it wise, prudent, or safe, to vest the powers of laying and collecting internal taxes in the general government, while imperfectly organized and inadequate? And to trust to amending it hereafter, and making it adequate to this purpose? It is not only unsafe but absurd to lodge power in a government before it is fitted to receive it. It is confessed that this power and representation ought to go together. Why give the power first? Why give the power to the few, who, when possessed of it, may have address enough to prevent the increase of representation? Why not keep the power, and, when necessary, amend the constitution, and add to its other parts this power, and a proper increase of representation at the same time? Then men who may want the power will be under strong inducements to let in the people, by their representatives, into the government, to hold their due proportion of this power. If a proper representation be impracticable, then we shall see this power resting in the states, where it at present ought to be, and not inconsiderately given up.

When I recollect how lately congress, conventions, legislatures, and people contended in the cause of liberty, and carefully weighed the importance of taxation, I can scarcely believe we are serious in proposing to vest the powers of laying and collecting internal taxes in a government so imperfectly organized for such purposes. Should the United States be taxed by a house of representatives of two hundred members, which would be about fifteen members for Connecticut, twenty-five for Massachusetts, etc., still the middle and lower classes of people could have no great share, in fact, in taxation. I am aware it is said, that the representation proposed by the new constitution is sufficiently numerous; it may be for many purposes; but to suppose that this branch is sufficiently numerous to guard the rights of the people in the administration of the government, in which the purse and sword is placed, seems to argue that we have forgot what the true meaning of representation is. . . .

In considering the practicability of having a full and equal representation of the people from all parts of the union, not only distances and different opinions, customs and views, common in extensive tracts of country, are to be taken into view, but many differences peculiar to Eastern, Middle, and Southern States. These differences are not so perceivable among the members of congress, and men of general information in the states, as among the men who would properly form the democratic branch. The Eastern states are very democratic, and composed chiefly of moderate freeholders; they have but few rich men and no slaves; the Southern states are composed chiefly of rich planters and slaves; they have but few moderate freeholders, and the prevailing influence in them is generally a dissipated aristocracy. The Middle states partake partly of the Eastern and partly of the Southern character. . . . I have no idea that the interests, feelings, and opinions of three or four millions of people, especially touching internal taxation, can be collected in such a house. In the nature of things, nine times in ten, men of the elevated classes in the community only can be chosen....

I am sensible also, that it is said that congress will not attempt to lay and collect internal taxes; that it is necessary for them to have the power, though it cannot probably be exercised. I admit that it is not probable that any prudent congress will attempt to lay and collect internal taxes, especially direct taxes: but this only proves, that the power would be improperly lodged in congress, and that it might be abused by imprudent and designing men.

I have heard several gentlemen, to get rid of objections to this part of the constitution, attempt to construe the powers relative to direct taxes, as those who object to it would have them; as to these, it is said, that congress will only have power to make requisitions, leaving it to the states to lay and collect them. I see but very little color for this construction, and the attempt only proves that this part of the plan cannot be defended. By this plan there can be no doubt, but that the powers of congress will be complete as to all kinds of taxes whatever. Further, as to internal taxes, the state governments will have concurrent powers with the general government, and both may tax the same objects in the same year; and the objection that the general government may
suspend a state tax, as a necessary measure for the promoting the collection of a federal tax, is not without foundation.

THE FEDERAL FARMER

ANTI-FEDERALIST PAPER NO. 37

Factions And The Constitution

.... To have a just idea of the government before us, and to show that a consolidated one is the object in view, it is necessary not only to examine the plan, but also its history, and the politics of its particular friends.

The confederation was formed when great confidence was placed in the voluntary exertions of individuals, and of the respective states; and the framers of it, to guard against usurpation, so limited, and checked the powers, that, in many respects, they are inadequate to the exigencies of the union. We find, therefore, members of congress urging alterations in the federal system almost as soon as it was adopted. It was early proposed to vest congress with powers to levy an impost, to regulate trade, etc., but such was known to be the caution of the states in parting with power, that the vestment even of these, was proposed to be under several checks and limitations.

During the war, the general confusion, and the introduction of paper money, infused in the minds of the people vague ideas respecting government and credit. We expected too much from the return of peace, and of course we have been disappointed. Our governments have been new and unsettled; and several legislatures, by making tender, suspension, and paper money laws, have given just cause of uneasiness to creditors. By these and other causes, several orders of men in the community have been prepared, by degrees, for a change of government. And this very abuse of power in the legislatures, which in some cases has been charged upon the democratic part of the community, has furnished aristocratical men with those very weapons, and those very means, with which, in great measure, they are rapidly effecting their favorite object. And should an oppressive government be the consequence of the proposed change, posterity may reproach not only a few overbearing, unprincipled men, but those parties in the states which have misused their powers.

The conduct of several legislatures, touching paper money, and tender laws, has prepared many honest men for changes in government, which otherwise they would not have thought of-when by the evils, on the one hand, and by the secret instigations of artful men, on the other, the minds of men were become sufficiently uneasy, a bold step was taken, which is usually followed by a revolution, or a civil war. A general convention for mere commercial purposes was moved for-the authors of this measure saw that the people's attention was turned solely to the amendment of the federal system; and that, had the idea of a total change been started, probably no state would have appointed members to the convention. The idea of destroying ultimately, the state government, and forming one consolidated system, could not have been admitted-a convention, therefore, merely for vesting in congress power to regulate trade was proposed. This was pleasing to the commercial towns; and the landed people had little or no concern about it. In September, 1786, a few men from the middle states met at Annapolis, and hastily proposed a convention to be held in May, 1787, for the purpose, generally, of amending the confederation.

This was done before the delegates of Massachusetts, and of the other states arrived-still not a word was said about destroying the old constitution, and making a new one. The states still unsuspecting, and not aware that they were passing the Rubicon, appointed members to the new convention, for the sole and express purpose of revising and amending the confederation-and, probably, not one man in ten thousand in the United States, till within these ten or twelve days,

had an idea that the old ship was to be destroyed, and be put to the alternative of embarking in the new ship presented, or of being left in danger of sinking. The States, I believe, universally supposed the convention would report alterations in the confederation, which would pass an examination in congress, and after being agreed to there, would be confirmed by all the legislatures, or be rejected. Virginia made a very respectable appointment, and placed at the head of it the first man in America. In this appointment there was a mixture of political characters; but Pennsylvania appointed principally those men who are esteemed aristocratical. Here the favorite moment for changing the government was evidently discerned by a few men, who seized it with address. Ten other states appointed, and tho' they chose men principally connected with commerce and the judicial department yet they appointed many good republican characters. Had they all attended we should now see, I am persuaded, a better system presented. The nonattendance of eight or nine men, who were appointed members of the convention, I shall ever consider as a very unfortunate event to the United States. Had they attended, I am pretty clear that the result of the convention would not have had that strong tendency to aristocracy now discernible in every part of the plan. There would not have been so great an accumulation of powers, especially as to the internal police of this country in a few hands as the constitution reported proposes to vest in them-the young visionary men, and the consolidating aristocracy, would have been more restrained than they have been. Eleven states met in the convention, and after four months close attention presented the new constitution, to be adopted or rejected by the people. The uneasy and fickle part of the community may be prepared to receive any form of government; but I presume the enlightened and substantial part will give any constitution presented for their adoption a candid and thorough examination.... We shall view the convention with proper respect-and, at the same time, that we reflect there were men of abilities and integrity in it, we must recollect how disproportionately the democratic and aristocratic parts of the community were represented. Perhaps the judicious friends and opposers of the new constitution will agree, that it is best to let it rely solely on its own merits, or be condemned for its own defects. . . .

This subject of consolidating the states is new. And because forty or fifty men have agreed in a system, to suppose the good sense of this country, an enlightened nation, must adopt it without examination, and though in a state of profound peace, without endeavoring to amend those parts they perceive are defective, dangerous to freedom, and destructive of the valuable principles of republican government -is truly humiliating. It is true there may be danger in delay; but there is danger in adopting the system in its present form.

And I see the danger in either case will arise principally from the conduct and views of two very unprincipled parties in the United States-two fires, between which the honest and substantial people have long found themselves situated. One party is composed of little insurgents, men in debt, who want no law, and who want a share of the property of others; these are called revellers, Shayites, etc. The other party is composed of a few, but more dangerous men, with their servile dependents; these avariciously grasp at all power and property; you may discover in all the actions of these men, an evident dislike to free and equal government, and they will go systematically to work to change, essentially, the forms of government in this country; these are called aristocrats, monarchists, etc. Between these two parties is the weight of the community; the men of middling property, men not in debt on the one hand, and men, on the other, content with republican governments, and not aiming at immense fortunes, offices, and power. In 1786,

the little insurgents, the revellers, came forth, invaded the rights of others, and attempted to establish governments according to their wills. Their movements evidently gave encouragement to the other party, which, in 1787, has taken the political field, and with its fashionable dependents, and the tongue and the pen, is endeavoring to establish in a great haste, a politer kind of government. These two parties, which will probably be opposed or united as it may suit their interests and views, are really insignificant, compared with the solid, free, and independent part of the community. It is not my intention to suggest, that either of these parties, and the real friends of the proposed constitution, are the same men. The fact is, these aristocrats support and hasten the adoption of the proposed constitution, merely because they think it is a stepping stone to their favorite object. I think I am well founded in this idea. I think the general politics of these men support it, as well as the common observation among them: That the proffered plan is the best that can be got at present, it will do for a few years, and lead to something better. The sensible and judicious part of the community will carefully weigh all these circumstances; they will view the late convention as a respectable body of men-America probably never will see an assembly of men, of a like number, more respectable. But the members of the convention met without knowing the sentiments of one man in ten thousand in these states respecting the new ground taken. Their doings are but the first attempts in the most important scene ever opened. Though each individual in the state conventions will not, probably, be so respectable as each individual in the federal convention, yet as the state conventions will probably consist of fifteen hundred or two thousand men of abilities, and versed in the science of government, collected from all parts of the community and from all orders of men, it must be acknowledged that the weight of respectability will be in them. In them will be collected the solid sense and the real political character of the country. Being revisers of the subject, they will possess peculiar advantages. To say that these conventions ought not to attempt, coolly and deliberately, the revision of the system, or that they cannot amend it, is very foolish or very assuming. . . .

THE FEDERAL FARMER

ANTI-FEDERALIST PAPER NO. 38

Some Reactions To Federalist Arguments

This was an essay by "BRUTUS JUNIOR" which appeared in The New-York Journal on November 8, 1787. Two articles by "A COUNTRYMAN" were written by DeWitt Clinton, and appeared also in the New York Journal on January 10 and February 14, 1788.

I have read with a degree of attention several publications which have lately appeared in favor of the new Constitution; and as far as I am able to discern, the arguments (if they can be so termed) of most weight, which are urged in its favor, may be reduced to the two following: 1st. That the men who formed it, were wise and experienced; that they were an illustrious band of patriots, and had the happiness of their country at heart; that they were four months deliberating on the subject, and therefore, it must be a perfect system.

2nd. That if the system be not received, this country will be without any government, and of consequence, will be reduced to a state of anarchy and confusion, and involved in bloodshed and carnage; and in the end, a government will be imposed upon us, not the result of reason and reflection, but of force and usurpation.

As I do not find ' that either Cato or the Centinel, Brutus, or the Old Whig, or any other writer against this constitution, have undertaken a particular refutation of this new species of reasoning, I take the liberty of offering to the public, through the channel of your paper, the few following animadversions on the subject; and, the rather, because I have discovered, that some of my fellow citizens have been imposed upon by it.

With respect to the first,-it will be readily perceived that it precludes all investigation of the merits of the proposed constitution, and leads to an adoption of the plan without inquiring whether it be good or bad. For if we are to infer the perfection of this system from the characters and abilities of the men who formed it, we may as well determine to accept it without any inquiry as with. A number of persons in this [New York] as well as the other states, have, upon this principle, determined to submit to it without even reading or knowing its contents.

But supposing the premises from which this conclusion is drawn to be just, it then becomes essential in order to give validity to the argument, to inquire into the characters of those who composed this body, that we may determine whether we can be justified in placing such unbounded confidence in them.

It is an invidious task, to call in question the characters of individuals, especially of such as are placed in illustrious stations. But when we are required implicitly to submit our opinions to those of others, from a consideration that they are so wise and good as not to be liable to err, and that too in an affair which involves in it the happiness of ourselves and our posterity, every honest man will justify a decent investigation of characters in plain language.

It is readily admitted that many individuals who composed this body were men of the first talents and integrity in the union. It is at the same time, well known to every man, who is but moderately acquainted with the characters of the members, that many of them are possessed of high aristocratic ideas, and the most sovereign contempt of the common people; that not a few were strongly disposed in favor of monarchy; that there were some of no small talents and of great influence, of consummate cunning and masters of intrigue, whom the war found poor or in embarrassed circumstances, and left with princely fortunes acquired in public employment....

that there were others who were young, ardent, and ambitious, who wished for a government corresponding with their feelings, while they were destitute of experience ... in political researches; that there were not a few who were gaping for posts of honor and emolument-these we find exulting in the idea of a change which will divert places of honor, influence and emolument, into a different channel, where the confidence of the people will not be necessary to their acquirement. It is not to be wondered at, that an assembly thus composed should produce a system liable to well founded objections, and which will require very essential alterations. We are told by one of themselves (Mr. [James] Wilson of Philadelphia) the plan was [a] matter of accommodation, and it is not unreasonable to suppose, that in this accommodation, principles might be introduced which would render the liberties of the people very insecure.

I confess I think it of no importance what are the characters of the framers of this government, and therefore should not have called them in question, if they had not been so often urged in print, and in conversation, in its favor. It ought to rest on its own intrinsic merit. If it is good, it is capable of being vindicated; if it is bad, it ought not to be supported. It is degrading to a freeman, and humiliating to a rational one, to pin his faith on the sleeve of any man, or body of men, in an affair of such momentous importance.

In answer to the second argument, I deny that we are in immediate danger of anarchy and commotions. Nothing but the passions of wicked and ambitious men will put us in the least danger on this head. Those who are anxious to precipitate a measure will always tell us that the present is the critical moment; now is the time, the crisis is arrived, and the present minute must be seized. Tyrants have always made use of this plea; but nothing in our circumstances can justify it.

The country is in profound peace, and we are not threatened by invasions from any quarter. The governments of the respective states are in the full exercise of their powers; and the lives, the liberty, and property of individuals are protected. All present exigencies are answered by them. It is true, the regulation of trade and a competent provision for the payment of the interest of the public debt is wanting; but no immediate commotion will arise from these; time may be taken for calm discussion and deliberate conclusions. Individuals are just recovering from the losses and embarrassment sustained by the late war. Industry and frugality are taking their station, and banishing from the community, idleness and prodigality. Individuals are lessening their private debts, and several millions of the public debt is discharged by the sale of the western territory.

There is no reason, therefore, why we should precipitately and rashly adopt a system, which is imperfect or insecure. We may securely deliberate and propose amendments and alterations. I know it is said we cannot change for the worse; but if we act the part of wise men, we shall take care that we change for the better. It will be labor lost, if after all our pains we are in no better circumstances than we were before.

I have seen enough to convince me very fully, that the new constitution is a very bad one, and a hundred-fold worse than our present government. And I do not perceive that any of the writers in favor of it (although some of them use a vast many fine words, and show a great deal of learning) are able to remove any of the objections which are made against it. Mr. [James] Wilson, indeed, speaks very highly of it, but we have only his word for its goodness; and nothing is more natural than for a mother to speak well of her own bantling, however ordinary it may be. He seems, however, to be pretty honest in one thing-where he says, "It is the nature of man to pursue his own interest, in preference to the public good"'-for they tell me he is a lawyer, and his interest then makes him for the new government, for it will be a noble thing for lawyers. Besides, he appears to have an eye to some high place under it, since he speaks with great pleasure of the places of honor and emolument being diverted to a new channel by this change of system. As to Mr. Publius [The Federalist], I have read a great many of his papers, and I really cannot find out what he would be at. He seems to me as if he was going to write a history, so I have concluded to wait and buy one of his books, when they come out. The only thing I can understand from him, as far as I have read, is that it is better to be united than divided-that a great many people are stronger than a few-and that Scotland is better off since the union with England than before. And I think, he proves too, very clearly, that the fewer nations there are in the world, the fewer disputes [there] will be about the law of nations-and the greater number that are joined in one government, the abler will they be to raise ships and soldiers, and the less need for fighting. But I do not learn that any body denies these matters, or that they have any thin- to do with the new constitution, Indeed I am at a loss to know, whether Mr. Publius means to persuade us to return back to the old government, and make ourselves as happy as Scotland has by its union, or to accept of the new constitution, and get all the world to join with us, so as to make one large government. It would certainly, if what he says is true, be very convenient for Nova-Scotia and Canada, and, for ought I know, his advice will have great weight with them. I have also read several other of the pieces, which appear to be wrote by some other little authors, and by people of little consequence, though they seem to think themselves men of importance, and take upon them grand names such as . . . Caesar,' . . . Now Mr. Caesar do[es] not depend so much on reasoning as upon bullying. He abuses the people very much, and if he spoke in our neighborhood as impudently as he writes in the newspapers, I question whether he would come off with whole bones. From the manner he talks of the people, he certainly cannot be one of them himself. I imagine he has lately come over from some old country, where they are all Lords and no common people. If so, it would be as well for him to go back again as to meddle himself with our business, since he holds such a bad opinion of us.

A COUNTRYMAN

The Federalist, as be terms himself, or Publius, puts one in mind of some of the gentlemen of the long robe, when hard pushed, in a bad cause, with a rich client. They frequently say a great deal which does not apply; but yet, if it will not convince the judge nor jury, may, perhaps, help to make them forget some part of the evidence, embarrass their opponent, and make the audience stare, besides increasing the practice.

A COUNTRYMAN

ANTI-FEDERALIST PAPER NO. 39

Appearance and Reality-the Form Is Federal; The Effect Is National

The following excerpt is from the essays of "A FARMER." It appeared in the Philadelphia Independent Gazetteer on April 15 and 22, 1788

.... The Freeman, in his second number, after mentioning in a very delusory manner diverse powers which remain with the states, says we shall find many other instances under the constitution which require or imply the existence or continuance of the sovereignty and severalty of the states. He, as well as all the advocates of the new system, take as their strong ground the election of senators by the state legislatures, and the special representation of the states in the federal senate, to prove that internal sovereignty still remains with the States. Therefore they say that the new system is so far from annihilating the state governments, that it secures them, that it cannot exist without them, that the existence of the one is essential to the existence of the other.

It is true that this particular partakes strongly of that mystery which is characteristic of the system itself. But if I demonstrate that this particular, so far from implying the continuance of the state sovereignties, proves in the clearest manner the want of it, I hope the other particular powers will not be necessary to dwell upon.

The State legislatures do not choose senators by legislative or sovereign authority, but by a power of ministerial agency as mere electors or boards of appointment. They have no power to direct the senators how or what duties they shall perform; they have neither power to censure the senators, nor to supersede them for misconduct. It is not the power of choosing to office merely that designates sovereignty, or else corporations who appoint their own officers and make their own by-laws, or the heads of department who choose the officers under them, such as commanders of armies, etc., may be called sovereigns, because they can name men to office whom they cannot dismiss therefrom. The exercise of sovereignty does not consist in choosing masters, such as the senators would be, who, when chosen, would be beyond control, but in the power of dismissing, impeaching, or the like, those to whom authority is delegated. The power of instructing or superseding of delegates to Congress under the existing confederation has never been complained of, although the necessary rotation of members of Congress has often been censured for restraining the state sovereignties too much in the objects of their choice. As well may the electors who are to vote for the president under the new constitution, be said to be vested with the sovereignty, as the State legislatures in the act of choosing senators. The senators are not even dependent on the States for their wages, but in conjunction with the federal representatives establish their own wages. The senators do not vote by States, but as individuals.

The representatives also vote as individuals, representing people in a consolidated or national government; they judge upon their own elections, and, with the Senate, have the power of regulating elections in time, place and manner, which is in other words to say, that they have the power of elections absolutely vested in them.

That the State governments have certain ministerial and convenient powers continued to them is not denied, and in the exercise of which they may support, but cannot control the general government, nor protect their own citizens from the exertion of civil or military tyranny-and this

ministerial power will continue with the States as long as two- thirds of Congress shall think their agency necessary. But even this will be no longer than two-thirds of Congress shall think proper to propose, and use the influence of which they would be so largely possessed to remove it.

But these powers of which the Freeman gives us such a profuse detail, and in describing which be repeats the same powers with only varying the terms, such as the powers of officering and training the militia, appointing State officers, and governing in a number of internal cases, do not any of them separately, nor all taken together, amount to independent sovereignty. They are powers of mere ministerial agency, which may, and in many nations of Europe are or have been vested, as before observed, in heads of departments, hereditary vassals of the crown, or in corporations; but not that kind of independent sovereignty which can constitute a member of a federal republic, which can enable a State to exist within itself if the general government should cease.

I have often wondered how any writer of sense could have the confidence to avow, or could suppose the people to be ignorant enough to believe that, when a State is deprived of the power not only of standing armies (this the members of a confederacy ought to be), but of commanding its own militia, regulating its elections, directing or superseding its representatives, or paying them their wages; who is, moreover, deprived of the command of any property, I mean source of revenue or taxation, or what amounts to the same thing, who may enact laws for raising revenue, but who may have these laws rendered nugatory, and the execution thereof superseded by the laws of Congress. [sic] This is not a strained construction, but the natural operation of the powers of Congress under the new constitution; for every object of revenues, every source of taxation, is vested in the general government. Even the power of making inspection laws, which, for obvious conveniency, is left with the several States, will be unproductive of the smallest revenue to the State governments; for, if any should arise, it is to be paid over to the officers of Congress.

Besides, the words "to make all laws necessary and proper for carrying into execution the foregoing powers," etc., give, without doubt, the power of repelling or forbidding the execution of any tax law whatever, that may interfere with or impede the exercise of the general taxing power, and it would not be possible that two taxing powers should be exercised on the same sources of taxation without interfering with each other. May not the exercise of this power of Congress, when they think proper, operate not only to destroy those ministerial powers which are left with the States, but even the very forms? May they not forbid the state legislatures to levy a shilling to pay themselves, or those whom they employ, days' wages?

The State governments may contract for making roads (except post-roads), erecting bridges, cutting canals, or any other object of public importance; but when the contract is performed or the work done, may not Congress constitutionally prevent the payment? Certainly; they may do all this and much more, and no man would have a right to charge them with breaking the law of their appointment. It is an established maxim, that wherever the whole power of the revenue or taxation is vested, there virtually is the whole effective, influential, sovereign power, let the forms be what they may. By this armies are procured, by this every other controlling guard is defeated. Every balance or check in government is only so far effective as it has a control over the revenue.

The State governments are not only destitute of all sovereign command of, or control over, the revenue or any part of it, but they are divested of the power of commanding or prescribing the duties, wages, or punishments of their own militia, or of protecting their life, property or characters from the rigors of martial law. The power of making treason laws is both a power and an important defense of sovereignty; it is relative to and inseparable from it; to convince the States that they are consolidated into one national government, this power is wholly to be assumed by the general government. All the prerogatives, all the essential characteristics of sovereignty, both of the internal and external kind, are vested in the general government, and consequently the several States would not be possessed of any essential power or effective guard of sovereignty. Thus I apprehend, it is evident that the consolidation of the States into one national government (in contra-distinction from a confederacy) would be the necessary consequence of the establishment of the new constitution, and the intention of its framers-and that consequently the State sovereignties would be eventually annihilated, though the forms may long remain as expensive and burdensome remembrances of what they were in the days when (although laboring under many disadvantages) they emancipated this country from foreign tyranny, humbled the pride and tarnished the glory of royalty, and erected a triumphant standard to liberty and independence.

A FARMER

ANTI-FEDERALIST PAPER NO. 40

On the Motivations And Authority Of The Founding Fathers

Anti-Federalist #40 is a compilation of articles.

It was a common saying among many sensible men in Great Britain and Ireland, in the time of the war, that they doubted whether the great men of America, who had taken an active part in favor of independence, were influenced by pure patriotism; that it was not the love of their country they had so much at heart, as their own private, interest; that a thirst after dominion and power, and not to protect the oppressed from the oppressor, was the great operative principle that induced these men to oppose Britain so strenuously. This seemingly illiberal sentiment was, however, generally denied by the well-hearted and unsuspecting friends of American liberty in Europe, who could not suppose that men would engage in so noble a cause thro' such base motives. But alas! The truth of the sentiment is now indisputably confirmed; facts are stubborn things, and these set the matter beyond controversy. The new constitution and the conduct of its despotic advocates, show that these men's doubts were really well founded. Unparalleled duplicity! That men should oppose tyranny under a pretence of patriotism, that they might themselves become the tyrants. How does such villainy disgrace human nature! Ah, my fellow citizens, you have been strangely deceived indeed; when the wealthy of your own country assisted you to expel the foreign tyrant, only with a view to substitute themselves in his stead...

But the members of the Federal Convention were men w e been all tried in the field of action, say some; they have fought for American liberty. Then the more to their shame be it said; curse on the villain who protects virgin innocence only with a view that he may himself become the ravisher; so that if the assertion were true, it only turns to their disgrace; but as it happens it is not truth, or at least only so in part. This was a scheme taken by the despots and their sycophants to bias the public mind in favor of the constitution. For the convention was composed of a variety of characters: ambitious men, Jesuits, tories, lawyers, etc., formed the majority, whose similitude to each other, consisted only in their determination to lord it over their fellow citizens; like the rays that converging from every direction meet in a point, their sentiments and deliberations concentered in tyranny alone; they were unanimous in forming a government that should raise the fortunes and respectability of the well born few, and oppress the plebeians.

PHILADELPHIENSIS

Does our soil produce no more Washington's? Is there none who would oppose the attempt to establish a government by force? Can we not call from the fields, the counters, the bar, and mechanics' shops, any more Generals? Is our soil exhausted? And does any one suppose that the Americans, like the Romans, will submit to an army merely because they have conquered a foreign enemy?...

AN AMERICAN

I revere the characters of some of the gentlemen that composed the convention at Philadelphia, yet I think they were human, and subject to imposition and error, as well as the rest of mankind.
You lost eight or ten years of your lives and labor by the last war, and you were left at last with your debts and encumbrances on you, and numbers of you were soon after the close of it, sued and harassed for them. Your persons have been put into a loathsome prison, and others of you have had your property sold for taxes, and sometimes for one tenth of its former and actual value and you now pay very grievous and heavy taxes, double and treble what you paid before the war; and should you adopt this new government, your taxes will be great, increased to support their..
. servants and retainers, who will be multiplied upon you to keep you in obedience, and collect their duties, taxes, impositions, and excises. Some of you may say the rich men were virtuous in the last war; yes, my countrymen, they had reason then to be so! Our liberty then was in dispute with a mighty and powerful tyrant, and it was for their interest to promote and carry on the

opposition, as long as they could stay at home and send the common people into the field to fight their battles. After the war began, they could not with decency recede, for the sword and enemy were at the very entrance of their gates. The case is greatly altered now; you conquered the enemy, and the rich men now think to subdue you by their wiles and arts, or make you, or persuade you, to do it yourselves. Their aim, I perceive, is now to destroy that liberty which you set up as a reward for the blood and treasure you expended in the pursuit of and establishment of it. They well know that open force will not succeed at this time, and have chosen a safer method, by offering you a plan of a new Federal Government, contrived with great art, and shaded with obscurity, and recommended to you to adopt; which if you do, their scheme is completed, the yoke is -fixed on your necks, and you will be undone, perhaps for ever, and your boasted liberty is but a sound, Farewell! Be wise, be watchful, guard yourselves against the dangers that are concealed in this plan of a new Federal Government.

A FARMER AND PLANTER

Make the best of this new government-say it is composed of any thing but inspiration-you ought to be extremely cautious, watchful, jealous of your liberty; for, instead of securing your rights, you may lose them forever. If a wrong step be now made, the republic may be lost forever. If this new government will not come up to the expectation of the people, and they shall be disappointed, their liberty will be lost, and tyranny must and will arise. I repeat it again, and I beg gentlemen to consider, that a wrong step, made now, will plunge us into misery, and our republic will be lost. It will be necessary for this [Virginia Ratifying] Convention to have a faithful historical detail of the facts that preceded the session of the federal Convention, and the reasons that actuated its members in proposing an entire alteration of government, and to demonstrate the dangers that awaited us. If they were of such awful magnitude as to warrant a proposal so extremely perilous as this, I must assert, that this Convention has an absolute right to a thorough discovery of every circumstance relative to this great event. And here I would make this inquiry of those worthy characters who composed a part of the late federal Convention. I am sure they were fully impressed with the necessity of forming a great consolidated government, instead of a confederation. That this is a consolidated government is demonstrably clear; and the danger of such a government is, to my mind, very striking. I have the highest veneration for those gentlemen; but, sir, give me leave to demand: What right had they to say, We, the people?
My political curiosity, exclusive of my anxious solicitude for the public welfare, leads me to ask: Who authorized them to speak the language of, We, the people, instead of, We, the states? States
are the characteristics and the soul of a confederation. If the states be not the agents of this compact, it must be one great, consolidated, national government, of the people of all the states. I have the highest respect for those gentlemen who formed the Convention, and, were some of them not here, I would express some testimonial of esteem for them. America had, on a former occasion, put the utmost confidence in them-a confidence which was well placed; and I am sure, sir, I would give up any thing to them; I would cheerfully confide in them as my representatives.
But, sir, on this great occasion, I would demand the cause of their conduct. Even from that illustrious man who saved us by his valor, I would have a reason for his conduct. . . . That they exceeded their power is perfectly clear. . . . The federal Convention ought to have amended the old system; for this purpose they were solely delegated; the object of their mission extended to no other consideration. You must, therefore, forgive the solicitation of one unworthy member to know what danger could have arisen under the present Confederation, and what are the causes of this proposal to change our government.

PATRICK HENRY

What then are we to think of the motives and designs of those men who are urging the implicit and immediate adoption of the proposed government; are they fearful, that if you exercise your good sense and discernment, you will discover the masqued aristocracy, that they are attempting to smuggle upon you under the suspicious garb of republicanism? When we find that the principal agents in this business are the very men who fabricated the form of government, it certainly ought to be conclusive evidence of their invidious design to deprive us of our liberties.
The circumstances attending this matter, are such as should in a peculiar manner excite your suspicion; it might not be useless to take a review of some of them.
In many of the states, particularly in this [Pennsylvania] and the northern states, there are aristocratic juntos of the well-horn few, who have been zealously endeavoring since the establishment of their constitutions, to humble that offensive upstart, equal liberty; but all their efforts were unavailing, the ill-bred churl obstinately kept his assumed station. . . .

Documents of Revolution

A comparison of the authority under which the convention acted, and their form of government, will show that they have despised their delegated power, and assumed sovereignty; that they have entirely annihilated the old confederation, and the particular governments of the several States, and instead thereof have established one general government that is to pervade the union; constituted on the most unequal principles, destitute of accountability to its constituents, and as despotic in its nature, as the Venetian aristocracy; a government that will give full scope to the magnificent designs of the well-horn, a government where tyranny may glut its vengeance on the low-born, unchecked by an odious bill of rights. . . ; and yet as a blind upon the understandings of the people, they have continued the forms of the particular governments, and termed the whole a confederation of the United States, pursuant to the sentiments of that profound, but corrupt politician Machiavel, who advises any one who would change the constitution of a state to keep as much as possible to the old forms; for then the people seeing the same officers, the same formalities, courts of justice and other outward appearances, are insensible of the alteration, and believe themselves in possession of their old government. Thus Caesar, when he seized the Roman liberties, caused himself to be chosen dictator (which was an ancient office), continued the senate, the consuls, the tribunes, the censors, and all other offices and forms of the
commonwealth; and yet changed Rome from the most free, to the most tyrannical government in the world. . . .
The late convention, in the majesty of its assumed omnipotence, have not even condescended to submit the plan of the new government to the confederation of the people, the true source of authority; but have called upon them by their several constitutions, to 'assent to and ratify' in toto, what they have been pleased to decree; just as the grand monarch of France requires the parliament of Paris to register his edicts without revision or alteration, which is necessary previous to their execution. . . .
If you are in doubt about the nature and principles of the proposed government, view the conduct of its authors and patrons: that affords the best explanation, the most striking comment.
The evil genius of darkness presided at its birth, it came forth under the veil of mystery, its true features being carefully concealed, and every deceptive art has been and is practicing to have this spurious brat received as the genuine offspring of heaven-born liberty. So fearful are its patrons that you should discern the imposition, that they have hurried on its adoption, with the greatest precipitation. . .
After so recent a triumph over British despots, after such torrents of blood and treasure have been spent, after involving ourselves in the distresses of an arduous war, and incurring such a debt for the express purpose of asserting the rights of humanity; it is truly astonishing that a set of men among ourselves should have the effrontery to attempt the destruction of our liberties.
But in this enlightened age to hope to dupe the people by the arts they are practicing is still more extraordinary. . .
The advocates of this plan have artfully attempted to veil over the true nature and principles of it with the names of those respectable characters that by consummate cunning and address they have prevailed upon to sign it; and what ought to convince the people of the deception and excite their apprehensions, is that with every advantage which education, the science of government and of law, the knowledge of history and superior talents and endowments, furnish the authors and advocates of this plan with, they have from its publication exerted all their power and influence to prevent all discussion of the subject, and when this could not be prevented they have constantly avoided the ground of argument and recurred to declamation, sophistry and personal abuse, but principally relied upon the magic of names. . . . Emboldened by the sanction of the august name of a Washington, that they have prostituted to their purpose, they have presumed to overleap the usual gradations to absolute power, and have attempted to seize at once upon the supremacy of dominion.

CENTINEL

. . . Another thing they tell us, that the constitution must be good, from the characters which composed the Convention that framed it. It is graced with the names of a Washington and a Franklin. Illustrious names, we know-worthy characters in civil society. Yet we cannot suppose them to be infallible guides; neither yet that a man must necessarily incur guilt to himself merely by dissenting from them in opinion. We cannot think the noble general has the same ideas with
ourselves, with regard to the rules of right and wrong. We cannot think he acts a very consistent part, or did through the whole of the contest with Great Britain. Notwithstanding he wielded the sword in defense of American liberty, yet at the same time was, and is to this day, living upon the labors of several hundreds of miserable Africans, as free born as himself; and some of them very likely, descended from parents who, in point of property and dignity in their own country, might cope with any man

in America. We do not conceive we are to be overborne by the weight of any names, however revered. "ALL MEN ARE BORN FREE AND EQUAL"......
THE YEOMANRY OF MASSACHUSETTS

ANTI-FEDERALIST PAPER NO. 41-43

(Part I)Richard Henry Lee "the Quantity Of Power The Union Must Possess Is One Thing; The Mode Of Exercising The Powers Given Is Quite A Different Consideration"

Taken from "THE FEDERAL FARMER,"
.... A federal republic in itself supposes state or local governments to exist, as the body or props, on which the federal bead rests, and that it cannot remain a moment after they cease. In erecting the federal government, and always in its councils, each state must be known as a sovereign body. But in erecting this government, I conceive, the legislature of the state, by the expressed or implied assent of the people, or the people of the state, under the direction of the government of it, may accede to the federal compact. Nor do I conceive it to be necessarily a part of a confederacy of states, that each have an equal voice in the general councils. A confederated republic being organized, each state must retain powers for managing its internal police, and all delegate to the union power to manage general concerns. The quantity of power the union must possess is one thing; the mode of exercising the powers given is quite a different consideration-and it is the mode of exercising them, that makes one of the essential distinctions between one entire or consolidated government, and a federal republic. That is, however the government may be organized, if the laws of the union, in most important concerns, as in levying and collecting taxes, raising troops, etc., operate immediately upon the persons and property of individuals, and not on states, extend to organizing the militia, etc., the government, as to its administration, as to making and executing laws, is not federal, but consolidated. To illustrate my idea: the union makes a requisition, and assigns to each state its quota of men or monies wanted; each state, by its own laws and officers, in its own way, furnishes its quota. Here the state governments stand between the union and individuals; the laws of the union operate only on states, as such, and federally. Here nothing can be done without the meetings of the state legislatures. But in the other case the union, though the state legislatures should not meet for years together, proceeds immediately by its own laws and officers to levy and collect monies of individuals, to enlist men, form armies, etc. Here the laws of the union operate immediately on the body of the people, on persons and property. In the same manner the laws of one entire consolidated government operate. These two modes are very distinct, and in their operation and consequences have directly opposite tendencies.... I am not for depending wholly on requisitions. Since the peace, and till the convention reported, the wisest men in the United States generally supposed that certain limited funds would answer the purposes of the union. And though the states are by no means in so good a condition as I wish they were, yet, I think, I may very safely affirm, they are in a better condition than they would be had congress always possessed the powers of taxation now contended for. The fact is admitted, that our federal government does not possess sufficient powers to give life and vigor to the political system; and that we experience disappointments, and several inconveniences. But we ought carefully to distinguish those which are merely the consequences of a severe and tedious war, from those which arise from defects in the federal system. There has been an entire revolution in the United States within thirteen years, and the least we can compute the waste of labor and property at, during that period, by the war, is three
hundred millions of dollars. Our people are like a man just recovering from a severe fit of sickness. It was the war that disturbed the course of commerce introduced floods of paper money, the stagnation of credit, and threw many valuable men out of steady business. From these sources our greatest evils arise. Men of knowledge and reflection must perceive it. But then, have we not done more in three or four years past, in repairing the injuries of the war, by repairing houses and estates, restoring industry, frugality, the fisheries, manufactures, etc., and thereby laying the foundation of good government, and of individual and political happiness, than any people ever did in a like time? We must judge from a view of the country and facts, and not from foreign newspapers, or our own, which are printed chiefly in the commercial towns, where imprudent living, imprudent importations, and many unexpected disappointments, have produced a despondency, and a disposition to view

everything on the dark side. Some of the evils we feel, all will agree, ought to be imputed to the defective administration of the governments.

From these and various considerations, I am very clearly of opinion that the evils we sustain merely on account of the defects of the confederation, ar but as a feather in the balance against a mountain, compared with those which would infallibly be the result of the loss of general liberty, and that happiness men enjoy under a frugal, free, and mild government.

Heretofore we do not seem to have seen danger any where, but in giving power to congress, and now no where but in congress wanting powers; and without examining the extent of the evils to be remedied, by one step we ar for giving up to congress almost all powers of any importance without limitation. The defects of the confederation are extravagantly magnified, an every species of pain we feel imputed to them; and hence it is inferred, the must be a total change of the principles, as well as forms of government And in the main point, touching the federal powers, we rest all on a logical inference, totally inconsistent with experience and sound political reasoning.

It is said, that as the federal head must make peace and war, and provide for the common defense, it ought to possess all powers necessary to that end. That powers unlimited, as to the purse and sword, to raise men and monies and form the militia, are necessary to that end; and therefore, the federal head ought to possess them. This reasoning is far more specious than solid.

It is necessary that these powers so exist in the body politic, as to be called into exercise whenever necessary for the public safety. But it is by no means true that the man, or congress of men, whose duty it more immediately is to provide for the common defense, ought to possess them without limitation. But clear it is, that if such men, or congress, be not in a situation to hold them without danger to liberty, he or they ought not to possess them. It has long been thought to be a well founded position, that the purse and sword ought not to be placed in the same hands in a free government. Our wise ancestors have carefully separated them-placed the sword in the hands of their king, even under considerable limitations, and the purse in the hands of the commons alone. Yet the king makes peace and war, and it is his duty to provide for the common defense of the nation. This authority at least goeth thus far-that a nation, well versed in the science of government, does not conceive it to be necessary or expedient for the man entrusted with the common defense and general tranquility, to possess unlimitedly the power in question, or even in any considerable degree. Could he, whose duty it is t defend the public, possess in himself independently, all the means of doing it consistent with the public good, it might be convenient. But the people o England know that their liberties and happiness would be in

infinitely great danger from the king's unlimited possession of these powers, than from al external enemies and internal commotions to which they might be exposed Therefore, though they have made it his duty to guard the empire, yet the have wisely placed in other hands, the hands of their representatives, the power to deal out and control the means. In Holland their high mightiness must provide for the common defense, but for the means they depend in considerable degree upon requisitions made on the state or local assemblies Reason and facts evince, that however convenient it might be for an executive magistrate, or federal head, more immediately charged with the national defense and safety, solely, directly, and independently to possess all the means, yet such magistrate or head never ought to possess them if thereby the public liberties shall be endangered. The powers in question never have been, by nations wise and free, deposited, nor can they ever be, with safety, any where out of the principal members of the national system. Where these form one entire government, as in Great Britain, they are separated and lodged in the principal members of it. But in a federal republic, there is quite a different organization; the people form this kind of government, generally, because their territories are too extensive to admit of their assembling in one legislature, or of executing the laws on free principles under one entire government. They Convene in their local assemblies, for local purposes, and for managing their internal concerns, and unite their states under a federal head for general purposes. It is the essential characteristic of a confederated republic, that this head be dependent on, and kept within limited bounds by the local governments; and it is because, in these alone, in fact, the people can be substantially assembled or represented. It is, therefore, we very universally see, in this kind of government, the congressional powers placed in a few hands, and accordingly limited, and specifically enumerated; and the local assemblies strong and well guarded, and composed of numerous members. Wise men will always place the controlling power where the people are substantially collected by their representatives. By the proposed system the federal head will possess, without limitation, almost every species of power that can, in its exercise, tend to change the government, or to endanger liberty; while in it, I think it has been fully shown, the people will have but the shadow of representation, and but the shadow of security for their rights and liberties. In a confederated republic, the division of representation, etc., in its nature, requires a correspondent division and deposit of powers, relative to taxes and military concerns. And I think the plan offered stands quite alone, in confounding the principles of governments in themselves totally distinct. I wish not to exculpate the states for their improper neglects in not paying their quotas of requisitions. But, in applying the remedy, we must be governed by reason and facts. It will not be denied that the people have a right to change the government when the majority choose it, if not restrained by some existing compact; that they have a right to displace their rulers, and consequently to determine when their measures are reasonable or not; and that they have a right, at any time, to put a stop to those measures they may deem prejudicial to them, by such forms and negatives as they may see fit to provide. From all these, and many other well founded considerations, I need not mention, a question arises, what powers shall there be delegated to the federal head, to insure safety, as well as energy, in the government? I think there is a safe and proper medium pointed out by experience, by reason, and facts. When we have organized the government, we ought to give power to the union, so far only as experience and present circumstances shall direct, with a reasonable regard to time to come. Should future circumstances, contrary to our expectations, require that further powers be transferred to the union, we can do it far more easily, than get back those we may now imprudently give. The system proposed is untried. Candid advocates and opposers admit, that it is in a degree, a mere experiment, and that its organization is weak and imperfect. Surely then,

the safe ground is cautiously to vest power in it, and when we are sure we have given enough for ordinary exigencies, to be extremely careful how we delegate powers, which, in common cases, must necessarily be useless or abused, and of very uncertain effect in uncommon ones. By giving the union power to regulate commerce, and to levy and collect taxes by imposts, we give it an extensive authority, and permanent productive funds, I believe quite as adequate to present demands of the union, as excises and direct taxes can be made to the present demands of the separate states. The state governments are now about four times as expensive as that of the union; and their several state debts added together, are nearly as large as that of the union. Our impost duties since the peace have been almost as productive as the other sources of taxation, and when under one general system of regulations, the probability is that those duties will be very considerably increased. Indeed the representation proposed will hardly justify giving to congress unlimited powers to raise taxes by imposts, in addition to the other powers the union must necessarily have. It is said, that if congress possess only authority to raise taxes by imposts, trade probably will be overburdened with taxes, and the taxes of the union be found inadequate to any uncommon exigencies. To this we may observe, that trade generally finds its own level, and will naturally and necessarily heave off any undue burdens laid upon it. Further, if congress alone possess the impost, and also unlimited power to raise monies by excises and direct taxes, there must be much more danger that two taxing powers, the union and states, will carry excises and direct taxes to an unreasonable extent, especially as these have not the natural boundaries taxes on trade have. However, it is not my object to propose to exclude congress from raising monies by internal taxes, except in strict conformity to the federal plan; that is, by the agency of the state governments in all cases, except where a state shall neglect, for an unreasonable time, to pay its quota of a requisition; and never where so many of the state legislatures as represent a majority of the people, shall formally determine an excise law or requisition is improper, in their next session after the same be laid before them. We ought always to recollect that the evil to be guarded against is found by our own experience, and the experience of others, to be mere neglect in the states to pay their quotas; and power in the union to levy and collect the neglecting states'

quotas with interest, is fully adequate to the evil. By this federal plan, with this exception mentioned, we secure the means of collecting the taxes by the usual process of law, and avoid the evil of attempting to compel or coerce a state; and we avoid also a circumstance, which never yet could be, and I am fully confident never can be, admitted in a free federal republic-I mean a permanent and continued system of tax laws of the union, executed in the bowels of the states by many thousand officers, dependent as to the assessing and collecting federal taxes solely upon the union. On every principle, then, we ought to provide that the union render an exact account of all monies raised by imposts and other taxes whenever monies shall be wanted for the purposes of the union beyond the proceeds of the impost duties; requisitions shall be made on the states for the monies so wanted; and that the power of laying and collecting shall never be exercised, except in cases where a state shall neglect, a given time, to pay its quota. This mode seems to be strongly pointed out by the reason of the case, and spirit of the government; and I believe, there is no instance to be found in a federal republic, where the congressional powers ever extended generally to collecting monies by direct taxes or excises. Creating all these restrictions, still the powers of the union in matters of taxation will be too unlimited; further checks, in my mind, are indispensably necessary. Nor do I conceive, that as full a representation as is practicable in the federal government, will afford sufficient security. The strength of the government, and the confidence of the people, must be collected principally in the local assemblies. . . . A government possessed of more power than its constituent parts will justify,

will not only probably abuse it, but be unequal to bear its own burden; it may as soon be destroyed by the pressure of power, as languish and perish for want of it.

There are two ways further of raising checks, and guarding against -undue combinations and influence in a federal system. The first is-in levying taxes, raising and keeping up armies, in building navies, in forming plans for the militia, and in appropriating monies for the support of the military-to require the attendance of a large proportion of the federal representatives, as two-thirds or three-fourths of them; and in passing laws, in these important cases, to require the consent of two-thirds or three- fourths of the members present. The second is, by requiring that certain important laws of the federal head-as a requisition or a law for raising monies by excise-shall be laid before the state legislatures, and if disapproved of by a given number of them, say by as many of them as represent a majority of the people, the law shall have no effect. Whether it would be advisable to adopt both, or either of these checks, I will not undertake to determine. We have seen them both exist in confederated republics. The first exists substantially in the confederation, and will exist in some measure in the plan proposed, as in choosing a president by the house, or in expelling members; in the senate, in making treaties, and in deciding on impeachments; and in the whole, in altering the constitution. The last exists in the United Netherlands, but in a much greater extent. The first is founded on this principle, that these important measures may, sometimes, be adopted by a bare quorum of members, perhaps from a few states, and that a bare majority of the federal representatives may frequently be of the aristocracy, or some particular interests, connections, or parties in the community, and governed by motives, views, and inclinations not compatible with the general interest. The last is founded on this principle, that the people will be substantially represented, only in their state or local assemblies; that their principal security must be found in them; and that, therefore, they ought to have ultimately a constitutional control over such interesting measures.
THE FEDERAL FARMER

ANTI-FEDERALIST PAPER NO. 41-43 (PART II) (RICHARD HENRY LEE)

"the Quantity Of Power The Union Must Possess Is One Thing; The Mode Of Exercising The Powers Given Is Quite A Different Consideration"

... In the present state of mankind, and of conducting war, the government of every nation must have power to raise and keep up regular troops. The question is, how shall this power be lodged?
In an entire government, as in Great-Britain, where the people assemble by their representatives in one legislature, there is no difficulty; it is of course properly lodged in that legislature. But in a confederated republic, where the organization consists of a federal head, and local governments, there is no one part in which it can be solely, and safely lodged. By Art. 1., Sect. 8., "congress shall have power to raise and support armies," etc. By Art. I., Sect. 10., "no state, without the consent of congress, shall keep troops, or ships of war, in time of peace." It seems fit the union should direct the raising of troops, and the union may do it in two ways: by requisitions on the states, or by direct taxes. The first is most conformable to the federal plan, and safest; and it may be improved, by giving the union power, by its own laws and officers, to raise the state's quota that may neglect, and to charge it with the expense; and by giving a fixed quorum of the state legislatures power to disapprove the requisition. There would be less danger in this power to raise troops, could the state governments keep a proper control over the purse and over the militia. But after all the precautions we can take, without evidently fettering the union too much, we must give a large accumulation of powers to it, in these and other respects. There is one check, which, I think may be added with great propriety-that is, no land forces shall be kept up, but by legislative acts annually passed by congress, and no appropriation of monies for their support shall be for a longer term than one year. This is the constitutional practice in Great Britain, and the reasons for such checks in the United States appear to be much stronger. We may also require that these acts be passed by a special majority, as before mentioned. There is another mode still more guarded, and which seems to be founded in the true spirit of a federal system: it seems proper to divide those powers we can with safety, lodge them in no one member of the government alone; yet substantially to preserve their use, and to insure duration to the government by modifying the

exercise of them-it is to empower congress to raise troops by direct levies, not exceeding a given number, say 2000 in time of peace, and 12,000 in a time of war, and for such further troops as may be wanted, to raise them by requisitions qualified ,as before mentioned. By the above recited clause no state shall keep troops, etc., in time of peace-this clearly implies it may do it in time of war. This must be on the principle that the union cannot defend all parts of the republic, and suggests an idea very repugnant to the general tendency of the system proposed, which is to disarm the state governments. A state in a long war may collect forces sufficient to take the field against the neighboring states. This clause was copied from the confederation, in which it was of more importance than in the plan proposed, because under this the separate states, probably, will have but small revenues.

By Article I., section 8., congress shall have power to establish uniform laws on the subject of bankruptcies throughout the United States. It is to be observed, that the separate states have ever been in possession of the power, and in the use of it, of making bankrupt-laws, militia laws, and

laws in some other cases, respecting which, the new constitution, when adopted, will give the union power to legislate, etc. But no words are used by the constitution to exclude the jurisdiction of the several states, and whether they will be excluded or not, or whether they and the union will have concurrent jurisdiction or not, must be determined by inference, and from the nature of the subject. If the power, for instance, to make uniform laws on the subject of bankruptcies, is in its nature indivisible, or incapable of being exercised by two legislatures independently, or by one in aid of the other, then the states are excluded, and cannot legislate at all on the subject, even though the union should neglect or find it impracticable to establish uniform bankrupt laws. How far the union will find it practicable to do this, time only can fully determine. When we consider the extent of the country, and the very different ideas of the different parts in it, respecting credit, and the mode of making men's property liable for paying their debts, we may, I think with some degree of certainty, conclude that the union never will be able to establish such laws. But if practicable, it does not appear to me, on further reflection, that the union ought to have the power. It does not appear to me to be a power properly incidental to a federal head, and, I believe, no one ever possessed it. It is a power that will immediately and extensively interfere with the internal police of the separate states, especially with their administering justice among their own citizens. By giving this power to the union, we greatly extend the jurisdiction of the federal judiciary, as all questions arising on bankrupt laws, being laws of the union . . .-[indeed], almost all civil causes-may be drawn into those courts. We must be sensible how cautious we ought to be in extending unnecessarily the jurisdiction of those courts for reasons I need not repeat. This article of power too, will considerably increase, in the hands of the union, an accumulation of powers, some of a federal and some of an unfederal nature, [already] too large without it. The constitution provides that congress shall have the sole and exclusive government of what is called the federal city, a place not exceeding ten miles square, and of all places ceded for forts, dock-yards, etc. I believe this is a novel kind of provision in a federal republic; it is repugnant to the spirit of such a government, and must be founded in an apprehension of a hostile disposition between the federal head and the state governments. And it is not improbable that the sudden retreat of congress from Philadelphia first gave rise to it. With this apprehension, we provide, the government of the union shall have secluded places, cities, and castles of defense, which no state laws whatever shall invade. When we attentively examine this provision in all its consequences, it opens to view scenes almost without bounds. A federal, or rather a national city, ten miles square, containing a hundred square miles, is about four times as large as London; and for forts, magazines, arsenals, dock yards, and other needful buildings, congress may possess a number of places or towns in each state. It is true, congress cannot have them unless the state legislatures cede them; but when once ceded, they never can be recovered. And though the general temper of the legislatures may be averse to such cessions, yet many opportunities and advantages may be taken of particular times and circumstances of complying assemblies, and of particular parties, to obtain them. it is not improbable, that some considerable towns or places, in some intemperate moments, or influenced by anti-republican principles, will petition to be ceded for the purposes mentioned in the provision. There are men, and even towns, in the best republics, which are often fond of withdrawing from the government of them, whenever occasion shall present. The case is still stronger. If the provision in question holds out allurements to attempt to withdraw, the people of a state must ever be subject to state as well as federal taxes; but the federal city and places will be subject only to the latter, and to them by no fixed proportion. Nor of the taxes raised in them, can the separate states demand any account of congress. These doors opened for withdrawing

from the state governments entirely, may, on other accounts, be very alluring and pleasing to those anti- republican men who prefer a place under the wings of courts.

If a federal town be necessary for the residence of congress and the public officers, it ought to be a small one, and the government of it fixed on republican and common law principles, carefully enumerated and established by the constitution. it is true, the states, when they shall cede places, may stipulate that the laws and government of congress in them shall always be formed on such principles. But it is easy to discern, that the stipulations of a state, or of the inhabitants of the place ceded, can be of but little avail against the power and gradual encroachments of the union.

The principles ought to be established by the federal constitution, to which all states are parties; but in no event can there be any need of so large a city and places for forts, etc., totally exempted from the laws and jurisdictions of the state governments. If I understand the constitution, the laws of congress, constitutionally made, will have complete and supreme jurisdiction to all federal purposes, on every inch of ground in the United States, and exclusive jurisdiction on the high seas, and this by the highest authority, the consent of the people. Suppose ten acres at West-Point shall be used as a fort of the union, or a sea port town as a dockyard: the laws of the union, in those places, respecting the navy, forces of the union, and all federal objects, must prevail, be noticed by all judges and officers, and executed accordingly. And I can discern no one reason for excluding from these places, the operation of state laws, as to mere state purpose for instance, for the collection of state taxes in them; recovering debts; deciding questions of property arising within them on state laws; punishing, by state laws, theft, trespasses, and offenses committed in them by mere citizens against the state law.

The city, and all the places in which the union shall have this exclusive jurisdiction, will be immediately under one entire government, that of the federal head, and be no part of any state, and consequently no part of the United States. The inhabitants of the federal city and places, will be as much exempt from the laws and control of the state governments, as the people of Canada or Nova Scotia will be. Neither the laws of the states respecting taxes, the militia, crimes of property, will extend to them; nor is there a single stipulation in the constitution, that the inhabitants of this city, and these places, shall be governed by laws founded on principles of freedom. All questions, civil and criminal, arising on the laws of these places, which must be the laws of congress, must be decided in the federal courts; and also, all questions that may, by such judicial fictions as these courts may consider reasonable, be supposed to arise within this city, or any of these places, may be brought into these courts. By a very common legal fiction, any personal contract may be supposed to have been made in any place. A contract made in Georgia may be supposed to have been made in the federal city; the courts will admit the fiction. . . .

Every suit in which an inhabitant of a federal district may be a party, of course may be instituted in the federal courts; also, every suit in which it may be alleged and not denied, that a party in it is an inhabitant of such a district; also, every suit to which a foreign state or subject, the union, a state, citizens of different states in fact, or by reasonable legal fictions, may be a party or parties.

And thus, by means of bankrupt laws, federal districts, etc., almost all judicial business, I apprehend may be carried into the federal courts, without essentially departing from the usual course of judicial proceedings. The courts in Great Britain have acquired their powers, and extended very greatly their jurisdictions by such :fiction and suppositions as I have mentioned.

The constitution, in these points, certainly involves in it principles, and almost hidden cases, which may unfold and in time exhibit consequences we hardly think of. The power of

naturalization, when viewed in connection with the judicial powers and cases, is, in my mind, of very doubtful extent. By the constitution itself, the citizens of each state will be naturalized citizens of every state, to the general purposes of instituting suits, claiming the benefits of the laws, etc. And in order to give the federal courts jurisdiction of an action, between citizens of the same state, in common acceptation- may not a court allow the plaintiff to say, he is a citizen of one state, and the defendant a citizen of another without carrying legal fictions so far, by any means, as they have been carried by the courts of King's Bench and Exchequer, in order to bring causes within their cognizance? Further, the federal city and districts, will be totally distinct from any state, and a citizen of a state will not of course be subject of any of them. And to avail himself of the privileges and immunities of them, must he not be naturalized by congress in them? And may not congress make any proportion of the citizens of the states naturalized subjects of the federal city and districts, and thereby entitle them to sue or defend, in all cases, in the federal courts? I have my doubts, and many sensible men, I find, have their doubts, on these points. And we ought to observe, they must be settled in the courts of law, by their rules, distinctions, and fictions. To avoid many of these intricacies and difficulties, and to avoid the undue and unnecessary extension of the federal judicial powers, it appears to me that no federal districts ought to be allowed, and no federal city or town-except perhaps a small town, in which the government shall be republican, but in which congress shall have no jurisdiction over the inhabitants of the states. Can the union want, in such a town, any thing more than a right to the soil to which it may set its buildings, and extensive jurisdiction over the federal buildings, and property, its own members, officers, and servants in it? As to all federal objects, the union will have complete jurisdiction over them of course any where, and every where. I still think that no actions ought to be allowed to be brought in the federal courts, between citizens of different states; at least, unless the cause be of very considerable importance. And that no action against a state government, by any citizen or foreigner, ought to be allowed; and no action, in which a foreign subject is party, at least, unless it be of very considerable importance, ought to be instituted in federal courts. I confess, I can see no reason whatever, for a foreigner, or for citizens of different states, carrying sixpenny causes into the federal courts. I think the state courts will be found by experience, to be bottomed on better principles, and to administer justice better than the federal courts. The difficulties and dangers I have supposed will result from so large a federal city, and federal districts, from the extension of the federal judicial powers, etc. are not, I conceive, merely possible, but probable. I think pernicious political consequences will follow from them, and from the federal city especially, for very obvious reasons, a few of which I will mention.

We must observe that the citizens of a state will be subject to state as well as federal taxes, and the inhabitants of the federal city and districts only to such taxes as congress may lay. We are not to suppose all our people are attached to free government, and the principles of the common law, but that many thousands of them will prefer a city governed not on republican principles. This city, and the government of it, must indubitably take their tone from the characters of the men, who from the nature of its situation and institution must collect there. This city will not be established for productive labor, for mercantile, or mechanic industry; but for the residence of government, its officers and attendants. If hereafter it should ever become a place of trade and industry, [yet] in the early periods of its existence, when its laws and government must receive their fixed tone, it must be a mere court, with its appendages-the executive, congress, the law courts, gentlemen of fortune and pleasure, with all the officers, attendants, suitors, expectants

and dependents on the whole. However brilliant and honorable this collection may be, if we expect it will have any sincere attachments to simple and frugal republicanism, to that liberty and mild government, which is dear to the laborious part of a free people, we must assuredly deceive ourselves. This early collection will draw to it men from all parts of the country, of a like political description. We see them looking towards the place already.

Such a city, or town, containing a hundred square miles, must soon be the great, the visible, and dazzling centre, the mistress of fashions, and the fountain of politics. There may be a free or shackled press in this city, and the streams which may issue from it may over flow the country, and they will be poisonous or pure, as the fountain may be corrupt or not. But not to dwell on a subject that must give pain to the virtuous friends of freedom, I will only add, can a free and enlightened people create a common head so extensive, so prone to corruption and slavery, as this city probably will be, when they have it in their power to form one pure and chaste, frugal and republican?
THE FEDERAL FARMER

ANTI-FEDERALIST PAPER NO. 44

What Congress Can Do; What A State Can Not

"DELIBERATOR" appeared in The Freeman's Journal; or, The North-American Intelligencer, February 20, 1788.
A writer in the Pennsylvania Packet, under the signature of A Freeman, has lately entered the lists as another champion for the proposed constitution. Particularly he has endeavored to show that our apprehensions of this plan of government being a consolidation of the United States into one government, and not a confederacy of sovereign independent states, is entirely groundless; and it must be acknowledged that he has advocated this cause with as much show of reason, perhaps, as the subject will admit.

The words states, several states, and united states are, he observes, frequently mentioned in the constitution. And this is an argument that their separate sovereignty and independence cannot be endangered! He has enumerated a variety of matters which, he says, congress cannot do; and which the states, in their individual capacity, must or may do, and thence infers their sovereignty and independence. In some of these, however, I apprehend he is a little mistaken.
1. "Congress cannot train the militia." This is not strictly true. For by the 1st Article they are empowered "to provide for organizing, arming, and disciplining" them; and tho' the respective states are said to have the authority of training the militia, it must be "according to the discipline prescribed by Congress." In this business, therefore, they will be no other than subalterns under Congress, to execute their orders; which, if they shall neglect to do, Congress will have constitutional powers to provide for, by any other means they shall think proper. They shall have power to declare what description of persons shall compose the militia; to appoint the stated times and places for exercising them; to compel personal attendance, whether when called for into actual service, or on other occasions, under what penalties they shall think proper, without regard to scruples of

conscience or any other consideration. Their executive officer may march and countermarch them from one extremity of the state to the other-and all this without so much as consulting the legislature of the particular states to which they belong! Where then is that boasted security against the annihilation of the state governments, arising from "the powerful military support" they will have from their militia?

2. "Congress cannot enact laws for the inspection of the produce of the country." Neither is this strictly true. Their power "to regulate commerce with foreign nations and among the several states, and to make all laws which shall be necessary and proper for carrying this power (among others vested in them by the constitution) into execution," most certainly extends to the enacting of inspection laws. The particular states may indeed propose such laws to them; but it is expressly declared, in the 1st article, that "all such laws shall be subject to the revision and control of the Congress."

3. "The several states can prohibit or impose duties on the importation of slaves into their own ports." Nay, not even this can they do, "without the consent of Congress," as is expressly

declared in the close of the 1st article. The duty which Congress may, and it is probable will lay on the importation of slaves, will form a branch of their revenue. But this impost, as well as all others, "must be uniform throughout the United States." Congress therefore cannot consent that one state should impose an additional duty on this article of commerce, unless all other states should do the same; and it is not very likely that some of the states will ever ask this favor.

4. "Congress cannot interfere with the opening of rivers and canals; the making or regulation of roads, except post roads; building bridges; erecting ferries; building lighthouses, etc." In one case, which may very frequently happen, this proposition also fails. For if the river, canal, road, bridge, ferry, etc., be common to two states, or a matter in which they may be both concerned, and consequently must both concur, then the interference and consent of Congress becomes absolutely necessary, since it is declared in the constitution that "no state shall, without the consent of Congress, enter into any agreement or compact with another state."

5. "The elections of the President, Vice President, senators and representatives are exclusively in the hands of the states-even as to filling vacancies." This, in one important part, is not true. For, by the 2d article, "in case of the removal of the President from office, or of his death, resignation, or inability to discharge the duties of the said office, the same shall devolve on the Vice President, and the Congress may by law provide for the case of removal, death, etc., both of the President and Vice President, declaring what officer shall then act as president, and such officer shall act accordingly, until the disability be removed, or a president shall be elected." But no such election is provided for by the constitution, till the return of the periodical election at the expiration of the four years for which the former president was chosen. And thus may the great powers of this supreme magistrate of the United States be exercised, for years together, by a man who, perhaps, never had one vote of the people for any office of government in his life.

6. "Congress cannot interfere with the constitution of any state." This has been often said, but alas, with how little truth-since it is declared in the 6th article that "this constitution and the laws of the United States which shall be made in pursuance thereof, and all treaties, etc., shall be the supreme law of the land, and every state shall be bound thereby, anything in the constitution or laws of any state to the contrary notwithstanding."

But, sir, in order to form a proper judgment of the probable effects of this plan of general government on the sovereignties of the several states, it is necessary also to take a view of what Congress may, constitutionally, do and of what the states may not do. This matter, however, the above writer has thought proper to pass over in silence. I would therefore beg leave in some measure, to supply this omission; and if in anything I should appear to be mistaken I hope he will take the same liberty with me that I have done with him-he will correct my mistake.

1. Congress may, even in time of peace, raise an army of 100,000 men, whom they may canton through the several states, and billet out on the inhabitants, in order to serve as necessary instruments in executing their decrees.

2. Upon the inhabitants of any state proving refractory to the will of Congress, or upon any other pretense whatsoever, Congress may can out even all the militia of as many states as they think

proper, and keep them in actual service, without pay, as long as they please, subject to the utmost rigor of military discipline, corporal punishment, and death itself not excepted.

3. Congress may levy and collect a capitation or poll tax, to what amount they shall think proper; of which the poorest taxable in the state must pay as much as the richest.

4. Congress may, under the sanction of that clause in the constitution which empowers them to regulate commerce, authorize the importation of slaves, even into those states where this iniquitous trade is or may be prohibited by their laws or constitutions.

5. Congress may, under the sanction of that clause which empowers them to lay and collect duties (as distinct from imposts and excises) impose so heavy a stamp duty on newspapers and other periodical publications, as shall effectually prevent all necessary information to the people through these useful channels of intelligence.

6. Congress may, by imposing a duty on foreigners coming into the country, check the progress of its population. And after a few years they may prohibit altogether, not only the emigration of foreigners into our country, but also that of our own citizens to any other country.

7. Congress may withhold, as long as they think proper, all information respecting their proceedings from the people.

8. Congress may order the elections for members of their own body, in the several states, to be held at what times, in what places, and in what manner they shall think proper. Thus, in Pennsylvania, they may order the elections to be held in the middle of winter, at the city of Philadelphia; by which means the inhabitants of nine-tenths of the state will be effectually (tho' constitutionally) deprived of the exercise of their right of suffrage.

9. Congress may, in their courts of judicature, abolish trial by jury in civil cases altogether; and even in criminal cases, trial by a jury of the vicinage is not secured by the constitution. A crime committed at Fort Pitt may be tried by a jury of the citizens of Philadelphia.

10. Congress may, if they shall think it for the "general welfare," establish an uniformity in religion throughout the United States. Such establishments have been thought necessary, and have accordingly taken place in almost all the other countries in the world, and will no doubt be thought equally necessary in this.

11. Though I believe it is not generally so understood, yet certain it is, that Congress may emit paper money, and even make it a legal tender throughout the United States; and, what is still worse, may, after it shall have depreciated in the hands of the people, call it in by taxes, at any rate of depreciation (compared with gold and silver) which they may think proper. For though no state can emit bills of credit, or pass any law impairing the obligation of contracts, yet the Congress themselves are under no constitutional restraints on these points.

12. The number of representatives which shall compose the principal branch of Congress is so small as to occasion general complaint. Congress, however, have no power to increase the number of representatives, but may reduce it even to one fifth part of the present arrangement.

13. On the other hand, no state can call forth its militia even to suppress any insurrection or domestic violence which may take place among its own citizens. This power is, by the constitution, vested in Congress.

14. No state can compel one of its own citizens to pay a debt due to a citizen of a neighboring state. Thus a Jersey-man will be unable to recover the price of a turkey sold in the Philadelphia market, if the purchaser shall be inclined to dispute, without commencing an action in one of the federal courts.

15. No state can encourage its own manufactures either by prohibiting or even laying a duty on the importation of foreign articles.

16. No state can give relief to insolvent debtors, however distressing their situation may be, since Congress will have the exclusive right of establishing uniform laws on the subject of bankruptcies throughout the United States; and the particular states are expressly prohibited from passing any law impairing the obligation of contracts.
DELIBERATOR

ANTI-FEDERALIST PAPER NO. 45

Powers Of National Government Dangerous To State Governments; New York As An Example

Robert Yates, a delegate to the 1787 convention from New York, left on July 10, 1787. He became an Antifederalist leader. Under the nome de plume "Sydney" he wrote in the New York Daily Patriotic Register, June 13 and 14, 1788.
TO THE CITIZENS OF THE STATE OF NEW YORK.
Although a variety of objections to the proposed new constitution for the government of the United States have been laid before the public by men of the best abilities, I am led to believe that representing it in a point of view which has escaped their observation may be of use, that is, by comparing it with the constitution of the State of New York.

Documents of Revolution

The following contrast is therefore submitted to the public, to show in what instances the powers of the state government will be either totally or partially absorbed, and enable us to determine whether the remaining powers will, from those kind of pillars, be capable of supporting the mutilated fabric of a government which even the advocates for the new constitution admit excels

"the boasted models of Greece or Rome, and those of all other nations, in having precisely marked out the power of the government and the rights of the people."

It may be proper to premise that the pressure of necessity and distress (and not corruption) had a principal tendency to induce the adoption of the state constitutions and the existing confederation; that power was even then vested in the rulers with the greatest caution; and that, as from every circumstance we have reason to infer that the Dew constitution does not originate from a pure source, we ought deliberately to trace the extent and tendency of the trust we are about to repose, under the conviction that a reassumption of that trust will at least be difficult, if not impracticable. If we take a retrospective view of the measures of Congress. . . . we can scarcely entertain a doubt but that a plan has long since been framed to subvert the confederation; that that plan has been matured with the most persevering industry and unremitted attention; and that the objects expressed in the preamble to the constitution, that is "to promote the general welfare and secure the blessings of liberty to ourselves and our posterity," were merely the ostensible, and not the real reasons of its framers. . .

The state governments are considered in . . . [the new constitution] as mere dependencies, existing solely by its toleration, and possessing powers of which they may be deprived whenever the general government is disposed so to do. If then the powers of the state governments are to be totally absorbed, in which all agree, and only differ as to the mode-whether it will be effected by a rapid progression, or by as certain, but slower, operations-what is to limit the oppression of the general government? Where are the rights, which are declared to be incapable of violation?

And what security have people against the wanton oppression of unprincipled governors? No constitutional redress is pointed out, and no express declaration is contained in it, to limit the

boundaries of their rulers. Beside which the mode and period of their being elected tends to take away their responsibility to the people over whom they may, by the power of the purse and the sword, domineer at discretion. Nor is there a power on earth to tell them, What dost thou? or, Why dost thou so? I shall now proceed to compare the constitution of the state of New York with the proposed federal government, distinguishing the paragraphs in the former, which are rendered nugatory by the latter; those which are in a great measure enervated, and such as are in the discretion of the general government to permit or not....

1 & 37

The 1st "Ordains, determines, and declares that no authority shall on any pretence whatever be exercised over the people or the members of this State, but such as shall be derived from and granted by them."

The 37th, "That no purchases or contracts for the sale of lands with or of the Indians within the limits of this state, shall be binding on the Indians, or deemed valid, unless made under the authority and with the consent of the legislature of this state."

. . . What have we reasonably to expect will be their conduct [i.e., the new national government]

when possessed of the powers "to regulate commerce with foreign nations, and among the several states, and with the Indian tribes," when they are armed with legislative, executive, and judicial powers, and their laws the supreme laws of the land. And when the states are prohibited, without the consent of Congress, to lay any "imposts or duties on imports," and if they do they shall be for the use of the Treasury of the United States-and all such laws subject to the revision and control of Congress.

It is . . . evident that this state, by adopting the new government, will enervate their legislative rights, and totally surrender into the hands of Congress the management and regulation of the Indian trade to an improper government, and the traders to be fleeced by iniquitous impositions, operating at one and the same time as a monopoly and a poll-tax. . . .

The 2nd provides "that the supreme legislative power within this state shall be vested in two separate and distinct bodies of men, the one to be called the assembly, and the other to be called the senate of the state of New York, who together shall form the legislature."

The 3rd provides against laws that may be hastily and inadvertently passed, inconsistent with the spirit of the constitution and the public good, and that "the governor, the chancellor and judges of the supreme court, shall revise all bills about to be passed into laws, by the legislature."

The 9th provides "that the assembly shall be the judge of their own members, and enjoy the same privileges, and proceed in doing business in like manner as the assembly of the colony of New York of right formerly did."

The 12th provides "that the senate shall, in like manner, be judges of their own members," etc.

Documents of Revolution

The 31st describes even the style of laws—that the style of all laws shall be as follows: "Be it enacted by the people of the state of New York represented in senate and assembly," and that all writs and proceedings shall run in the name of the people of the state of New York, and tested in the name of the chancellor or the chief judge from whence they shall issue.

The powers vested in the legislature of this state by these paragraphs will be weakened, for the proposed new government declares that "all legislative powers therein granted shall be vested in a congress of the United States, which shall consist of a senate and a house of representatives,"

and it further prescribes, that "this constitution and the laws of the United States, which shall be made in pursuance thereof; and all treaties made, or which shalt be made under the authority of the United States, shall be the supreme law of the land, and the judges in every state shall be bound thereby, anything in the constitution or laws of any state to the contrary notwithstanding; and the members of the several state legislatures, and all executive and judicial officers, both of the United States and of the several states, shall be bound by oath or affirmation to support this constitution."

Those who are full of faith, suppose that the words "in pursuance thereof" are restrictive, but if they reflect a moment and take into consideration the comprehensive expressions of the instrument, they will find that their restrictive construction is unavailing, and this is evidenced by 1st art., 8th sect., where this government has a power "to lay and collect all taxes, duties, imposts and excises, to pay the debts, and provide for the common defense and general welfare of the United States," and also "to make all laws which shall be necessary and proper for carrying into execution the foregoing powers vested by this constitution in the government of the United States, or in any department or office thereof."

.... To conclude my observation on this head, it appears to me as impossible that these powers in the state constitution and those in the general government can exist and operate together, as it would be for a man to serve two masters whose interests clash, and secure the approbation of both. Can there at the same time and place be and operate two supreme legislatures, executives, and judicials? Will a "guarantee of a republican form of government to every state in the union" be of any avail, or secure the establishment and retention of state rights?

If this guarantee had remained, as it was first reported by the committee of the whole house, to wit, "that a republican constitution, and its existing laws, ought to be guaranteed to each state by the United States," it would have been substantial; but the changing the word constitution into the word form bears no favorable appearance. . . .

13, 35, 41

By the 13th paragraph "no member of this State shall be disfranchised, or deprived of any of the rights or privileges secured to the subjects of the State by the constitution, unless by the law of the land, or judgment of its peers."

The 35th adopts, under certain exceptions and modifications, the common law of England, the statute law of England and Great Britain, and the acts of the legislature of the colony, which together formed the law on the 19th of April, 1775.

The 41st provides "that the trial by jury remain inviolate forever; that no acts of attainder shall be passed by the legislature of this State for crimes other than those committed before the termination of the present war. And that the legislature shall at no time hereafter institute any new courts but such as shall proceed according to the course of the common law.

There can be no doubt that if the new government be adopted in all its latitude, every one of these paragraphs will become a dead letter. Nor will it solve any difficulties, if the United States guarantee "to every state in the union a republican form of government;" we may be allowed the form and not the substance, and that it was so intended will appear from the changing the word constitution to the word form and the omission of the words, and its existing laws. And I do not even think it uncharitable to suppose that it was designedly done; but whether it was so or not, by leaving out these words the jurisprudence of each state is left to the mercy of the new government....

17, 18, 19, 20, 21, 27, 40

The 17th orders "That the supreme executive power and authority of this State shall be vested in a governor."

By the 18th he is commander-in-chief of the militia and admiral of the navy of the State; may grant pardons to all persons convicted of crimes; he may suspend the execution of the sentence in treason or murder.

By the 19th paragraph he is to see that the laws and resolutions of the legislature be faithfully executed.

The 20th and 21st paragraphs give the lieutenant-governor, on the death, resignation, removal from office, or impeachment of the governor, all the powers of a governor.

By the 27th he [the Governor] is president of the council of appointment, and has a casting vote and the commissioning of all officers.

The 40th paragraph orders that the militia at all times, both in peace and war, shall be armed and disciplined, and kept in readiness; in what manner the Quakers shall be excused; and that a magazine of warlike stores be forever kept at the expense of the State, and by act of the legislature, established, maintained, and continued in every county in the State.

Documents of Revolution

Whoever considers the following powers vested in the [national] government, and compares them with the above, must readily perceive they are either all enervated or annihilated.

By the 1st art., 8th sec., 15th, 16th and 17th clauses, Congress will be empowered to call forth the militia to execute the laws of the union, suppress insurrections and repel invasions; to provide for organizing, arming and disciplining the militia, for the governing such part of them as may be employed in the service of the United States, and for the erection of forts, magazines, etc.

And by the 2nd art., 2nd sec., "The president shall be commander- in-chief of the army and navy of the United States, and of the militia of the several States when called into actual service of the United States. . . . except in cases of impeachment."

And by the 6th art., "The members of the several state legislatures, and all the executive and judicial officers; both of the United States, and of the several states, shall be bound by oath or affirmation to support the constitution."

Can this oath be taken by those who have already taken one under the constitution of this state?

... From these powers lodged in Congress and the powers vested in the states, it is clear that there must be a government within a government; two legislative, executive, and judicial powers. The power of raising an army in time of peace, and to command the militia, will give the president ample means to enforce the supreme laws of the land. . . .

42

This paragraph provides "that it shalt be in the discretion of the legislature to naturalize all such persons and in such manner as they shall think proper."

The 1st art., 8th sec., 4th clause, give to the new government power to establish a uniform rule of naturalization. And by the 4th art., 2nd sec., "the citizens of each state shall be entitled to all the privileges and immunities of citizens in the several states," whereby the clause is rendered entirely nugatory.

From this contrast it appears that the general government, when completely organized, will absorb all those powers of the state which the framers of its constitution had declared should be only exercised by the representatives of the people of the state; that the burdens and expense of supporting a state establishment will be perpetuated; but its operations to ensure or contribute to any essential measures promotive of the happiness of the people may be totally prostrated, the general government arrogating to itself the right of interfering in the most minute objects of internal police, and the most trifling domestic concerns of every state, by possessing a power of passing laws "to provide for the general welfare of the United States," which may affect life, liberty and property in every modification they may think expedient, unchecked by cautionary reservations, and unrestrained by a declaration of any of those rights which the wisdom and prudence of America in the year 1776 held ought to be at all events protected from violation.

In a word, the new constitution will prove finally to dissolve all the power of the several state legislatures, and destroy the rights and liberties of the people; for the power of the first will be all in all, and of the latter a mere shadow and form without substance, and if adopted we may (in imitation of the Carthagenians) say, Delenda vit America.

SYDNEY

ANTI-FEDERALIST PAPER NO. 46

"Where Then Is The Restraint?"

This essay by "AN OLD WHIG" (see AFP #'s Nos. 18-20, 49, 50, and 70) appeared in the Maryland Gazette and Baltimore Advertiser on Nov. 2, 1788.

Let us look to the first article of the proposed new constitution, which treats of the legislative powers of Congress; and to the eighth section, which pretends to define those powers. We find here that the Congress in its legislative capacity, shall have the power to lay and collect taxes, duties, and excises; to borrow money; to regulate commerce; to fix the rule for naturalization and the laws of bankruptcy; to coin money; to punish counterfeiters; to establish post offices and post roads; to secure copy rights to authors; to constitute tribunals; to define and punish piracies; to declare war; to raise and support armies; to provide and support a navy; to call forth the militia; to organize, arm and discipline the militia; to exercise absolute power over a district ten miles square, independent of all the State legislatures, and to be alike absolute over all forts, magazines, arsenals, dock-yards, and other needful buildings thereunto belonging. This is a short abstract of the powers given to Congress. These powers are very extensive, but I shall not stay at present to inquire whether these express powers were necessary to be given to Congress?

Whether they are too great or too small?

My object is to consider that undefined, unbounded and immense power which is comprised in the following clause - "And to make all laws which shall be necessary and proper for carrying into execution the foregoing powers, and all other powers vested by this constitution in the government of the United States; or in any department or offices thereof." Under such a clause as this, can anything be said to be reserved and kept back from Congress? Can it be said that the Congress have no power but what is expressed? "To make all laws which shall be necessary and proper" - or, in other words, to make all such laws which the Congress shall think necessary and proper - for who shalt judge for the legislature what is necessary and proper? Who shall set themselves above the sovereign? What inferior legislature shall set itself above the supreme legislature? To me it appears that no other power on earth can dictate to them, or control them, unless by force; and force, either internal or external, is one of those calamities which every good man would wish his country at all times to be delivered from. This generation in America have seen enough of war, and its usual concomitants, to prevent all of us from wishing to see any more of it-all except those who make a trade of war. But to the question - without force what can restrain the Congress from making such laws as they please? What limits are there to their authority? I fear none at all. For surely it cannot be justly said that they have no power but what is expressly given to them, when by the very terms of their creation they are vested with the powers of making laws in all cases -necessary and proper; when from the nature of their power, they must necessarily be the judges what laws are necessary and proper.

The British act of Parliament, declaring the power of Parliament to make laws to bind America in all cases whatsoever, was not more extensive. For it is as true as a maxim, that even the British Parliament neither could nor would pass any law in any case in which they did not either deem it necessary and proper to make such a law, or pretend to deem it so. And in such cases it is not of a farthing consequence whether they really are of opinion that the law is necessary and proper, or only pretend to think so, for who can overrule their pretensions? No one; unless we had a Bill of

Rights, to which we might appeal and under which we might contend against any assumption of undue power, and appeal to the judicial branch of the government to protect us by their judgments. This reasoning, I fear, is but too just. And yet, if any man should doubt the truth of it, let me ask him one other question: What is the meaning of the latter part of the clause which vests the Congress with the authority of making all laws which shall be necessary and proper for carrying into execution all other powers (besides the foregoing powers vested, etc., etc.)? Was it thought that the foregoing powers might perhaps admit of some restraint, in their construction as to what was necessary and proper to carry them into execution? Or was it deemed right to add still further that they should not be restrained to the powers already named? Besides the powers already mentioned, other powers may be assumed hereafter as contained by implication in this constitution. The Congress shall judge of what is necessary and proper in all these cases, and in all other cases-in short, in all cases whatsoever.

Where then is the restraint? How are Congress bound down to the powers expressly given? What is reserved, or can be reserved? Yet even this is not all. As if it were determined that no doubt should remain, by the sixth article of the Constitution it is declared that "this Constitution and the laws of the United States which shall be made in pursuance thereof, and all treaties made, or which shall be made, under the authority of the United States, shalt be the supreme law of the land, and the judges in every state shall be bound thereby, any thing in the Constitutions or laws of any State to the contrary notwithstanding." The Congress are therefore vested with the supreme legislative power, without control. In giving such immense, such unlimited powers, was there no necessity of a Bill of Rights, to secure to the people their liberties?

Is it not evident that we are left wholly dependent on the wisdom and virtue of the men who shall from time to time be the members of Congress? And who shall be able to say seven years hence, the members of Congress will be wise and good men, or of the contrary character?

ANTI-FEDERALIST PAPER NO. 47

"balance" Of Departments Not Achieved Under New Constitution

This essay is made up of of excerpts from "CENTINEL's," letters of October 5 and 24, 1787.

Documents of Revolution

Taken from The Independent Gazetteer,

I am fearful that the principles of government inculcated in Mr. [John] Adams' treatise [Defence of the Constitutions of Government of the United States of America], and enforced in the numerous essays and paragraphs in the newspapers, have misled some well designing members of the late Convention. But it will appear in the sequel, that the construction of the proposed plan of government is infinitely more extravagant.

I have been anxiously expecting that some enlightened patriot would, ere this, have taken up the pen to expose the futility, and counteract the baneful tendency of such principles. Mr. Adams'

sine qua non of a good government is three balancing powers; whose repelling qualities are to produce an equilibrium of interests, and thereby promote the happiness of the whole community.

He asserts that the administrators of every government, will ever be actuated by views of private interest and ambition, to the prejudice of the public good; that therefore the only effectual method to secure the rights of the people and promote their welfare, is to create an opposition of interests between the members of two distinct bodies, in the exercise of the powers of government, and balanced by those of a third. This hypothesis supposes human wisdom competent to the task of instituting three co-equal orders in government, and a corresponding weight in the community to enable them respectively to exercise their several parts, and whose views and interests should be so distinct as to prevent a coalition of any two of them for the destruction of the third. Mr. Adams, although he has traced the constitution of every form of government that ever existed, as far as history affords materials, has not been able to adduce a single instance of such a government. He indeed says that the British constitution is such in theory, but this is rather a confirmation that his principles are chimerical and not to be reduced to practice. If such an organization of power were practicable, how long would it continue? Not a day–for there is so great a disparity in the talents, wisdom and industry of mankind, that the scale would presently preponderate to one or the other body, and with every accession of power the means of further increase would be greatly extended. The state of society in England is much more favorable to such a scheme of government than that of America. There they have a powerful hereditary nobility, and real distinctions of rank and interests; but even there, for want of that perfect equality of power and distinction of interests in the three orders of government, they exist but in name. The only operative and efficient check upon the conduct of administration, is the sense of the people at large.

Suppose a government could be formed and supported on such principles, would it answer the great purposes of civil society? If the administrators of every government are actuated by views of private interest and ambition, how is the welfare and happiness of the community to be the result of such jarring adverse interests?

Therefore, as different orders in government will not produce the good of the whole, we must recur to other principles. I believe it will be found that the form of government, which holds

those entrusted with power in the greatest responsibility to their constituents, the best calculated for freemen. A republican, or free government, can only exist where the body of the people are virtuous, and where property is pretty equally divided. In such a government the people are the sovereign and their sense or opinion is the criterion of every public measure. For when this ceases to be the case, the nature of the government is changed, and an aristocracy, monarchy or despotism will rise on its ruin. The highest responsibility is to be attained in a simple structure of government, for the great body of the people never steadily attend to the operations of government, and for want of due information are liable to be imposed on. If you complicate the plan by various orders, the people will be perplexed and divided in their sentiment about the source of abuses or misconduct; some will impute it to the senate, others to the house of representatives, and so on, that the interposition of the people may be rendered imperfect or perhaps wholly abortive. But if, imitating the constitution of Pennsylvania, you vest all the legislative power in one body of men (separating the executive and judicial) elected for a short period, and necessarily excluded by rotation from permanency, and guarded from precipitancy and surprise by delays imposed on its proceedings, you will create the most perfect responsibility. For then, whenever the people feel a grievance, they cannot mistake the authors, and will apply the remedy with certainty and effect, discarding them at the next election. This tie of responsibility will obviate all the dangers apprehended from a single legislature, and will the best secure the rights of the people.

Having premised this much, I shall now proceed to the examination of the proposed plan of government, and I trust, shall make it appear to the meanest capacity, that it has none of the essential requisites of a free government; that it is neither founded on those balancing restraining powers, recommended by Mr. Adams and attempted in the British constitution, or possessed of that responsibility to its constituents, which, in my opinion, is the only effectual security for the liberties and happiness of the people. But on the contrary, that it is a most daring attempt to establish a despotic aristocracy among freemen, that the world has ever witnessed....

Documents of Revolution

Thus we see, the house of representatives are on the part of the people to balance the senate, who I suppose will be composed of the better sort, the well born, etc. The number of the representatives (being only one for every 30,000 inhabitants) appears to be too few, either to communicate the requisite information of the wants, local circumstances and sentiments of so extensive an empire, or to prevent corruption and undue influence, in the exercise of such great powers; the term for which they are to be chosen, too long to preserve a due dependence and accountability to their constituents; and the mode and places of their election not sufficiently ascertained, for as Congress have the control over both, they may govern the choice, by ordering the representatives of a whole State, to be elected in one place, and that too may be the most inconvenient.

The senate, the great efficient body in this plan of government, is constituted on the most unequal principles. The smallest State in the Union has equal weight with the great States of Virginia, Massachusetts, or Pennsylvania. The senate, besides its legislative functions, has a very considerable share in the executive; none of the principal appointments to office can be made without its advice and consent. The term and mode of its appointment will lead to permanency.

The members are chosen for six years, the mode is under the control of Congress, and as there is no exclusion by rotation, they may be continued for life, which, from their extensive means of

influence, would follow of course. The President, who would be a mere pageant of State, unless he coincides with the views of the senate, would either become the head of the aristocratic junto in that body, or its minion; besides, their influence being the most predominant, could the best secure his re-election to office. And from his power of granting pardons, he might screen from punishment the most treasonable attempts on the liberties of the people, when instigated by the senate....

Mr. [James] Wilson asserts that never was charge made with less reason, than that which predicts the institution of a baneful aristocracy in the federal Senate.' In my first number, I stated that this body would be a very unequal representation of the several States, that the members being appointed for the long term of six years, and there being no exclusion by rotation, they might be continued for life, which would follow of course from their extensive means of influence, and that possessing a considerable share in the executive as well as the legislative, it would become a permanent aristocracy, and swallow up the other orders in the government.

That these fears are not imaginary, a knowledge of the history of other nations, where the powers of government have been injudiciously placed, will fully demonstrate. Mr. Wilson says, "the senate branches into two characters; the one legislative and the other executive. In its legislative character it can effect no purpose, without the co-operation of the house of representatives, and in its executive character it can accomplish no object without the concurrence of the president.

Thus fettered, I do not know any act which the senate can of itself perform, and such dependence necessarily precludes every idea of influence and superiority." This I confess is very specious, but experience demonstrates that checks in government, unless accompanied with adequate power and independently placed, prove merely nominal, and will be inoperative. Is it probable, that the President of the United States, limited as he is in power, and dependent on the will of the senate, in appointments to office, will either have the firmness or inclination to exercise his prerogative of a conditional control upon the proceedings of that body, however injurious they may be to the public welfare? It will be his interest to coincide with the views of the senate, and thus become the head of the aristocratic junto. The king of England is a constituent part in the legislature, but although an hereditary monarch, in possession of the whole executive power, including the unrestrained appointment to offices, and an immense revenue, enjoys but in name the prerogative of a negative upon the parliament. Even the king of England, circumstanced as he is, has not dared to exercise it for near a century past. The check of the house of representatives upon the senate will likewise be rendered nugatory for want of due weight in the democratic branch, and from their constitution they may become so independent of the people as to be indifferent of its interests. Nay, as Congress would have the control over the mode and place of their election, by ordering the representatives of a whole state to be elected at one place, and that too the most inconvenient, the ruling powers may govern the choice, and thus the house of representatives may be composed of the creatures of the senate. Still the semblance of checks may remain, but without operation.

This mixture of the legislative and executive moreover highly tends to corruption. The chief improvement in government, in modern times, has been the complete separation of the great distinctions of power; placing the legislative in different hands from those which hold the executive; and again severing the judicial part from the ordinary administrative. "When the legislative and executive powers (says Montesquieu) are united in the same person or in the same body of magistrates, there can be no liberty."

CENTINEL

ANTI-FEDERALIST PAPER NO. 48

No Separation Of Departments Results In No Responsibility

"LEONIDAS," from London, obviously did not understand Article II Section I of the proposed new Constitution. But his works were welcomed in the London Times, and either The Freeman's Journal, or The North-American Intelligencer on July 30, 1788. In the new constitution for the future government of the thirteen United States of America, the President and Senate have all the executive and two thirds of the Legislative power.

This is a material deviation from those principles of the English constitution, for which they fought with us; and in all good governments it should be a fundamental maxim, that, to give a proper balance to the political system, the different branches of the legislature should be unconnected, and the legislative and executive powers should be separate. By the new constitution of America this union of the executive and legislative bodies operates in the most weighty matters of the state. They jointly make all treaties; they jointly appoint all officers civil and military; and, they jointly try all impeachments, either of their own members, or the officers appointed by themselves.

In this formidable combination of power, there is no responsibility. And where there is power without responsibility, how can there be liberty?

The president of the United States is elected for four years, and each of the thirteen states has one vote at his election; which vote is not of the people, but of electors two degrees from the people.

The senate is a body of six years duration; and as in the choice of presidents, the largest state has but one vote, so it is in the choice of senators. Now this shows, that responsibility is as little to be apprehended from amenability to constituents, as from the terror of impeachment; for to the members of the senate it is clear, that trial by impeachment is nothing but parade.

From such an union in governments, it requires no great depth of political knowledge to prophesy, that monarchy or aristocracy must be generated, and perhaps of the most grievous kind. The only check in favor of the democratic principle is the house of representatives; but its smallness of number, and great comparative disparity of power, render that house of little effect to promote good or restrain bad government.

The power given to this ill-constructed senate is, to judge of what may be for the general welfare; and such engagements, when made the acts of Congress, become the supreme laws of the land.

This is a power co-extensive with every possible object of human legislation. Yet there is no restraint, no charter of rights, no residuum of human privileges, not intended to be given up to society. The rights of conscience, the freedom of the press, and trial by jury, are at the mercy of this senate. Trial by jury has been already materially injured. The trial in criminal cases is not by twelve men of the vicinage, or of the county, but of the state; and the states are from fifty to seven hundred miles in extent! In criminal cases this new system says, the trial shall be by jury.

On civil cases it is silent. There it is fair to infer, that as in criminal cases it has been materially impaired, in civil cases it may be altogether omitted. But it is in truth, strongly discountenanced in civil cases; for this new system gives the supreme court in matters of appeal, jurisdiction both of law and fact.

This being the beginning of American freedom, it is very clear the ending will be slavery, for it cannot be denied that this constitution is, in its first principles, highly and dangerously oligarchical; and it is every where agreed, that a government administered by a few, is, of all governments, the worst.

LEONIDAS

ANTI-FEDERALIST PAPER NO. 49

(PART I) ON CONSTITUTIONAL CONVENTIONS

The following essay is in two parts: the first is by "MASSACHUSETTENSIS," and is reprinted from The Massachusetts Gazette of January 29, 1788; the second part was written by "AN OLD WHIG," and is taken from The New-York Journal of November 27, 1787.

That the new constitution cannot make a union of states, but only of individuals, and purposes the beginning of one new society, one new government in all matters, is evident from these considerations, viz: It marks no line of distinction between separate state matters, and what would of right come under the control of the powers ordained in a union of states. To say that no line could be drawn, is giving me the argument. For what can be more absurd than to say, that states are united where a general power is established that extends to all objects of government, i.e., all that exist among the people who make the compact? And is it not clear that Congress have the right (by the constitution), to make general laws for proving all acts, records, proceedings, and the effect thereof, in what are now called the states? Is it possible after this that any state act can exist, or any public business be done, without the direction and sanction of Congress, or by virtue of some subordinate authority? If not, how in the nature of things can there be a union of states? Does not the uniting of states, as states, necessarily imply the existence of separate state powers?

Again, the constitution makes no consistent, adequate provision for amendments to be made to it by states, as states. Not they who drew up the amendments (should any be made), but they who ratify them, must be considered as making them. Three fourths of the legislatures of the several states, as they are now called, may ratify amendments-that is, if Congress see fit, but not without.

Where is then any independent state authority recognized in the plan? And if there is no independent state authority, how can there be a union of states? But is it not a question of importance why the states in their present capacity, cannot ratify the original? I mean, why the legislatures of the several states cannot do this business? I wish to be informed where to find the regular exercise and legal sanction of state power, if the legislative authority of the state is set aside. Have the people some other constitutional means by which they can give their united voice in state affairs? This leads me to observe, that should the new constitution be received as it stands, it can never be proved that it originated from any proper state authority; because there is no such authority recognized either in the form of it, or in the mode fixed upon for its ratification. It says, "We the people of the United States," etc., make this constitution; but does this phrase, "We the people of the United States," prove that the people are acting in state character, or that the several states must of necessity exist with separate governments? Who that understands the subject will believe either? ...

The plan does not acknowledge any constitutional state authority as necessary in the ratification of it. This work is to be done by a mere convention, only in consequence of mere recommendation; which does by no means amount to a proper state act. As no state act can exist independent of the supreme authority of the state, and this authority is out of the question in the ratification of the new constitution, it clearly follows that the ratifying of it, by a mere convention, is no proper state business. To conclude, the people may make the original, but the people have no right to alter it. Congress may order this matter just as they please, and consequently have whom they please elected for governors or representatives, not of the states but of the people; and not of the people as men but as property. . . .

MASSACHUSETTENSIS

It appears to me that I was mistaken in supposing that we could so very easily make trial of this constitution, and again change it at our pleasure. The conventions of the several states cannot propose any alterations-they are only to give their assent and ratification. And after the constitution is once ratified, it must remain fixed until two thirds of both the houses of Congress shall deem it necessary to propose amendments; or the legislatures of two thirds of the several states shall make application to Congress for the calling a convention for proposing amendments

Documents of Revolution

- which amendments shall not be valid until they are ratified by the legislatures of three fourths of the several states, or by conventions in three fourths thereof, as one or the other mode of ratification may be proposed by Congress. This appears to me to be only a cunning way of saying that no alteration shall ever be made; so that whether it is a good constitution or a bad constitution, it will remain forever unamended. Lycurgus, when he promulgated his laws to the Spartans, made them swear that they would make no alterations in them until he should return from a journey which he was then about to undertake. He chose never to return, and therefore no alteration could be made in his laws. The people were made to believe that they could make trial of his laws for a few months or years, during his absence, and as soon as he returned they could continue to observe them or reject at pleasure. Thus this celebrated republic was in reality established by a trick. In like manner the proposed constitution holds out a prospect of being subject to be changed if it be found necessary or convenient to change it; but the conditions upon which an alteration can take place, are such as in all probability will never exist. The consequence will be that when the constitution is once established it never can be altered or amended without some violent convulsion or civil war. The conditions, I say, upon which any alterations can take place, appear to me to be such as never will exist. Two thirds of both houses of congress, or the legislatures of two thirds of the states, must agree in desiring a convention to be called. This will probably never happen. But if it should happen, then the convention may agree to the amendments or not, as they think right; and after all three fourths of the states must ratify the amendments. Before all this labyrinth can be traced to a conclusion, ages will revolve, and perhaps the great principles upon which our late glorious revolution was founded, will be totally forgotten. If the principles of liberty are not firmly fixed and established in the present constitution, in vain may we hope for retrieving them hereafter. People once possessed of power are always loathe to part with it; and we shall never find two thirds of a Congress voting or proposing anything which shall derogate from their own authority and importance, or agreeing to give back to the people any part of those privileges which they have once parted with-so far from it, that the greater occasion there may be for a reformation, the less likelihood will there be of accomplishing it. The greater the abuse of power, the more obstinately is it always persisted in. As to any expectation of two thirds of the legislatures concurring in such a request, it is if possible still more remote. The legislatures of the states will be but forms and shadows, and it will be the height of arrogance and presumption in them, to turn their thoughts to such high subjects. After this constitution is once established, it is too evident that we shall be obliged to fill up the offices of assemblymen and councillors, as we
do those of constables, by appointing men to serve whether they will or not, and fining them if they refuse. The members thus appointed, as soon as they can hurry through a law or two for repairing highways, or impounding cattle, will conclude the business of their sessions as suddenly as possible, that they may return to their own business. Their heads will not be perplexed with the great affairs of state. We need not expect two thirds of them ever to interfere in so momentous a question as that of calling a continental convention. The different legislatures will have no communication with one another, from the time of the new constitution being ratified to the end of the world. Congress will be the great focus of power as well as the great and only medium of communication from one state to another. The great and the wise and the mighty will be in possession of places and offices; they will oppose all changes in favor of liberty; they will steadily pursue the acquisition of more and more power to themselves and their adherents....

AN OLD WHIG

ANTI-FEDERALIST PAPER NO. 50

(Part II) On Constitutional Conventions

Antifederalists sought a second constitutional convention immediately after conclusion of the first. This essay by "AN OLD WHIG," is from either The Freeman's Journal or The North-American Intelligencer, of November 28, 1787.

It is true that the Continental Convention have directed their proposed constitution to be laid before a Convention of Delegates to be chosen in each state "for their assent and ratification,"

which seems to preclude the idea of any power in the several Conventions of proposing any alterations; or, indeed, even of rejecting the plan proposed if they should disapprove of it. Still, however, the question recurs, what authority the late Convention had to bind the people of the United States to any particular form of government, or to forbid them to adopt such form of government, as they should think fit. I know it is a language frequent in the mouths of some heaven-born Phaetons among us-who, like the son of Apollo, think themselves entitled to guide the chariot of the sun-that common people have no right to judge of the affairs of government; that they are not fit for it; that they should leave these matters to their superiors. This, however, is not the language of men of real understanding, even among the advocates for the proposed Constitution; but these still recognize the authority of the people, and will admit, at least in words, that the people have a right to be consulted. Then I ask, if the people in the different states have a right to be consulted in the new form of continental government, what authority could the late Convention have to preclude them from proposing amendments to the plan they should offer? Had the Convention any right to bind the people to the form of government they should propose? Let us consider this matter.

The late Convention were chosen by the General Assembly of each state. They had the sanction of Congress. For what? To consider what alterations were necessary to be made in the articles of Confederation. What have they done? They have made a new Constitution for the United States.

I will not say that in doing so they have exceeded their authority; but, on the other hand, I trust that no man of understanding among them will pretend to say that anything they did, or could do, was of the least avail to lessen the right of the people to judge for themselves in the last resort.

This right is perhaps unalienable; but, at all events, there is no pretense for saying that this right was ever meant to be surrendered up into the hands of the late Continental Convention. The people have an undoubted right to judge of every part of the government which is offered to them. No power on earth has a right to preclude them; and they may exercise this choice either by themselves or their delegates legally chosen in the state Convention. I venture to say that no man, reasoning upon Revolution principles, can possibly controvert this right.

Indeed, very few go so far as to controvert the right of the people to propose amendments. But we are told the thing is impracticable; that if we begin to propose amendments there will be no end to them; that the several states will never agree in their amendments; that we shall never unite in any plan; that if we reject this, we shall either have a worse one or none at all; that we ought therefore to adopt this at once without alteration or amendment. Now, these are very kind gentlemen who insist upon doing so much good for us, whether we will or not. Idiots and maniacs ought certainly to be restrained from doing themselves mischief, and ought to be

compelled to that which is for their own good. Whether the people of America are to be considered in this light and treated accordingly, is a question which deserves, perhaps, more consideration than it has yet received. A contest between the patients and their doctors, which are mad or which are fools, might possibly be a very unhappy one. I hope at least that we shall be able to settle this important business without so preposterous a dispute. What then would you have us do, it may be asked? Would you have us adopt the proposed constitution or reject it? The method I would propose is this:

1. Let the conventions of each state, as they meet, after considering the proposed constitution, state their objections and propose their amendments. So far from these objections and amendments clashing with each other in irreconcilable discord, as it has too often been suggested they would do, that from what has been hitherto published in the different states in opposition to the proposed constitution we have a right to expect that they will harmonize in a very great degree. The reason I say so is that about the same time, in very different parts of the continent, the very same objections have been made, and the very same alterations proposed by different writers, who I verily believe know nothing at all of each other and were very far from acting

by a premeditated concert; and that others who have not appeared as writers in the newspapers in the different states, have appeared to act and speak in perfect unison with those objections and amendments, particularly in the article of a bill of rights; that in short, the very same sentiments seem to have been echoed from the different parts of the continent by the opposers of the proposed constitution. And these sentiments have been very little contradicted by its friends, otherwise than by suggesting their fears that by opposing the constitution at present proposed, we might be disappointed of any federal government, or receive a worse one than the present. It would be a most delightful surprise to find ourselves all of one opinion at last. And I cannot forbear hoping that when we come fairly to compare our sentiments, we shalt find ourselves much more nearly agreed, than in the hurry and surprise in which we have been involved on this subject, we ever suffered ourselves to imagine.

2. When the conventions have stated these objections and amendments, let them transmit them to congress, and adjourn, praying that congress will direct another convention to be called from the different states, to consider of these objections and amendments, and pledging themselves to abide by whatever decision shall be made by such future convention on the subject whether it be to amend the proposed constitution or to reject any alterations, and ratify it as it stands.

3. If a new convention of the United States should meet, and revise the proposed constitution, let us agree to abide by their decision. It is past a doubt that every good citizen of America pants for an efficient federal government. T have no doubt we shall concur at last in some plan of continental government, even if many people could imagine exceptions to it. But if the exceptions which are made at present shall be maturely considered, and even be pronounced by our future representatives as of no importance (which I trust they will not), even in that case I have no doubt that almost every man will give up his own private opinion and concur in that decision.

4. If, by any means, another continental convention should fail to meet, then let the conventions of the several states again assemble and at last decide the great solemn question, whether we shall adopt the constitution now proposed or reject it. And whenever it becomes necessary to

decide upon this point one, at least, who from the beginning has been invariably anxious for the liberty and independence of this country, will concur in adopting and supporting this constitution, rather than none; though, I confess, I could easily imagine some other form of confederation which I should think better entitled to my hearty approbation, and indeed I am not afraid of a worse.

AN OLD WHIG

ANTI-FEDERALIST PAPER NO. 51

Do Checks And Balances Really Secure The Rights Of The People?

This satire is from a pamphlet of "ARISTOCROTIS," The Government of Nature Delineated; Or An Exact Picture of the New Federal Constitution (Carlisle, PA, 1788)

The present is an active period. Europe is in a ferment breaking their constitutions; America is in a similar state, making a constitution. For this valuable purpose a convention was appointed, consisting of such as excelled in wisdom and knowledge, who met in Philadelphia last May. For my own part, I was so smitten with the character of the members, that I had assented to their production, while it was yet in embryo. And I make no doubt but every good republican did so too. But how great was my surprise, when it appeared with such a venerable train of names annexed to its tail, to find some of the people under different signatures-such as Centinel, Old Whig, Brutus, etc. - daring to oppose it, and that too with barefaced arguments, obstinate reason and stubborn truth. This is certainly a piece of the most extravagant impudence to presume to contradict the collected wisdom of the United States; or to suppose a body, who engrossed the whole wisdom of the continent, was capable of erring. I expected the superior character of the convention would have secured it from profane sallies of a plebeian's pen; and its inherent infallibility debarred the interference of impertinent reason or truth. It was too great an act of condescension to permit the people, by their state conventions, "to assent and ratify," what the grand convention prescribed to them; but to inquire into its principles, or investigate its properties, was a presumption too daring to escape resentment. Such licentious conduct practised by the people, is a striking proof of our feeble governments, and calls aloud for the pruning knife, i.e., the establishment of some proper plan of discipline. This the convention, in the depth of their united wisdom hath prescribed, which when established, will certainly put a stop to the growing evil. A consciousness of this, is, no doubt, the cause which stimulates the people to oppose it with so much vehemence. They deprecate the idea of being confined within their proper sphere; they cannot endure the thought of being obliged to mind their own business, and leave the affairs of government to those whom nature hath destined to rule. I say nature, for it is a fundamental principle, as clear as an axiom, that nature hath placed proper degrees and subordinations amongst mankind and ordained a few(1) to rule, and many to obey. I am not obliged to prove this principle because it would be madness in the extreme to attempt to prove a self- evident truth.

(1) If any person is so stupidly dull as not to discern who these few are, I would refer such to nature herself for information. Let them observe her ways and be wise. Let them mark those men whom she hath endued with the necessary qualifications of authority; such as the dictatorial air, the magisterial voice, the imperious tone, the haughty countenance, the lofty look, the majestic mien. Let them consider those whom she hath taught to command with authority, but comply with disgust; to be fond of sway, but impatient of control; to consider themselves as Gods, and all the rest of mankind as two legged brutes. Now it is evident that the possessors of these divine qualities must have been ordained by nature to dominion and empire; for it would be blasphemy against her supreme highness to suppose that she confers her gifts in vain. Fortune hath also distinguished those upon whom nature hath imprinted the lineaments of authority. She hath heaped her favors and lavished her gifts upon those very persons whom nature delighteth to

honor. Indeed, instinct hath taught those men that authority is their natural right, and therefore they grasp at it with an eagerness bordering on rapacity.

But with all due submission to the infallible wisdom of the grand convention, let me presume to examine whether they have not, in the new plan of government, inviolably adhered to this supreme principle. . . .

In article first, section first, of the new plan, it is declared that "all legislative powers herein granted shall be vested in a Congress of the United States which shall consist of a Senate"-very right, quite agreeable to nature and House of Representatives"-not quite so right. This is a palpable compliance with the humors and corrupt practices of the times. But what follows in section 2 is still worse: "The House of Representatives shall be composed of members chosen every second year by the people of the several states." This is a most dangerous power, and must soon produce fatal and pernicious consequences, were it not circumscribed and poised by proper checks and balances. But in this is displayed the unparalleled sagacity of the august convention: that when such bulwarks of prejudice surrounded the evil, so as to render it both difficult and dangerous to attack it by assault and storm, they have invested and barricaded it so closely as will certainly deprive it of its baneful influence and prevent its usual encroachments. They have likewise stationed their miners and sappers so judiciously, that they will certainly, in process of time, entirely reduce and demolish this obnoxious practice of popular election. There is a small thrust given to it in the body of the conveyance itself. The term of holding elections is every two years; this is much better than the detestable mode of annual elections, so fatal to energy.

However, if nothing more than this were done, it would still remain an insupportable inconvenience. But in section 4 it is provided that congress by law may alter and make such regulations with respect to the times, places, and manner of holding elections, as to them seemeth fit and proper. This is certainly a very salutary provision, most excellently adapted to counterbalance the great and apparently dangerous concessions made to the plebeians in the first and second sections. With such a prudent restriction as this they are quite harmless: no evil can arise from them if congress have only the sagacity and fortitude to avail themselves of the power they possess by this section. For when the stated term (for which the primary members was elected) is nigh expired, congress may appoint [the] next election to be held in one place in each state; and so as not to give the rabble needless disgust, they may appoint the most central place for that purpose. They can never be at a loss for an ostensible reason to vary and shift from place to place until they may fix it at any extremity of the state it suits. This will be the business of the senate, to observe the particular places in each state, where their influence is most extensive, and where the inhabitants are most obsequious to the will of their superiors, and there appoint the elections to be held. By this means, such members will be returned to the house of representatives (as it is called) as the president and senate shall be pleased to recommend; and they no doubt will recommend such gentlemen only as are distinguished by some peculiar federal feature-so that unanimity and concord will shine conspicuous through every branch of government. This section is ingeniously calculated, and must have been intended by the convention, to exterminate electioneering entirely. For by putting the time of election in the hands of congress they have thereby given them a power to perpetuate themselves when they shall find it safe and convenient to make the experiment. For though a preceding clause says,

"that representatives shall be chosen for two years, and senators for six years," yet this clause being subsequent annuls the former, and puts it in the power of congress, (when some favorable

juncture intervenes) to alter the time to four and twelve years. This cannot be deemed an unconstitutional stretch of power, for the constitution in express terms puts the time of holding elections in their power, and certainly they are the proper judges when to exert that power. Thus by doubling the period from time to time, its extent will soon be rendered coeval with the life of man. And it is but a very short and easy transition from this to hereditary succession, which is most agreeable to the institutions of nature, who in all her works, hath ordained the descendant of every species of beings to succeed its immediate progenitor, in the same actions, ends and order.

The indefatigable laborious ass never aspires to the honors, nor assumes the employment of the sprightly warlike steed, nor does he ever pretend that it is his right to succeed him in all his offices and dignities, because he bears some resemblance to the defunct in his figure and nature.

The llama, though useful enough for the purposes for which he was intended by nature, is every way incompetent to perform the offices of the elephant; nor does he ever pretend to usurp his elevated station. Every species of beings, animate and inanimate, seem fully satisfied with the station assigned them by nature. But perverse, obstinate man, he alone spurns at her institutions, and inverts her order.' He alone repines at his situation, and endeavors to usurp the station of his superiors. But this digression has led me from the subject in hand. . . .

(2) This is only to be understood of the inferior class of mankind. The superior order have aspiring feelings given them by nature, such as ambition, emulation, etc., which makes it their duty to persevere in the pursuit of gratifying these refined passions.

The next object that presents itself is the power which the new constitution gives to congress to regulate the manner of elections. The common practice of voting at present is by ballot. By this mode it is impossible for a gentleman to know how he is served by his dependent, who may be possessed of a vote. Therefore this mode must be speedily altered for that viva voce, which will secure to a rich man all the votes of his numerous dependents and friends and their dependents.

By this means he may command any office in the gift of the people, which he pleases to set up for. This will answer a good end while electioneering exists; and will likewise contribute something towards its destruction. A government founded agreeable to nature must be entirely independent; that is, it must be beyond the reach of annoyance or control from every power on earth, Now in order to render it thus, several things are necessary.

Documents of Revolution

The next object that presents itself is the power which the new constitution gives to congress to regulate the manner of elections. The common practice of voting at present is by ballot. By this mode it is impossible for a gentleman to know how he is served by his dependent, who may be possessed of a vote. Therefore this mode must be speedily altered for that viva voce, which will secure to a rich man all the votes of his numerous dependents and friends and their dependents.

By this means he may command any office in the gift of the people, which he pleases to set up for. This will answer a good end while electioneering exists; and will likewise contribute something towards its destruction. A government founded agreeable to nature must be entirely independent; that is, it must be beyond the reach of annoyance or control from every power on earth, Now in order to render it thus, several things are necessary.

2dly. It will create and diffuse a spirit of industry among the people. They will then be obliged to labor for money to pay their taxes. There will be no trifling from time to time, as is done now.

The new government will have energy sufficient to compel immediate payment.

3dly. This will make the people attend to their own business, and not be dabbling in politics -

things they are entirely ignorant of; nor is it proper they should understand. But it is very probable that the exercise of this power may be opposed by the refractory plebeians, who (such is the perverseness of their natures) often refuse to comply with what is manifestly for their advantage. But to prevent all inconvenience from this quarter the congress have power to raise and support armies. This is the second thing necessary to render government independent. The creatures who compose these armies are a species of animals, wholly at the disposal of government; what others call their natural rights they resign into the hands of their superiors-even the right of self-preservation (so precious to all other beings) they entirely surrender, and put their very lives in the power of their masters. Having no rights of their own to care for, they become naturally jealous and envious of those possessed by others. They are therefore proper instruments in the hands of government to divest the people of their usurped rights. But the capital business of these armies will be to assist the collectors of taxes, imposts, and excise, in raising the revenue; and this they will perform with the greatest alacrity, as it is by this they are supported; but for this they would be in a great measure useless; and without this they could not exist. . . .

From these remarks, I think it is evident, that the grand convention hath dexterously provided for the removal of every thing that hath ever operated as a restraint upon government in any place or age of the world. But perhaps some weak heads may think that the constitution itself will be a check upon the new congress. But this I deny, for the convention has so happily worded themselves, that every part of this constitution either bears double meaning, or no meaning at all; and if any concessions are made to the people in one place, it is effectually cancelled in another-so that in fact this constitution is much better and gives more scope to the rulers than they durst safely take if there was no constitution at all. For then the people might contend that the power was inherent in them, and that they had made some implied reserves in the original grant. But now they cannot, for every thing is expressly given away to government in this plan. Perhaps some people may think that power which the house of representatives possesses, of impeaching the officers of government, will be a restraint upon them. But this entirely vanishes, when it is considered that the senate hath the principal say in appointing these officers, and that they are the sole judges of all impeachments. Now it would be absurd to suppose that they would remove their own servants for performing their secret orders. . . . For the interest of rulers and the ruled will then be two distinct things. The mode of electing the president is another excellent regulation, most wisely calculated to render him the obsequious machine of congress. He is to be chosen by electors appointed in such manner as the state legislators shall direct. But then the highest in votes cannot be president, without he has the majority of all the electors; and if none have this majority, then the congress is to choose the president out of the five highest on the return. By this means the congress will always have the making of the president after the first election. So that if the reigning president pleases his masters, he need be under no apprehensions of being turned out for any severities used to the people, for though the congress may not have influence enough to procure him the majority of the votes of the electoral college, yet they will always be able to prevent any other from having such a majority; and to have him returned

among the five highest, so that they may have the appointing of him themselves. All these wise regulations, prove to a demonstration, that the grand convention was infallible. The congress having thus disentangled themselves from all popular checks and choices, and being supported by a well disciplined army and active militia, will certainly command dread and respect abroad, obedience and submission at home. They will then look down with awful dignity and tremendous majesty from the pinnacle of glory to which fortune has raised them upon the insignificant creatures, their subjects, whom they have reduced to that state of vassalage and servile submission, for which they were primarily destined by nature. America will then be great amongst the nations(3) and princess amongst the provinces. Her fleets will cover the deserts of the ocean and convert it into a popular city; and her invincible armies overturn the thrones of princes. The glory of Britain (4) shall fall like lightning

before her puissant arm; when she ariseth to shake the nations, and take vengeance on all who dare oppose her. O! thou most venerable and august congress! with what astonishing ideas my mind is ravished! when I contemplate thy rising grandeur, and anticipate thy future glory! Happy thy servants! happy thy vassals! and happy thy slaves, which fit under the shade of thy omnipotent authority, and behold the glory of thy majesty! for such a state who would not part with ideal blessings of liberty? who would not cheerfully resign the nominal advantages of freedom? the dazzling splendor of Assyrian, Persian, Macedonian and Roman greatness will then be totally eclipsed by the radiant blaze of this glorious western luminary! These beautiful expressions, aristocracy, and oligarchy, upon which the popular odium hath fixed derision and contempt, will then resume their natural emphasis; their genuine signification will be perfectly understood, and no more perverted or abused.
ARISTOCROTIS

(3) That is, if we may credit the prognostications with which our federal news-papers and pamphlets daily teem.

(4) Britain once the supreme ruler of this country, but her authority was rejected. Not, as a great many believe, because her claims were tyrannical and oppressive, but because her dominion excluded those from monopolizing the government into their own hands, whom nature had qualified to rule. It is certainly no more than the natural right of rulers "to bind their subjects, in all cases whatsoever." This power is perfectly synonymous with that clause in the constitution which invests congress with power to make all laws which shall be "necessary and proper for carrying into execution the foregoing powers and all other powers," etc., and that which says "the constitution, laws, and treaties of congress shall be the supreme law of the land; any thing in the constitutions or laws of any of the states to the contrary notwithstanding." But nothing less would satisfy Britain, than a power to bind the natural rulers as well as subjects.

Anti-Federalist Paper No. 52

On The Guarantee Of Congressional Biennial Elections

The following essay was signed by Consider Arms, Malichi Maynard, and Samuel Field. It was taken from The Hampshire Gazette of April 9, 1788.

We the subscribers being of the number, who did not assent to the ratification of the federal constitution, under consideration in the late state convention, held at Boston, to which we were called by the suffrages of the corporations to which we respectively belong-beg leave, through the channel of your paper, to lay before the public in general, and our constituents in particular, the reasons of our dissent, and the principles which governed us in our decision of this important question.

Fully convinced, ever since the late revolution, of the necessity of a firm, energetic government, we should have rejoiced in an opportunity to have given our assent to such a one; and should in the present case, most cordially have done it, could we at the same time been happy to have seen the liberties of the people and the rights of mankind properly guarded and secured. We conceive that the very notion of government carries along with it the idea of justice and equity, and that the whole design of instituting government in the world, was to preserve men's properties from rapine, and their bodies from violence and bloodshed.

These propositions being established, we conceive must of necessity produce the following consequence: That every constitution or system, which does not quadrate with this original design, is not government, but in fact a subversion of it. Having premised thus much, we proceed to mention some things in this constitution to which we object, and to enter into an inquiry, whether, and how far they coincide with those simple and original notions of government before mentioned.

In the first place, as direct taxes are to be apportioned according to the numbers in each state, and as Massachusetts has none in it but what are declared free men, so the whole, blacks as well as whites, must be numbered; this must therefore operate against us, as two-fifths of the slaves in the southern states are to be left out of the numeration. Consequently, three Massachusetts infants will increase the tax equal to five sturdy full-grown Negroes of theirs, who work every day in the week for their masters, saving the Sabbath, upon which they are allowed to get something for their own support. We can see no justice in this way of apportioning taxes. Neither can we see any good reason why this was consented to on the part of our delegates.

We suppose it next to impossible that every individual in this vast continental union, should have his wish with regard to every single article composing a frame of government. And therefore, although we think it More agreeable to the principles of republicanism, that elections should be annual, yet as the elections in our own state government are so, we did not view it so dangerous to the liberties of the people, that we should have rejected the constitution merely on account of the biennial

elections of the representatives-had we been sure that the people have any security even of this. But this we could not find. For although it is said, that "the House of
Representatives shall be chosen every second year, by the people of the several states," etc., and that "the times, places and manner of holding elections for senators and representatives, shall be prescribed in each state by the legislature thereof," yet all this is wholly superseded by a subsequent provision, which empowers Congress at any time to enact a law, whereby such regulations may be altered, except as to the places of choosing senators. Here we conceive the people may be very materially injured, and in time reduced to a state of as abject vassalage as any people were under the control of the most mercenary despot that ever tarnished the pages of history. The depravity of human nature, illustrated by examples from history, will warrant us to say, it may be possible, if not probable, that the congress may be composed of men, who will wish to burden and oppress the people. In such case, will not their inventions be fruitful enough to devise occasions for postponing the elections? And if they can do this once, they can twice; if they can twice, they can thrice, so by degrees render themselves absolute and perpetual. Or, if they choose, they have another expedient. They can alter the place of holding elections. They can say, whatever the legislature of this state may order to the contrary, that all the elections of our representatives shall be made at Mechias, or at Williamstown. Consequently, nine-tenths of the people will never vote. And if this should be thought a measure favorable to their reelection, or the election of some tool for their mercenary purposes, we doubt not it will be thus ordered. But says the advocates for the constitution, "it is not likely this will ever happen; we are not to expect our rulers will ever proceed to a wanton exercise of the powers given them." But what reason have we more than past ages, to expect that we shall be blessed with impeccable rulers? We think not any. Although it has been said that every generation grows wiser and wiser, yet we have no reason to think they grow better and better. And therefore the probability lies upon the dark side. Does not the experience of past ages leach, that men have generally exercised all the powers they had given them, and even have usurped upon them, in order to accomplish their own sinister and avaricious designs, whenever they thought they could do it with impunity? This we presume will not be denied. And it appeared to us that the arguments made use of by the favorers of the constitution, in the late convention at Boston, proceeded upon the plan of righteousness in those who are to rule over us, by virtue of this new form of government. But these arguments, we confess, could have no weight with us, while we judge them to be founded altogether upon a slippery perhaps.

We are sensible, that in order to the due administration of government, it is necessary that certain powers should be delegated to the rulers from the people. At the same time, we think they ought carefully to guard against giving so much as will enable those rulers, by that means, at once, or even in process of time, to render themselves absolute and despotic. This we think is the case with the form of government lately submitted to our consideration. We could not, therefore, acting uprightly, consulting our own good and the good of our constituents, give our assent unto it. We could not then and we still cannot see, that because people are many times guilty of crimes and deserving of punishment, that it from thence follows the authority ought to have power to punish them when they are not guilty, or to punish the innocent with the guilty without discrimination, which amounts to the same thing. But this we think in fact to be the case as to this federal constitution. For the congress, whether they have provocation or not, can at any time order the elections in any or all the states to be conducted in such manner as wholly to defeat and render entirely nugatory the intention of those elections, and convert that which was considered and intended to be the palladium of the liberties of the people-the grand bulwark against any invasion upon them-into a formidable engine, by which to overthrow them all, and
thus involve them in the depth of misery and distress. But it was pled by some of the ablest advocates of the constitution, that if congress should exercise such powers to the prejudice of the people (and they did not deny but they could if they should be disposed) they (the people) would not suffer it. They would have recourse to the ultima ratio, the dernier resort of the oppressed-the sword.

But it appeared to us a piece of superlative incongruity indeed, that the people, whilst in the full and indefeasible possession of their liberties and privileges, should be so very profuse, so very liberal in the disposal of them, as consequently to place themselves in a predicament miserable to an extreme. So wretched indeed, that they may at once be reduced to the sad alternative of yielding themselves vassals into the hands of a venal and corrupt administration, whose only wish may be to aggrandize themselves and families-to wallow in luxury and every species of dissipation, and riot upon the spoils of the community; or take up the sword and involve their country in all the horrors of a civil war-the consequences of which, we think, we may venture to augur will more firmly rivet their shackles and end in the entailment of vassalage to their posterity. We think this by no means can fall within the description of government before mentioned. Neither can we think these suggestions merely chimerical, or that they proceed from an overheated enthusiasm in favor of republicanism; neither yet from an illplaced detestation of aristocracy; but from the apparent danger the people are in by establishing this constitution.

When we take a forward view of the proposed congress-seated in the federal city, ten miles square, fortified and replenished with all kinds of military stores and every implement; with a navy at command on one side, and a land army on the other-we say, when we view them thus possessed of the sword in one hand and the purse strings of the people in the other, we can see no security left for them in the enjoyment of their liberties, but what may proceed from the bare possibility that this supreme authority of the nation may be possessed of virtue and integrity sufficient to influence them in the administration of equal justice and equity among those whom they shall govern. But why should we voluntarily choose to trust our all upon so precarious a tenure as this? We confess it gives us pain to anticipate the future scene: a scene presenting to view miseries so complicated and extreme, that it may be part of the charms of eloquence to extenuate, or the power of art to remove.
CONSIDER ARMS
MALICHI MAYNARD
SAMUEL FIELD

ANTI-FEDERALIST PAPER NO. 53

A Plea For The Right Of Recall

"AMICUS" appeared in the Columbian Herald, August 28, 1788.

Some time before a Convention of the United States was held, I mentioned in a paragraph which was published in one of the Charlestown papers, that it would be acting wisely in the formation of a constitution for a free government, to enact, that the electors should recall their representatives when they thought proper, although they should be chosen for a certain term of years; as a right to appoint (where the right of appointing originates with the appointees) implies a right to recall. As the persons appointed are meant to act for the benefit of the appointees, as well as themselves, they, if they mean to act for their mutual benefit, can have no objection to a proposal of this kind. But if they have any sinister designs, they will certainly oppose it, foreseeing that their electors will displace them as soon as they begin to act contrary to their interest. I am therefore glad to find that the state of New York has proposed an amendment of this kind to the federal constitution, viz: That the legislatures of the respective states may recall their senators, or either of them, and elect others in their stead, to serve the remainder of the time for which the senators so recalled were appointed. I wish this had been extended to the representatives in both houses, as it is as prudent to have a check over the members of one house as of the other.

Some persons as object to this amendment, in fact say, that it is safer to give a man an irrevocable power of attorney, than a revocable one; and that it is right to let a representative ruin us, rather than recall him and put a real friend of his country, and a truly honest man in his place, who would rather suffer ten thousand deaths than injure his country, or sully his honor and reputation. Such persons seem to say, that power ought not to originate with the people (which is the wish, I fear, of some among us); and also that we are not safe in trusting our own legislature with the power of recalling such senators as will not abide by such instructions - as shall be either given them, when chosen, or sent to them afterwards, by the legislature of this or any other state, or by the electors that chose them, although they should have met together in a body for the purpose of instructing or sending them instructions on a matter on which the salvation of the state depends. That we should insist on the amendment respecting this matter taking place, which the state of New York has proposed, appears to me to be absolutely necessary, the security of each state may be almost said to rest on it. For my own part, I would rather that this amendment should take place and give the new government unlimited powers to act for the public good, than give them limited powers, and at the same time put it out of our power, for a certain term of years, to recall our representatives, although we saw they were exceeding their powers, and were bent on making us miserable and themselves, by means of a standing army-a perpetual and absolute government. For power is a very intoxicating thing, and has made many a man do unwarrantable actions, which before he was invested with it, he had no thoughts of doing. I hope by what I have said I shall not be thought to cast even the shadow of a reflection on the principles of either of the members of the federal convention-it is far from being my intention. I wish for nothing more than a good government and a constitution under which our liberties will be perfectly safe. To preserve which, I think the wisest conduct will be to keep the staff of power in our own hands as much as possible, and not wantonly and inconsiderately give up a greater
share of our liberties with a view of contributing to the public good, than what the necessity of the case requires.

Documents of Revolution

For our own sakes we shall keep in power those persons whose conduct pleases us as long as we can, and shall perhaps sometimes wish (when we meet with a person of an extra worthy character and abilities) that we could keep him in power for life. On the other hand, we shall dismiss from our employ as soon as possible, such persons as do not consult our interest and will not follow our instructions. For there are, I fear, a few persons among us, so wise in their own eyes, that they would if they could, pursue their own will and inclinations, in opposition to the instructions of their constituents. In so doing, they may perhaps, once in a hundred times, act for the interest of those they represent, more than if they followed the instructions given them. But I wish that we would never suffer any person to continue our representative that obeyed not our instructions, unless something unforeseen and unknown by us turned up, which he knew would alter our sentiments, if we were made acquainted with it; and which would make his complying with our will highly imprudent. In every government matter, on which our representatives were not instructed, we should leave them to act agreeable to their own judgment; on which account we should always choose men of integrity, honor and abilities to represent us. But when we did instruct them, as they are our representatives and agents, we should insist on their acting and voting conformable to our directions. But as they would each of them be a member of the community, they should have a right to deliver to the houses of representatives of which they were members, their own private sentiments so that if their private sentiments contained cogent reasons for acting contrary to the instructions given them-the other members of said houses who would not be bound by said instructions, would be guided by them; in which case, that would take place which would be most for the public good, which ought to be the wish of all of us.
AMICUS

ANTI-FEDERALIST PAPER NO. 54

APPORTIONMENT AND SLAVERY: NORTHERN AND SOUTHERN VIEWS

This four part essay shows both northern and southern dissatisfaction with "the Great Compromise"
The first is taken from the third essay of "BRUTUS."
The second: from the speeches of Rawlins Lowndes to the South Carolina ratifying convention on January 16, 17, and 18, 1788.
The third: from the sixth essay by "CATO."
The fourth: from an essay by "A GEORGIAN," appearing in The Gazette of the State of Georgia on November 15, 1787.
"Representatives and direct taxes shall be apportioned among the several States, which may be included in this Union, according to their respective numbers, which shall be determined by adding to the whole number of free persons, including those bound to service for a term of years, and excluding Indians not taxed, three-fifths of all other persons." What a strange and unnecessary accumulation of words are here used to conceal from the public eye what might have been expressed in the following concise manner: Representatives are to be proportioned among the States respectively, according to the number of freemen and slaves inhabiting them, counting five slaves for three freemen.
"In a free State," says the celebrated Montesquieu, "every man, who is supposed to be a free agent, ought to be concerned in his own government, therefore the legislature should reside in the whole body of the people, or their representatives." But it has never been alleged that those who are not free agents can, upon any rational principle, have anything to do in government, either by themselves or others. If they have no share in government, why is the number of members in the assembly to be increased on their account? Is it because in some of the States, a considerable part of the property of the inhabitants consists in a number of their fellow-men, who are held in bondage, in defiance of every idea of benevolence, justice and religion, and contrary to all the principles of liberty which have been publicly avowed in the late Glorious Revolution?
If this be a just ground for representation, the horses in some of the States, and the oxen in others, ought to be represented-for a great share of property in some of them consists in these animals; and they have as much control over their own actions as these poor unhappy creatures, who are intended to be described in the above recited clause, by the words, "all other persons." By this mode of apportionment, the representatives of the different parts of the Union will be extremely unequal; in some of the Southern States the slaves are nearly equal in number to the free men; and for all these slaves they will be entitled to a proportionate share in the legislature; this will give them an unreasonable weight in the government, which can derive no additional strength, protection, nor defense from the slaves, but the contrary. Why, then, should they be represented? What

385

adds to the evil is, that these States are to be permitted to continue the inhuman traffic of importing slaves until the year 1808-and for every cargo of these unhappy

people which unfeeling, unprincipled, barbarous and avaricious wretches may tear from their country, friends and tender connections, and bring into those States, they are to be rewarded by having an increase of members in the General Assembly....
BRUTUS

.... six of the Eastern States formed a majority in the House of Representatives. In the enumeration he passed Rhode Island, and included Pennsylvania. Now, was it consonant with reason, with wisdom, with policy, to suppose, in a legislature where a majority of persons sat whose interests were greatly different from ours, that we had the smallest chance of receiving adequate advantages? Certainly not. He believed the gentlemen that went from this state, to represent us in Convention, possessed as much integrity, and stood as high in point of character, as any gentlemen that could have been selected; and he also believed that they had done every thing in their power to procure for us a proportionate share in this new government; but the very little they had gained proved what we may expect in future-that the interest of the Northern States would so predominate as to divest us of any pretensions to the title of a republic. In the first place, what cause was there for jealousy of our importing Negroes? Why confine us to twenty years, or rather why limit us at all? For his part, he thought this trade could be justified on the principles of religion, humanity, and justice; for certainly to translate a set of human beings from a bad country to a better, was fulfilling every part of these principles. But they don't like our slaves, because they have none themselves, and therefore want to exclude us from this great advantage. Why should the Southern States allow of this, without the consent of nine states? ...

We had a law prohibiting the importation of Negroes for three years, a law he greatly approved of; but there was no reason offered why the Southern States might not find it necessary to alter their conduct, and open their ports.

Without Negroes, this state would degenerate into one of the most contemptible in the Union; and he cited an expression that fell from General Pinckney on a former debate, that whilst there remained one acre of swampland in South Carolina, he should raise his voice against restricting the importation of Negroes. Even in granting the importation for twenty years, care had been taken to make us pay for this indulgence, each negro being liable, on importation, to pay a duty not exceeding ten dollars; and, in addition to this, they were liable to a capitation tax. Negroes were our wealth, our only natural resource; yet behold how our kind friends in the north were determined soon to tie up our hands, and drain us of what we had! The Eastern States drew their means of subsistence, in a great measure, from their shipping; and, on that head, they had been particularly careful not to allow of any burdens: they were not to pay tonnage or duties; no, not even the form of clearing out: all ports were free and open to them! Why, then, call this a reciprocal bargain, which took all from one party, to bestow it on the other!

Major [Pierce] BUTLER observed, that they were to pay five per cent impost.

This, Mr. LOWNDES proved, must fall upon the consumer. They are to be the carriers; and, we being the consumers, therefore all expenses would fall upon us. A great number of gentlemen were captivated with this new Constitution, because those who were in debt would be compelled to pay; others pleased themselves with the reflection that no more confiscation laws would be passed; but those were small advantages, in proportion to the evils that might be apprehended from the laws that might be passed by Congress, whenever there was a majority of representatives from the Eastern States, who were governed by prejudices and ideas extremely different from ours. . . .

Great stress was laid on the admirable checks which guarded us, under the new Constitution, from the encroachments of tyranny; but too many checks in a political machine must produce the same mischief as in a mechanical one-that of throwing all into confusion. But supposing we considered ourselves so much aggrieved as to reduce us to the necessity of insisting on redress, what probability had we of relief? Very little indeed. In the revolving on misfortune, some little gleams of comfort resulted from a hope of being able to resort to an impartial tribunal for redress; but pray what reason was there for expectancy that, in Congress, the interest of five Southern States would be considered in a preferable point of view to the nine Eastern ones?

.... the mode of legislation in the infancy of free communities was by the collective body, and this consisted of free persons, or those whose age admitted them to the right of mankind and citizenship, whose sex made them capable of protecting the state, and whose birth may be denominated Free Born; and no traces can be found that ever women, children, and slaves, or those who were not sui juris, in the early days of legislation, met with the free members of the community to deliberate on public measures; hence is derived this maxim in free governments, that representation ought to bear a proportion to the number of free inhabitants in a community; this principle your own state constitution, and others, have observed in the establishment of a future census, in order to apportion the representatives, and to increase or diminish the representation to the ratio of the increase or diminution of electors. But, what aid can the community derive from the assistance women, infants and slaves, in their deliberation, or in their defense? What motives, therefore, could the convention have in departing from just and rational principle of representation, which is the governing prince of this state and of all America?

CATO

Article 1, section 2. This section mentions that, within three years after the first meeting of the Congress of the United States, an enumeration shall take place, the number of representatives not to exceed one member for every 30,000. This article I believe to be inadmissable. First, it affords to small a representation, (supposing 48 at the highest calculation) and especially in the southern states, their climate, soil, and produce, . . . not being capable of that population as in the northern states. Would it not therefore be better to increase the number of representatives, say one member for every 20,000 for the states north of Virginia, and one for every 15,000 south of the said state, itself included? Or, secondly, divide the states into districts which shall choose the representatives, by which every part of a state will have an equal chance, without being liable to parties or factions? Should it be said it will increase the expense, it will be money well laid out, and the more so if we retain the paying them out of our own bands. And, supposing the voting in the house of representatives was continued as heretofore by states, would it not be more equal still? At any rate I would strenuously recommend to vote by states, and not individually, as it will be accommodating the idea of equality, which should ever be observed in a republican form of government. Or, thirdly, if it was in proportion to the quotas of the states, as rated in taxation, then the number of members would increase with the proportion of tax, and at that rate there

would always be an equality in the quota of tax as well as representation; for what chance of equality according to the constitution in question, can a state have that has only one or two votes, when others have eight or ten, (for it is evident that each representative, as well as senator, is meant to have a vote, as it mentions no other mode but in choosing the president), and as it is generally allowed that the United States are divided into two natural divisions, the northern as far as Virginia, the latter included forms the southern? This produces a wide difference in climate, soil, customs, manners of living, and the produce of the land, as well as trade, also in population, to which it is well observed the latter is not so favorable as the former, and never can nor will be, nature itself being the great obstacle. And when taxation is in agitation, as also many other points, it must produce differences in sentiments; and, in such dispute, how is it likely to be decided? According to the mode of voting, the number of members north of Virginia the first three years is 42, and the southern, Virginia included, 23....

Is human nature above self interest? If the northern states do not horde the southern in taxation, it would appear then really that they are more disinterested men than we know of.

ANTI-FEDERALIST PAPER NO. 55

(PART I)Will The House Of Representatives Be Genuinely Representative?

Following are four essays by "THE FEDERAL FARMER"

.... It being impracticable for the people to assemble to make laws, they must elect legislators, and assign men to the different departments of the government. In the representative branch we must expect chiefly to collect the confidence of the people, and in it to find almost entirely the force of persuasion. In forming this branch, therefore, several important considerations must be attended to. It must possess abilities to discern the situation of the people and of public affairs, a disposition to sympathize with the people, and a capacity and inclination to make laws congenial to their circumstances and condition. It must afford security against interest combinations, corruption and influence. It must possess the confidence, and have the voluntary support of the people.

I think these positions will not be controverted, nor the one I formerly advanced, that a fair and equal representation is that in which the interests, feelings, opinions and views of the people are collected, in such manner as they would be were the people all assembled. Having made these general observations, I shall proceed to consider further my principal position, viz. that there is no substantial representation of the people provided for in a government, in which the most essential powers, even as to the internal police of the country, are proposed to be lodged; and to propose certain amendments as to the representative branch.... The representation is insubstantial and ought to be increased. In matters where there is much room for opinion, you will not expect me to establish my positions with mathematical certainty; you must only expect my observations to be candid, and such as are well founded in the mind of the writer. I am in a field where doctors disagree; and as to genuine representation, though no feature in government can be more important, perhaps, no one has been less understood, and no one that has received so imperfect a consideration by political writers. The ephori in Sparta, and the tribunes in Rome, were but the shadow; the representation in Great Britain is unequal and insecure. In America we have done more in establishing this important branch on its true principles, than, perhaps, all the world besides. Yet even here, I conceive, that very great improvements in representation may be made. In fixing this branch, the situation of the people must be surveyed, and the number of representatives and forms of election apportioned to that situation. When we find a numerous people settled in a fertile and extensive country, possessing equality, and few or none of them oppressed with riches or wants, it ought to be the anxious care of the constitution and laws, to arrest them from national depravity, and to preserve them in their happy condition. A virtuous people make just laws, and good laws tend to preserve unchanged a virtuous people. A virtuous and happy people by laws uncongenial to their characters, may easily be gradually changed into servile and depraved creatures. Where the people, or their representatives, make the laws, it is probable they will generally be fitted to the national character and circumstances, unless the representation be partial, and the imperfect substitute of the people. However the people may be electors, if the representation be so formed as to give one

or more of the natural classes of men in society an undue ascendancy over others, it is imperfect; the former will gradually become masters, and the latter slaves. It is the first of all among the political balances, to preserve in its proper station each of these classes. We talk of balances in the legislature, and among the departments of government; we ought to carry them to the body of the people. Since I advanced the idea of balancing the several orders of men in a community, in forming a genuine representation, and seen that idea considered as chimerical, I have been sensibly struck with a sentence in the Marquis Beccaria's treatise. This sentence was quoted by Congress in 1774, and is as follows:-"In every society there is an effort continually tending to confer on one part the height of power and happiness, and to reduce the others to the extreme of weakness and misery; the intent of good laws is to oppose this effort, and to diffuse their influence universally and equally." Add to this Montesquieu's opinion, that "in a free state every man, who is supposed to be a free agent, ought to be concerned in his own government: therefore, the legislative should reside in the whole body of the people, or their representatives."

It is extremely clear that these writers had in view the several orders of men in society, which we call aristocratical, democratical, mercantile, mechanics etc., and perceived the efforts they are constantly, from interested and ambitious views, disposed to make to elevate themselves and oppress others. Each order must have a share in the business of legislation actually and efficiently. It is deceiving a people to tell them they are electors, and can choose their legislators, if they cannot, in the nature of things, choose men from among themselves, and genuinely like themselves. I wish you to take another idea along with you. We are not only to balance these natural efforts, but we are also to guard against accidental combinations; combinations founded in the connections of offices and private interests, both evils which are increased in proportion as the number of men, among which the elected must be, are decreased. To set this matter in a proper point of view, we must form some general ideas and descriptions of the different classes of men, as they may be divided by occupation and politically. The first class is the aristocratical.

There are three kinds of aristocracy spoken of in this country-the first is a constitutional one, which does not exist in the United States in our common acceptation of the word. Montesquieu, it is true, observes that where part of the persons in a society, for want of property, age, or moral character, are excluded any share in the government, the others, who alone are the constitutional electors and elected, form this aristocracy. This, according to him, exists in each of the United States, where a considerable number of persons, as all convicted of crimes, under age, or not possessed of certain property, are excluded any share in the government. The second is an aristocratic faction, a junto of unprincipled men, often distinguished for their wealth or abilities, who combine together and make their object their private interests and aggrandizement. The existence of this description is merely accidental, but particularly to be guarded against. The third is the natural aristocracy; this term we use to designate a respectable order of men, the line between whom and the natural democracy is in some degree arbitrary. We may place men on one side of this line, which others may place on the other, and in all disputes between the few and the many, a considerable number are wavering and uncertain themselves on which side they are, or ought to be. In my idea of our natural aristocracy in the United States, I include about four or five thousand men; and among these I reckon those who have been placed in the offices of governors, of members of Congress, and state senators generally, in the principal officers of the army and militia, the superior judges, the most eminent professional men, etc., and men of large property. The other persons and orders in the community form the natural democracy; this includes in general, the yeomanry, the subordinate officers, civil and military, the fishermen, mechanics and traders, many of the merchants and professional men. It is easy to perceive that men of these two classes, the aristocratical and democratical, with views equally honest, have sentiments widely different, especially respecting public and private expenses, salaries, taxes, etc. Men of the first class associate more extensively, have a high sense of honor, possess abilities, ambition, and general knowledge; men of the second class are not so much used to combining great objects; they possess less ambition, and a larger share of honesty; their dependence is principally on middling and small estates, industrious pursuits, and hard labor, while that of the former is principally on the emoluments of large estates, and of the chief offices of government. Not only the efforts of these two great parties are to be balanced, but other interests and parties also, which do not always oppress each other merely for want of power, and for fear of the consequences; though they, in fact, mutually depend on each other. Yet such are their general views, that the merchants alone would never fail to make laws favorable to themselves and oppressive to the farmers. The farmers alone would act on like principles; the former would tax the land, the latter the trade. The manufacturers are often disposed to contend for monopolies; buyers make every exertion to lower prices; and sellers to raise them. Men who live by fees and salaries endeavor to raise them; and the part of the people who pay them, endeavor to lower them; the public creditors to augment the taxes, and the people at large to lessen them. Thus, in every period of society, and in all the transactions of men, we see parties verifying the observation made by the Marquis; and those classes which have not their centinels in the government, in proportion to what they have to gain or lose, must infallibly be ruined.

Efforts among parties are not merely confined to property. They contend for rank and distinctions; all their passions in turn are enlisted in political controversies. Men, elevated in society, are often disgusted with the changeableness of the democracy, and the latter are often agitated with the passions of jealousy and envy. The yeomanry possess a large share of property and strength, are nervous and firm in their opinions and habits; the mechanics of towns are ardent and changeable-honest and credulous, they are inconsiderable for numbers, weight and strength, not always sufficiently stable for supporting free governments; the fishing interest partakes partly of the strength and stability of the landed, and partly of the changeableness of the mechanic interest. As to merchants and traders, they are our agents in almost all money transactions, give activity to government, and possess a considerable share of influence in it. It has been observed by an able writer, that frugal industrious merchants are generally advocates for liberty. It is an observation, I believe, well founded, that the schools produce but few advocates for republican forms of government. Gentlemen of the law, divinity, physic, etc., probably form about a fourth part of the people; yet their political influence, perhaps, is equal to that of all the other descriptions of men. If we may judge from the appointments to Congress, the legal characters will often, in a small representation, be the majority; but the more the representatives are increased, the more of the farmers, merchants, etc., will be found to be brought into the government.

These general observations will enable you to discern what I intend by different classes, and the general scope of my ideas, when I contend for uniting and balancing their interests, feelings, opinions, and views in the legislature. We may not only so unite and balance these as to prevent a change in the government by the gradual exaltation of one part to the depression of others, but we may derive many other advantages from the combination and full representation. A small representation can never be well informed as to the circumstances of the people. The members of it must be too far removed from the people, in general, to sympathize with them, and too few to

communicate with them. A representation must be extremely imperfect where the representatives are not circumstanced to make the proper communications to their constituents, and where the constituents in turn cannot, with tolerable convenience, make known their wants, circumstances, and opinions to their representatives. Where there is but one representative to 30,000 or 40,000

inhabitants, it appears to me, he can only mix and be acquainted with a few respectable characters among his constituents. Even double the general representation, and then there must be a very great distance between the representatives and the people in general represented. On the proposed plan, the state of Delaware, the city of Philadelphia, the state of Rhode Island, the province of Maine, the county of Suffolk in Massachusetts, will have one representative each.

There can be but little personal knowledge, or but few communications, between him and the people at large of either of those districts. It has been observed that mixing only with the respectable men, he will get the best information and ideas from them; he will also receive impressions favorable to their purposes particularly....

Could we get over all our difficulties respecting a balance of interests and party efforts, to raise some and oppress others, the want of sympathy, information and intercourse between the representatives and the people, an insuperable difficulty will still

remain. I mean the constant liability of a small number of representatives to private combinations. The tyranny of the one, or the licentiousness of the multitude, are, in my mind, but small evils, compared with the factions of the few. It is a consideration well worth pursuing, how far this house of representatives will be liable to be formed into private juntos, how far influenced by expectations of appointments and offices, how far liable to be managed by the president and senate, and how far the people will have confidence in them....
THE FEDERAL FARMER

ANTI-FEDERALIST PAPER NO. 56

(PART II) Will The House Of Representatives Be Genuinely Representative?

.... Why in England have the revolutions always ended in stipulations in favor of general liberty, equal laws, and the common rights of the people, and in most other countries in favor only of a few influential men? The reasons, in my mind, are obvious. In England the people have been substantially represented in many respects; in the other countries it has not been so. Perhaps a small degree of attention to a few simple facts will illustrate this. In England, from the oppressions of the Norman Kings to the revolution in 1688, during which period of two or three hundred years, the English liberties were ascertained and established, the aristocratic part of that nation was substantially represented by a very large number of nobles, possessing similar interests and feelings with those they represented. The body of the people, about four or five millions, then mostly a frugal landed people, were represented by about five hundred representatives, taken not from the order of men which formed the aristocracy, but from the body of the people, and possessed of the same interests and feelings. De Lolme, speaking of the British representation, expressly founds all his reasons on this union; this similitude of interests, feelings, views and circumstances. He observes the English have preserved their liberties, because they and their leaders or representatives have been strictly united in interests, and in contending for general liberty. Here we see a genuine balance founded in the actual state of things. The whole community, probably, not more than two-fifths more numerous than we now are, were represented by seven or eight hundred men; the barons stipulated with the common people, and the king with the whole. Had the legal distinction between lords and commons been broken down, and the people of that island been called upon to elect forty-five senators, and one hundred and twenty representatives, about the proportion we propose to establish, their whole legislature evidently would have been of the natural aristocracy, and the body of the people would not have had scarcely a single sincere advocate. Their interests would have been neglected, general and equal liberty forgot, and the balance lost. Contests and conciliations, as in most other countries, would have been merely among the few, and as it might have been necessary to serve their purposes, the people at large would have been flattered or threatened, and probably not a single stipulation made in their favor. In Rome the people were miserable, though they bad three orders, the consuls, senators, and tribunes, and approved the laws, and all for want of a genuine representation. The people were too numerous to assemble, and do any thing properly themselves. The voice of a few, the dupes of artifice, was called the voice of the people. It is difficult for the people to defend themselves against the arts and intrigues of the great, but by selecting a suitable number of men fixed to their interests to represent them, and to oppose ministers and senators. . . . [Much] depends on the number of the men selected, and the manner of doing it. To be convinced of this, we need only attend to the reason of the case, the conduct of the British commons, and of the Roman tribunes. Equal liberty prevails in England, because there was a representation of the people, in fact and reality, to establish it. Equal liberty never prevailed in Rome because there was but the shadow of a representation. There were consuls in Rome annually elected to execute the laws; several hundred senators represented the great families; the body of the people annually chose tribunes from among themselves to defend them and to secure their rights; I think the number of tribunes annually chosen never exceeded
ten. This representation, perhaps, was not proportionally so numerous as the representation proposed in the new plan; but the difference will not appear to be so great, when it shall be recollected, that these tribunes were chosen annually, that the great patrician families were not admitted to these offices of tribunes, and that the people of Italy who elected the tribunes were a long while, if not always, a small people compared with the people of the United States. What was the consequence of this trifling representation? The people of Rome always elected for their tribunes men conspicuous for their riches, military commands, professional popularity, etc., great commoners, between whom and the noble families there was only the shadowy

difference of legal distinction. Among all the tribunes the people chose for several centuries, they had scarcely five real friends to their interests. These tribunes lived, felt and saw, not like the people, but like the great patrician families, like senators and great officers of state, to get into which it was evident by their conduct, was their sole object. These tribunes often talked about the rights and prerogatives of the people, and that was all; for they never even attempted to establish equal liberty. So far from establishing the rights of the people, they suffered the senate, to the exclusion of the people, to engross the powers of taxation; those excellent and almost only real weapons of defense even the people of England possess. The tribunes obtained that the people should be eligible to some of the great offices of state, and marry, if they pleased, into the noble families; these were advantages in their nature, confined to a few elevated commoners, and of trifling importance to the people at large. Nearly the same observations may be made as to the ephori of Sparta.

We may amuse ourselves with names; but the fact is, men will be governed by the motives and temptations that surround their situation. Political evils to be guarded against are in the human character, and not in the name of patrician or plebeian. Had the people of Italy, in the early period of the republic, selected yearly or biennially, four or five hundred of their best informed men, emphatically from among themselves, these representatives would have formed an honest respectable assembly, capable of combining in them the views and exertions of the people and their respectability would have procured them honest and able leaders, and we should have seen equal liberty established. True liberty stands in need of a fostering band,- from the days of Adam she has found but one temple to dwell in securely. She has laid the foundation of one, perhaps her last in America; whether this is to be completed and have duration, is yet a question. Equal liberty never yet found many advocates among the great. It is a disagreeable truth that power perverts men's views in a greater degree than public employments inform their understandings.

They become hardened in certain maxims, and more lost to fellow feelings. Men may always be too cautious to commit alarming and glaring iniquities; but they, as well as systems, are liable to be corrupted by slow degrees. Junius well observes, we are not only to guard against what men will do, but even against what they may do. Men in high public offices are in stations where they gradually lose sight of the people, and do not often think of attending to them, except when necessary to answer private purposes.

The body of the people must have this true representative security placed some where in the nation. And in the United States, or in any extended empire, I am fully persuaded [it] can be placed no where, but in the forms of a federal republic, where we can divide and place it in several state or district legislatures, giving the people in these the means of opposing heavy internal taxes and oppressive measures in the proper stages. A great empire contains the amities and animosities of a world within itself. We are not like the people of England, one people
compactly settled on a small island, with a great city filled with frugal merchants, serving as a common centre of liberty and union. We are dispersed, and it is impracticable for any but the few to assemble in one place. The few must be watched, checked, and often resisted. Tyranny has ever shown a predilection to be in close amity with them, or the one man. Drive it from kings and it flies to senators, to decemviri, to dictators, to tribunes, to popular leaders, to military chiefs, etc.

De Lolme well observes, that in societies, laws which were to be equal to all are soon warped to the private interests of the administrators, and made to defend the usurpations of a few. The English, who had tasted the sweets of equal laws, were aware of this, and though they restored their king, they carefully delegated to parliament the advocates of freedom.

I have often lately heard it observed that it will do very well for a people to make a constitution and ordain that at stated periods they will choose, in a certain manner, a first magistrate, a given number of senators and representatives, and let them have all power to do as they please. This doctrine, however it may do for a small republic-as Connecticut, for instance, where the people may choose so many senators and representatives to assemble in the legislature, [representing] in an eminent degree, the interests, the views, feelings, and genuine sentiments of the people themselves - can never be admitted in an extensive country. And when this power is lodged in the hands of a few, not to limit the few is but one step short of giving absolute power to one man.

In a numerous representation the abuse of power is a common injury, and has no temptation; among the few, the abuse of power may often operate to the private emolument of those who abuse it.

THE FEDERAL FARMER

ANTI-FEDERALIST PAPER NO. 57

(PART III) Will The House Of Representatives Be Genuinely Representative?

.... But "the people must elect good men." Examine the system-is it practicable for them to elect fit and proper representatives where the number is so small? "But the people may choose whom they please." This is an observation, I believe, made without due attention to facts and the state of the community, To explain my meaning, I will consider the descriptions of men commonly presented to the people as candidates for the offices of representatives. We may rank them in three classes.

1. The men who form the natural aristocracy, as before defined.
2. Popular demagogues-these men also are often politically elevated, so as to be seen by the people through the extent of large districts; they often have some abilities, fare] without principle, and rise into notice by their noise and arts.
3. The substantial and respectable part of the democracy- they are a numerous and valuable set of men, who discern and judge well, but from being generally silent in public assemblies are often overlooked. They are the most substantial and best informed men in the several towns, who occasionally fill the middle grades of offices, etc., who hold not a splendid, but respectable rank in private concerns. These men are extensively diffused through all the counties, towns and small districts in the union; even they, and their immediate connections, are raised above the majority of the people, and as representatives are only brought to a level with a more numerous part of the community, the middle orders, and a degree nearer the mass of the people. Hence it is, that the best practical representation, even in a small state, must be several degrees more aristocratical than the body of the people. A representation so formed as to admit but few or none of the third class, is in my opinion, not deserving of the name. Even in armies, courts-martial are so formed as to admit subaltern officers into them. The true idea is, so to open and enlarge the representation as to let in a due proportion of the third class with those of the first. Now, my opinion is, that the representation proposed is so small as that ordinarily very few or none of them can be elected. And, therefore, after all the parade of words and forms, the government must possess the soul of aristocracy, or something worse, the spirit of popular leaders.

I observed in a former letter, that the state of Delaware, of Rhode Island, the Province of Maine, and each of the great counties in Massachusetts, etc., would have one member, and rather more than one when the representatives shall be increased to one for each 30,000 inhabitants. In some districts the people are more dispersed and unequal than in others. In Delaware they are compact, in the Province of Maine dispersed; how can the elections in either of those districts be regulated so that a man of the third class can be elected? Exactly the same principles and motives, the same uncontrollable circumstances, must govern the elections as in the choice of the governors. Call upon the people of either of those districts to choose a governor, and it will probably never happen that they will not bestow a major part, or the greatest number, of their votes on some very conspicuous or very popular character. A man that is known among a few thousands of people,

may be quite unknown among thirty or forty thousand. On the whole it appears to me to be almost a self- evident position, that when we call on thirty or forty thousand inhabitants to unite in giving their votes for one man it will be uniformly impracticable for them to unite in any men, except those few who have become eminent for their civil or military rank, or their popular legal abilities. It will be found totally impracticable for men in the private walks of life, except in the profession of the law, to become conspicuous enough to attract the notice of so many electors and have their suffrages.

But if I am right, it is asked why so many respectable men advocate the adoption of the proposed system. Several reasons may be given. Many of our gentlemen are attached to the principles of monarchy and aristocracy; they have an aversion to democratic republics. The body of the people have acquired large powers and substantial influence by the revolution. In the unsettled state of things, their numerous representatives, in some instances, misused their powers, and have induced many good men suddenly to adopt ideas unfavorable to such republics, and which ideas they will discard on reflection. Without scrutinizing into the particulars of the proposed system, we immediately perceive that its general tendency is to collect the powers of government, now in the body of the people in reality, and to place them in the higher orders and fewer hands; no wonder then that all those of and about these orders are attached to it. They feel there is something in this system advantageous to them. On the other hand, the body of the people evidently feel there is something wrong and disadvantageous to them. Both descriptions perceive there is something tending to bestow on the former the height of power and happiness, and to reduce the latter to weakness, insignificance, and misery. The people evidently feel all this though they want expressions to convey their ideas. Further, even the respectable part of the democracy have never yet been able to distinguish clearly where the fallacy lies. They find there are defects in the confederation; they see a system presented; they think something must be done; and, while their minds are in suspense, the zealous advocates force a reluctant consent. Nothing can be a stronger evidence of the nature of this system, than the general sense of the several orders in the community respecting its tendency. The parts taken generally by them proves my position, that notwithstanding the parade of words and forms, the government must possess the soul of aristocracy.

Congress, heretofore, have asked for moderate additional powers. The cry was give them-be federal. But the proper distinction between the cases that produce this disposition, and the system proposed, has not been fairly made and seen in all its consequences. We have seen some of our state representations too numerous and without examining a medium we run to the opposite extreme. It is true, the proper number of federal representatives, is matter of opinion in some degree; but there are extremes which we immediately perceive, and others which we clearly discover on examination. We should readily pronounce a representative branch of 15 members small in a federal government, having complete powers as to taxes, military matters, commerce, the coin, etc. On the other hand, we should readily pronounce a federal representation as numerous as those of the several states, consisting of about 1,500 representatives, unwieldy and totally improper. It is asked, has not the wisdom of the convention found the medium? Perhaps not. The convention was divided on this point of numbers. At least some of its ablest members urged, that instead of 65 representatives there ought to be 130 in the first instance. They fixed one representative for each 40,000 inhabitants, and at the close of the work, the president suggested that the representation appeared to be too small and without debate, it was put at, not

exceeding one for each 30,000. I mention these facts to show, that the convention went on no fixed data. In this extensive country it is difficult to get a representation sufficiently numerous.

Necessity, I believe, will oblige us to sacrifice in some degree the true genuine principles of representation. But this sacrifice ought to be as little as possible. How far we ought to increase the representation I will not pretend to say; but that we ought to increase it very considerably, is clear-to double it at least, making full allowances for the state representations. And this we may evidently do and approach accordingly towards safety and perfection without encountering any inconveniences. It is with great difficulty the people can unite these different interests and views even tolerably, in the state senators, who are more than twice as numerous as the federal representatives, as proposed by the convention; even these senators are considered as so far removed from the people, that they are not allowed immediately to hold their purse strings. The principal objections made to the increase of the representation are, the expense and difficulty in getting the members to attend. The first cannot be important; the last, if founded, is against any federal government. As to the expense, I presume the house of representatives will not be in sessions more than four months in the year. We find by experience that about two-thirds of the members of representative assemblies usually attend; therefore, of the representation proposed by the convention, about forty-five members probably will attend. Doubling their number, about 90 will probably attend. Their pay, in one case, at four dollars a day each (which is putting it high enough) will amount to, yearly, 21,600 dollars; in the other case, 43,200 dollars-[a] difference [of] 21,600 dollars. Reduce the state representatives from 1,500 down to 1,000 and thereby save the attendance of two-thirds of the 500, say three months in a year, at one dollar and a quarter a day each [would amount to] 37,125 dollars. Thus we may leave the state representations sufficient large, and yet save enough by the reduction nearly to support exceeding well the whole federal representation I propose. Surely we -never can be so unwise as to sacrifice, essentially, the all- important principles of representation for so small a sum as 21,600 dollars a year for the United States. A single company of soldiers would cost this sum. It is a fact that can easily be shown, that we expend three times this sum every year upon useless inferior offices and very trifling concerns. It is also a fact which can be shown that the United States in the late war suffered more by a faction in the federal government, then the pay of the federal representation will amount to for twenty years.

As to the attendance-can we be so unwise as to establish an unsafe and inadequate representative branch, and give it as a reason, that we believe only a few members will be induced to attend?

We ought certainly to establish an adequate representative branch, and adopt measures to induce an attendance. I believe that a due proportion of 130 or 140 members may be induced to attend.

There are various reasons for the non-attendance of the members of the present congress; it is to be presumed that these will not exist under the new system...

Documents of Revolution

In the second place, it is said the members of congress must return home, and share in the burdens they may impose; and, therefore, private motives will induce them to make mild laws, to support liberty, and ease the burdens of the people, This brings us to a mere question of interest under this head. I think these observations will appear, on examination, altogether fallacious; because this individual interest, which may coincide with the rights and interests of the people, will be far more than balanced by opposite motives and opposite interests. If, on a fair calculation, a man will gain more by measures oppressive to others than he will lose by them, he is interested in their adoption. It is true, that those who govern generally, by increasing the public burdens, increase their own share of them; but by this increase they may, and often do, increase their salaries, fees, and emoluments, in a tenfold proportion, by increasing salaries, forming armies and navies, and by making offices. If it shall appear the members of congress will have these temptations before them, the argument is on my side. They will view the account, and be induced continually to make efforts advantageous to themselves and connections, and oppressive to others. We must examine facts. Congress, in its present form, have but few offices to dispose of worth the attention of the members, or of men of the aristocracy. Yet from 1774 to this time, we find a large proportion of those offices assigned to those who were or had been members of congress; and though the states choose annually sixty or seventy members, many of them have been provided for. But few men are known to congress in this extensive country, and, probably, but few will be to the president and senate, except those who have or shall appear as members of congress, or those whom the members may bring forward. The states may now choose yearly ninety-one members of congress; under the new constitution they will have it in their power to choose exactly the same number, perhaps afterwards, one hundred and :fifteen, but these must be chosen once in two and six years. So that, in the course of ten years together, not more than two-thirds so many members of congress will be elected and brought into view, as there now are under the confederation in the same term of time. But at least there will be five, if not ten times, as many offices and places worthy of the attention of the members, under the new constitution, as there are under the confederation. Therefore, we may fairly presume, that a very great proportion of the members of congress, especially the influential ones, instead of returning to private life, will be provided for with lucrative offices, in the civil or military department; and not only the members, but many of their sons, friends, and connections. These offices will be in the constitutional disposition of the president and senate, and, corruption out of the question, what kind of security can we expect in a representation so many of the members of which may rationally feel themselves candidates for these offices? Let common sense decide. It is true, that members chosen to offices must leave their seats in congress; and to some few offices they cannot be elected till the time shall be expired for which they were elected members. But this scarcely will effect the bias arising from the hopes and expectations of office....

But it is asked how shall we remedy the evil, so as to complete and perpetuate the temple of equal laws and equal liberty? Perhaps we never can do it. Possibly we never may be able to do it in this immense country, under any one system of laws however modified. Nevertheless, at present, I think the experiment worth making. I feel an aversion to the disunion of the states, and to separate confederacies; the states have fought and bled in a common cause, and great dangers too may attend these confederacies. I think the system proposed capable of very considerable degrees of perfection, if we pursue first principles. I do not think that De Lolme, or any writer I have seen, has sufficiently pursued the proper inquiries and efficient means for making representation and balances in government more perfect. It is our task to do this in America. Our object is equal liberty, and equal laws diffusing their influence among all orders of men. To obtain this we must guard against the bias of interest and passions, against interested combinations, secret or open. We must aim at a balance of efforts and strength. Clear it is, by increasing the representation we lessen the prospects of each member of congress being provided for in public offices. We proportionably lessen official influence, and strengthen his prospects of becoming a private citizen, subject to the common burdens, without the compensation of the emoluments of office. By increasing the representation we make it more difficult to corrupt and influence the members. We diffuse them more extensively among the body of the people, perfect the balance, multiply information, strengthen the confidence of the people, and consequently support the laws on equal and free principles. There are two other ways, I think, of obtaining in some degree the security we want; the one is, by excluding more extensively the members from being appointed to offices; the other is, by limiting some of their powers. These two I shall examine hereafter.

THE FEDERAL FARMER

ANTI-FEDERALIST PAPER NO. 58

(PART IV)Will The House Of Representatives Be Genuinely Representative?

It is said that our people have a high sense of freedom, possess power, property, and the strong arm; meaning, I presume, that the body of the people can take care of themselves, and awe their rulers; and, therefore, particular provision in the constitution for their security may not be essential. When I come to examine these observations, they appear to me too trifling and loose to deserve a serious answer.

To palliate for the smallness of the representation, it is observed, that the state governments in which the people are fully represented, necessarily form a part of the system. This idea ought to be fully examined. We ought to inquire if the convention have made the proper use of these essential parts. The state governments then, we are told, will stand between the arbitrary exercise of power and the people. True they may, but armless and helpless, perhaps, with the privilege of making a noise when hurt. This is no more than individuals may do. Does the constitution provide a single check for a single measure by which the state governments can constitutionally and regularly check the arbitrary measures of congress? Congress may raise immediately fifty thousand men and twenty millions of dollars in taxes, build a navy, model the militia, etc., and all this constitutionally. Congress may arm on every point, and the state governments can do no more than an individual, by petition to congress, suggest their measures are alarming and not right.

I conceive the position to be undeniable, that the federal government will be principally in the hands of the natural aristocracy, and the state governments principally in the hands of the democracy, the representatives of the body of the people. These representatives in Great Britain hold the purse, and have a negative upon all laws. We must yield to circumstances and depart something from this plan, and strike out a new medium so as to give efficacy to the whole system, supply the wants of the union, and leave the several states, or the people assembled in the state legislatures, the means of defense.

It has been often mentioned that the objects of congress will be few and national, and require a small representation; that the objects of each state will be many and local, and require a numerous representation. This circumstance has not the weight of a feather in my mind. It is certainly inadvisable to lodge in 65 representatives, and 26 senators, unlimited power to establish systems of taxation, armies, navies, model the militia, and to do every thing that may essentially tend soon to change, totally, the affairs of the community; and to assemble 1500 state representatives, and 160 senators, to make fence laws and laws to regulate the descent and conveyance of property, the administration of justice between man and man, to appoint militia officers, etc.

It is not merely the quantity of information I contend for. Two taxing powers may be inconvenient; but the point is, congress, like the senate of Rome, will have taxing powers, and the people no check. When the power is abused, the people may complain and grow angry, so

may the state governments; they may remonstrate and counteract, by passing laws to prohibit the collection of congressional taxes. But these will be acts of the people, acts of sovereign power, the dernier resort unknown to the constitution; acts operating in terrorem, acts of resistance, and not the exercise of any constitutional power to stop or check a measure before matured. A check properly is the stopping, by one branch in the same legislature, a measure proposed by the other in it. In fact the constitution provides for the states no check, properly speaking, upon the measures of congress. Congress can immediately enlist soldiers, and apply to the pockets of the people.

These few considerations bring us to the very strong distinction between the plan that operates on federal principles, and the plan that operates on consolidated principles. A plan may be federal or not as to its organization each state may retain its vote or not; the sovereignty of the state may be represented, or the people of it. A plan may be federal or not as to its operation-federal when it requires men and monies of the states, and the states as such make the laws for raising the men and monies; not federal when it leaves the states' governments out of the question, and operates immediately upon the persons and property of the citizens. The first is the case with the confederation; the second with the new plan. In the first the state governments may be [a] check; in the last none at all. . . .

It is also said that the constitution gives no more power to congress than the confederation, respecting money and military matters; that congress under the confederation, may require men and monies to any amount, and the states are bound to comply. This is generally true; but, I think

... that the states have well founded checks for securing their liberties. I admit the force of the observation that all the federal powers, by the confederation, are lodged in a single assembly.

However, I think much more may be said in defense of the leading principles of the confederation. I do not object to the qualifications of the electors of representatives, and I fully agree that the people ought to elect one branch.

Further, it may be observed, that the present congress is principally an executive body, which ought not to be numerous; that the house of representatives will be a mere legislative branch, and being the democratic on ought to be numerous. It is one of the greatest advantages of a government of different branches, that each branch may be conveniently made conformable to the nature of the business assigned it, and all be made conformable to the condition of the several orders of the people. After all the possible checks and limitations we can devise, the powers of the union must be very extensive; the sovereignty of the nation cannot produce the object in view, the defense and tranquility of the whole, without such powers, executive and judicial. I dislike the present congress-a single assembly-because it is impossible to fit it to receive those powers. The executive and judicial powers, in the nature of things, ought to be lodged in a few hands; the legislature in many hands. Therefore, want of safety and unavoidable hasty measures out of the question, they never can all be lodged in one assembly properly-it, in its very formation, must imply a contradiction.

In objection to increasing the representation, it has also been observed that it is difficult to assemble a hundred men or more without making the tumultuous and a mere mob. Reason and experience do not support this observation. The most respectable assemblies we have any knowledge of and the wisest, have been those, each of which consisted of several hundred members - as the senate of Rome, of Carthage, of Venice, the British Parliament, etc. I think I may, without hazarding much, affirm that our more numerous state assemblies and conventions have universally discovered more wisdom, and as much order, as the less numerous ones. There must be also a very great difference between the characters of two or three hundred men assembled from a single state, and the characters of that number or half the number assembled from all the united states. It is added, that on the proposed plan the house of representatives in fifty or a hundred years will consist of several hundred members. The plan will begin with sixty-five, and we have no certainty that the number ever will increase, for this plain reason-that all that combination of interests and influence which has produced this plan, and supported [it] so far, will constantly oppose the increase of the representation, knowing that thereby the government will become more free and democratic. But admitting, after a few years, there will be a member for each 30,000 inhabitants, the observation is trifling; the government is in a considerable measure to take its tone from its early movements, and by means of a small representation it may in half of 50 or 100 years, get moved from its basis, or at least so far as to be incapable of ever being recovered. We ought, therefore, ... now to fix the government on proper principles, and fit to our present condition. When the representation shall become too numerous, alter it. Or we may now make provision, that when the representation shall be increased to a given number, that then there shall be one for each given number of inhabitants, etc.

Another observation is, that congress will have no temptations to do wrong. The men that make it must be very uninformed, or suppose they are talking to children. In the first place, the members will be governed by all those motives which govern the conduct of men, and have before them all the allurements of offices and temptations to establish unequal burdens, before described. In the second place, they and their friends, probably, will find it for their interests to keep up large armies, navies, salaries, etc., and in laying adequate taxes. In the third place, we have no good grounds to presume, from reason or experience, that it will be agreeable to their characters or views, that the body of the people should continue to have power effectually to interfere in the affairs of government. But it is confidently added, that congress will not have it in their power to oppress or enslave the people; that the people will not bear it. It is not supposed that congress will act the tyrant immediately, and in the face of daylight. It is not supposed congress will adopt important measures without plausible pretenses, especially those which may tend to alarm or produce opposition. We are to consider the natural progress of things-that men unfriendly to republican equality will go systematically to work, gradually to exclude the body of the people from any share in the government, first of the substance, and then of the forms. The men who will have these views will not be without their agents and supporters. When we reflect, that a few years ago we established democratic republics, and fixed the state governments as the barriers between congress and the pickets of the people, what great progress has been made in less than seven years to break down those barriers, and essentially to change the principles of our governments, even by the armless few-is it chimerical to suppose that in fifteen or twenty years to come, that much more can be performed, especially after the adoption of the constitution, when the few will be so much better armed with power and influence, to continue the struggle?

Probably they will be wise enough never to alarm, but gradually prepare the minds of the people for one specious change after another, till the final object shall be obtained. Say the advocates, these are only possibilities. They are probabilities a wise people ought to guard against; and the address made use of to keep the evils out of sight, and the means to prevent them, confirm my opinion.

But to obviate all objections to the proposed plan in the last resort, it is said our people will be free, so long as they possess the habits of freemen, and when they lose them, they must receive some other forms of government. To this I shall only observe, that this is very humiliating language, and can, I trust, never suit a manly people who have contended nobly for liberty, and declared to the world they will be free.

THE FEDERAL FARMER

ANTI-FEDERALIST PAPER NO. 59

The Danger of Congressional Control Of Elections

Alexander Hamilton, in Federalist #59, addresses this same topic from an opposing viewpoint.

This essay was written anonymously by "VOX POPULI," and appeared in The Massachusetts Gazette on October 30, 1787.

. . I beg leave to Jay before the candid public the first clause in the fourth section of the first article of the proposed Constitution:

"The times, places and manner of holding elections, for senators and representatives, shall be prescribed in each state by the legislature thereof; but the Congress may, at any time, by law, make or alter such regulations except as to the places of choosing senators."

By this clause, the time, place and manner of choosing representatives is wholly at the disposal of Congress.

Why the Convention who formed the proposed Constitution wished to invest Congress with such a power, I am by no means capable of saying; or why the good people of this commonwealth [Massachusetts] should delegate such a power to them, is no less hard to determine. But as the subject is open for discussion, I shall make a little free inquiry into the matter.

And, first. What national advantage is there to be acquired by giving them such a power?

The only advantage which I have heard proposed by it is, to prevent a partial representation of the several states in Congress; "for if the time, manner and place were left wholly in the hands of the state legislatures, it is probable they would not make provision by appointing time, manner and place for an election; in which case there could be no election, and consequently the federal government weakened."

But this provision is by no means sufficient to prevent an evil of that nature. For will any reasonable man suppose-that when the legislature of any state, who are annually chosen, are so corrupt as to break thro' that government which they have formed, and refuse to appoint time, place and manner of choosing representatives-I say, can any person suppose, that a state so corrupt would not be full as likely to neglect, or even refuse, to choose representatives at the time and place and in the manner prescribed by Congress? Surely they would. So it could answer no good national purpose on that account; and I have not heard any other national advantage proposed thereby.

We will now proceed, in the next place, to consider why the people of this commonwealth should vest Congress with such a power.

No one proposes that it would be any advantage to the people of this state. Therefore, it must be considered as a matter of indifference, except there is an opportunity for its operating to their disadvantage-in which case, I conceive it ought to be disapprobated.

Whether there is danger of its operating to the good people's disadvantage, shall now be the subject of our inquiry.

Supposing Congress should direct, that the representatives of this commonwealth should be chosen all in one town, (Boston, for instance) on the first day of March - would not that be a very injurious institution to the good people of this commonwealth? Would not there be at least nine-tenths of the landed interest of this commonwealth entirely unrepresented? Surely one may reasonably imagine there would. What, then, would be the case if Congress should think proper to direct, that the elections should be held at the north-west, south-west, or north-east part of the state, the last day of March? How many electors would there attend the business? And it is a little remarkable, that any gentleman should suppose, that Congress could possibly be in any measure as good judges of the time, place and manner of elections as the legislatures of the several respective states.

These as objections I could wish to see obviated. And I could wish the public inquiry might extend to a consideration, whether or not it would not be more conducive, to prevent a partial representation, to invest Congress with power to levy such a fine as they might think proper on states not choosing representatives, than by giving them this power of appointing time, manner and place.

It is objected by some, that Congress could not levy, or at least, could not collect, such a fine of a delinquent state. If that is the case, Congress could not collect any tax they might think proper to levy, nor execute any order whatever; but at any time any state might break through the national compact, dissolve the federal constitution, and set the whole structure afloat on the ocean of chaos.

It is, therefore, proposed to the public to consider, whether the said clause in the fourth section of the first article can answer the only purposes for which it is said to have been provided, or any other which will prove any advantage either to the nation or state.

VOX POPULI

ANTI-FEDERALIST PAPER NO. 60

Will the Constitution Promote The Interests Of Favorite Classes?

John F. Mercer of Maryland was the author of this essay, taken from his testimony to members of the ratifying conventions of New York and Virginia, 1788, (From the Etting Collection of the Historical Society of Pennsylvania.)

We have not that permanent and fixed distinction of ranks or orders of men among us, which unalterably separating the interests and views, produces that division in pursuits which is the great security of the mixed Government we separated from and which we now seem so anxiously to copy. If the new Senate of the United States will be really opposite in their pursuits and views from the Representatives, have they not a most dangerous power of interesting foreign nations by Treaty [to] support Their views?-for instance, the relinquishment of the navigation of [the]

Mississippi-and yet where Treaties are expressly declared paramount to the Constitutions of the several States, and being the supreme law, [the Senate] must of course control the national legislature, if not supersede the Constitution of the United States itself. The check of the President over a Body, with which he must act in concert-or his influence and power be almost annihilated-can prove no great constitutional security. And even the Representative body itself . .

. are not sufficiently numerous to secure them from corruption. For all governments tend to corruption, in proportion as power concentrating in the hands of the few, tenders them objects of corruption to Foreign Nations and among themselves.

For these and many other reasons we are for preserving the rights of the State governments, where they must not be necessarily relinquished for the welfare of the Union. And, where so relinquished, the line should be definitely drawn. If under the proposed Constitution the States exercise any power, it would seem to be at the mercy of the General Government. For it is remarkable that the clause securing to them those rights not expressly relinquished in the old Confederation, is left out in the new Constitution. And we conceive that there is no power which Congress may think necessary to exercise for the general welfare, which they may not assume under this Constitution. And this Constitution, and the laws made under it, are declared paramount even to the unalienable rights which have heretofore been secured to the citizens of these States by their constitutional compacts. . . .

Moreover those very powers, which are to be expressly vested in the new Congress, are of a nature most liable to abuse. They are those which tempt the avarice and ambition of men to a violation of the rights of their fellow citizens, and they will be screened under the sanction of an undefined and unlimited authority. Against the abuse and improper exercise of these special powers, the people have a right to be secured by a sacred Declaration, defining the rights of the individual, and limiting by them the extent of the exercise. The people were secured against the abuse of those powers by fundamental laws and a Bill of Rights, under the government of Britain and under their own Constitution. That government which permits the abuse of power, recommends it, and will deservedly experience the tyranny which it authorizes; for the history of mankind establishes the truth of this political adage-that in government what may be done will be done.

The most blind admirer of this Constitution must in his heart confess that it is as far inferior to the British Constitution, of which it is an imperfect imitation, as darkness is to light. In the British Constitution the rights of men, the primary object of the social compact, are fixed on an immoveable foundation and clearly defined and ascertained by their Magna Charta, their Petition of Rights, their Bill of Rights, and their effective administration by ostensible Ministers secures responsibility. In this new Constitution a complicated system sets responsibility at defiance and the rights of men neglected and undefined are left at the mercy of events. We vainly plume ourselves on the safeguard alone of representation, forgetting that it will be a representation on principles inconsistent with true and just representation; that it is but a delusive shadow of representation, proffering in theory what can never be fairly reduced to practice. And, after all, government by representation (unless confirmed in its views and conduct by the constant inspection, immediate superintendence, and frequent interference and control of the people themselves on one side, or an hereditary nobility on the other, both of which orders have fixed and permanent views) is really only as one of perpetual rapine and confusion. Even with the best checks it has failed in all the governments of Europe, of which it was once the basis, except that of England.

When we turn our eyes back to the zones of blood and desolation which we have waded through to separate from Great Britain, we behold with manly indignation that our blood and treasure have been wasted to establish a government in which the interest of the few is preferred to the rights of the many. When we see a government so every way inferior to that we were born under, proposed as the reward of our sufferings in an eight years calamitous war, our astonishment is only equaled by our resentment. On the conduct of Virginia and New York, two important States, the preservation of liberty in a great measure depends. The chief security of a Confederacy of Republics was boldly disregarded, and the Confederation violated, by requiring 9 instead of 13 voices to alter the Constitution. But still the resistance of either of these States in the present temper of America (for the late conduct of the party here [Maryland] must open the eyes of the people in Massachusetts with respect to the fate of their amendment) will secure all that we mean to contend for-the natural and unalienable rights of men in a constitutional manner.

At the distant appearance of danger to these, we took up arms in the late Revolution. And may we never have cause to look back with regret on that period when connected with the Empire of Great Britain, we were happy, secure and free.

ANTI-FEDERALIST PAPER NO. 61

Questions And Comments On The Constitutional Provisions Regarding The Election Of Congressmen

.... It is well observed by Montesquieu, that in republican governments the forms of elections are fundamental; and that it is an essential part of the social compact, to ascertain by whom, to whom, when, and in what manner, suffrages are to be given. Wherever we find the regulation of elections have not been carefully fixed by the constitution, or the principles of them, we constantly see new legislatures modifying ... [their] own form, and changing the spirit of the government to answer partial purposes.

By the proposed plan it is -fixed, that the qualifications of the electors of the federal representatives shall be the same as those of the electors of state representatives; though these vary some in the several states the electors are fixed and designated. The qualifications of the representatives are also fixed and designated, and no person under 25 years of age, not an inhabitant of the state, and not having been seven years a citizen of the United States, can be elected. The clear inference is, that all persons 25 years of age, and upwards, inhabitants of the state, and having been, at any period or periods, seven years citizens of the United States, may be elected representatives. They have a right to be elected by the constitution, and the electors have a right to choose them. This is fixing the federal representation, as to the elected, on a very broad basis. It can be no objection to the elected, that they are Christians, Pagans, Mahometans, or Jews; that they are of any color, rich or poor, convict or not. Hence many men may be elected, who cannot be electors. Gentlemen who have commented so largely upon the wisdom of the constitution, for excluding from being elected young men under a certain age, would have done well to have recollected, that it positively makes pagans, convicts, etc., eligible. The people make the constitution; they exclude a few persons, by certain descriptions, from being elected, and all not thus excluded are clearly admitted. Now a man 25 years old, an inhabitant of the state, and having been a citizen of the states seven years, though afterwards convicted, may be elected, because not within any of the excluding clauses; the same of a beggar, an absentee, etc.

The right of the electors, and eligibility of the elected, being fixed by the people, they cannot be narrowed by the state legislatures, or congress. It is established, that a man being (among other qualifications) an inhabitant of the state, shall be eligible. Now it would be narrowing the right of the people to confine them in their choice to a man, an inhabitant of a particular county or district in the state. Hence it follows, that neither the state legislatures nor congress can establish district elections; that is, divide the state into districts, and confine the electors of each district to the choice of a man resident in it. If the electors could be thus limited in one respect, they might in another be confined to choose a man of a particular religion, of certain property, etc., and thereby half of the persons made eligible by the constitution be excluded. All laws, therefore, for regulating elections must be made on the broad basis of the constitution.

Next, we may observe, that representatives are to be chosen by the people of the state. What is a choice by the people of the state? If each given district in it choose one, will that be a choice within the meaning of the constitution? Must the choice be by plurality of votes, or a majority?

Documents of Revolution

In connection with these questions, we must take the 4th Sect., Art I., where it is said the state legislatures shall prescribe the times, places, and manner of holding elections; but congress may make or alter such regulations. By this clause, I suppose, the electors of different towns and districts in the state may be assembled in different places, to give their votes; but when so assembled, by another clause they cannot, by congress or the state legislatures, be restrained from giving their votes for any man an inhabitant of the state, and qualified as to age, and having been a citizen the time required. But I see nothing in the constitution by which to decide, whether the choice shall be by a plurality or a majority of votes. This, in my mind, is by far the most important question in the business of elections. When we say a representative shall be chosen by the people, it seems to imply that he shall be chosen by a majority of them; but states which use the same phraseology in this respect, practice both ways. I believe a majority of the states choose by pluralities; and, I think it probable, that the federal house of representatives will decide that a choice of its members by pluralities is constitutional. A man who has the most votes is chosen in Great Britain. It is this, among other things, that gives every man fair play in the game of influence and corruption. I believe that not much stress was laid upon the objection that congress may assemble the electors at some out of the way place. However, the advocates seem to think they obtain a victory of no small glory and importance, when they can show, with some degree of color, that the evil is rather a possibility than a probability. . .

It is easy to perceive that there is an essential difference between elections by pluralities and by majorities, between choosing a man in a small or limited district, and choosing a number of men promiscuously by the people of a large state. And while we are almost secure of judicious unbiased elections by majorities in such districts, we have no security against deceptions, influence and corruption in states or large districts in electing by pluralities. When a choice is made by a plurality of votes, it is often made by a very small part of the electors, who attend and give their votes; when by a majority, never by so few as one half of them. The partialities and improprieties attending the former mode may be illustrated by a case that lately happened in one of the middle states. Several representatives were to be chosen by a large number of inhabitants compactly settled, among whom there were four or five thousand voters. Previous to the time of election a number of lists of candidates were published, to divide and distract the voters in general. About half a dozen men of some influence, who had a favorite list to carry, met several times, fixed their list, and agreed to hand it about among all who could probably be induced to adopt it, and to circulate the other lists among their opponents, to divide them. The poll was opened, and several hundred electors, suspecting nothing, attended and put in their votes. The list of the half dozen was carried, and men were found to be chosen, some of whom were very disagreeable to a large majority of the electors. Though several hundred electors voted, men on that list were chosen who had only 45, 43, 44, etc., votes each. They had a plurality, that is, more than any other persons. The votes generally were scattered, and those who made even a feeble combination succeeded in placing highest upon the list several very unthought of and very unpopular men. This evil never could have happened in a town where all the voters meet in one place, and consider no man as elected unless he have a majority, or more than half of all the votes. Clear it is, that the man on whom thus but a small part of the votes are bestowed cannot possess the confidence of the people, or have any considerable degree of influence over them.

But as partial, as liable to secret influence, and corruption as the choice by pluralities may be, I think, we cannot avoid it, without essentially increasing the federal representation, and adopting the principle of district elections. There is but one case in which the choice by the majority is practicable, and that is, where districts are formed of such moderate extent that the electors in each can conveniently meet in one place, and at one time, and proceed to the choice of a representative; when, if no man have a majority or more than half of all the votes the first time, the voters may examine the characters of those brought forward, accommodate, and proceed to repeat their votes till some one shall have that majority. This, I believe, cannot be a case under the constitution proposed in its present form. To explain my ideas, take Massachusetts, for instance. She is entitled to eight representatives. She has 370,000 inhabitants, about 46,000 to one representative. If the elections be so held that the electors throughout the state meet in their several towns or places, and each elector puts in his vote for eight representatives, the votes of the electors will ninety-nine times in a hundred, be so scattered that on collecting the votes from the several towns or places, no men will be found, each of whom have a majority of the votes, and therefore the election will not be made .... I might add many other observations to evince the superiority and solid advantages of proper district elections, and a choice by a majority, and to prove that many evils attend the contrary practice. These evils we must encounter as the constitution now stands. I see no way to fix elections on a proper footing, and to render tolerably equal and secure the federal representation, but by increasing the representation, so as to have one representative for each district in which the electors may conveniently meet in one place, and at one time, and choose by a majority. Perhaps this might be effected pretty generally, by fixing one representative for each twelve thousand inhabitants; dividing, or fixing the principles for dividing the states into proper districts; and directing the electors of each district to the choice, by a majority, of some men having a permanent interest and

residence in it. I speak of a representation tolerably equal, etc., because I am still of opinion, that it is impracticable in this extensive country to have a federal representation sufficiently democratic, or substantially drawn from the body of the people. The principles just mentioned may be the best practical ones we can expect to establish. By thus increasing the representation we not only make it more democratical and secure, strengthen the confidence of the people in it, and thereby render it more nervous and energetic; but it will also enable the people essentially to change, for the better, the principles and forms of elections. To provide for the people's wandering throughout the state for a representative may sometimes enable them to elect a more brilliant or an abler man, than by confining them to districts; but generally this latitude will be used to pernicious purposes, especially connected with the choice by plurality-when a man in the remote part of the state, perhaps obnoxious at home, but ambitious and intriguing, may be chosen to represent the people in another part of the state far distant, and by a small part of them, or by a faction, or by a combination of some particular description of men among them. This has been long the case in Great Britain; it is the case in several states; nor do I think that such pernicious practices will be merely possible in our federal concerns, but highly probable. By establishing district elections, we exclude none of the best men from being elected; and we fix what, in my mind, is of far more importance than brilliant talents-I mean a sameness, as to residence and interests, between the representative and his constituents. And by the election by a majority, he is sure to be the man, the choice of more than half of them....
THE FEDERAL FARMER

ANTI-FEDERALIST PAPER NO. 62

(PART I) On the Organization And powers of the Senate

Taken from the 16th essay of "Brutus" from The New York Journal of April 10, 1788.
The following things may be observed with respect to the constitution of the Senate.
1st. They are to be elected by the legislatures of the States and not by the people, and each State is to be represented by an equal number.
2d. They are to serve for six years, except that one third of those first chosen are to go out of office at the expiration of two years, one third at the expiration of four years, and one third at the expiration of six years, after which this rotation is to be preserved, but still every member will serve for the term of six years.
3d. If vacancies happen by resignation or otherwise, during the recess of the legislature of any State, the executive is authorised to make temporary appointments until the next meeting of the legislature.
4. No person can be a senator who had not arrived to the age of thirty years, been nine years a citizen of the United States, and who is not at the time he is elected an inhabitant of the State for which he is elected.
The apportionment of members of the Senate among the States is not according to numbers, or the importance of the States, but is equal. This, on the plan of a consolidated government, is unequal and improper; but is proper on the system of confederation - on this principle I approve of it. It is indeed the only feature of any importance in the constitution of a confederated government. It was obtained after a vigorous struggle of that part of the Convention who were in favor of preserving the state governments. It is to be regretted that they were not able to have infused other principles into the plan, to have secured the government of the respective states, and to have marked with sufficient precision the line between them and the general government.
The term for which the senate are to be chosen, is in my judgment too long, and no provision being made for a rotation will, I conceive, be of dangerous consequence.
It is difficult to fix the precise period for which the senate should be chosen. It is a matter of opinion, and our sentiments on the matter must be formed, by attending to certain principles.
Some of the duties which are to be performed by the Senate, seem evidently to point out the propriety of their term of service being extended beyond the period of that of the assembly.
Besides, as they are designed to represent the aristocracy of the country, it seems fit they should possess more stability, and so continue a longer period then that branch who represent the democracy. The business of making treaties and some other which it will be proper to commit to the senate, requires that they should have experience, and therefore that they should remain

some time in office to acquire it. But still it is of equal importance that they should not be so long in office as to be likely to forget the hand that formed them, or be insensible of their interests. Men

long in office are very apt to feel themselves independent; to form and pursue interests separate from those who appointed them. And this is more likely to be the case with the senate, as they will for the most part of the time be absent from the state they represent, and associate with such company as will possess very little of the feelings of the middling class of people. For it is to be remembered that there is to be a federal city, and the inhabitants of it will be the great and the mighty of the earth. For these reasons I would shorten the term of their service to four years. Six years is a long period for a man to be absent from his home; it would have a tendency to wean him from his constituents.

A rotation in the senate would also in my opinion be of great use. It is probable that senators once chosen for a state will, as the system now stands, continue in office for life. The office will be honorable if not lucrative. The persons who occupy it will probably wish to continue in it, and therefore use all their influence and that of their friends to continue in office. Their friends will be numerous and powerful, for they will have it in their power to confer great favors-, besides it will before long be considered as disgraceful not to be reelected. It will therefore be considered as a matter of delicacy to the character of the senator not to return him again. Everybody acquainted with public affairs knows how difficult it is to remove from office a person who is long been in it. It is seldom done except in cases of gross misconduct. It is rare that want of competent ability procures it. To prevent this inconvenience I conceive it would be wise to determine, that a senator should not be eligible after he had served for the period assigned by the constitution for a certain number of years; perhaps three would be sufficient. A further benefit would be derived from such an arrangement; it would give opportunity to bring forward a greater number of men to serve their country, and would return those, who had served, to their state, and afford them the advantage of becoming better acquainted with the condition and politics of their constituents. It further appears to me proper, that the legislatures should retain the right which they now hold under the confederation, of recalling their members. It seems an evident dictate of reason that when a person authorises another to do a piece of business for him, he should retain the power to displace him, when he does not conduct according to his pleasure. This power in the state legislatures, under confederation, has not been exercised to the injury of the government, nor do I see any danger of its being so exercised under the new system. It may operate much to the public benefit.

These brief remarks are all I shall make on the organization of the senate. The powers with which they are invested will require a more minute investigation.

This body will possess a strange mixture of legislative, executive, and judicial powers, which in my opinion will in some cases clash with each other.

1. They are one branch of the legislature, and in this respect will possess equal powers in all cases with the house of representatives; for I consider the clause which gives the house of representatives the right of originating bills for raising a revenue as merely nominal, seeing the senate . . . [has the power] to propose or concur with amendments.

2. They are a branch of the executive in the appointment of ambassadors and public ministers, and in the appointment of all other officers, not otherwise provided for. Whether the forming of

treaties, in which they are joined with the president, appertains to the legislative or the executive part of the government, or to neither, is not material.

3. They are a part of the judicial, for they form the court of impeachments.

It has been a long established maxim, that the legislative, executive and judicial departments in government should be kept distinct. It is said, I know, that this cannot be done. And therefore that this maxim is not just, or at least that it should only extend to certain leading features in a government. I admit that this distinction cannot be perfectly preserved. In a due balanced government, it is perhaps absolutely necessary to give the executive qualified legislative powers, and the legislative or a branch of them judicial powers in the last resort. It may possibly also, in some special cases, be advisable to associate the legislature, or a branch of it, with the executive, in the exercise of acts of great national importance. But still the maxim is a good one, and a separation of these powers should be sought as far as is practicable. I can scarcely imagine that any of the advocates of the system will pretend, that it was necessary to accumulate all these powers in the senate. There is a propriety in the senate's possessing legislative powers. This is the principal end which should be held in view in their appointment. I need not here repeat what has so often and ably been advanced on the subject of a division of the legislative power into two branches. The arguments in favor of it I think conclusive. But I think it equally evident, that a branch of the legislature should not be invested with the power of appointing officers. This power in the senate is very improperly lodged for a number of reasons - These shall be detailed in a future number.

BRUTUS

ANTI-FEDERALIST PAPER NO. 63

(PART II) On the Organization and Powers Of The Senate

.... The senate is an assembly of 26 members, two from each state; though the senators are apportioned on the federal plan, they will vote individually. They represent the states, as bodies politic, sovereign to certain purposes. The states being sovereign and independent, are all considered equal, each with the other in the senate. In this we are governed solely by the ideal equalities of sovereignties; the federal and state governments forming one whole, and the state governments an essential part, which ought always to be kept distinctly in view, and preserved. I feel more disposed, on reflection, to acquiesce in making them the basis of the senate, and thereby to make it the interest and duty of the senators to preserve distinct, and to perpetuate the respective, sovereignties they shall represent. . . .

The senate, as a legislative branch, is not large, but as an executive branch quite too numerous. It is not to be presumed that we can form a genuine senatorial branch in the United States, a real representation of the aristocracy and balance in the legislature, any more than we can form a genuine representation of the people. Could we separate the aristocratical and democratical interest, compose the senate of the former, and the house of assembly of the latter, they are too unequal in the United States to produce a balance. Form them on pure principles, and leave each to be supported by its real weight and connections, the senate would be feeble and the house powerful. I say, on pure principles; because I make a distinction between a senate that derives its weight and influence from a pure source-its numbers and wisdom, its extensive property, its extensive and permanent connections -and a senate composed of a few men, possessing small property, and small and unstable connections, that derives its weight and influence from a corrupt or pernicious source: that is, merely from the power given it by the constitution and laws, to dispose of the public offices, and the annexed emoluments, and by those means to interest officers, and the hungry expectants of offices, in support of its measures. I wish the proposed senate may not partake too much of the latter description.

To produce a balance and checks, the constitution proposes two branches in the legislature. But they are so formed, that the members of both must generally be the same kind of men-men having similar interests and views, feelings and connections -men of the same grade in society, and who associate on all, occasions (probably, if there be any difference, the senators will be the most democratic.) Senators and representatives thus circumstanced, as men, though convened in two rooms to make laws, must be governed generally by the same motives and views, and therefore pursue the same system of politics. The partitions between the two branches will be merely those of the building in which they fit. There will not be found in them any of those genuine balances and checks, among the real different interests, and efforts of the several classes of men in the community we aim at. Nor can any such balances and checks be formed in the present condition of the United States in any considerable degree of perfection. . .

Though I conclude the senators and representatives will not form in the legislature those balances and checks which correspond with the actual state of the people, yet I approve of two branches,

because we may notwithstanding derive several advantages from them. The senate, from the mode of its appointment, will probably be influenced to support the state governments; and, from its periods of service will produce stability in legislation, while frequent elections may take place in the other branch. There is generally a degree of competition between two assemblies even composed of the same kind of men; and by this, and by means of every law passing a revision in the second branch, caution, coolness, and deliberation are produced in the business of making laws. By means of a democratic branch we may particularly secure personal liberty; and by means of a senatorial branch we may particularly protect property. By the division, the house becomes the proper body to impeach all officers for misconduct in office, and the senate the proper court to try them; and in a country where limited powers must be lodged in the first magistrate, the senate, perhaps, may be the most proper body to be found to have a negative upon him in making treaties, and managing foreign affairs.

Though I agree the federal senate, in the form proposed, may be useful to many purposes, and that it is not very necessary to alter the organization, modes of appointment, and powers of it in several respects; yet, without alterations in others, I sincerely believe it will, in a very few years, become the source of the greatest evils. Some of these alterations, I conceive, to be absolutely necessary and some of them at least advisable.

Documents of Revolution

1. By the confederation the members of congress are chosen annually. By Art. 1. Sect. 2. of the constitution, the senators shall be chosen for six years. As the period of service must be, in a considerable degree, matter of opinion on this head, I shall only make a few observations, to explain why I think it more advisable to limit it to three or four years.

The people of this country have not been accustomed to so long appointments in their state governments. They have generally adopted annual elections. The members of the present congress are chosen yearly, who, from the nature and multiplicity of their business, ought to be chosen for longer periods than the federal senators. Men six years in office absolutely contract callous habits, and cease, in too great a degree, to feel their dependence, and for the condition of their constituents. Senators continued in offices three or four years, will be in them longer than any popular erroneous opinions will probably continue to actuate their electors. Men appointed for three or four years will generally be long enough in office to give stability, and amply to acquire political information. By a change of legislators, as often as circumstances will permit, political knowledge is diffused more extensively among the people, and the attention of the electors and elected more constantly kept alive-circumstances of infinite importance in a free country. Other reasons might be added, but my subject is too extensive to admit of my dwelling upon less material points.

2. When the confederation was formed, it was considered essentially necessary that the members of congress should at any time be recalled by their respective states, when the states should see fit, and others be sent in their room. I do not think it is less necessary that this principle should be extended to the members of congress under the new constitution, and especially to the senators. I have had occasion several times to observe, that let us form a federal constitution as extensively, and on the best principles in our power, we must, after all, trust a vast deal to a few men, who, far removed from their constituents, will administer the federal government. There is but little danger these men will feel too great a degree of dependence. The necessary and important object

to be attended to, is to make them feel dependent enough. Men elected for several years, several hundred miles distant from their states, possessed of very extensive powers, and the means of paying themselves, will not, probably, be oppressed with a sense of dependence and responsibility.

The senators will represent sovereignties, which generally have, and always ought to retain, the power of recalling their agents. The principle of responsibility is strongly felt in men who are liable to be recalled and censured for their misconduct; and, if we may judge from experience, the latter will not abuse the power of recalling their members; to possess it will at least be a valuable check. It is in the nature of all delegated power, that the constituents should retain the right to judge concerning the conduct of their representatives. They must exercise the power, and their decision itself, their approving or disapproving that conduct implies a right, a power to continue in office, or to remove from it. But whenever the substitute acts under a constitution, then it becomes necessary that the power of recalling him be expressed. The reasons for lodging a power to recall are stronger, as they respect the senate, than as they respect the representatives.

The latter will be more frequently elected, and changed of course, and being chosen by the people at large, it would be more difficult for the people than for the legislatures to take the necessary measures for recalling. But even the people, if the powers will be more beneficial to them than injurious, ought to possess it. The people are not apt to wrong a man who is steady and true to their interests. They may for a while be misled by party representations, and leave a good man out of office unheard; but every recall supposes a deliberate decision, and a fair hearing.

And no man who believes his conduct proper, and the result of honest views, will be the less useful in his public character on account of the examination his actions may be liable to. A man conscious of the contrary conduct ought clearly to be restrained by the apprehensions of a trial. I repeat it, it is interested combinations and factions we are particularly to guard against in the federal government, and all the rational means that can be put into the hands of the people to prevent them ought to be provided and furnished for them. Where there is a power to recall, trusty sentinels among the people, or in the state legislatures will have a fair opportunity to become useful. If the members in congress from the states join in such combinations, or favor them, or pursue a pernicious line of conduct, the most attentive among the people or in the state legislatures may formally charge them before their constituents. The very apprehensions of such constitutional charge may prevent many of the evils mentioned; and the recalling the members of a single state, a single senator or representative, may often prevent many more. Nor do 1, at present, discover any danger in such proceedings, as every man who shall move for a recall will put his reputation at stake, to show he has reasonable grounds for his motion. It is not probable such motions will be made unless there be good apparent grounds for succeeding. Nor can the charge or motion be anything more than the attack of an individual or individuals unless a majority of the constituents shall see cause to go into the inquiry. Further, the circumstances of such a power being lodged in the constituents will tend continually to keep up their watchfulness, as well as the attention and dependence of the federal senators and representatives.

3. By the confederation it is provided, that no delegate shall serve more than three years in any term of six years; and thus, by the forms of the government a rotation of members is produced. A like principle has been adopted in some of the state governments, and also in some ancient and modern republics. Whether this exclusion of a man for a given period, after he shall have served a given time, ought to be ingrafted into a constitution or not is a question, the proper decision [of which] materially depends upon the leading features of the government. Some governments are so formed as to produce a sufficient fluctuation and change of members; in the ordinary course of elections proper numbers of new members are from time to time brought into the legislature, and a proportionate number of old ones go out, mix, and become diffused among the people.

This is the case with all numerous representative legislatures, the members of which are frequently elected, and constantly within the view of their constituents. This is the case with our state governments, and in them a constitutional rotation is unimportant. But in a government consisting of but a few members, elected for long periods, and far removed from the observation of the people, but few changes in the ordinary course of elections take place among the members.

They become in some measure a fixed body, and often inattentive to the public good, callous, selfish, and the fountain of corruption. To prevent these evils, and to force a principle of pure animation into the federal government, which will be formed much in this last manner mentioned, and to produce attention, activity, and a diffusion of knowledge in the community, we ought to establish among others the principle of rotation. Even good men in office, in time, imperceptibly lose sight of the people, and gradually fall into measures prejudicial to them. It is only a rotation among the members of the federal legislature I shall contend for. Judges and officers at the heads of the judicial and executive departments are in a very different situation. Their offices and duties require the information and studies of many years for performing them in a manner advantageous to the people. These judges and officers must apply their whole time to the detail business of their offices, and depend on them for their support. Then, they always act under masters or superiors, and may be removed from office for misconduct. They pursue a certain round of executive business; their offices must be in all societies confined to a few men, because but few can become qualified to fill them. And were they, by annual appointments, open to the people at large, they are offices of such a nature as to be of no service to them. They must leave these offices in the possession of the few individuals qualified to fill them, or have them badly filled. In the judicial and executive departments also, the body of the people possess a large share of power and influence, as jurors and subordinate officers, among whom there are many and frequent rotations. But in every free country the legislatures are all on a level, and legislation becomes partial whenever, in practice, it rests for any considerable time in a few hands. It is the true republican principle to diffuse the power of making the laws among the people and so to modify the forms of the government as to draw in turn the well informed of every class into the legislature. To determine the propriety or impropriety of this rotation, we must take the inconveniencies as well as the advantages attending it into view. On the one hand by this rotation, we may sometimes exclude good men from being elected. On the other hand, we guard against those pernicious connections, which usually grow up among men left to continue long periods in office. We increase the number of those who make the laws and return to their constituents; and thereby spread information, and preserve a spirit of activity and investigation among the people. Hence a balance of interests and exertions are preserved, and the ruinous measures of actions rendered more impracticable. I would not urge the principle of rotation, if I believed the consequence would be an uninformed federal legislature; but I have no apprehension of this in this enlightened country. The members of congress, at any one time, must be but very few compared with the respectable well informed men in the United States; and I have no idea there will be any want of such men for members of congress, though by a principle of rotation the constitution should exclude from being elected for two years those federal legislators, who may have served the four years immediately preceding, or any four years in the six preceding years. If we may judge from experience and fair calculations, this principle will

never operate to exclude at any one period a fifteenth part even of those men who have been members of congress. Though no man can sit in congress by the confederation more than three years in any term of six years, yet not more than three, four, or five men in any one state have been made ineligible at any one period. And if a good man happens to be excluded by this rotation, it is only for a short time. All things considered, the inconveniencies of the principle must be very inconsiderable compared with the many advantages of it. It will generally be expedient for a man who has served four years in congress to return home, mix with the people, and reside some time with them. This will tend to reinstate him in the interests, feelings, and views similar to theirs, and thereby confirm in him the essential qualifications of a legislator.

Even in point of information, it may be observed, the useful information of legislators is not acquired merely in studies in offices, and in meeting to make laws from day to day. They must learn the actual situation of the people by being among them, and when they have made laws, return home and observe how they operate. Thus occasionally to be among the people, is not

only necessary to prevent or banish the callous habits and self-interested views of office in legislators, but to afford them necessary information, and to render them useful. Another valuable end is answered by it, sympathy, and the means of communication between them and their constituents, is substantially promoted. So that on every principle legislators, at certain periods, ought to live among their constituents. Some men of science are undoubtedly necessary in every legislature; but the knowledge, generally, necessary for men who make laws, is a knowledge of the common concerns, and particular circumstances of the people. In a republican government seats in the legislature are highly honorable. I believe but few do, and surely none ought to, consider them as places of profit and permanent support. Were the people always properly attentive, they would, at proper periods, call their lawmakers home, by sending others in their room. But this is not often the case; and therefore, in making constitutions, when the people are attentive, they ought cautiously to provide for those benefits, those advantageous changes in the administration of their affairs, which they are often apt to be inattentive to in practice. On the whole, to guard against the evils, and to secure the advantages I have mentioned, with the greatest degree of certainty, we ought clearly in my opinion, to increase the federal representation, to secure elections on proper principles, to establish a right to recall members, and a rotation among them.
THE FEDERAL FARMER

ANTI-FEDERALIST PAPER NO. 64

(PART III) On the Organization and Powers of The Senate

Taken from the New York Journal, Nov. 22, 1787 by "CINCINNATUS" It appears to have been written in answer to James Wilson's Antifederalist # 12)
I come now, sir, to the most exceptionable part of the Constitution-the Senate. In this, as in every other part, you [James Wilson of Pennsylvania] are in the line of your profession Law], and on that ground assure your fellow citizens, that-"perhaps there never was a charge made with less reason, than that which predicts the institution of a baneful aristocracy in the Federal Senate."
And yet your conscience smote you, sir, at the beginning, and compelled you to prefix a perhaps to this strange assertion. The senate, you say, branches into two characters-the one legislative and the other executive. This phraseology is quaint, and the position does not state the whole truth. I am very sorry, sir, to be so often obliged to reprehend the suppression of information at the moment that you stood forth to instruct your fellow citizens, in what they were supposed not to understand. In this character, you should have abandoned your professional line, and told them, not only the truth, but the whole truth. The whole truth then is, that the same body, called the senate, is vested with legislative, executive and judicial powers. The two first you acknowledge; the last is conveyed in these words, sec. 3d.: "The Senate shall have the sole power to try all impeachments." On this point then we are to come to issue-whether a senate so constituted is likely to produce a baneful aristocracy, which will swallow up the democratic rights and liberties of the nation. To judge on this question, it is proper to examine minutely into the constitution and powers of the senate; and we shall then see with what anxious and subtle cunning it is calculated for the proposed purpose. 1st. It is removed from the people, being chosen by the legislatures-and exactly in the ratio of their removal from the people do aristocratic principles constantly infect the minds of man. 2nd. They endure, two thirds for four, and one third for six years, and in proportion to the duration of power, the aristocratic exercise of it and attempts to extend it, are invariably observed to increase. 3rd. From the union of the executive with the legislative functions, they must necessarily be longer together, or rather constantly assembled; and in proportion to their continuance together, they will be able to form effectual schemes for extending their own power, and reducing that of the democratic branch. If any one would wish to see this more fully illustrated, let him turn to the history of the Decemviri in Rome. 4th. Their advice and consent being necessary to the appointment of all the great officers of state, both at home and abroad, will enable them to win over any opponents to their measures in the house of representatives, and give them the influence which, we see, accompanies this power in England; and which, from the nature of man, must follow it every where. 5th. The sole power of impeachment being vested in them, they have it in their power to control the representative in this democratic right; to screen from punishment, or rather from conviction, all high offenders, being their creatures, and to keep in awe all opponents to their power in high office. 6th. The union established between them and the vice president, who is made one of the corps, and will therefore be highly animated

with the aristocratic spirit of it, furnishes them a powerful shield against popular suspicion and inquiry, he being the second man in the United States who stands highest in the confidence and estimation of the people. And lastly, the right of altering or amending money-bills, is a high additional power given them as a branch of the legislature, which their analogous branch, in the English parliament, could never

obtain because it has been guarded by the representatives of the people there, with the most strenuous solicitude as one of the vital principles of democratic liberty.

Is a body so vested with means to soften and seduce-so armed with power to screen or to condemn-so fortified against suspicion and inquiry-so largely trusted with legislative powers-so independent of and removed from the people-so tempted to abuse and extend these powers-is this a body which freemen ought ever to create, or which freemen can ever endure? Or is it not a monster in the political creation, which we ought to regard with horror? Shall we thus forget our own fetters? Shall we set up the idol, before which we shall soon be obliged, however reluctantly, to bow? Shall we consent to see a proud aristocracy erect his domineering crest in triumph over our prostrate liberties?

But we shall yet see more clearly, how highly favored this senate has been, by taking a similar view of the representative body. This body is the true representative of the democratic part of the system; the shield and defense of the people. . . . Its transcendent and incommunicable power of impeachment-that high source of its dignity and control-in which alone the majesty of the people feels his sceptre, and bears aloft his fasces-is rendered ineffectual, by its being triable before its rival branch, the senate, the patron and prompter of the measures against which it is to sit in judgment. It is therefore most manifest, that from the very nature of the constitution the right of impeachment apparently given, is really rendered ineffectual. And this is contrived with so much art, that to discover it you must bring together various and distant parts of the constitution, or it will not strike the examiner, that the same body that advises the executive measures of government which are usually the subject of impeachment, are the sole judges on such impeachments. They must therefore be both party and judge, and must condemn those who have executed what they advised. Could such a monstrous absurdity have escaped men who were not determined, at all events, to vest all power in this aristocratic body? Is it not plain, that the senate is to be exalted by the humiliation of the democracy? A democracy which, thus bereft of its powers, and shorn of its strength, will stand a melancholy monument of popular impotence. . . .

"When the legislative and executive powers are united in the same person, or in the same corps,"

[says Montesquieu] "there can be no liberty. Because, it may be feared, that the same monarch or senate will make tyrannical laws, that they may execute them tyrannically." I am aware that this great man is speaking of a senate being the whole legislature; whereas the one before us is but a branch of the proposed legislature. But still the reason applies, inasmuch as the legislative power of the senate will enable it to negative all bills that are meant to control the executive; and from being secure of preventing any abridgment, they can watch every pliant hour of the representative body to promote an enlargement of the executive powers. One thing at least is certain, that by making this branch of the legislature participant in the executive, you not only prevent the legislature from being a check upon the executive, but you inevitably prevent its being checked or controlled by the other branch.

To the authority of Montesquieu, I shall add that of Mr. De Lolme, whose disquisition on government is allowed to be deep, solid, and ingenious. . . . "It is not only necessary," [says he]

"to take from the legislature the executive power which would exempt them from the laws; but they should not have even a hope of being ever able to arrogate to themselves that power." To remove this hope from their expectation, it would have been proper, not only to have previously

laid down, in a declaration of rights, that these powers should be forever separate and incommunicable; but the frame of the proposed constitution should have had that separation religiously in view, through all its parts. It is manifest this was not the object of its framers; but, that on the contrary there is a studied mixture of them in the senate as necessary to erect it into that potent aristocracy which it must infallibly produce. In pursuit of this daring object, than which no greater calamity can be brought upon the people, another egregious error in constitutional principles is committed. I mean that of dividing the executive powers between the senate and president. Unless more harmony and less ambition should exist between these two executives than ever yet existed between men in power, or than can exist while human nature is as it is, this absurd division must be productive of constant contentions for the lead, must clog the execution of government to a mischievous, and sometimes to a disgraceful degree; and if they should unhappily harmonize in the same objects of ambition, their number and their combined power would preclude all fear of that responsibility, which is one of the great securities of good, and restraints on bad governments. Upon these principles Mr. DeLolme has foreseen that "the effect of a division of the executive power is the establishment of absolute power in one of continual contention;" he therefore lays it down, as a general rule . . . "for the tranquility of the state it is necessary that the executive power should be in one." I will add, that this singlehood of the executive is indispensably necessary to effective execution, as well as to the responsibility and rectitude of him to whom it is entrusted.

By this time I hope it is evident from reason and authority, that in the constitution of the senate there is much cunning and little wisdom; that we have much to fear from it, and little to hope, and then it must necessarily produce a baneful aristocracy, by which the democratic rights of the people will be overwhelmed.

It was probably upon this principle that a member of the convention, of high and unexceeded reputation for wisdom and integrity, is said to have emphatically declared, that he would sooner lose his right hand, than put his name to such a constitution.

CINCINNATUS

ANTI-FEDERALIST PAPER NO. 65

(PART IV) On the Organization and Powers Of The Senate

(by Gilbert Livingston and John Lansing delivered on June 24, 1788 to the New York ratifying convention)

Mr. G[ilbert] LIVINGSTON rose, and addressed the chair.

He, in the first place, considered the importance of the Senate as a branch of the legislature, in three points of view:-
First, they would possess legislative powers coextensive with those of the House of Representatives except with respect to originating revenue laws; which, however, they would have power to reject or amend, as in the case of other bills. Secondly, they would have an importance, even exceeding that of the representative house, as they would be composed of a smaller number, and possess more firmness and system. Thirdly, their consequence and dignity would still further transcend those of the other branch, from their longer continuance in office.

These powers, Mr. Livingston contended, rendered the Senate a dangerous body.

He went on, in the second place, to enumerate and animadvert on the powers with which they were clothed in their judicial capacity, and in their capacity of council to the President, and in the forming of treaties. In the last place, as if too much power could not be given to this body, they were made, he said, a council of appointment, by whom ambassadors and other officers of state were to be appointed. These are the powers, continued he, which are vested in this small body of twenty-six men; in some cases, to be exercised by a bare quorum, which is fourteen; a majority of which number, again, is eight. What are the checks provided to balance this great mass of power? Our present Congress cannot serve longer than three years in six: they are at any time subject to recall. These and other checks were considered as necessary at a period which I choose to honor with the name of virtuous. Sir, I venerate the spirit with which every thing was done at the trying time in which the Confederation was formed. America had then a sufficiency of this virtue to resolve to resist perhaps the first nation in the universe, even unto bloodshed. What was her aim? Equal liberty and safety. What ideas had she of this equal liberty? Read them in her Articles of Confederation. True it is, sir, there are some powers wanted to make this glorious compact complete. But, sir, let us be cautious that we do not err more on the other hand, by giving power too profusely, when, perhaps, it will be too late to recall it. Consider, sir, the great influence which this body, armed at all points, will have. What will be the effect of this? Probably a security of their reelection, as long as they please. Indeed, in my view, it will amount nearly to an appointment for life. What will be their situation in a federal town? Hallowed ground! Nothing so unclean as state laws to enter there, surrounded, as they will be, by an impenetrable wall of adamant and gold, the wealth of the whole country flowing into it. [Here a member, who did not fully understand, called out to know what WALL the gentleman meant; on which be turned, and replied, "A wall of gold-of adamant, which will flow in from all parts of the continent." At which flowing metaphor, a great laugh in the house.] The gentleman continued: Their attention to their various business will probably require their constant attendance. In this Eden will they reside with their families, distant from the observation of the people. In such a situation, men are apt to forget their dependence, lose their sympathy, and contract selfish habits.

Factions are apt to be formed, if the body becomes permanent. The senators will associate only with men of their own class, and thus become strangers to the condition of the common people.

Documents of Revolution

They should not only return, and be obliged to live with the people, but return to their former rank of citizenship, both to revive their sense of dependence, and to gain a knowledge of the country. This will afford opportunity to bring forward the genius and information of the states, and will be a stimulus to acquire political abilities. It will be the means of diffusing a more general knowledge of the measures and spirit of the administration. These things will confirm the people's confidence in government. When they see those who have been high in office residing among them as private citizens, they will feel more forcibly that the government is of their own choice. The members of this branch having the idea impressed on their minds, that they are soon to return to the level whence the suffrages of the people raised them,-this good effect will follow: they will consider their interests as the same with those of their constituents, and that they legislate for themselves as well as others. They will not conceive themselves made to receive, enjoy, and rule, nor the people solely to earn, pay, and submit.

Mr. Chairman, I have endeavored, with as much perspicuity and candor as I am master of, shortly to state my objections to this clause. I would wish the committee to believe that they are not raised for the sake of opposition, but that I am very sincere in my sentiments in this important investigation. The Senate, as they are now constituted, have little or no check on them. Indeed, sir, too much is put into their hands. When we come to that part of the system which points out their powers, it will be the proper time to consider this subject more particularly.

I think, sir, we must relinquish the idea of safety under this government, if the time for services is not further limited, and the power of recall [not] given to the state legislatures. I am strengthened in my opinion by an observation made yesterday, by an honorable member from New York, to this effect "that there should be no fear of corruption of the members in the House of Representatives; especially as they are, in two years, to return to the body of the people." I therefore move that the committee adopt the following resolution, as an amendment to this clause:-

"Resolved, That no person shall be eligible as a senator for more than six years in any term of twelve years, and that it shall be in the power of the legislatures of the several states to recall their senators, or either of them, and to elect others in their stead, to serve for the remainder of the time for which such senator or senators, so recalled, were appointed."

Hon. Mr. [John] LANSING. I beg the indulgence of the committee, while I offer some reasons in support of the motion just made; in doing which, I shall confine myself to the point, and shall hear with attention, and examine with candor, the objections which may be opposed to it. . .

Sir, I am informed by gentlemen who have been conversant in public affairs, and who have had seats in Congress, that there have been, at different times, violent parties in that body-an evil that a change of members has contributed, more than any other thing, to remedy. If, therefore, the power of recall should be never exercised, if it should have no other force than that of a check to the designs of the bad, and to destroy party spirit, certainly no harm, but much good, may result from adopting the amendment. If my information be true, there have been parties in Congress which would have continued to this day, if the members had not been removed. No inconvenience can follow from placing the powers of the Senate on such a foundation as to make them feel their dependence. It is only a check calculated to make them more attentive to the objects for which they were appointed. Sir, I would ask, Is there no danger that the members of the Senate will sacrifice the interest of their state to their own private views? Every man in the United States ought to look with anxious concern to that body. Their number is so exceedingly small, that they may easily feel their interests distinct from those of the community. This smallness of number also renders them subject to a variety of accidents, that may be of the highest disadvantage. If one of the members is sick, or if one or both are prevented occasionally from attending, who are to take care of the interests of their state?

Sir, we have frequently observed that deputies have been appointed for certain purposes, who have not punctually attended to them, when it was necessary. Their private concerns may often require their presence at home. In what manner is this evil to be corrected? The amendment provides a remedy. It is the only thing which can give the states a control over the Senate. It will be said, there is a power in Congress to compel the attendance of absent members; but will the members from the other states be solicitous to compel such attendance, except to answer some particular view, or promote some interest of their own? If it be the object of the senators to protect the sovereignty of their several states, and if, at any time, it be the design of the other states to make encroachments on the sovereignty of any one state, will it be for their interest to compel the members from this state to attend, in order to oppose and check them? This would be strange policy indeed....

Sir, it is true there have been no instances of the success of corruption under the old Confederation; and may not this be attributed to the power of recall, which has existed from its first formation? It has operated effectually, though silently. It has never been exercised, because no great occasion has offered. The power has by no means proved a discouragement to individuals, in serving their country. A seat in Congress has always been considered a distinguished honor, and a favorite object of ambition. I believe no public station has been sought with more avidity. If this power has existed for so many years, and through so many scenes of difficulty and danger, without being exerted, may it not be rationally presumed that it never will be put in execution, unless the indispensable interest of a state shall require it? I am perfectly convinced that, in many emergencies, mutual concessions are necessary and proper; and that, in some instances, the smaller interests of the states should be sacrificed to great national objects. But when a delegate makes such sacrifices as tend to political destruction or to reduce sovereignty to subordination, his state ought to have the power of defeating his design, and reverting to the people. It is observed, that the appropriation of money is not in the power of the Senate alone; but, sir, the exercise of certain powers, which constitutionally and necessarily involve the disposal of money, belongs to the Senate. They have, therefore, a right of disposing of the property of the United States. If the Senate declare war, the lower house must furnish the supplies.

It is further objected to this amendment, that it will restrain the people from choosing those who are most deserving of their suffrages, and will thus be an abridgment of their rights. I cannot suppose this last inference naturally follows. The rights of the people will be best supported by checking, at a certain point, the current of popular favor, and preventing the establishment of an

influence which may leave to elections little more than the form of freedom. The Constitution of this state says, that no man shall hold the office of sheriff or coroner beyond a certain period.

Does any one imagine that the rights of the people are infringed by this provision? The gentlemen, in their reasoning on the subject of corruption, seem to set aside experience and to consider the Americans as exempt from the common vices and frailties of human nature. It is unnecessary to particularize the numerous ways in which public bodies are accessible to corruption. The poison always finds a channel, and never wants an object. Scruples would be impertinent arguments would be in vain, checks would be useless, if we were certain our rulers would be good men; but for the virtuous government is not instituted. Its object is to restrain and punish vice; and all free constitutions are for with two views-to deter the governed from crime, and the governors from tyranny.

ANTI-FEDERALIST PAPER NO. 66

From North Carolina

Mr. JOSEPH TAYLOR objected to the provision made for impeaching. He urged that there could be no security from it, as the persons accused were triable by the Senate, who were a part of the legislature themselves; that, while men were fallible, the senators were liable to errors, especially in a case where they were concerned themselves....

Mr. [Timothy] BLOODWORTH wished to be informed, whether this sole power of impeachment, given to the House of Representatives, deprived the state of the power of impeaching any of its members....

Mr. JOSEPH TAYLOR. Mr. Chairman, the objection is very strong. If there be but one body to try, where are we? If any tyranny or oppression should arise, how are those who perpetrated such oppression to be tried and punished? By a tribunal consisting of the very men who assist in such tyranny. Can any tribunal be found, in any community, who will give judgment against their own actions? Is it the nature of man to decide against himself? I am obliged to the worthy member from New Hanover for assisting me with objections. None can impeach but the representatives; and the impeachments are to be determined by the senators, who are one of the branches of power which we dread under this Constitution.... the words "sole power of impeachment" were so general, and might admit of such a latitude of construction, as to extend to every legislative member upon the continent, so as to preclude the representatives of the different states from impeaching....

Mr. [William] PORTER wished to be informed, if every officer, who was a creature of that Constitution, was to be tried by the Senate-whether such officers, and those who had complaints against them, were to go from the extreme parts of the continent to the seat of government, to adjust disputes....

Mr. J. TAYLOR. Mr. Chairman, I conceive that, if this Constitution be adopted, we shall have a large number of officers in North Carolina under the appointment of Congress. We shall undoubtedly, for instance, have a great number of tax-gatherers. If any of these officers shall do wrong, when we come to fundamental principles, we find that we have no way to punish them but by going to Congress, at an immense distance, whither we must carry our witnesses. Every gentlemen must see, in these cases, that oppressions will arise. I conceive that they cannot be tried elsewhere. I consider that the Constitution will be explained by the word "sole." If they did not mean to retain a general power of impeaching, there was no occasion for saying the "sole power." I consider therefore that oppressions will arise. If I am oppressed, I must go to the House of Representatives to complain. I consider that, when mankind are about to part with rights, they ought only to part with those rights which they can with convenience relinquish, and not such as must involve them in distresses....

I observe that, when these great men are met in Congress, in consequence of this power, they will have the power of appointing all the officers of the United States. My experience in life shows me that the friends of the members of the legislature will get the offices. These senators and members of the House of Representatives will appoint their friends to all offices. These officers will be great men, and they will have numerous deputies under them. The receiver-general of the taxes of North Carolina must be one of the greatest men in the country. Will he come to me for his taxes? No. He will send his deputy, who will have special instructions to oppress me. How am I to be redressed? I shall be told that I must go to Congress, to get him impeached. This being the case, whom am I to impeach? A friend of the representatives of North Carolina. For, unhappily for us, these men will have too much weight for us; they will have friends in the government who will be inclined against us, and thus we may be oppressed with impunity.

ANTI-FEDERALIST PAPER NO. 67

Various Fears Concerning the Executive Department

From the "CATO" letters of George Clinton, taken from The New-York Journal of November 8, 1787.

I shall begin with observations on the executive branch of this new system; and though it is not the first in order, as arranged therein, yet being the chief, is perhaps entitled by the rules of rank to the first consideration. The executive power as described in the 2d article, consists of a president and vice-president, who are to hold their offices during the term of four years; the same article has marked the manner and time of their election, and established the qualifications of the president; it also provides against the removal, death, or inability of the president and vice-president - regulates the salary of the president, delineates his duties and powers; and, lastly, declares the causes for which the president and vice-president shall be removed from office.

Notwithstanding the great learning and abilities of the gentlemen who composed the convention, it may be here remarked with deference, that the construction of the first paragraph of the first section of the second article is vague and inexplicit, and leaves the mind in doubt as to the election of a president and vice-president, after the expiration of the election for the first term of four years; in every other case, the election of these great officers is expressly provided for; but there is no explicit provision for their election which is to set this political machine in motion; no certain and express terms as in your state constitution, that statedly once in every four years, and as often as these offices shall become vacant, by expiration or otherwise, as is therein expressed, an election shall be held as follows, etc.; this inexplicitness perhaps may lead to an establishment for life.

It is remarked by Montesquieu, in treating of republics, that in all magistracies, the greatness of the power must be compensated by the brevity of the duration, and that a longer time than a year would be dangerous. It is, therefore, obvious to the least intelligent mind to account why great power in the hands of a magistrate, and that power connected with considerable duration, may be dangerous to the liberties of a republic. The deposit of vast trusts in the hands of a single magistrate enables him in their exercise to create a numerous train of dependents. This tempts his ambition, which in a republican magistrate is also remarked, to be pernicious, and the duration of his office for any considerable time favors his views, gives him the means and time to perfect and execute his designs; he therefore fancies that he may be great and glorious by oppressing his fellow citizens, and raising himself to permanent grandeur on the ruins of his country. And here it may be necessary to compare the vast and important powers of the president, together with his continuance in office, with the foregoing doctrine-his eminent magisterial situation will attach many adherents to him, and he will be surrounded by expectants and courtiers. His power of nomination and influence on all appointments; the strong posts in each state comprised within his superintendence, and garrisoned by troops under his direction; his control over the army, militia, and navy; the unrestrained power of granting pardons for treason, which may be used to screen from punishment those whom he had secretly instigated to commit the crime, and thereby prevent a discovery of his own guilt; his duration in office for four years-these, and various other principles evidently prove the truth of the position, that if the president is possessed of ambition, he has power and time sufficient to ruin his country.

Though the president, during the sitting of the legislature, is assisted by the senate, yet he is without a constitutional council in their recess. He will therefore be unsupported by proper information and advice, and will generally be directed by minions and favorites, or a council of state will grow out of the principal officers of the great departments, the most dangerous council in a free country. . . . The language and the manners of this court will be what distinguishes them from the rest of the community, not what assimilates them to it; and in being remarked for a behavior that shows they are not meanly born, and in adulation to people of fortune and power.

The establishment of a vice-president is as unnecessary as it is dangerous. This officer, for want of other employment, is made president of the senate, thereby blending the executive and legislative powers, besides always giving to some one state, from which he is to come, an unjust pre-eminence.

It is a maxim in republics that the representative of the people should be of their immediate choice; but by the manner in which the president is chosen, he arrives to this office at the fourth or fifth hand. Nor does the highest vote, in the way he is elected, determine the choice-for it is only necessary that he should be taken from the highest of five, who may have a plurality of votes. . . .

And wherein does this president, invested with his powers and prerogatives, essentially differ from the king of Great Britain (save as to name, the creation of nobility, and some immaterial incidents, the offspring of absurdity and locality)? The direct prerogatives of the president, as springing from his political character, are among the following: It is necessary, in order to distinguish him from the rest of the community, and enable him to keep, and maintain his court, that the compensation for his services, or in other words, his revenue, should be such as to enable him to appear with the splendor of a prince. He has the power of receiving ambassadors from, and a great influence on their appointments to foreign courts; as also to make treaties, leagues, and alliances with foreign states, assisted by the Senate, which when made becomes the supreme law of land. He is a constituent part of the legislative power, for every bill which shall pass the House of Representatives and Senate is to be presented to him for approbation. If he approves of it he is to sign it, if he disapproves he is to return it with objections, which in many cases will amount to a complete negative; and in this view he will have a great share in the power of making peace, coining money, etc., and all the various objects of legislation, expressed or implied in this Constitution. For though it may be asserted that the king of Great Britain has the express power of making peace or war, yet he never thinks it prudent to do so without the advice of his Parliament, from whom be is to derive his support -and therefore these powers, in both president and king, are substantially the same. He is the generalissimo of the nation, and of course has the command and control of the army, navy and militia; he is the general conservator of the peace of the union-he may pardon all offenses, except in cases of impeachment, and the principal fountain of all offices and employments. Will not the exercise of these powers therefore tend either to the establishment of a vile and arbitrary aristocracy or monarchy? The safety of the people in a republic depends on the share or proportion they have in the government; but experience ought to teach you, that when a man is at the head of an elective government invested

with great powers, and interested in his re-election, in what circle appointments will be made; by which means an imperfect aristocracy bordering on monarchy may be established. You must, however, my countrymen, beware that the advocates of this new system do not deceive you by a fallacious resemblance between it and your own state government [New York] which you so much prize; and, if you examine, you will perceive that the chief magistrate of this state is your immediate choice, controlled and checked by a just and full representation of the people, divested of the prerogative of influencing war and peace, making treaties, receiving and sending embassies, and commanding standing armies and navies, which belong to the power of the confederation, and will be convinced that this government is no more like a true picture of your own than an Angel of Darkness resembles an Angel of Light.

CATO

ANTI-FEDERALIST PAPER NO. 68

On the Mode of Electing the President

From a speech by William Grayson given to the Virginia ratifying convention on June 18, 1788.

Mr. [William] GRAYSON. Mr. Chairman, one great objection with me is this: If we advert to.....
[the] democratical, aristocratical, or executive branch, we shall find their powers are perpetually varying and fluctuating throughout the whole. Perhaps the democratic branch would be well constructed, were it not for this defect. The executive is still worse, in this respect, than the democratic branch. He is to be elected by a number of electors in the country; but the principle is changed when no person has a majority of the whole number of electors appointed, or when more than one have such a majority, and have an equal number of votes; for then the lower house is to vote by states. It is thus changing throughout the whole. It seems rather founded on accident than any principle of government I ever heard of. We know that there scarcely ever was an election of such an officer without the interposition of foreign powers. Two causes prevail to make them intermeddle in such cases:-one is, to preserve the balance of power; the other, to preserve their trade. These causes have produced interferences of foreign powers in the election of the king of Poland. All the great powers of Europe have interfered in an election which took place not very long ago, and would not let the people choose for themselves. We know how much the powers of Europe have interfered with Sweden. Since the death of Charles XII, that country has been a republican government. Some powers were willing it should be so; some were willing her imbecility should continue; others wished the contrary; and at length the court of France brought about a revolution, which converted it into an absolute government. Can America be free from these interferences? France, after losing Holland, will wish to make America entirely her own. Great Britain will wish to increase her influence by a still closer connection. It is the interest of Spain, from the contiguity of her possessions in the western hemisphere to the United States, to be in an intimate connection with them, and influence their deliberations, if possible. I think we have every thing, to apprehend from such interferences. It is highly probable the President will be continued in office for life. To gain his favor, they will support him. Consider the means of importance he will have by creating officers. If he has a good understanding with the Senate, they will join to prevent a discovery of his misdeeds. . . .

This quadrennial power cannot be justified by ancient history. There is hardly an instance where a republic trusted its executive so long with much power; nor is it warranted by modern republics. The delegation of power is, in most of them, only for one year.

When you have a strong democratical and a strong aristocratical branch, you may have a strong executive. But when those are weak, the balance will not be preserved, if you give the executive extensive powers for so long a time. As this government is organized, it would be dangerous to trust the President with such powers. How will you punish him if he abuse his power? Will you call him before the Senate? They are his counsellors and partners in crime. Where are your checks? We ought to be extremely cautious in this country. If ever the government be changed, it will probably be into a despotism. The first object in England was to destroy the monarchy; but the aristocratic branch restored him, and of course the government was organized on its ancient principles. But were a revolution to happen here, there would be no means of restoring the government to its former organization. This is a caution to us not to trust extensive powers. I have an extreme objection to the mode of his election. I presume the seven Eastern States will always elect him. As he is vested with the power of making treaties, and as there is a material distinction between the carrying and productive states, the former will be disposed to have him to themselves. He will accommodate himself to their interests in forming treaties, and they will continue him perpetually in office. Thus mutual interest will lead them reciprocally to support one another. It will be a government of a faction, and this observation will apply to every part of it; for, having a majority, they may do what they please. I have made an estimate which shows with what facility they will be able to reelect him. The number of electors is equal to the number of representatives and senators; viz., ninety-one. They are to vote for two persons. They give, therefore, one hundred and eighty-two votes. Let there be forty-five votes for four different candidates, and two for the President. He is one of the five highest, if he have but two votes, which he may easily purchase. In this case, by the 3d clause of the 1st section of the 2d article, the election is to be by the representatives, according to states. Let New Hampshire be for him,-a majority of its . . . . .

3 representatives is 2
Rhode Island 1 1

Connecticut 5 3
New Jersey 4 3
Delaware 1 1
Georgia 3 2
North Carolina 5 3
A majority of seven states is 15
Thus the majority of seven states is but 15, while the minority amounts to 50.
The total number of voices (91 electors and 65 representatives) is . . 156
Voices in favor of the President are, 2 state electors and 15 representatives 17
139
So that the President may be reelected by the voices of 17 against 139.
It may be said that this is an extravagant case, and will never happen. In my opinion, it will often happen. A person who is a favorite of Congress, if he gets but two votes of electors, may, by the subsequent choice of 15 representatives, be elected President. Surely the possibility of such a case ought to be excluded.

ANTI-FEDERALIST PAPER NO. 69

The Character Of The Executive Office By Richard Henry Lee

The great object is, in a republican government, to guard effectually against perpetuating any portion of power, great or small, in the same man or family. This perpetuation of power is totally uncongenial to the true spirit of republican governments. On the one hand the first executive magistrate ought to remain in office so long as to avoid instability in the execution of the laws; on the other, not so long as to enable]him to take any measures to establish himself. The convention, it seems, first agreed that the president should be chosen for seven years, and never after to be eligible. Whether seven years is a period too long or not, is rather a matter of opinion; but clear it is, that this mode is infinitely preferable to the one finally adopted. When a man shall get the chair, who may be reelected from time to time, for life, his greatest object will be to keep it; to gain friends and votes, at any rate; to associate some favorite son with himself, to take office after him. Whenever he shall have any prospect of continuing the office in himself and family, he will spare no artifice, no address, and no exertions, to increase the powers and importance of it. The servile supporters of his wishes will be placed in all offices, and tools constantly employed to aid his views and sound his praise. A man so situated will have no permanent interest in the government to lose, by contests and convulsions in the state; but always much to gain, and frequently the seducing and flattering hope of succeeding. If we reason at all on the subject, we must irresistibly conclude that this will be the case with nine tenths of the presidents. We may have, for the first president, and perhaps, one in a century or two afterwards (if the government should withstand the attacks of others) a great and good man, governed by superior motives; but these are not events to be calculated upon in the present state of human nature. A man chosen to this important office for a limited period and always afterwards rendered, by the constitution, ineligible, will be governed by very different considerations. He can have no rational hopes or expectations of retaining his office after the expiration of a known limited time, or of continuing the office in his family, as by the constitution there must be a constant transfer of it from one man to another, and consequently from one family to another. No man will wish to be a mere cypher at the bead of the government. The great object of each president then will be to render his government a glorious period in the annals of his country.

When a man constitutionally retires from office, he retires without pain; he is sensible he retires because the laws direct it, and not from the success of his rivals, nor with that public disapprobation which being left out, when eligible, implies. It is said that a man knowing that at a given period he must quit his office, will unjustly attempt to take from the public, and lay in store the means of support and splendor in his retirement. There can, I think, be but very little in this observation. The same constitution that makes a man eligible for a given period only, ought to make no man eligible till he arrive to the age of forty or forty-five years. If he be a man of fortune, be will retire with dignity to his estate; if not, he may, like the Roman consuls, and other eminent characters in republics, find an honorable support and employment in some respectable office. A man who must, at all events, thus leave his office, will have but few or no temptations to fill its dependent offices with his tools, or any particular set of men; whereas the man constantly looking forward to his future elections, and perhaps, to the aggrandizement of his family, will have every inducement before him to fill all places with his own props and

dependents. As to public monies, the president need handle none of them, and he may always rigidly be made to account for every shilling he shall receive.

On the whole, it would be, in my opinion, almost as well to create a limited monarchy at once, and give some family permanent power and interest in the community, and let it have something valuable to itself to lose in convulsions in the state, and in attempts of usurpation, as to make a first magistrate eligible for life, and to create hopes and expectations in him and his family of obtaining what they have not. In the latter case, we actually tempt them to disturb the state, to foment struggles and contests, by laying before them the flattering prospect of gaining much without risking anything.

The constitution provides only that the president shall hold his office during the term of four years; that, at most, only implies, that one shall be chosen every fourth year. It also provides that in case of the removal, death, resignation, or inability, both of the president and vice-president, congress may declare what officer shall act as president; and that such officers shall act accordingly, until the disability be removed, or a president shall be elected. It also provides that congress may determine the time of choosing electors, and the day on which they shall give their votes. Considering these clauses together, I submit this question-whether in case of a vacancy in the office of president, by the removal, death, resignation, or inability of the president and vice president, and congress should declare that a certain officer, as secretary of foreign affairs, for instance, shall act as president, and suffer such officer to continue several years, or even for his life, to act as president, by omitting to appoint the time for choosing electors of another president, it would be any breach of the constitution? There appears to me to be an intended provision for supplying the office of president-not only for any remaining portion of the four years, but in cases of emergency-until another president shall be elected. . . . [But] we do not know that it is impossible; we do not know that it is improbable, in case a popular officer should thus be declared the acting president, that he might continue for life, and without any violent act, but merely by neglects and delays on the part of congress. . .

THE FEDERAL FARMER

ANTI-FEDERALIST PAPER NO. 70

The Powers And Dangerous Potentials Of His Elected Majesty

"AN OLD WHIG's" essay from The New-York Journal of December 11, 1787.

.... In the first place the office of president of the United States appears to me to be clothed with such powers as are dangerous. To be the fountain of all honors in the United States-commander in chief of the army, navy, and militia; with the power of making treaties and of granting pardons; and to be vested with an authority to put a negative upon all laws, unless two thirds of both houses shall persist in enacting it, and put their names down upon calling the yeas and nays for that purpose-is in reality to be a king, as much a king as the king of Great Britain, and a king too of the worst kind: an elective king. If such powers as these are to be trusted in the hands of any man, they ought, for the sake of preserving the peace of the community, at once to be made hereditary. Much as I abhor kingly government, yet I venture to pronounce, where kings are admitted to rule they should most certainly be vested with hereditary power. The election of a king whether it be in America or Poland, will be a scene of horror and confusion; and I am perfectly serious when I declare, that, as a friend to my country, I shall despair of any happiness in the United States until this office is either reduced to a lower pitch of power, or made perpetual and hereditary. When I say that our future president will be as much a king as the king of Great Britain, I only ask of my readers to look into the constitution of that country, and then tell me what important prerogative the king of Great Britain is entitled to which does not also belong to the president during his continuance in office. The king of Great Britain, it is true, can create nobility which our president cannot; but our president will have the power of making all the great men, which comes to the same thing. All the difference is, that we shall be embroiled in contention about the choice of the man, while they are at peace under the security of an hereditary succession. To be tumbled headlong from the pinnacle of greatness and be reduced to a shadow of departed royalty, is a shock almost too great for human nature to endure. It will cost a man many struggles to resign such eminent powers, and ere long, we shall find some one who will be very unwilling to part with them. Let us suppose this man to be a favorite with his army, and that they are unwilling to part with their beloved commander in chief-or to make the thing familiar, let us suppose a future president and commander in chief adored by his army and the militia to as great a degree as our late illustrious commander in chief; and we have only to suppose one thing more, that this man is without the virtue, the moderation and love of liberty which possessed the mind of our late general-and this country will be involved at once in war and tyranny. So far is it from its being improbable that the man who shall hereafter be in a situation to make the attempt to perpetuate his own power, should want the virtues of General Washington, that it is perhaps a chance of one hundred millions to one that the next age will not furnish an example of so disinterested a use of great power. We may also suppose, without trespassing upon the bounds of probability, that this man may not have the means of supporting, in private life, the dignity of his former station; that like Caesar, he may be at once ambitious and poor, and deeply involved in debt. Such a man would die a thousand deaths rather than sink from the heights of splendor and power, into obscurity and wretchedness. We are certainly about giving our president too much or too little; and in the course of less than twenty years we shall find that we have given him enough to enable him to take all. It would be infinitely more prudent to give him at once as much as would content him, so that we might be able to retain the rest in

peace, for if once power is seized by violence, not the least fragment of liberty will survive the shock. I would therefore advise my countrymen seriously to ask themselves this question: Whether they are prepared to receive a king? If they are, to say so at once, and make the kingly office hereditary; to frame a constitution that should set bounds to his power, and, as far as possible, secure the liberty of the subject. If we are not prepared to receive a king, let us call another convention to revise the proposed constitution, and form it anew on the principles of a confederacy of free republics; but by no means, under pretense of a republic, to lay the foundation for a military government, which is the worst of all tyrannies.
AN OLD WHIG

ANTI-FEDERALIST PAPER NO. 71

The Presidential Term Of Office

Part 1: Luther Martin, The Genuine Information
Part 2: An excerpt from the 18th letter of "AGRIPPA" appearing in The Massachusetts Gazette on February 5, 1788.
Part 3: From by "A CUSTOMER" in the Maine Cumberland Gazette, March 13, 1788.

.... The second article relates to the executive-his mode of election, his powers, and the length of time he should continue in office.

On this subject there was a great diversity of sentiment [at the Philadelphia constitutional convention]. Many of the members were desirous that the President should be elected for seven years, and not to be eligible a second time. Others proposed that he should not be absolutely ineligible, but that he should not be capable of being chosen a second time, until the expiration of a certain number of years. The supporters of the above proposition went upon the idea that the best security for liberty was a limited duration, and a rotation of office, in the chief executive department.

There was a party who attempted to have the President appointed during good behavior, without any limitation as to time; and, not being able to succeed in that attempt, they then endeavored to have him reeligible without any restraint. It was objected that the choice of a President to continue in office during good behavior, would at once be rendering our system an elective monarchy; and that, if the President was to be reeligible without any interval of disqualification, it would amount nearly to the same thing, since, from the powers that the President is to enjoy, and the interests and influence with which they will be attended, he will be almost absolutely certain of being reelected from time to time, as long as he lives. As the propositions were reported by the committee of the whole house, the President was to be chosen for seven years, and not to be eligible at any time after. In the same manner, the proposition was agreed to in Convention; and so it was reported by the committee of detail, although a variety of attempts were made to alter that part of the system by those who were of a contrary opinion, in which they repeatedly failed; but, sir, by never losing sight of their object, and choosing a proper time for their purpose, they succeeded, at length, in obtaining the alteration, which was not made until within the last twelve days before the Convention adjourned....

Resolved, that the constitution lately proposed for the United States be received only upon the following conditions. . . .
The president shall be chosen annually and shall serve but one year, and shall be chosen successively from the different states, changing every year....

AGRIPPA

I have one difficulty in my mind respecting our admirable Constitution, which I hope somebody will attempt to remove. Art. 3, sect. 1: "The executive power shall be vested in a President of the United States of America. He shall hold his office during the term of four years." Here is no
declaration that a new one shall be chosen at the expiration of that time. "Congress may determine the time of choosing the electors; and the day on which they shall give their votes."

But suppose they should think it for the public good, after the first election, to appoint the first Tuesday of September, in the year two thousand, for the purpose of choosing the second President; and by law empower the Chief Justice of the Supreme Judicial Court to act as President until that time. However disagreeable it might be to the majority of the States, I do not see but that they are left without a remedy, provided four States should be satisfied with the measure. The President elected is not to receive any other emolument; yet the Chief Justice is not disqualified as a Judge. Why did our worthy Chief Justice, at Cambridge the year past, in his address to the Grand Jury, call upon them to support "that free and excellent Constitution, which it has cost the blood of thousands of our friends and fellow citizens to establish; that Constitution which has carefully separated and distinguished the principal departments of power, that they might never combine against the liberty of the subject"-if it is not a necessary article in a constitution? If necessary in a State constitution, why not in one for the whole people? Was it not as easy to have said the President should be chosen every fourth year, as to have said the Representatives shall be chosen every second year? The celebrated Mr. King observes that this is not a confederation of States-for the style is in the name of the people. Therefore, it appears to me, the rights of the people should be as well guarded, on this point, here, as in the constitution of a State....

A CUSTOMER

ANTI-FEDERALIST PAPER NO. 72

On The Electoral College; On Reeligibility Of The President

By an anonymous writer "REPUBLICUS," appearing in The Kentucky Gazette on March 1, 1788.

. . I go now to Art. 2, Sec. 1, which vest the supreme continental executive power in a president-in order to the choice of whom, the legislative body of each state is empowered to point out to their constituents some mode of choice, or (to save trouble) may choose themselves, a certain number of electors, who shall meet in their respective states, and vote by ballot, for two persons, one of whom, at least, shall not be an inhabitant of the same state with themselves. Or in other words, they shall vote for two, one or both of whom they know nothing of. An extraordinary refinement this, on the plain simple business of election; and of which the grand convention have certainly the honor of being the first inventors; and that for an officer too, of so much importance as a president - invested with legislative and executive powers; who is to be commander in chief of the army, navy, militia, etc.; grant reprieves and pardons; have a temporary negative on all bills and resolves; convene and adjourn both houses of congress; be supreme conservator of laws; commission all officers; make treaties; and who is to continue four years, and is only removable on conviction of treason or bribery, and triable only by the senate, who are to be his own council, whose interest in every instance runs parallel with his own, and who are neither the officers of the people, nor accountable to them. Is it then become necessary, that a free people should first resign their right of suffrage into other hands besides their own, and then, secondly, that they to whom they resign it should be compelled to choose men, whose persons, characters, manners, or principles they know nothing of? And, after all (excepting some such change as is not likely to happen twice in the same century) to intrust Congress with the final decision at last? Is it necessary, is it rational, that the sacred rights of mankind should thus dwindle down to Electors of electors, and those again electors of other electors? This seems to be degrading them even below the prophetical curse denounced by the good old patriarch, on the offspring of his degenerate son: "servant of servants". . .

Again I would ask (considering how prone mankind are to engross power, and then to abuse it) is it not probable, at least possible, that the president who is to be vested with all this demi omnipotence - who is not chosen by the community; and who consequently, as to them, is irresponsible and independent-that he, I say, by a few artful and dependent emissaries in Congress, may not only perpetuate his own personal administration, but also make it hereditary?

By the same means, he may render his suspensive power over the laws as operative and permanent as that of G. the 3d over the acts of the British parliament; and under the modest title of president, may exercise the combined authority of legislation and execution, in a latitude yet unthought of. Upon his being invested with those powers a second or third time, he may acquire such enormous influence-as added to his uncontrollable power over the army, navy, and militia; together with his private interest in the officers of all these different departments, who are all to be appointed by himself, and so his creatures, in the true political sense of the word; and more especially when added to all this, he has the power of forming treaties and alliances, and calling

them to his assistance-that he may, I say, under all these advantages and almost irresistible temptations, on some pretended pique, haughtily and contemptuously, turn our poor lower house (the only shadow of liberty we shall have left) out of doors, and give us law at the bayonet's point. Or, may not the senate, who are nearly in the same situation, with respect to the people, from similar motives and by similar means, erect themselves easily into an oligarchy, towards which they have already attempted so large a stride? To one of which channels, or rather to a confluence of both, we seem to be fast gliding away; and the moment we arrive at it-farewell liberty. . . .

To conclude, I can think of but one source of right to government, or any branch of it-and that is THE PEOPLE. They, and only they, have a right to determine whether they will make laws, or execute them, or do both in a collective body, or by a delegated authority. Delegation is a positive actual investiture. Therefore if any people are subjected to an authority which they have not thus actually chosen-even though they may have tamely submitted to it-yet it is not their legitimate government. They are wholly passive, and as far as they are so, are in a state of slavery. Thank heaven we are not yet arrived at that state. And while we continue to have sense enough to discover and detect, and virtue en(>ugh to detest and oppose every attempt, either of force or fraud, either from without or within, to bring us into it, we never will.

Let us therefore continue united in the cause of rational liberty. Let unity and liberty be our mark as well as our motto. For only such an union can secure our freedom; and division will inevitably destroy it. Thus a mountain of sand may peace meal [sic] be

removed by the feeble hands of a child; but if consolidated into a rock, it mocks the united efforts of mankind, and can only fall in a general wreck of nature.
REPUBLICUS

ANTI-FEDERALIST PAPER NO. 73

Does the Presidential Veto Power Infringe On The Separation Of Departments?

"WILLIAM PENN," an anonymous writer appeared in the [Philadelphia] Independent Gazetteer on January 3, 1788.
... I believe that it is universally agreed upon in this enlightened country, that all power residing originally in the people, and being derived from them, they ought to be governed by themselves only, or by their immediate representatives. I shall not spend any time in explaining a principle so well and so generally understood, but I shall proceed immediately to that which I conceive to be the next in order.

The next principle, without which it must be clear that no free government can ever subsist, is the DIVISION OF POWER among those who are charged with the execution of it. It has always been the favorite maxim of princes, to divide the people, in order to govern them. It is now time that the people should avail themselves of the same maxim, and divide powers among their rulers, in order to prevent their abusing it. The application of this great political truth, has long been unknown to the world, and yet it is grounded upon a very plain natural principle. If, says Montesquieu, the same man, or body of men, is possessed both of the legislative and executive power, there is NO LIBERTY, because it may be feared that the same monarch, or the same senate, will enact tyrannical laws, in order to execute them in a tyrannical manner. Nothing can be clearer, and the natural disposition of man to ambition and power makes it probable that such would be the consequence. Suppose for instance, that the same body, which has the power of raising money by taxes, is also entrusted with the application of that money, they will very probably raise large sums, and apply them to their own private uses. If they are empowered to create offices, and appoint the officers, they will take that opportunity of providing for themselves, and their friends, and if they have the power of inflicting penalties for offenses, and of trying the offenders, there will be no bounds to their tyranny. Liberty therefore can only subsist, where the powers of government are properly divided, and where the different jurisdictions are inviolably kept distinct and separate.

(1) I shall illustrate this doctrine by an example. A burgher of a certain borough of Switzerland was elected Bailiff, or Chief Magistrate, for one year, according to the constitution of the place.

Shortly after his appointment, he sent for one of his neighbors, and ordered him to pull off his boots. The honest neighbor was astonished, and attempted to remonstrate, but the bailiff was determined to exert his authority, and threatened to send him to jail, if he did not yield him an immediate obedience. The poor man was forced to comply, for the bailiff was vested with power, both legislative and executive. He pulled off his worship's boots, but said to him, "When I am appointed bailiff in my turn, you shall pull off my boots and clean them too."

The first and most natural division of the powers of government are into the legislative and executive branches. These two should never be suffered to have the least share of each other's jurisdiction, or to intermeddle with it in any manner. For whichever of the two divides its power

with the other, will certainly be subordinate to it; and if they both have a share of each other's authority, they will be in fact but one body. Their interest as well as their powers will be the same, and they will combine together against the people.

It is therefore a political error of the greatest magnitude, to allow the executive power a negative, or in fact any kind of control over the proceedings of the legislature. The people of Great Britain have been so sensible of this truth, that since the days of William III, no king of England has dared to exercise the negative over the acts of the two houses of parliament, to which he is clearly entitled by his prerogative.

This doctrine is not novel in America; it seems on the contrary to be everywhere well understood and admitted beyond controversy. In the bills of rights or constitutions of New-Hampshire, Massachusetts, Maryland, Virginia, North-Carolina and Georgia, it is expressly declared, "That the legislative, executive and judicial departments, shall be forever separate and distinct from each other." In Pennsylvania and Delaware, they are effectually separated without any particular declaration of the principle. In the other states indeed, the executive branch possesses more or less of the executive power. And here it must

Documents of Revolution

appear singular that the state of Massachusetts-where the doctrine of a separate jurisdiction is most positively established, and in whose bill of rights these remarkable words are to be found, "The executive shall never exercise the legislative and judicial powers, or either of them, to the end it may be a government of laws and not of men" (sect. 30) -yet in that commonwealth and New-Hampshire, the executive branch, which consists of a single magistrate, has more control over the legislature than in any other state. For there, if the governor refuses his assent to a bill, it cannot be passed into a law, unless two thirds of the house afterwards concur. In New York the same power is given to a Council of Revision, consisting of the Governor, the Chancellor and judges of the Supreme Court, or any three of them, of which the Governor is to be one. In Rhode-Island and Connecticut, whose governments were established before the revolution, the Governor has a single vote as a member of the upper house, and New Jersey has adopted this part of their constitution. In Georgia the laws are to be revised by the Governor and Council, but they can do no more than give their opinion upon them. In Maryland the bills are to be signed by the Governor before they can be enacted; and in South-Carolina they are to be sealed with the great seal, which is in the Governor's custody. But in the first of these states, the constitution prescribes that the Governor shall sign the bills; and in the latter, a joint committee of both houses of legislature is to wait upon the chief magistrate to receive and return the great seat, which implies that he is bound to deliver it to them, for the special purpose of affixing it to the laws of the state. Pennsylvania has proceeded upon a much more rational ground, their legislature having a particular seal of their own, and their laws requiring only to be signed by the speaker. It in Maryland or South-Carolina a difference should ever arise between the legislature and the Governor, and the latter should refuse to sign the laws, or to deliver the great seal, the most fatal consequences might ensue. Here then we see the great leading principle of the absolute division of the legislative from the executive jurisdiction, admitted in almost every one of the American states as a fundamental maxim in the politics of a free country. The theory of this general doctrine is everywhere established, though a few states have somewhat swerved from it in the practice. From whence we must conclude, that even the knowledge and full conviction of a new political truth will not always immediately conquer inveterate habits and prejudices. The idea of the negative, which the

constitution of England gives to the monarch over the proceedings of the other branches of parliament, although it has so long become obsolete, has had an effect upon timid minds, and upon the minds of those who could not distinguish between the form and spirit of the British constitution. They would not grant to the executive branch an absolute negative over the legislature, but yet they tried every method to introduce something similar to it. They reprobated the doctrine in the most express words, and yet they could not bear to part entirely with it. It is curious to observe how many different ways they have endeavored to conciliate truth with prejudice. Of those states who have allowed the executive branch to intermeddle with the proceedings of the legislature, no two (New Hampshire and Massachusetts excepted) have done it exactly in the same manner. They have tried every possible medium, but having lost sight of the original principle which they had already established, and which alone could have been their safest guide, they groped about in the dark, and could not find any solid ground on which to establish a general rule. Like Noah's dove, being once out of the ark of truth, they could not find elsewhere a place to rest their feet.

These facts will no doubt afford an interesting page in the history of the contradictions of the human mind. Unfortunately, they do not stand single, and this is not the only instance that we find in the constitutions of the different states, of a general principle being expressly declared as a part of the natural rights of the citizens, and afterwards being as expressly contradicted in the practice. Thus we find it declared in every one of our bills of rights, "that there shall be a perfect liberty of conscience, and that no sect shall ever be entitled to a preference over the others." Yet in Massachusetts and Maryland, all the officers of government, and in Pennsylvania the members of the legislature, are to be of the Christian religion; in New-Jersey, North-Carolina, and Georgia, the Protestant, and in Delaware, the trinitarian sects, have an exclusive right to public employment; and in South-Carolina the constitution goes so far as to declare the creed of the established church. Virginia and New-York are the only states where there is a perfect liberty of conscience. I cannot say any thing as to Connecticut and Rhode-Island, as their constitutions are silent on the subject, and I have not been informed of their practice.

Whether these religious restrictions are right or wrong, it is not my intention, nor is it my object to examine in the course of these disquisitions. I only meant to show, that in laying down a political system it is safer to rely on principles than upon precedents, because the former are -

fixed and immutable, while the latter vary with men, places, times and circumstances.

WILLIAM PENN

ANTI-FEDERALIST PAPER NO. 74

The President as Military King

"PHILADELPHIENSIS," who was influenced by Thomas Paine (in "Common Sense), wrote the following selection. It is taken from 3 essays which appearing February 6 & 20, and April 9 of 1788 in either The Freeman's Journal or, The North-American Intelligencer.

Before martial law is declared to be the supreme law of the land, and your character of free citizens be changed to that of the subjects of a military king-which are necessary consequences of the adoption of the proposed constitution - let me admonish you in the name of sacred liberty, to make a solemn pause. Permit a freeman to address you, and to solicit your attention to a cause wherein yourselves and your posterity are concerned. The sun never shone upon a more important one. It is the cause of freedom of a whole continent of yourselves and of your fellow men....

A conspiracy against the freedom of America, both deep and dangerous, has been formed by an infernal junto of demagogues. Our thirteen free commonwealths are to be consolidated into one despotic monarchy. Is not this position obvious? Its evidence is intuitive.... Who can deny but the president general will be a king to all intents and purposes, and one of the most dangerous kind too-a king elected to command a standing army. Thus our laws are to be administered by this tyrant; for the whole, or at least the most important part of the executive department is put in his hands.

A quorum of 65 representatives, and of 26 senators, with a king at their head, are to possess powers that extend to the lives, the liberties, and property of every citizen of America. This novel system of government, were it possible to establish it, would be a compound of monarchy and aristocracy, the most accursed that ever the world witnessed. About 50 (these being a quorum) of the well born, and a military king, with a standing army devoted to his will, are to have an uncontrolled power....

There is not a tincture of democracy in the proposed constitution, except the nominal elections of the president general and the illustrious Congress be supposed to have some color of that nature.

But this is a mere deception, invented to gull the people into its adoption. Its framers were well aware that some appearance of election ought to be observed, especially in regard to the first Congress; for without such an appearance there was not the smallest probability of their having it organized and set in operation. But let the wheels of this government be once cleverly set in motion, and I'll answer for it, that the people shall not be much troubled with future elections, especially in choosing their king-the standing army will do that business for them.

The thoughts of a military officer possessing such powers, as the proposed constitution vests in the president general, are sufficient to excite in the mind of a freeman the most alarming apprehensions; and ought to rouse him to oppose it at all events. Every freeman of America ought to hold up this idea to himself: that he has no superior but God and the laws. But this tyrant will be so much his superior, that he can at any time he thinks proper, order him out in the militia to exercise, and to march when and where he pleases. His officers can wantonly inflict the most disgraceful punishment on a peaceable citizen, under pretense of disobedience, or the smallest neglect of militia duty....

The President-general, who is to be our king after this government is established, is vested with powers exceeding those of the most despotic monarch we know of in modern times. What a handsome return have these men [the authors of the Constitution made to the people of America for their confidence! Through the misconduct of these bold conspirators we have lost the most glorious opportunity that any country ever had to establish a free system of government. America under one purely democratical, would be rendered the happiest and most powerful nation in the universe. But under the proposed one composed of an elective king and a standing army, officered by his sycophants, the starvelings of the Cincinnati, and an aristocratical Congress of the well-born-an iota of happiness, freedom, or national strength cannot exist. What a pitiful figure will these ungrateful men make in history; who, for the hopes of obtaining some lucrative employment, or of receiving a little more homage from the rest of their fellow creatures, framed a system of oppression that must involve in its consequences the misery of their own offspring....

Some feeble attempts have been made by the advocates of this system of tyranny, to answer the objections made to the smallness of the number of representatives and senators, and the improper powers delegated to them. But, as far as I recollect, no one has been found bold enough to stand forth in defense of that dangerous and uncontrolled officer, the President-General, or more properly, our new King.

A few pieces under the signature of An American Citizen' were published immediately after the Constitution broke the shell, and the hydra made its way from the dark conclave into the open light. In the first number the writer, in touching on the

President, endeavored to conceal his immense powers, by representing the King of Great Britain as possessed of many hereditary prerogatives, rights and powers that he was not possessed of; that is, he shows what he is not, but neglects to show what he really is. But so flimsy a palliative could scarce escape the censure of the most ignorant advocate for such an officer; and since [then] we hear of no further attempts to prove the necessity of a King being set over the freemen of America.

The writer of these essays has clearly proven, that the President is a King to all intents and purposes, and at the same time one of the most dangerous kind too - an elective King, the commander in chief of a standing army, etc. And to those add, that he has a negative power over the proceedings of both branches of the legislature. And to complete his uncontrolled sway, he is neither restrained nor assisted by a privy council, which is a novelty in government. I challenge the politicians of the whole continent to find in any period of history a monarch more absolute...

PHILADELPHIENSIS

ANTI-FEDERALIST PAPER NO. 75

A NOTE PROTESTING THE TREATY MAKING PROVISIONS OF THE CONSTITUTION

The following essay was penned anonymously by "HAMPDEN," and it appeared in The Pittsburgh Gazette on February 16, 1788.

.... It may be freely granted, that from a mistaken zeal in favor of that political liberty which was so recently purchased at so costly a rate, even good men may give it [the constitution]
unreasonable opposition; but such men cannot be reasonably charged with sordid personal interest as their motive-because it is great and sudden changes which produces opportunities of preferment. But that class of men-who either prompted by their own ambition or desperate fortunes, are expecting employments under the proposed plan; or those weak and ardent men who always expect to be gainers by revolutions, and who are never contented, but always hastening from one difficulty to another-may be expected to ascribe every excellence to the proposed system, and to urge a thousand reasons for our real or supposed distresses, to induce our adopting thereof. Such characters may also be expected to promise us such extravagantly flattering advantages to arise from it, as if it was accompanied with such miraculous divine energy as divided the Red Sea, and spoke with thunder on Mount Sinai....

The first clause of the constitution assures us, that the legislative powers shall be vested in a Congress, which shall consist of a senate and house of representatives; and in the second clause of the second article, it is declared that the president, by and with the consent of the senate, is to make treaties. Here the supreme executive magistrate is officially connected with the highest branch of the legislature. And in article sixth, clause second, we find that all treaties made, or which shall be made, under the authority of the United States, shall be the supreme law of the land, and the judges in every state shall be bound thereby, anything in the constitution or laws of any state to the contrary notwithstanding. When we consider the extent of treaties-that in filing the tariff of trade, the imposts and port duties generally are or may be fixed by a large construction which interested rulers are never at a less to give to any constitutional power-treaties may be extended to almost every legislative object of the general government. Who is it that does not know, that by treaties in Europe the succession and constitution of many sovereign states, has been regulated. The partition treaty, and the war of the grand alliance, respecting the government of Spain, are well remembered; nor is it long since three neighboring powers established a nobleman of that nation upon the throne and regulated and altered the fundamental laws of that country, as well as divided the territory thereof, and all this was done by treaty. And from this power of making treaties, the house of representatives, which has the best chance of possessing virtue, and public confidence, is entirely excluded. Indeed, I see nothing to hinder the president and senate, at a convenient crisis, to declare themselves hereditary and supreme, and the lower house altogether useless, and to abolish what shadow of the state constitutions remain by this power alone; and as the president and senate have all that influence which arises from the creating and appointing of all offices and officers, who can doubt but at a proper occasion they will succeed in such an attempt? And who can doubt but that men will arise who will attempt it?

Will the doing so be a more flagrant breach of trust, or a greater degree of violence and perfidy, than has already been practised in order to introduce the proposed plan?... Of the same kind, and full as inconsistent and dangerous, is the first clause of the second article, compared with the second clause of the second section. We first find the president fully and absolutely vested with the executive power, and presently we find the most important and most influential portion of the executive power-e.g., the appointment of all officers-vested in the senate, with whom the president only acts as a nominating member. It is on this account that I have said above, that the greatest degree of virtue may be expected in the house of representatives; for if any considerable part of the executive power be joined with the legislature, it will as surely corrupt that branch with which it is combined, as poison will the human body. Therefore, though the small house of representatives will consist of the natural aristocracy of the country, as well as the senate, yet not being dangerously combined with the executive branch, it has not such certain influential inducements to corruption...

It will be asked, no doubt, who is this that dares so boldly to arraign the conduct and censure the production of a convention composed of so chosen a band of patriots? To this I answer, that I am a freeman, and it is the character of freemen to examine and judge for themselves. They know that implicit faith respecting politics is the handmaid to slavery; and that the greatness of those names who frame a government, cannot sanctify its faults, nor prevent the evils that result from its imperfections.... With respect to the majority, I do not doubt the testimony of a dignified supporter of the system, that they were all, or nearly all, eminent lawyers; but I do doubt the patriotism and political virtue of several of the most eminently active of them. But it is not with the men, but with the plan to which they gave birth, we have to contend, and to contend with such a degree of moderation and firmness, as will best promote political security, shall be the endeavor of HAMPDEN

Anti-Federalist Paper No. 76-77

AN ANTIFEDERALIST VIEW OF THE APPOINTING POWER UNDER THE CONSTITUTION

by Richard Henry Lee

.... In contemplating the necessary officers of the union, there appear to be six different modes in which, in whole or in part, the appointments may be made. 1. by the legislature; 2. by the president and the senate; 3. by the president and an executive council; 4. by the president alone; 5. by the heads of the departments; 6. by the state governments. Among all these, in my opinion, there may be an advantageous distribution of the power of appointments.

In considering the legislators, in relation to the subject before us, two interesting questions particularly arise: 1. whether they ought to be eligible to hold any offices whatever during the period for which they shall be elected to serve, and even for some time afterwards. 2. how far they ought to participate in the power of appointments. As to the first, it is true that legislators in foreign countries, or in our state governments, are not generally made ineligible to office. There are good reasons for it. In many countries the people have gone on without ever examining the principles of government. There have been but few countries in which the legislators have been a particular set of men periodically chosen. But the principal reason is, that which operates in the several states, viz., the legislators are so frequently chosen, and so numerous, compared with the number of offices for which they can reasonably consider themselves as candidates, that the chance of any individual member's being chosen, is too small to raise his hopes or expectations, or to have any considerable influence upon his conduct. Among the state legislators, one man in twenty may be appointed in some committee business, etc., for a month or two; but on a fair computation, not one man in a hundred sent to the state legislatures is appointed to any permanent office of profit. Directly the reverse of this will evidently be found true in the federal administration. Throughout the United States, about four federal senators, and thirty-three representatives, averaging the elections, will be chosen in a year. These few men may rationally consider themselves as the fairest candidates for a very great number of lucrative offices, which must become vacant in the year; and pretty clearly a majority of the federal legislators, if not excluded, will be mere expectants for public offices. I need not adduce further arguments to establish a position so clear. I need only call to your recollection my observations in a former letter, wherein I endeavored to show the fallacy of the argument, that the members must return home and mix with the people. It is said, that men are governed by interested motives, and will not attend as legislators, unless they can, in common with others, be eligible to offices of honor and profit. This will undoubtedly be the case with some men, but I presume only with such men as never ought to be chosen legislators in a free country. An opposite principle will influence good men. Virtuous patriots, and generous minds, will esteem it a higher honor to be selected as the guardians of a free people. They will be satisfied with a reasonable compensation for their time and service; nor will they wish to be within the vortex of influence. The valuable effects of this principle of making legislators ineligible to offices for a given time, has never yet been sufficiently attended to or considered. I am assured that it was established by the convention after long debate, and afterwards, on an unfortunate change of a few members, altered. Could the federal legislators be excluded in the manner proposed, I think it would be an important point gained; as to themselves, they would be left to act much more from motives consistent with the public good. In considering the principle of rotation I had occasion to distinguish the condition of a legislator from that of a mere official man. We acquire certain habits, feelings, and opinions, as men and citizens-others, and very different ones, from a long continuance in office. It is, therefore, a valuable observation in many bills of rights, that rulers ought frequently to return and mix with the people. A legislature, in a free country, must be numerous; it is in some degree a periodical assemblage of the people, frequently formed. The principal officers in the executive and judicial departments must have more permanency in office. Hence it may be inferred, that the legislature will remain longer uncorrupted and virtuous; longer congenial to the people, than the officers of those departments. If it is not, therefore in our power to preserve republican principles for a series of ages, in all the departments of government, we may a long while preserve them in a well formed legislature. To this end we ought to take every precaution to prevent legislators becoming mere office-men; choose them frequently, make them recallable, establish rotation among them, make them ineligible to offices, and give them as small a share as possible in the disposal of them. Add to this, a legislature in the nature of things is not formed for the detail business of appointing officers, there is also generally an impropriety in the same men making offices and filling them, and a still greater impropriety in their impeaching and trying the officers they appoint. For these and other reasons, I conclude the legislature is not a proper body for the appointment of officers in general. But having gone through with the different modes of appointment, I shall endeavor to show what share in the distribution of the power of appointments the legislature must, from necessity, rather than from propriety, take.

2. Officers may be appointed by the president and senate. This mode, for general purposes, is clearly not defensible. All the reasoning touching the legislature will apply to the senate. The senate is a branch of the legislature, which ought to be kept pure and unbiased. It has a part in trying officers for misconduct, and in creating offices it is too numerous for a council of appointment, or to feel any degree of responsibility. If it has an advantage of the legislature, in being the least numerous, it has a disadvantage in being more unsafe; add to this, the senate is to have a share in the important branch of power respecting treaties. Further, this sexennial senate of 26 members, representing 13 sovereign states, will not in practice be found to be a body to advise, but to order and dictate in fact; and the president will be a mere primus inter pares. The consequence will be that the senate, with these efficient means of influence, will not only dictate, probably, to the president, but manage the house, as the constitution now stands; and under appearances of a balanced system, in reality govern alone. There may also, by this undue connection, be particular periods when a very popular president may have a very improper influence upon the senate and upon the legislature. A council of appointment must very probably sit all, or near all, the year. The senate will be too important and too expensive a body for this.

By giving the senate, directly or indirectly, an undue influence over the representatives, and the improper means of fettering, embarrassing, or controlling the president or executive, we give the government in the very outset a fatal and pernicious tendency to . . . aristocracy. When we, as a circumstance not well to be avoided, admit the senate to a share of power in making treaties, and in managing foreign concerns, we certainly progress full far enough towards this most undesirable point in government. For with this power, also, I believe, we must join that of appointing ambassadors, other foreign ministers, and consuls, being powers necessarily connected. In every point of view, in which I can contemplate this subject, it appears extremely clear to me, that the senate ought not generally to be a council of appointment. The legislature, after the people, is the great fountain of power, and ought to be kept as pure and uncorrupt as

possible, from the hankerings, biases, and contagion of offices. Then the streams issuing from it will be less tainted with those evils. It is not merely the number of impeachments, that are to be expected to make public officers honest and attentive in their business. A general opinion must pervade the community, that the house, the body to impeach them for misconduct, is disinterested, and ever watchful for the public good; and that the judges who shall try impeachments, will not feel a shadow of bias. Under such circumstances men will not dare transgress, who, not deterred by such accusers and judges, would repeatedly misbehave. We have already suffered many and extensive evils, owing to the defects of the confederation, in not providing against the misconduct of public officers. When we expect the law to be punctually executed, not one man in ten thousand will disobey it. It is the probable chance of escaping punishment that induces men to transgress. It is one important means to make the government just and honest, rigidly and constantly to hold before the eyes of those who execute it, punishment and dismissal from office for misconduct. These are principles no candid man who has just ideas of the essential features of a free government will controvert. They are, to be sure, at this period, called visionary, speculative and anti-governmental-but in the true style of courtiers, selfish politicians, and flatterers of despotism. Discerning republican men of both parties see their value. They are said to be of no value by empty boasting advocates for the constitution, who, by their weakness and conduct, in fact, injure its cause much more than most of its opponents. From their high sounding promises, men are led to expect a defense of it, and to have their doubts removed. When a number of long pieces appear, they, instead of the defense, etc., they expected, see nothing but a parade of names; volumes written without ever coming to the point; cases quoted between which and ours there is not the least similitude; and partial extracts made from histories and governments, merely to serve a purpose. Some of them, like the true admirers of royal and senatorial robes, would fain prove, that nations who have thought like free-men and philosophers about government, and endeavored to be free, have often been the most miserable. If a single riot in the course of five hundred years happened in a free country; if a salary or the interest of a public or private debt was not paid at the moment-they seem to lay more stress upon these trifles (for trifles they are in a free and happy country), than upon the oppressions of despotic government for ages together. As to the lengthy writer in New York, I have attentively examined his pieces. He appears to be a candid good hearted man, to have a good style and some plausible ideas. But when we carefully examine his pieces, to see where the strength of them lies-when the mind endeavors to fix on those material parts, which ought to be the essence of all voluminous productions-we do not find them. The writer appears constantly to move on a smooth surface, the part of his work like the parts of a cob-house, are all equally strong and all equally weak, and all like those works of the boys, without an object. His pieces appear to have but little relation to the great question, whether the constitution is fitted to the condition and character of this people or not.

But to return. 3. Officers may be appointed by the president and an executive council. When we have assigned to the legislature the appointment of a few important officers; to the president and senate the appointment of those concerned in managing foreign affairs; to the state governments the appointment of militia officers; and authorise the legislature, by legislative acts, to assign to the president alone, to the heads of the departments, and courts of law respectively, the appointment of many inferior officers-we shall then want to lodge some where a residuum of power, a power to appoint all other necessary officers, as established by law. The fittest receptacle for this residuary power is clearly, in my opinion, the first executive magistrate, advised and directed by an executive council of seven or nine members, periodically chosen from such proportional districts as the union may for the purpose be divided into. The people may give their votes for twice the number of counsellors wanted, and the federal legislature take twice the number also from the highest candidates, and from among them choose the seven or nine, or number wanted. Such a council may be rationally formed for the business of appointments; whereas the senate, created for other purposes, never can be. Such councils form a feature in some of the best executives in the union. They appear to be essential to every first magistrate, who may frequently want advice.

To authorise the president to appoint his own council would be unsafe. To give the sole appointment of it to the legislature would confer an undue and unnecessary influence upon that branch. Such a council for a year would be less expensive than the senate for four months. The president may nominate, and the counsellors always be made responsible for their advice and opinions, by recording and signing whatever they advise to be done. They and the president, to many purposes, will properly form an independent executive branch; have an influence unmixed with the legislative, which the executive never can have while connected with a powerful branch of the legislature. And yet the influence arising from the power of appointments be less dangerous, because in less dangerous hands-hands properly adequate to possess it. Whereas the senate, from its character and situation, will add a dangerous weight to the power itself, and be far less capable of responsibility, than the council proposed. There is another advantage: the residuum of power as to appointments, which the president and council need possess, is less than that the president and senate must have. And as such a council would render the sessions of the senate unnecessary many months in the year, the expenses of the government would not be increased, if they would not be lessened by the institution of such a council. I think I need not dwell upon this article, as the fitness of this mode of appointment will perhaps amply appear by the evident unfitness of the others.

4. Officers may be appointed by the president alone. It has been almost universally found, when a man has been authorized to exercise power alone, he has never done it alone; but, generally,

[was] aided [in] his determinations by, and rested on the advice and opinions of others. And it often happens when advice is wanted, the worst men, the most interested creatures obtrude themselves, the worst advice is at hand, and misdirects the mind of him who would be informed and advised. It is very seldom we see a single executive depend on accidental advice and assistance; but each single executive has, almost always, formed to itself a regular council, to be assembled and consulted on

important occasions. This proves that a select council, of some kind is, by experience, generally found necessary and useful. But in a free country, the exercise of any considerable branch of power ought to be under some checks and controls. As to this point, I think the constitution stands well. The legislature may, when it shall deem it expedient, from time to time, authorise the president alone to appoint particular inferior officers; and when necessary, to take back the power. His power, therefore, in this respect, may always be increased or decreased by the legislature, as experience, the best instructor, shall direct-always keeping him, by the constitution, within certain bounds. Officers, in the fifth place, may be appointed by the heads of departments or courts of law. Art. 2., Sect. 2., respecting appointments, goes on-

"But congress may by law vest the appointment of such inferior officers as they think proper in the president alone, in the courts of law, or in the heads of departments." The probability is, as the constitution now stands, that the Senate, a branch of the legislature, will be tenacious of the

power of appointment, and much too sparingly part with a share of it to the courts of law, and heads of departments. Here again the impropriety appears of the senate's having, generally, a share in the appointment of officers. We may fairly assume, that the judges and principal officers in the departments will be able well informed men in their respective branches of business; that they will, from experience, be best informed as to proper persons to fill inferior offices in them; that they will feel themselves responsible for the execution of their several branches of business, and for the conduct of the officers they may appoint therein. From these, and other considerations, I think we may infer, that impartial and judicious appointments of subordinate officers will, generally, be made by the courts of law, and the heads of departments. This power of distributing appointments, as circumstances may require, into several hands, in a well formed disinterested legislature, might be of essential service not only in promoting beneficial appointments, but also in preserving the balance in government. A feeble executive may be strengthened and supported by placing in its hands more numerous appointments; an executive too influential may be reduced within proper bounds, by placing many of the inferior appointments in the courts of law, and heads of departments; nor is there much danger that the executive will be wantonly weakened or strengthened by the legislature by thus shifting the appointments of inferior officers. Since all must be done by legislative acts which cannot be passed without the consent of the executive, or the consent of two-thirds of both branches, a good legislature will use this power to preserve the balance and perpetuate the government. Here again we are brought to our ultimatum-is the legislature so constructed as to deserve our confidence?

6. Officers may be appointed by the state governments. By Art. 1., Sect. S., the respective states are authorised exclusively to appoint the militia officers. This not only lodges the appointments in proper places, but it also tends to distribute and lodge in different executive hands the powers of appointing to offices, so dangerous when collected into the hands of one or a few men. It is a good general rule, that the legislative, executive, and judicial powers, ought to be kept distinct. But this, like other general rules, has its exceptions; and without these exceptions we cannot form a good government, and properly balance its parts. And we can determine only from reason, experience and a critical inspection of the parts of the government, how far it is proper to intermix those powers. Appointments, I believe, in all mixed governments, have been assigned to different hands- some are made by the executive, some by the legislature, some by the judges, and some by the people. It has been thought advisable by the wisest nations-that the legislature should so far exercise executive and judicial powers as to appoint some officers judge of the elections of its members, and impeach and try officers for misconduct; that the executive should have a partial share in legislation; and that judges should appoint some subordinate officers, and regulate so far as to establish rules for their own proceedings. Where the members of the government, as the house, the senate, the executive, and judiciary, are strong and complete, each in itself, the balance is naturally produced; each party may take the powers congenial to it, and we have less need to be anxious about checks, and the subdivision of powers.

If after making the deductions already alluded to, from the general power to appoint federal officers, the residuum shall be thought to be too large and unsafe, and to place an undue influence in the hands of the president and council, a further deduction may be made, with many advantages and perhaps with but a few inconveniencies-and that is, by giving the appointment of

a few great officers to the legislature-as of the commissioners of the treasury, of the comptroller, treasurer, master coiner, and some of the principal officers in the money department; of the sheriffs or marshalls of the United States; of states attorneys, secretary of the home department, and secretary of war; perhaps of the judges of the supreme court; of major generals and admirals.

The appointments of these officers, who may be at the heads of the great departments of business, in carrying into execution the national system, involve in them a variety of considerations. They will not often occur and the power to make them ought to remain in safe hands. Officers of the above description are appointed by the legislatures in some of the states, and in some not. We may, I believe, presume that the federal legislature will possess sufficient knowledge and discernment to make judicious appointments. However, as these appointments by the legislature tend to increase a mixture of power, to lessen the advantages of impeachments and responsibility, I would by no means contend for them any further than it may be necessary for reducing the power of the executive within the bounds of safety.

THE FEDERAL FARMER

ANTI-FEDERALIST PAPER NO. 78-79

(PART I) The Power Of The Judiciary

Part I is taken from the first part of the "Brutus's" 15th essay of The New-York Journal on March 20, 1788;
Part II is part one of his 16th of the New York Journal of April 10, 1788.

The supreme court under this constitution would be exalted above all other power in the government, and subject to no control. The business of this paper will be to illustrate this, and to show the danger that will result from it. I question whether the world ever saw, in any period of it, a court of justice invested with such immense powers, and yet placed in a situation so little responsible. Certain it is, that in England, and in the several states, where we have been taught to believe the courts of law are put upon the most prudent establishment, they are on a very different footing.

The judges in England, it is true, hold their offices during their good behavior, but then their determinations are subject to correction by the house of lords; and their power is by no means so extensive as that of the proposed supreme court of the union. I believe they in no instance assume the authority to set aside an act of parliament under the idea that it is inconsistent with their constitution. They consider themselves bound to decide according to the existing laws of the land, and never undertake to control them by adjudging that they are inconsistent with the constitution-much less are they vested with the power of giv[ing an] equitable construction to the constitution.

The judges in England are under the control of the legislature, for they are bound to determine according to the laws passed under them. But the judges under this constitution will control the legislature, for the supreme court are authorised in the last resort, to determine what is the extent of the powers of the Congress. They are to give the constitution an explanation, and there is no power above them to set aside their judgment. The framers of this constitution appear to have followed that of the British, in rendering the judges independent, by granting them their offices during good behavior, without following the constitution of England, in instituting a tribunal in which their errors may be corrected; and without adverting to this, that the judicial under this system have a power which is above the legislative, and which indeed transcends any power before given to a judicial by any free government under heaven.

I do not object to the judges holding their commissions during good behavior. I suppose it a proper provision provided they were made properly responsible. But I say, this system has followed the English government in this, while it has departed from almost every other principle of their jurisprudence, under the idea, of rendering the judges independent; which, in the British constitution, means no more than that they hold their places during good behavior, and have fixed salaries . . . [the authors of the constitution] have made the judges independent, in the fullest sense of the word. There is no power above them, to control any of their decisions. There is no authority that can remove them, and they cannot be controlled by the laws of the legislature. In short, they are independent of the people, of the legislature, and of every power under heaven. Men placed in this situation will generally soon feel themselves independent of heaven itself. Before I proceed to illustrate the truth of these reflections, I beg liberty to make one remark. Though in my opinion the judges ought to hold their offices during good behavior, yet I think it is clear, that the reasons in favor of this establishment of the judges in England, do by no means apply to this country.

The great reason assigned, why the judges in Britain ought to be commissioned during good behavior, is this, that they may be placed in a situation, not to be influenced by the crown, to give such decisions as would tend to increase its powers and prerogatives. While the judges held their places at the will and pleasure of the king, on whom they depended not only for their offices, but also for their salaries, they were subject to every undue influence. If the crown wished to carry a favorite point, to accomplish which the aid of the courts of law was necessary, the pleasure of the king would be signified to the judges. And it required the spirit of a martyr for the judges to determine contrary to the king's will. They were absolutely dependent upon him both for their offices and livings. The king, holding his office during life, and transmitting it to his posterity as an inheritance, has much stronger inducements to increase the prerogatives of his office than those who hold their offices for stated periods or even for life. Hence the English nation gained a great point, in favor of liberty, when they obtained the appointment of the judge, during good behavior. They got from the crown a concession which deprived it of one of the most powerful engines with which it might enlarge the boundaries of the royal prerogative and encroach on the liberties of the people. But these reasons do not apply to this country. We have no hereditary monarch; those who appoint the judges do not hold their offices for life, nor do they descend to their children. The same arguments, therefore, which will conclude in favor of the tenure of the judge's offices for good behavior, lose a considerable part of their weight when applied to the state and condition of America. But much less can it be shown, that the nature of our government requires that the courts should be placed beyond all account more independent, so much so as to be above control.

I have said that the judges under this system will be independent in the strict sense of the word.

To prove this I will show that there is no power above them that can control their decisions, or correct their errors. There is no authority that can remove them from office for any errors or want of capacity, or lower their salaries, and in many cases their power is superior to that of the legislature.

1st. There is no power above them that can correct their errors or control their decisions. The adjudications of this court are final and irreversible, for there is no court above them to which appeals can lie, either in error or on the merits. In this respect it differs from the courts in England, for there the house of lords is the highest court, to whom appeals, in error, are carried from the highest of the courts of law.

2nd. They cannot be removed from office or suffer a diminution of their salaries, for any error in judgment [due] to want of capacity. It is expressly declared by the constitution, "That they shall at stated times receive a compensation for their services which shall not be diminished during their continuance in office."

The only clause in the constitution which provides for the removal of the judges from offices, is that which declares, that "the president, vice- president, and all civil officers of the United States,

shall be removed from office, on impeachment for, and conviction of treason, bribery, or other high crimes and misdemeanors." By this paragraph, civil officers, in which the judges are included, are removable only for crimes. Treason and bribery are named, and the rest are included under the general terms of high crimes and misdemeanors. Errors in judgment, or want of capacity to discharge the duties of the office, can never be supposed to be included in these words, high crimes and misdemeanors. A man may mistake a case in giving judgment, or manifest that he is incompetent to the discharge of the duties of a judge, and yet give no evidence of corruption or want of integrity. To support the charge, it will be necessary to give in evidence some facts that will show, that the judges committed the error from wicked and corrupt motives.

3d. The power of this court is in many cases superior to that of the legislature. I have showed, in a former paper, that this court will be authorised to decide upon the meaning of the constitution; and that, not only according to the natural and obvious meaning of the words, but also according to the spirit and intention of it. In the exercise of this power they will not be subordinate to, but above the legislature. For all the departments of this government will receive their powers, so far as they are expressed in the constitution, from the people immediately, who are the source of power. The legislature can only exercise such powers as are given them by the constitution; they cannot assume any of the rights annexed to the judicial; for this plain reason, that the same authority which vested the legislature with their powers, vested the judicial with theirs. Both are derived from the same source; both therefore are equally valid, and the judicial hold their powers independently of the legislature, as the legislature do of the judicial. The supreme court then have a right, independent of the legislature, to give a construction to the constitution and every part of it, and there is no power provided in this system to correct their construction or do it away. If, therefore, the legislature pass any laws, inconsistent with the sense the judges put upon the constitution, they will declare it void; and therefore in this respect their power is superior to that of the legislature. In England the judges are not only subject to have their decisions set aside by the house of lords, for error, but in cases where they give an explanation to the laws or constitution of the country contrary to the sense of the parliament -though the parliament will not set aside the judgment of the court-yet, they have authority, by a new law, to explain the former one, and by this means to prevent a reception of such decisions. But no such power is in the legislature. The judges are supreme and no law, explanatory of the constitution, will be binding on them.

When great and extraordinary powers are vested in any man, or body of men, which in their exercise, may operate to the oppression of the people, it is of high importance that powerful checks should be formed to prevent the abuse of it.

Perhaps no restraints are more forcible, than such as arise from responsibility to some superior power. Hence it is that the true policy of a republican government is, to frame it in such manner, that all persons who are concerned in the government, are

made accountable to some superior for their conduct in office. This responsibility should ultimately rest with the people. To have a government well administered in all its parts, it is requisite the different departments of it should be separated and lodged as much as may be in different hands. The legislative power should be in one body, the executive in another, and the judicial in one different from either. But still each of these bodies should be accountable for their conduct. Hence it is impracticable, perhaps, to maintain a perfect distinction between these several departments. For it is difficult, if not impossible, to call to account the several officers in government, without in some degree mixing the legislative and judicial. The legislature in a free republic are chosen by the people at stated periods, and their responsibility consists, in their being amenable to the people. When the term for which they are chosen shall expire, who (the people) will then have opportunity to displace them if they disapprove of their conduct. But it would be improper that the judicial should be elective, because their business requires that they should possess a degree of law knowledge, which is acquired only by a regular education; and besides it is fit that they should be placed, in a certain degree in an independent situation, that they may maintain firmness and steadiness in their decisions. As the people therefore ought not to elect the judges, they cannot be amenable to them immediately, some other mode of amenability must therefore be devised for these, as well as for all other officers which do not spring from the immediate choice of the people. This is to be effected by making one court subordinate to another, and by giving them cognizance of the behavior of all officers. But on this plan we at last arrive at some supreme, over whom there is no power to control but the people themselves. This supreme controlling power should be in the choice of the people, or else you establish an authority independent, and not amenable at all, which is repugnant to the principles of a free government. Agreeable to these principles I suppose the supreme judicial ought to be liable to be called to account, for any misconduct, by some body of men, who depend upon the people for their places; and so also should all other great officers in the State, who are not made amenable to some superior officers....
BRUTUS

ANTI-FEDERALIST PAPER NO. 80

(PART II)The Power Of The Judiciary

From the 11th essay of "Brutus" taken from The New-York Journal, January 31, 1788.
The nature and extent of the judicial power of the United States, proposed to be granted by the constitution, claims our particular attention.
Much has been said and written upon the subject of this new system on both sides, but I have not met with any writer who has discussed the judicial powers with any degree of accuracy. And yet it is obvious, that we can gain but very imperfect ideas of the manner in which this government will work, or the effect it will have in changing the internal police and mode of distributing justice at present subsisting in the respective states, without a thorough investigation of the powers of the judiciary and of the manner in which they will operate. This government is a complete system, not only for making, but for executing laws. And the courts of law, which will be constituted by it, are not only to decide upon the constitution and the laws made in pursuance of it, but by officers subordinate to them to execute all their decisions. The real effect of this system of government, will therefore be brought home to the feelings of the people, through the medium of the judicial power. It is, moreover, of great importance, to examine with care the nature and extent of the judicial power, because those who are to be vested with it, are to be placed in a situation altogether unprecedented in a free country. They are to be rendered totally independent, both of the people and the legislature, both with respect to their offices and salaries.
No errors they may commit can be corrected by any power above them, if any such power there be, nor can they be removed from office for making ever so many erroneous adjudications.
The only causes for which they can be displaced, is, conviction of treason, bribery, and high crimes and misdemeanors.
This part of the plan is so modelled, as to authorize the courts, not only to carry into execution the powers expressly given, but where these are wanting or ambiguously expressed, to supply what is wanting by their own decisions.
That we may be enabled to form a just opinion on this subject, I shall, in considering it, 1st.
Examine the nature and extent of the judicial powers, and 2nd. Inquire, whether the courts who are to exercise them, are so constituted as to afford reasonable ground of confidence, that they will exercise them for the general good.

Documents of Revolution

With a regard to the nature and extent of the judicial powers, I have to regret my want of capacity to give that full and minute explanation of them that the subject merits. To be able to do this, a man should be possessed of a degree of law knowledge far beyond what I pretend to. A number of hard words and technical phrases are used in this part of the system, about the meaning of which gentlemen learned in the law differ. Its advocates know how to avail themselves of these phrases. In a number of instances, where objections are made to the powers given to the judicial, they give such an explanation to the technical terms as to avoid them.

Though I am not competent to give a perfect explanation of the powers granted to this department of the government, I shall yet attempt to trace some of the leading features of it, from which I presume it will appear, that they will operate to a total subversion of the state judiciaries, if not to the legislative authority of the states.

In article 3d, sect. 2d, it is said, "The judicial power shall extend to all cases in law and equity arising under this constitution, the laws of the United States, and treaties made, or which shall be made, under their authority, etc." The first article to which this power extends is, all cases in law and equity arising under this constitution.

What latitude of construction this clause should receive, it is not easy to say. At first view, one would suppose, that it meant no more than this, that the courts under the general government should exercise, not only the powers of courts of law, but also that of courts of equity, in the manner in which those powers are usually exercised in the different states. But this cannot be the meaning, because the next clause authorises the courts to take cognizance of all cases in law and equity arising under the laws of the United States; this last article, I conceive, conveys as much power to the general judicial as any of the state courts possess.

The cases arising under the constitution must be different from those arising under the laws, or else the two clauses mean exactly the same thing. The cases arising under the constitution must include such, as bring into question its meaning, and will require an explanation of the nature and extent of the powers of the different departments under it. This article, therefore, vests the judicial with a power to resolve all questions that may arise on any case on the construction of the constitution, either in law or in equity.

lst. They are authorised to determine all questions that may arise upon the meaning of the constitution in law. This article vests the courts with authority to give the constitution a legal construction, or to explain it according to the rules laid down for construing a law. These rules give a certain degree of latitude of explanation. According to this mode of construction, the courts are to give such meaning to the constitution as comports best with the common, and generally received acceptation of the words in which it is expressed, regarding their ordinary and popular use, rather than their grammatical propriety. Where words are dubious, they will be explained by the context. The end of the clause will be attended to, and the words will be understood, as having a view to it; and the words will not be so understood as to bear no meaning or a very absurd one.

2nd. The judicial are not only to decide questions arising upon the meaning of the constitution in law, but also in equity. By this they are empowered, to explain the constitution according to the reasoning spirit of it, without being confined to the words or letter. "From this method of interpreting laws (says Blackstone) by the reason of them, arises what we call equity"; which is thus defined by Grotius, "the correction of that, wherein the law, by reason of its universality, is deficient; for since in laws all cases cannot be foreseen, or expressed, it is necessary, that when the decrees of the law cannot be applied to particular cases, there should somewhere be a power vested of defining those circumstances, which had they been foreseen the legislator would have expressed. . . ." The same learned author observes, "That equity, thus depending essentially upon each individual case, there can be no established rules and fixed principles of equity laid down, without destroying its very essence, and reducing it to a positive law."

From these remarks, the authority and business of the courts of law, under this clause, may be understood.

They [the courts] will give the sense of every article of the constitution, that may from time to time come before them. And in their decisions they will not confine themselves to any fixed or established rules, but will determine, according to what appears to them, the reason and spirit of the constitution. The opinions of the supreme court, whatever they may be, will have the force of law; because there is no power provided in the constitution that can correct their errors, or control their adjudications. From this court there is no appeal. And I conceive the legislature themselves, cannot set aside a judgment of this court, because they are authorised by the constitution to decide in the last resort. The legislature must be controlled by the constitution, and not the constitution by them. They have therefore no more right to set aside any judgment pronounced upon the construction of the constitution, than they have to take from the president, the chief command of the army and navy, and commit it to some other person. The reason is plain; the judicial and executive derive their authority from the same source, that the legislature do theirs; and therefore in all cases, where the constitution does not make the one responsible to, or controllable by the other, they are altogether independent of each other.

Documents of Revolution

The judicial power will operate to effect, in the most certain, but yet silent and imperceptible manner, what is evidently the tendency of the constitution: I mean, an entire subversion of the legislative, executive and judicial powers of the individual states. Every adjudication of the supreme court, on any question that may arise upon the nature and extent of the general government, will affect the limits of the state jurisdiction. In proportion as the former enlarge the exercise of their powers, will that of the latter be restricted.

That the judicial power of the United States, will lean strongly in favor of the general government, and will give such an explanation to the constitution, as will favor an extension of its jurisdiction, is very evident from a variety of considerations.

1st. The constitution itself strongly countenances such a mode of construction. Most of the articles in this system, which convey powers of any considerable importance, are conceived in general and indefinite terms, which are either equivocal, ambiguous, or which require long definitions to unfold the extent of their meaning. The two most important powers committed to any government, those of raising money, and of raising and keeping up troops, have already been considered, and shown to be unlimited by any thing but the discretion of the legislature. The clause which vests the power to pass all laws which are proper and necessary, to carry the powers given into execution, it has been shown, leaves the legislature at liberty, to do everything, which in their judgment is best. It is said, I know, that this clause confers no power on the legislature, which they would not have had without it-though I believe this is not the fact, Yet, admitting it to be, it implies that the constitution is not to receive an explanation strictly according to its letter; but more power is implied than is expressed. And this clause, if it is to be considered as explanatory of the extent of the powers given, rather than giving a new power, is to be understood as declaring that in construing any of the articles conveying power, the spirit,

intent and design of the clause should be attended to, as welt as the words in their common acceptation.

This constitution gives sufficient color for adopting an equitable construction, if we consider the great end and design it professedly has in view. These appear from its preamble to be, "to form a more perfect union, establish justice, insure domestic tranquility, provide for the common defense, promote the general welfare, and secure the blessings of liberty to ourselves and posterity." The design of this system is here expressed, and it is proper to give such a meaning to the various parts, as will best promote the accomplishment of the end; this idea suggests itself naturally upon reading the preamble, and will countenance the court in giving the several articles such a sense, as will the most effectually promote the ends the constitution had in view. How this manner of explaining the constitution will operate in practice, shall be the subject of future inquiry.

2nd. Not only will the constitution justify the courts in inclining to this mode of explaining it, but they will be interested in using this latitude of interpretation. Every body of men invested with office are tenacious of power; they feel interested, and hence it has become a kind of maxim, to hand down their offices, with all its rights and privileges, unimpaired to their successors. The same principle will influence them to extend their power, and increase their rights; this of itself will operate strongly upon the courts to give such a meaning to the constitution in all cases where it can possibly be done, as will enlarge the sphere of their own authority. Every extension of the power of the general legislature, as well as of the judicial powers, will increase the powers of the courts; and the dignity and importance of the judges, will be in proportion to the extent and magnitude of the powers they exercise. I add, it is highly probable the emolument of the judges will be increased, with the increase of the business they will have to transact and its importance.

From these considerations the judges will be interested to extend the powers of the courts, and to construe the constitution as much as possible, in such a way as to favor it; and that they will do it, appears probable.

3rd. Because they [the courts] will have precedent to plead, to justify them in it [extending their powers]. It is well known, that the courts in England, have by their authority, extended their jurisdiction far beyond the limits set them in their original institution, and by the laws of the land.

The court of exchequer is a remarkable instance of this. It was originally intended principally to recover the king's debts, and to order the revenues of the crown. It had a common law jurisdiction, which was established merely for the benefit of the king's accountants. We learn from Blackstone, that the proceedings in this court are grounded on a writ called quo minus, in which the plaintiff suggests, that he is the king's farmer or debtor, and that the defendant hath done him the damage complained of, by which he is less able to pay the king. These suits, by the statute of Rutland, are expressly directed to be confined to such matters as specially concern the king, or his ministers in the exchequer. And by the articuli super cartas, it is enacted, that no common pleas be thenceforth held in the exchequer contrary to the form of the great charter. But now any person may sue in the exchequer. The surmise of being debtor to the king being matter of form, and mere words of course, the court is open to all the nation.

When the courts will have a precedent before them of a court which extended its jurisdiction in opposition to an act of the legislature, is it not to be expected that they will extend theirs, especially when there is nothing in the constitution expressly against it? And they are authorised to construe its meaning, and are not under any control.

This power in the judicial, will enable them to mould the government, into any shape they please. The manner in which this may be effected we will hereafter examine.

BRUTUS

ANTI-FEDERALIST PAPER NO. 81

(PART III)The Power Of The Judiciary

Part I: from the 12th essay by "Brutus" from the February 7th & 14th (1788) issues of The New-York Journal
Part II: Taken from the first half of the 14th essay February 28, 1788.
In my last, I showed, that the judicial power of the United States under the first clause of the second section of article eight, would be authorised to explain the constitution, not only according to its letter, but according to its spirit and intention; and having this power, they would strongly incline to give it such a construction as to extend the powers of the general government, as much as possible, to the diminution, and finally to the destruction, of that of the respective states.
I shall now proceed to show how this power will operate in its exercise to effect these purposes. .
. . First, let us inquire how the judicial power will effect an extension of the legislative authority.
Perhaps the judicial power will not be able, by direct and positive decrees, ever to direct the legislature, because it is not easy to conceive how a question can be brought before them in a course of legal discussion, in which they can give a decision, declaring, that the legislature have certain powers which they have not exercised, and which, in consequence of the determination of the judges, they will be bound to exercise. But it is easy to see, that in their adjudication they may establish certain principles, which being received by the legislature will enlarge the sphere of their power beyond all bounds.
It is to be observed, that the supreme court has the power, in the last resort, to determine all questions that may arise in the course of legal discussion, on the meaning and construction of the constitution. This power they will hold under the constitution, and independent of the legislature.
The latter can no more deprive the former of this right, than either of them, or both of them together, can take from the president, with the advice of the senate, the power of making treaties, or appointing ambassadors.
In determining these questions, the court must and will assume certain principles, from which they will reason, in forming their decisions. These principles, whatever they may be, when they become fixed by a course of decisions, will be adopted by the legislature, and will be the rule by which they will explain their own powers. This appears evident from this consideration, that if the legislature pass laws, which, in the judgment of the court, they are not authorised to do by the constitution, the court will not take notice of them; for it will not be denied, that the constitution is the highest or supreme law. And the courts are vested with the supreme and uncontrollable power, to determine in all cases that come before them, what the constitution means. They cannot, therefore, execute a law, which in their judgment, opposes the constitution, unless we can suppose they can make a superior law give way to an inferior. The legislature, therefore, will not go over the limits by which the courts may adjudge they are confined. And there is little room to doubt but that they will come up to those bounds, as often as occasion and opportunity may offer, and they may judge it proper to do it. For as on the one hand, they will not readily
pass taws which they know the courts will not execute, so on the other, we may be sure they will not scruple to pass such as they know they will give effect, as often as they may judge it proper.
From these observations it appears, that the judgment of the judicial, on the constitution, will become the rule to guide the legislature in their construction of their powers.
What the principles are, which the courts will adopt, it is impossible for us to say. But taking up the powers as I have explained them in my last number, which they will possess under this clause, it is not difficult to see, that they may, and probably will, be very liberal ones.
We have seen, that they will be authorized to give the constitution a construction according to its spirit and reason, and not to confine themselves to its letter.

Documents of Revolution

To discover the spirit of the constitution, it is of the first importance to attend to the principal ends and designs it has in view. These are expressed in the preamble, in the following words, viz., "We, the people of the United States, in order to form a more perfect union, establish justice, insure domestic tranquility, provide for the common defense, promote the general welfare, and secure the blessings of liberty to ourselves and our posterity, do ordain and establish this constitution," etc. If the end of the government is to be learned from these words, which are clearly designed to declare it, it is obvious it has in view every object which is embraced by any government. The preservation of internal peace-the due admission of justice-and to provide for the defense of the community-seems to include all the objects of government. But if they do not, they are certainly comprehended in the words, "to provide for the general welfare." If it be further considered, that this constitution, if it is ratified, will not be a compact entered into by states, in their corporate capacities, but an agreement of the people of the United States as one great body politic, no doubt can remain but that the great end of the constitution, if it is to be collected from the preamble, in which its end is declared, is to constitute a government which is to extend to every case for which any government is instituted, whether external or internal. The courts, therefore, will establish this as a principle in expounding the constitution, and will give every part of it such an explanation as will give latitude to every department under it, to take cognizance of every matter, not only that affects the general and national concerns of the union, but also of such as relate to the administration of private justice, and to regulating the internal and local affairs of the different parts.

Such a rule of exposition is not only consistent with the general spirit of the preamble, but it will stand confirmed by considering more minutely the different clauses of it.

The first object declared to be in view, is "To form a more perfect union." It is to be observed, it is not an union of states or bodies corporate; had this been the case the existence of the state governments might have been secured. But it is a union of the people of the United States considered as one body, who are to ratify this constitution if it is adopted. Now to make a union of this kind perfect, it is necessary to abolish all inferior governments, and to give the general one complete legislative, executive and judicial powers to every purpose. The courts therefore will establish it as a rule in explaining the constitution; to give it such a construction as will best tend to perfect the union or take from the state governments every power of either making or executing laws. The second object is "to establish justice." This must include not only the idea of instituting the rule of justice, or of making laws which shall be the measure or rule of right, but also of providing for the application of this rule or of administering justice under it. And under this the courts will in their decisions extend the power of the government to all cases they possibly can, or otherwise they will be restricted in doing what appears to be the intent of the constitution they should do, to wit, pass laws and provide for the execution of them, for the general distribution of justice between man and man. Another end declared is "to insure domestic tranquility." This comprehends a provision against all private breaches of the peace, as well as against all public commotions or general insurrections; and to attain the object of this clause fully, the government must exercise the power of passing laws in these subjects, as well as of appointing magistrates with authority to execute them. And the courts will adopt these ideas in their expositions. I might proceed to the other clause, in the preamble, and it would appear by a consideration of all of them separately, as it does by taking them together, that if the spirit of this system is to be known from its declared end and design in the preamble, its spirit is to subvert and abolish all the powers of the state governments, and to embrace every object to which any government extends.

As it sets out in the preamble with this declared intention, so it proceeds in the different parts with the same idea. Any person, who will peruse the 5th section with attention, in which most of the powers are enumerated, will perceive that they either expressly or by implication extend to almost every thing about which any legislative power can be employed. If this equitable mode of construction is applied to this part of the constitution, nothing can stand before it.

This will certainly give the first clause in that article a construction which I confess I think the most natural and grammatical one, to authorise the Congress to do any thing which in their judgment will tend to provide for the general welfare, and this amounts to the same thing as general and unlimited powers of legislation in all cases.

This same manner of explaining the constitution, will fix a meaning, and a very important one too, to the 12th clause of the same section, which authorises the Congress to make all laws which shall be proper and necessary for carrying into effect the foregoing powers, etc. A voluminous writer in favor of this system, has taken great pains to convince the public, that this clause means nothing: for that the same powers expressed in this, are implied in other parts of the constitution.

Perhaps it is so, but still this will undoubtedly be an excellent auxiliary to assist the courts to discover the spirit and reason of the constitution, and when applied to any and every of the other clauses granting power, will operate powerfully in extracting the spirit from them.

I might instance a number of clauses in the constitution, which, if explained in an equitable manner, would extend the powers of the government to every case, and reduce the state legislatures to nothing. But, I should draw out my remarks to an undue length, and I presume enough has been said to show, that the courts have sufficient ground in the exercise of this power, to determine, that the legislature have no bounds set to them by this constitution, by any supposed right the legislatures of the respective states may have to regulate any of their local concerns.

I proceed, 2nd, to inquire, in what manner this power will increase the jurisdiction of the courts.

I would here observe, that the judicial power extends, expressly, to all civil cases that may arise save such as arise between citizens of the same state, with this exception to those of that description, that the judicial of the United States have cognizance of cases between citizens of the same state, claiming lands -under grants of different states. Nothing more, therefore, is necessary to give the courts of law, under this constitution, complete jurisdiction of all civil causes, but to comprehend cases between citizens of the same state not included in the foregoing exception.

I presume there will be no difficulty in accomplishing this. Nothing more is necessary than to set forth in the process, that the party who brings the suit is a citizen of a different state from the one against whom the suit is brought and there can be little doubt but that the court will take cognizance of the matter. And if they do, who is to restrain them? Indeed, I will freely confess, that it is my decided opinion, that the courts ought to take cognizance of such causes under the powers of the constitution. For one of the great ends of the constitution is, "to establish justice."

This supposes that this cannot be done under the existing governments of the states; and there is certainly as good reason why individuals, living in the same state, should have justice, as those who live in different states. Moreover, the constitution expressly declares, that "the citizens of each state shall be entitled to all the privileges and immunities of citizens in the several states," It will therefore be no fiction, for a citizen of one state to set forth, in a suit, that he is a citizen of another; for he that is entitled to all the privileges and immunities of a country, is a citizen of that country. And in truth, the citizen of one state will, under this constitution, be a citizen of every state....

It is obvious that these courts will have authority to decide upon the validity of the laws of any of the states, in all cases where they come in question before them. Where the constitution gives the general government exclusive jurisdiction, they will adjudge all laws made by the states, in such cases, void ab inilio. Where the constitution gives them concurrent jurisdiction, the laws of the United States must prevail, because they are the supreme law. In such cases, therefore, the laws of the state legislatures must be repealed, restricted, or so construed, as to give full effect to the laws of the union on the same subject. From these remarks it is easy to see, that in proportion as the general government acquires power and jurisdiction, by the liberal construction which the judges may give the constitution, those of the states will lose their rights, until they become so trifling and unimportant, as not to be worth having. I am much mistaken, if this system will not operate to effect this with as much celerity, as those who have the administration of it will think prudent to suffer it. The remaining objections of the judicial power shall be considered in a future paper.

The second paragraph of sect. 2, art. 3, is in these words: "In all cases affecting ambassadors, other public ministers and consuls, and those in which a state shall be a party, the supreme court shall have original jurisdiction. In all the other cases before mentioned, the supreme court shall have appellate jurisdiction, both as to law and fact, with such exceptions, and under such regulations as the Congress shall make."

Although it is proper that the courts of the general government should have cognizance of all matters affecting ambassadors, foreign ministers, and consuls, yet I question much the propriety of giving the supreme court original jurisdiction in all cases of this kind.

Ambassadors, and other public ministers, claim, and are entitled by the law of nations, to certain privileges, and exemptions, both for their persons and their servants. The meanest servant of an ambassador is exempted by the law of nations from being sued for debt. Should a suit be brought against such an one by a citizen, through inadvertency or want of information, he will be subject to an action in the supreme court. All the officers concerned in issuing or executing the process will be liable to like actions. Thus may a citizen of a state be compelled, at great expense and inconveniency, to defend himself against a suit, brought against him in the supreme court, for inadvertently commencing an action against the most menial servant of an ambassador for a just debt.

The appellate jurisdiction granted to the supreme court, in this paragraph, has justly been considered as one of the most objectionable parts of the constitution. Under this power, appeals may be had from the inferior courts to the supreme, in every case to which the judicial power extends, except in the few instances in which the supreme court will have original jurisdiction. By this article, appeals will lie to the supreme court, in all criminal as well as civil causes. This I know, has been disputed by some; but I presume the point will appear clear to any one, who will attend to the connection of this paragraph with the one that precedes it. In the former, all the cases, to which the power of the judicial shall extend, whether civil or criminal, are enumerated.

Documents of Revolution

There is no criminal matter, to which the judicial power of the United States will extend, but such as are included under some one of the cases specified in this section. For this section is intended to define all cases, of every description, to which the power of the judicial shall reach.

But in all these cases it is declared, the supreme court shall have appellate jurisdiction, except in those which affect ambassadors, other public ministers and consuls, and those in which a state shall be a party. If then this section extends the power of the judicial, to criminal cases, it allows appeals in such cases. If the power of the judicial is not extended to criminal matters by this section, I ask, by what part of this system does it appear, that they have any cognizance of them?

I believe it is a new and unusual thing to allow appeals in criminal matters. It is contrary to the sense of our laws, and dangerous to our lives and liberties. . . . As our taw now stands, a person charged with a crime has a right to a fair and impartial trial by a jury of his country, and their verdict is final. If be is acquitted no other court can call upon him to answer for the same crime.

But by this system, a man may have had ever so fair a trial, have been acquitted by ever so respectable a jury of his country, and still the officer of the government who prosecutes may appeal to the supreme court. The whole matter may have a second hearing. By this means, persons who may have disobliged those who execute the general government, may be subjected to intolerable oppression. They may be kept in long and ruinous confinement, and exposed to heavy and insupportable charges, to procure the attendance of witnesses, and provide the means of their defense, at a great distance from their places of residence. I can scarcely believe there can be a considerate citizen of the United States that will approve of this appellate jurisdiction, as extending to criminal cases, if they will give themselves time for reflection.

Whether the appellate jurisdiction as it respects civil matters, will not prove injurious to the rights of the citizens, and destructive of those privileges which have ever been held sacred by

Americans, and whether it will not render the administration of justice intolerably burdensome, intricate, and dilatory, will best appear, when we have considered the nature and operation of this power.

It has been the fate of this clause, as it has of most of those against which unanswerable objections have been offered, to be explained different ways, by the advocates and opponents to the constitution. I confess I do not know what the advocates of the system would make it mean, for I have not been fortunate enough to see in any publication this clause taken up and considered. It is certain however, they do not admit the explanation which those who oppose the constitution give it, or otherwise they would not so frequently charge them with want of candor, for alleging that it takes away the trial by jury. Appeals from an inferior to a superior court, as practised in the civil law courts, are well understood. In these courts, the judges determine both on the law and the fact; and appeals are allowed from the inferior to the superior courts, on the whole merits; the superior tribunal will re-examine all the facts as well as the law, and frequently new facts will be introduced, so as many times to render the cause in the court of appeals very different from what it was in the court below.

If the appellate jurisdiction of the supreme court, be understood in the above sense, the term is perfectly intelligible. The meaning then is, that in an the civil case enumerated, the supreme court shall have authority to reexamine the whole merits of the case, both with respect to the facts and the law which may arise under it, without the intervention of a jury; that this is the sense of this part of the system appears to me clear, from the express words of it, "in all the other cases before mentioned, the supreme court shall have appellate jurisdiction, both as to law and fact, etc." Who are the supreme court? Does it not consist of the judges? . . . They will therefore have the same authority to determine the fact as they will have to determine the law, and no room is left for a jury on appeals to the supreme court.

If we understand the appellate jurisdiction in any other way, we shall be left utterly at a loss to give it a meaning. The common law is a, stranger to any such jurisdiction: no appeals can lie from any of our common law courts, upon the merits of the case. The only way in which they can go up from an inferior to a superior tribunal is by habeas corpus before a hearing, or by certiorari, or writ of error, after they are determined in the subordinate courts. But in no case, when they are carried up, are the facts re-examined, but they are always taken as established in the inferior court.

BRUTUS

ANTI-FEDERALIST PAPER NO. 82

(PART IV) The Power of The Judiciary

Part I: Part II of "Brutus'" 14th essay (from the March 6, 1788, New-York Journal) Part II: The final segment of the 15th essay (March 20, 1788 New York Journal) It may still be insisted that this clause [on appellate jurisdiction] does not take away the trial by jury on appeals, but that this may be provided for by the legislature, under that paragraph which authorises them to form regulations and restrictions for the court in the exercise of this power.

The natural meaning of this paragraph seems to be no more than this, that Congress may declare, that certain cases shall not be subject to the appellate jurisdiction, and they may point out the mode in which the court shall proceed in bringing up the causes before them, the manner of their taking evidence to establish the facts, and the method of the court's proceeding. But I presume they cannot take from the court the right of deciding on the fact, any more than they can deprive them of the right of determining on the law, when a cause is once before them; for they have the same jurisdiction as to fact, as they have as to the law. But supposing the Congress may under this clause establish the trial by jury on appeals. It does not seem to me that it will render this article much less exceptionable. An appeal from one court and jury, to another court and jury, is a thing altogether unknown in the laws of our state [New York], and in most of the states in the union. A practice of this kind prevails in the eastern states: actions are there commenced in the inferior courts, and an appeal lies from them on the whole merits to the superior courts. The consequence is well known. Very few actions are determined in the lower courts; it is rare that a case of any importance is not carried by appeal to the supreme court, and the jurisdiction of the inferior courts is merely nominal; this has proved so burdensome to the people in Massachusetts, that it was one of the principal causes which excited the insurrection in that state, in the year past. [There are] very few sensible and moderate men in that state but what will admit, that the inferior courts are almost entirely useless, and answer very little purpose, save only to accumulate costs against the poor debtors who are already unable to pay their just debts.

But the operation of the appellate power in the supreme judicial of the United States, would work infinitely more mischief than any such power can do in a single state.

The trouble and expense to the parties would be endless and intolerable. No man can say where the supreme court are to hold their sessions; the presumption is, however, that it must be at the seat of the general government. In this case parties must travel many hundred miles, with their witnesses and lawyers, to prosecute or defend a suit. No man of middling fortune, can sustain the expense of such a law suit, and therefore the poorer and middling class of citizens will be under the necessity of submitting to the demands of the rich and the lordly, in cases that will come under the cognizance of this court. If it be said, that to prevent this oppression, the supreme court will sit in different parts of the union, it may be replied, that this would only make the oppression somewhat more tolerable, but by no means so much as to give a chance of justice to the poor and middling class. It is utterly impossible that the supreme court can move into so many different parts of the Union, as to make it convenient or even tolerable to attend before them with witnesses to try causes from every part of the United States. If to avoid the expense and

inconvenience of calling witnesses from a great distance, to give evidence before the supreme court, the expedient of taking the deposition of witnesses in writing should be adopted, it would not help the matter. It is of great importance in the distribution of justice that witnesses should be examined face to face, that the parties should have the fairest opportunity of cross examining them in order to bring out the whole truth. There is something in the manner in which a witness delivers his testimony which can not be committed to paper, and which yet very frequently gives a complexion to his evidence, very different from what it would bear if committed to writing.

Besides, the expense of taking written testimony would be, enormous. Those who are acquainted with the costs that arise in the courts, where all the evidence is taken in writing, well know that they exceed beyond all comparison those of the common law courts, where witnesses are examined viva voce.

The costs accruing in courts generally advance with the grade of the courts. Thus the charges attending a suit in our common pleas, is much less than those in the supreme court, and these are much lower than those in the court of chancery. Indeed, the costs in the last mentioned court, are in many cases so exorbitant and the proceedings so dilatory that the suitor had almost as well give up his demand as to prosecute his suit. We have just reason to suppose, that the costs in the supreme general court will exceed either of our courts. The officers of the general court will be more dignified than those of the states, the lawyers of the most ability will practice in them, and the trouble and expense of attending them will be greater. From all these considerations, it appears, that the expense attending suits in the supreme court will be so great, as to put it out of the power of the poor and middling class of citizens to contest a suit in it.

From these remarks it appears, that the administration of justice under the powers of the judicial will be dilatory; that it will be attended with such an heavy expense as to amount to little short of a denial of justice to the poor and middling class of people who in every government stand most in need of the protection of the law; and that the trial by jury, which has so justly been the boast of our forefathers as well as ourselves is taken away under them.

These extraordinary powers in this court are the more objectionable, because there does not appear the least necessity for them, in order to secure a due and impartial distribution of justice.

The want of ability or integrity, or a disposition to render justice to every suitor, has not been objected against the courts of the respective states. So far as I have been informed, the courts of justice in all the states have ever been found ready to administer justice with promptitude and impartiality according to the laws of the land. It is true in some of the states, paper money has been made, and the debtor authorised to discharge his debts with it, at a depreciated value; in others, tender laws have been passed, obliging the creditor to receive on execution other property than money in discharge of his demand; and in several of the states laws have been made unfavorable to the creditor and tending to render property insecure.

But these evils have not happened from any defect in the judicial departments of the states. The courts indeed are bound to take notice of these laws, and so will the courts of the general government be under obligation to observe the laws made by the general legislature not repugnant to the constitution. But so far have the judicial been from giving undue latitude of construction to laws of this kind, that they have invariably strongly inclined to the other side. All

the acts of our legislature, which have been charged with being of this complexion, have uniformly received the strictest construction by the judges, and have been extended to no cases but to such as came within the strict letter of the law. In this way, have our courts, I will not say evaded the law, but so limited its operation as to work the least possible injustice. The same thing has taken place in Rhode-Island, which has justly rendered herself infamous, by tenaciously adhering to her paper money system. The judges there gave a decision, in opposition to the words of the statute, on this principle: that a construction according to the words of it would contradict the fundamental maxims of their laws and constitution.

No pretext therefore can be formed, from the conduct of the judicial courts [of the states], which will justify giving such powers to the supreme general court. For their decisions have been such as to give just ground of confidence in them, that they will finally adhere to the principles of rectitude; and there is no necessity of lodging these powers in the [federal] courts, in order to guard against the evils justly complained of, on the subject of security of property under this constitution. For it has provided, "that no state shall emit bills of credit, or make any thing but gold and silver coin a tender in payment of debts." It has also declared, that "no state shall pass any law impairing the obligation of contracts." These prohibitions give the most perfect security against those attacks upon property which I am sorry to say some of the states have but too wantonly made, . . . For "this constitution will be the supreme law of the land, and the judges in every state will be bound thereby; any thing in the constitution and laws of any state to the contrary notwithstanding."

The courts of the respective states might therefore have been securely trusted with deciding all cases between man and man, whether citizens of the same state or of different states, or between foreigners and citizens. Indeed, for ought I see, every case that can arise under the constitution or laws of the United States ought in the first instance to be tried in the court of the state, except those which might arise b@tween states, such as respect ambassadors, or other public ministers, and perhaps such as call in question the claim of lands under grants from different states. The state courts would be under sufficient control, if writs of error were allowed from the state courts to the supreme court of the union, according to the practice of the courts in England and of this state, on all cases in which the laws of the union are concerned, and perhaps to all cases in which a foreigner is a party.

This method would preserve the good old way of administering justice, would bring justice to every man's door, and preserve the inestimable right of trial by jury. It would be following, as near as our circumstances will admit, the practice of the courts in England, which is almost the only thing I would wish to copy in their government.

But as this system now stands, there is to be as many inferior courts as Congress may see fit to appoint, who are to be authorised to originate and in the first instance to try all the cases falling under the description of this article. There is no security that a trial by jury shall be had in these courts, but the trial here will soon become, as it is in Massachusetts' inferior courts, [a] mere matter of form; for an appeal may be had to the supreme court on the whole merits. This court is to have power to determine in law and in equity, on the law and the fact, and this court is exalted above all other power in the government, subject to no control; and so fixed as not to be removable, but upon impeachment, which is much the same thing as not to be removable at all.

To obviate the objections made to the judicial power, it has been said, that the Congress, in forming the regulations and exceptions which they are authorised to make respecting the appellate jurisdiction, will make provision against all the evils which are apprehended from this article. On this I would remark, that this way of answering the objection made to the power, implies an admission that the power is in itself improper without restraint; and if so, why not restrict it in the first instance. The just way of investigating any power given to a government, is to examine its operation supposing it to be put in exercise. If upon inquiry, it appears that the power, if exercised, would be prejudicial, it ought not to be given. For to answer objections made to a power given to a government, by saying it will never be exercised, is really admitting that the power ought not to be exercised, and therefore ought not to be granted.

I have, in the course of my observation on this constitution, affirmed and endeavored to show, that it was calculated to abolish entirely the state governments, and to melt down the states into one entire government, for every purpose as well internal and local, as external and national. In this opinion the opposers of the system have generally agreed - and this has been uniformly denied by its advocates in public. Some individuals indeed, among them, will confess that it has this tendency, and scruple not to say it is what they wish; and I will venture to predict, without the spirit of prophecy, that if it is adopted without amendments, or some such precautions as will insure amendments immediately after its adoption, that the same gentlemen who have employed their talents and abilities with such success to influence the public mind to adopt this plan, will employ the same to persuade the people, that it will be for their good to abolish the state governments as useless and burdensome. Perhaps nothing could have been better conceived to facilitate the abolition of the state governments than the constitution of the judicial. They will be able to extend the limits of the general government gradually, and by insensible degrees, and to accommodate themselves to the temper of the people. Their decisions on the meaning of the constitution will commonly take place in cases which arise between individuals, with which the public will not be generally acquainted. One adjudication will form a precedent to the next, and this to a following one.

These cases will immediately affect individuals only, so that a series of determinations will probably take place before even the people will be informed of them. In the meantime all the art and address of those who wish for the change will be employed to make converts to their opinion. The people will be told that their state officers, and state legislatures, are a burden and expense without affording any solid advantage; that all the laws passed by them might be equally well made by the general legislature. If to those who will be interested in the change, be added those who will be under their influence, and such who will submit to almost any change of government which they can be persuaded to believe will ease them of taxes, it is easy to see the party who will favor the abolition of the state governments would be far from being inconsiderable. In this situation, the general legislature might pass one law after another, extending the general and abridging the state jurisdictions, and to sanction their proceedings would have a course of decisions of the judicial to whom the constitution has committed the power of explaining the constitution. If the states remonstrated, the constitutional mode of deciding upon the validity of the law is with the supreme court; and neither people, nor state legislatures, nor the general legislature can remove them or reverse their decrees. Had the

construction of the constitution been less [more?] with the legislature, they would have explained it at their peril. If they exceed[ed] their powers, or sought to find in the spirit of the constitution, more than was expressed in the letter, the people from whom they derived their power could remove them, . . . Indeed, I can see no other remedy that the people can have against their rulers for encroachments of this nature. A constitution is a compact of a people with their rulers; if the rulers break the compact, the people have a right and ought to remove them and do themselves justice. But in order to enable them to do this with the greater facility, those whom the people choose at stated periods should have the power in the last resort to determine the sense of the compact. If they determine contrary to the understanding of the people, an appeal will lie to the people at the period when the rulers are to be elected, and they will have it in their power to remedy the evil. But when this power is lodged in the hands of men independent of the people, and of their representatives, and who are not constitutionally accountable for their opinions, no way is left to control them but with a high hand and an outstretched arm.
BRUTUS

Documents of Revolution

ANTI-FEDERALIST PAPER NO. 83

The Federal Judiciary and The Issue Of Trial By Jury By Luther Martin Of Maryland

.... in all those cases, where the general government has jurisdiction in civil questions, the proposed Constitution not only makes no provision for the trial by jury in the first instance, but, by its appellate jurisdiction, absolutely takes away that inestimable privilege, since it expressly declares the Supreme Court shall have appellate jurisdiction both as to law and fact. Should, therefore, a jury be adopted in the inferior court, it would only be a needless expense, since, on an appeal, the determination of that jury, even on questions of fact, however honest and upright, is to be of no possible effect. The Supreme Court is to take up all questions of fact; to examine the evidence relative thereto; to decide upon them, in the same manner as if they had never been tried by a jury. Nor is trial by jury secured in criminal cases. It is true that, in the first instance, in the inferior court, the trial is to be by jury. In this, and in this only, is the difference between criminal and civil cases. But, sir, the appellate jurisdiction extends, as I have observed, to cases criminal, as well as civil, and on the appeal the court is to decide not only on the law but on the fact. If, therefore, even in criminal cases, the general government is not satisfied with the verdict of the jury, its officer may remove the prosecution to the Supreme Court; and there the verdict of the jury is to be of no effect, but the judges of this court are to decide upon the fact as well as the law, the same as in civil cases.

Thus, sir, jury trials, which have ever been the boast of the English constitution-which have been by our several state constitutions so cautiously secured to us-jury trials, which have so long been considered the surest barrier against arbitrary power, and the palladium of liberty, with the loss of which the loss of our freedom may be dated, are taken away by the proposed form of government, not only in a great variety of questions between individual and individual, but in every case, whether civil or criminal, arising under the laws of the United States, or the execution of those laws. It is taken away in those very cases where, of all others, it is most essential for our liberty to have it sacredly guarded and preserved: in every case, whether civil or criminal, between government and its officers on the one part, and the subject or citizen on the other. Nor was this the effect of inattention, nor did it arise from any real difficulty in establishing and securing jury trials by the proposed Constitution if the Convention had wished to do so; but the same reason influenced here as in the case of the establishment of the inferior courts. As they could not trust state judges, so would they not confide in state juries. They alleged that the general government and the state governments would always be at variance-that the citizens of the different states would enter into the views and interests of their respective states, and therefore ought not to be trusted in determining causes in which the general government was any way interested, without giving the general government an opportunity, if it disapproved the verdict of the jury, to appeal, and to have the facts examined into again, and decided upon by its own judges, on whom it was thought a reliance might be had by the general government, they being appointed under its authority. Thus, sir, in consequence of this appellate jurisdiction, and its extension to facts as well as to law, every arbitrary act of the general government, and every oppression of all that variety of officers appointed under its authority for the collection of taxes, duties, impost, excise, and other purposes, must be submitted to by the

individual, or must be opposed with little prospect of success, and almost a certain prospect of ruin, at least in those cases where the middle and common class of citizens are interested. Since, to avoid that oppression, or to obtain redress, the application must be made to one of the courts of the United States-by good fortune, should this application be in the first instance attended with success, and should damages be recovered equivalent to the injury sustained, an appeal lies to the Supreme Court, in which case the citizen must at once give up his cause, or he must attend to it at the distance, perhaps, of more than a thousand miles from the place of his residence, and must take measures to procure before that court, on the appeal, all the evidence necessary to support his action, which, even if ultimately prosperous, must be attended with a loss of time, a neglect of business, and an expense, which will be greater than the original grievance, and to which men in moderate circumstances would be utterly unequal.

ANTI-FEDERALIST PAPER NO. 84

On the Lack Of A Bill Of Rights

By "BRUTUS"

When a building is to be erected which is intended to stand for ages, the foundation should be firmly laid. The Constitution proposed to your acceptance is designed, not for yourselves alone, but for generations yet unborn. The principles, therefore, upon which the social compact is founded, ought to have been clearly and precisely stated, and the most express and full declaration of rights to have been made. But on this subject there is almost an entire silence.

If we may collect the sentiments of the people of America, from their own most solemn declarations, they hold this truth as self-evident, that all men are by nature free. No one man, therefore, or any class of men, have a right, by the law of nature, or of God, to assume or exercise authority over their fellows. The origin of society, then, is to be sought, not in any natural right which one man has to exercise authority over another, but in the united consent of those who associate. The mutual wants of men at first dictated the propriety of forming societies: and when they were established, protection and defense pointed out the necessity of instituting government. In a state of nature every individual pursues his own interest; in this pursuit it frequently happened, that the possessions or enjoyments of one were sacrificed to the views and designs of another; thus the weak were a prey to the strong, the simple and unwary were subject to impositions from those who were more crafty and designing. In this state of things, every individual was insecure; common interest, therefore, directed that government should be established, in which the force of the whole community should be collected, and under such directions, as to protect and defend every one who composed it. The common good, therefore, is the end of civil government, and common consent, the foundation on which it is established. To effect this end, it was necessary that a certain portion of natural liberty should be surrendered, in order that what remained should be preserved. How great a proportion of natural freedom is necessary to be yielded by individuals, when they submit to government, I shall not inquire. So much, however, must be given, as will be sufficient to enable those to whom the administration of the government is committed, to establish laws for the promoting the happiness of the community, and to carry those laws into effect. But it is not necessary, for this purpose, that individuals should relinquish all their natural rights. Some are of such a nature that they cannot be surrendered. Of this kind are the rights of conscience, the right of enjoying and defending life, etc. Others are not necessary to be resigned in order to attain the end for which government is instituted; these therefore ought not to be given up. To surrender them, would counteract the very end of government, to wit, the common good. From these observations it appears, that in forming a government on its true principles, the foundation should be laid in the manner I before stated, by expressly reserving to the people such of their essential rights as are not necessary to be parted with. The same reasons which at first induced mankind to associate and institute government, will operate to influence them to observe this precaution. If they had been disposed to conform themselves to the rule of immutable righteousness, government would not have been requisite. It was because one part exercised fraud, oppression and violence, on the other, that men came together, and agreed that certain rules should be formed to regulate the conduct of all, and the power of the whole community lodged in the hands of rulers to enforce an obedience to them. But rulers have the same propensities as other men; they are as likely to use the power

with which they are vested, for private purposes, and to the injury and oppression of those over whom they are placed, as individuals in a state of nature are to injure and oppress one another. It is therefore as proper that bounds should be set to their authority, as that government should have at first been instituted to restrain private injuries.

This principle, which seems so evidently founded in the reason and nature of things, is confirmed by universal experience. Those who have governed, have been found in all ages ever active to enlarge their powers and abridge the public liberty. This has induced the people in all countries, where any sense of freedom remained, to fix barriers against the encroachments of their rulers.

The country from which we have derived our origin, is an eminent example of this. Their magna charta and bill of rights have long been the boast, as well as the security of that nation. I need say no more, I presume, to an American, than that this principle is a fundamental one, in all the Constitutions of our own States; there is not one of them but what is either founded on a declaration or bill of rights, or has certain express reservation of rights interwoven in the body of them. From this it appears, that at a time when the pulse of liberty beat high, and when an appeal was made to the people to form Constitutions for the government of themselves, it was their universal sense, that such declarations should make a part of their frames of government. It is, therefore, the more astonishing, that this grand security to the rights of the people is not to be found in this Constitution.

It has been said, in answer to this objection, that such declarations of rights, however requisite they might be in the Constitutions of the States, are not necessary in the general Constitution, because, "in the former case, every thing which is not reserved is given; but in the latter, the reverse of the proposition prevails, and every thing which is not given is reserved." It requires but little attention to discover, that this mode of reasoning is rather specious than solid. The powers, rights and authority, granted to the general government by this Constitution, are as complete, with respect to every object to which they extend, as that of any State government-it reaches to every thing which concerns human happiness-life, liberty, and property are under its control. There is the same reason, therefore, that the exercise of power, in this case, should be restrained within proper limits, as in that of the State governments. To set this matter in a clear light, permit me to instance some of the articles of the bills of rights of the individual States, and apply them to the case in question.

For the security of life, in criminal prosecutions, the bills of rights of most of the States have declared, that no man shall be held to answer for a crime until he is made fully acquainted with the charge brought against him; he shall not be compelled to accuse, or furnish evidence against himself-the witnesses against him shall be brought face to face, and he shall be fully heard by himself or counsel. That it is essential to the security of life and liberty, that trial of facts be in the vicinity where they happen. Are not provisions of this kind as necessary in the general government, as in that of a particular State? The powers vested in the new Congress extend in many cases to life; they are authorized to provide for the punishment of a variety of capital crimes, and no restraint is laid upon them in its exercise, save only, that "the trial of all crimes, except in cases of impeachment, shall be by jury; and such trial shall be in the State where the said crimes shall have been committed." No man is secure of a trial in the county where he is charged to have committed a crime; he may be brought from Niagara to New York, or carried from Kentucky to Richmond for trial for an offense supposed to be committed. What security is

there, that a man shall be furnished with a full and plain description of the charges against him?

That he shall be allowed to produce all proof he can in his favor? That he shall see the witnesses against him face to face, or that he shall be fully heard in his own defense by himself or counsel?

For the security of liberty it has been declared, "that excessive bail should not be required, nor excessive fines imposed, nor cruel or unusual punishments inflicted. That all warrants, without oath or affirmation, to search suspected places, or seize any person, his papers or property, are grievous and oppressive."

These provisions are as necessary under the general government as under that of the individual States; for the power of the former is as complete to the purpose of requiring bail, imposing fines, inflicting punishments, granting search warrants, and seizing persons, papers, or property, in certain cases, as the other.

For the purpose of securing the property of the citizens, it is declared by all the States, "that in all controversies at law, respecting property, the ancient mode of trial by jury is one of the best securities of the rights of the people, and ought to remain sacred and inviolable."

Does not the same necessity exist of reserving this right under their national compact, as in that of the States? Yet nothing is said respecting it. In the bills of rights of the States it is declared, that a well regulated militia is the proper and natural defense of a free government; that as standing armies in time of peace are dangerous, they are not to be kept up, and that the military should be kept under strict subordination to, and controlled by, the civil power.

The same security is as necessary in this Constitution, and much more so; for the general government will have the sole power to raise and to pay armies, and are under no control in the exercise of it; yet nothing of this is to be found in this new system.

I might proceed to instance a number of other rights, which were as necessary to be reserved, such as, that elections should be free, that the liberty of the press should be held sacred; but the instances adduced are sufficient to prove that this argument is without foundation. Besides, it is evident that the reason here assigned was not the true one, why the framers of this Constitution omitted a bill of rights; if it had been, they would not have made certain reservations, while they totally omitted others of more importance. We find they have, in the ninth section of the first article declared, that the writ of habeas corpus shall not be suspended, unless in cases of rebellion,-that no bill of attainder, or ex post facto law, shall be passed,-that no title of nobility shall be granted by the United States, etc. If every thing which is not given is reserved, what propriety is there in these exceptions? Does this Constitution any where grant the power of suspending the habeas corpus, to make ex post facto laws, pass bills of attainder, or grant titles of nobility? It certainly does not in express terms. The only answer that can be given is, that these are implied in the general powers granted. With equal truth it may be said, that all the powers which the bills of rights guard against the abuse of, are contained or implied in the general ones granted by this Constitution.

So far is it from being true, that a bill of rights is less necessary in the general Constitution than in those of the States, the contrary is evidently the fact. This system, if it is possible for the

people of America to accede to it, will be an original compact; and being the last wilt, in the nature of things, vacate every former agreement inconsistent with it. For it being a plan of government received and ratified by the whole people, all other forms which are in existence at the time of its adoption, must yield to it. This is expressed in positive and unequivocal terms in the sixth article: "That this Constitution, and the laws of the United States which shall be made in pursuance thereof, and all treaties made, or which shall be made, under the authority of the United States, shall be the supreme law of the land; and the judges in every State shall be bound thereby, any thing in the Constitution, or laws of any State, to the contrary notwithstanding."

"The senators and representatives before-mentioned, and the members of the several State legislatures, and all executive and judicial officers, both of the United States, and of the several States, shall be bound, by oath or affirmation, to support this Constitution."

It is therefore not only necessarily implied thereby, but positively expressed, that the different State Constitutions are repealed and entirely done away, so far as they are inconsistent with this, with the laws which shall be made in pursuance thereof, or with treaties made, or which shall be made, under the authority of the United States. Of what avail will the Constitutions of the respective States be to preserve the rights of its citizens? Should they be pled, the answer would be, the Constitution of the United States, and the laws made in pursuance thereof, is the supreme law, and all legislatures and judicial officers, whether of the General or State governments, are bound by oath to support it. No privilege, reserved by the bills of rights, or secured by the State governments, can limit the power granted by this, or restrain any laws made in pursuance of it. It stands, therefore, on its own bottom, and must receive a construction by itself, without any reference to any other. And hence it was of the highest importance, that the most precise and express declarations and reservations of rights should have been made.

This will appear the more necessary, when it is considered, that not only the Constitution and laws made in pursuance thereof, but alt treaties made, under the authority of the United States, are the supreme law of the land, and supersede the Constitutions of all the States. The power to make treaties, is vested in the president, by and with the advice and consent of two-thirds of the senate. I do not find any limitation or restriction to the exercise of this power. The most important article in any Constitution may therefore be repealed, even without a legislative act.

Ought not a government, vested with such extensive and indefinite authority, to have been restricted by a declaration of rights? It certainly ought.

So clear a point is this, that I cannot help suspecting that persons who attempt to persuade people that such reservations were less necessary under this Constitution than under those of the States, are wilfully endeavoring to deceive, and to lead you into an absolute state of vassalage.

BRUTUS

ANTI-FEDERALIST PAPER NO. 85

Concluding Remarks: Evils Under Confederation Exaggerated; Constitution Must Be Drastically Revised Before Adoption

By Melancthon Smith (a "PLEBIAN")

.... It is agreed, the plan is defective-that some of the powers granted are dangerous-others not well defined-and amendments are necessary why then not amend it? Why not remove the cause of danger, and, possible, even the apprehension of it? The instrument is yet in the hands of the people; it is not signed, sealed, and delivered, and they have power to give it any form they please.

But it is contended, adopt it first, and then amend it. I ask, why not amend, and then adopt it?

Most certainly the latter mode of proceeding is more consistent with our ideas of prudence in the ordinary concerns of life If men were about entering into a contract respecting their private concerns it would be highly absurd in them to sign and seal an instrument containing stipulations which are contrary to their interests and wishes, under the expectation, that the parties, after its execution, would agree to make alteration agreeable to their desire. They would insist upon the exceptionable clause being altered before they would ratify the contract. And is a compact for the government of ourselves and our posterity of less moment than contract between individuals?

Certainly not. But to this reasoning, which at first vie would appear to admit of no reply, a variety of objections are made, and number of reasons urged for adopting the system, and afterwards proposing amendments. Such as have come under my observation, I shall state, an remark upon.

It is insisted, that the present situation of our country is such, as not t admit of a delay in forming a new government, or of time sufficient to deliberate and agree upon the amendments which are proper, without involving ourselves in a state of anarchy and confusion.

On this head, all the powers of rhetoric, and arts of description, ar employed to paint the condition of this country, in the most hideous an frightful colors. We are told, that agriculture is without encouragement trade is languishing; private faith and credit are disregarded, and public credit is prostrate; that the laws and magistrates are condemned and set at naught; that a spirit of licentiousness is rampant, and ready to break over every bound set to it by the government; that private embarrassments and distresses invade the house of every man of middling property, and insecurity threatens every man in affluent circumstances: in short, that we are in a state of the most grievous calamity at home, and that we are contemptible abroad, the scorn of foreign nations, and the ridicule of the world. From this high wrought picture, one would suppose that we were in a condition the most deplorable of any people upon earth. But suffer me, my countrymen, to call your attention to a serious and sober estimate of the situation in which you are placed, while I trace the embarrassments under which you labor, to their true sources, What is your condition? Does not every man sit under his own vine and under his own fig-tree, having none to make him afraid? Does not every one follow his calling without impediments and receive the reward of his well-earned industry? The farmer cultivates his land, and reaps the fruit

which the bounty of heaven bestows on his honest toil. The mechanic is exercised in his art, and receives the reward of his labor. The merchant drives his commerce, and none can deprive him of the gain he honestly acquires; all classes and callings of men amongst us are protected in their various pursuits, and secured by the laws in the possession and enjoyment of the property obtained in those pursuits. The laws are as well executed as they ever were, in this or any other country. Neither the hand of private violence, nor the more to be dreaded hand of legal oppression, are reached out to distress us.

It is true, many individuals labor under embarrassments, but these are to be imputed to the unavoidable circumstances of things, rather than to any defect in our governments. We have just emerged from a long and expensive war. During its existence few people were in a situation to increase their fortunes, but many to diminish them. Debts contracted before the war were left unpaid while it existed, and these were left a burden too heavy to be borne at the commencement of peace. Add to these, that when the war was over, too many of us, instead of reassuming our old habits of frugality, and industry, by which alone every country must be placed in a prosperous condition, took up the profuse use of foreign commodities. The country was deluged with articles imported from abroad, and the cash of the country has been sent to pay for them, and still left us laboring under the weight of a huge debt to persons abroad. These are the true sources to which we are to trace all the private difficulties of individuals. But will a new government relieve you from these? ... Your present condition is such as is common to take place after the conclusion of a war. Those who can remember our situation after the termination of the war preceding the last, will recollect that our condition was similar to the present, but time and industry soon recovered us from it. Money was scarce, the produce of the country much lower than it has been since the peace, and many individuals were extremely embarrassed with debts; and this happened although we did not experience the ravages, desolations, and loss of property, that were suffered during the late war.

With regard to our public and national concerns, what is there in our condition that threatens us with any immediate danger? We are at peace with all the world; no nation menaces us with war; nor are we called upon by any cause of sufficient importance to attack any nation. The state governments answer the purposes of preserving the peace, and providing for present exigencies.

Our condition as a nation is in no respect worse than it has been for several years past. Our public debt has been lessened in various ways, and the western territory, which has been relied upon as a productive fund to discharge the national debt has at length been brought to market, and a considerable part actually applied to its reduction. I mention these things to show, that there is nothing special, in our present situation, as it respects our national affairs, that should induce us to accept the proffered system, without taking sufficient time to consider and amend it.

I do not mean by this, to insinuate, that our government does not stand in need of reform. It is admitted by all parties, that alterations are necessary in our federal constitution, but the circumstances of our case do by no means oblige us to precipitate this business, or require that we should adopt a system materially defective. We may safely take time to deliberate and amend, without in the meantime hazarding a condition, in any considerable degree, worse than the present.

But it is said that if we postpone the ratification of this system until the necessary amendments are first incorporated, the consequence will be a civil war among the states.... The idea of [New York] being attacked by the other states, will appear visionary and chimerical, if we consider that tho' several of them have adopted the new constitution, yet the opposition to it has been numerous and formidable. The eastern states from whom we are told we have most to fear, should a civil war be blown up, would have full employ to keep in awe those who are opposed to it in their own governments. Massachusetts, after a long and dubious contest in their convention, has adopted it by an inconsiderable majority, and in the very act has marked it with a stigma in its present form. No man of candor, judging from their public proceedings, will undertake to say on which side the majority of the people are. Connecticut, it is true, have acceded to it, by a large majority of their convention; but it is a fact well known, that a large proportion of the yeomanry of the country are against it. And it is equally true, that a considerable part of those who voted for it in the convention, wish to see it altered. In both these states the body of the common people, who always do the fighting of a country, would be more likely to fight against than for it.

Can it then be presumed, that a country divided among themselves, upon a question where even the advocates for it, admit the system they contend for needs amendments, would make war upon a sister state? ... The idea is preposterous...

The reasonings made use of to persuade us, that no alterations can be agreed upon previous to the adoption of the system, are as curious as they are futile. It is alleged, that there was great diversity of sentiments in forming the proposed constitution; that it was the effect of mutual concessions and a spirit of accommodation, and from hence it is inferred, that further changes cannot be hoped for. I should suppose that the contrary inference was the fair one. If the convention, who framed this plan, were possessed of such a spirit of moderation and condescension, as to be induced to yield to each other certain points, and to accommodate themselves to each other's opinions, and even prejudices, there is reason to expect, that this same spirit will continue and prevail in a future convention, and produce an union of sentiments on the points objected to. There is more reason to hope for this, because the subject has received a full discussion, and the minds of the people much better known than they were when the convention sat. Previous to the meeting of the convention, the subject of a new form of government had been little thought of, and scarcely written upon at all. It is true, it was the general opinion, that some alterations were requisite in the federal system. This subject had been contemplated by almost every thinking man in the union. It had been the subject of many well-written essays, and it was the anxious wish of every true friend to America. But it was never in the contemplation of one in a thousand of those who had reflected on the matter, to have an entire change in the nature of our

Documents of Revolution

federal government-to alter it from a confederation of states, to that of one entire government, which will swallow up that of the individual states. I will venture to say, that the idea of a government similar to the one proposed, never entered the minds of the legislatures who appointed the convention, and of but very few of the members who composed it, until they had assembled and heard it proposed in that body: much less had the people any conception of such a plan until after it was promulgated, While it was agitated, the debates of the convention were kept an impenetrable secret, and no opportunity was given for well informed men to offer their sentiments upon the subject. The system was therefore never publicly discussed, nor indeed could be, because it was not known to the people until after it was proposed. Since then, it has been the object of universal attention-it has been thought of by every reflecting man-been discussed in a public and private manner, in conversation and in print; its defects have been pointed out, and every objection to it stated; able advocates have written in its favor, and able opponents have written against it. And what is the result? It cannot be denied but that the general opinion is, that it contains material errors, and requires important amendments. This then being the general sentiment, both of the friends and foes of the system, can it be doubted, that another convention would concur in such amendments as would quiet the fears of the opposers, and effect a great degree of union on the subject? -- An event most devoutly to be wished. But it is further said, that there can be no prospect of procuring alterations before it is acceded to, because those who oppose it do not agree among themselves with respect to the amendments that are necessary. To this I reply, that this may be urged against attempting alterations after it is received, with as much force as before; and therefore, if it concludes anything, it is that we must receive any system of government proposed to us, because those who object to it do not entirely concur in their objections. But the assertion is not true to any considerable extent. There is a remarkable uniformity in the objections made to the constitution, on the most important points. It is also worthy of notice, that very few of the matters found fault with in it, are of a local nature, or such as affect any particular state; on the contrary, they are such as concern the principles of general liberty, in which the people of New Hampshire, New York and Georgia are equally interested. . . .

It has been objected too that the new system . . . is calculated to and will effect such a consolidation of the States, as to supplant and overturn the state governments....

It has been said that the representation in the general legislature is too small to secure liberty, or to answer the intention of representation. In this there is an union of sentiments in the opposers.

The constitution has been opposed, because it gives to the legislature an unlimited power of taxation both with respect to direct and indirect taxes, a right to lay and collect taxes, duties, imposts and excises of every kind and description, and to any amount. In this there has been as general a concurrence of opinion as in the former.

The opposers to the constitution have said that it is dangerous, because the judicial power may extend to many cases which ought to be reserved to the decision of the State courts, and because the right of trial by jury is not secured in the judicial courts of the general government, in civil cases. All the opposers are agreed in this objection.

The power of the general legislature to alter and regulate the time, place and manner of holding elections, has been stated as an argument against the adoption of the system. The opposers to the constitution universally agree in this objection. . .

The mixture of legislative, judicial, and executive powers in the Senate; the little degree of responsibility under which the great officers of government will be held; and the liberty granted by the system to establish and maintain a standing army without any limitation or restriction, are also objected to the constitution; and in these there is a great degree of unanimity of sentiment in the opposers. . . .

You have heard that both sides on this great question, agree, that there are in it great defects; yet the one side tell you, choose such men as will adopt it, and then amend it-while the other say, amend previous to its adoption. I have stated to you my reasons for the latter, and I think they are unanswerable. Consider, you the common people, the yeomanry of the country, for to such I

principally address myself, you are to be the principal losers, if the constitution should prove oppressive. When a tyranny is established, there are always masters as well as slaves; the great and well-born are generally the former, and the middling class the latter. Attempts have been made, and will be repeated, to alarm you with the fear of consequences; but reflect there are consequences on both sides, and none can be apprehended more dreadful, than entailing on ourselves and posterity a government which will raise a few to the height of human greatness and wealth, while it will depress the many to the extreme of poverty and wretchedness.

Consequences are under the control of that all-wise and all-powerful being, whose providence conducts the affairs of all men. Our part is to act right, and we may then have confidence that the consequences will be favorable. The path in which you should walk is plain and open before you; be united as one man, and direct your choice to such men as have been uniform in their opposition to the proposed system in its present form, or without proper alterations. In men of this description you have reason to place confidence, while on the other hand, you have just cause to distrust those who urge the adoption of a bad constitution, under the delusive expectation of making amendments after it is acceded to. Your jealousy of such characters should be the more excited, when you consider that the advocates for the constitution have shifted their ground. When men are uniform in their opinions, it affords evidence that they are sincere. When they are shifting, it gives reason to believe, they do not change from conviction. It must be recollected, that when this plan was first announced to the public, its supporters cried it up as the most perfect production of human wisdom, It was represented either as having no defects, or if it had, they were so trifling and inconsiderable, that they served only, as the shades in a fine picture, to set off the piece to the greater advantage. One gentleman in Philadelphia went so far in the ardor of his enthusiasm in its favor, as to pronounce, that the men who formed it were as really under the guidance of Divine Revelation, as was Moses, the Jewish lawgiver.

Their language is now changed; the question has been discussed; the objections to the plan ably stated, and they are admitted to be unanswerable. The same men who held it almost perfect, now admit it is very imperfect; that it is necessary it should be amended. The only question between us, is simply this@hall we accede to a bad constitution, under the uncertain prospect of getting it amended, after we have received it, or shall we amend it before we adopt it? Common sense will point out which is the most rational, which is the most secure line of conduct. May heaven inspire you with wisdom, union, moderation and firmness, and give you hearts to make a proper estimate of your invaluable privileges, and preserve them to you, to be transmitted to your posterity unimpaired, and may they be maintained in this our country, while Sun and Moon endure.

A Plebeian

The End

* * *

THE CONSTITUTION OF THE UNITED STATES OF AMERICA, 1787

We the people of the United States, in Order to form a more perfect Union, establish Justice, insure domestic Tranquility, provide for the common defence, promote the general Welfare, and secure the Blessings of Liberty to ourselves and our Posterity, do ordain and establish this Constitution for the United States of America.

ARTICLE I

Section 1. All legislative Powers herein granted shall be vested in a Congress of the United States, which shall consist of a Senate and House of Representatives.

Section 2. The House of Representatives shall be composed of Members chosen every second Year by the People of the several States, and the electors in each State shall have the qualifications requisite for electors of the most numerous branch of the State legislature.

No Person shall be a Representative who shall not have attained to the Age of twenty five Years, and been seven Years a citizen of the United States, and who shall not, when elected, be an Inhabitant of that State in which he shall be chosen.

Representatives and direct Taxes shall be apportioned among the several States which may be included within this Union, according to their respective Numbers, which shall be determined by adding to the whole number of free Persons, including those bound to Service for a Term of Years, and excluding Indians not taxed, three fifths of all other Persons. The actual Enumeration shall be made within three Years after the first Meeting of the Congress of the United States, and within every subsequent Term of ten Years, in such Manner as they shall by law Direct. The number of Representatives shall not exceed one for every thirty

Thousand, but each State shall have at least one Representative; and until such enumeration shall be made, the State of New Hampshire shall be entitled to chuse three, Massachusetts eight, Rhode Island and Providence Plantations one, Connecticut five, New York six, New Jersey four, Pennsylvania eight, Delaware one, Maryland six, Virginia ten, North Carolina five, South Carolina five, and Georgia three.

When vacancies happen in the Representation from any State, the Executive Authority thereof shall issue Writs of Election to fill such Vacancies.

The House of Representatives shall chuse their Speaker and other Officers; and shall have the sole Power of Impeachment.

Section 3. The Senate of the United States shall be composed of two Senators from each State, chosen by the legislature thereof, for six Years; and each Senator shall have one Vote.

Immediately after they shall be assembled in Consequence of the first Election, they shall be divided as equally as may be into three Classes. The Seats of the Senators of the first Class shall be vacated at the expiration of the second Year, of the second Class at the expiration of the fourth Year, and of the third Class at the expiration of the sixth Year, so that one third may be chosen every second Year; and if vacancies happen by Resignation, or otherwise, during the recess of the Legislature of any State, the Executive thereof may make temporary Appointments until the next meeting of the Legislature, which shall then fill such Vacancies.

No person shall be a Senator who shall not have attained to the Age of thirty Years, and been nine Years a Citizen of the United States, and who shall not, when elected, be an Inhabitant of that State for which he shall be chosen.

The Vice-President of the United States shall be President of the Senate, but shall have no Vote, unless they be equally divided.

The Senate shall choose their other Officers, and also a President pro tempore, in the Absence of the Vice-President, or when he shall exercise the Office of President of the United States.

The Senate shall have the sole Power to try all Impeachments. When sitting for that Purpose, they shall be on Oath or Affirmation. When the President of the United States is tried, the Chief Justice shall preside: And no Person shall be convicted without the Concurrence of two thirds of the Members present.

Judgment in cases of Impeachment shall not extend further than to removal from Office, and disqualification to hold and enjoy any Office of honor, Trust or Profit under the United States: but the Party convicted shall nevertheless be liable and subject to Indictment, Trial, Judgment and Punishment, according to Law.

Section 4. The Times, Places and Manner of holding Elections for Senators and Representatives, shall be prescribed in each State by the Legislature thereof; but the Congress may at any time by Law make or alter such Regulations, except as to the Places of chusing Senators.

The Congress shall assemble at least once in every Year, and such Meeting shall be on the first Monday in December, unless they shall by law appoint a different Day.

Section 5. Each House shall be the Judge of the Elections, Returns and Qualifications of its own Members, and a Majority of each shall constitute a Quorum to do Business; but a smaller Number may adjourn from day to day, and may be authorized to compel the Attendance of absent Members, in such Manner, and under such Penalties as each House may provide.

Each house may determine the Rules of its Proceedings, punish its Members for disorderly Behavior, and, with the Concurrence of two-thirds, expel a Member.

Each house shall keep a Journal of its Proceedings, and from time to time publish the same, excepting such Parts as may in their Judgment require Secrecy; and the Yeas and Nays of the Members of either House on any question shall, at the Desire of one fifth of those Present, be entered on the Journal.

Neither House, during the Session of Congress, shall, without the Consent of the other, adjourn for more than three days, nor to any other Place than that in which the two Houses shall be sitting.

Section 6. The Senators and Representatives shall receive a Compensation for their Services, to be ascertained by Law, and paid out of the Treasury of the United States. They shall in all Cases, except Treason, Felony and Breach of the Peace, be privileged from Arrest during their Attendance at the Session of their respective Houses, and in going to and returning from the same; and for any Speech or Debate in either House, they shall not be questioned in any other Place.

No Senator or Representative shall, during the Time for which he was elected, be appointed to any civil Office under the authority of the United States, which shall have been created, or the Emoluments whereof shall have been increased during such time; and no Person holding any Office under the United States, shall be a Member of either House during his Continuance in Office.

Section 7. All Bills for raising Revenue shall originate in the House of Representatives; but the Senate may propose or concur with Amendments as on other Bills.

Every Bill which shall have passed the House of Representatives and the Senate, shall, before it become a Law, be presented to the President of the United States; If he approve he shall sign it, but if not he shall return it, with his Objections to that House in which it shall have originated, who shall enter the Objections at large on their Journal, and proceed to reconsider it. If after such Reconsideration two thirds of that house shall agree to pass the Bill, it shall be sent, together with the Objections, to the other House, by which it shall likewise be reconsidered, and if approved by two thirds of that House, it shall become a law. But in all such Cases the Votes of both Houses shall be determined by Yeas and Nays, and the Names of the Persons voting for and against the Bill shall be entered on the Journal of each House respectively. If any Bill shall not be returned by the President within ten Days (Sundays excepted) after it shall have been presented to him, the Same shall be a Law, in like Manner as if he had signed it, unless the Congress by their Adjournment prevent its Return, in which case it shall not be a Law.

Every Order, Resolution, or Vote to which the Concurrence of the Senate and House of Representatives may be necessary (except on a question of Adjournment) shall be presented to the President of the United States; and before the Same shall take Effect, shall be approved by him, or being disapproved by him, shall be repassed by two thirds of the Senate and House of Representatives, according to the Rules and Limitations prescribed in the Case of a Bill.

Section 8. The Congress shall have Power to lay and collect Taxes, Duties, Imposts and Excises, to pay the Debts and provide for the common Defence and general Welfare of the United States; but all Duties, Imposts and Excises shall be uniform throughout the United States;

To borrow Money on the credit of the United States;

To regulate Commerce with foreign Nations, and among the several States, and with the Indian Tribes;

To establish an uniform Rule of Naturalization, and uniform Laws on the subject of Bankruptcies throughout the United States;

To coin Money, regulate the Value thereof, and of foreign Coin, and fix the Standard of Weights and Measures;

To provide for the Punishment of counterfeiting the Securities and current Coin of the United States;

To establish Post Offices and Post Roads;

To promote the Progress of Science and useful Arts, by securing for limited Times to Authors and Inventors the exclusive Right to their respective Writings and Discoveries;

To constitute Tribunals inferior to the supreme Court;

To define and punish Piracies and Felonies committed on the high Seas, and Offenses against the Law of Nations;

To declare War, grant Letters of Marque and Reprisal, and make Rules concerning Captures on Land and Water;

To raise and support Armies, but no Appropriation of Money to that Use shall be for a longer term than two Years;

To provide and maintain a Navy;

To make Rules for the Government and Regulation of the land and naval Forces;

To provide for calling forth the Militia to execute the Laws of the Union, suppress Insurrections and repel Invasions;

To provide for organizing, arming, and disciplining, the Militia, and for governing such Part of them as may be employed in the Service of the United States, reserving to the States respectively, the Appointment of the Officers, and the Authority of training the militia according to the discipline prescribed by Congress;

To exercise exclusive Legislation in all Cases whatsoever, over such District (not exceeding ten Miles square) as may, by Cession of particular States, and the Acceptance of Congress, become the Seat of the Government of the United States, and to exercise like Authority over all Places purchased by the Consent of the Legislature of the State in which the Same shall be, for the Erection of Forts, Magazines, Arsenals, Dockyards, and other needful Buildings;—And

To make all Laws which shall be necessary and proper for carrying into Execution the foregoing Powers, and all other Powers vested by this Constitution in the Government of the United States, or in any Department or Officer thereof.

Section 9. The Migration or Importation of such Persons as any of the States now existing shall think proper to admit, shall not be prohibited by the Congress prior to the Year one thousand eight hundred and eight, but a Tax or Duty may be imposed on such Importation, not exceeding ten dollars for each Person.

The Privilege of the Writ of Habeas Corpus shall not be suspended, unless when in Cases of Rebellion or Invasion the public Safety may require it.

No Bill of Attainder or ex post facto Law shall be passed.

No Capitation, or other direct, Tax shall be laid, unless in Proportion to the Census or Enumeration herein before directed to be taken.

No Tax or Duty shall be laid on Articles exported from any State.

No Preference shall be given by any Regulation of Commerce or Revenue to the Ports of one State over those of another: nor shall Vessels bound to, or from, one State, be obliged to enter, clear, or pay Duties in another.

No Money shall be drawn from the Treasury, but in Consequence of Appropriations made by Law; and a regular Statement and Account of the Receipts and Expenditures of all public Money shall be published from time to time.

No Title of Nobility shall be granted by the United States; and no Person holding any Office of Profit or Trust under them, shall, without the Consent of the Congress, accept of any present, Emolument, Office, or Title, of any kind whatever, from any King, Prince, or foreign State.

Section 10. No State shall enter into any Treaty, Alliance, or Confederation; grant Letters of Marque and Reprisal; coin Money; emit Bills of Credit; make any Thing but gold and silver Coin a Tender in Payment of Debts; pass any Bill of Attainder, ex post facto Law, or Law impairing the Obligation of Contracts, or grant any Title of Nobility.

No State shall, without the Consent of the Congress, lay any Imposts or Duties on Imports or Exports, except what may be absolutely necessary for executing it's inspection Laws: and the net Produce of all Duties and Imposts, laid by any State on Imports or Exports, shall be for the Use of the Treasury of the United States; and all such Laws shall be subject to the Revision and Controul of the Congress.

No State shall, without the Consent of Congress, lay any Duty of Tonnage, keep Troops, or Ships of War in time of Peace, enter into any Agreement or Compact with another State, or with a foreign Power, or engage in War, unless actually invaded, or in such imminent Danger as will not admit of delay.

ARTICLE II

Section 1. The executive Power shall be vested in a President of the United States of America. He shall hold his Office during the Term of four Years, and, together with the Vice President chosen for the same Term, be elected, as follows:

Each State shall appoint, in such Manner as the Legislature thereof may direct, a Number of Electors, equal to the whole Number of Senators and Representatives to which the State may be entitled in the Congress: but no Senator or Representative, or Person holding an Office of Trust or Profit under the United States, shall be appointed an Elector.

The Electors shall meet in their respective States, and vote by Ballot for two Persons, of whom one at least shall not be an Inhabitant of the same State with themselves. And they shall make a List of all the Persons voted for, and of the Number of Votes for each; which List they shall sign and certify, and transmit sealed to the Seat of the Government of the United States, directed to the President of the Senate. The President of the Senate shall, in the Presence of the Senate and House of Representatives, open all the Certificates, and the Votes shall then be counted. The Person having the greatest Number of Votes shall be the President, if such Number be a Majority of the whole Number of Electors appointed; and if there be more than one who have such Majority, and have an equal Number of votes, then the House of Representatives shall immediately chuse by Ballot one of them for President; and if no Person have a Majority, then from the five highest on the List the said House shall in like Manner chuse the President. But in chusing the President, the Votes shall be taken by States, the Representation from each State having one Vote; a Quorum for this Purpose shall consist of a Member or Members from two thirds of the States, and a Majority of all the States shall be necessary to a Choice. In every Case, after the Choice of the President, the Person having the greatest Number of Votes of the Electors shall be the Vice President. But if there should remain two or more who have equal Votes, the Senate shall chuse from them by Ballot the Vice President.

The Congress may determine the Time of chusing the Electors, and the Day on which they shall give their Votes; which Day shall be the same throughout the United States.

No Person except a natural born Citizen, or a Citizen of the United States, at the time of the Adoption of this Constitution, shall be eligible to the Office of President; neither shall any Person be eligible to that Office who shall not have attained to the Age of thirty five Years, and been fourteen Years a Resident within the United States.

In Case of the Removal of the President from Office, or of his Death, Resignation, or Inability to discharge the Powers and Duties of the said Office, the Same shall devolve on the Vice President, and the Congress may by Law provide for the Case of Removal, Death, Resignation or Inability, both of the President and Vice President, declaring what Officer shall then act as President, and such Officer shall act accordingly, until the Disability be removed, or a President shall be elected.

The President shall, at stated Times, receive for his Services, a Compensation, which shall neither be encreased nor diminished during the Period for which he shall have been elected, and he shall not receive within that Period any other Emolument from the United States, or any of them.

Before he enter on the Execution of his Office, he shall take the following Oath or Affirmation:—"I do solemnly swear (or affirm) that I will faithfully execute the Office of President of the United States, and will to the best of my Ability, preserve, protect and defend the Constitution of the United States."

Section 2. The President shall be Commander in Chief of the Army and Navy of the United States, and of the Militia of the several States, when called into the actual Service of the United States; he may require the Opinion, in writing, of the principal Officer in each of the executive Departments, upon any Subject relating to the Duties of their respective Offices, and he shall have Power to grant Reprieves and Pardons for Offenses against the United States, except in Cases of impeachment.

He shall have Power, by and with the Advice and Consent of the Senate, to make Treaties, provided two thirds of the Senators present concur; and he shall nominate, and by and with the Advice and Consent of the Senate, shall appoint Ambassadors, other public Ministers and Consuls, Judges of the supreme Court, and all other Officers of the United States, whose Appointments are not herein otherwise provided for, and which shall be established by Law: but the Congress may by Law vest the Appointment of such inferior Officers, as they think proper, in the President alone, in the Courts of Law, or in the Heads of Departments.

The President shall have Power to fill up all Vacancies that may happen during the Recess of the Senate, by granting Commissions which shall expire at the End of their next session.

Section 3. He shall from time to time give to the Congress Information of the State of the Union, and recommend to their Consideration such Measures as he shall judge necessary and expedient; he may, on extraordinary Occasions, convene both Houses, or either of them, and in Case of Disagreement between them, with Respect to the Time of Adjournment, he may adjourn them to such Time as he shall think proper; he shall receive Ambassadors and other public Ministers; he shall take Care that the Laws be faithfully executed, and shall Commission all the Officers of the United States.

Section 4. The President, Vice President and all civil Officers of the United States, shall be removed from Office on Impeachment for, and Conviction of, Treason, Bribery, or other high Crimes and Misdemeanors.

ARTICLE III

Section 1. The judicial Power of the United States, shall be vested in one supreme Court, and in such inferior Courts as the Congress may from time to time ordain and establish. The Judges, both of the supreme and inferior Courts, shall hold their Offices during good behavior, and shall, at stated Times, receive for their Services, a Compensation, which shall not be diminished during their Continuance in Office.

Section 2. The judicial Power shall extend to all Cases, in Law and Equity, arising under this Constitution, the Laws of the United States, and Treaties made, or which shall be made, under their Authority;—to all Cases affecting Ambassadors, other public Ministers and Consuls;—to all Cases of admiralty and maritime Jurisdiction;—to Controversies to which the United States shall be a Party;—to Controversies between two or more States;—between a State and Citizens of another State;—between Citizens of different States; —between Citizens of the same State claiming Lands under Grants of different States, and between a State, or the Citizens thereof, and foreign States, Citizens or Subjects.

In all cases affecting Ambassadors, other public Ministers and Consuls, and those in which a State shall be Party, the supreme Court shall have original Jurisdiction. In all the other Cases before mentioned, the supreme Court shall have appellate Jurisdiction, both as to Law and Fact, with such Exceptions, and under such Regulations as the Congress shall make.

The Trial of all Crimes, except in Cases of Impeachment, shall be by Jury; and such Trial shall be held in the State where the said Crimes shall have been committed; but when not committed within any State, the Trial shall be at such Place or Places as the Congress may by Law have directed.

Section 3. Treason against the United States, shall consist only in levying War against them, or in adhering to their Enemies, giving them Aid and Comfort. No Person shall be convicted of Treason unless on the Testimony of two Witnesses to the same overt Act, or on Confession in open Court.

The Congress shall have power to declare the punishment of Treason, but no Attainder of Treason shall work Corruption of Blood, or Forfeiture except during the Life of the Person attainted.

ARTICLE IV

Section 1. Full Faith and Credit shall be given in each State to the public Acts, Records, and judicial Proceedings of every other State. And the Congress may by general Laws prescribe the Manner in which such Acts, Records, and Proceedings shall be proved, and the Effect thereof.

Section 2. The Citizens of each State shall be entitled to all Privileges and Immunities of Citizens in the several States.

A Person charged in any State with Treason, Felony, or other Crime, who shall flee from Justice, and be found in another State, shall on Demand of the executive Authority of the State from which he fled, be delivered up, to be removed to the State having Jurisdiction of the Crime.

No person held to Service or Labor in one State, under the Laws thereof, escaping into another, shall, in Consequence of any Law or Regulation therein, be discharged from such Service or Labor, But shall be delivered up on Claim of the Party to whom such Service or Labor may be due.

Section 3. New States may be admitted by the Congress into this Union; but no new States shall be formed or erected within the Jurisdiction of any other State; nor any State be formed by the Junction of two or more States, or Parts of States, without the Consent of the Legislatures of the States concerned as well as of the Congress.

The Congress shall have Power to dispose of and make all needful Rules and Regulations respecting the Territory or other Property belonging to the United States; and nothing in this Constitution shall be so construed as to Prejudice any Claims of the United States, or of any particular State.

Section 4. The United States shall guarantee to every State in this Union a Republican Form of Government, and shall protect each of them against Invasion; and on Application of the Legislature, or of the Executive (when the Legislature cannot be convened) against domestic Violence.

ARTICLE V

The Congress, whenever two thirds of both Houses shall deem it necessary, shall propose Amendments to this Constitution, or, on the Application of the Legislatures of two thirds of the several States, shall call a Convention for proposing Amendments, which, in either Case, shall be valid to all Intents and Purposes, as Part of this Constitution, when ratified by the Legislatures of three fourths of the several States, or by Conventions in three fourths thereof, as the one or the other Mode of Ratification may be proposed by the Congress; Provided that no Amendment which may be made prior to the Year one thousand eight hundred and eight shall in any Manner affect the first and fourth Clauses in the ninth Section of the first Article; and that no State, without its Consent, shall be deprived of it's equal Suffrage in the Senate.

ARTICLE VI

All Debts contracted and Engagements entered into, before the Adoption of this Constitution, shall be as valid against the United States under this Constitution, as under the Confederation.

This Constitution, and the Laws of the United States which shall be made in Pursuance thereof; and all Treaties made, or which shall be made, under the Authority of the United States, shall be the supreme Law of the Land; and the Judges in every State shall be bound thereby, any Thing in the Constitution or Laws of any State to the Contrary notwithstanding.

The Senators and Representatives before mentioned, and the Members of the several State Legislatures, and all executive and judicial Officers, both of the United States and of the several States, shall be bound by Oath or Affirmation, to support this Constitution; but no religious Test shall ever be required as a Qualification to any Office or public Trust under the United States.

ARTICLE VII

The Ratification of the Conventions of nine States, shall be sufficient for the Establishment of this Constitution between the States so ratifying the Same.

Done in Convention by the Unanimous Consent of the States present the Seventeenth Day of September in the Year of our Lord one thousand seven hundred and eighty seven and of the Independence of the United States of America the Twelfth. In Witness whereof We have hereunto subscribed our Names,

Go. WASHINGTON—

Presid. and deputy from Virginia

New Hampshire

John Langdon

Nicholas Gilman

Massachusetts

Nathaniel Gorham

Rufus King

Documents of Revolution

Connecticut

Wm. Saml. Johnson

Roger Sherman

New York

Alexander Hamilton

New Jersey

Wil: Livingston

David Brearley

Wm. Paterson

Jona: Dayton

Pennsylvania

B Franklin

Thomas Mifflin

Robt Morris

Geo. Clymer

Thos FitzSimons

Jared Ingersoll

James Wilson

Gouv Morris

Delaware

Geo: Read

Gunning Bedford jun

John Dickinson

Richard Bassett

Jaco: Broom

Maryland

James Mchenry

Dan of St Thos. Jenifer

Danl Carroll

Virginia

John Blair—

James Madison Jr.

North Carolina

Wm. Blount

Rich'd Dobbs Spaight

Hu Williamson

South Carolina

J. Rutledge

Charles Cotesworth Pinckney

Charles Pinckney

Pierce Butler

Georgia

William Few

Abr Baldwin

Attest:

William Jackson, Secretary

THE UNITED STATES BILL OF RIGHTS.

The Ten Original Amendments to the Constitution of the United States
Passed by Congress September 25, 1789
Ratified December 15, 1791

I

Congress shall make no law respecting an establishment of religion, or prohibiting the free exercise thereof; or abridging the freedom of speech, or of the press, or the right of the people peaceably to assemble, and to petition the Government for a redress of grievances.

II

A well-regulated militia, being necessary to the security of a free State, the right of the people to keep and bear arms, shall not be infringed.

III

No soldier shall, in time of peace be quartered in any house, without the consent of the owner, nor in time of war, but in a manner to be prescribed by law.

IV

The right of the people to be secure in their persons, houses, papers, and effects, against unreasonable searches and seizures, shall not be violated, and no Warrants shall issue, but upon probable cause, supported by oath or affirmation, and particularly describing the place to be searched, and the persons or things to be seized.

V

No person shall be held to answer for a capital, or otherwise infamous crime, unless on a presentment or indictment of a Grand Jury, except in cases arising in the land or naval forces, or in the Militia, when in actual service in time of War or public danger; nor shall any person be subject for the same offense to be twice put in jeopardy of life or limb; nor shall be compelled in any criminal case to be a witness against himself, nor be deprived of life, liberty, or property, without due process of law; nor shall private property be taken for public use without just compensation.

VI

In all criminal prosecutions, the accused shall enjoy the right to a speedy and public trial, by an impartial jury of the State and district wherein the crime shall have been committed, which district shall have been previously ascertained by law, and to be informed of the nature and cause of the accusation; to be confronted with the witnesses against him; to have compulsory process for obtaining witnesses in his favor, and to have the assistance of counsel for his defense.

VII

In suits at common law, where the value in controversy shall exceed twenty dollars, the right of trial by jury shall be preserved, and no fact tried by a jury shall be otherwise re-examined in any court of the United States, than according to the rules of the common law.

VIII

Excessive bail shall not be required nor excessive fines imposed, nor cruel and unusual punishments inflicted.

IX

The enumeration in the Constitution, of certain rights, shall not be construed to deny or disparage others retained by the people.

X

The powers not delegated to the United States by the Constitution, nor prohibited by it to the States, are reserved to the States respectively, or to the people.

Made in the USA
Middletown, DE
06 January 2024